Third Edition

FOUNDATIONS OF ADDICTIONS COUNSELING

David Capuzzi
Walden University
Johns Hopkins University
Professor Emeritus, Portland State University

Mark D. Stauffer
Walden University

Boston Columbus Indianapolis New York San Francisco Hoboken Amsterdam
Cape Town Dubai London Madrid Milan Munich Paris Montreal Toronto Delhi Mexico City
Sao Paulo Sydney Hong Kong Seoul Singapore Taipei Tokyo

Vice President and Editorial Director: Jeffery W. Johnston
Vice President and Publisher: Kevin M. Davis
Editorial Assistant: Caitlin Griscom
Executive Field Marketing Manager: Krista Clark
Senior Product Marketing Manager: Christopher Barry
Project Manager: Lauren Carlson
Procurement Specialist: Deidra Skahill
Cover Art: Balazs Kovacs Images / Shutterstock
Full-Service Project Management: Jogender Taneja/Aptara®, Inc.
Composition: Aptara®, Inc.
Printer/Binder: LSC Communications
Cover Printer: LSC Communications
Text Font: Minion Pro

Credits and acknowledgments for material borrowed from other sources and reproduced, with permission, in this textbook appear on the appropriate page within the text.

Every effort has been made to provide accurate and current Internet information in this book. However, the Internet and information posted on it are constantly changing, so it is inevitable that some of the Internet addresses listed in this textbook will change.

Copyright © 2016, 2012, 2008 by Pearson Education, Inc. or its affiliates. All Rights Reserved. Manufactured in the United States of America. This publication is protected by Copyright, and permission should be obtained from the publisher prior to any prohibited reproduction, storage in a retrieval system, or transmission in any form or by any means, electronic, mechanical, photocopying, recording, or likewise. For information regarding permissions, request forms, and the appropriate contacts within the Pearson Education Global Rights & Permissions department, please visit www.pearsoned.com/permissions.

PEARSON and ALWAYS LEARNING are exclusive trademarks in the U.S. and/or other countries owned by Pearson Education, Inc. or its affiliates.

Library of Congress Cataloging-in-Publication Data
Foundations of addictions counseling / [edited by] David Capuzzi Walden University, Professor Emeritus, Portland State University, Mark D. Stauffer, Walden University. – Third edition.
    pages cm
  Includes bibliographical references and index.
  ISBN 978-0-13-399864-1 – ISBN 0-13-399864-9
 1. Drug abuse counseling.   I. Capuzzi, Dave.   II. Stauffer, Mark D.
RC564.F69 2016
362.29—dc23   2014041656

ISBN 10:   0-13-399864-9
ISBN 13: 978-0-13-399864-1

PREFACE

Whether you are entering the field of addictions counseling or are a counselor who wants to be prepared for the screening, assessment, and treatment of addiction in your practice, this text provides a foundational basis. *Foundations of Addictions Counseling* addresses real-life clinical concerns while providing the necessary information to keep up to date with field trends. It also addresses the evolving standards of professional organizations, accrediting bodies, licensure boards, and graduate programs and departments. Counselors in school, mental health, rehabilitation, hospital, private practice, and a variety of other settings must be thoroughly prepared to support clients in their quest to be healthy and unimpaired. As the addictions profession has matured, more and more emphasis has been placed on the importance of preparing counselors to work holistically and synthesize knowledge domains from mental health, developmental, and addiction perspectives. The authors provide this knowledge in support of your work on behalf of various clients and diverse communities.

Counselors can expect some of their clients to want to address concerns connected with the use of substances and the development of addictive behavior. This book draws on the specialized knowledge for each contributed chapter. It is written for use in graduate-level preparation programs for counselors. Because of the clarity of the writing and the use of case studies, it may also be adopted in some undergraduate and community college courses. Requirements of the Council for the Accreditation of Counseling and Related Educational Programs (CACREP) and other certification associations have led most university programs in counselor education to require an addictions course for all students, regardless of specialization (school, community, rehabilitation, couples, marriage and family, student personnel, etc.). Addictions counseling is also being offered for CADC I and II certifications, which require undergraduate coursework related to addictions counseling.

NEW TO THIS EDITION

- A new chapter dedicated to the process of rehabilitation in both inpatient and outpatient settings
- A major revision of Chapter 16 so that prevention across the life span is addressed in this edition
- Additional case studies to further illustrate points and enliven class discussion
- Informational sidebars to encourage the visual learner and reader contemplation
- Integration of updated and current research from the field's peer-reviewed journals
- Instructor's manual that includes updated journaling exercises, group work, PowerPoints, and experiential exercises for the online as well as face-to-face classroom.
- Connection to Pearson's *MyCounselingLab* videos, assignments, and certification practice.

It is our hope that this third edition of *Foundations of Addictions Counseling* will provide the beginning student counselor with the basics needed for follow-up courses and supervised practice in the arena of addictions counseling.

Although the text addresses the history, theories, and research related to addictions counseling, at least half of the book's emphasis is on techniques and skills needed by the practitioner. In addition, guidelines for addictions counseling in family, rehabilitation, and school settings are addressed as are topics connected with cross-cultural counseling and addictions. Some of the topics that make the book engaging and of high interest to readers:

- Concrete reference to assessment tools
- Outpatient and inpatient treatment
- Maintenance and relapse prevention
- Counseling with addicted/recovering clients
- Counseling couples and families that are coping with addictions issues
- Addictions prevention programs for children, adolescents, and college students

Writers experienced in addictions counseling were asked to contribute so that the reader is provided with not only theory and research but also with those applications so pertinent to the role of the practicing, licensed, and certified addictions counselor. This book also reflects the view of the editors that counselors must be prepared in a holistic manner, since addiction issues are so often the reason clients seek the assistance of a professional counselor.

The book is unique in both format and content. The contributing authors' format provides state-of-the-art information by experts nationally recognized for their expertise, research, and publications related to addictions counseling. The content looks at areas not always addressed in introductory texts. Examples include chapters on professional issues in addictions counseling, process addictions, and gender and addictions counseling. Chapters focused on addictions counseling with gay, lesbian, bisexual, transgender, and questioning clients; on engaging ethnic diversity; and on pharmacotherapy provide perspectives often overlooked in texts of this kind. The format and content enhance readability and interest and should engage and motivate graduate students in counseling and aligned professions as well as those enrolled in lower division courses.

The book is designed for students taking a preliminary course in addictions counseling. It presents a comprehensive overview of the foundations of addictions counseling, the skills and techniques needed for addictions counseling, and addictions counseling in specific settings. As editors, we know that one text cannot adequately address all the complex and holistic factors involved in assisting clients who present with issues related to addictive behavior. We have, however, attempted to provide our readers with a broad perspective based on current professional literature and the rapidly changing world we live in at this juncture of the new millennium. The following overview highlights the major features of the text.

OVERVIEW

The format for the co-edited textbook is based on the contributions of authors who are recognized for their expertise, research, and publications. With few exceptions, each chapter contains case studies illustrating practical applications of the concepts presented. Most chapters refer the reader to websites containing supplemental information. Students will find it helpful to use the study material on the website maintained by Pearson Publishing. Professors may want to make use of the PowerPoints developed for each chapter, as well as the test manual that can be used to develop quizzes and exams on the book's content.

The text is divided into the following four parts with the new rehabilitation chapter capping the textbook: (1) Introduction to Addictions Counseling; (2) The Treatment of Addictions; (3) Addictions in Family Therapy, Rehabilitation, and School Settings; and (4) Cross-Cultural Counseling in Addictions.

PART 1 Introduction to Addictions Counseling (Chapters 1 through 6), begins with information on the historical perspectives and etiological models that serve as the foundation for current approaches to addictions counseling, and provides the reader with the contextual background needed to assimilate subsequent chapters. Chapters focused on substance and process addictions, professional issues, an introduction to assessment, and assessment and diagnosis of addictions are included as well.

PART 2 The Treatment of Addictions (Chapters 7 through 13) presents information about motivational interviewing, other psychotherapeutic approaches, comorbid disorders, group work, pharmacotherapy, 12-step programs, and maintenance and relapse prevention. All chapters provide overviews and introduce readers to the skills and techniques used in the addictions counseling process.

PART 3 Addictions in Family Therapy, Rehabilitation, and School Settings (Chapters 14 through 16) presents information relative to addiction and families, persons with disabilities, and children, adolescents, and college students. These chapters highlight information that has relevance and application to diverse contexts.

PART 4 Cross-Cultural Counseling in Addictions (Chapters 17 through 19) discusses ethnic diversity, gender and addictions, and gay, lesbian, bisexual, transgender, questioning affirmative addictions treatment.

An Epilogue with a new, final chapter on inpatient and outpatient rehabilitation provides the readership with even more information than in the second edition of the text. We think the additional case studies included in this third edition along with the use of sidebars enliven the content and make the text even more user friendly and practitioner oriented.

Every attempt has been made by the editors and contributors to provide the reader with current information in each of the 19 areas of focus. It is our hope that this third edition of *Foundations of Addictions Counseling* will provide the beginning student counselor with the basics needed for follow-up courses and supervised practice in the arena of addictions counseling with clients.

ACKNOWLEDGMENTS

We would like to thank the 35 authors who contributed their expertise, knowledge, and experience in the development of this textbook. We would also like to thank our families, who provided us with the freedom and encouragement to make this endeavor possible. Our thanks are also directed to members of the Pearson production team for their encouragement and assistance with copyediting and, ultimately, the publication of the book.

Special thanks are extended to Cass Dykeman, professor of Counselor Education at Oregon State University, for his suggestions on content areas included in this book. Thanks to his input, readers of *Foundations of Addictions Counseling* will benefit from a more comprehensive overview of counseling with clients experiencing addictions issues.

We would like to thank the reviewers of our manuscript for their comments and insights: Edward F. Hudspeth, Henderson State University; Kimberly Tran, Fayetteville State University; and Kent B. Provost, Argosy University, Chicago.

CONTRIBUTORS

MEET THE EDITORS

David Capuzzi, PhD, NCC, LPC, is a counselor educator and member of the core faculty in clinical mental health counseling at Walden University and professor emeritus at Portland State University. Previously, he served as an affiliate professor in the Department of Counselor Education, Counseling Psychology, and Rehabilitation Services at Pennsylvania State University and Scholar in Residence in counselor education at Johns Hopkins University. He is past president of the American Counseling Association (ACA), formerly the American Association for Counseling and Development, and past chair of both the ACA Foundation and the ACA Insurance Trust.

From 1980 to 1984, Dr. Capuzzi was editor of *The School Counselor*. He has authored a number of textbook chapters and monographs on the topic of preventing adolescent suicide, and is co-editor and author with Dr. Larry Golden of *Helping Families Help Children: Family Interventions with School Related Problems* (1986) and *Preventing Adolescent Suicide* (1988). He coauthored and edited with Douglas R. Gross *Youth at Risk: A Prevention Resource for Counselors, Teachers, and Parents* (1989, 1996, 2000, 2004, 2008, and 2014); *Introduction to the Counseling Profession* (1991, 1997, 2001, 2005, 2009, and 2013); *Introduction to Group Work* (1992, 1998, 2002, 2006, and 2010); and *Counseling and Psychotherapy: Theories and Interventions* (1995, 1999, 2003, 2007, and 2011). Other texts are *Approaches to Group Work: A Handbook for Practitioners* (2003), *Suicide Across the Life Span* (2006), *Foundations of Couples, Marriage, and Family Counseling* (2015), *Human Development Across the Life Span; Applications for Counselors* (2016), and *Sexuality Issues in Counseling,* the last coauthored and edited with Larry Burlew. He has authored or coauthored articles in a number of ACA-related journals.

A frequent speaker and keynoter at professional conferences and institutes, Dr. Capuzzi has also consulted with a variety of school districts and community agencies interested in initiating prevention and intervention strategies for adolescents at risk for suicide. He has facilitated the development of suicide prevention, crisis management, and postvention programs in communities throughout the United States; provides training on the topics of youth at risk and grief and loss; and serves as an invited adjunct faculty member at other universities as time permits.

An ACA fellow, he is the first recipient of ACA's Kitty Cole Human Rights Award and a recipient of Leona Tyler Award in Oregon. In 2010, he received ACA's Gilbert and Kathleen Wrenn Award for a Humanitarian and Caring Person. In 2011, he was named a Distinguished Alumni of the College of Education at Florida State University.

Mark D. Stauffer, PhD, NCC, is a core faculty member in the clinical mental health counseling program at Walden University. He specialized in couples, marriage, and family counseling during his graduate work in the Counselor Education Program at Portland State University, where he received his master's degree. He received his doctoral degree from Oregon State University, Department of Teacher and Counselor Education.

Dr. Stauffer is the immediate past co-chair of the American Counseling Association International Committee with Dr. Sachin Jain. He was a Chi Sigma Iota International fellow and was awarded the ACA's Emerging Leaders Training Grant. He is a member of the International Association of Marriage and Family Counseling (IAMFC).

As a clinician, Dr. Stauffer has worked in the Portland Metro Area in Oregon at crises centers and other nonprofit organizations working with low-income individuals, couples, and families. He has studied and trained in the Zen tradition, and presents locally and nationally on meditation and mindfulness-based therapies in counseling. His research focus has centered on Eastern methods and East–West collaboration. In private practice, Dr. Stauffer worked with couples and families from a family systems perspective.

He has co-edited five textbooks in the counseling field with Dr. David Capuzzi: *Introduction to Group Work* (2010); *Career Counseling: Foundations, Perspectives, and Applications* (2006, 2012), *Foundations of Addictions Counseling* (2008, 2012), *Foundations of Couples, Marriage, and Family Counseling* (2015), and *Human Development across the Life Span: Applications for Counselors* (2016).

MEET THE CONTRIBUTORS

Lisa Aasheim, PhD, is an associate professor of Counselor Education and Coordinator of the School Counseling Program and the Director of the Community Counseling Training Clinic at Portland State University. She specializes in clinical supervision and counselor development, focusing most significantly on bridging the gap between counselor training and professional practice. She is the author of the internationally adopted book, *Practical Clinical Supervision for Counselors: An Experiential Guide,* and provides trainings and consultation to supervisors around the United States.

Currently, Dr. Aasheim teaches master's-, doctoral-, and postgraduate-level courses focusing on clinical supervision, addictions counseling, and counselor education. She also provides professional-level trainings for counselors, social workers, and helping professionals throughout the Pacific Northwest in topics such as motivational interviewing, the therapeutic alliance, agency dynamics, and relational change strategies in agency work.

Kelly Aissen, PhD, earned her PhD in counselor education in mental health counseling from the University of Florida. She is a Licensed Mental Health Counselor (LMHC) in private practice and a Qualified Clinical Supervisor in Florida. Dr. Aissen is contributing faculty in the School of Counseling at Walden University, teaching Addiction Counseling, Psychopharmacology, Diagnosis & Treatment, Crisis & Trauma, and Couples counseling. She has also presented at several local, regional, and national conferences on impaired professionals, addiction treatment strategies, and communication skill development. Her current clinical, teaching, and research interests encompass women's issues, the family disease of addiction, life transitions, and interpersonal relationships.

In addition to her teaching and current practice, Dr. Aissen has worked in inpatient and outpatient psychiatric and substance abuse treatment programs and residential group homes for the developmentally disabled, taught independent living skills to foster care children and teens, and ran coping skill and relapse prevention groups for clients in recovery from addiction.

Malvika Behl, MA, is a licensed school counselor in Missouri, a counselor trainee in Ohio, and a chemical dependency counselor assistant in Ohio. She has experience in working at a college setting as a counseling intern in an individual, couple, and group setting. She currently provides counseling service at the University Counseling Center as an extern with undergraduate and graduate students. She is interested in working as a chemical dependency counselor. She also has an interest in working with children and adolescents who have suffered trauma.

Malvika is a first-year doctoral student at the University of Toledo in Counselor Education where she teaches undergraduate counseling courses on substance abuse like models of substance abuse treatment and substance abuse prevention. Her research interests include behavioral supervision, substance abuse counseling in school systems, diagnosing qualification for school counselors, embedded therapy, and trauma focused cognitive behavioral therapy.

Malachy Bishop, PhD, CRC, is Professor of Rehabilitation Counseling and Rehabilitation Counseling and Doctoral Program Coordinator with the Department of Early Childhood, Special Education, and Rehabilitation Counseling at the University of Kentucky. He obtained his master's in rehabilitation counseling at Portland State University and his PhD in rehabilitation psychology from the University of Wisconsin—Madison. He conducts research in employment and psychosocial aspects of chronic neurological conditions, including epilepsy, multiple sclerosis, and brain injury, and adaptation to chronic illness and disability.

Dr. Bishop serves on the editorial board of several professional rehabilitation journals. He has authored over 85 articles and book chapters on rehabilitation counseling and health care, edited three books, and made research and training presentations throughout the United States and internationally. He served on the Institute of Medicine's Committee on Public Health dimensions of the Epilepsies. Dr. Bishop has received the American Rehabilitation Counseling Association's Research Award five times and was the 2005 recipient of the National Council on Rehabilitation Education's New Career Award.

Cynthia A. Briggs, PhD, LPC (NC), NCC, is a core faculty member in clinical mental health counseling at Walden University. In addition to her primary teaching role, she maintains a small counseling and coaching private practice, provides corporate training on interpersonal dynamics and leadership, and is a published author of creative nonfiction essays. In the past, she served as an adjunct professor for Wake Forest University, University of North Carolina—Charlotte, and Guilford College. She also served as the Addiction Counseling Program Coordinator at Winona State University, developing and implementing a certificate program for graduate students of addiction counseling.

She is the coauthor of the landmark text *Women, Girls, and Addiction: Celebrating the Feminine in Addiction Treatment and Recovery*, published in 2009 by Routledge. Her current research interests include qualitative methodology (oral history and autoethnography). She is in the process of collecting oral histories and retrospectives of World War II veterans.

Stephanie A. Calmes, PhD, received her doctorate in counselor education and supervision from the University of Toledo. She is a Licensed Professional Clinical Counselor with Supervisory endorsement (PCC-S) in the state of Ohio and a Licensed Independent Chemical Dependency Counselor—Clinical Supervisor (LICDC-CS). Her research interests include chemical dependency counseling and supervision, dual diagnosis, trauma, and resiliency.

Dr. Calmes has experience working in dual diagnosis treatment, as well as in both outpatient and residential chemical dependency treatment programs. She is the current Director of Clinical Services and Professional Development at COMPASS Corporation for Recovery Services in Toledo, Ohio.

Richard Cicchetti, PhD, LPC, CRC, SATP-C, is a core faculty member in the clinical mental health counseling program at Walden University. He graduated from Old Dominion University with a doctorate in counselor education and supervision, and holds a master's degree in rehabilitation counseling from Northeastern Illinois University and a certification for treatment of sexual addictions from Mid America Nazarene University. He is a member of the Association for Humanistic Counseling, the Illinois Counseling Association, and the American Counseling Association. He serves on committees for the ACA, AHA, and ICA and maintains a private practice with ex-felons and veterans who experience issues with readjustment, clients who experience issues with substance abuse, compulsive gambling, sexual addictions, shoplifting, hoarding, and marital issues.

Dr. Cicchetti has published a book chapter on sexual addictions, articles related to grief and disability, and has conducted presentations and seminars to ex-felons and ex-military members about readjustment issues, jobs skills and training, and process addictions. He has held positions at Old Dominion University and Adler School of Professional Psychology.

Pamela A. Cingel, PhD, earned her doctorate from the University of Toledo in 1992. She has been a full-time counselor educator and psychology instructor for 24 years and has taught courses at the undergraduate, master's, and doctoral levels. She has over 16 years of clinical experience as a counselor. She was the manager of an inpatient chemical dependency unit for adolescents and provided clinical supervision to various community agencies and currently serves as the faculty advisor for Psi Chi.

Dr. Cingel is currently a professor and director of the Psychology Program at St. Thomas University in Miami, Florida. She is working on the establishment of a new psychology program, Psychology Fellows, with the emphasis Change the Brain, Change the World. She is the director of the Student and Faculty Research Center, which is currently celebrating the 13th Annual Undergraduate Research Symposium. Her research interests include emotional intelligence, adolescents, change in faculty expectations, and gender studies.

Chris Cook, FRC Psych, is a professor in the Department of Theology & Religion at Durham University, England, and an Honorary Consultant Psychiatrist with Tees, Esk & Wear Valleys NHS Foundation Trust. He trained at St. George's Hospital Medical School, London, and has worked in the psychiatry of substance misuse for over 25 years. He was professor of the Psychiatry of Alcohol Misuse at the University of Kent from 1997 to 2003. He was ordained as an Anglican priest in Canterbury Cathedral in 2001 and is now an Honorary Minor Canon at Durham Cathedral.

Dr. Cook is interested in spirituality, theology, and health, and his publications include *Alcohol, Addiction and Christian Ethics* (Cook, CCH, Cambridge University Press, 2006) and *Spirituality, Theology & Mental Health* (Ed Cook CCH, SCM, 2013). He was chair of the Special Interest Group in Spirituality and Psychiatry at the Royal College of Psychiatrists from 2009 to 2013.

Cass Dykeman, PhD, is an associate professor of counselor education at Oregon State University. He is a Master Addictions Counselor (MAC), National Certified Counselor (NCC), and National Certified School Counselor (NCSC). Dr. Dykeman received a master's in counseling from the University of Washington and a doctorate in counselor education from the University of Virginia. He served as principal investigator for a $1.5 million federal school-to-work research project. In addition, he is the author of numerous books, book chapters, and scholarly journal articles.

Dr. Dykeman is past president of both the Washington State Association for Counselor Education and Supervision and the Western Association for Counselor Education and Supervision. He is also past chairperson of the School Counseling Interest Network of the Association for Counselor Education and Supervision. His current research interests include psychopharmacology and addiction counseling.

Ellyn Joan Essic, PhD, LPC (retired), was the 2009–2010 president of the International Association of Addiction and Offender Counselors (IAAOC) Division of ACA. She received a master's degree in 1987 from Wake Forest University and a doctorate from University of North Carolina—Greensboro in 1999 in counselor education. She is a practitioner with more than 25 years of counseling experience in addictions, interpersonal violence, trauma, gender issues, and stress management.

Dr. Essic served from 2000 to 2007 as program director and then clinical director of a large alcohol and drug treatment program located in rural Alaska for a Native Health Consortium. She taught counselor educators and others over the years in a number of university settings, and has presented nationally and internationally on native issues, domestic violence, and addiction, as well as other topics. She currently lives in Lewisville, North Carolina, and is trained as a Disaster Relief worker for the American Red Cross and as an Air Disaster Counselor.

Abbe' Finn, PhD, is the program coordinator for the School and Mental Health Counseling Programs in the College of Health Professions and Social Work at Florida Gulf Coast University.

She received her doctorate from the University of New Orleans Counselor Education Program, has an MA from Loyola University in New Orleans, an MEd from Tulane University in early childhood education, and a bachelor's degree in speech pathology and audiology from Tulane University.

She has worked extensively in the mental health field with individuals as well as groups in counseling. Before joining the university faculty full-time, she was an employee assistance counselor with United States Postal Service Employees Assistance Program and worked at a residential treatment facility. Dr. Finn specialized in working with groups in crisis response, survivors of childhood sexual trauma, and clients in addiction recovery. Her areas of research include group counseling with people with addictions, suicide prevention, violence prevention, and addiction prevention.

Scott E. Gillig, PhD, earned his doctorate from the University of Toledo in 1988. He has been a full-time university professor for 24 years with an additional five years of part-time university teaching. He has over 20 years of clinical experience as a counselor. He has worked with chemically dependent adolescents and adults in a dual diagnosis chemical dependency treatment residential unit. He is currently a professor and coordinator of the Educational Leadership Master's Program at St. Thomas University in Miami, Florida. He teaches both master's and doctoral courses. He has successfully chaired numerous dissertation committees. His research interests include counseling outcomes, depression, chemical dependency, treatment planning, and student mentoring.

Dr. Gillig is the founding faculty advisor for the St. Thomas University chapter of Phi Delta Kappa, Educational Academic & Professional Society International. Dr. Gillig has an interest in the psychology of photography and photographs wildlife, sports, weddings, people, and events. He has won several photography awards, has had his photographs displayed at art exhibits, and hosts a website with over 6,000 St. Thomas University sporting event photos. He has photographed every class he has taught since coming to St. Thomas University in 2006.

Sarah H. Golden, MA, received her master's degree in counselor education from Western Michigan University and completed her undergraduate work at Hope College. She is currently working on her doctorate in counselor education and supervision with a concentration in consultation from Walden University. Golden is a Limited Licensed Professional Counselor in Michigan and a credentialed school counselor in California. She is presently working in Los Angeles with diverse populations at University of Southern California Hybrid High School, an urban college preparatory charter high school that emphasizes positive multigenerational change. She has also been the consulting counselor for an online/onsite blended learning charter school, where she saw a need for a counseling program so developed and implemented counseling services. In addition to the school roles, Golden is also a Disaster Mental Health Volunteer for the American Red Cross. Her other professional interests include working with marginalized populations, consultation, crisis intervention, program development, and multicultural counseling.

In addition to her career, Golden is an enthusiast for volunteer work and giving back to the community. She is passionate about international work and has done short-term volunteering with youth in Rwanda, Africa. These projects included working with youth from preschool to high school ages in various capacities. She is striving to develop counseling programs for youth through platforms of athletics or creative outlets in order to promote physical and mental health, positive personal growth, empowerment, and team building. Dr. Golden is an avid runner and marathoner, and has been a cross country and track coach. She has also taught marathon classes. Dr. Golden is passionate about utilizing her education, passions, and skills to create and promote change.

Laura R. Haddock, PhD, received her doctorate in counselor education from the University of Mississippi and currently serves as Core Faculty and Coordinator of the PhD program in Counselor Education and Supervision at Walden University. Dr. Haddock has been a counselor educator since 2005, supported by more than 20 years as a mental health counselor. Her clinical practice includes work with a variety of populations, with particular interest in adults with serious mental illness. She is a licensed professional counselor, national certified counselor, and approved clinical supervisor.

Dr. Haddock is an active counseling professional and has served on the Mississippi Licensed Professional Counselors Board of Examiners and the executive boards for Mississippi Counseling Association and Mississippi Licensed Professional Counselors Association. Dr. Haddock routinely presents research on the state, national, and international levels as well as publishing scholarly writings for professional counseling journals and textbooks. She serves as an editorial board member for multiple professional counseling journals and is a two-time winner of outstanding research awards by state counseling organizations. Her research interests include counselor wellness and secondary trauma, sexuality, cultural diversity, and supervision.

Melinda Haley, PhD, received her master's in counselor education at Portland State University (Portland, Oregon) and her doctorate in counseling psychology from New Mexico State University (Las Cruces, New Mexico) and was an assistant professor at the University of Texas, El Paso, in the Counseling and Guidance program for 5years. Dr. Haley currently works as a core faculty member in the Counselor Education and Supervision Doctoral program at Walden. She has written numerous book chapters and journal articles on diverse topics related to counseling. She has extensive applied experience working with adults, adolescents, children, inmates, domestic violence offenders, and culturally diverse populations in the areas of assessment, diagnosis, treatment planning, crisis management, and intervention.

Dr. Haley's research interests include multicultural issues in teaching and counseling, personality development over the lifespan, personality disorders, the psychology of criminal and serial offenders, trauma and post-traumatic stress disorder, bias and racism, and social justice issues.

Debra A. Harley, PhD, CRC, is a Provost's Distinguished Service Professor in the Department of Early Childhood, Special Education and Rehabilitation Counseling at the University of

Kentucky. She completed her doctoral study at Southern Illinois University—Carbondale in special education and rehabilitation. She is past editor of the *Journal of Applied Rehabilitation Counseling* and the *Journal of Rehabilitation Administration*. She is co-editor of a book on contemporary mental health issues among African Americans. Her research interests include substance abuse, cultural diversity, and gender issues.

Misty K. Hook, PhD, received her master's degree in counseling psychology from the University of Kansas. Her doctorate is in counseling psychology from Ball State University with special emphasis on couples and family counseling. Dr. Hook was a professor of psychology for 5 years at Texas Woman's University where she taught counseling and family psychology courses. During that time, she cofounded the Mothering Caucus for the Association for Women in Psychology and participated in organizations dedicated to the study and service of women and families.

Dr. Hook is currently a psychologist in private practice where she sees families, couples, and individuals. In addition to her clinical work, Dr. Hook writes extensively about psychology, public policy, popular culture, gender, and issues concerning families. She has written many book chapters and columns; for two years she wrote a weekly column and Q&A section for an international website about counseling. Dr. Hook currently has her own blog and is working on other writing projects.

Adrianne L. Johnson, PhD, PCC, NCC, received her doctorate from the University of Arkansas in 2007 and is an Associate Professor of Clinical Mental Health Counseling at Wright State University. Her clinical and professional experience includes community mental health, crisis intervention, substance abuse treatment, counseling with the Latino population, and higher education leadership. She has published and presented internationally on psychoanalysis, video game addiction, substance abuse treatment, clinical practice with disabilities, aging and technology, and polyamory. She is certified in online course learning and design, and promotes course design focusing on evidence-based practice.

Dr. Johnson advocates for social justice and excellence in practice through various organizational memberships. Her advocacy efforts include professional development in education and clinical training, bias awareness in teaching and clinical practice, and the promotion of diversity inclusion in practice and education. Additional advocacy efforts include working with Wright Patterson Air Force Base on military sexual assault prevention and active involvement in Wright State University's partnerships with local school districts.

Pamela S. Lassiter, PhD, received her doctorate in Counseling from Georgia State University in 2004. She is an Associate Professor in the Counseling Department at the University of North Carolina at Charlotte. She has over 25 years of work experience as a counselor, clinical supervisor, and administrator in substance abuse treatment and community mental health settings. Her areas of research include multicultural counseling and supervision; lesbian, gay, bisexual, transgender, and questioning (LGBTQ) issues in counseling; LGBT parenting issues; substance abuse counseling; and women's issues.

She served as coordinator of the Substance Abuse Program at UNCC for 7 years and is past president of the International Association of Addictions and Offender Counseling (IAAOC), where she served as an officer for 5 years. Her presidential initiatives were focused on multicultural competencies and substance abuse counseling and supervision. She is the past recipient of the Dr. Mary Thomas Burke Mentoring Award given by the North Carolina Counseling

Association of Spiritual, Ethical, and Religious Values in Counseling and the Jo Anna White Founder's Award given by the Chi Epsilon Chapter of Chi Sigma Iota International.

Melissa M. Lugo, MSEd, PEL-School Counselor is a doctoral student in the Department of Counseling, Adult and Higher Education at Northern Illinois University (NIU). She teaches introduction to the counseling profession as well as coteaches ethics, human sexuality counseling, school counseling curriculum, and LGBT issues. She completed her master's degree in school counseling from Northern Illinois University.

Ms. Lugo has experience providing counseling to children, adolescents, and adults, as well as working in student affairs. She has provided individual and group counseling at the middle-school level and has experience in academic advising. She is a Student Success Specialist at NIU, where she focuses on retention for the university and specializes in the College of Business and College of Health and Human Sciences.

James W. McMullen, MSEd, LPCA, NCC, is a doctoral student at the University of North Carolina at Charlotte. He earned his master's in counseling from Old Dominion University. He has clinical experience in school counseling, college counseling, and performing brief counseling interventions with trauma patients at Carolinas Medical Center in Charlotte, North Carolina.

Mr. McMullen currently serves as the president of the Mu Tau Beta Chapter of Chi Sigma Iota, the international honor society for counseling. In addition to his interest in addictions counseling, he has researched and advocated extensively for underserved clients as well as for counselor professional identity development. His research interests have led to both national and regional presentations and publications.

Regina Moro, PhD, is an assistant professor of counseling at Barry University in Miami Shores, Florida. She is a Licensed Clinical Addiction Specialist (LCAS) in North Carolina and a National Certified Counselor (NCC). Her professional interests include substance abuse prevention and intervention, crisis and trauma in medical settings, and multiculturalism and social justice issues in counseling. Regina has served as a Chi Sigma Iota Leadership Fellow, on the leadership team of the International Association of Addiction and Offenders Counseling, and most recently as the president of the North Carolina Association for Humanistic Counseling.

Dr. Moro focused on severe risk and dependent drinkers in her dissertation research analyzing beneficial responses to alcohol screening and brief interventions associated with The Teachable Moment. She has presented her findings at international (INEBRIA 2012, Barcelona, and INEBRIA 2013, Rome), national, and state organizations. Her clinical experiences include college mental health, college career counseling, and work in medical settings (i.e., primary care and trauma).

Rochelle Moss, PhD, is currently an associate professor in the Department of Counseling at Henderson State University in Arkadelphia, Arkansas. She taught previously at the University of Mississippi and Texas A&M—Commerce. She also was employed as a school counselor for 15 years and has worked in private practice since 2000. She is a Licensed Professional Counselor and Supervisor in the state of Arkansas and has worked extensively with adolescents, young adults, and college athletes as well as cancer patients and their families.

Dr. Moss is an active member of the American Counseling Association, Association of Counselor Education and Supervision, and past president of Arkansas Association of Counselor Education and Supervision. Her current research interests include women's issues, health and wellness counseling, and neuroscience and counseling.

Cynthia J. Osborn, PhD, is professor of counseling and human development services at Kent State University in Kent, Ohio, where she routinely teaches the two addictions counseling courses offered. She is licensed in Ohio as a Professional Clinical Counselor with Supervisory Endorsement (LPCC-S) and an Independent Chemical Dependency Counselor (LICDC). Her clinical background is in substance abuse counseling, primarily servicing an adult population with co-occurring disorders (i.e., mental health and substance use concerns) in rural Appalachia.

Dr. Osborn is a member of the Motivational Interviewing Network of Trainers (MINT), is a former co-editor (with John D. West) of the journal *Counselor Education and Supervision*, and is coauthor (with Dennis L. Thombs) of the fourth edition of *Introduction to Addictive Behaviors*. Her research, publications, and presentations have focused on solution-focused counseling, counselor supervision, motivational interviewing, college alcohol use, and leadership in the counseling profession.

Dilani Perera-Diltz, PhD, is a counselor educator at Cleveland State University, Ohio. She is licensed in Ohio as a Professional Clinical Counselor (PCC-s), Licensed Independent Chemical Dependency Counselor (LICDC), and a School Counselor. Prior to academia, she worked as a substance abuse counselor at Western Ohio Regional Habilitation and Treatment Center and St. Rita's Hospital in Lima, Ohio. She worked as a mental health counselor at Psychosocial Associates in Columbus Grove, Ohio. She also worked as an Employee Assistance Program Counselor at Behavioral Connections in Bowling Green, Ohio.

Among her research interests are substance abuse, trauma, counselor training, and international mental health. Her publications include psychometrics of a variety of psychological instruments, online teaching, and school counselor issues. She is an editorial board member of the *Journal of Addictions and Offender Counseling*. She loves animals and currently provides a home for four cats and a dog.

Jane E. Rheineck, PhD, LCPC, NCC, earned her doctorate in counselor education and supervision from the University of Arkansas, is an associate professor in the department of Counseling, Adult and Higher Education at NIU, where she has taught classes in clinical skills, counseling ethics, and LGBT issues. Dr. Rheineck has an ongoing program of research and scholarship that focuses on a variety of LGBT issues. Dr. Rheineck has authored or coauthored several articles published in the *Journal of Mental Health Counseling*, *ADULTSPAN*, and the *Wisconsin Counseling Journal*. She has also published several book chapters addressing lesbian health issues that are nationally recognized within the field of LGBT counseling practices. Dr. Rheineck's scholarly work also includes over 30 presentations, most of which are at the national level.

The scope of Dr. Rheineck's service is broad. She is the CACREP liaison, serves on college and university committees, and has a presence and holds leadership roles at the national level. Her national contributions include, but are not limited to, organizing career network services for the *Association for Counselor Education & Supervision* and the *Southern Association for Counselor Education & Supervision*.

Jennifer L. Rogers, PhD, NCC, is an assistant professor in counseling at Wake Forest University. She earned her PhD in counseling and counselor education from Syracuse University in 2013. Her dissertation examined the impact of patient- and intervention-level variables on post intervention drinking patterns of alcohol-using trauma patients analyzing data from The Teachable Moment.

Dr. Rogers has clinical experience in intensive outpatient, university mental health, and primary care settings, including performing alcohol screenings and brief counseling interventions with trauma patients at Wake Forest University Baptist Medical Center.

Chelsea Sharpe, MS, is currently a multisystemic therapy therapist contracted with the Department of Juvenile Justice in Athens, Georgia. She is a group facilitator and mentor for the Adopted Teen Empowerment & Mentoring Program at the University of Georgia. Ms. Sharpe has received a management award for collaborating with community stakeholders within juvenile justice, courts, and school systems. She is certified in working with victims of commercial and sexual exploitation of children and youth mental health first aid.

Ms. Sharpe is a doctoral student at Walden University majoring in counselor education and supervision with a specialization in trauma and crisis. Her clinical interests include working with at-risk youth and adults in the areas of substance abuse, aggression, grief and loss, relationships issues, and childhood sexual abuse. She has presented at an Association for Assessment and Research in Counseling national conference. Her research interests include substance abuse, veterans, divorce, childhood sexual abuse, and parenting styles.

Donna S. Sheperis, PhD, earned her doctorate in counselor education from the University of Mississippi. An associate professor at Lamar University (Dr. Sheperis just started this new position). A core faculty member in the Mental Health Counseling Program of Walden University, Dr. Sheperis is a Licensed Professional Counselor, National Certified Counselor, Certified Clinical Mental Health Counselor, and Approved Clinical Supervisor with over 20 years of experience in clinical mental health counseling settings. She has served as co-chair of the ACA Ethics Committee and is involved with the Association for Assessment and Research in Counseling, the Association for Humanistic Counseling, and the Association for Counselor Education and Supervision.

Dr. Sheperis is the editor of the textbook *Clinical Mental Health Counseling: Fundamentals of Applied Practice* and has authored numerous articles in peer-reviewed journals. Dr. Sheperis presents regularly on topics related to all aspects of clinical mental health counseling and has received several awards for her teaching, scholarship, and research. Her primary areas of interest include clinical mental health counselor development, assessment of mental health and coping, counseling ethics, and supervision.

Anneliese A. Singh, PhD, LPC, is an Associate Professor in the Department of Counseling and Human Development Services at The University of Georgia. Her clinical, research, and advocacy interests include LGBTQ youth, Asian American/Pacific Islander counseling and psychology, multicultural counseling and social justice training, qualitative methodology with historically marginalized groups (e.g., people of color, LGBTQ, immigrants), feminist theory and practice, and empowerment interventions with survivors of trauma.

Dr. Singh is a past president of the Association of Lesbian, Gay, Bisexual, and Transgender Issues in Counseling (ALGBTIC), where her Presidential Initiatives included the development of counseling competencies for working with transgender clients in counseling, supporting queer people of color, and ensuring safe schools for LGBTQ youth. She is a founder of the Georgia Safe Schools Coalition, an organization that works at the intersection of heterosexism, racism, sexism, and other oppressions to create safe school environments in Georgia. She is the recipient of the 2007 Ramesh and Vijaya Bakshi Community Change Award and the 2008 O'Hana award from Counselors for Social Justice of the American Counseling Association for her organizing work with LGBTQ youth.

G. Michael Szirony, PhD, NCC, CRC, is a core faculty member in the clinical mental health counseling education and supervision program at Walden University. Having graduated from Kent State University with a doctorate in counseling and human development and a master's degree in rehabilitation counseling, he completed his training in medical hypnoanalysis at Northeast Ohio Medical University and his doctoral internship at Western Reserve Psychiatric Hospital in Sagamore Hills, Ohio. He is a recipient of the National Rehabilitation Association's JPD Research Award and has served in leadership positions in academia and counseling associations; in addition, he is a member of the American Counseling Association and the Humanistic Counseling Association, having studied at the Gestalt Institute.

Dr. Szirony has published articles and book chapters on rehabilitation, neuropsychology, and distance education, has presented at national and state conferences, and serves on the editorial board of the journal, *Work*. He has held faculty positions at Kent State University, Penn State, the University of Arkansas at Little Rock, and Ohio University, and worked in private practice for several years.

Lebogang Tiro, MEd, is a doctoral student in rehabilitation counseling at the University of Kentucky. She received her Master of Education in Counseling and Human Services from the University of Botswana. She has a bachelor's degree in special education with an emphasis in visual impairment and early childhood education. Ms. Tiro has taught as a lecturer at the University of Botswana. Presently, her interests are related to gaining more information on neurological conditions such as multiple sclerosis, traumatic brain injury and spinal cord injuries. She is also interested in chronic illnesses like diabetes, high blood pressure, and cancer.

Prior to being a lecturer, Ms. Tiro was an educator for 13 years in a primary school, where she also became head of the department for learning disabilities. She was involved in formulating strategies for helping students who had problems in reading and writing, a skill she attained during her bachelor's degree. She is intending to publish more on areas related to disability.

Jennifer Vasquez, BS, is enrolled in the MEd School Counseling program at Cleveland State University. She will complete her degree May 2015 and is currently providing school counseling services at Villa Angela-St. Joseph's High School and Eastlake North High School as part of her practicum. She is interested in working with high school students to promote understanding of the emotional and physical dangers of substance use and abuse. She plans, in her school counseling practice, to help students identify resource people in the school/community and how to seek their help as well as learn safe coping skills for managing life events and peer pressure.

Ms. Vasquez's interests in working with children include Strength-Based Counseling Services Promoting Resiliency in all areas of school counseling, developing student strengths to help them overcome disadvantage and adversity. She is specifically interested in how learning environments can be structured to promote protective factors, life skills, and resilience for at-risk/at-promise students.

Laura J. Veach, PhD, LPC, LCAS, CCS, NCC, has her PhD in counselor education from the University of New Orleans and her master's in counseling from Wake Forest University. She is an associate professor and director of the CACREP-accredited Addictions Counseling Track in the Department of Counseling at the University of North Carolina at Charlotte, North Carolina. With her research, she also has a joint faculty appointment as associate professor in the Department of Surgical Sciences at the Wake Forest School of Medicine in Winston-Salem, North Carolina. Dr. Veach also serves as principal investigator of a Childress Institute for Pediatric

Trauma study on brief counseling interventions with violently injured youth and was coprincipal investigator with the Level I Trauma Center at Wake Forest Baptist Medical for a Robert Wood Johnson Foundation Grant, The Teachable Moment, researching best practices with alcohol screening and brief counseling interventions in a 3-year, prospective clinical trial comparing two counseling interventions. Dr. Veach is an active member of IAAOC and the international screening and brief intervention research organization, INEBRIA. She specializes in addictions and substance abuse counseling and has over 30 years of clinical, management, and start-up experience in counseling settings.

Dr. Veach also provides clinical services for the Red Cross with specialized training in Disaster Mental Health response and served in Louisiana and at Virginia Tech. She was the 2006 President of the International Association of Addictions and Offender Counseling (IAAOC). She was awarded the IAAOC Counselor Educator Award in March 2007, the WFU Graduate Faculty Award for excellence in teaching at Wake Forest University May 2007, the ACA Counselor Education Advocacy Award March 2008, and in North Carolina was named the 2010 recipient of the Dr. Mary Thomas Burke Professional Award (The Mentoring Award).

BRIEF CONTENTS

PART 1 Introduction To Addictions Counseling
- **Chapter 1** History and Etiological Models of Addiction   1
- **Chapter 2** Substance Addictions   18
- **Chapter 3** Process Addictions   48
- **Chapter 4** Important Professional Issues in Addiction Counseling   66
- **Chapter 5** Introduction to Assessment   89
- **Chapter 6** Assessment and Diagnosis of Addictions   119

PART 2 The Treatment of Addictions
- **Chapter 7** Motivational Interviewing   147
- **Chapter 8** Psychotherapeutic Approaches   165
- **Chapter 9** Treatment of Comorbid Disorders   192
- **Chapter 10** Group Therapy for Treatment of Addictions   217
- **Chapter 11** Addiction Pharmacotherapy   240
- **Chapter 12** 12-Step Facilitation of Treatment   263
- **Chapter 13** Maintenance and Relapse Prevention   285

PART 3 Addictions in Family Therapy, Rehabilitation, and School Settings
- **Chapter 14** Alcohol Addiction and Families   305
- **Chapter 15** Persons with Disabilities and Substance-Related and Addictive Disorders   328
- **Chapter 16** Substance Abuse Prevention Programs Across the Life Span   353

PART 4 Cross-Cultural Counseling in Addictions
- **Chapter 17** Cross-Cultural Counseling: Engaging Ethnic Diversity   383
- **Chapter 18** Gender, Sex, and Addictions   406
- **Chapter 19** Lesbian, Gay, Bisexual, Transgender, and Queer Affirmative Addictions Treatment   428

EPILOGUE Some Additional Perspectives
- **Chapter 20** Inpatient and Outpatient Addiction Treatment   449

CONTENTS

Preface   iii
Acknowledgments   vi
Contributors   vii

PART 1   Introduction to Addictions Counseling

Chapter 1   HISTORY AND ETIOLOGICAL MODELS OF ADDICTION   1
by David Capuzzi, Mark D. Stauffer, and Chelsea Sharpe

Approaches to the Prevention of Addiction in the United States   2
Current Policies Influencing Prevention   5
Models for Explaining the Etiology of Addiction   6
  The Moral Model   7
  Psychological Models   7
  Family Models   9
  The Disease Model   10
  The Public Health Model   10
  The Developmental Model   11
  Biological Models   11
  Sociocultural Models   12
  Multicausal Models   13
    Summary and Some Final Notations   14 • Useful Websites   15 • References   16

Chapter 2   SUBSTANCE ADDICTIONS   18
by Laura J. Veach, Jennifer L. Rogers, Regina R. Moro, and E. J. Essic

Neurobiology and the Physiology of Addiction   19
Substances of Addiction   26
  Depressants   26
  Opioids   34
  Stimulants   35
  Cannabinoids   41
  Hallucinogens and Other Psychedelics   41
    Summary and Some Final Notations   43 • Useful Websites   44 • References   44

Chapter 3 PROCESS ADDICTIONS 48
by Laura J. Veach, Jennifer L. Rogers, Regina M. Moro, E. J. Essic, and James W. McMullen
Sexual Addiction 50
    Case Study 51
Gambling Addiction 52
    Case Study 1 54
    Case Study 2 54
Work Addiction 56
    Case Study 59
Compulsive Buying 59
    Case Study 60
Food Addiction and Disordered Eating 60
    Case Study 62
        Summary and Some Final Notations 62 • Useful Websites 63
        • References 63

Chapter 4 IMPORTANT PROFESSIONAL ISSUES IN ADDICTION COUNSELING 66
by Melinda Haley and Sarah H. Golden
Professional Issues Pertaining to Counselors 66
    Counselor Competence 67
    Credentialing 76
Treatment and Research Issues 80
    Managed Care, Treatment Funding, and Provider Reimbursement 80
    Measuring Outcomes and Efficacy of Treatment 81
Future Trends 83
        Summary and Some Final Notations 83 • Useful Websites 84
        • References 84

Chapter 5 INTRODUCTION TO ASSESSMENT 89
by Mark D. Stauffer, David Capuzzi, and Kelly Aissen
Philosophical Foundations of Addictions Counseling 90
    Hope 90
    Strength-Based Approaches 91
    A Whole Person Approach 92
    Motivation 93
    Client Collaboration in Addictions Counseling 94
    Multidisciplinary Approach 94
    Advocacy 94

The Role of an Addictions Assessor 95
Points to Remember About Human Assessment Measures 95
    Protect Client Welfare and Information 95
    Be Competent to Use a Given Assessment Instrument 96
    Recognize Uniqueness and Diversity 96
    Keep Empathic Connection Alive 97
    Use Multiple Methods 97
    Continue to Assess Over Time and in Relation to Stage of Treatment 97
    Be Skilled When Communicating About Assessment Procedures and Results 98
Flow of Addictions Assessment 98
    Screening 99
    Crisis Intervention 100
Operationalizing Assessment Interviews 100
    Structured, Semistructured, and Unstructured Interviews 100
    Assessment Dimensions Related to Level of Care 101
Gathering Background and Contextual Information 103
    Client Presentation and Functioning 104
Treatment-Specific Assessment Information 108
    Readiness for Change 108
    Stage of Change Theory 108
    Prior Treatment Related to Addiction 109
    Other Background Information 110
    Family Systems and Peer Relationships 110
        Summary and Some Final Notations 113 • Useful Websites 113 • References 114

Chapter 6 ASSESSMENT AND DIAGNOSIS OF ADDICTIONS 119
by John M. Laux, Dilani M. Perera-Diltz, Stephanie A. Calmes, Malvika Behl, and Jennifer Vasquez

Why Use Standardized Assessments? 121
Philosophical Underpinning of Instrument Construction 122
Screening, Assessment, and Diagnosis 123
Evaluating Substance Abuse Screens and Assessments 123
    Sensitivity and Specificity 123
    Reliability and Validity 124
    Cost-Efficiency 124
Diagnosis 124

Self-Administered, Stand-Alone Screening Instruments 126
    Substance Abuse Subtle Screening Inventory-3 (SASSI-3) 126
    The Michigan Alcoholism Screening Test (MAST) 127
    The CAGE 128
    Alcohol Use Disorders Identification Test (AUDIT) 129
    Alcohol Use Inventory (AUI) 130

Substance Abuse Scales Found on Personality Assessment Instruments 130
    Minnesota Multiphasic Personality Inventory—2 (MMPI-2) 131
    Personality Assessment Inventory (PAI) 133
    Millon Clinical Multiaxial Inventory—III (MCMI-III) 134

Counselor-Initiated Comprehensive Substance Abuse Assessment 135
    The Addiction Severity Index (ASI) 136

Instruments Designed to Assess Alcohol Misuse During Pregnancy 137
    T-ACE 137
    TWEAK 138
        Summary and Some Final Notations 139 • *Useful Websites* 141 • *References* 141

PART 2 The Treatment of Addictions

Chapter 7 MOTIVATIONAL INTERVIEWING 147
by Lisa Langfuss Aasheim

Overview: Motivational Interviewing 147

The Stages of Change Model 148

Change and Resistance 151
    Change 151
    Resistance 151

Motivational Interviewing: Helping Clients Achieve Change 152
    The Primary Principles of Motivational Interviewing 153

Motivational Interviewing Techniques: Early in the Change Process 154
    Five Techniques to Use Early and Often 154

The Role of Resistance in the Change Process 157
    The Many Forms of Resistance 158
    Reducing Resistance 158

Guiding the Change Process: More Motivational Interviewing Techniques 161

Enhancing Confidence 161
Strengthening Commitment 162

Advantages and Disadvantages of Motivational Interviewing 162

Summary and Some Final Notations 163 • Useful Websites 163 • References 164

Chapter 8 PSYCHOTHERAPEUTIC APPROACHES 165

by Cynthia J. Osborn

Counselor Beliefs and Behaviors 165

Empirically Supported Treatment Approaches 166

Behavioral and Cognitive-Behavioral Assumptions and Practices 168

Functional Analysis 169
Cognitive-Behavioral Interventions that Target Triggers 170
Contingency Management and Behavior Contracting 172
Community Reinforcement Approach 173
Mindfulness-Based Relapse Prevention 174

Brief Interventions 175

Solution-Focused Counseling 176

Encouragement from Research 177
Solution-Focused Integration 179
Solution-Focused Assumptions and Practices Useful in Substance Abuse Counseling 180

▶ CASE STUDY: A Reframe for Exceptional Anton 182

Harm Reduction 184

Summary and Some Final Notations 187 • Useful Websites 187 • References 188

Chapter 9 TREATMENT OF COMORBID DISORDERS 192

by Scott E. Gillig and Pamela A. Cingel

History of How Mental Health Systems Have Adapted to Meet the Needs of Clients with Multiple Disorders 192

Prevalence of Comorbidity 193

▶ CASE STUDY 195

Assessment 197

Cultural Issues Related to Assessment 198

Treatment and Care Needs 200

▶ CASE STUDY 201

Comorbid Treatment Models 202

Disease Concept Model 202
▶ **CASE STUDY** 203
Alternative Models 204
Other Treatment Issues 205
Multidisciplinary Treatment Team 205
A Brief Description of the Counseling Process that Leads to Treatment Planning 206
▶ **CASE STUDY:** A Case Study of Dwayne 208
Summary and Final Notations 214 • Useful Websites 214 • References 215

Chapter 10 GROUP THERAPY FOR TREATMENT OF ADDICTIONS 217
by Laura R. Haddock and Donna S. Sheperis

Theory Behind Group Work 217
Group Treatment of Addiction 218
An Overview of Types of Groups 219
Psychoeducational Groups 219
Psychotherapeutic Groups 220
Self-Help Groups 222
Ethical and Legal Issues with Groups 223
Competence of the Leader 224
Screening of Participant 224
Informed Consent 225
Confidentiality 225
Voluntary Versus Involuntary Participation 226
Group Conflict 227
Managing Diversity in Group Settings 227
Ethnicity 228
Gender 228
Sexuality 229
Type of Addiction 230
Group Counseling for Family Members of Addicts 230
▶ **CASE STUDIES:** Case Study I: Development of a Six-Session Alcohol and Drug Education Group 231
Case Study II: Psychotherapeutic Group, Open Focus 233
Strategies for Effective Group Treatment 236
Summary and Some Final Notations 237 • Useful Websites 237 • References 238

Chapter 11 ADDICTION PHARMACOTHERAPY 240
by Cass Dykeman

Rationale for a Chapter on Pharmacotherapy of Addiction 240

Terms and Concepts 241

    Key Pharmacotherapy Terms 241

Key Concepts of Neurology in Pharmacotherapy 241

Diversity and Pharmacotherapy 243

    ▶ **PHARMACOTHERAPY CASE STUDY I:** Generalized Anxiety Disorder (DSM 5 300.02), Alcohol Use Disorder (DSM 5 303.90 Severe), and Sedative, Hypnotic, or Anxiolytic Dependence Use Disorder (DSM 5 304.10 Moderate) 245

Key Concepts of Neurotransmitters in Pharmacotherapy 246

Key Concepts of Pharmacokinetics in Pharmacotherapy 247

Key Concepts of Pharmacodynamics in Pharmacotherapy 247

A Biological Theory of Craving 248

The Professional Counselor's Role in Addiction Pharmacotherapy 250

Application Example: Pharmacotherapy of Alcohol Use Disorder 251

    Aversion Treatment, First-Line: Disulfiram (Antabuse) 251

    Alcohol Withdrawal Treatment 251

    First-Line: Diazepam (Valium) and the Other Longer Half-Life Benzodiazepines 252

    ▶ **PHARMACOTHERAPY CASE STUDY II:** Alcohol Withdrawal (DSM 5 291.81) and Alcohol Use Disorder (DSM 5 303.90 Severe) in a Pregnant Patient (ICD-10-CM O99.3) 252

    Second-Line: Baclofen (Lioresal) 253

    Second-Line: Carbamazepine (Tegretol) 253

    Anticraving Treatment: Overview 253

    Anticraving Treatment: First-Line: Acamprosate (Campral) 253

    Anticraving Treatment: First-Line: Naltrexone (ReVia, Depade) 253

    Alcohol Withdrawal and Anticraving Treatment: Second-Line: Sodium Oxybate-SMO (Xyrem) 254

    ▶ **PHARMACOTHERAPY CASE STUDY III:** Alcohol Use Disorder (DSM 5 305.00 Mild) and Major Depressive Disorder—Moderate (DSM 5 296.22) 254

    Anticraving Treatment: Second-Line: Lamotrigine (Lamictal) 255

    Anticraving Treatment: Alternative Medications 255

Glossary of Pharmacotherapy Terms 256

    Summary and Some Final Notations 258 • Useful Websites 259 • References 259

Chapter 12 12-STEP FACILITATION OF TREATMENT 263
by Adrianne L. Johnson

History: Development of 12-Step Groups 263
- Alcoholics Anonymous 263
- Al-Anon 265
- Co-Dependents Anonymous 265
- Narcotics Anonymous 265
- Alateen 266
- Other Support Groups 266

The Group Process: How 12-Step Groups Work 267
- Goals 267
- The Twelve Steps and Twelve Traditions 268
- Group Dynamics as Applied to 12-Step Groups 269

The Role of Sponsors in Recovery 269
Do 12-Step Programs Really Work? 270
Specific Advantages and Disadvantages of 12-Step Groups 271
- Advantages 271
- Disadvantages 272

Using the 12-Step Group as Part of Treatment 274
- The Role of the Counselor 275

How Can I Learn More About Groups? 279
- *Summary and Some Final Notations* 279 • *Useful Websites* 280 • *References* 281

Chapter 13 MAINTENANCE AND RELAPSE PREVENTION 285
by Rochelle Moss and Christopher C. H. Cook

Introduction 285
Relapse Prevention for Addictive Behaviors 285
Relapse Prevention Model 287
- Self-Efficacy 287
- Outcome Expectancies 288
- Craving 288
- Coping 288
- Motivation 289
- Emotional States 289
- Social Support 289

High-Risk Situations 290
Seemingly Irrelevant Decisions (SIDs) 292
The Abstinence Violation Effect 293

Lifestyle Change 294
Developing a Management Plan 296
Case Study of Relapse Prevention 296
  Self-Assessment of HRSs 297
  Coping Strategies 298
  Lapse and Relapse Prevention Techniques 298
  Support Systems and Lifestyle Changes 299
  Other Lifestyle Changes 301
The Reality of Relapse Prevention 301
  Summary and Some Final Notations 302 • Useful Websites 302 • References 302

PART 3 Addictions in Family Therapy, Rehabilitation, and School Settings

Chapter 14 ALCOHOL ADDICTION AND FAMILIES 305
by Misty K. Hook

Addiction and the Family 306
  Family Counseling 306
  Stages in Addicted Family Systems 310
  Parenting in an Addicted Family System 311
Addiction and the Couple 312
  The Impact of Alcohol on Couple Relationships 312
Addiction and the Children 315
  Behavioral Outcomes 317
  Psychosocial Outcomes 317
Counseling Addicted Family Systems 319
  Efficacy of Couples and Family Counseling 319
  Assessment of Addicted Family Systems 319
  Treatment Strategies for Addicted Family Systems 320
    Summary and Some Final Notations 322 • Useful Websites 322 • References 323

Chapter 15 PERSONS WITH DISABILITIES AND SUBSTANCE-RELATED AND ADDICTIVE DISORDERS 328
by Debra A. Harley, Malachy Bishop, and Lebogang Tiro

Introduction 328
Characteristics and Status of People with Disabilities and Addictions 332
  ▶ CASE STUDY: The Case of Rita 334

Risk Factors for Persons with Disabilities 335
   Health and Medical Risk Factors 336
   Psychological Risk Factors 336
   Interpersonal and Social Risk Factors 337
   Economic and Employment Risk Factors 337
   Access Risk Factors 338
   ▶ **CASE STUDY:** The Case of Abram 339
   Sociocultural Factors 340
Treatment Utilization and Outcomes 341
Intervention Strategies in Rehabilitation Settings 343
   Summary and Some Final Notations 347 • Useful Websites 348 • References 348

Chapter 16 SUBSTANCE ABUSE PREVENTION PROGRAMS ACROSS THE LIFE SPAN 353

by Abbé Finn

The Need for Prevention Programs Across the Life Span 353
Public Health Prevention Program Model 357
   Primary Prevention Programs 357
   Secondary Prevention Programs 358
   Tertiary Prevention Programs 358
Evidenced-Based Prevention Programs 358
   Program Needs Assessment 359
Types of Substance Abuse Prevention Programs 359
   Prevention Program Strategies 359
Prevention Programs Targeting All Age Groups 360
   Restriction of Access to Drugs 360
Substance Abuse Prevention Programs for Children and Adolescents and Young Adults 360
   Early Diagnosis and Treatment of Emotional Problems 360
   Juvenile Drug Court Diversionary Programs 361
   School-Based Substance Abuse Prevention Programs 362
D.A.R.E. 363
   Evaluative Reviews of D.A.R.E 363
   Early Action Against Teen Drug Use 364
   In-School Drug Testing 365
   Multimodal Programs 366
   Harm Reduction Programs 368

Brief Alcohol Screening and Intervention for College Students (BASICS) 369

Mass Media Campaigns Aimed at Young Adult Population 369

Risk Reduction and Protective Programs 370

Prevention and Treatment Programs for Pregnant Adolescents and Adults 371

Home Visit Programs 372

Addiction Prevention Programs for Military Personnel, Veterans, and Their Families 373

Military Personnel 373

Veterans 374

Prevention Programs for Senior Adults 374

Substance Abuse Prevention Outcomes 375

Summary and Some Final Notations 376 • *Useful Websites 377* • *References 377*

PART 4 Cross-Cultural Counseling in Addictions

Chapter 17 CROSS-CULTURAL COUNSELING: ENGAGING ETHNIC DIVERSITY 383

by Jane E. Rheineck and Melissa M. Lugo

Why Does Culture Matter in Substance Abuse Treatment? 384

Definitions 385

How Did We Get to This Point? 385

Treatment Needs and Issues for Racial and Ethnic Minorities 387

Disparities in Use and Access to Treatment 387

Racial and Ethnic Minorities 387

Theoretical Frameworks 393

Racial and Cultural Identity Models 393

Association of Multicultural Counseling and Development (AMCD) Multicultural Counseling Competencies 394

▶ **CASE SCENARIOS:**

Lawrence 396

Jorgé 396

LaDonna 396

Carl 397

Alicia 397

Summary and Some Final Notations 401 • *Useful Websites 401* • *References 401*

Chapter 18 GENDER, SEX, AND ADDICTIONS 406
   by Cynthia A. Briggs
   Introduction 406
   Gender, Alcohol, and Drug Use and Abuse in the United States 407
   Women and Addiction 410
   　Biological Considerations 410
   　　▶ **CASE STUDY: Introducing Sandra 411**
   　Psychological Considerations 411
   　　▶ **CASE STUDY: Sandra 412**
   　Social Considerations 412
   　Special Considerations for Addicted Women 413
   　　▶ **CASE STUDY: Sandra 415**
   Men and Addiction 415
   　Biological Considerations 415
   　　▶ **CASE STUDY: Tom 416**
   　Psychological Considerations 416
   　　▶ **CASE STUDY: Tom 417**
   　Social Considerations 417
   　　▶ **CASE STUDY: Tom 418**
   Treatment Considerations 418
   　Treatment Overview and History 418
   　Gender-Specific Treatment Needs: Women 419
   　　▶ **CASE STUDIES: Sandra and Tom 420**
   　Gender-Specific Treatment Needs: Men 421
   　Gender-Specific Treatment Needs: Transgendered Clients 423
   　Gender-Specific Treatment Needs: Intersex Clients 423
   　Treatment Outcomes and Relapse Prevention 424
   　　Summary and Some Final Notations 424 • Useful Websites 424 • References 425

Chapter 19 LESBIAN, GAY, BISEXUAL, TRANSGENDER, AND QUEER AFFIRMATIVE ADDICTIONS TREATMENT 428
   by Anneliese A. Singh and Pamela S. Lassiter
   Common Terms for and Myths About LGBTQ People 430
   Coming Out, Cultural Differences, and Addiction 431
   　　▶ **CASE STUDY: Coming Out and Cultural Issues in Addictions Treatment 433**

xxxii Contents

LGBQT-Affirmative Addiction Treatment and Assessment 433
LGBQT-Specific Assessment of Addiction 434
▶ **CASE STUDY:** Lesbian Client Coming Out in a Support Group 437
LGBTQ-Specific Treatment of Addiction 437
Modality Issues 438
Relapse Prevention 439
▶ **CASE STUDY:** A Gay Transgender Man with a Relapse Crisis 439
Role of Addictions Counselors Working with LGBTQ Clients 440
Creating a Safe Environment for LGBTQ People 441
How to Be an Advocate for LGBTQ-Affirmative Treatment 442
▶ **CASE STUDY:** The Story of Sonali 444
Summary and Some Final Notations 445 • Useful Websites 445 • References 446

EPILOGUE Some Additional Perspectives

CHAPTER 20 INPATIENT AND OUTPATIENT ADDICTION TREATMENT 449
by Richard Cicchetti and G. Michael Szirony

Introduction 449

Inpatient Treatment 450
Levels of Care 450
Types of Inpatient Services 454
Clinician Determination of Inpatient Treatment 455
Use of Motivational Interviewing to Assess Readiness to Change 456
Challenges Facing Rehabilitation Centers 457
Client Inpatient Experience 458
▶ **CASE STUDY** 460

Outpatient Treatment 460
Drug and Alcohol Legislation Affecting Treatment 461
Residential Drug Abuse Program 466
Advocacy 469
Summary and Some Final Notations 470 • Useful Websites 470 • References 471

INDEX 474

Chapter 1

History and Etiological Models of Addiction

David Capuzzi
Walden University
Mark D. Stauffer
Walden University

Chelsea Sharpe
Multisystemic Therapy Therapist
Athens, Georgia

The specialists serving the highest proportion of clients with a primary addiction diagnosis are professional counselors (20%), not social workers (7%), psychologists (6%), or psychiatrists (3%)
(Lee, Craig, Fetherson, & Simpson, 2013, p. 2)

The history of addictions counseling, a specialization within the profession of counseling, follows a pattern of evolution similar to that witnessed in many of the helping professions (social work, psychology, nursing, medicine). Early practitioners had more limited education and supervision (Astromovich & Hoskins, 2013; Iarussi, Perjessy, & Reed, 2013), were not licensed by regulatory boards, did not have well defined codes of ethics upon which to base professional judgments, may not have been aware of the values and needs of diverse populations, and did not have access to a body of research that helped define best practices and treatment plans (Hogan, Gabrielsen, Luna, & Grothaus, 2003).

It is interesting to watch the evolution of a profession and specializations within a profession. For example, in the late 1950s, the profession of counseling was energized by the availability of federal funds to prepare counselors. The impetus for the U.S. government to provide funds for both graduate students and university departments was Russia's launching of *Sputnik*. School counselors were needed to help prepare students for academic success, especially in math and science, so the United States could "catch up" with its "competitors."

As noted by Fisher and Harrison (2000), in earlier times, barbers who also did "bloodletting" practiced medicine, individuals who were skilled at listening to others and making suggestions for problem resolution became known as healers, and those who could read and write and were skilled at helping others do so became teachers with very little formal education or preparation to work with others in such a capacity. Fifty years ago nursing degrees were conferred without completing a baccalaureate (today a baccalaureate is minimal and a master's degree is rapidly becoming the standard), a teacher could become a school counselor with 12 to 18 credits of coursework (today a two-year master's is the norm), and 20 years ago an addictions counselor was an alcoholic or addict in recovery who used his or her prior experience with drugs as the basis for the addictions counseling done with clients.

Until the middle 1970s, there was no such thing as licensure for counselors, and those wishing to become counselors could often do so with less than a master's degree. In 1976, Virginia became the first state to license counselors and outline a set of requirements that had to be met in order to obtain a license as a counselor. It took 33 years for all 50 states to pass licensure laws for counselors; this achievement took place in 2009 when the state of California passed its licensure law for counselors.

The purpose of this chapter is threefold: first, to provide an overview of the history of substance abuse prevention in the United States; second, to describe the most common models for explaining the etiology of addiction; and third, to overview and relate the discussion of the history of prevention and the models for understanding the etiology of addiction to the content of the text.

APPROACHES TO THE PREVENTION OF ADDICTION IN THE UNITED STATES

Alcoholic beverages have been a part of this nation's past since the landing of the Pilgrims. Early colonists had a high regard for alcoholic beverages because alcohol was regarded as a healthy substance with preventive and curative capabilities rather than as an intoxicant. Alcohol played a central role in promoting a sense of conviviality and community until, as time passed, the production and consumption of alcohol caused enough concern to precipitate several versions of the "temperance" movement (Center for Substance Abuse Prevention, 1993). The first of these began in the early 1800s, when clergymen took the position that alcohol could corrupt both mind and body and asked people to take a pledge to refrain from the use of distilled spirits.

In 1784, Dr. Benjamin Rush argued that alcoholism was a disease, and his writings marked the initial development of the temperance movement. By 1810, Rush called for the creation of a "sober house" for the care of what he called the "confirmed drunkard."

The temperance movement's initial goal was the replacement of excessive drinking with more moderate and socially approved levels of drinking. Between 1825 and 1850, thinking about the use of alcohol began to change from temperance-as-moderation to temperance-as-abstinence (White, 1998). Six artisans and workingmen started the "Washingtonian Total Abstinence Society" in a Baltimore tavern on April 2, 1840. Members went to taverns to recruit members and, in just a few years, precipitated a movement that inducted several hundred thousand members. The Washingtonians were key in shaping future self-help groups because they introduced the concept of sharing experiences in closed, alcoholics only meetings. Another version of the temperance movement occurred later in the 1800s with the emergence of the Women's Christian Temperance Movement and the mobilization of efforts to close down saloons. Societies such as the Daughters of Rechab, the Daughters of Temperance, and the Sisters of Sumaria are examples of such groups. (Readers are referred to White's discussion of religious conversion as a remedy for alcoholism for more details about the influence of religion in America on the temperance movement.) These movements contributed to the growing momentum to curtail alcohol consumption and the passage of the Volstead Act and prohibition in 1920 (Hall, 2010).

It is interesting to note that the United States was not alone during the first quarter of the 20th century in adopting prohibition on a large scale; other countries enacting similar legislation included Iceland, Finland, Norway, both czarist Russia and the Soviet Union, the Canadian provinces, and Canada's federal government. A majority of New Zealand voters approved national prohibition two times but never got the legislation to be effected (Blocker, 2006). Even though Prohibition was successful in reducing per capita consumption of alcohol, the law created such social turmoil and defiance that it was repealed in 1933.

Shortly after the passage of the Volstead Act in 1920, "speakeasies" sprang up all over the country in defiance of prohibition. The locations of these establishments were spread by "word of mouth" and people were admitted to "imbibe and party" only if they knew the password. Local police departments were kept busy identifying the locations of such speakeasies and made raids and arrests whenever possible. Often the police were paid so that raids did not take place and so patrons would feel more comfortable in such establishments.

Following the repeal of Prohibition, all states restricted the sale of alcoholic beverages in some way or another to prevent or reduce alcohol-related problems. In general, however, public policies and the alcoholic beverage industry took the position that the problems connected with the use of alcohol existed because of the people who used it and not because of the beverage itself. This view of alcoholism became the dominant view and force for quite some time and influenced, until recently, many of the prevention and early treatment approaches used in this country.

Paralleling the development of attitudes and laws for the use of alcohol, the nonmedical use of drugs, other than alcohol, can be traced back to the early colonization and settlement of the United States. Like alcohol, attitudes toward the use of certain drugs, and the laws passed declaring them legal or illegal, have changed over time and often have had racial/ethnic or class associations based on prejudice and less than accurate information. Prohibition was in part a response to the drinking patterns of European immigrants who became viewed as the lower class. Cocaine and opium were legal during the 19th century and favored by the middle and upper class, but cocaine became illegal when it was associated with African Americans following the Reconstruction era in the United States. The use of opium was first restricted in California during the latter part of the 19th century when it became associated with Chinese immigrant workers. Marijuana was legal until the 1930s when it became associated with Mexican immigrants. LSD, legal in the 1950s, became illegal in 1967 when it became associated with the counterculture.

It is interesting to witness the varying attitudes and laws concerning the use of marijuana. Many view marijuana as a "gateway" drug and disapprove of the medical use of marijuana; others think that the use of marijuana should be legalized and that access should be unlimited and use monitored only by the individual consumer.

It is interesting to note that it was not until the end of the 19th century (Center for Drug Abuse Prevention, 1993) that concern arose with respect to the use of drugs in patent medicines and products sold over the counter (cocaine, opium, and morphine were common ingredients in many potions). Until 1903, believe it or not, cocaine was an ingredient in some soft drinks. Heroin was even used in the 19th century as a nonaddicting treatment for morphine addiction and alcoholism. Gradually, states began to pass control and prescription laws and, in 1906, the U.S. Congress passed the Pure Food and Drug Act designed to control addiction by requiring labels on drugs contained in products, including opium, morphine, and heroin. The Harrison Act of 1914 resulted in the taxation of opium and coca products with registration and record-keeping requirements.

Current drug laws in the United States are derived from the 1970 Controlled Substance Act (Center for Drug Abuse Prevention, 1993), under which drugs are classified according to their medical use, potential for abuse, and possibility of creating dependence. Increases in per capita consumption of alcohol and illegal drugs raised public concern so that by 1971 the National Institute on Alcohol Abuse and Alcoholism (NIAAA) was established; by 1974, the National Institute on Drug Abuse (NIDA) had also been created. Both of these institutes conducted research and had strong prevention components as part of their mission. To further prevention efforts, the Anti-Drug Abuse Prevention Act of 1986 created the U.S. Office for Substance Abuse Prevention (OSAP); this office consolidated alcohol and other drug prevention initiatives under the Alcohol, Drug Abuse, and Mental Health Administration (ADAMHA). ADAMHA mandated that states set aside 20% of their alcohol and drug funds for prevention efforts while the remaining 80% could be used for treatment programs. In 1992, OSAP was changed to the Center for Substance Abuse Prevention (CSAP) and became part of the new Substance Abuse and Mental Health Services Administration (SAMSHA) and retained its major program areas. The research institutes of NIAAA and NIDA were then transferred to the National Institutes of Health (NIH). The Office of National Drug Control Policy (ONDCP) was also a significant development when it was established through the passage of the Anti-Drug Abuse Act of 1988. It focused on dismantling drug trafficking organizations, on helping people to stop using drugs, on preventing the use of drugs in the first place, and on preventing minors from abusing drugs.

Time passed, and Congress declared that the United States would be drug free by 1995; that "declaration" has not been fulfilled. Since the mid-1990s, there have been efforts to control the recreational and nonmedical use of prescription drugs and to restrict the flow of drugs into the country. In 2005, Congress budgeted $6.63 billion for U.S. government agencies directly focused on the restriction of illicit drug use. However, as noted later in this text, 13–18 metric tons of heroin is consumed yearly in the United States (Department of Health and Human Services [DHHS], 2004). In addition, there has been a dramatic increase in the abuse of prescription opioids since the mid-1990s, largely due to initiation by adolescents and young adults. As noted by Rigg and Murphy (2013), the incidence of prescription painkiller abuse increased by more than 400%, from 628,000 initiates in 1990 to 2.7 million in 2000.

There has been an attempt to restrict importation by strengthening the borders and confiscating illegal substances before they enter the United States. There has also been an attempt to reduce importation. The U.S. government uses foreign aid to pressure drug producing countries to stop cultivating, producing, and processing illegal substances. Some of the foreign aid is tied to judicial reforms, antidrug programs, and agricultural subsidies to grow legal produce (DHHS, 2004).

In an attempt to reduce drug supplies, the government has incarcerated drug suppliers. Legislators have mandated strict enforcement of mandatory sentences, resulting in a great increase in prison populations. As a result, the arrest rate of juveniles for drug-related crimes has doubled in the past 10 years while arrest rates for other crimes have declined by 13%. A small minority of these offenders (2 out of every 1,000) will be offered Juvenile Drug Court (JDC) diversionary programs as an option to prison sentences (CASA, 2004).

During the last few years, there has been much media attention focused on the drug cartels in Mexico and the drug wars adjacent to the U.S. border near El Paso, Texas. In April of 2010, the governor of Arizona signed into law legislation authorizing the police to stop anyone suspected of being an illegal immigrant and demand proof of citizenship.

CURRENT POLICIES INFLUENCING PREVENTION

> *Addiction today remains as formidable a reality as it ever was, with 23 million Americans in substance abuse treatment and over $180 billion a year consumed in addiction-related expenditure in the United States (Hammer, Dingel, Ostergren, Nowakowski, & Koenig, 2012, pp. 713–714).*

There are a number of current policies influencing the prevention of addiction that should be noted (McNeese & DiNitto, 2005) and are listed below.

- All states in the United States set a minimum age for the legal consumption of alcohol and prescribe penalties for retailers who knowingly sell alcohol to minors and underage customers. There are some states that penalize retailers even when a falsified identification is used to purchase liquor.
- Even though the Twenty-First Amendment repealed prohibition, the "dry" option is still open to individual states and some states, mainly in the South, do have dry counties.

Even though a few states still have "dry" counties, residents of those counties can often consume alcohol in restaurants that allow patrons to enter the establishment with a bottle of alcohol, usually wrapped or "bagged." The restaurant then charges a fee for opening the bottle and allowing the liquor to be served. In addition, some counties allow liquor stores to be located just outside the county line, perhaps in a waterway accessed by a short walk across a connecting boardwalk or foot bridge.

- Many state governments influence the price of alcohol through taxation and through the administration of state-owned liquor stores.
- As part of the initial training of U.S. Air Force and Navy recruits, alcohol and tobacco use is forbidden during basic training and for a short time during advanced and technical training. This is because use of these substances usually has a negative effect on military readiness and performance (Bray et al., 2010).
- Besides taxation and the operation of state-owned liquor stores, government can attempt to regulate consumption by controlling its distribution. It accomplishes this through adopting policies regulating the number, size, location, and hours of business for outlets as well as regulating advertising.
- Perhaps no other area of alcohol policy has been as emotionally charged as the setting of the minimum legal age for consuming alcoholic beverages. Most states have adopted the age of 21 as the minimum legal age for unrestricted purchase of alcohol. This is a point of contention among many because at age 18 the young are eligible for military service.
- When a legally intoxicated individual (someone with a blood alcohol content [BAC] of 0.08 to 0.10) drives an automobile, in most states, a crime has been committed. Penalties can range from suspension of the driver's license to a mandatory jail sentence, depending on the frequency of convictions.

- Insurance and liability laws can also be used to influence lower consumption of alcohol because those drivers with DUI convictions may face higher insurance premiums or may be unable to purchase insurance. In addition, in a majority of states, commercial establishments that serve alcoholic beverages are civilly liable to those who experience harm as a result of an intoxicated person's behavior.
- Public policies regarding the use of illicit drugs have not reached the same level of specificity as those regulating the use of alcohol (and, for that matter, tobacco). Since 1981 and the election of Ronald Reagan as president, federal policy has been more concerned with preventing recreational use of drugs than with helping habitual users. The approach chosen by the George H. Bush administration was one of zero tolerance. The George H. Bush administration did increase treatment funding by about 50%. Simultaneously, the administration continued to focus its attention on casual, middle-class drug use rather than with addiction or habitual use. In 1992, the presidential candidates, George H. Bush and Bill Clinton, rarely mentioned the drug issue except as related to adolescent drug use. In the year 2000, the major issue in the campaign of George W. Bush was whether Mr. Bush ever used cocaine. The administration of George W. Bush made very few changes in drug policy.
- Of major significance is the fact that SAMHSA was reauthorized in the year 2000 (Bazelon Center for Mental Health Law, 2000). That reauthorization created a number of new programs, including funding for integrated treatment programs for co-occurring disorders for individuals with both mental illness and a substance abuse disorder.
- Currently, a very controversial option for policy is being considered and discussed by policy makers (Fish, 2013). In short, replacing current assumptions and causal models underlying the war on drugs and punishment of drug users with alternative points of view could lead to a different way of understanding drug use and abuse and to different drug policy options. These alternatives could include refocusing our primary emphasis from attacking drugs to shrinking the black market through a targeted policy of legalization for adults, and differentiating between problem users (who should be offered help) and nonproblem users (who should be left alone). We could shift from a policy of punishing and marginalizing problem users to one of harm reduction and reintegration into society and shifting from a mandatory treatment policy to one of voluntary treatment. Abstention need not be the only acceptable treatment outcome because many (but not all) problem users can become occasional, nonproblematic users.

MODELS FOR EXPLAINING THE ETIOLOGY OF ADDICTION

> *Historically, addiction has been understood in various ways—a sin, a disease, a bad habit—each a reflection of a variety of social, cultural, and scientific conceptions (Hammer et al., 2012, p. 713).*

Substance use and abuse has been linked to a variety of societal issues and problems (crime and violence, violence against women, child abuse, difficulties with mental health, risks during pregnancy, sexual risk-taking, fatal injury, etc.). Given the impact the abuse of substances can have on society in general and the toll it often levies on individuals and families, it seems reasonable to attempt to understand the etiology or causes of addiction so that diagnosis and treatment plans can be as efficacious as possible. There are numerous models for explaining the etiology of addiction (McNeese & DiNitto, 2005); these models are not always mutually exclusive and none are presented as the correct way of understanding the phenomena of addiction. The moral, psychological, family, disease, public health, developmental, biological, sociocultural, and some multicausal models will be described in the subsections that follow.

The Moral Model

The moral model is based on beliefs or judgments of what is right or wrong, acceptable or unacceptable. Those who advance this model do not accept that there is any biological basis for addiction; they believe that there is something morally wrong with people who use drugs heavily.

The moral model explains addiction as a consequence of personal choice, and individuals who are engaging in addictive behaviors are viewed as being capable of making alternative choices. This model has been adopted by certain religious groups and the legal system in many states. For example, in states in which violators are not assessed for chemical dependency and in which there is no diversion to treatment, the moral model guides the emphasis on "punishment." In addition, in communities in which there are strong religious beliefs, religious intervention might be seen as the only route to changing behavior. The moral model for explaining the etiology of addiction focuses on the sinfulness inherent in human nature (Ferentzy & Turner, 2012). Since it is difficult to establish the sinful nature of human beings through empirically based research, this model has been generally discredited by present-day scholars. It is interesting to note, however, that the concept of addiction as sin or moral weakness continues to influence many public policies connected with alcohol and drug abuse (McNeese & DiNitto, 2005). This may be part of the reason why needle/syringe exchange programs have so often been opposed in the United States.

Although the study of the etiology of alcoholism and other addictions has made great strides in moving beyond the moral model, alcoholics are not immune to social stigma, and other types of addiction have yet to be widely viewed as something other than a choice. But as we move further away from the idea that addiction is the result of moral failure, we move closer to providing effective treatment and support for all those who suffer.

Psychological Models

Another explanation for the reasons people crave alcohol and other mind-altering drugs has to do with explanations dealing with a person's mind and emotions. There are several different psychological models for explaining the etiology of alcoholism and drug addiction, including cognitive-behavioral, learning, psychodynamic, and personality theory models.

COGNITIVE-BEHAVIORAL MODELS Cognitive-behavioral models suggest a variety of motivations and reinforcers for taking drugs. One explanation suggests that people take drugs to experience variety (Weil & Rosen, 1993). Drug use might be associated with a variety of experiences such as self-exploration, religious insights, altering moods, escape from boredom or despair, and enhancement of creativity, performance, sensory experience, or pleasure (Lindgren, Mullins, Neighbors, & Blayney, 2010). If we assume that people enjoy variety, then it can be understood why they repeat actions that they enjoy (positive reinforcement).

> The use of mind-altering drugs received additional media attention in the 1960s, when "flower children" sang and danced in the streets of San Francisco and other cities, sometimes living together in communities they created. Much press was given to the use of drugs to enhance sensory experience in connection with some of the encounter groups led by facilitators in southern California.

The desire to experience pleasure is another explanation connected with the cognitive-behavioral model. Alcohol and other drugs are chemical surrogates of natural reinforcers such as eating and sex. Social drinkers and alcoholics often report using alcohol to relax even though studies show that alcohol causes people to become more depressed, anxious, and nervous (NIAAA, 1996). Dependent behavior with respect to the use of alcohol and other drugs is maintained by the degree of reinforcement the person perceives as occurring; alcohol and other drugs may be perceived as being more powerful reinforcers than natural reinforcers and set the stage for addiction. As time passes, the brain adapts to the presence of the drug or alcohol, and the person experiences unpleasant withdrawal symptoms (e.g., anxiety, agitation, tremors, increased blood pressure, seizures). To avoid such unpleasant symptoms, the person consumes the substance anew and the cycle of avoiding unpleasant reactions (negative reinforcement) occurs and a repetitive cycle is established. In an interesting review of the literature on the etiology of addiction (Lubman, Yucel, & Pantelis, 2004), it was proposed that in chemically addicted individuals, maladaptive behaviors and high relapse rates may be conceptualized as compulsive in nature. The apparent loss of control over drug-related behaviors suggests that individuals who are addicted are unable to control the reward system in their lives and that addiction may be considered a disorder of compulsive behavior very similar to obsessive compulsive disorder.

LEARNING MODELS Learning models are closely related and somewhat overlap the explanations provided by cognitive-behavioral models. Learning theory assumes that alcohol or drug use results in a decrease in uncomfortable psychological states such as anxiety, stress, or tension, thus providing positive reinforcement to the user. This learned response continues until physical dependence develops and, like the explanation provided within the context of cognitive-behavioral models, the aversion of withdrawal symptoms becomes a reason and motivation for continued use. Learning models provide helpful guidelines for treatment planning because, as pointed out by Bandura (1969), what has been learned can be unlearned; the earlier the intervention occurs the better, since there will be fewer behaviors to unlearn.

PSYCHODYNAMIC MODELS Psychodynamic models link addiction to ego deficiencies, inadequate parenting, attachment disorders, hostility, homosexuality, masturbation, and so on. As noted by numerous researchers and clinicians, such models are difficult to substantiate through research since they deal with concepts difficult to operationalize and with events that occurred many years prior to the development of addictive behavior. A major problem with psychodynamic models is that the difficulties linked to early childhood development are not specific to alcoholism or addiction, but are reported by nonaddicted adults with a variety of other psychological problems (McNeese & DiNitto, 2005). Nevertheless, current thinking relative to the use of psychodynamic models as a potential explanation for the etiology of addiction has the following beliefs in common (Dodgen & Shea, 2000):

1. Substance abuse can be viewed as symptomatic of more basic psychopathology.
2. Difficulty with an individual's regulation of affect can be seen as a core problem or difficulty.
3. Disturbed object relations may be central to the development of substance abuse.

Readers are referred to Chapter 12 of *Slaying the Dragon: The History of Addiction Treatment and Recovery in America* by William L. White (1998) for a more extensive discussion of psychodynamic models in the context of the etiology of addiction.

PERSONALITY THEORY MODELS These theories make the assumption that certain personality traits predispose the individual to drug use. An "alcoholic personality" is often described by traits such as dependent, immature, impulsive, highly emotional, having low frustration tolerance, unable to express anger, and confused about their sex role orientation (Catanzaro, 1967; Milivojevic et al., 2012; Schuckit, 1986).

Although many tests have been constructed to attempt to identify the personality traits of a drug-addicted person, none have consistently distinguished the traits of the addicted individual from those of the nonaddicted individual. One of the subscales of the Minnesota Multiphasic Personality Inventory does differentiate alcoholics from the general population, but it may only be detecting the results of years of alcoholic abuse rather than underlying personality traits (MacAndrew, 1979). The consensus among those who work in the addictions counseling arena seems to be that personality traits are not of much importance in explaining addiction because an individual can become drug dependent irrespective of personality traits (Raistrick & Davidson, 1985).

Family Models

As noted in Chapter 14, during the infancy of the field of addictions counseling, addictions counselors were used to working only with the addict. Family members were excluded. However, it soon became clear that family members were influential in motivating the addict to get sober or in preventing the addict from making serious changes.

There are at least three models of family-based approaches to understanding the development of substance abuse (Dodgen & Shea, 2000).

BEHAVIORAL MODELS A major theme of the behavioral model is, that within the context of the family, there is a member (or members) who reinforces the behavior of the abusing family member. A spouse or significant other, for example, may make excuses for the family member or even prefer the behavior of the abusing family member when that family member is under the influence of alcohol or another drug. Some family members may not know how to relate to a particular family member when he or she is not "under the influence."

FAMILY SYSTEMS There have been many studies demonstrating the role of the family in the etiology of drug abuse (Baron, Abolmagd, Erfan, & El Rakhawy, 2010). As noted in Chapter 14, the family systems model focuses on the way roles in families interrelate (Tafa & Baiocco, 2009). Some family members may feel threatened if the person with the abuse problem shows signs of wanting to recover since caretaker roles, for example, would no longer be necessary within the family system if the member began behaving more responsibly. The possibility of adjusting roles could be so anxiety producing that members of the family begin resisting all attempts of the "identified patient" to shift relationships and change familiar patterns of day-to-day living within the family system.

FAMILY DISEASE This model is based on the idea that the entire family has a disorder or disease, and all must enter counseling or therapy for improvement to occur within the addicted family member. This is very different from approaches to family counseling in which the counselor is willing to work with whichever family members will come to the sessions, even though every family member is not present.

The Disease Model

The disease concept follows the medical model and posits addiction as an inherited disease that chemically alters the body in such a way that the individual is permanently ill at a genetic level (Lee et al., 2013, p. 4).

E. M. Jellinek (1960) is generally credited with introducing this controversial and initially popular model of addiction in the late 1930s and early 1940s (Stein & Foltz, 2009). However, it is interesting to note that, as early as the later part of the 18th century, the teachings and writings of Benjamin Rush, the Surgeon General of George Washington's revolutionary armies, actually precipitated the birth of the American disease concept of alcoholism as an addiction (White, 1998). In the context of this model, addiction is viewed as a primary disease rather than being secondary to another condition (reference the discussion, earlier in this chapter, of psychological models). Jellinek's disease model was originally applied to alcoholism but has been generalized to addiction to other drugs. In conjunction with his work, Jellinek also described the progressive stages of the disease of alcoholism and the symptoms connected with each stage. These stages (prodromal, middle or crucial, and chronic) were thought to be progressive and not reversible. Consistent with this concept of irreversibility is the belief that addictive disease is chronic and incurable. Once the individual has this disease, according to the model, it never goes away, and there is no treatment method that will enable the individual to use again without the high probability that the addict will revert to problematic use of the drug of choice. One implication of this philosophy is that the goal for an addict must be abstinence, which is the position taken by Alcoholics Anonymous (Fisher & Harrison, 2005). In addition, the idea that addiction is both chronic and incurable is the reason that addicts who are maintaining sobriety refer to themselves as "recovering" rather than as "recovered."

The vocabulary of *recovery* was first used by Alcoholics Anonymous in 1939. It is significant because we use the term *recovery* in the context of disease or illness rather than in connection with moral failure or character deficits. This reinforces the disease model to explain the etiology of addiction.

Interestingly, although Jellinek's disease model of addiction has received wide acceptance (Ferentzy & Turner, 2012), the research from which he derived his conclusions has been questioned. Jellinek's data were gathered from questionnaires. Of the 158 questionnaires distributed, 60 were discarded; no questionnaires from women were used. The questions about the original research, which led to the conceptualization of the "disease" model, have led to controversy. On the one hand, the articulation of addiction as a disease removes the moral stigma attached to addiction and replaces it with an emphasis on treatment of an illness, results in treatment coverage by insurance carriers, and sometimes encourages the individual to seek assistance much like that requested for diabetes, hypertension, or high cholesterol. On the other hand, the progressive, irreversible progression of addiction through stages does not always occur as predicted, and the disease concept may promote the idea for some individuals that one is powerless over the disease, is not responsible for behavior, may relapse after treatment, or may engage in criminal behavior to support the "habit."

The Public Health Model

It is interesting to note that the public health model was not originally conceptualized to focus on psychobehavioral ailments since, from its early beginnings, the emphasis has been on promoting healthy behaviors. As noted by Ferentzy and Turner (2012), the 20th-century psychiatrist Paul Lemkau, founding chairperson of the Mental Hygiene department in the Johns Hopkins

University School of Public Health, was one of the first to apply a public health model to mental disorders. Lemkau promoted the establishment of community, rather than residential, treatment centers because he believed that mental health, including the treatment of addiction, was a public rather than a private issue. Lemkau believed that when individuals did not engage in healthy behaviors and became addicted, it was because of the impact of social issues. He viewed addiction as a societal disease, in direct contrast to the more dominant, individualistic conceptions associated with the disease model.

The Developmental Model

As noted by Sloboda, Glantz, and Tarter (2012), the etiology of addiction can also be explicated by applying a developmental framework to understand the factors that increase or decrease risks for the individual to use or misuse drugs. They posited that vulnerability is never static or unchanging, but varies across the life span. Sloboda and her colleagues examined some of the key developmental competencies associated with the following developmental stages: prenatal through early childhood, middle childhood, adolescence, late adolescence/early adulthood, and adulthood. This research provided detailed examples of competencies that must be mastered during each of these developmental stages to decrease the possibility of engaging in risky behavior that includes the use and misuse of drugs. Readers interested in exploring the developmental model for understanding the etiology of addiction will find the Sloboda et al. (2012) an article excellent starting point for additional study.

Biological Models

Biophysiological and genetic theories assume that addicts are constitutionally predisposed to develop dependence on drugs. These theories or models support a medical model of addiction, apply disease terminology, and often place the responsibility for treatment under the purview of physicians, nurses, and other medical personnel. Usually, biological explanations branch into genetic and neurobiological discussions.

GENETIC MODELS Although genetic factors have never really been established as a definitive cause of alcoholism, the statistical associations between genetic factors and alcohol abuse are very strong. For example, it has been established that adopted children more closely resemble their biological parents than their adoptive parents when it comes to their use of alcohol (Dodgen & Shea, 2000; Goodwin, Hill, Powell, & Viamontes, 1973); alcoholism occurs more frequently in some families than others (Cotton, 1979); concurrent alcoholism rates are higher in monozygotic twin pairs than in dizygotic pairs (Kaij, 1960); and children of alcoholics can be as much as seven times more likely to be addicted than children whose parents are not alcoholic (Koopmans & Boomsina, 1995). Because of such data, some genetic theorists have posited that an inherited metabolic defect may interact with environmental elements and lead, in time, to alcoholism. Some research points to an impaired production of enzymes within the body and yet other lines of inquiry point to the inheritance of genetic traits that result in a deficiency of vitamins (probably the vitamin B complex), which leads to a craving for alcohol as well as the accompanying cellular or metabolic changes.

There have been numerous additional lines of inquiry that have attempted to establish a genetic marker that predisposes a person toward alcoholism or other addictions (Bevilacqua & Goldman, 2010). Studies that examined polymorphisms in gene products and DNA, the D2 receptor gene, and even color blindness as factors have all been conducted and then later more or less discounted. Genetic research on addiction shows potential, but is a complex activity given the fact that each individual carries genes located on 23 pairs of chromosomes. The Human

Genome Project, which is supported by the National Institutes of Health and the U.S. Department of Energy, is conducting some promising studies (NIAAA, 2000).

NEUROBIOLOGICAL MODELS Neurobiological models are complex (Jacob, 2013) and have to do with the neurotransmitters in the brain that serve as the chemical messengers of our brain (Hammer et al., 2012); Kranzler & Li, 2008; Wilcox, Gonzales, & Miller, 1998). Almost all addictive drugs, as far as we know, seem to have primary transmitter targets for their actions. The area of the brain in which addiction occurs is the limbic system or the emotional part of the brain. The limbic part of the brain refers to an inner margin of the brain just outside the cerebral ventricles, and the transmitter dopamine is key in its activity in the limbic system and the development of addiction. As a person begins to use a drug, changes in brain chemistry in the limbic system begin to occur and lead to addiction. Current thinking is that these changes can also be reversed by the introduction of other drugs in concert with counseling and psychotherapy.

Sociocultural Models

Sociocultural models have been formulated by making observations of the differences and similarities between cultural groups and subgroups. As noted by Goode (1972), the social context of drug use strongly influences drug definitions, drug effects, drug-related behavior, and the drug experience. These are contextual models and can only be understood in relation to the social phenomena surrounding drug use. A person's likelihood of using drugs, according to these models, the way he/she behaves, and the way abuse and addiction are defined are all influenced by the sociocultural system surrounding the individual.

SUPRACULTURAL MODELS The classic work of Bales (1946) provided some hypotheses connecting culture, social organization, and the use of alcohol. He believed that cultures that create guilt, suppress aggression and sexual tension, and that support the use of alcohol to relieve those tensions will probably have high rates of alcoholism. Bales also hypothesized that the culture's collective attitude toward alcohol use could influence the rate of alcoholism. Interestingly, he categorized these attitudes as favoring (1) abstinence, (2) ritual use connected with religious practices, (3) convivial drinking in a social setting, and (4) utilitarian drinking (drinking for personal reasons). The fourth attitude (utilitarian) in a culture that produces high levels of tension is the most likely to lead to high levels of alcoholism; the other three attitudes lessen the probability of high alcoholism rates. Another important aspect of Bales' thinking is the degree to which the culture offers alternatives to alcohol use to relieve tension and to provide a substitute means of satisfaction. A culture that emphasizes upward economic or social mobility will frustrate individuals who are unable to achieve at such high levels and increase the possibility of high alcoholism rates.

In 1974, Bacon theorized that high rates of alcoholism were likely to exist in cultures that combine a lack of indulgence toward children with demanding attitudes toward achievement and negative attitudes toward dependent behavior in adults. An additional important factor in supracultural models is the degree of consensus in the culture regarding alcohol and drug use. In cultures in which there is little agreement, a higher rate of alcoholism and other drug use can be expected. Cultural ambivalence regarding the use of alcohol and drugs can result in the weakening of social controls, which allows the individual to avoid being looked upon in an unfavorable manner.

CULTURE-SPECIFIC MODELS Culture-specific models of addiction are simultaneously fascinating and hampered by the possibilities inherent in promoting stereotypes and overgeneralizing about the characteristics of those who "seem" to fit the specific culture under consideration. For example, there are many similarities between the French and Italian cultures since both cultures are profoundly Catholic and both cultures support wineries and have populations that consume alcohol quite freely (Levin, 1989). The French drink both wine and spirits, with meals and without, at home as well as away from the family. The French often consider it bad manners to refuse a drink, and the attitudes toward drinking too much are usually quite liberal. The Italians drink mostly wine, with meals and at home, and they strongly disapprove of public misconduct due to the overconsumption of wine. They do not pressure others into accepting a drink.

In some Italian American families children over the age of about 10 can drink wine with dinner, but are admonished never to drink large amounts of wine; wine is to be enjoyed in social situations and is never to be consumed in excess. As a result, these children usually become adults who drink wine in moderation and never have problems derived by too much consumption of alcoholic beverages.

As the reader might expect from prior discussion, the rate of alcoholism in France is much more problematic than that which exists in Italy. Although the authors would agree that the prevailing customs and attitudes relating to the consumption of alcohol in a specific culture can provide insight and have usefulness as a possible explanation of the etiology of addiction in the culture under consideration, readers should be cautious about cultural stereotyping and make every attempt to address diversity issues in counseling as outlined in the current version of the Code of Ethics of the American Counseling Association (ACA) as well as the ACA guidelines for culturally competent counseling practices. (See the ACA website at www.counseling.org.)

SUBCULTURAL MODELS   It should also be briefly noted that there have been many investigations of both sociological and environmental causes of addiction and alcoholism at the subcultural level. Factors related to age, gender, ethnicity, socioeconomic class, religion, and family background can create different patterns within specific cultural groups (McNeese & DiNitto, 2005; White, 1998). They also can be identified as additional reasons why counselors and other members of the helping professions must vigilantly protect the rights of clients to be seen and heard for who they really are rather than who they might be assumed to resemble.

Multicausal Models

The great challenge to understanding the etiology of drug use and drug use disorders is the complexity of the phenomenon itself (Sloboda et al., 2012, p. 954).

At this point in your reading you may be wondering which of these etiological models or explanations of addiction is the correct model. As you may have already surmised, although all of these models are helpful and important information for counselors beginning their studies in addiction counseling, no single model adequately explains why some individuals become addicted to a substance and others do not. An important advance in the study of addiction is the realization that addiction is probably not caused by a single factor, and the most likely models for increasing our understanding and our development of treatment options are multivariate (Buu et al., 2009; McNeese & DiNitto, 2005; Stevens & Smith, 2005). Even though there may be some similarities in all addicted individuals, the etiology and motivation for the use of drugs varies from person to person. For some individuals, there may be a genetic predisposition or some kind of a physiological reason for use and later addiction to a drug. For others, addiction may be a result of an irregularity or disturbance of some kind in their personal development without a known genetic predisposition or physiological dysfunction. The possible debate over which model is the correct model is valuable only because it assists the practitioner to see the importance of adopting an interdisciplinary or multicausal model.

An interesting example of a multicausal model that has been proposed is the *syndrome model* of addiction (Shaffer et al., 2004). This model suggests that the current research pertaining to excessive eating, gambling, sexual behaviors, shopping, substance abuse, and so on does not adequately capture the origin, nature, and processes of addiction. The researchers believe that the current view of addictions is very similar to the view held during the early days of AIDS awareness when rare diseases were not recognized as opportunistic infections of an underlying immune deficiency syndrome. The syndrome model of addiction suggests that there are multiple and interacting antecedents of addiction that can be organized in at least three primary areas: (1) shared neurobiological antecedents, (2) shared psychosocial antecedents, and (3) shared experiences and consequences. Another promising example of a multicausal model is the *integral model* (Amodia, Cano, & Eliason, 2005). This integral approach examines substance abuse etiology and treatment from a four-quadrant perspective adapted from the work of Ken Wilbur. It also incorporates concepts from integrative medicine and transpersonal psychology. Readers are referred to the references cited in this subsection for more complete information about both the syndrome and integral models.

The multicausal model is similar to the public health model recently adopted by health care and other human service professionals. This model conceptualizes the problem of addiction as an interaction among three factors: the "agent" or drug, the "host" or person, and the "environment," which may be comprised of a number of entities. When the agent or drug interacts with the host, it is important to realize that there are a variety of factors within the host, including the person's genetic composition, cognitive structure and expectations about drug experiences, family background, and personality traits, that must be taken into consideration as a treatment plan is developed. Environmental factors that need to be considered include social, political, cultural, and economic variables. When a counselor or therapist uses a multicausal model to guide the diagnosis and treatment planning process, the complex interaction of several variables must be taken into consideration.

Summary and Some Final Notations

This chapter provided an overview of the historical evolution of approaches to the prevention of addiction in the United States. It chronicled the movement from the rudimentary and unregulated approaches of early practitioners to the more carefully regulated, credentialed, and evidence-based methods in use today. The social and political influences on the attitudes toward the use of drugs for both recreational and medical purposes were also addressed. A brief review of the federal government's role in funding agencies focused on the prevention of drug abuse as well as the provision of treatment for addicted individuals provided the background for some of the current policies influencing the prevention of addiction. Descriptions of the moral, psychological, family, disease, public health, developmental, biological, sociocultural, and multicausal models for understanding the etiology of addiction provided the reader with the background to understand topics covered in subsequent chapters of the text.

In addition to the first chapter on history and etiological models of addiction, Part I of our text, *Introduction to Addictions Counseling*, includes chapters on substance and process addictions, professional issues, interviewing clients, and assessment and diagnosis of addiction. These introductory chapters provide the background for Part II, *The Treatment of Addictions*, which provides a thorough examination of current treatment modalities. The seven chapters in this section address motivational interviewing, psychotherapeutic approaches, co-occurring disorders and addictions treatment, group work and addictions, pharmacological treatment of addictions, 12-step facilitation of treatment, and maintenance and relapse prevention. Part III, *Addictions in Family Therapy*,

Rehabilitation, and School Settings, provides the reader with needed perspective regarding variations in treatment modalities so necessary for competent counseling in specific settings. The chapters in this section discuss interventions with couples and families, persons with disabilities and addictions, and prevention programs for children, adolescents, and college settings. Part IV, *Cross-Cultural Counseling in Addictions*, addresses ethnic diversity, gender and addictions, and gay, lesbian, bisexual affirmative addiction treatment.

The final epilogue chapter presents an interesting discussion of the characteristics and issues connected with both inpatient and outpatient treatment of addiction.

Although it is impossible to include every conceivable topic that would be helpful to a counselor or therapist beginning the study of addictions counseling in a single text, we believe the information in this text is comprehensive enough in scope and sufficiently detailed to provide an excellent foundation for follow-up courses as well as supervised practicum and internship experiences for those wishing to develop a specialization in addictions counseling.

MyCounselingLab

Visit the MyCounselingLab site for *Foundations of Addictions Counseling*, Third Edition to enhance your understanding of concepts. You'll have the opportunity to practice your skills through video- and case-based exercises. You will find sets of questions to help you prepare for your certification exam with *Licensure Quizzes*. There is also a Video Library that provides taped counseling sessions, ethical scenarios, and interviews with helpers and clients.

Useful Websites

The following websites provide additional information relating to the chapter topics:

FUNDING OPPORTUNITIES

NIMH
www.nimh.nih.gov/

NIDA Extramural Affairs
www.drugabuse.gov/funding/

NIAAA
www.niaaa.nih.gov/

NIH Grants and Funding Opportunities
grants.nih.gov/grants/index.cfm
Enhancing Practice Improvement in Community-Based Care for Prevention and Treatment of Drug Abuse or Co-occurring Drug Abuse and Mental Disorders.
grants.nih.gov/grants/guide/rfa-files/RFA-DA-06-001.html

HRSA
www.hrsa.gov/grants/default.htm

FUNDING SOURCES FOR PREVENTION PROGRAMS

The Catalog of Federal Domestic Assistance (CFDA)
www.cfda.gov/
A database of all federal programs available to state and local governments (including the District of Columbia); federally recognized Indian tribal governments; territories (and possessions) of the United States; domestic public, quasi-public, and private profit and nonprofit organizations and institutions; specialized groups; and individuals.

Federal Register (FR)
www.gpoaccess.gov/fr/index.html
The Federal Register is the official daily publication for all federal agency funding notices. The bound version can be viewed at a local or university library.

The Foundation Center
www.fdncenter.org/
The Foundation Center's mission is to support and improve institutional philanthropy by promoting public understanding of the field and helping grantseekers succeed.

Foundations & Grantmakers Directory
www.foundations.org/grantmakers.html
This directory lists foundations and grantmakers by name.

The Grantsmanship Center
www.tgcigrantproposals.com
This resource is designed to help nonprofit organizations and government agencies write better grant proposals and develop better programs.

A starting point for accessing grant-related information and resources on the Internet.

GuideStar
www.guidestar.org/
GuideStar is a free information service on the programs and finances of more than 600,000 charities and nonprofit organizations. The database of nonprofit organizations is searchable by several different criteria. The site also offers news on philanthropy and other resources for donors and volunteers.

The Research Assistant
www.theresearchassistant.com/funding/index.asp
Resources for new and minority drug abuse researchers.

The Robert Wood Johnson Foundation (RWJF)
www.rwjf.org/index.jsp
RWJF, the largest U.S. foundation devoted to improving the health and health care of all Americans, funds grantees through both multisite national programs and single-site projects.

U.S. Department of Education (DOE)
www.ed.gov/topics/topics.jsp?&top=Grants+%26+Contracts
DOE only posts those grants currently open for competition at this site.

U.S. Department of Housing and Urban Development
www.hud.gov/grants/index.cfm

References

Amodia, D. S., Cano, C., & Eliason, M. J. (2005). An integral approach to substance abuse. *Journal of Psychoactive Drugs, 37*(4), 363–371.

Astramovich, R. L., & Hoskins, W. J. (2013). Evaluating addictions counseling programs: Promoting best practices, accountability, and advocacy. *Journal of Addictions & Offender Counseling, 34*(2), 114–124. doi:10.1002/j.2161-1874.2013.00019.x

Bacon, M. K. (1974). The dependency-conflict hypothesis and the frequency of drunkenness. *Quarterly Journal of Studies on Alcohol, 40,* 863–876.

Bales, R. F. (1946). Cultural differences in rates of alcoholism. *Quarterly Journal of Studies on Alcohol, 6,* 480–499.

Bandura, A. (1969). *Principles of behavior modification.* New York, NY: Holt, Rinehart, and Winston.

Baron, D., Abolmagd, S., Erfan, S., & El Rakhawy, M. (2010). Personality of mothers of substance dependent patients. *Journal of Multidisciplinary Healthcare, 3,* 29–32.

Bazelon Center for Mental Health Law. (2000). Legislative Update: 2000 SAMHSA reauthorization. Retrieved January 2006 from http://www.bazelon.org/takeaction/alerts/10-17-00samhsa.htm

Bevilacqua, L., & Goldman, D. (2010). Geonomics of addiction. *Current Psychiatry Reviews, 6,* a22–134.

Blocker, J. S. (2006). Did prohibition really work? Alcohol prohibition as a public health innovation. *American Journal of Public Health, 96*(2), 233–243.

Bray, R. M., Brown, J. M., Jones, S. B., Pemberton, M. R., Vandermaas-Peeler, R., & Williams, J. (2010, January). Alcohol use after forced abstinence in basic training among United States Navy and Air Force trainees. *Journal of Studies on Alcohol and Drugs, 71*(1), 15+.

Buu, A., DiPiazza, C., Wang, J., Puttler, L. I., Fitzgerald, H. E., & Zucker, R. A. (2009). *Journal of Studies of Alcohol and Drugs, 70,* 489–498.

CASA: National Center on Addiction and Substance Abuse at Columbia University. (2004). *Criminal neglect: Substance abuse, juvenile justice and the children left behind.* New York, NY: Author.

Catanzaro, P. (1967). Psychiatric aspects of alcoholism. In D. J. Pittman (Ed.), *Alcoholism.* New York, NY: Harper & Row.

Center for Substance Abuse Prevention. (1993). *Prevention primer: An encyclopedia of alcohol, tobacco and other drug prevention terms* (DHHS Publication No. SMA 2060). Rockville, MD: National Clearing House for Alcohol and Drug Information.

Cotton, N. A. (1979). The familial incidence of alcoholism. *Journal of Studies on Alcohol, 40,* 89–116.

Department of Health and Human Services. (2004). *National drug control strategy.* Washington, DC: Government Printing Office.

Dodgen, C. E., & Shea, W. M. (2000). *Substance use disorders: Assessment and treatment.* San Diego, CA: Academic Press.

Ferentzy, P., & Turner, N. E. (2012). Morals, medicine, metaphors, and the history of the disease model of problem gambling. *Journal of Gambling Issues, 27,* 1–27. doi:10.4309/jgi.2012.27.4

Fish, J. M. (2013). Rethinking drug policy assumptions. *Humanist, 73*(2), 12–15.

Fisher, G. L., & Harrison, T. C. (2000). *Substance abuse: Information for school counselors, social workers, therapists and counselors* (2nd ed.). Boston, MA: Allyn & Bacon.

Fisher, G. L., & Harrison, T. C. (2005). *Substance abuse: Information for school counselors, social workers, therapists and counselors* (3rd ed.). Boston, MA: Allyn & Bacon.

Goode, E. (1972). *Drugs in American society.* New York, NY: Alfred A. Knopf.

Goodwin, D. W., Hill, S., Powell, B., & Viamontes, J. (1973). The effect of alcohol on short-term memory in alcoholics. *British Journal of Psychiatry, 122,* 93–94.

Hall, W. (2010). What are the policy lessons of National Alcohol Prohibition in the United States, 1920–1933? *Addiction (Abingdon, England), 105*(7), 1164–1173. doi:10.1111/j.1360-0443.2010.02926.x

Hammer, R. R., Dingel, M. J., Ostergren, J. E., Nowakowski, K. E., & Koenig, B. A. (2012). The experience of addiction as told by the addicted: Incorporating biological understandings into self-story. *Culture, Medicine and Psychiatry, 36*(4), 712–734. doi:10.1007/s11013-012-9283-x

Hogan, J. A., Gabrielsen, K. R., Luna, N., & Grothaus, D. (2003). *Substance abuse prevention: The intersection of science and practice.* Boston, MA: Allyn & Bacon.

Iarussi, M. M., Perjessy, C. C., & Reed, S. W. (2013). Addiction-specific CACREP Standards in clinical mental health counseling programs: How are they met? *Journal of Addictions & Offender Counseling, 34*(2), 99–113. doi:10.1002/j.2161-1874.2013.00018.x

Jacob, C. (2013). Peter Riederer "70th birthday" neurobiological foundations of modern addiction treatment. *Journal of Neural Transmission, 120*(1), 55–64. doi:10.1007/s00702-012-0886-8

Jellinek, E. M. (1960). *The disease concept of alcoholism.* New Haven, CT: Hillhouse Press.

Kaij, L. (1960). *Alcoholism in twins: Studies on the etiology and sequels of abuse of alcohol.* Stockholm, Sweden: Almquist and Wiskell.

Koopmans, J. R., & Boomsina, D. L. (1995). *Familiar resemblances in alcohol use: Genetic or cultural transmission.* Amsterdam, The Netherlands: Department of Psychonomics, Vriji Univeriteit.

Kranzler, H. R., & Li, T. (2008). What is addiction? *Alcohol Research and Health, 31,* 93–95.

Lee, T. K., Craig, S. E., Fetherson, B. T. L., & Simpson, C. D. (2013). Addiction competencies in the 2009 CACREP Clinical Mental Health Counseling Program Standards. *Journal of Addictions & Offender Counseling, 34*(1), 2–15. doi:10.1002/j.2161-1874.2013.00010.x

Levin, J. D. (1989). *Alcoholism: A bio-social approach.* New York, NY: Hemisphere.

Lindgren, K. P., Mullins, P. M., Neighbors, C., & Blayney, J. A. (2010). Curiosity killed the cocktail? Curiosity, sensation seeking, and alcohol-related problems in college women. *Addictive Behaviors, 35,* 513–516.

Lubman, D. L., Yucel, M., & Pantelis, C. (2004). Addiction, a condition of compulsive behaviour? Neuroimaging and neuropsychological evidence of inhibitory dysregulation. *Society for the Study of Addiction, 99,* 1491–1502.

MacAndrew, C. (1979). On the possibility of the psychometric detection of persons who are prone to the abuse of alcohol and other substances. *Journal of Addictive Behaviors, 4,* 11–20.

McNeese, C. A., & DiNitto, D. M. (2005). *Chemical dependency: A systems approach* (3rd ed.). Boston, MA: Allyn & Bacon.

Milivojevic, D., Milovanovic, S. D., Jovanovic, M., Svrakic, D. M., Svrakic, N. M., Svrakic, S. M., & Cloninger, C. R. (2012). Temperament and character modify risk of drug addiction and influence choice of drugs. *The American Journal on Addictions, 21*(5), 462–467. doi:10.1111/j.1521-0391.2012.00251.x

National Institute on Alcohol Abuse and Alcoholism. (1996). *Alcohol alert* (no. 33). Washington, DC: U.S. Government Printing Office.

National Institute on Alcohol Abuse and Alcoholism (2000). *Tenth special report on alcohol and health to the U.S. Congress.* Washington, DC: U.S. Government Printing Office.

Raisitrick, D., & Davidson, R. (1985). *Alcoholism and drug addiction.* New York, NY: Churchill and Livingstone.

Rigg, K. K., & Murphy, J. W. (2013). Understanding the etiology of prescription opioid abuse: Implications for prevention and treatment. *Qualitative Health Research, 23*(7), 963–975. doi:10.1177/1049732313488837

Schuckit, M. A. (1986). Etiological theories on alcoholism. In N. J. Estes & M. E. Heinemann (Eds.), *Alcoholism; Development, consequences, and interventions* (3rd ed., pp. 15–30). St. Louis, MO: C. V. Mosby.

Shaffer, H. J., LaPlante, D. A., LaBrie, R. A., Kidman, R. C., Donato, A. N., & Stanton, M. V. (2004). Toward a syndrome model of addiction: Multiple expressions, common etiology. *Harvard Review of Psychiatry, 12,* 367–374.

Sloboda, Z., Glantz, M. D., & Tarter, R. E. (2012). Revisiting the concepts of risk and protective factors for understanding the etiology and development of substance use and substance use disorders: Implications for prevention. *Substance Use & Misuse, 47*(8/9), 944–962. doi:10.3109/10826084.2012.663280

Stein, D. B., & Foltz, R. (2009). The need to operationally define "disease" in psychiatry and psychology. *Ethical Human Psychology and Psychiatry, 11,* 120–141.

Stevens, P., & Smith, R.L. (Eds.). (2005). *Substance abuse counseling: Theory and practice.* Upper Saddle River, NJ: Merrill/Prentice Hall.

Tafa, M., & Baiocco, R. (2009). Addictive behavior and family functioning during adolescence. *The American Journal of Family Therapy, 37,* 388–395.

Weil, A., & Rosen, W. (1993). *Alcoholism: The nutritional approach.* Austin, TX: The University of Texas Press.

White, W. L. (1998). *Slaying the dragon: The history of addiction treatment and recovery in America.* Bloomington, IL: Chestnut Health Systems.

Wilcox, R. E., Gonzales, R. A., & Miller, J. D. (1998). Introduction to neurotransmitters, receptors, signal transduction and second messengers. In C. H. Nemeroff & A. E. Schatzberg (Eds.), *Textbook of psychopharmacology* (pp. 3–36). Washington, DC: American Psychiatric Press.

Chapter 2

Substance Addictions

Laura J. Veach
Wake Forest School of Medicine
Jennifer L. Rogers
Wake Forest University

Regina R. Moro
Barry University
E. J. Essic
Professional Counselor

Many tears are shed by those struggling with addiction. Tears are often accompanied by anger, frustration, fear, guilt, love, and loss. Think of this composite case: Jerry died too young struggling with addiction that eventually cost him his life and brought such grief to his splintered family, which was torn apart by an illness not yet grasped. Jerry had been a star athlete, kind brother, great son—now gone at 21, lost to our world. So many questions remain: Why did he get addicted? Why didn't he recover? Why couldn't we help him? So many whys, yet so few answers for many in our nation. The nature of addiction continues to baffle us, not only for Jerry's surviving loved ones but for many other loved ones who have lost so much because addiction took lives. It is equally baffling to differentiate key recovery predictors related to individuals who recover from individuals who do not. Looking for answers brings us to this chapter, where we search for knowledge about drugs, the brain, and addiction disorders.

Current estimates indicate that the extent of addiction disorders, with the exclusion of tobacco addiction, involves approximately 32 million Americans (James & Gilliland, 2005). The American Psychiatric Association (APA, 2013) estimates that in any given year approximately 8.5% of Americans aged 18 years or older meet new diagnostic criteria for an alcohol use disorder, 1.5% for cannabis use disorder, and approximately 0.3% for cocaine stimulant use disorders, for example. Throughout history, humans have used drugs to achieve desired changes of experiences; even ancient warriors "fortified themselves with alcohol before battle to boost their courage and decrease sensitivity to pain" (Weil & Rosen, 1983, p. 20). For some people, the ingestion of chemicals results in substance, or ingestive, addiction, which will be discussed at length in this chapter. For others, certain behaviors or processes, such as gambling, trigger process addiction, which will be reviewed in Chapter 3. Physical dependence is perhaps the most well known of the many features of the addictive process; as used in this chapter, the term *addiction* comprises all of these features. Recent emphasis among addiction specialists highlights the clarity provided by the term *addiction* rather than *dependency* or *habit*: "By emphasizing the behavioral aspects of compulsive substance use, addiction captures the chronic, relapsing, and compulsive nature of substance use that occurs despite the associated negative consequences" (Kranzler & Li, 2008, p. 93).

To better inform and prepare counselors, this chapter provides comprehensive information about the neurobiological and physiological factors regarding addiction. Tolerance and withdrawal aspects will also be reviewed. In addition, we also examine substances of addiction. First, we will discuss biological factors.

NEUROBIOLOGY AND THE PHYSIOLOGY OF ADDICTION

Records indicate that people sought help for drinking problems in Egypt approximately 5,000 years ago (White, 1998). Although substantial research exists today, many questions remain regarding addiction. Research continues to provide novel insights into the biology and treatment of addiction. However, there is to date no known single biological factor or explanation of addiction. Indeed, most addiction experts agree that "alcoholism and other addictions are complex, multiply-determined disorders in which biological and environmental factors interact to enhance personal vulnerability" (White, 1998, p. 289). Nevertheless, what has become increasingly clear is that "addictive behaviors are not the same as enhanced habits" (Yin, 2008, p. 342).

The organ of the body perhaps most researched in addiction is the brain. This research is referred to as neurobiology, and it is very complex. Consider the following: There are more than 100 billion neurons, or nerve cells, in the brain, with at least 40,000 connections, or synapses, for every neuron (Amen, 2005). Put differently, "the size of a grain of sand contains a hundred thousand neurons and one billion synapses, all 'talking' to one another" (Amen, 2005, p. 20). It is thought that while our neurons simply age over time, our synapses are different: they can change depending on our experiences—not only the experiences of our bodies, but also the experiences of our neurons, between which chemical messengers exchange information. For example, injuries to our brains, such as a stroke, cause permanent changes to neurons and synapses; it is thought that recovery in the brain often involves *brain plasticity*, the brain's ability to "repair, replace, and retrain its neural circuitry" (Taylor, 2006, p. 35).

Another experience that causes permanent damage to the brain is addiction, which can be thought of as a hijacking of the brain that causes many changes in the connections between neurons (Amen, 2005; Lubman, Yücel, & Pantelis, 2004). It has been likened to "Trojan horses that sneak into the nerve cells and take control" (Moyers & Ketcham, 2006, p. 278). Compelling neurobiology studies, which have contributed to a better understanding of the brain and its complex functions pertaining to addiction, have enabled specialists to begin to take back control. The National Institute on Drug Abuse (NIDA), a key leader in addiction research, considers addiction a brain disease that can be successfully treated (NIDA, 2010a). Researchers have identified specific areas within the brain most prone to the effects of euphoria-producing connections, chemicals, or processes. These areas have been studied closely with the goal of ascertaining how the addictive cycle is triggered. Currently, a number of brain studies show that "a common element

Neuroscience of the 12 Steps

Addiction is considered to be a chronic, or lifelong, disease by both the medical establishment and programs like Alcoholics Anonymous. There is increasing neuroscientific data suggesting that 12-step programs may help addicts achieve and maintain sobriety by protecting and enhancing the prefrontal cortex of the brain (Schnabel, 2009). The prefrontal cortex—which controls complex activities like self-monitoring, social thinking, abstract thought, and moral behavior—seems to be impaired in persons struggling with addiction. The processes of attending meetings (involving social interaction) and "working the steps" (involving abstract thought and moral behavior) may strengthen the prefrontal cortex to allow for abstinence (self-monitoring). According to Nora Volkow, director of the National Institute on Drug Abuse, "A lot of the treatment programs out there are targeting these systems without necessarily knowing that they are doing it."

Source: Schnabel, J. (2009). Neuroscience: Rethinking rehab. *Nature, 458* (7234), 25–27.

across these studies is the identification of [brain] regions whose impaired function perturbs the balance between reward and executive control networks" (Volkow & Baler, 2013, p. 662). Many addiction experts agree that the neurobiology of addiction is complex and remains challenging, even as we better understand how the brain changes with the onset of addiction.

A basic concept of the neurobiology of addiction is the "reward pathway," which comprises the areas of the brain most involved in addiction. The brain's limbic system is home to the areas of the brain thought to make up the reward pathway—the ventral tegmental area (VTA), nucleus accumbens, and the prefrontal cortex as shown in Figure 2.1 (NIDA, 2007). When stimuli activate these particular areas of the brain, pleasurable sensations are produced. Chemical messengers, called *neurotransmitters*, play critical roles in transmitting information between neurons through specialized gaps, or synapses. A synapse measures between 20 and 50 nanometers; a communication between neurons at the synapse happens within milliseconds (Lovinger, 2008). Dopamine is an important neurotransmitter involved in pleasurable sensations (Lubman et al., 2004). Curiously, dopamine is "made by very few cells in the brain and acts mainly within a subset of brain regions . . . and [it] seems to have a disproportionately large impact on brain function" (Lovinger, 2008, p. 204). In Figure 2.2, an illustration shows how cocaine, for example, interferes with the normal action of dopamine by blocking the removal, or reuptake, of this important neurotransmitter (NIDA, 2010b). For example, it is with the normal "reuptake," or removal, of dopamine with which cocaine interferes. The result is an increase of dopamine at the neurons and an overstimulation of receiving neurons called "neuroreceptors"—experienced by the user as pleasurable euphoria. An addict seeks to continue reexperiencing the euphoric sensation resulting from an abundance of powerful neurotransmitters, including dopamine. In the brain, this "dopaminergic transmission and reward pathway" is a primary feature of addiction (Lovinger, 2008; Lubman et al., 2004; NIDA, 2010b). Other important neurotransmitters, such as gamma-amino butyric acid (GABA) and glutamate, are identified in current research as significant when examining the brain's response to alcohol (Spirito, 2009). It is believed that advanced research will unlock more keys to understand GABA's special roles in inhibiting or slowing the dopaminergic surge (Riegal & Kalivas, 2010); intoxication, such as uncoordinated motor activity (stumbling, unsteady movements); anti-anxiety

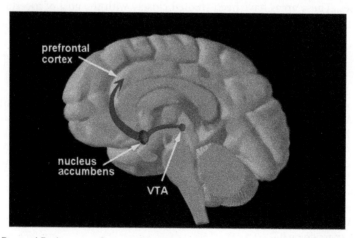

FIGURE 2.1 Reward Pathway   *Source:* National Institute on Drug Abuse. (2007). Retrieved from http://www.drugabuse.gov/publications/teaching-packets/understanding-drug-abuse-addiction/section-i/4-reward-pathway

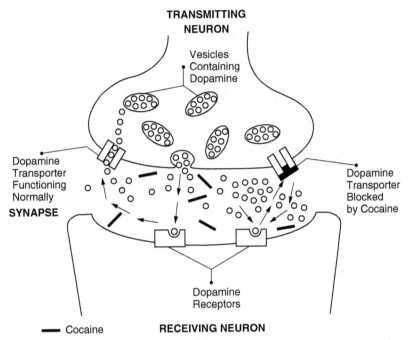

FIGURE 2.2 Cocaine Interfering with Neurons. *Source*: National Institute on Drug Abuse. (2005). Retrieved from http://science.education.nih.gov/supplements/nih2/addiction/guide/lesson3-1.htm

properties contributing to disinhibition, such as dancing on tables; and alcohol withdrawal complications (Lovinger, 2008). Glutamate, the predominant excitatory neurotransmitter in the brain, functions in many key aspects of the brain's operations such as learning and memory; alcohol's memory-impairing actions are thus better understood since, as only one of many of its effects on glutamate, alcohol interferes with the actions of this key neurotransmitter (Lovinger, 2008).

Brain researchers can test and assess living brain activity through the use of neuroimaging technology (Oscar-Berman & Marinkovic, 2004; Taylor, 2006). One such technique, positron emission tomography (PET), has further aided researchers by allowing them to visualize the effects of addictive chemicals and how brain activity differs between those using and those not using mood-altering substances.

In addition to understanding the role of the reward pathway in the addicted brain, neurobiology research is also investigating another complex hallmark of addiction, loss of control, described as continued drug use despite significant adverse consequences. Scientists have identified two frontal areas of the brain, the anterior cingulated cortex (ACC) and the orbitofrontal cortex (OFC), for this important neurological area of study; these areas are thought to be key components of another aspect of the brain, the inhibitory pathway. According to Lubman and colleagues (2004), for example, neuroimaging studies suggest that "compulsive behavior, as seen in both intractable addiction and OCD [obsessive-compulsive disorder], requires dysfunction within two highly interconnected cortical systems (ACC and OFC) critically involved in self-regulation (i.e., the inhibitory system)" (p. 1497).

Additional areas of intense study that address the compulsive nature of addiction and continued use despite adverse consequences (i.e., an inability to stop using even after major family, job, or integrity losses) involve another part of the brain, the cortico-basal ganglia network. Within this network lies the dorsal striatum, where substantial excitatory and inhibitory neurotransmitters work that are primarily involved in controlling behavior. The brain pathway that begins "from the VTA to the dorsal striatum is often referred to as the habit circuit, because of its vital role in conditioned learning" (Witkiewitz, Lustyk, & Bowen, 2013, p. 354). Yin notes "it is possible that all addictive drugs, including alcohol, can affect the capacity for change (i.e., plasticity) in the cortico-basal ganglia networks, thereby altering normal learning processes that are critical for selecting and controlling actions" (2008, p. 323). Mindfulness training and neuroimaging studies, also referred to as contemplative neuroscience, have produced other exciting outcomes that point to future directions for addiction treatment and brain healing (Witkiewitz et al., 2013). One specific new approach, termed *mindfulness-based relapse prevention* (MBRP), targets reduction of cravings and relapse; MBRP shows promise as an effective method to add in addiction counseling (Witkiewitz et al., 2013). Critical research suggests that as compulsive using and drinking continue, the brain sustains physical damage and becomes less capable of unlearning. Continued emphasis on brain circuitry alteration can assist counselors in improving their understanding and empathy when the addict cannot "just learn to stop" (Riegal & Kalivas, 2010).

At present, it is significant that researchers can now study, with neuroimaging equipment, the effect of drugs on the brain's functioning, both while under the influence of drugs and long after the drug has been eliminated from the body (NIDA, 2010a, 2010b). Notably, one neuropsychiatrist using scanning equipment for a number of years in addiction treatment notes that alcoholics "have some of the worst brains of all" (Amen, 2005, p. 81). Estimates indicate about half of approximately 20 million alcoholics in America have brain damage to some degree (Oscar-Berman & Marinkovic, 2004). Volkow and Baler (2013) highlight imaging studies that determined "relapsers show increased atrophy in bilateral orbitofrontal cortex and in the right medial prefrontal cortex and ACC, brain areas associated with error monitoring" (p. 663). Researchers have determined that some alcoholics seem to exhibit more damage to the right hemisphere of the brain than the left hemisphere (Oscar-Berman & Marinkovic, 2004). Research also suggests significant brain volume shrinkage (Crews, 2008; Sullivan & Pfefferbaum, 2005). Strikingly, "depending on age, the brain of the detoxified alcoholic can appear as ravaged as that of a patient with Alzheimer's disease. . ." (Sullivan & Pfefferbaum, p. 583). Additionally, substantial changes have been noted in the hippocampus of youth engaged in binge drinking (Taffe et al., 2010).

Cutting-edge neurobiology research now suggests that new brain cells may be created from the division of neural stem cells, a process called *neurogenesis*. It has been discovered that alcohol can significantly disrupt neurogenesis (Crews, 2008; Taffe et al., 2010). Accordingly, promising new approaches in the treatment of cocaine addiction, for example, may involve neurosurgical procedures such as deep brain stimulation, which is currently in use with certain patients with Parkinson's disease. Rouaud and colleagues (2009) examined the effect of deep brain stimulation in the subthalamic nucleus of rats and found evidence of a decrease in motivation for further cocaine. Extensive research with PET scans and other neuroimaging technology will add to the knowledge of the causes, effects, and treatment of addiction. These imaging tools, such as PET scans, are increasingly adding to the addiction specialist's treatment tools and "may make it possible to develop biomarkers to predict disease trajectories and therapeutic outcomes that are necessary for individualized medicine and optimal patient care" (Volkow & Baler, 2013, p. 663). Another exciting area of research has been enabled by the ability of modern computers to more quickly analyze and compare large amounts of data. Known as bioinformatics, or data mining, this powerful tool helps researchers synthesize findings (Hitzemann & Overbeck, 2008). One such tool, the GeneNetwork (Williams & Lu, 2008), focuses on gene expression arrays.

Other physiological factors, such as tolerance and withdrawal symptoms, are important to our understanding of addiction. Tolerance, the brain and central nervous system's neuroadaptation to continual surges of neurotransmitters, has often been misunderstood (NIDA, 2010a). Many drinkers, including those who binge drink, mistakenly believe that they are somehow less at risk of addiction if they demonstrate greater tolerance. For example, heavy drinkers may brag that they "can drink others under the table" and show little impairment. In fact, studies indicate that a high metabolic and pharmacodynamic tolerance yields a greater risk for alcohol dependency—the body is already doing something different in metabolizing a neurotoxin (National Institute on Alcohol Abuse and Alcoholism [NIAAA], 2005; van Wormer & Davis, 2013). When the body becomes more efficient in processing and eliminating a mood-altering substance, the term *metabolic tolerance* is accurate (Doweiko, 2015). Thus, those who drink heavily are at higher risk for developing substance use disorders and display tolerance. Tolerance is one of the first signs of physical dependency (Doweiko, 2015), and the counselor is well advised to address binge drinking or drug-abusing patterns earlier rather than later. As molecular scientists conduct extensive laboratory research into the neural mechanisms involved in tolerance and addiction, there is increasing evidence supporting the involvement of complex molecular and genetic influences pertaining to alcohol tolerance (Lovinger, 2008; Pietrzykowski & Treistman, 2008).

Tolerance helps explain why approximately 11% of the drinking population consumes over 50% of the alcohol in this country (Knapp, 1996; van Wormer & Davis, 2013). It takes increasing amounts of mood-altering chemicals or processes to achieve the desired effect when tolerance develops. For example, ongoing research focused on increasing trends of risky drinking patterns of college athletes. Researchers noted that nearly 60% (59.4%) of those surveyed reported patterns of heavy drinking, consuming at least five or more drinks at any one sitting (National Collegiate Athletic Association [NCAA], 2006). Of importance is the finding that slightly more than 18% of the athletes who drink report drinking 10 or more drinks at any one drinking occasion, thus demonstrating markedly increased tolerance (NCAA, 2006).

To further illustrate this, let us look at a sample case. Susan is a 20-year-old student athlete in college. Now in her junior year, she is a strong competitor on her college swim team. Susan began drinking in her freshman year of college and would feel euphoric effects after one drink. With continued drinking, perhaps on weekends, Susan noticed after 3 months that she could have four drinks and experience minimal euphoria, so she increased her intake to achieve the desired effect. In this example, Susan found that having five or six drinks during any one drinking episode was not unusual for her, yet for a female, four or more drinks per drinking episode is defined as abusive drinking. For males, binge drinking is defined as the consumption during any one drinking episode of five or more drinks (NIAAA, 2005; Watson, 2002). With continued drinking over multiple years, Susan saw her tolerance increase. She now reports drinking at least six drinks on any one occasion, with minimal effects.

Because of a recent arrest for Driving Under the Influence (DUI), Susan goes to a counselor. The counselor should note that heavy alcohol use in women increases the chances of osteoporosis (NIAAA, 2005), a serious condition, and one of major concern to a physically active individual like Susan. The counselor should also understand that recent research indicates that women have a greater incidence of complications from alcohol use and experience more physical damage with less alcohol in a shorter time frame than males (Miller, 2004; NIAAA, 2005). Although some studies have shown that one drink daily, and no more, may have cardiovascular benefits, there is also evidence that for women, such daily consumption may increase breast cancer risks (NIAAA, 2005). It is important for the beginning counselor to also attend to issues regarding tolerance and possible physical withdrawal from drugs, especially alcohol. Fortunately, Susan agrees to continue counseling to address her drinking issues. How will you determine whether Susan is a risky drinker or alcohol dependent? What counseling approach do you think

TABLE 2.1 Commonly Abused Drugs (NIDA, 2012a)

NIDA — NATIONAL INSTITUTE ON DRUG ABUSE

Commonly Abused Drugs
Visit NIDA at www.drugabuse.gov

National Institutes of Health
U.S. Department of Health and Human Services
NIH... Turning Discovery Into Health

Substances: Category and Name	Examples of Commercial and Street Names	DEA Schedule*/How Administered**	Acute Effects/Health Risks
Tobacco			
Nicotine	Found in cigarettes, cigars, bidis, and smokeless tobacco (snuff, spit tobacco, chew)	Not scheduled/smoked, snorted, chewed	Increased blood pressure and heart rate/chronic lung disease, cardiovascular disease, stroke; cancers of the mouth, pharynx, larynx, esophagus, stomach, pancreas, cervix, kidney, bladder and acute myeloid leukemia; adverse pregnancy outcomes; addiction
Alcohol			
Alcohol (ethyl alcohol)	Found in liquor, beer, and wine	Not scheduled/swallowed	In low doses, euphoria, mild stimulation, relaxation, lowered inhibitions; in higher doses: drowsiness, slurred speech, nausea, emotional volatility, loss of coordination, visual distortions, impaired memory, sexual dysfunction, loss of consciousness/ increased risk of injuries, violence, fetal damage (in pregnant women); depression; neurologic deficits; hypertension, liver and heart disease; addiction, fatal overdose
Cannabinoids			
Marijuana	Blunt, dope, ganja, grass, herb, joint, bud, Mary Jane, pot, reefer, green, trees, smoke, sinsemilla, skunk, weed	I/smoked, swallowed	Euphoria, relaxation, slowed reaction time, distorted sensory perception, impaired balance and coordination, increased heart rate and appetite; impaired learning, memory; anxiety, panic attacks, psychosis/cough; frequent respiratory infections; possible mental health decline; addiction
Hashish	Boom, gangster, hash, hash oil, hemp	I/smoked, swallowed	
Opioids			
Heroin	Diacetylmorphine: smack, horse, brown sugar, dope, H, junk, skag, skunk, white horse, China white; cheese (with OTC cold medicine and antihistamine)	I/injected, smoked, snorted	Euphoria; drowsiness; impaired coordination; dizziness; confusion; nausea; sedation; feeling of heaviness in the body; slowed or arrested breathing/constipation; endocarditis; hepatitis; HIV; addiction; fatal overdose
Opium	Laudanum, paregoric: big O, black stuff, block, gum, hop	II, III, V/swallowed, smoked	
Stimulants			
Cocaine	Cocaine hydrochloride: blow, bump, C, candy, Charlie, coke, crack, flake, rock, snow, toot	II/snorted, smoked, injected	Increased heart rate, blood pressure, body temperature, metabolism; feelings of exhilaration; increased energy, mental alertness; tremors; reduced appetite; irritability; anxiety; panic, paranoid, violent behavior; psychosis/weight loss; insomnia; cardiac or cardiovascular complications; stroke; seizures; addiction
Amphetamine	Biphetamine, Dexedrine: bennies, black beauties, crosses, hearts, LA turnaround, speed, truck drivers, uppers	II/swallowed, snorted, smoked, injected	Also, for cocaine—nasal damage from snorting
Methamphetamine	Desoxyn: meth, ice, crank, chalk, crystal, fire, glass, go fast, speed	II/swallowed, snorted, smoked, injected	Also, for methamphetamine—severe dental problems
Club Drugs			
MDMA (methylenedioxymethamphetamine)	Ecstasy, Adam, clarity, Eve, lover's speed, peace, uppers	I/swallowed, snorted, injected	MDMA—mild hallucinogenic effects; increased tactile sensitivity, empathic feelings; lowered inhibition, anxiety, chills, sweating, teeth clenching, muscle cramping/sleep disturbances; depression; impaired memory; hyperthermia; addiction
Flunitrazepam***	Rohypnol: forget-me pill, Mexican Valium, R2, roach, Roche, roofies, roofinol, rope, rophies	IV/swallowed, snorted	Flunitrazepam—sedation; muscle relaxation; confusion; memory loss; dizziness; impaired coordination/addiction
GHB***	Gamma-hydroxybutyrate: G, Georgia home boy, grievous bodily harm, liquid ecstasy, soap, scoop, goop, liquid X	I/swallowed	GHB—drowsiness; nausea; headache; disorientation, loss of coordination, memory loss/unconsciousness; seizures; coma
Dissociative Drugs			
Ketamine	Ketalar SV: cat Valium, K, Special K, vitamin K	III/injected, snorted, smoked	Feelings of being separate from one's body and environment; impaired motor function/anxiety; tremors; numbness; memory loss; nausea
PCP and analogs	Phencyclidine: angel dust, boat, hog, love boat, peace pill	I, II/swallowed, smoked, injected	Also, for ketamine—analgesia; impaired memory; delirium; respiratory depression and arrest; death
Salvia divinorum	Salvia, Shepherdess's Herb, Maria Pastora, magic mint, Sally-D	Not scheduled/chewed, swallowed, smoked	Also, for PCP and analogs—analgesia, psychosis, aggression; violence; slurred speech; loss of coordination; hallucinations
Dextromethorphan (DXM)	Found in some cough and cold medications: Robotripping, Robo, Triple C	Not scheduled/swallowed	Also, for DXM—euphoria; slurred speech; confusion; dizziness; distorted visual perceptions
Hallucinogens			
LSD	Lysergic acid diethylamide: acid, blotter, cubes, microdot, yellow sunshine, blue heaven	I/swallowed, absorbed through mouth tissues	Altered states of perception and feeling; hallucinations; nausea
Mescaline	Buttons, cactus, mesc, peyote	I/swallowed, smoked	Also, for LSD and mescaline—increased body temperature, heart rate, blood pressure; loss of appetite, sweating; sleeplessness; numbness; dizziness; weakness; tremors; impulsive behavior, rapid shifts in emotion
Psilocybin	Magic mushrooms, purple passion, shrooms, little smoke	I/swallowed	Also, for LSD—Flashbacks, Hallucinogen Persisting Perception Disorder
			Also, for psilocybin—nervousness; paranoia; panic
Other Compounds			
Anabolic steroids	Anadrol, Oxandrin, Durabolin, Depo-Testosterone, Equipoise: roids, juice, gym candy, pumpers	III/injected, swallowed, applied to skin	Steroids—no intoxication effects/hypertension; blood clotting and cholesterol changes; liver cysts; hostility and aggression; acne; in adolescents—premature stoppage of growth; in males—prostate cancer, reduced sperm production, shrunken testicles, breast enlargement; in females—menstrual irregularities, development of beard and other masculine characteristics
Inhalants	Solvents (paint thinners, gasoline, glues); gases (butane, propane, aerosol propellants, nitrous oxide); nitrites (isoamyl, isobutyl, cyclohexyl): laughing gas, poppers, snappers, whippets	Not scheduled/inhaled through nose or mouth	Inhalants (varies by chemical)—stimulation; loss of inhibition; headache; nausea or vomiting; slurred speech; loss of motor coordination; wheezing/cramps; muscle weakness; depression; memory impairment; damage to cardiovascular and nervous systems; unconsciousness; sudden death

TABLE 2.1 Commonly Abused Drugs (NIDA, 2012a)

Substances: Category and Name	Examples of Commercial and Street Names	DEA Schedule*/ How Administered**	Acute Effects/Health Risks
Prescription Medications			
CNS Depressants	For more information on prescription medications, please visit http://www.nida.nih.gov/DrugPages/PrescripDrugsChart.html		
Stimulants			
Opioid Pain Relievers			

* Schedule I and II drugs have a high potential for abuse. They require greater storage security and have a quota on manufacturing, among other restrictions. Schedule I drugs are available for research only and have no approved medical use. Schedule II drugs are available only by prescription (unrefillable) and require a form for ordering. Schedule III and IV drugs are available by prescription, may have five refills in 6 months, and may be ordered orally. Some Schedule V drugs are available over the counter.

** Some of the health risks are directly related to the route of drug administration. For example, injection drug use can increase the risk of infection through needle contamination with staphylococci, HIV, hepatitis, and other organisms.

*** Associated with sexual assaults.

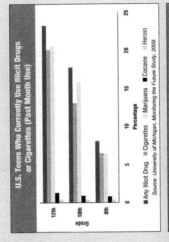

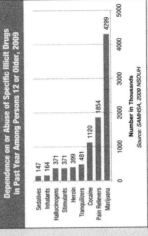

Principles of Drug Addiction Treatment

More than three decades of scientific research show that treatment can help drug-addicted individuals stop drug use, avoid relapse and successfully recover their lives. Based on this research, 13 fundamental principles that characterize effective drug abuse treatment have been developed. These principles are detailed in NIDA's *Principles of Drug Addiction Treatment: A Research-Based Guide*. The guide also describes different types of science-based treatments and provides answers to commonly asked questions.

1. **Addiction is a complex but treatable disease that affects brain function and behavior.** Drugs alter the brain's structure and how it functions, resulting in changes that persist long after drug use has ceased. This may help explain why abusers are at risk for relapse even after long periods of abstinence.

2. **No single treatment is appropriate for everyone.** Matching treatment settings, interventions, and services to an individual's particular problems and needs is critical to his or her ultimate success.

3. **Treatment needs to be readily available.** Because drug-addicted individuals may be uncertain about entering treatment, taking advantage of available services the moment people are ready for treatment is critical. Potential patients can be lost if treatment is not immediately available or readily accessible.

4. **Effective treatment attends to multiple needs of the individual, not just his or her drug abuse.** To be effective, treatment must address the individual's drug abuse and any associated medical, psychological, social, vocational, and legal problems.

5. **Remaining in treatment for an adequate period of time is critical.** The appropriate duration for an individual depends on the type and degree of his or her problems and needs. Research indicates that most addicted individuals need at least 3 months in treatment to significantly reduce or stop their drug use and that the best outcomes occur with longer durations of treatment.

6. **Counseling—individual and/or group—and other behavioral therapies are the most commonly used forms of drug abuse treatment.** Behavioral therapies vary in their focus and may involve addressing a patient's motivations to change, building skills to resist drug use, replacing drug-using activities with constructive and rewarding activities, improving problem solving skills, and facilitating better interpersonal relationships.

7. **Medications are an important element of treatment for many patients, especially when combined with counseling and other behavioral therapies.** For example, methadone and buprenorphine are effective in helping individuals addicted to heroin or other opioids stabilize their lives and reduce their illicit drug use. Also, for persons addicted to nicotine, a nicotine replacement product (nicotine patches or gum) or an oral medication (bupropion or varenicline), can be an effective component of treatment when part of a comprehensive behavioral treatment program.

8. **An individual's treatment and services plan must be assessed continually and modified as necessary to ensure it meets his or her changing needs.** A patient may require varying combinations of services and treatment components during the course of treatment and recovery. In addition to counseling or psychotherapy, a patient may require medication, medical services, family therapy, parenting instruction, vocational rehabilitation and/or social and legal services. For many patients, a continuing care approach provides the best results, with treatment intensity varying according to a person's changing needs.

9. **Many drug-addicted individuals also have other mental disorders.** Because drug abuse and addiction—both of which are mental disorders—often co-occur with other mental illnesses, patients presenting with one condition should be assessed for the other(s). And when these problems co-occur, treatment should address both (or all), including the use of medications as appropriate.

10. **Medically assisted detoxification is only the first stage of addiction treatment and by itself does little to change long-term drug abuse.** Although medically assisted detoxification can safely manage the acute physical symptoms of withdrawal, detoxification alone is rarely sufficient to help addicted individuals achieve long-term abstinence. Thus, patients should be encouraged to continue drug treatment following detoxification.

11. **Treatment does not need to be voluntary to be effective.** Sanctions or enticements from family, employment settings, and/or the criminal justice system can significantly increase treatment entry, retention rates, and the ultimate success of drug treatment interventions.

12. **Drug use during treatment must be monitored continuously, as lapses during treatment do occur.** Knowing their drug use is being monitored can be a powerful incentive for patients and can help them withstand urges to use drugs. Monitoring also provides an early indication of a return to drug use, signaling a possible need to adjust an individual's treatment plan to better meet his or her needs.

13. **Treatment programs should assess patients for the presence of HIV/AIDS, hepatitis B and C, tuberculosis, and other infectious diseases, as well as provide targeted risk-reduction counseling to help patients modify or change behaviors that place them at risk of contracting or spreading infectious diseases.** Targeted counseling specifically focused on reducing infectious disease risk can help patients further reduce or avoid substance-related and other high-risk behaviors. Treatment providers should encourage and support HIV screening and inform patients that highly active antiretroviral therapy (HAART) has proven effective in combating HIV, including among drug-abusing populations.

This chart may be reprinted. Citation of the source is appreciated.

Source: National Institute on Drug Abuse. (2012). *Commonly abused drugs.* Retrieved from http://www.drugabuse.gov

would be most helpful for this athlete? How would you gauge your rapport and empathy with her? What will you do if she continues risky drinking?

Substance withdrawal refers to the physiological changes that occur when a substance leaves the body. These changes, depending on their severity, can provide evidence that pharmacodynamic tolerance is present. Most withdrawal symptoms, which are usually the opposite of the drug effects, can begin within 4 hours of last use and may continue for varying lengths of time, usually 3–7 days, depending on the substance, degree of physical dependence, genetic factors, and overall health of the person (Doweiko, 2015). At its most benign, a hangover after an episode of heavy drinking is one example of substance withdrawal. In its more complicated progression, withdrawal, depending on the drug use, can manifest as mild to extreme tremors; nausea or vomiting; mood disturbances such as pronounced anxiety, depressed mood, and increased irritability, or *anhedonia*; neurological disturbances such as delusions, headaches, sleep disturbance, mild to severe seizures, or delirium tremens involving visual, auditory, or tactile hallucinations; physiological conditions such as diarrhea, goose bumps, fever, or rhinitis; and cardiac complications including elevated blood pressure, pulse, and cardiac arrhythmias (Doweiko, 2015; van Wormer & Davis, 2013). Complicated alcohol withdrawal, for example, is one of the most serious life-threatening types of withdrawal and nearly 15% of alcohol-dependent individuals can have withdrawal seizures if not medically detoxified.

SUBSTANCES OF ADDICTION

There are a number of chemical substances with addictive properties. The most recent data in the United States regarding patterns of illicit drug use point toward increasing use (NIDA, 2014a). To better understand these substances, they are classified into the following categories: depressants, opioids, stimulants, cannabinoids, and hallucinogens. Table 2.1 shows commonly abused illicit and prescription drugs, the Drug Enforcement Agency (DEA) Schedule regulating drugs, route of administration, drug effects, and health risks in a chart prepared by the National Institute on Drug Abuse (NIDA, 2012a). History shows a pattern of increasing concentration levels to better achieve maximum euphoric effects.

Depressants

ALCOHOL It is important to understand the most commonly abused substances that jeopardize the health and well-being of an individual. By far, the most abused mood-altering substance today is ethanol, or ethyl alcohol, with approximately 71% of people in the United States over age 18 reporting alcohol consumption within the previous 12 months in 2012 (NIAAA, 2014), and nearly a quarter of drinkers reported binge drinking within the recent month (Substance Abuse and Mental Health Services Administration [SAMHSA], 2013). Note the alcohol consumption per capita values displayed in Table 2.2. The Centers for Disease Control and Prevention (CDC) and NIAAA note that excessive drinking is the primary risk factor leading to injury, and a major cause of death, ranking third in the United States (NIAAA, 2014). This translates to one preventable fatality that is alcohol related every 48 minutes and nearly 51 billion dollars in total costs for alcohol-related crashes (CDC, 2013). Alcohol is "humanity's oldest domesticated drug" (Siegal & Inciardi, 2004, p. 78), and no one is immune from its potential for addiction. Regarding its effects and attraction, Knapp writes that alcohol is "the drink of deception: alcohol gives you power and robs you of it in equal measure" (1996, p. 95).

TABLE 2.2 Apparent Per Capita Alcohol Consumption: National, State, and Regional Trends, 1977–2011

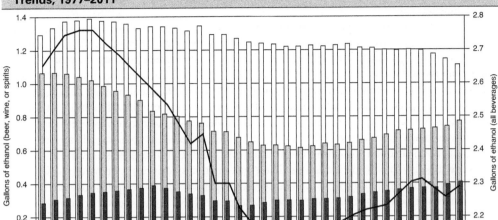

Source: LaVallee, R. A., LeMay, H. A., & Yi, H.-Y. (2013). *Surveillance Report #97*. Retrieved from http://pubs.niaaa.nih.gov/publications/survelliance97/CONS11.htm

Alcohol has certainly been evident in anthropological records for centuries, although it is not clear how it was first discovered. Historians generally believe it was about 10,000 years ago, after berries or fruits left too long in the sun began fermenting, resulting in a crude version of wine (Erickson, 2001; Siegal & Inciardi, 2004). Distilling alcohol to get higher potency began around 800 A.D. in Arabia. Jabir ibn Hayyan, otherwise known as Geber, in searching for an alchemy formula, burned impurities in wine and thus discovered distilled spirits (Spicer, 1993). Distillation, however, was not popular until the 13th century, when a university professor in France, Arnauld de Villeneuve, promoted this new type of alcohol as a cure for diseases (Spicer, 1993).

Alcohol is classified as a depressant to the central nervous system. As such, it often was used as an anesthetic or sleep aid. Drinking to achieve relaxation and euphoria contributed to the reputation of alcohol as a desirable social lubricant due to its disinhibition and relaxation effects. However, alcohol is also a powerful neurotoxin, and alcoholism leads to critical areas of damage to key executive brain functioning with a "profound untoward effect on the cerebrum and cerebellum" (Sullivan & Pfefferbaum, 2005, p. 590).

Many addiction specialists and addiction counselor educators emphasize that the critical ingredient in alcohol is ethanol, whether a person consumes beer, wine, or distilled liquor. It is important for those counselors working with clients discussing information about alcohol use to address the common misconception that some alcoholic beverages are safer or less addicting than others. Some individuals have rationalized that since beer, for example, is only 5% ethanol, it is less harmful, and hence less addicting. What is important to understand is that "the same quantity of alcohol is consumed if someone drinks either a 12-ounce can or bottle of beer, a three- to four-ounce glass of wine, or a mixed drink made with one and one-half ounces of distilled spirits" (Siegal & Inciardi, 2004, p. 75). Although the overall sizes of the drinks vary, the amount of ethanol is equivalent, and it is ethanol that is the significant addicting agent in alcoholic beverages.

To better determine the potency of ethanol, the term *proof* is used to indicate the beverage's strength or, in other words, the percentage of pure ethanol in the beverage. Using the standard formula, one roughly doubles the percentage of ethanol to determine potency; for example, wine is generally around 7% alcohol, equating to 14 proof; the same is true for over-the-counter cough and cold preparations containing alcohol, such as popular brands that may be 20% alcohol, or surprisingly, 40 proof. Conversely, to determine the percentage of ethyl alcohol in a beverage, one can divide by half the designated proof, for example, 151-proof rum is 75.5% ethanol.

Physiologically, when alcoholic beverages are consumed, ethanol is readily absorbed into the bloodstream through the lining of the stomach and small intestine, so its mood-altering effects are usually felt within 20 minutes. The effect of ethanol can be moderated by a variety of factors such as food in the stomach, total body weight, gender, and the response to alcohol (tolerance). There are notable gender differences. Researchers have established that women achieve higher blood alcohol content (BAC) levels when consuming the exact same amount of alcohol as males (NIAAA, 2005; Oscar-Berman & Marinkovic, 2004). Explanations of this difference point out that women experience higher alcohol concentrations due to lower dilution rates, since women have less water weight per pound than men (NIAAA, 2005). Because several researchers noted women show more severe consequences, faster progression through the stages of alcohol dependency, and higher BACs, the term *telescoping* is often used when describing women's responses to alcohol (Gilbertson, Prather, & Nixon, 2008). Questions remain whether this telescoping effect is due to gender differences, as neuroscientists using neuroimaging have observed micro- and macrostructural brain damage differences between male and female alcoholics (Gilbertson et al., 2008). Gender issues pertaining to substances are also discussed in greater detail in Chapter 18.

The effects of alcohol are experienced biologically for as long as the ethanol remains in the body. The liver is the major organ responsible for eliminating, or detoxifying, alcohol. The main job of the liver is to metabolize or excrete toxins, processing ethanol as a toxin to the system (Doweiko, 2015)—hence the appropriate term, *intoxicated*. The liver processes ethanol at relatively the same speed and rate for most people. Myths of drinking pots of hot coffee or taking frequent cold showers do not speed the rate at which the liver metabolizes ethanol (van Wormer & Davis, 2013). No substance exists that can accelerate the rate of breakdown of ethanol (Siegal & Inciardi, 2004). Of particular note to the counselor regarding ethanol-metabolizing rates are the number of young people who die each year as a direct result of alcohol poisoning (Falkowski, 2000). Often those with little experience drinking alcohol do not understand that overintoxication can be fatal. Since death due to overintoxication occurs infrequently, awareness of this danger is often limited, so it is important that counselors stress the risk one takes when consuming large quantities of alcohol quickly. Respiratory arrest or aspiration of vomit have been the leading fatal factors in recent high-profile deaths of inexperienced young college drinkers after imbibing large quantities of alcohol in a short time period (Falkowski, 2000).

An additional important concept for the counselor to understand is the method of measuring the amount of alcohol in one's body. To determine the amount of alcohol in the bloodstream, a BAC is often measured either by a breathalyzer or a blood sample. There are a number of portable, easy-to-use breathalyzer instruments available for measuring BAC. Ordinarily a BAC level is best obtained within 12 hours after drinking as the ethanol may be eliminated from the body after this time period. The relatively short elimination time for alcohol is one of the main reasons a breathalyzer is the preferred measuring method, as opposed to a urine drug screen, the preferred method for measuring other drug levels.

Hospital emergency rooms and trauma units are the most likely setting to obtain blood samples for alcohol levels, often due to alcohol-related injuries such as falls, burns, and motor vehicle crashes. The National Highway Traffic Safety Administration (NHTSA, 2012) estimates that a person dies every 51 minutes in an alcohol-related crash in the United States. Further, new reports of deaths from impaired driving find that less than 20% of impairment is due to additional other drugs (CDC, 2013); alcohol is the primary drug involved in impaired-driver fatalities. Health care costs are extensive when trauma injury, such as injuries received in a motor vehicle crash, are alcohol related. Alcohol screening for risky drinking and brief counseling intervention (ASBCI) studies in trauma settings have recently demonstrated such efficacy that the American College of Surgeons' Standards now require ASBCI services in all Level I Trauma Centers in the United States (American College of Surgeons, 2006). This innovative policy mandates that Level I Trauma Centers use the "teachable moment" generated by traumatic alcohol-related injury (approximately 45–50% of trauma patients) as a gateway to effective prevention of future alcohol abuse, especially with underage and young adult drinkers, and to decrease or delay the onset of alcohol use disorders (SAMHSA, 2007). Nationally, many Level 1 and 2 hospital trauma centers are increasing routine alcohol screenings and brief counseling interventions in concentrated efforts to reduce trauma recidivism and impact risky drinking patterns (SAMHSA, 2007; Schermer, 2005). The use of an evidence-based screening tool, such as a positive finding of binge drinking, is used to help identify risky drinkers (SAMHSA, 2007). This new prevention strategy indicates that a brief counseling intervention has a powerful impact that facilitates changes in future behavior (Dunn et al., 2008; Leontiva et al., 2009; O'Brien, Reboussin, Veach, & Miller, 2012; Toumbourou et al., 2007) and reduces hospital trauma recidivism by 50% (Crawford et al., 2004; Gentilello et al., 1999). One study examining youth aged 12–18 admitted to a hospital with major injuries found that alcohol counseling during their hospitalization reduced alcohol consumption in addition to further injury (Dunn et al., 2008). By far, those deemed risky drinkers (approximately 30% of drinkers) have a favorable response to ASBCI, may delay or prevent alcohol dependency by changing risky drinking patterns, and improve their overall health. More than 50% of alcohol-impaired drivers involved in a fatal automobile crash have a BAC at or above .15 (NHTSA, 2012). Currently all 50 states and the District of Columbia have enacted .08 BAC laws stating that any driver with a BAC at or above .08 would be charged with operating a vehicle illegally, commonly referred to as DUI (NHTSA, 2012). Drivers aged 21–25 were reporting driving under influence (26.1%) at more than twice the average rate in the United States (12.4%; 30.9 million individuals) (SAMHSA, 2009).

Employers are also affected by alcohol-related trauma: The total cost to employers related to automobile crashes where at least one driver was alcohol impaired is more than $9 billion annually and of that total, $3.1 billion is directly related to alcohol impairment on the job (NHTSA, 2004). Recent data further indicated that in 2008, 56.2% of whites aged 12 and above reported current alcohol use, followed by 43.3% of persons identified as American Indians or Alaska Natives, 43.2% for persons of Hispanic descent, 41.9% of African-Americans, and 37% of persons identified as Asian (SAMHSA, 2009). The SAMHSA data further showed the highest rate of binge drinking patterns was noted in the Hispanic population (25.6%). Youth are not immune to alcohol-related trauma. Toumbourou et al. (2007) examined current studies regarding patterns of alcohol use worldwide and noted "hazardous alcohol use alone has been estimated to cause 31.5% of all deaths in 15–29 year old men in the developed world and 86% of the 3.6 million substance-related deaths of 15–29 year old men and women worldwide" (p. 1391).

Their findings also show that harmful use and abuse rather than dependence make up the majority of problems in substance use among adolescents. Miller, Levy, Spicer, and Taylor (2006) calculated that in the United States, alcohol use by minors accounted for approximately 16% of all alcohol sales in 2001. Their findings further illustrated cost by calculating that 3,170 deaths, 2 million other harmful events, $5.4 billion in medical costs, $14.9 billion from loss of work or other resources, for a total cost of $41.6 billion in lost quality of living, were all attributed to underage drinking. The findings noted that alcohol-related violent acts and motor vehicle crashes were primary factors in the cost analysis. The CDC also identified patterns of alcohol use among high school students (9th–12th graders) in its biannual Youth Risk Behavior Surveillance Survey (YRBSS); in 2007, three-fourths (75%) of students reported consuming one or more alcoholic beverages in their lifetime, with slightly over one-fourth (26%) indicating a pattern of heavy drinking as defined by five or more drinks during any one drinking occasion on at least one day in the month preceding the survey (2009). On closer examination, it is of particular note that just under half (40.4%) of male 12th graders indulged in binge drinking in the month prior to the survey, far exceeding the next highest percentage of binge drinkers (26.1%) who were 18–24 years of age (CDC, 2009). Further comparison data indicate, for example, that less than a tenth (7.8%) of those aged 55–64 reported similar binge drinking patterns (Centers for Disease Control and Prevention, 2009). College students aged 18–22 were found to have the highest binge drinking rates (40.5%), with approximately 16% deemed heavy drinkers (SAMHSA, 2009).

Case Study. In an informal survey done by a student reporter for the high school newspaper, it was reported that almost 20% of the student body used either cigarettes or smokeless tobacco (which were viewed as much safer than cigarettes). While the numbers for most illicit drug use was low, 1 in 15 students reported recreational use of prescription drugs ranging from OxyContin to Ritalin. Almost 70% of the 300 students surveyed reported alcohol use within the past 6 months, with 41% reporting semiregular binge drinking (30% of 11th and 12th graders and 11% of 9th and 10th graders).

What major issues should the school counselor and faculty be concerned about, and how might they go about effectively addressing these issues? Which behaviors offer the highest risks and why? Which behaviors, and with whom, would you address first? Discuss how you think these students compare to national averages, including illicit drug use.

In summary, alcohol abuse, addiction, and risky drinking create significant problems for many people. The addiction counselor benefits from increased knowledge and awareness about

Addiction, Mental Health, and Childhood Trauma

In a recent study examining traumatic childhood events among persons diagnosed with both substance use and mental health disorders who were being treated in an in-patient setting, 65.9% of the 402 participants reported emotional abuse and neglect during their childhood (Wu, Schairer, Dellor, & Grella, 2010). Physical abuse was reported by 49.3%, sexual abuse was reported by 48%, and family violence was reported by 56%. The severity of childhood traumatic events was scored on a 6-point scale. Each unit increase in severity of trauma increased the risk of lifetime alcohol dependence by 18% and tobacco use by 16%. As has been found in previous research, there is strong correlation between substance use, mental health diagnoses, and childhood trauma, suggesting the ecological complexity of substance abuse.

Source: Wu, N. S., Schairer, L. C., Dellor, E., & Grella, C. (2010). Childhood trauma and health outcomes in adults with comorbid substance abuse and mental health disorders. *Addictive Behaviors, 35*(1), 68–71.

the most commonly abused substance, alcohol, which impacts far more individuals in a negative way than any other mood-altering chemical substance.

Case Study. Because several members of Ellen's family, including both parents, were alcoholic, she abstained from alcohol until she was 29, when she began drinking socially. Six years later, her drinking began affecting her job. An increasing pattern of absenteeism, tardiness, and attitude problems resulted in a confrontation with her boss, who required she get an assessment and follow any recommendation made. The results indicated a high degree of tolerance, and a multitude of social and physical problems related to her drinking. She insists that she drinks only wine, not hard liquor, does not drink every day, and never before evening, so she is certain that alcohol is not a problem.

What areas of her life need more exploration? What kinds of data and counseling techniques might a counselor use to help break through Ellen's denial and increase her motivation to address the issues alcohol is causing in her life?

Counseling in a Hospital Trauma Center: A Doctoral Counseling Student's Perspective

When someone is admitted to a trauma center in America, there is around a 50% chance that the incident that brought him or her there will have involved alcohol consumption. It is no wonder, then, that Level I Trauma Centers in the United States are required to provide patients with both alcohol screening and brief counseling intervention, when problem drinking is indicated. The manner in which those services are delivered varies across institutions. Currently, only a few use professional counselors. One of these is the Wake Forest Baptist Medical Center (WFBMC) trauma center. This vignette offers one counselor's observations about the alcohol screening and brief counseling intervention done there, drawn from the writer's experience over the course of about one year. It is an experience that has been overwhelmingly positive.

The setting at the WFBMC trauma center is dynamic and fast paced. Mornings begin with surgery rounds, during which each patient's plan of care is reviewed with a multidisciplinary care team. Amid a cacophony of ringing phones and buzzing pagers, medical professionals engage in intense conversations, exploring, inquiring, and debating one another in an effort to ensure provision of the best care. The counselor's contributions to the discussion are critical: sharing each patient's blood alcohol level upon admittance; recommending, when necessary, a Clinical Institute Withdrawal Assessment (CIWA); noting other important mental health concerns she may have gleaned during a visit with a patient in recent days.

The trauma center is not a traditional counseling setting. At any moment, a physician may call requesting a session with a patient with a substance abuse history or a nurse may pull me aside in the hall with concerns about a patient. Moreover, the patients do not present as traditional clients. A trauma patient does not schedule an appointment. Each and every one bears the fresh physical and emotional wounds of the terrible incident that put them where they lay: a gunshot, a stabbing, a serious fall, a crushing car accident. Some are lucky even to have survived. All likely are in one of the most vulnerable states, both physically and emotionally, they ever have been.

It is the counselor who is equipped to assist such patients as they struggle with a trauma fresh in their minds. It is the counselor, sitting at their bedside, to whom they express frustration, sadness, and confusion. Many, in such moments, recognize that addiction or substance abuse led them to this frightening place. It is through counseling that these individuals are able to consider the risks associated with their behavior. And, often, it is through counseling that they may decide to make a change.

Many of the patients I visited not only were willing to discuss their concerns about their drinking habits, but eager. While some express ambivalence, many hope for a better future and desperately crave a new beginning. It is the honor and privilege of the counselor to assist them as they begin their journey, even if only for a brief time. My experience in the WFBMC trauma center has provided a valuable new perspective on counseling and what it means to be a counselor. The work is challenging, compelling, and rewarding. It has afforded the unique opportunities both of learning, first hand, the inner workings of a hospital setting and of collaborating with interdisciplinary teams. The physicians, medical students, physician assistants, and nurses alongside whom I work have shown an appreciation for and understanding of the complex psychosocial issues with which their patients have presented. It is evident that WFBMC trauma center values providing high-quality, integrated care. Counselors have been included as a part of the team. From this counselor's perspective, their inclusion has proven vital.

Leigh Zick Dongre, M.A., LPCA, NCC, is a Ph.D. student in Counselor Education and Supervision at the University of North Carolina at Charlotte. She is a Graduate Assistant for the Trauma Service and Burn Unit at Wake Forest Baptist Medical Center from May 2013 to the present.

Counseling in a Hospital Trauma Center: A Master's Student Reflecting on Her Practicum

When I began my graduate studies in counseling at Wake Forest University, I had been out of school for a quarter of a century. I felt a sense of urgency when picking my practicum site, knowing that my experiences during the semester's placement would be the foundation on which I would build my professional career. I felt called to serve at a site that would stretch my abilities and challenge my confidence, and my experience in the trauma unit at WFBMC has afforded me countless opportunities to take what I have learned so far in my coursework and translate it into action. No patient on the trauma floor has *chosen* to spend time in the hospital. Removed from the normality of day-to-day life, patients often feel isolated, confused, and overwhelmed by the sights and sounds of a trauma ward. In addition to the physical stresses of injury following a traumatic event, there is a sense of emotional vulnerability that is palpable as I enter into a patient's room. While my first responsibility is to provide support, I also have the opportunity to conduct alcohol screening and brief interventions with patients who meet the criteria, and have discovered, much to my initial surprise, that a hospital bed is fertile ground for self-assessment and is often where decisions to change are born. Recovering from trauma, patients are often very willing to look at their lifestyle and behaviors regarding their use of alcohol, and I have been astounded at the eagerness many patients demonstrate when considering their drinking habits. Taking the opportunity to conduct an Alcohol Use Disorder Identification Test (AUDIT) inventory with patients provides them a lens through which they may assess their choices and consider whether changes in those choices may positively impact their lives. I have been humbled by the openness and meaningful self-assessment that I have witnessed during my time on "Reynolds 11." No matter where I go in my professional and academic career, I *will* encounter clients struggling with addiction. Having this opportunity to see what change can look like in patients who have endured a physical trauma has been a true privilege.

Sara W. Bailey is a Graduate Student in the Counseling Department of Wake Forest University. She is the 2014–2015 WFU Counseling Department Anderson Fellow at the Memory Assessment Clinic Counseling Center at Wake Forest Baptist Medical Center.

The **Teachable Moment**, focused on alcohol screening, brief counseling interventions, and policy implications in a Level I Trauma Center at Wake Forest University Baptist Medical Center in North Carolina, is a 3-year prospective clinical trial research study funded by the Substance Abuse Policy Research Program of The Robert Wood Johnson Foundation. Principal Investigator: **Mary Claire O'Brien**, M.D.; Co-Investigators: **Laura J. Veach**, Ph.D., Preston Miller, M.D., and **Beth Reboussin**, Ph.D.

Janeé R. Avent, Ph.D. *(Assistant Professor of Counseling, University of Texas San Antonio; former student, University of North Carolina at Greensboro):* One of the most stressful times for a counseling graduate student is finding an internship site. As always, I chose to embark on something that was both new and seemingly quite challenging. I selected a new internship in the Trauma Center of Wake Forest University Baptist Medical Center. I did not know what to expect coming into this internship. When I began my internship, I had limited counseling experience and had never worked in a hospital setting.

This learning experience has been both challenging and rewarding. Challenging in that it is never an easy task to walk unexpectedly into a client's hospital room in the trauma center to talk with them about their alcohol use. Challenging in that it is difficult to ask concerned family members to step out of the room while I talk with their loved one in confidence about risky drinking. There is also a personal emotional challenge that comes with witnessing someone in such physical and affective pain concurrently.

Nonetheless, for every measure of challenge, there is an even greater sense of reward. It is so easy to view oneself as the expert, but it never ceases to amaze me how much the clients teach me—they teach me about strength, determination, and humility. Many are willing to be vulnerable and discuss personal issues surrounding alcohol and related injuries because they are willing to do whatever is necessary to make healthy changes in their lifestyles. Even the clients who are not ready to discuss change remind me that I am here to plant a seed and hopefully one day that seed will grow.

Due to the support and respect I receive from the entire Trauma community, this experience has been very rewarding. The learning curve has been very steep and there has been a significant amount to process at one time, but it has been manageable because of the trust and reassurance I gain from the Trauma surgeons and staff, my clinical supervisors, and the Teachable Moment research team. If internship is the time when one is shaping clinical approach and preparing for a future career in counseling, then I can only be excited about the possibilities that exist not only for me but for the counseling profession. There are new opportunities that unfold every day, and I have the ability to work with populations that I had not anticipated, but I have come to appreciate and greatly enjoy.

Janeé R. Avent is an Assistant Professor at the University of Texas San Antonio. She was the Counseling Intern for the Trauma Service and Burn Unit of Wake Forest Baptist Medical Center June 2009–May 2010.

SEDATIVES/HYPNOTICS Another classification of drugs that depress the central nervous system is sedative/hypnotic drugs. The most common drugs in this group are benzodiazepines, barbiturates, and nonbarbiturates. Currently, benzodiazepines, sometimes referred to as tranquilizers, are frequently prescribed for a wide range of symptoms, from sleeplessness, anxiety, and muscular strain, to seizures (Erickson, 2001). They are of particular risk for women. For instance, findings show women are 55% more likely to be prescribed benzodiazepines than are men (NIDA, 2005). With their discovery in the 1960s, many heralded them as a much safer alternative to barbiturates in the belief that no addictive potential existed. Decades later, researchers found that benzodiazepines, such as Valium (diazepam) or Xanax (alprazolam), are highly addictive with long-term use and often have serious withdrawal complications requiring medical detoxification. Researchers also note that benzodiazepines, even taken as prescribed by a physician, are toxic to the brain, as evidenced with brain scanning techniques showing "an overall diminished or dehydrated pattern of activity, just as with drugs of abuse" (Amen, 2005, p. 79). Benzodiazepines are often prescribed as the initial drug for treating anxiety despite research showing limited effectiveness with long-term use, in part due to tolerance issues. Short-term use (4–8 weeks) may show maximum effect for anxiety, but other medications, such as antidepressants with anti-anxiety actions, are far more effective for long-term anxiety management without the addictive potential as seen with benzodiazepines (Doweiko, 2015).

Concerns about benzodiazepine abuse and addiction are growing. For example, trend analyses note a 41% increase (from 71,609 to 100,784) in benzodiazepine-related emergency department visits between 1995 and 2002 (Crane & Lemanski, 2004). Addiction treatment admissions in which tranquilizers were the primary drug of addiction climbed 79% over a 10-year period, 1992–2002 (SAMHSA, 2005). For women, it is a particularly troublesome pattern when "men lead women in numbers of addicts for every substance except prescription medications" (Briggs & Pepperell, 2009, p. 20).

Another concern about benzodiazepines is their potential for use as a date-rape drug. Rohypnol (flunitrazepam), a benzodiazepine with amnesiac properties that is approximately 10 times more potent than Valium, has been used in sexual assault crimes (Falkowski, 2000).

Central nervous system depressants also include barbiturates, such as Tuinal (amobarbital with secobarbital) or Nembutal (pentobarbital). Barbiturates use was most prevalent during the 1950s through the 1970s when, at that time, they were second only to alcohol as a drug of abuse (Erickson, 2001). Barbiturates are fast-acting. Within the brain, neurotransmitters and depolarizing activity decreases, thereby further depressing the central nervous system and thus making barbiturates dangerous in their potential for lethal overdose, especially if combined with other central nervous system depressants (Erickson, 2001).

Nonbarbiturates include drugs such as Quaalude (methaqualone) and have much the same physiological profile as barbiturates. Because of accidental overdosing dangers associated with both barbiturates and nonbarbiturates, their use, fortunately, has declined.

Case Study. Daphne, a 35-year-old African-American married mother of two, has struggled with anxiety since she was young, but has done well and graduated with a master's degree in nursing 2 years ago. This year she was hired to teach nursing students in a hospital program. Due to her anxiety, her physician prescribed Valium. She loves her job, but feels that the stress of being "on stage" can only be managed with the help of her medication. For 6 months, her physician continued to prescribe the sedative, but has refused to prescribe it any longer because she is demanding more and stronger dosages in order to cope. Daphne has come to you in hopes of convincing the psychiatrist in your practice to prescribe Valium for her.

What are the issues here, and how would you address them? If she continues to work with you, what kind of treatment plan would you create with her, and what are some of the modalities you might employ?

Opioids

Opium is "the parent of all narcotic drugs" (Weil & Rosen, 1983, p. 80) and contains 20 different drugs, the primary one being morphine. Opioids, derivatives of opium compounds, are abused because of their ability to affect the brain's reward pathway dramatically and produce a longer-lasting euphoria that includes initial sensations compared often to orgasm, followed by drowsy bliss-like states. Opioid use disorders continue to have a profound impact in our culture. Morphine was used extensively in the Civil War and the resulting addictive patterns became known as "soldier's disease" (Stevens, 2009).

Heroin, more potent than morphine, was not extracted from opium until 1895 and heralded because it reduced the side effects associated with morphine (Stevens, 2009). In the United States, for decades, many prevention and addiction specialists focused on heroin abuse and addiction due to its highly addictive nature and potency.

Intravenous injection is the preferred route of administration in heroin addiction; however, recent trends indicate an increase in the use of heroin by snorting and smoking, possibly due to higher grade potency in recent years and heightened awareness of HIV infection risks (Dziegielewski & Suris, 2005). One addict's case example describes the heroin addictive cycle aptly as "a shot of heroin and all that pain and suffering gets instantly traded in for rainbows, warm sunshine, and laughter. . . . [F]ear of withdrawal combined with the easy access of high purity heroin is what keeps so many addicted" (Dziegielewski & Suris, 2005, p. 155).

Long-term efforts to recover from heroin addiction may include use of a slower-acting opioid, such as methadone, to assist the heroin addict in harm reduction. After three decades of methadone maintenance programs, methadone is generally regarded as effective in harm reduction for opioid and heroin addiction treatment (Dziegielewski & Suris, 2005). A newer, slow-acting synthetic opiate, buprenorphine, is also gaining in use as an alternative to methadone (Doweiko, 2015) and is used in treating opioid addiction. One study by Horton et al. (2009) stressed that even past use of heroin, found in as many as 1 in 4 of those seeking residential substance abuse treatment, indicates a greater tendency for riskier behaviors, poorer outcomes, and higher relapse potential, possibly related to clinical dissociation patterns. Horton and colleagues encourage better screening for dissociative disorders among clients with a history of heroin use in addition to continued research.

OxyContin is the trade name for one synthetic opioid that has received extensive media attention due to its abuse potential and addictive features. Recent information, for example, indicates that in 2001 more than 7.2 million prescriptions were written for OxyContin, resulting in sales of $1.45 billion, increasing the next year to sales of $1.59 billion (Inciardi & Goode, 2004). From 1994 to 2002, NIDA (2005) noted a 450% increase in oxycodone-related medical emergencies. The continued search for other pain management medications in lieu of opioids because of their serious addictive properties remains important. Overall, addiction specialists view opiate abuse and addiction with significant concern. More research is needed to better understand the neurobiology of opiate addiction to develop more effective treatment resources.

Case Study. Injured in an accident, Peter, a 23-year-old separated white male, was hospitalized for several weeks and given morphine for pain. Upon discharge, OxyContin was prescribed. Two months after release, Peter continues to describe high levels of pain. He has seen his physician twice to request more and stronger dosages of OxyContin. Today he made a third appointment and his estranged wife called the physician to discuss her concerns over Peter's continued pain, as well as his changing behavior, including irritability, work absenteeism, and his often groggy appearance. Peter told her that he is having flashbacks about the accident and that the medication seems to help alleviate these as well as his physical pain.

As a counselor, discuss how you and the doctor can help Peter deal with his emotional and physical issues. Discuss the complications of the addictive and medical issues present, and how addiction theory and practice can be put to use in this example.

Stimulants

TOBACCO The primary mood-altering substance in tobacco products is nicotine, a mild stimulant. It is believed that the indigenous people of the Americas used tobacco long before the first white Europeans arrived. The resulting history and expansion of the use of tobacco has had profound effects. Tobacco addiction is associated with the deaths of 100 million people in the 20th century (NIDA, 2010a). It is important to examine trends among youth since substantial prevention efforts have been implemented to reduce tobacco use. In 2008, adolescents aged 12–17 showed a declining trend of tobacco use since 2002, decreasing from 15.2 to 11.4%, with most of that decline attributed to decreasing cigarette use (SAMHSA, 2009). However, slightly over one-fifth of adults continue to smoke despite evidence of serious health risks associated with smoking (Stevens, 2009).

Cigarette use is associated with those addicted to other substances. In 2008, one survey found that heavy alcohol intake was associated with tobacco use; 58% of heavy drinkers also smoked cigarettes in the same month (SAMHSA, 2009).

In an effort to find the benefits of nicotine without the dangers associated with becoming a smoker, some rationalized that chewing or smokeless tobacco might be less dangerous to one's health; adolescent trends have remained relatively stable, with approximately 2% of 12- to 17-year-olds reporting monthly use of smokeless tobacco (SAMHSA, 2009). More evidence indicates that smokeless tobacco, for example, carries significant health risk for hypertension, coronary artery disease, oral cancer, oral lesions, and tumors (Doweiko, 2015; Prentice, 2003). Medications such as Bupropion, Varenicline, and nicotine replacement aids are increasingly utilized to treat tobacco addiction (NIDA, 2010a).

Case Study. Many studies have shown a high concurrent use of cigarettes with alcohol and other substance use. Many treatment centers have instituted no-smoking policies, believing that in addition to the risks posed by nicotine addiction, continued tobacco use may heighten the likelihood of relapse for recovering alcoholics and drug addicts. Others believe that forcing a nicotine-dependent person to stop smoking when he or she is in substance abuse treatment may cause that person to drop out of treatment, thus lessening the chances of recovery from the primary addiction. A new treatment center, ChangeNOW, is totally smoke-free.

When consulting with this new treatment center, what conceptual views would you support and why? How would you address these issues with both the counselors you are consulting with (several of whom smoke) and with a new client, a heavy smoker, who really wants a referral from you to this new facility?

What About Caffeine Addiction?

Many people have had the experience of having ingested too much or too little coffee in the morning. Among mood-altering drugs, caffeine is the most widely used worldwide. It is regularly consumed by over 85% of children and adults in the United States. The DSM-5 describes diagnostic criteria for four caffeine-related conditions: caffeine intoxication, caffeine withdrawal, other caffeine-induced disorders (e.g., sleep-related, anxiety), and unspecified caffeine-related disorder. Also, Caffeine Use Disorder is included in the DSM-5's Section III—indicating that more research is required to ascertain whether it is a clinically significant disorder. Researchers at American University recently developed the Caffeine Withdrawal Symptom Questionnaire (CWSQ), the first validated measure of caffeine withdrawal symptoms. In their rigorously designed double-blind study, seven major types of symptoms emerged: (1) fatigue/drowsiness, (2) low alertness/difficulty concentrating, (3) mood disturbances, (4) low sociability/motivation to work, (5) nausea/upset stomach, (6) flu-like feelings, and (7) headache. The researchers hope that their ongoing work refining this instrument will serve to help in the assessment, diagnosis, and understanding of caffeine withdrawal.

Sources: American Psychiatric Association. (2013). *Diagnostic and statistical manual of mental disorders* (5th ed.). Arlington, VA: American Psychiatric Publishing.

Juliano, L. M., Huntley, E. D., Harrell, P. T., & Westerman, A. T. (2012). Development of the Caffeine Withdrawal Symptom Questionnaire: Caffeine withdrawal symptoms cluster into 7 factors. *Drug and Alcohol Dependence, 124*(3), 229–234.

EPHEDRINE, AMPHETAMINES, AND AMPHETAMINE-LIKE MEDICATIONS Other types of stimulants include ephedrine, amphetamines, and amphetamine-like medications (e.g., Ritalin, Concerta). Unlike many other mood-altering substances that are primarily used for the euphoria produced by the drug, amphetamines are often used for the euphoric experience and to enhance productivity. Although, as Weil and Rosen point out, "instead of automatically improving physical and mental performance, stimulants sometimes just make people do poor work faster" (1983, p. 38).

Abuse of Prescription Stimulants by Young People

Researchers identified 21 studies representing a total of 113,104 subjects in a recent systemic review of the medical literature examining the prevalence of nonprescribed stimulant medication use among children and young adults (Wilens et al., 2008). According to the research, 5–9% of grade school and high school students reported taking nonprescribed stimulant medications (i.e., Ritalin, Adderall) in the last year. The reported rates among college-age persons ranged from 5 to 35%. Among those people who had a prescription for stimulants, 16–29% had been asked to give, trade, or sell their medications. Reasons stated for using nonprescribed stimulants included improving alertness and concentration, experimenting, and getting high. Persons at the highest risk for misusing and diverting stimulants included whites, members of fraternities and sororities, individuals with lower grade point averages, those prescribed immediate-release compared to extended-release preparations, and individuals who reported attention deficit hyperactivity disorder (ADHD) symptoms.

Source: Wilens, T., Adler, L., Adams, J., Sgambati, S., Rotrosen, J., Sawtelle, R., Utzinger, L., & Fusillo, S. (2008). Misuse and diversion of stimulants prescribed for ADHD: A systematic review of the literature. *Journal of the American Academy of Child and Adolescent Psychiatry, 47*(1), 21–31.

Ancient Chinese medicine began using plants containing ephedrine over 5,000 years ago; more recent medical refinement resulted in extensive use in the United States after 1930 for problems mainly affecting the respiratory system. The legal ban in 2004 of ephedrine (Hall, 2004) was a result of a drug fraught with significant side effects. Almost 70 years ago efforts to find a synthetic alternative to ephedrine with fewer side effects (such as anxiety) and better outcomes resulted in the pharmaceutical development of amphetamines.

Several addiction experts note that *speed* (a slang term for amphetamines) was used extensively by military personnel during wartime in the 1940s to improve endurance and alertness (Miller, 2004; Weil & Rosen, 1983). In the 1950s, it was injected as a treatment to stop heroin addiction (Miller, 2004). Amphetamine use in the 1960s and 1970s spiraled, with "approximately 10 billion amphetamine tablets manufactured in the United States in the year 1970" (Doweiko, 2009, p. 118). With such extensive amphetamine use, many of the negative side effects such as agitation with severe anxiety, cardiovascular damage, paranoia, severe depression, drug-induced psychosis, and withdrawal-induced suicidal ideation were discovered. Warnings about the abuse and addiction potential of speed were commonplace in the early 1970s with slogans such as "Speed Kills" (Johnston, 2010). Overall, the illicit use of amphetamines has been problematic, highlighted by increasing methamphetamine-related episodes; NIDA (2014b) documented that substantial brain changes can be observed with imaging studies showing both chemical and cellular changes in the brains of chronic and prolonged methamphetamine abuse. Current research shows an increasing overall usage rate of amphetamines among athletes (4.1%), including greater use of stimulants by females as compared to male athletes, and higher rates of use in white athletes as compared to their non-white peers (NCAA, 2006).

Current research shows an increasing overall usage rate of amphetamines among athletes (4.1%) including greater use of stimulants by females as compared to male athletes, and higher rates of use in white athletes as compared to their nonwhite peers (NCAA, 2006). Methamphetamine ("meth") is often the preferred stimulant of abuse and can be taken by mouth, snorted, smoked, or most problematically, injected. Recovering amphetamine addicts show continued slower physical movement and impaired memory even after ceasing any methamphetamine use for 9 months, and researchers are further concerned that addicts may have an increased risk for other neurodegenerative diseases (Zickler, 2002). The methamphetamine manufacturer cautions in the *Physician's Desk Reference* (PDR) that "methamphetamine has a high potential for abuse . . . [that] may lead to drug dependence" (*Physician's Desk Reference*, 2002, p. 440). Tolerance to methamphetamine develops quickly, which can exacerbate the addictive cycle. Often, end-stage addiction includes intravenous administration and severe withdrawal, profound weight loss, extreme dental complications, severe risk of contracting HIV and hepatitis B and C, intense craving patterns, brain damage, and often, significant cardiac complications (NIDA, 2014c). Culturally, a primary diagnosis of a methamphetamine/amphetamine use disorder is most often seen in non-Hispanic white individuals (66%); next, individuals of Hispanic origin (21%); and lastly 3%, respectively, in Asian/Pacific Island or non-Hispanic black individuals (APA, 2013). Encouraging data from 2008 show the rates of monthly use of methamphetamine decreased over 50% between 2006 and 2008 in the United States (SAMHSA, 2009). Further, reports by the DEA (2013) cite a 67% reduction in methamphetamine use by teens from 2000 through 2012.

Alternatives to pharmaceutically produced amphetamines are illicit amphetamines. One example is a form of methamphetamine known as "ice" and, more recently, methcathinone or "Kat." Both Kat and ice produce stimulant effects and have many of the same risks and side effects as amphetamines; because of the lowered cost associated with illicit amphetamines—averaging $15 per gram—combined with the relative ease of manufacturing the drug, illegal methamphetamine labs remain a significant concern in many communities (Stevens, 2009). One report, in an effort to educate individuals to better detect illegal methamphetamine-making labs, stressed that a variety of toxic chemicals are often present—such as lye, rock salt, lithium from batteries, pool acid, iodine, antifreeze, paint thinner, and lighter fluid—and are detectable during manufacturing, particularly with items "such as phosphine, ether, ammonia, battery acid, and acetone, [because they] have distinctive smells . . . phosphine smells like garlic, sulfur smells like rotten eggs, ammonia smells like cat urine, and acetone smells like nail polish remover" (Scott, 2002, p. 29). In 2012, the DEA (2013) reported a continued reduction in meth lab incidents involving explosions, dump sites, and raids, citing just over 11,000 for the year while seizing the largest annual amount of methamphetamine of nearly 4,000 kilograms. Efforts to reduce the illegal manufacture of methamphetamine continue in the United States, but children and individuals remain at risk from the toxic chemical spills and explosions associated with such labs.

Other stimulants of particular focus for the counselor are amphetamine-like stimulants, such as Ritalin or its generic name, methylphenidate. For a number of years, methylphenidate has been used extensively for the treatment of ADHD. Its main action in the brain involves blocking dopamine reuptake, which results in behavior changes of improved concentration and tracking of information (Doweiko, 2015). Ritalin also exhibits side effects that include weight and appetite loss, insomnia, nausea, hypertension, anemia, or perseveration (Doweiko, 2015). Newer research points to complications such as liver damage, decreasing seizure thresholds, growth hormone disruption, visual hallucinations, cardiac arrhythmias, and heart tissue damage in some individuals; of note, youth can be sensitive to problematic side effects (Breggin & Cohen, 2007; Doweiko, 2015). Unfortunately, more reports indicate Ritalin is also being abused by illegally diverting the drug to individuals without a prescription. Breggin and Cohen (2007) further point out that Ritalin (methylphenidate) and other amphetamines (dextroamphetamine, dexamphetamine [Adderall], methamphetamine [Desoxyn]), often prescribed for young people in the treatment of ADHD, were required by the Federal Drug Administration in 2006 to be labeled with a warning against prescribing them to individuals with heart problems, due to an increasing number of reports about sudden death in children and adults prescribed these stimulants. Continued research into the long-term effects of Ritalin and other stimulants prescribed for ADHD remains a needed priority.

Case Study. Bailey, 21, is a gay biracial single male and has been through treatment four times for his methamphetamine addiction, the last one a 7-day program followed by a 4-week intensive outpatient program (IOP). After this last attempt, he was able to stay clean for only 2 weeks before relapsing, despite being highly motivated. While high, he was arrested for stealing $34 from a convenience store. He was referred to drug court, and the judge has agreed to give him one last try at treatment before incarcerating him.

What treatment level, modalities, length, and aftercare plans do you think would be most likely to help Bailey attain and maintain sobriety? Discuss the difficulties a meth addict faces in maintaining recovery that differ from those of many other substances. What, if any, other issues might the counselor want to consider?

COCAINE Cocaine is also classified as a stimulant, as is crack cocaine, the smokeable, concentrated form of cocaine. History shows, as with many mood-altering drugs, increasing efforts to produce more concentrated forms of the drug to achieve maximum euphoric effect. Note in Table 2.3 the history of methods used to increase the concentration of cocaine (Inaba & Cohen, 2007). Current trends show a steady decline in use of cocaine since the mid-1990s. For example, a 2012 report indicated cocaine use by U.S. workers dropped by nearly 40% in the years 2008–2012 (DEA, 2013).

Epidemics of cocaine abuse and addiction occurred in the late 1800s and again in the early 1900s, which helped lead to its prohibition of nonmedical use with legislation of the Harrison Act of 1914 (Doweiko, 2015). By the late 1970s, many stimulant abusers and addicts were seeking a safer alternative to amphetamines—hence, the rise in cocaine use began again. This time a new, more powerful form of cocaine, crack, was synthesized, and its distribution was rampant throughout all socioeconomic strata in the 1980s and early 1990s (Stevens, 2009). Currently, it is estimated that cocaine-use disorder among adults 18 years old and higher is 0.3% of the U.S. population (APA, 2013). Since smoking a substance is the fastest route into the bloodstream, usually in approximately 4 seconds, intense cravings accompany the pattern of abuse and increasing doses are often sought by the user. Addiction can develop quickly, within weeks to months (APA, 2013). In one addict's account, the initial experience with crack is aptly described as an all-encompassing experience: "In seconds my brain exploded. . . . My heart felt as if it would explode with light, with love. Nothing else mattered except reaching that peak of rapture over and over again" (Moyers & Ketchum, 2006, pp. 101–102). Many celebrities and professional athletes were featured in media segments about their cocaine and crack addictions, while many prevention specialists organized to combat the deleterious consequences of cocaine abuse and dependency. At one time it was believed that cocaine users were only at risk for habituation or psychological dependence; however, it is now clear that physical dependence

TABLE 2.3 History of Cocaine: Methods to Increase Potency

Time Period	Methods to Increase the Potency of Cocaine	Time for Euphoric Effect to Reach Brain
Peru, 1450s	Chew coca leaf with charred oyster shells (slow absorption rate).	20–30 minutes
Europe & United States, 1900s	Snort powder cocaine (snuff); increased absorption rate via mucosa in nasal passages via snorting.	3–5 minutes
	Liquify cocaine in liquid products claiming improved health such as tonics or soft drinks, such as Coca-Cola.	15–30 minutes
	Injecting cocaine either intravenously (IV) or intramuscularly (IM); increased absorption rapidly with intense euphoric effect.	30 seconds (IV) 3–5 minutes (IM)
United States, 1970s	Smoking cocaine known as "freebasing" (complicated mixing of highly flammable ethyl ether with cocaine to produce more concentrated form of cocaine via heating in a pipe). Addiction potential appeared in diagnostic literature.	5–8 seconds
United States, 1980s	Smoking "crack" cocaine, readily packaged concentrated form of cocaine in smokeable form (simple and expedient path to intoxication peak). Highest risk for addiction because of most rapid delivery and easily concealed packaging also led to ease of sales and distribution resulting in crack epidemic.	5–8 seconds

Source: Inaba, D. S., & Cohen, W. E. (2007). *Uppers, downers, all-arounders* (6th ed.). Medford, OR: CNS Productions, Inc.

can occur, as evidenced by tolerance and withdrawal symptomatology (APA, 2013). Cocaine's effect on the brain involves many of the same brain regions in the reward pathway, particularly sexual desire, complicating recovery efforts, again because of intense cravings. One writer, who struggled in recovery from crack addiction, described the cravings that led to yet one more relapse, after a 3-year abstinence, as "a 'physiological imperative' . . . evoking a howling internal torment that overrides the need for food, for water, for sleep, for love" (Moyers & Ketcham, 2006, p. 278).

In summary, stimulant drugs often result in a strong potential for abuse and dependency, with physical and psychological complications thwarting recovery efforts.

Case Study. Bette is a 34-year-old Latina woman with two children aged 10 and 4. She began using cocaine recreationally with friends a few months ago. She has become rapidly dependent on the drug and is now using rock cocaine as well. She vanished from home for 4 days after emptying the family bank account of $14,000. She reports wanting to stop, but has tried three previous times (two of them short in-patient stays) to quit and has relapsed within a few days each time. Explain what is happening in terms of addiction theory and discuss the components of a treatment plan that could be developed as an effective intervention.

Cannabinoids

Marijuana, possibly one of the most controversial illicit drugs, is in a drug class all by itself. Marijuana "is an ancient drug, used since prehistoric times in parts of the Old World" (Weil & Rosen, 1983, p. 113). It often acts like a stimulant; at other times it is similar to a depressant and it resembles a mild psychedelic drug. It is in its own classification as a cannabinoid because of its many unique properties. It is considered to be the most commonly abused illegal drug (APA, 2013). The latest data trends indicated that those aged 50 and older are showing increased use of illicit drugs. For example, in 2002, 1.9% of those aged 55–59 reported illicit drug use, whereas in 2008 that percentage increased to 5% (SAMHSA, 2009).

For a number of years, experts questioned whether one could develop a dependency on marijuana. However, by 1983 experts in drug issues noted that tolerance, withdrawal, and dependence occurred with regular marijuana use. It became increasingly clear that the pattern of dependency is different: "[A]t its worst marijuana dependence consists of chain smoking, from the moment of getting up in the morning to the time of falling asleep . . . but dramatic withdrawal syndromes don't occur . . . and craving for the drug is not nearly as intense as for tobacco, alcohol, or narcotics" (Weil & Rosen, 1983, p. 119). Diagnostic categories for marijuana dependence are included as a substance-use disorder in the widely accepted diagnostic manual of mental disorders; the cannabis-use disorder is considered severe if 6 or more of the 11 diagnostic criteria are met; moderate if 4–5 criteria are met; and mild if there are 2–3 of the criteria present (APA, 2013). For teens, it is noted that use before age 15 is a "robust predictor of the development of cannabis use disorder and other types of substance use disorders and mental disorders during young adulthood" (APA, 2013, p. 513).

The negative physical effects of smoking marijuana on a frequent basis are seen with the reduced lung capacity estimated between 15% and 40% (Prentice, 2003). Other concerns include lowered testosterone levels, increased exercising pulse rates upwards of 20%, and decreased muscle strength (Prentice, 2003). Brain changes, especially in short-term memory and executive functioning, the capacity to learn, and focused attention are also associated with negative effects of continued marijuana abuse (APA, 2013). Recently, the APA recognized withdrawal complications and included, for the first time in the *Diagnostic Statistical Manual* (5th edition; DSM-5), important guidance as follows: "abrupt cessation of daily or near-daily cannabis use often results in the onset of a cannabis withdrawal syndrome . . . [causing] significant distress and contribute to difficulty quitting or relapse" (2013, p. 511). Also, newer analyses note an association between the use of marijuana and psychosis-related complications. One recent in-depth examination, using sibling pair analysis of over 3,000 individuals since birth, found at the 21-year follow-up significant patterns that support mounting evidence that "longer duration since first cannabis use was associated with multiple psychosis-related outcomes in young adults" (McGrath et al., 2010, p. E5). These psychosis-related outcomes include diagnoses of schizophrenia, persistent delusional disorder, or acute psychotic disorders, for example; these diagnoses were seen at a much higher rate in those individuals who reported at least 6 years of marijuana use. These outcomes could not be better explained by factors such as family mental illness, environmental concerns, or genetics (McGrath et al., 2010). Promising new research will continue to yield a better understanding of the unique properties and health effects of marijuana.

Hallucinogens and Other Psychedelics

Another classification of commonly abused drugs includes hallucinogens. Examples of hallucinogens include lysergic acid derivatives (LSD) or psilocybin, indole-type hallucinogens, and phencyclidine (PCP), a phenylethylamine-type hallucinogen, also referred to as a dissociative anesthetic. Hallucinogens range in their effect on the brain; for example, LSD alters the

Legalization of Marijuana

Growing support for the legalization and regulation of medical marijuana is evidenced by recent changes in state marijuana laws. At the time of this writing, 20 states and the District of Columbia have enacted laws to legalize medical marijuana, and 13 states have pending legislation or ballot measures regarding the legalization of medical marijuana. States require a recommendation from a physician stating that a patient would benefit from medical marijuana use. Physicians may prescribe marijuana for many different conditions, including multiple sclerosis and cancer. Parental consent must be provided for patients under the age of 18. Alabama and Indiana have not legalized medical marijuana, but they have enacted pro-medical marijuana legislation. Additionally, 15 states have recently enacted legislation that decriminalizes first-time possession of small amounts of marijuana for personal use. While the specific amount limit varies state to state, offenders receive no prison time or personal criminal record as long as there is no intent to distribute or sell. Research examining decriminalization of marijuana suggests that it has had little to no impact on people's decisions to use the drug, has contributed to the reduction of juvenile offenses, and lessens expenses related to arrests and prosecution of marijuana convictions. Currently, Washington and Colorado are the only states that have legalized marijuana for recreational use. Commerce of recreational marijuana is regulated by state laws, similar to the laws that regulate alcohol sales. Colorado officially legalized recreational marijuana on January 1, 2014. While it is too early to see the full effects, budget numbers predict that more than $100 million in revenue for the state was generated from taxes and reduced criminal costs. Although state laws differ regarding the use and possession of marijuana, federal laws prohibit its use, even for medicinal purposes. Possession of marijuana can be classified as a misdemeanor depending on the number of offenses, but the cultivation and sale of marijuana or any associated paraphernalia is considered a felony. The incongruence between state and federal laws regarding this substance will likely continue to garner attention in the legislature, courts, and public discourse on this controversial matter.

Sources: Healy, J. (2014, February 20). Colorado expects to reap tax bonanza from legal marijuana sales. *The New York Times.* Retrieved from http://www.nytimes.com/2014/02/21/us/colorado-expects-to-reap-tax-bonanza-from-legal-marijuana-sales.html

Lyman, R. (2014, February 26). Pivotal point is seen as more states consider legalizing marijuana. *The New York Times.* Retrieved from http://www.nytimes.com/2014/02/27/us/momentum-is-seen-as-more-states-consider-legalizing-marijuana.html

NORML. (n.d.) *Federal laws and penalties.* Retrieved from http://norml.org/laws/item/federal-penalties-2

NORML. (n.d.). *Marijuana decriminalization and its impact on use.* Retrieved from http://norml.org/aboutmarijuana/item/marijuana-decriminalization-its-impact-on-use-2

NORML. (n.d.). *States that have decriminalized.* Retrieved from http://norml.org/aboutmarijuana/item/states-that-have-decriminalized

Procon.org. (n.d.). *13 states with pending legislation to legalize marijuana.* Retrieved from http://medicalmarijuana.procon.org/view.resource.php?resourceID=002481

Procon.org. (n.d.). *20 legal medical marijuana states and DC: Laws, fees, and possession limits.* Retrieved from http://medicalmarijuana.procon.org/view.resource.php?resourceID=000881

---

neurotransmitter serotonin, and PCP blocks major neurotransmission reuptake and disrupts neuro-electrical impulses (Erickson, 2001). Currently, 1.1 million people were identified as hallucinogen users within the recent month they were surveyed. Rates of reported use remain relatively unchanged in the past decade (SAMHSA, 2013).

Other psychoactive drugs that are not technically hallucinogens but have perception-altering properties—psychedelics—include MDMA (commonly known as "ecstasy" as a pill or "Molly" when in pure-powder form). The most popular psychedelic of the 1990s, MDMA, also designated as 3,4-methylenedioxymethamphetamine, is a synthesized psychoactive drug with stimulant properties. Its chemical makeup is a "synthetic compound related to both mescaline and the amphetamines" (Inciardi & McElrath, 2004, p. 286). In recent years, two major drugs that have psychedelic effects—synthetic cathinones and pure powder-form MDMA—have seen increasing abuse. Synthetic cathinones have emerged in recent years because they are being marketed as "bath salts." As such, they were able to be sold legally in gas stations, in convenience stores, and on the Internet (Wiedland, Halter, & Levine, 2012). Users report seeking synthetic cathinones for their amphetamine-like properties (Prosser & Nelson, 2012); however, users also report psychedelic effects such as hallucinations, paranoia, and psychosis (Wiedland et al., 2012). The dangerous adverse effects from using synthetic cathinones led to a drastic surge in emergency department visits and calls to poison control centers (NIDA, 2012b). Pure powder-form MDMA, or "Molly," has typically been associated as a party drug due to the resulting effects of euphoria, empathy toward others, and sensory distortions felt for approximately 3–6 hours after use (NIDA, 2013). Many users seek Molly from the belief that it is free from additives and therefore safer than other drugs of abuse (Kahn, Ferraro, & Benveniste, 2012). However, in a sample of Molly pills obtained and tested in the southeastern United States, hundreds of the pills contained methylone, one of the synthetic cathinones found in "bath salts" (NIDA, 2014b). In addition, cocaine and heroin have also been found. Users seeking Molly are often unaware that the pure drug they think they are using is actually a dangerous mix of substances.

In addition, hallucinogens and other psychedelic drugs may often be used with other addictive drugs, but are not regarded as having physiologically addicting properties such as tolerance or withdrawal syndromes. Psychological dependency, however, has been noted with hallucinogens and other psychedelics. Complications from traumatic experiences and emotions are noted as unpredictable responses to hallucinogens (NIDA, 2010a).

Summary and Some Final Notations

Most current research and treatment approaches point to the multiple genetic and environmental factors in attempting to better understand all addictions, and emphasize treating the whole person (Center for Substance Abuse Treatment [CSAT], 2008). Although promising genetic research into addiction (Conner et al., 2005) has been conducted in the previous decade, researchers have not yet defined a single physiological or neurobiological marker as the key link to predicting or diagnosing addiction (Doweiko, 2015; Volkow & Baler, 2013).

This chapter provided the reader with information to better inform and prepare him-or herself to be an effective counselor. Comprehensive information about the neurobiology and physiological factors regarding addiction indicate how much progress has been made in our understanding of addiction. In addition, various substances of addiction were examined. Finally, it is important to conclude that continued evidence-based research remains key for providing effective addictions counseling.

MyCounselingLab

Visit the MyCounselingLab site for *Foundations of Addictions Counseling,* Third Edition to enhance your understanding of concepts. You'll have the opportunity to practice your skills through video- and case-based exercises. You will find sets of questions to help you prepare for your certification exam with *Licensure Quizzes.* There is also a Video Library that provides taped counseling sessions, ethical scenarios, and interviews with helpers and clients.

Useful Websites

The following websites provide additional information relating to the chapter topics:

Al-Anon and Alateen
www.al-anon.org/

Alcoholics Anonymous World Services, Inc.
www.alcoholics-anonymous.org/

Center for Substance Abuse Treatment (CSAT)
www.samhsa.gov

Cocaine Anonymous World Services, Inc.
www.ca.org/

Genetic Bioinformatics
genenetwork.org

Information on the Links Between HIV/AIDS and Drug Use
HIV.drugabuse.gov

Motivational Interviewing Information
www.motivationalinterview.org/

Narcotics Anonymous
www.na.org/

National Clearinghouse for Alcohol and Drug Information (NCADI)
ncadi.samhsa.gov/

National Council on Alcoholism and Drug Dependence, Inc. (NCADD)
www.ncadd.org

National Institute on Alcohol Abuse and Alcoholism (NIAAA)
www.niaaa.nih.gov

National Institute on Drug Abuse (NIDA)
www.nida.nih.gov

NIDA for Teens—The Science Behind Drug Abuse
www.teens.drugabuse.gov

Office of National Drug Control Policy (ONDCP)
www.whitehousedrugpolicy.gov

Screening and Brief Interventions
beta.samhsa.gov/sbirt

Substance Abuse and Mental Health Services Administration (SAMHSA), Department of Health and Human Services
www.samhsa.gov/

References

Amen, D. G. (2005). *Making a good brain great: The Amen Clinic program for achieving and sustaining optimal mental performance.* New York, NY: Harmony Books.

American College of Surgeons. (2006). *Resources for optimal care of the injured patient: 2006.* Chicago, IL: Author.

American Psychiatric Association. (2000). *Diagnostic and statistical manual of mental disorders* (4th ed., text rev.). Washington, DC: Author.

American Psychiatric Association. (2013). *Diagnostic and statistical manual of mental disorders* (5th ed.). Arlington, VA: American Psychiatric Publishing.

Breggin, P. R., & Cohen, D. (2007). *Your drug may be your problem: How and why to stop taking psychiatric medications* (rev. ed.). Philadelphia, PA: Da Capo Press.

Briggs, C. A., & Pepperell, J. L. (2009). *Women, girls, and addiction: Celebrating the feminine in counseling treatment and recovery.* New York, NY: Routledge.

Center for Substance Abuse Treatment. (2008). *Managing depressive symptoms in substance abuse clients during early recovery. Treatment Improvement Protocol (TIP) Series 48* (DHHS Publication No. SMA 08–4353). Rockville, MD: SAMHSA.

Centers for Disease Control and Prevention. (2009). *The issue: Excessive drinking and injuries.* Retrieved from http://www.cdc.gov/injuryresponse/alcohol-screening/

Centers for Disease Control and Prevention. (2013). *Impaired driving: Get the facts.* Retrieved from http://www.cdc.gov/Motorvehiclesafety/Impaired_Driving/impaired-drv_factsheet.html

Conner, B. T., Noble, E. T., Berman, S. M., Oskaragoz, T., Ritchie, T., Antolin, T., & Sheen, C. (2005). DRD2 genotypes and substance use in adolescent children of alcoholics. *Drug and Alcohol Dependence, 79,* 379–387.

Crane, E. H., & Lemanski, N. (2004). *Benzodiazepines in drug abuse-related emergency department visits: 1995–2002, The DAWN Report.* Rockville, MD: Office of Applied Studies, Substance Abuse & Mental Health Services Administration.

Crawford, M. J., Patton, R., Touquet, R., Drummond, C., Byford, S., Barrett, B., . . . , Henry, J. A. (2004). Screening and referral for brief intervention of alcohol-misusing patients in an emergency department: A pragmatic randomized controlled trial. *Lancet, 364*, 1334–1339.

Crews, F. T. (2008). Alcohol-related neurodegeneration and recovery. *Alcohol Research & Health, 31*(3), 377–388.

Doweiko, H. E. (2009). *Concepts of chemical dependency* (7th ed.). Belmont, CA: Thomson Brooks/Cole.

Doweiko, H. E. (2015). *Concepts of chemical dependency* (9th ed.). Belmont, CA: Brooks/Cole.

Drug Enforcement Agency. (2013). *Successes in the fight against drugs*. Retrieved from www.justice.gov/dea/resource-center/2012_successes.pdf

Dunn, C., Rivara, F. P., Donovan, D., Fan, M. Y., Russo, J., Jurkovich, G., & Zatzick, D. (2008). Predicting adolescent alcohol drinking patterns after major injury. *The Journal of Trauma: Injury, Infection, and Critical Care, 65*(3), 736–740.

Dziegielewski, S. F., & Suris, N. (2005). Heroin and other opiates. In S. F. Dziegielewski (Ed.), *Understanding substance addictions: Assessment and intervention* (pp. 150–173). Chicago, IL: Lyceum Books, Inc.

Erickson, S. (2001). Etiological theories of substance abuse. In P. Stevens & R. L. Smith (Eds.), *Substance abuse counseling: Theory and practice* (2nd ed., pp. 77–112). Upper Saddle River, NJ: Prentice-Hall.

Falkowski, C. L. (2000). *Dangerous drugs: An easy-to-use reference for parents and professionals*. Center City, MN: Hazelden.

Gentilello, L., Rivara, F., Donovan, D., Jurkovich, G. J., Daranciang, E., Dunn, C. W., . . . , Ries, R. R. (1999). Alcohol interventions in a trauma center as a means of reducing the risk of injury recurrence. *Annals of Surgery, 230*, 473–483.

Gilbertson, R., Prather, R., & Nixon, S. J. (2008). The role of selected factors in the development and consequences of alcohol dependency. *Alcohol Research & Health, 31*, 389–399.

Hall, J. (2004, May 18). Ephedrine ban has holes. *The Free Lance-Star*. Retrieved from http://www.freelancestar.com/News/FLS/2004/052004/05182004/1360590

Healy, J. (2014, February 20). Colorado expects to reap tax bonanza from legal marijuana sales. *The New York Times*. Retrieved from http://www.nytimes.com/2014/02/21/us/colorado-expects-to-reap-tax-bonanza-from-legal-marijuana-sales.html

Hitzemann, R., & Oberbeck, D. (2008). Strategies to study the neuroscience of alcoholism: Introduction. *Alcohol Health & Research, 31*, 231–232.

Horton, E. G., Diaz, N., Peluso, P. R., Mullaney, D., Weiner, M., & McIlveen, J. W. (2009). Relationships between trauma, posttraumatic stress disorder symptoms, dissociative symptoms, and lifetime heroin use among individuals who abuse substances in residential treatment. *Journal of Addictions & Offender Counseling, 29*, 81–95.

Inaba, D. S., & Cohen, W. E. (2007). *Uppers, downers, all-arounders* (6th ed.). Medford, OR: CNS Productions, Inc.

Inciardi, J. A., & Goode, J. L. (2004). OxyContin: Miracle medicine or problem drug? In J. C. Inciardi & K. McElrath (Eds.), *The American drug scene* (4th ed., pp. 163–173). Los Angeles, CA: Roxbury Publishing.

Inciardi, J. A., & McElrath, K. (Eds.). (2004). *The American drug scene* (4th ed.). Los Angeles, CA: Roxbury Publishing.

James, R. K., & Gilliland, B. E. (2005). *Crisis intervention strategies*. Belmont, CA: Thomson Brooks/Cole.

Johnston, L. D. (2010). *Monitoring the future: National survey results on drug use, 1975–2008: Volume II: College students*. Darby, PA: DIANE Publishing.

Juliano, L. M., Huntley, E. D., Harrell, P. T., & Westerman, A. T. (2012). Development of the Caffeine Withdrawal Symptom Questionnaire: Caffeine withdrawal symptoms cluster into 7 factors. *Drug and Alcohol Dependence, 124*(3), 229–234.

Kahn, D. E., Ferraro, N., & Benveniste, R. J. (2012). 3 cases of primary intracranial hemorrhage associated with "molly," a purified form of 3,4-methylenedioxymethamphetamine (MDMA). *Journal of the Neurological Sciences, 323*(1-2), 257–260. doi: 10.1016/j.jns.2012.08.031

Knapp, C. (1996). *Drinking: A love story*. New York, NY: Dell Publishing.

Kranzler, H. R., & Li, T.-K. (2008). What is addiction? *Alcohol Research & Health, 31*, 93–95.

Leontiva, L., Horn, K., Helmkamp, J., Furbee, M., Jarrett, T., & Williams, J. (2009). Counselors' reflections on the administration of screening and brief intervention for alcohol problems in the emergency department and 3-month follow-up outcome. *Journal of Critical Care, 24*, 273–279.

Lovinger, D. M. (2008). Communication networks in the brain: Neurons, receptors, neurotransmitters and alcohol. *Alcohol Research & Health, 31*, 196–214.

Lubman, D. I., Yücel, M., & Pantelis, C. (2004). Addiction, a condition of compulsive behaviour? Neuroimaging and neuropsychological evidence of inhibitory dysregulation. *Addiction, 99*, 1491–1502.

Lyman, R. (2014, February 26). Pivotal point is seen as more states consider legalizing marijuana. *The New York Times*. Retrieved from http://www.nytimes.com/2014/02/27/us/momentum-is-seen-as-more-states-consider-legalizing-marijuana.html

McGrath, J., Welham, J., Scott, J., Varghese, D., Degenhardt, L., Hayatbakhsh, M. R., . . . , Najman, J. M. (2010). Association between cannabis use and psychosis-related outcomes using sibling pair analysis in a cohort of young adults. *Archives of General Psychiatry, 67,* E1–E8. doi:10.1001/archgenpsychiatry.2010.6

Miller, M. A. (2004). History and epidemiology of amphetamine abuse in the United States. In J. C. Inciardi & K. McElrath (Eds.), *The American drug scene* (4th ed., pp. 252–266). Los Angeles, CA: Roxbury Publishing.

Miller, T. R., Levy, D. T., Spicer, R. S., & Taylor, D. M. (2006). Societal costs of underage drinking. *Journal of Studies on Alcohol, 67,* 519–528.

Moyers, W. C., & Ketcham, K. (2006). *Broken: My story of addiction and redemption.* New York, NY: Penguin Books Ltd.

National Collegiate Athletic Association. (2001). *NCAA study of substance use habits of college student-athletes.* Indianapolis, IN: Author.

National Collegiate Athletic Association. (2006). *NCAA study of substance use of college student-athletes.* Indianapolis, IN: Author.

National Highway Traffic Safety Administration. (2004, January 15). *The economic burden of traffic crashes on employers.* Retrieved from http://www.nhtsa.dot.gov/people/injury/airbags/EconomicBurden/index.html

National Highway Traffic Safety Administration. (2012). *Traffic safety facts: Alcohol-impaired driving.* Retrieved from http://www-nrd.nhtsa.dot.gov/Pubs/811700.pdf

National Institute on Alcohol Abuse and Alcoholism. (2005). *Alcohol: A women's health issue* (NIH Publication No. 03–4956). Rockville, MD: Author.

National Institute on Alcohol Abuse and Alcoholism. (2014, February). *Alcohol facts and statistics.* Retrieved from http://niaaa.nih.gov/alcohol-health/overview-alcohol-consumption/alcohol-facts-and-statistics

National Institute on Drug Abuse. (2005). *Prescription drugs: Abuse and addiction.* Research Report Series. Retrieved from http://www.drugabuse.gov/ResearchReports/Prescription/prescription.html

National Institute on Drug Abuse. (2006). *Medical consequences of drug abuse.* Retrieved from http://www.drugabuse.gov/consequences/

National Institute on Drug Abuse. (2007). *The reward pathway.* Retrieved from http://www.drugabuse.gov/publications/teaching-packets/understanding-drug-abuse-addiction/section-i/4-reward-pathway

National Institute on Drug Abuse. (2010a). *Drugs, brains, and behavior: The science of addiction* (NIH Pub. No. 10-5605). Retrieved from www.nida.nih.gov/scienceofaddiction

National Institute on Drug Abuse. (2010b). *Drugs change the ways neurons communicate.* Retrieved from http://science.education.nih.gov/supplements/nih2/addiction/guide/lesson3-1.htm

National Institute on Drug Abuse. (2012a). *Commonly abused drugs.* Retrieved from http://www.drugabuse.gov/DrugPages/DrugsofAbuse.html

National Institute on Drug Abuse. (2012b). *Drug facts: Synthetic cathinones ("bath salts").* Retrieved from http://www.drugabuse.gov/publications/drugfacts/synthetic-cathinones-bath-salts

National Institute on Drug Abuse. (2013). *Drug facts: MDMA (ecstasy or molly).* Retrieved from http://www.drugabuse.gov/publications/drugfacts/mdma-ecstasy-or-molly

National Institute on Drug Abuse. (2014a). *Drug facts: Nationwide trends.* Retrieved from http://www.drugabuse.gov/publications/drugfacts/nationwide-trends

National Institute on Drug Abuse. (2014b). *Emerging trends.* Retrieved from http://www.drugabuse.gov/drugs-abuse/emerging-trends

National Institute on Drug Abuse. (2014c). *Methamphetamine.* Research Report Series Drug Facts. Retrieved from http://www.drugabuse.gov/sites/default/files/drugfactsmeth.pdf

O'Brien, M. C., Reboussin, B., Veach, L. J., & Miller, P. R. (2012). *Robert Wood Johnson Grant # 65032: The Teachable Moment Study.* Unpublished research report.

Oscar-Berman, M., & Marinkovic, K. (2004). *Alcoholism and the brain: An overview.* Retrieved from http://pubs.niaaa.nih.gov/publications/arh27-2/125-133.pdf

Physician's desk reference (56th ed.). (2002). Montvale, NJ: Thomson PDR.

Pietrzykowski, A. Z., & Treistman, S. N. (2008). The molecular basis of tolerance. *Alcohol Research & Health, 31*(4), 298–309.

Prentice, W. E. (2003). *Arnheim's principles of athletic training: A competency-based approach* (11th ed.). New York, NY: McGraw Hill.

Procon.org. (n.d.). *13 states with pending legislation to legalize marijuana.* Retrieved from http://medicalmarijuana.procon.org/view.resource.php?resourceID=002481

Procon.org. (n.d.). *20 legal medical marijuana states and DC: Laws, fees, and possession limits.* Retrieved from http://medicalmarijuana.procon.org/view.resource.php?resourceID=000881

Prosser, J. M., & Nelson, L. S. (2012). The toxicology of bath salts: A review of synthetic cathinones. *Journal of Medical Toxicology, 8*(1), 33–42. doi:10.1007/s13181-011-0193-z

Riegel, A. C., & Kalivas, P. W. (2010). Neuroscience: Lack of inhibition leads to abuse. *Nature, 463,* 743–744. doi:10.1038/463743a

Rouaud, T., Lardeux, S., Panayotis, N., Paleressompoulle, D., Cador, M., & Baunez, C. (2009). Reducing the desire for cocaine with subthalamic nucleus deep brain stimulation. *Proceedings of the National Academy of Sciences, 107*(3), 1196–1200. Retrieved from http://www.pnas.org/cgi/doi/10.1073/pnas.0908189107

Schermer, C. R. (2005). Feasibility of alcohol screening and brief intervention. *The Journal of Trauma: Injury, Infection, and Critical Care, 59*(3), S119–S123.

Schnabel, J. (2009). Neuroscience: Rethinking rehab. *Nature, 458*(7234), 25–27.

Scott, M. S. (2002). Clandestine drug labs. *Problem-Oriented Guides for Police, No 16*. Washington, DC: U.S. Department of Justice.

Siegal, H. A., & Inciardi, J. A. (2004). A brief history of alcohol. In J. C. Inciardi & K. McElrath (Eds.), *The American drug scene* (4th ed., pp. 74–79). Los Angeles, CA: Roxbury Publishing.

Spicer, J. (1993). *The Minnesota Model: The evolution of the multi-disciplinary approach to addiction recovery.* Center City, MN: Hazelden Educational Materials.

Spirito, A. (2009). Alcohol Education Inventor—Revised: What every mental health professional should know about alcohol. *Journal of Substance Abuse Treatment, 37*, 41–53.

Stevens, P. (2009). Introduction to substance abuse counseling. In P. Stevens & R. L. Smith (Eds.), *Substance abuse counseling* (4th ed., pp. 1–30). Upper Saddle River, NJ: Pearson Education, Inc.

Substance Abuse and Mental Health Services Administration. (2005). Characteristics of primary tranquilizer admissions: 2002. *The DASIS Report*. Rockville, MD: Office of Applied Studies, SAMHSA. Retrieved from http://www.oas.samhsa.gov/2k5/tranquilizerTX/tranquilizerTX.htm

Substance Abuse and Mental Health Services Administration. (2007). *Alcohol screening and brief intervention for trauma patients: Committee on Trauma quick guide* (DHHS Publication No SMA 07-4266). Rockville, MD: SAMHSA.

Substance Abuse and Mental Health Services Administration. (2009, October 15). *The NSDUH Report: Trends in tobacco use among adolescents: 2002 to 2008*. Rockville, MD: Office of Applied Studies, SAMHSA.

Substance Abuse and Mental Health Services Administration. (2013). *Results from the 2012 National Survey on Drug Use and Health: Summary of National Findings* (NSDUH Series H-46, HHS Publication No. SMA 13-4795). Rockville, MD: SAMHSA.

Sullivan, E. V., & Pfefferbaum, A. (2005). Neurocircuitry in alcoholism: A substrate of disruption and repair [Electronic version]. *Psychopharmacology, 180*, 583–594.

Taffe, M. A., Kotzebue, R. W., Crean, R. D., Crawford, E. F., Edwards, S., & Mandyam, C. D. (2010). Long-lasting reduction in hippocampal neurogenesis by alcohol consumption in adolescent nonhuman primates. *Proceedings of the National Academy of Science, 107*(24), 11104–11109.

Taylor, J. B. (2006). *My stroke of insight: A brain scientist's personal journey*. New York, NY: Viking.

Toumbourou, J. W., Stockwell, T., Neighbors, C., Marlatt, G. A., Sturge, J., & Rehm, J. (2007). Interventions to reduce harm associated with adolescent substance use. *The Lancet, 369*, 1391–1401.

van Wormer, K., & Davis, D. R. (2013). *Addiction treatment: A strengths perspective* (3rd ed.). Pacific Grove, CA: Brooks/Cole.

Volkow, N. D., & Baler, R. D. (2013). Brain imaging biomarkers to predict relapse in alcohol addiction. *JAMA Psychiatry, 70*, 661–663.

Watson, J. C. (2002). Assessing the potential for alcohol-related issues among college student-athletes. *Athletic Insight, 4*(3). Retrieved from http://www.athleticinsight.com/Vol4Iss3/AlcoholAssessment.htm

Weil, A., & Rosen, W. (1983). *Chocolate to morphine*. Boston, MA: Houghton Mifflin.

White, W. L. (1998). *Slaying the dragon: The history of addiction treatment and recovery in America*. Bloomington, IL: Chestnut Health Systems.

Wiedland, D. M., Halter, M. J., & Levine, C. (2012). Bath salts: They are not what you think. *Journal of Psychosocial Nursing and Mental Health Services, 50*(2), 17–21.

Wilens, T., Adler, L., Adams, J., Sgambati, S., Rotrosen, J., Sawtelle, R., . . . , Fusillo, S. (2008). Misuse and diversion of stimulants prescribed for ADHD: A systematic review of the literature. *Journal of the American Academy of Child and Adolescent Psychiatry, 47*(1), 21–31.

Williams, R. W., & Lu, L. (2008). Integrative genetic analyses of alcohol dependence using the GeneNetwork Web resources. *Alcohol Research & Health, 31*, 275–277.

Witkiewitz, K., Lustyk, M. K., & Bowen, S. (2013). Retraining the brain: A review of hypothesized neurobiological mechanisms of mindfulness-based relapse prevention. *Psychology of Addictive Behaviors, 27*, 351–365.

Wu, N. S., Schairer, L. C., Dellor, E., & Grella, C. (2010). Childhood trauma and health outcomes in adults with comorbid substance abuse and mental health disorders. *Addictive Behaviors, 35*(1), 68–71.

Yin, H. H. (2008). From action to habits: Neuroadaptations leading to dependence. *Alcohol Research & Health, 31*, 340–344.

Zickler, P. (2002). Methamphetamine abuse linked to impaired cognitive and motor skills despite recovery of dopamine transporters. *NIDA Research Findings, 17*(1), 4–6.

Chapter 3

Process Addictions

Laura J. Veach
Wake Forest School of Medicine
Jennifer L. Rogers
Wake Forest University
Regina R. Moro
Barry University

E. J. Essic
Professional Counselor
James W. McMullen
University of North Carolina at Charlotte

Addiction may be further defined in terms of ingestive or process addictions. Chemical dependence is classified as an ingestive addiction due to the taking in of mood-altering chemicals, like alcohol or other drugs (AOD), whereas process addictions encompass behavior patterns (for example, gambling or sexual addictions) or processes that produce euphoria without the use of mood-altering AOD. Addiction specialists rarely debate that addiction is a biopsychosocial disease, but many continue to challenge the nature of addiction with questions about substance versus process addictions.

The term *process addiction*—an addiction to a behavior, process, or action—is still contentiously debated. It was not until the 1970s and 1980s that the addiction field began to formally discuss the idea that a behavior could be diagnosed as an addictive disorder. Sussman and Sussman (2011) provide a review of addiction research studies since 1948 to ascertain key elements in understanding addiction, whether substance or process, and highlight the following: "[W]hen contemplating addiction, one often thinks of it in terms of a process" (p. 4026). Hagedorn and Juhnke (2005) cite a need for a universal definition of an addictive disorder to "[create a] common clinical language, a legitimization of the disorder for the purposes of third-party reimbursement, and a step toward a standardized treatment protocol" (p. 70). Past research on addiction focused on the presence of physical dependence to the substance or behavior as demonstrated by tolerance and withdrawal, but current research claims physical dependence is no longer necessary to diagnose an addiction to a substance or behavior (Hagedorn & Juhnke, 2005). In fact, the older *Diagnostic Statistical Manual* (4th ed., text rev.; DSM-IV-TR) explicitly states that "neither tolerance nor withdrawal is necessary or sufficient for a diagnosis of Substance Dependence" (American Psychiatric Association [APA], 2000, p. 194). In addition, newer research using sophisticated brain imaging techniques continues to add compelling evidence that the brain reward and inhibitory systems of process addicts resemble brains of ingestive addicts (Ahmed, Guillem, & Vandaele, 2013; Clark & Limbrick-Oldfield, 2013). Yet researchers and experts continue to debate whether a behavior can be diagnosed under the same criteria as a substance use disorder.

A number of addiction specialists, including the International Association of Addictions and Offender Counselors Committee on Process Addictions, advocated that the newly published *Diagnostic and Statistical Manual* (DSM-5; APA, 2013) include diagnostic categories of addictive disorders containing subtypes for gambling, sex, spending, work, exercise, Internet, and eating (Hagedorn, 2009). However, gambling was the only disorder included in the revised section on addictive disorders in the newly released DSM-5 (APA, 2013). At present there remains a lack of agreement regarding common terminology throughout the multidisciplinary field of addictions counseling, especially language pertaining to process addiction (Kranzler & Li, 2008; Petry & O'Brien, 2013; Sussman & Sussman, 2011).

According to addiction specialists, the importance of screening and assessment in the treatment of process addiction is paramount. Additional assessment information is reviewed in later chapters, but it is important to stress the following as we begin our examination of process addictions: (1) that understanding the addictive elements in compulsive and obsessive patterns with addictive elements and the associated negative consequences is critical; and (2) that assessing the loss of the ability to abstain from harmful processes, or behaviors, is often thought of as one of the hallmarks of addiction, including tolerance and withdrawal patterns, if any. Further, it is critical for the counselor to distinguish a process addiction from other types of behavior that may lead to negative consequences, for example, displaying undesirable social behavior. A person struggling with an addiction, whether it be process or substance, is engaging in behaviors marked by obsession, compulsion, and significant life (career, relationship, health) impairment. Someone engaged in violating a social taboo, such as discussing sexual practices in social settings or eating certain foods, may experience awkward silences and social regrets, but this is not addiction. If, however, an individual experiences euphoria while compulsively and obsessively discussing sexual practices in social settings, even after an ongoing pattern of adverse consequences related to this behavior (for example, arguments with spouse/partner or disciplinary action by an employer), then the counselor would be advised to evaluate further for an addictive pattern. Marked impairment of functioning, accompanied by a continuance of the behavior despite serious adverse consequences, are part of the inherent nature of addiction, thereby separating these patterns from being mere social habits or taboos. Addiction is a complex diagnosis, leading to clinically significant impairment. Process addictions warrant further discussion.

The debate continues as to whether behavioral addictions should be classified as an addictive disorder. As a result, the concept of what we classify and diagnose as an addiction is still evolving. Whether we are speaking of a process or substance addiction, addictions interfere with people's ability to truly know themselves, their spirituality, and the world around them (Schaef, 1990). In this chapter we will discuss five of the most prominent and researched process addictions to date: sex, gambling, working, compulsive buying, and food.

It is important to note that frequently, addiction to one substance or process is accompanied or replaced by addiction to another substance or process (e.g., a female with an eating disorder is also struggling with substance abuse or dependence; a male recovering from a sexual addiction develops a gambling addiction). Comorbidity, or multiple addictions occurring at once, is quite common whether a person is suffering from a substance or a process addiction (National Association of Anorexia Nervosa and Associated Disorders [ANAD], 2014; Fassel & Schaef, 1989; Grilo, Sinha, & O'Malley, 2002; Hagedorn, 2009; Hagedorn & Juhnke, 2005; Mitchell et al., 2001). As Schaef (1990) aptly points out, "the addiction changes behavior, distorts reality and fosters self-centeredness . . . [and] no one has only one addiction. As addicts begin recovering from their primary addiction and achieve some sobriety, other addictions emerge" (p. 18).

The prevalence of process addictions is not clearly known since currently there is a lack of agreement as to what precise criteria can be used to define the various types of process addictions. Some believe that process addictions are rampant in our society. As an example of possible prevalence, Hagedorn (2009) extrapolated from various data and reported that each sexual addiction treatment center in operation would need to serve 1.08 million persons struggling with sexual addiction; for gambling addiction, there is one treatment facility for every 250,000 individuals suffering; and for those struggling with Internet addiction, one treatment facility exists per 2.9 million clients. Similar to substance addiction, warning signs of process addiction can include a greater sense of isolation, less social interaction, less attention to personal hygiene, increased legal difficulties, changes in eating and sleeping patterns, increased irritability, and wariness of changing compulsive behavior (Zamora, 2003).

SEXUAL ADDICTION

Experts in the field of addiction did not really start talking about sex addiction until the early 1980s, when Patrick Carnes introduced the idea that sexual behavior, rather than a drug, could be addicting (Schneider, 2004). The prevalence of sexual addiction is estimated, conservatively, at 3% of U.S. adults (Sussman, Lisha, & Griffiths, 2011). An estimated 20–25% of sexual addicts are women (Carnes, 2011). Additionally, a range of 20–40% of sex addicts are thought to be struggling with another addiction, such as alcoholism (Sussman et al., 2011). The incidence of sexual addiction is on the rise because of increased affordability, easy access to sexual materials, and anonymity of the Internet (Hagedorn & Juhnke, 2005). Love, or relationship, addiction pertains to different behaviors and often may involve the spouse or partner of addicts, but is not focused primarily on compulsive sexual behaviors and thus is excluded from this section on sexual addiction. More information can be found in materials related to codependency (Co-Dependents Anonymous, Inc., 2010; S-Anon International Family Groups, 2013).

There are varying definitions of sexual addiction. Sexaholics Anonymous, Inc. (SA) defines a *sexaholic* as someone who is addicted to lust. The sexaholic can no longer determine what is right or wrong, has lost control, lost the power of choice, and is not free to stop sexual behavior despite adverse consequences, such as threats of job or family loss (Sexaholics Anonymous, Inc., 2010). Common characteristics of male and female sexaholics include marked isolation, prevalent guilt, marked depression, and a deep feeling of emptiness. Typical behaviors of a sexaholic include compulsively fantasizing about sexual desires; remaining in harmful codependent relationships; engaging in compulsive masturbation; obsessive and compulsive use of pornography, including on the Internet; repeatedly engaging in promiscuous sexual relationships; conducting adulterous affairs; and compulsively pursuing exhibitionism or sexually abusive relationships, regardless of legal, career, or family consequences (Sexaholics Anonymous, Inc., 2010).

According to Bailey and Case with the American Association for Marriage and Family Therapy (AAMFT), sex addicts experience unhealthy abuse of sex in a downward compulsive cycle (2014). For some it may begin with masturbation, pornography, or a relationship, but progresses in an obsessive and compulsive pattern to increasingly dangerous behaviors and greater risks. *Cybersex*, another term often referenced when discussing sex addiction, involves "Internet-related sexually oriented chat rooms, message boards, and pornography" (Long, Burnett, & Thomas, 2006, p. 218). Long et al. (2006) further identify pornography and telephone sex with dependence patterns.

Denial is the undertone of all addictions. Sexual addiction can be the primary, secondary, or simultaneous disorder along with other substance or process addictions such as chemical dependency, eating disorders, work addiction, compulsive buying, or compulsive gambling. Additionally, sexual addiction often coexists with other psychiatric issues such as depression, anxiety, personality disorder, relationship issues, or bipolar disorder (Seegers, 2003). For example, increased buying, spending, and sexual behaviors often accelerate during manic episodes but do not warrant a diagnosis of sex addiction. Conversely, in some cases, without adequate knowledge about addiction, a client may be misdiagnosed with bipolar disorder when the primary focus of clinical attention is a process addiction. Differential diagnoses add complications since sex addiction can resemble other disorders, for example, a manic or hypomanic episode with hypersexual behaviors. It is recommended that counselors evaluate carefully and obtain adequate psychosocial history before making a final diagnosis. There are few empirical studies regarding the comorbidity of sexual addiction and another psychiatric disorder or addiction (Miller, 2005; Sussman et al., 2011). Zapf, Greiner, and Carroll (2008) found that relational anxiety and avoidance behaviors were more prevalent in sexually addicted men in their recent study, noting "sexually addicted men are nearly 50% less likely to relate to their partners in a secure manner than nonaddicted men . . ." (p. 169). More research is needed to investigate sexually impulsive and out of control behaviors (Bancroft & Vukadinovic, 2004; Sussman et al., 2011).

Parkinson's Disease and Impulse Control

Parkinson's disease is a disorder of the central nervous system. It is a degenerative condition that usually impairs a person's speech, motor skills, and other functions. Persons suffering from Parkinson's disease may experience tremors, joint stiffness, and a decline in the executive functioning of the brain. A relationship between Parkinson's disease and impulse control disorders is currently being examined by researchers (Ceravolo, Frosini, Rossi, & Bonuccelli, 2010). Dopamine receptor agonists, a type of drug used to treat Parkinson's, is associated with compulsive gambling, sex, eating, and shopping. Changes in medication doses usually result in improvement in these behaviors.

As of now there are no diagnostic criteria or classifications for sexual addiction (American Psychiatric Association, 2013) in the new edition of the *Diagnostic and Statistical Manual of Mental Disorders* (DSM-5). Considerable review occurred in the revision of the current DSM-5; however, "subcategories as 'sex addiction,' 'exercise addiction,' or 'shopping addiction,' are not included because at this time there is insufficient peer-reviewed evidence to establish the diagnostic criteria and course descriptions needed to identify these behaviors as mental disorders" (Clark & Limbrick-Oldfield, 2013, p. 481). There are, however, DSM-5 diagnoses (and DSM-5 estimated prevalence) for sexual disorders, also known as paraphilic disorders, that can involve compulsivity, obsessions, and harm to others such as voyeurism (concerning perhaps 12% of males and 4% of females), pedophilia (estimated to involve 3–5% of men and a smaller number of women), sexual sadism (estimated range of perhaps 2–30% of individuals), sexual masochism (involving an unknown number of people), and exhibitionism (affecting possibly 2–4% of men) (APA, 2013). Screening for sex addiction is an important step for the counselor; first, the counselor's reluctance and discomfort regarding explicit sexual information, if present, can cause difficulty in developing the necessary nonjudgmental relationship (Zmuda, 2014). A briefer screening tool, PATHOS, developed by Patrick Carnes and associates, utilizes six items and may be an important way for both the counselor and the client to begin to assess for sexual addiction (Zmuda, 2014). Often treatment for sexual addictions involves many treatment approaches used for substance addictions, such as cognitive behavioral therapy; however, additional biological approaches, such as hormonal therapy involving antiandrogens or certain libido-inhibiting antidepressants, may also be used (Long et al., 2006).

Case Study

Kevin's Alcoholic Anonymous sponsor has insisted he come talk with you about his "sex addiction." He reports being highly sexed and sleeping with several women in the program "just as any other healthy male might." Upon deeper exploration, he reports having slept with over 500 women in the last 2 years and that when he is not able to have regular and frequent sexual contact, he gets depressed and really wants to drink. He is proud of his sexual prowess and feels that his behavior is to be envied rather than a source of concern. He says that he thinks sex is a much healthier outlet than drinking, and that it is fun, not an addiction.

Discuss whether Kevin's behaviors seem addictive and why. What red flags do you see? Discuss how he may fit on the addiction spectrum. Conceptually, what is happening? What theories/methods might you employ in his treatment? What leads you to differentiate Kevin's behavior as addictive rather than in the normal range of healthy sexual behavior?

GAMBLING ADDICTION

Gambling continues to rise with the increase in casinos, lotteries, and Internet gambling sites (Buck & Amos, 2000; Suissa, 2007). There is evidence that gambling can be traced back thousands of years, with Egyptian evidence of shell games dating from 2,500 B.C. (Suissa, 2007).

To reflect new research that demonstrates similarities between the reward systems activated by both substance-abuse disorders and behaviors related to gambling, as shown in Figure 3.1, the DSM-5 made substantial changes and now designates gambling as a disorder under the Non-Substance-Related Disorders section of Substance-Related and Addictive Disorders (APA, 2013)—the first of the process addictions to be so designated. A gambling disorder diagnosis requires that an individual show four or more of the nine gambling behaviors that are persistent and problematic in a 12-month period. Some of the descriptors for a person with a gambling disorder indicate that the person "needs to gamble with increasing amounts of money in order to achieve the desired excitement; lies to conceal the extent of involvement with gambling; and relies on others to provide money to relieve desperate financial situations" (APA, 2013, p. 585). Gamblers do not ingest a substance to experience their "high," and yet researchers have found that disordered gambling is related to neuroadaptation, or tolerance, and withdrawal symptoms (Shaffer & Kidman, 2003). In a study that looked at Internet gambling behavior (McBride & Derevensky, 2009), 23% of participants (N=563) that included males between the ages of 18 and

DSM-IV-TR (2000)	DSM-5 (2013)
Classified as an impulse control disorder	Classified as a nonsubstance related disorder
No levels; only specified between pathological gambling vs. social and professional gambling	Severity in 3 levels: mild, moderate, & severe
To be diagnosed, needed to meet 5 of the criteria (over unspecified amount of time)	To be diagnosed, need to meet 4 or more of the criteria in a 12-month period
Diagnostic Criteria A, defined as persistent and recurrent "maladaptive" gambling behavior	Diagnostic Criteria A, defined as persistent and recurrent "problematic" gambling behavior *leading to clinically significant impairment or distress*
Diagnostic Criteria A has 10 parts	Diagnostic Criteria A has 9 parts: removed #8 of DSM-IV; "Committed illegal acts such as forgery, fraud, theft, or embezzlement to finance gambling"

FIGURE 3.1 Gambling Disorder: New Diagnostic Changes

over 65 identified as problem gamblers. Problem gamblers were more likely to exhibit behaviors such as consuming alcohol or drugs while gambling on the Internet. Men evidence more gambling-related problems and comorbidities, although research indicates the trends show an increasing number of women involved in gambling (Rainone, Marel, Gallati, & Gargon, 2007), and the relationship between trauma and female gambling further complicates treatment (Nixon, Evans, Kalischuk, Solowoniuk, McCallum, & Hagen, 2013). For the women interviewed in this qualitative study, trauma that was experienced in life played a significant role in their entrance into the world of gambling (Nixon et al., 2013).

According to the DSM-5, the lifetime prevalence rate of adult disordered gambling ranges from 0.4% to 1% (APA, 2013) and a 12-month incidence of 0.2–0.3%, yet a review of 83 addiction studies by Sussman and colleagues (2011) calculated a 12-month gambling addiction prevalence of 2%. The prevalence rate is higher for youth and middle-aged individuals than the older population (APA, 2013).

Internet Gaming Disorder

There is debate in the field as to whether compulsive online gaming will eventually be acknowledged as a process addiction. Researchers suggest that appropriate diagnostic criteria for the disorder may be similar to those used to identify pathological gambling (Young, 2009). Currently, the DSM-5 includes Internet Gaming Disorder as a condition for further study and offers proposed diagnostic criteria that involve many of the addictive criteria, but does not endorse a diagnosis at this time. However, it does note the following: "Internet gaming has been reportedly defined as an 'addiction' by the Chinese government, and a treatment system has been set up" (APA, 2013, p. 796). For example, the overuse of Massively Multiplayer Online Role Playing Games (MMORPGs) is growing worldwide, especially among college students, and researchers are exploring means by which to both operationalize the phenomenon and predict problematic use (Hsu, Wen, & Wu, 2009). This growing area of addictions research will perhaps stretch conceptualizations of addictions in the 21st century.

Source: Hsu, S., Wen, M., & Wu, M. (2009). Exploring user experiences as predictors of MMORPG addiction. *Computers & Education, 53*(3), 990–999. doi:10.1016/j.compedu.2009.05.016

Source: Young, K. (2009). Internet addiction: Diagnosis and treatment considerations. *Journal of Contemporary Psychotherapy, 39*(4), 241–246. doi:10.1007/s10879-009-9120-x

Gambling involves an aspect of risk to get something greater in return, such as the euphoria often referenced by recovering gamblers (APA, 2013). Signs of gambling addiction can include "secretiveness and excessive time with phone calls and Internet access, unaccounted time away from work or home, unexplained preoccupation, increased debt and worry over finances, extravagant expenditures, and increased alcohol, drug consumption or both" (Buck & Amos, 2000, p. 5). Other disorders, such as substance use, depressive, anxiety, and personality disorders are often present in comorbidity with gambling disorders, which is to be taken into consideration during treatment (APA, 2013). The National Council on Problem Gambling (NCPG, 2014) has reported costs up to $7 billion related to gambling when factoring in bankruptcies, job loss, and criminal justice actions. Early intervention and treatment is urged by NCPG. Other national data is lacking, but an involved household survey in New York yielded important trends concerning the need for intervention and treatment. One finding indicated 67% of adults within the state had engaged in one or more gambling activities within the past year, and of those, approximately 5% reported problem gambling symptoms that could benefit from addiction counseling services (Rainone, Marel, Gallati, & Gargon, 2007). As knowledge about the prevalence of gambling addiction improves, more is also known about cultural considerations. Further, some helping professionals in the United States are recognizing gambling addiction as a hidden problem within Asian-American communities. One study found gambling problems at rates far greater in Asian-American clients than in the general population (Fong & Tsuang, 2007). A recent report suggests Asian Americans may choose gambling as a leisure activity, but more problematic within the community are those affected by gambling addiction (Forng & Tsuang, 2007). Literature and outreach videos have been prepared with a specific focus on Mandarin, Cantonese, and Vietnamese communities in the United States, to separate moderate gambling social activity from serious problem gambling (Massachusetts Council on Compulsive Gambling, National Problem Gambling Awareness Week, 2009).

Other helpful approaches advocate adaption of a harm reduction model with an emphasis on self-empowerment (Suissa, 2007) and avoiding a model of individual pathology that claims individuals are vulnerable for life (Suissa, 2011). The number of Gamblers Anonymous (GA) meetings has increased since their beginnings in 1957 (Suissa, 2007). Gambling addictions continue to create significant financial, family, and legal problems, and continued research is needed. Counselors benefit from specialized counseling training and may want to investigate national certification in this area as outlined by the National Council on Problem Gambling (NCPG, 2014).

Case Study 1

Marilyn reports that the major difficulty in her marriage is due to Du Nguyen's constant gambling. Family savings are gone, and the couple is 3 months behind on mortgage payments. Du Nguyen, embarrassed for seeking counseling, says that he has tried stopping because he is worried about his marriage. He says he wants to quit and feels shameful and guilty, but when faced with an opportunity to bet on sports or horses, his impulses overcome his reason. He has tried a number of unsuccessful strategies to control himself, and he wants help in order to save his marriage. He says he wants to understand his urges and be able to control them.

How can you help this couple understand the addiction process? What resources can you draw on to help them? What modalities might you use in working with them? How will you approach Du Nguyen's desire to "control" his gambling addiction? Would you diagnose with the new DSM-5?

Case Study 2

Jonathan is a computer analyst struggling at work focusing on his daily tasks. He reports that rather than focusing on his job, he consistently signs on to his favorite gambling website throughout the workday as well as when he gets home. When his supervisor asks him about the projects he is working on, he lies and states that issues arose in the project that resulted in it taking more time than usual. Jonathan turned down a promotion 6 months ago that would have made him the head of a team within the company. He says that this promotion would have cut into his ability to shift his focus between gambling online and his work.

What criteria are present for gambling disorder to be identified? How would you begin to work with Jonathan as his counselor? What options for treatment would you consider?

Technology Addiction

Technology addiction (TA), a new term encompassing technological use comprehensively, is an advancing phenomenon that continues to affect society through individuals' heavy reliance on euphoria-producing technological devices. Easy access offered by constant advances in technology and instant gratification may trigger addictive behaviors among vulnerable individuals. With the development of a specific technology (e.g., cell phones), more drivers are becoming distracted while driving as they are texting and talking on their phones. Research conducted by the Centers for Disease Control and Prevention ([CDC], 2011) found that 31% of adult drivers aged 18–64 had been reading or sending text or email messages while driving within 30 days of the CDC survey. The annual statistics continue to show rising trends of distracted driving related to technology. These findings indicate a need for more research to be conducted to investigate the addictive tendencies of technology.

Within the limits of current literature, there is a notable gap in the current definition and understanding of this phenomenon as the use of a device defines technology addiction rather than the addictive tendencies of the pleasure-seeking behavior for each specific subset, such as smartphone or Internet addiction. To better understand technology addiction, it is important to examine its biological, psychological, and sociological components. In other words, utilization of the biopsychosocial model may help us gain a better awareness of the addictive properties of technology. Acosta (2013) conducted a study to examine at-risk technology users and gain an in-depth understanding of those individuals' lived experiences. The results of the study suggest that participants identify both positive and negative effects of their technology use. After assessing participants' responses with the help of the biopsychosocial model, there were several themes that were described to influence participants' experiences with technology. Participants report being influenced by a cultural need to utilize technology, both externally (e.g., work) and internally (e.g., personal need). In other words, individuals experience pressures from their external world as well as their own internal world to use euphoria-producing technologies.

Additionally, several factors that motivate use of technology were discovered. One of the factors is the need for social connections and interpersonal relationships. Furthermore, the participants identified enmeshment of the functionality of technology, which means the device itself is not the object of the use; rather, it is the seeking behavior such as searching the Internet, which can be accessed from multiple devices. Convenience and awareness of personal benefits were also identified as factors that motivate use of technology. On the other hand, negative consequences that were the results of technology use such as utilizing technology for longer than intended, disruptions in interpersonal relationships, and having physical problems due to their use such as eye strain were also reported to influence participants' experiences with technology (Acosta, 2013).

The results of the study indicate that individuals who use technological devices may be vulnerable to risks associated with technology use. To assist the client with further investigation of the potential technology use hazards, the professional counselor might benefit from conducting a brief screening during therapy session with the help of TECH (Acosta, Lainas & Veach, 2013). If clients respond "yes" to at least one of the questions on the TECH screening instrument, it indicates a positive finding and counselors can start a discussion with the client about that person's patterns of technology use and factors that contribute and affect his or her behaviors related to technology. To date, "reSTART" is the only treatment center that exists in the United States that specializes in technology addiction treatment. Additionally, counselors and clients might find the following websites informative and helpful for exploration and better understanding of technology use and its risks: www.netaddictionrecovery.com, www.congressoftechnologyaddiction.org, and www.netaddictionanon.org

Source: Acosta, K. M., Lainas, H., & Veach, L. J. (2013). An emerging trend: Becoming aware of technology addiction. *NC Perspectives, 8,* 5–11.

Source: Acosta, K. M. (2013). *Understanding at-risk technology users: A phenomenological approach* [Doctoral dissertation]. Retrieved from ProQuest Digital Dissertations.

WORK ADDICTION

While the term *workaholism* is commonly used, there is no recognized diagnosis in current diagnostic manuals such as the DSM-5 (American Psychiatric Association, 2013). There is little data available on the actual prevalence of workaholism, but Sussman (2013) notes as many as one-third of workers, or about 18% of the population, may self-identify as workaholics; however, 10% may be a more conservative estimate. Additionally, the oftentimes secretive nature of the addiction, as well as the societal acceptance and even reward of workaholism, limits the availability of accurate data. According to Bonebright, Clay, and Ankenmann (2000), Oates first coined the term *workaholism* more than 25 years ago, and since then many researchers define workaholism differently. Seybold and Salamone (1994) describe workaholism as an excessive commitment to work that results in the neglect of important aspects of life. "In the narrowest sense, workaholism is an addiction to action; but the action takes many forms . . . the type of action may vary, but the process is the same: You leave yourself" (Fassel, 1990, p. 4). Chamberlain and Zhang (2009) describe work addiction as a dependence on work despite adverse consequences, with their research focusing on areas of increased somatic complaints, psychological symptoms, and poor self-acceptance. Recent research adds complications from perfectionism, which is often tied closely to workaholism (Stoeber, Davis, & Townley, 2013). Sussman (2013) points out that the number of hours worked weekly may be one important indicator of workaholism if the hours worked exceeds 50 hours per week.

The primary characteristics of workaholics include "multiple addictions, denial, self-esteem problems, external referenting, inability to relax, and obsessiveness" (Fassel, 1990, p. 27), as well as out-of-control behavior and an escape from personal issues or relationship intimacy (Buck & Amos, 2000; Sussman, 2013). These characteristics can be the result of a need to control one's life, an overly competitive drive to succeed, being raised by a workaholic parent or role model, and low self-esteem or self-image (Buck & Amos, 2000). In Figure 3.2, the stages of work addiction are examined utilizing a biopsychosocial approach depicting the progressive nature of addiction.

Workaholics do things in excess. They keep a frenetic pace and do not feel satisfied with themselves unless they are always doing something. As a result, workaholics tend to have more than one addiction, perhaps as many as 20% (Sussman et al., 2011). Often they smoke, drink, or do drugs as a way to cope with stress. They may have strict eating and exercise regimes in order to have enough energy to sustain such a fast-paced lifestyle. These efforts to cope help hide what is truly going on and prolong the individual's denial (Fassel & Schaef, 1989). Family, friends, and coworkers are thought to also experience negative effects of workaholism (Bonebright et al., 2000; Chamberlain & Zhang, 2009).

Operationalizing "Workaholism"

New research conducted in Japan and the Netherlands assessed the validity of new scales to measure two aspects of work addiction: working excessively hard and working compulsively. Workaholics who worked excessively hard and compulsively showed a high risk of burnout. While more research in this area is needed, the hypothesized two-factor construct fit the data in both countries and may prove a valuable means by which to better understand this process addiction.

Source: Schaufeli, W. B., Shimazu, A., & Taris, T. W. (2009). Being driven to work excessively hard: The evaluation of a two-factor measure of workaholism in the Netherlands and Japan. *Cross-Cultural Research, 43*(4), 320–348.

Work Addiction Stages	Symptoms	Organizational Response
Early Stage Time span: 5–8 years on average	*Bio:* Stress-related symptoms first noticed: frequent headaches, generalized anxiety (especially pertaining to work), digestive problems, minimal sleep problems, or mild irritability. *Psycho:* Increased hours thinking about or being at work, seeking additional projects/assignments, greater emphasis being placed on external recognition, decreased ability to self-validate (e.g., "I did a good job, I can stop now and continue this tomorrow"), increased self-criticism (e.g., "I should do more, spend more time at the office; I'm afraid I'm not working hard enough; It's got to be done better"). *Social:* Late arrival at home or social events due to increased work activity; increasing work at home or at social events via cell phone, texting, or Internet communication; increasing heated discussions with partner about time spent on work.	Promotions, recognition from peers & management, increased pay, bonuses, increased workload/assignments, favorable job reviews & evaluations.
Middle Stage Time span: 8–12 years on average	*Bio:* Increased stress-related symptoms; sleep disorders—insomnia/hypersomnia; pronounced weight loss/gain, or weight fluctuations; increased use of medications for sleep, anxiety, depression, increased use of mood-altering chemicals or processes (e.g. extramarital affairs, sexual promiscuity, gambling) to achieve pleasure or relaxation due to frequent tension and increased difficulty relaxing. *Psycho:* Increasing hours spent on work (both on and off site); perfectionism increasing; decreased tolerance of mistakes (self or colleagues); preoccupation with work products, projects, or outcomes. *Social:* Less leisure pursuits and/or decreased time spent in established leisure outlets, greater identity associated with workplace, title, or role; work–family conflicts experienced, minimal marital/partner separation may occur; intermittent experiences of significant job dissatisfaction leading to geographic escape from "this demanding job" to new locations.	Promotions, greater responsibilities assigned, management opportunities, possible relocation, increased travel, increased recognition and community service encouraged; job changes, seeking advancement, which may be due to varying productivity or employer/supervisee conflicts.
Late Stage Time span: 10–15 years on average	*Bio:* Stress-related physical complications such as cardiac events, e.g., heart attack or stroke, brought on by poor physical care with inability to successfully manage intense stress; probable activation of co-occurring addiction to mood-altering chemicals or processes (pathological gambler, alcoholism, or food addict). *Psycho:* Working continually or "bingeing" resulting in sustained work activity with *reduced* accomplishment; less productivity but more time spent on work; greater job dissatisfaction; increased agitation; workplace conflicts increasing; complaints by co-workers/supervisees; poor risk-taking with job assignments. *Social:* Minimal leisure activity; increased strife with work–family conflicts, impending divorce or estranged, poor communication with family/loved ones, withdrawn from family and social events.	Varied: Possible advancement due to long history of products OR demotions, reduction in force (RIF), job termination; mandatory supervisory referral to Executive Coach or Employee Assistance Program Counselor.

FIGURE 3.2 Stages of Work Addiction, Biopsychosocial Model (L. J. Veach)

A compounding problem of workaholism is that our fast-paced, performance-driven society readily supports, encourages, and rewards it (Fassel, 1990). In fact, many people are self-proclaimed workaholics. A common myth about workaholics is that since they work longer hours they are more productive; research, however, indicates otherwise (Bonebright et al., 2000; Fassel & Schaef, 1989). Workaholics tend to be less productive than the more relaxed worker who keeps regular hours. The workaholism–perfectionism connection is highlighted by research findings that show "workaholism is mainly driven by personal aspects of perfectionism rather than social aspects" (Stoeber et al., 2013, p. 737). The irony is that the workaholic's perfectionist tendencies and inability to delegate tasks to others can reduce efficiency and flexibility and decrease progress in the workplace (Bonebright et al., 2000). Numerous studies suggest that there is a relationship between workaholism and many difficulties (Brady, Vodanovich, & Rotunda, 2008; Bonebright et al., 2000; Chamberlain & Zhang, 2009; Sussman, 2013). Although it is difficult to pinpoint accurate numbers, the estimated cost of stress-related issues to companies is $150 million per year. These costs include workers' compensation for stress, burnout, hiring and retraining new employees, and legal fees when companies get sued by employees for stress-related illnesses (Fassel & Schaef, 1989). Sussman (2013) highlights several studies, of the few conducted, that illustrate negative workaholism consequences, such as driving sleep deprived or driving while working using mobile devices.

Bonebright et al. (2000) claim there are three "causal explanations" for why individuals choose to dedicate so many hours to their work. First, they truly find enjoyment and satisfaction in their work. Second, they have an uncontrollable desire to work, even if they do not enjoy the task. Third, they receive a euphoric high from accumulating the rewards of their hard work. Eventually, their desire to receive these accolades, the workaholic's euphoria, interferes with their health, relationships, family, and other activities, which is indicative of the addictive cycle.

Research supports that workaholics compared to nonworkaholics have greater anxiety, stress, anger, and depression. Likewise, workaholics perceive themselves as having more job stress, perfectionism, anxiety, health complaints, and less willingness to delegate job responsibilities to others (Robinson, 1998). In their recent work, Chamberlain and Zhang (2009) reported significant findings—namely, that workaholism negatively affects physical health, psychological well-being, and self-acceptance. These researchers also noted that adult children of workaholics were predominantly self-described workaholics, suggesting the parent's work addiction is often mirrored in their children. It is of particular concern with the reported low self-acceptance patterns of workaholics that "this nonaccepting attitude toward oneself could transfer to being overly critical and demanding of others" (Chamberlain & Zhang, 2009, p. 167). Brady et al. (2008) added empirical knowledge with an extensive study examining workaholism and work–family conflict, job satisfaction, and leisure among university faculty and staff in one sample along with employees in various community work settings in a different sample. These researchers noted that in both samples: first, high workaholism scores were significant predictors of heightened work–family conflict; next, higher drive scores, or ambition-driven behaviors, led to lower job satisfaction findings, particularly in the university employees; and finally, less enjoyment of leisure was significantly found in workaholics (Brady et al., 2008). Lastly, studies indicate that an individual's work addiction, as is true with other addictions, has a severe impact on others, producing marital conflict, dysfunction within the family, and strained social relationships (Brady et al., 2008; Robinson, 1998). Children of workaholics may be prone to developing workaholic tendencies of poor self-acceptance, increased physical complaints, or full-blown workaholism as a result of being raised in a workaholic family environment (Chamberlain & Zhang, 2009; Robinson, 1998). Treatment considerations may need to stress family counseling, self-talk, and reviewing with clients their individual reinforcement patterns, as outlined by Chamberlain and Zhang (2009). More research is needed in the area of diagnosing and effectively treating work addiction, as well as closer examination of the stages of work addiction in order to assess whether, as with other addictions, the adverse consequences of workaholism are progressive. Brief screening of behaviors described by Sussman (2013) such as frequent hurrying and rushing, overcontrolling, perfectionism, work bingeing, work-related exhaustion, hyperfocus on work leading to poor concentration and recall, compulsive checking on work, and poor self-care can assist the counselor with earlier exploration of possible workaholic patterns and interventions. Treatment approaches may include those based on other addiction treatment approaches including 12-step support groups, such as Workaholics Anonymous begun in 1983 (Sussman, 2013). Many researchers also emphasize the need to examine extensive data, the cost of workaholism to organizations, especially when higher incidences of hypercritical, inefficient, negative, and overcontrolling behaviors or increased complaints by supervisees occur (Brady et al., 2008; Sussman, 2013; Vodanovich & Piotrowski, 2006).

Case Study

Bryant, a married 48-year-old African-American male, is an associate professor at a midsized university. Recently, he has been experiencing marital discord and his only child, a 15-year-old son, has been experiencing pronounced anxiety accompanied by panic attacks at school. Bryant has recently been considering the offer of a promotion into university administration as an Associate Provost. He has an active research agenda, has published numerous textbooks and publications, and his professional service has received outstanding reviews in his field. He knows he is spending less and less time with his family and on leisure activities, and had a negative encounter with a colleague where he lost his temper, but believes he deserves this next step up since he has worked so hard. He wonders if he should pursue this prestigious offer and seeks career counseling with you, his Employee Assistance Program Counselor. What particular areas would you address? How would you begin to explore workaholism?

COMPULSIVE BUYING

The incidence of compulsive buying is estimated at 6% of the U.S population (Sussman et al., 2011). Since most of the data on compulsive buyers come from self-selected samples, it is difficult to know the true prevalence of this disorder. *Compulsive shopping, uncontrolled buying, addictive buying, addictive consumption, shopaholism,* and *spendaholism* are all names for compulsive buying (Lee & Mysyk, 2004). Compulsive buying (CB) has been described as a condition caused by chronic failures at self-regulation that becomes self-reinforcing over time, as persons move through antecedent, internal/external trigger, buying, and postpurchase phases (Kellet, 2009; Williams & Grisham, 2012). In its literature, Debtors Anonymous (2014) describes debt aptly for those suffering from compulsive buying, a process addiction, and equates debt with alcohol, food, or gambling for alcoholics, anorexics, and gamblers, respectively. Sometimes referred to as *oniomania*, a term used first in 1915, it is often comorbid with substance use, eating and impulse control disorders, and mood disorders (Filomensky et al., 2012). In clinical samples, women make up the majority of subjects, yet experts report a 1:1 male-to-female ratio (Filomensky et al., 2012).

Compulsive buying has been defined as consistent, repetitive purchasing that becomes the first response to negative or stressful life events or feelings. Compulsive buyers try to fill the meaninglessness, unhappiness, and void in their lives by purchasing items to relieve these negative feelings. Compulsive buying takes a toll on the individual, family, and society, and it can lead to "overspending, indebtedness, and bankruptcy" (Lee & Mysyk, 2004, p. 1710).

Recent studies note that impulsive behaviors predominate in compulsive buying and, as such, CB might be diagnosed as an impulse control disorder (Filomensky et al., 2012; Williams & Grisham, 2012). In addition, "kleptomania may be associated with compulsive buying" (APA, 2013, p. 479). Findings in a comprehensive study by Filomensky and colleagues (2012) substantiated that CB participants consistently showed impulsivity and acquiring behaviors on several measures, but minimal hoarding, bipolar, or obsessive-compulsive disorder-related behaviors. Psychosocial, cognitive behavioral, and pharmacotherapy (Filomensky et al., 2012; Kellet, 2009) treatment modalities have been suggested by the literature. In addition, twelve-step groups, such as Debtors Anonymous (2014), offer steps to regain financial health and recovery. Lee and Mysyk (2004) examine the larger social context of what it means to be a compulsive buyer in today's society. They point out that it is important to keep in mind, when examining and diagnosing a compulsive buyer, that we live in a consumer-driven society fueled by powerful messages urging buyers to spend. These messages tell us that buying things will enhance our self-esteem, make us happy, and increase social status. Strategies such as teaching individuals how to resist powerful marketing messages and examine the social forces at work may be useful. Lee and Mysyk (2004) do not rationalize the behavior of compulsive buyers, but do point out that the social forces behind purchasing in our society, including the media, the state of the economy, and easy access to credit, can also fuel the compulsive buyer. It is important to continue to gather data regarding prevalence and patterns associated with compulsive buying in order to better understand this process addiction.

Case Study

Gina is a recovering alcoholic whose husband died last year. She has struggled with depression and has withdrawn from most normal activities, including meetings. She began watching and ordering from one of the shopping networks a few months ago. Over the last 2 months her daughter has become increasingly concerned and brought her in for counseling because Gina has spent almost $10,000 on items she does not use or need. Sometimes, Gina admits, she may not even want the item, but feels good when she orders from her "family at the shopping network." She is angry at being confronted and says that it is her money and her choice. Considering information about process addictions and spending, and Gina's circumstances, do you consider this behavior problematic? Addictive? Discuss what you think may be happening with Gina, the danger signals you see, and how you would approach counseling with her.

FOOD ADDICTION AND DISORDERED EATING

Some addiction experts claim that—similar to alcohol or drugs—food can be addictive (Ahmed et al., 2013; Avena, Rada, & Hoebel, 2008; Clark & Saules, 2013; Gearhardt, White, Masheb, & Grilo, 2013; Gearhardt, Corbin, & Brownell, 2009b; Gearhardt, Corbin, & Brownell, 2009a; Gold, Graham, Cocores, & Nixon, 2009; Sheppard, 1993; Sinha & Jastrehoff, 2013; von Deneen, Gold, & Liu, 2009), while others continue to debate the issue (APA, 2013; von Ranson, McGue, & Iacono, 2003). Experts who claim that eating disorders (including anorexia, bulimia, and binge eating) are addictions argue that individuals suffering with these disorders often share common traits with those addicted to alcohol or drugs, such as obsession, compulsion, denial, tolerance, withdrawal symptoms, and cravings (Ahmed et al., 2013; Clark & Saules, 2013; Gearhardt et al., 2013;

Sheppard, 1993). Researchers are exploring the possible addictive qualities of certain types of foods, including foods with high fat and/or sugar content (Ahmed et al., 2013; Gold et al., 2009). For example, sugar releases opioids and dopamines in the brain, causing neurochemical changes and suggesting possible addictive qualities (Avena et al., 2008). The roles of hormones and genes that may be related to whether a person is likely to develop addictive eating patterns are also being investigated (von Deneen et al., 2009). Gold et al. (2009) assert that our nation's obesity epidemic alone suggests that certain foods may promote a loss of control and continued use despite negative consequences, which are among the diagnostic criterion for substance abuse and dependence. The existence of 12-step recovery programs for disordered eating, modeled after Alcoholics Anonymous's Twelve Steps and Traditions, perhaps indicates growing support among both the population and professionals for the treatment of eating disorders as addictions (von Ranson et al., 2003). Such programs include Overeaters Anonymous, Inc., Food Addicts in Recovery Anonymous, Anorexics Anonymous, and Bulimics Anonymous.

The debate about whether eating disorders are addictions continues as researchers learn more about the causes and best treatment for eating disorders and food addiction. There is still a great deal to learn about the causes of eating disorders. What is known is that eating disorders are complex, involving long-term psychological, behavioral, emotional, interpersonal, familial, biological, spiritual, and social factors (ANAD, 2014; National Eating Disorders Association [NEDA], 2014). In fact, although people with eating disorders are preoccupied with food, appearance, and weight, they also often struggle with issues of control, acceptance, and self-esteem. Regardless of the potential causes of eating disorders, they can create a self-perpetuating cycle of physical and emotional abuse that requires professional help.

Anorexia nervosa is typified by compulsive self-starvation and excessive weight loss. Some of the symptoms can include refusal to maintain a normal body weight for height, body type, age, and activity level; intense fear of weight gain; loss of menstrual periods; continuing to feel "fat" despite extreme weight loss; and extreme obsessive concern with body weight and shape (NEDA, 2014). ANAD (2014) states that symptoms of anorexia nervosa include weighing 15% below what is expected for age and height. An individual with anorexia nervosa may have a low tolerance for change and new situations, may fear growing up and taking charge of his or her own life, and be overly dependent on parents and family. Dieting may represent avoidance of and ineffective attempts at coping with the demands of new stages of life (ANAD, 2014).

Bulimia nervosa is typified by a compulsive cycle of binge eating and then purging. An individual with bulimia eats a large amount of food in a short period of time and then gets rid of the food and calories through vomiting, laxative abuse, or excessive exercise. Some of the symptoms of bulimia include repeated cycles of bingeing and purging, frequent dieting, extreme concern with body weight and shape, and feeling out of control during a binge, as well as eating beyond the point of fullness. Impulse control can be a problem for those with bulimia and lack of control may also extend to risky behaviors such as shoplifting, sexual adventurousness, and alcohol and other drug abuse (ANAD, 2014).

Binge eating disorder is a recognized disorder in the new diagnostic manual (APA, 2013) and is differentiated from bulimia nervosa in that there are episodes of uncontrollable, impulsive bingeing but there is no purging. An individual with binge eating disorder engages in random fasting and diets and feels extreme shame and self-hatred after bingeing. Individuals with binge eating disorder tend to eat rapidly and secretly, and be depressed and obese. Other eating disorders include a combination of symptoms from anorexia, bulimia, purging, night eating, and binge eating disorders and the symptoms, if severe enough, can be considered a clinical disorder (APA, 2013).

Case Study

Maggie is an 18-year-old college freshman. During high school, she was an honor roll student and athlete, participating on the soccer and swim teams. Maggie is very driven to succeed at college, and is feeling the strains of being in a new place with high academic standards. She began to gravitate to comforting favorite foods in the cafeteria, such as pizza, French fries, and soft serve ice cream. She soon began to notice that her clothes were getting tight. Maggie became very scared of gaining the "freshman fifteen" and started working out and eating more healthfully. After she lost the few pounds she had gained, however, she decided she could stand to lose a few more. She began getting up at 6 A.M. to fit in a long gym workout before class, and began to make rules about which foods in the cafeteria she was allowed to eat. Maggie comes to see you at the university counseling center because she is "stressed" and "anxious." During your assessment, you notice that she is very thin, and you learn that she has lost 20 pounds since she began what she describes as "just eating better and working out to be healthier."

What are the most important concerns to focus on first as her counselor? How would you begin to explore your concerns about her eating patterns, or would you? What levels of care might you consider: outpatient, intensive outpatient, and/or residential? Explain. How would you discuss the addictive nature of her eating patterns? Or, would you mention addiction?

According to the DSM-5, the lifetime prevalence rate of anorexia nervosa among females is 0.4% and one-tenth of that for men (APA, 2013). In the last 20 years the occurrence of anorexia nervosa has increased. The 12-month prevalence of bulimia nervosa among women is 1–1.53% and the prevalence for men is roughly one-tenth of that of females (APA, 2013). According to ANAD (2014), 1% of female adolescents suffer from anorexia nervosa and 1.1–4.2% of women suffer from bulimia nervosa during their life. Other estimates highlight that 5–15% of individuals suffering from anorexia and bulimia are male (ANAD, 2014). NEDA (2014) reports roughly 30 million are struggling with eating disorders. Because physicians are not required to report eating disorders to a health agency, and because the nature of the disorder is secretive, we only have estimates of how many people in this country are affected by eating disorders (ANAD, 2014; NEDA, 2014).

Summary and Some Final Notations

In summary, "to recognize the underlying addictive process is to acknowledge that society itself operates addictively; its institutions perpetuate the addictive process. It does not merely encourage addictions; it regards them as normal" (Schaef, 1990, p. 18). This chapter provides counselors with comprehensive introductory information about process addictions. It is imperative that counselors continue their education about the new scientific discoveries as well as the intricate and complex issues surrounding addiction.

MyCounselingLab

Visit the MyCounselingLab site for *Foundations of Addictions Counseling,* Third Edition to enhance your understanding of concepts. You'll have the opportunity to practice your skills through video- and case-based exercises. You will find sets of questions to help you prepare for your certification exam with *Licensure Quizzes.* There is also a Video Library that provides taped counseling sessions, ethical scenarios, and interviews with helpers and clients.

Useful Websites

The following websites provide additional information relating to the chapter topics:

Anorexia Nervosa and Related Disorders, Inc.
www.anad.org/

Anorexics and Bulimics Anonymous
www.aba12steps.org

CoDependents Anonymous
www.codependents.org

Debtors Anonymous
debtorsanonymous.org/

Food Addicts in Recovery Anonymous
www.foodaddicts.org

Gamblers Anonymous
www.GamblersAnonymous.org

Gambling, National Council on Problem Gambling
www.ncpgambling.org

National Eating Disorders Association
www.nationaleatingdisorders.org

Overeaters Anonymous
www.oa.org

S-Anon (for family and friends of sexually addicted people)
www.sanon.org

Sex Addicts Anonymous
www.saa-recovery.org

Sexaholics Anonymous
www.sa.org

Sex and Love Addicts Anonymous
www.slaafws.org

Stopping Over Shopping
www.shopaholicnomore.com/

References

Acosta, K. M. (2013). *Understanding at-risk technology users: A phenomenological approach* [Doctoral dissertation]. Retrieved from ProQuest Digital Dissertations.

Acosta, K. M., Lainas, H., & Veach, L. J. (2013). An emerging trend: Becoming aware of technology addiction. *NC Perspectives, 8,* 5–11.

Ahmed, S. H., Guillem, K., & Vandaele, Y. (2013). Sugar addiction: Pushing the drug-sugar analogy to the limit. *Current Opinion in Clinical Nutrition and Metabolic Care, 16,* 434–439.

American Psychiatric Association. (2000). *Diagnostic and statistical manual of mental disorders* (4th ed., text revision). Washington, DC: Author.

American Psychiatric Association. (2013). *Diagnostic and statistical manual of mental disorders* (5th ed.). Washington, DC: Author.

Avena, N. M., Rada, P., & Hoebel, B. G. (2008). Evidence for sugar addiction: Behavioral and neurochemical effects of intermittent, excessive sugar intake. *Neuroscience & Biobehavioral Reviews, 32*(1), 20–39. doi:10.1016/j.neubiorev.2007.04.019

Bailey, C. E., & Case, B. (2014). *Sexual addiction.* Retrieved from http://www.aamft.org/imis15/aamft/Content/Consumer_Updates/Sexual_Addiction.aspx

Bancroft, J., & Vukadinovic, Z. (2004). Sexual addiction, sexual compulsivity, sexual impulsivity, or what? Toward a theoretical model. *The Journal of Sex Research, 41,* 225–234.

Bonebright, C. A., Clay, D. L., & Ankenmann, R. D. (2000). The relationship of workaholism with work-life conflict, life satisfaction, and purpose in life. *Journal of Counseling Psychology, 47,* 469–477.

Brady, B. R., Vodanovich, S. J., & Rotunda, R. (2008). The impact of workaholism on work-family conflict, job satisfaction, and perception of leisure activities. *The Psychologist-Manager Journal, 11,* 241–263. doi:10.1080/10887150802371781

Buck, T., & Amos, S. (2000). *Related addictive disorders* (Report No. CG030040). U.S. Department of Education, Office of Educational Research and Improvement. (ERIC Document Reproduction Service No. ED440345)

Carnes, P. J. (2011). What is sex addiction? Retrieved from http://www.sexhelp.com/sex-education/what-is-sex-addiction-faqs

Centers for Disease Control and Prevention. (2011). Mobile device use while driving—United States and seven European countries. *MMWR, 62,* 177–182.

Ceravolo, R., Frosini, D., Rossi, C., & Bonuccelli, U. (2010). Impulse control disorders in Parkinson's disease: Definition, epidemiology, risk factors, neurobiology and management. *Parkinsonism and Related Disorders, 15*(Suppl. 4), S111–S115.

Chamberlain, C. M., & Zhang, N. (2009). Workaholism: Health and self-acceptance. *Journal of Counseling & Development, 87,* 159–169.

Clark, L., & Limbrick-Oldfield, E. H. (2013). Disordered gambling: A behavioural addiction. *Current Opinion in Neurobiology, 23,* 655–659.

Clark, S. M., & Saules, K. K. (2013). Validation of the Yale Food Addiction Scale among a weight-loss surgery population. *Eating Behaviors, 14,* 216–219.

Co-Dependents Anonymous, Inc. (1995). *Co-Dependents Anonymous*. Dallas, TX: CoDA Resource Publishing.

Debtors Anonymous. (2014). About Debtors Anonymous. Retrieved from http://debtorsanonymous.org/about/about.htm

Fassel, D. (1990). *Working ourselves to death*. New York, NY: HarperCollins.

Fassel, D., & Schaef, A. W. (1989, January). The high cost of workaholism. *Business & Health, 21,* 38–42.

Filomensky, T. Z., Almeida, K. M., Nogueira, M. C. C., Diniz, J. B., Lafer, B., Borcato, S. & Tavares, H. (2012). Neither bipolar nor obsessive-compulsive disorder: Compulsive buyers are impulsive acquirers. *Comprehensive Psychiatry, 53,* 554–561.

Fong, T. W., & Tsuang, J. (2007, November). Asian-Americans, addictions, and barriers to treatment. *Psychiatry,* pp. 51–58.

Gearhardt, A. N., Corbin, W. R., & Brownell, K. D. (2009a). Food addiction: An examination of the diagnostic criteria for dependence. *Journal of Addiction Medicine, 3*(1), 1–7. doi:10.1097/ADM.0b013e318193c993

Gearhardt, A. N., Corbin, W. R., & Brownell, K. D. (2009b). Preliminary validation of the Yale Food Addiction Scale. *Appetite, 52*(2), 430–436. doi:10.1016/j.appet.2008.12.003

Gearhardt, A. N., White, M. A., Masheb, R. M., & Grilo, C. M. (2013). An examination of food addiction in a racially diverse sample of obese patients with binge eating disorder in primary care settings. *Comprehensive Psychiatry, 54,* 500–505.

Gold, M. S., Graham, N. A., Cocores, J. A., & Nixon, S. J. (2009). Food addiction? *Journal of Addiction Medicine, 3*(1), 42–45. doi:10.1097/ADM.0b013e318199cd20

Grilo, C. M., Sinha, R., & O'Malley, S. S. (2002). Eating disorders and alcohol use disorders. *Alcohol Research & Health, 26*(2), 151–160.

Hagedorn, W. B. (2005). Sexual addiction as a precursor to chemical addiction. In V. A. Kelly & G. A. Juhnke (Eds.), *Critical incidents in addictions counseling* (pp. 25–33). Alexandria, VA: American Counseling Association.

Hagedorn, W. B. (2009). The call for a new *Diagnostic and Statistical Manual of Mental Disorders* diagnosis: Addictive disorders. *Journal of Addictions & Offender Counseling, 29,* 110–127.

Hagedorn, W. B., & Juhnke, G. A. (2005). Treating the sexually addicted client: Establishing a need for increased counselor awareness. *Journal of Addictions & Offender Counseling, 25,* 66–86.

Hsu, S., Wen, M., & Wu, M. (2009). Exploring user experiences as predictors of MMORPG addiction. *Computers & Education, 53*(3), 990–999. doi:10.1016/j.compedu.2009.05.016

Kellett, S. (2009). Compulsive buying: A cognitive-behavioural model. *Clinical Psychology Psychotherapy, 16*(2), 83.

Kranzler, H. R., & Li, T.-K. (2008). What is addiction? *Alcohol Research & Health, 31,* 93–95.

Lambert, L. T. K. (2013). Internet sex addiction. *Journal of Addiction Medicine, 7,* 145–146.

Lee, S., & Mysyk, A. (2004). The medicalization of compulsive buying. *Social Science & Medicine, 58,* 1709–1718.

Long, L. L., Burnett, J. A., & Thomas, R. V. (2006). *Sexuality counseling: An integrative approach*. Upper Saddle River, NJ: Pearson Education, Inc.

Massachusetts Council on Compulsive Gambling, National Problem Gambling Awareness Week 2009. (2009, February 27). MCCG Asian awareness Cantonese, Mandarin and Vietnamese [Video file]. Retrieved from http://youtube/9gB_pu4m44s

McBride, J., & Derevensky, J. (2009). Internet gambling behavior in a sample of online gamblers. *International Journal of Mental Health and Addiction, 7*(1), 149–167. doi:10.1007/s11469-008-9169-x

Miller, G. (2005). *Learning the language of addiction counseling*. Hoboken, NJ: John Wiley & Sons.

Mitchell, J. E., Redlin, J., Wonderlich, S., Crosby, R., Faber, R., Miltenberger, R., Smith, J., . . ., Lancaster, K. (2001). The relationship between compulsive buying and eating disorders. Retrieved from http://www.interscience.wiley.com

National Association of Anorexia Nervosa and Associated Eating Disorders. (2014). Eating disorder statistics. Retrieved from http://www.anad.org

National Council on Problem Gambling. (2014). National Council on Problem Gambling [Web log post]. Retrieved from http://www.ncpgambling.org

National Eating Disorders Association. (2014). Retrieved from http://www.nationaleatingdisorders.org

Petry, N. M., & O'Brien, C. P. (2013). Internet gaming disorder and the DSM-5. *Addiction Journal, 108,* 1186–1187.

Rainone, G., Marel, R., Gallati, R. J., & Gargon, N. (2007). *Gambling behaviors and problem gambling among adults in New York State: Initial findings from the 2006 OASAS Household Survey.* New York State Office of Alcoholism and State Services. Retrieved from http://www.gaming.ny.gov/gaming/20140409forum/OtherMaterials/OASAS,GamblinginNewYorkState(2006).pdf

Robinson, B. E. (1998). The workaholic family: A clinical perspective. *The American Journal of Family Therapy, 26,* 65–75.

Schaef, A. W. (1990, January 3–10). Is the church an addictive organization? *The Christian Century, 107*(1), 18–21.

Schaufeli, W. B., Shimazu, A., & Taris, T. W. (2009). Being driven to work excessively hard: The evaluation of a two-factor measure of Workaholism in the Netherlands and Japan. *Cross-Cultural Research, 43*(4), 320–348.

Schneider, J. P. (2004). Sexual addiction & compulsivity: Twenty years of the field, ten years of the journal [Editorial]. *Sexual Addiction & Compulsivity, 11,* 3–5.

Seegers, J. A. (2003). The prevalence of sexual addiction symptoms on the college campus. *Sexual Addiction & Compulsivity, 10,* 247–258.

S-Anon. (2013). What is S-Anon? Retrieved from http://www.sanon.org/whatissanon.html

Sexaholics Anonymous, Inc. (2010). What is a sexaholic and what is sexual sobriety? Retrieved from http://www.sa.org/sexaholic.php

Seybold, K. C., & Salamone, P. R. (1994). Understanding workaholism: A review of causes and counseling approaches. *Journal of Counseling & Development, 73*(1), 4–10.

Shaffer, H. J., & Kidman, R. (2003). Shifting perspectives on gambling and addiction. *Journal of Gambling Studies, 19*(1), 1–6.

Sheppard, K. (1993). *Food addiction: The body knows* (rev. ed.). Deerfield Beach, FL: Health Communications, Inc.

Sinha, R. & Jastreboff, A. M. (2013). Stress as a common risk factor for obesity and addiction. *Biological Psychiatry, 73,* 827–835.

Stoeber, J., Davis, C. R., & Townley, J. (2013). Perfectionism and workaholism in employees: The role of work motivation. *Personality and Individual Differences, 55,* 733–738.

Suissa, A. J. (2007). Gambling addiction as a pathology: Some markers for empowerment. *Journal of Addictions Nursing, 18,* 93–101. doi:10.1080/10884600701334952

Suissa, A. J. (2011). Vulnerability and gambling addictions: Psychosocial benchmarks and avenues for intervention. *International Journal of Mental Health and Addiction, 9,* 12–23. doi:10.1007/s11469-009-9248-7

Sussman, S. (2013). Workaholism: A review. *Journal of Addiction Research & Therapy, Supplement 6.* doi:10.4172/2155-6105.S6-001

Sussman, S., Lisha, N., & Griffiths, M. (2011). Prevalence of the addictions: A problem of the majority or the minority? *Evaluation & the Health Professions, 34,* 3–56. doi:10.1177/0163278710380124

Sussman, S., & Sussman, A. N. (2011). Considering the definition of addiction. *International Journal of Environmental Research and Public Health, 8,* 4025–4038. doi:10.3390/ijerph8104025

Vodanovich, S. J., & Piotrowski, C. (2006). Workaholism: A critical but neglected factor in O.D. *Organizational Development Journal, 24,* 55–60.

von Deneen, K. M., Gold, M. S., & Liu, Y. (2009). Food addiction and cues in Prader-Willi syndrome. *Journal of Addiction Medicine, 3*(1), 19–25. doi:10.1097/ADM.0b013e31819a6e5f

von Ranson, K. M., McGue, M., & Iacono, W. G. (2003). Disordered eating and substance use in an epidemiological sample: II. Associations within families. *Psychology of Addictive Behaviors, 17*(3). Retrieved from PsychARTICLES database.

Williams, A. D., & Grisham, J. R. (2012). Impulsivity, emotion regulation, and mindful attentional focus in compulsive buying. *Cognitive Therapy and Research, 36,* 451–457. doi: 10.1007/s10608-011-9384-9

Young, K. (2009). Internet addiction: Diagnosis and treatment considerations. *Journal of Contemporary Psychotherapy, 39*(4), 241–246. doi:10.1007/s10879-009-9120-x

Zamora, D. (2003). *Internet to sex: Defining addiction.* WebMD. Retrieved from http://my.webmd.com/content/Article/76/90153.htm

Zapf, J. L., Greiner, J., & Carroll, J. (2008). Attachment styles and male sex addiction. *Sexual Addiction & Compulsivity, 15,* 158–175. doi: 10.1080/10720160802 035832

Zmuda, N. (2014). Assessment and treatment of co-occurring substance use disorders and process addictions. In S. L. A. Straussner (Ed.), *Clinical work with substance-abusing clients* (3rd ed., pp. 520–536). New York, NY: Guilford Press.

Chapter 4

Important Professional Issues in Addiction Counseling

Melinda Haley
Sarah H. Golden
Walden University

Professional issues in addiction counseling are those topics attended to for the ethical, legal, and competent treatment of individuals suffering from substance use and addictive disorders. There are many issues that could be discussed within such an extensive topic—in fact, entire books have been written on many of the topics covered in this chapter. However, due to space and practical constraints, the discussion will focus on two broad areas related to addiction counseling: professional issues pertaining to counselors and treatment and research issues.

These are difficult subjects to write about because addiction counselors, although united in the professional treatment of clients with substance use and addiction disorders, may differ both in professional affiliation and ethical code. To add to this diversity, states have different laws regulating the addiction profession. Therefore, every attempt has been made to point out both differences and similarities where applicable. It is the responsibility of addiction professionals to know, understand, and practice under the specific state and federal laws, and the specific ethical code of the credentialing agency through which they have obtained their certification or licensing.

One unique aspect of the addiction field is that it is multidimensional and multidisciplinary. Those providing treatment for individuals with substance use and addictive disorders can be physicians, psychiatrists, psychologists, social workers, clergy, family therapists, or addiction counselors (Chandler, Balkin, & Perepiczka, 2011; Najavits, Kivlahan, & Kosten, 2011). While some might consider this a drawback, others find the diversity within the field essential (Madden et al., 2008). Because so many professions are involved in treating people with substance use and addictive disorders, there are many titles for these individuals, such as addiction counselors, substance abuse and dependence counselors, chemical dependency counselors, alcohol and other drug (AOD) counselors, and so on. To be consistent, the terms used to describe this profession within this chapter will be *addiction counselor* or *counselor*.

PROFESSIONAL ISSUES PERTAINING TO COUNSELORS

Addiction counselors have responsibilities to clients, the addiction field, other professionals, the public, and their employers (Rieckmann, Farentinos, Tillotson, Kocarnik, & McCarty, 2011). This section on professional issues pertaining to addiction counselors will review topics related to counselor competence and credentialing.

Counselor Competence

We are all limited in our practice as counselors. No one person is fully competent in all areas of mental health care or in addiction counseling. It is up to the addiction counselor to recognize his or her limitations with respect to the types of services he or she can offer. This section will review counselor competence within the following issues: (a) comorbidity; (b) specific populations; (c) clinical knowledge of polysubstance abuse and dependence; (d) knowledge of theory, treatment, and recovery models; (e) boundary violation issues; (f) multiculturalism; (g) education; (h) counselors in recovery; (i) counselors who have never been users; (j) self-care; and (k) continuing education.

COMORBIDITY The prevalence of comorbidity has been identified as posing various challenges due to the complexities of the disorders and trends in substance abuse treatment programs, which may not adequately meet the needs of both disorders (Langås, Malt, & Opjordsmoen, 2011; Matthews, Kelly, & Deane, 2011). The revised *Diagnostic Statistical Manual* (5th ed., DSM-5) provided an update for substance-related and addictive disorders, combining substance dependence and abuse into a singular category: Substance use disorder with subcategories (American Psychiatric Association, 2013). This change was a reflection of research that demonstrated separating abuse from dependence was problematic (Jones, Gill, & Ray, 2012). When experiencing comorbidity, substance-related disorders are accompanied by additional diagnoses, thus necessitating treatments to attend to each diagnosis.

The National Institute on Drug Abuse (NIDA, 2010) suggested that there are various factors that impact the pervasiveness of comorbidity among substance users, such as gender, type of disorder, and mental illness. An example of comorbidity is evidenced by the commonality of substance abuse accompanied by anxiety and mood disorders (NIDA, 2010). Dual or multiple diagnoses may pose challenges for accurate diagnosis; therefore, it is necessary for counselors to utilize assessment tools that encompass a broad spectrum of screening processes (NIDA, 2010). The duality of a mental health disorder with substance abuse necessitates the use of treatment programs and therapies that attend to the dynamics of both, thus attending to the individual and overlapping challenges that occur concurrently (Cridland, Deane, Hsu, & Kelly, 2012; Langås et al., 2011; Matthews et al., 2011; NIDA, 2010).

To further impress the need to attend to both components of a dual diagnosis, it has been found that various types of mental health disorders may prove to be a predictor for the onset and development of substance abuse or addiction (Swendsen et al., 2010). Treating clients with a comorbid condition offers a unique challenge to the competency of the addiction counselor, especially in cases where he or she does not have training or experience working with individuals with a particular mental disorder. The National Association of Addiction Professionals (NAAP, 2013) code of ethics indicates that addiction counselors are not ethically allowed to diagnose mental disorders without the proper mental health licensing; therefore, addiction counselors need to be cognizant of their limitations within their scope of practice and must refer when necessary.

There are many challenges with the diagnosis of substance abuse and mental health conditions. It is thus essential for counselors to consider various facets and consult when necessary. Based on the American Counseling Association (ACA, 2005) code of ethics, it is a counselor's responsibility to ensure competent treatment; therefore, if a substance abuse counselor is not trained in working with the diagnosis beyond substance abuse, collaborative action may be necessary (ACA, 2005). While the cause of either the mental health disorder or the substance abuse may be perplexing to isolate, counselors should be cognizant of various factors that may be related to the prevalence of comorbidity (NIDA, 2010). Examples may suggest that one leads to the other. For example, mental illness such as anxiety or depression may lead to self-medicating behaviors and substance addiction (NIDA, 2010). Recognizing the need for more training and competency for comorbid conditions, the National Association of Alcoholism and Drug Abuse Counselors (NAADAC) will be offering a credential in "co-occurring competency" (Brys, 2013).

SPECIFIC POPULATIONS While it is beyond the scope of this chapter to outline every specific population that might struggle with addiction concerns, one unique population that has garnered increased attention by addiction professionals in recent years has been minors (e.g., adolescents and children) seeking treatment for substance abuse or addiction. There are a number of legal and ethical questions that arise when working with minors. Compared to adult populations, adolescents have a unique set of needs pertaining to substance abuse treatment and experience specific challenges related to recovery and relapse prevention (Acri, Gogel, Pollock, & Wisdom, 2012; Gonzales, Anglin, Beattie, Ong, & Glik, 2012). For example, when treating minors, counselors need to attend to the various needs of youth, including their rationale behind the substance use, the diversity among individuals, and the motivational determinants for recovery (Dow & Kelly, 2013). Similarly, successful adolescent recovery and relapse prevention may necessitate support and inclusion of activities that promote drug-free lifestyles, such as helping the adolescent find a job to enhance stability (Acri et al., 2012). With these considerations in mind, it is essential for addiction counselors to gain the appropriate training and skills specific to this population.

In addition to the issue of competence in provision of services, counselors also have to consider whether the child or adolescent with whom they are working can legally provide consent for his or her own treatment, especially if he or she is attempting to access services without the knowledge of parents. The age at which minors can legally enter into financial, service, or relationship contracts varies from state to state. In addition, the legal mandates for working with youth may vary as well. Under federal law (42 C.F.R. §2.14), a minor of 12 years of age or older has the legal authority to sign himself or herself into treatment and execute written consent to disclose confidential information without the parent's or guardian's consent. However, the fact that minors can sign into legal agreements and consent to treatment poses an ethical dilemma for addiction counselors. For example, what if a minor discloses to an addiction counselor a pattern of ongoing alcohol and other drug use that is a clear danger to the youth him- or herself or others?

The NAADAC's code of ethics (2011b) necessitates that counselors remain aware of the implications of the client's culture, including age, and how it impacts treatment and interventions to ultimately act in the best interest of the client. Therefore, if facts are revealed relative to the potential harm to the life or physical well-being of the minor, counselors are mandated both by law and ethics to act in their client's best interest, even if that means the counselor breaks confidentiality. From an ethical perspective, counselors should get supervised experience when working with special populations with whom they have no prior experience, because there may be numerous ethical, legal, and treatment issues specific to these groups.

CLINICAL KNOWLEDGE OF POLYSUBSTANCE ABUSE AND DEPENDENCE Within the United States, there continues to be a high incidence rate of substance and polysubstance abuse especially among adolescents and young adults (Olthuis, Darredeau, & Barrett, 2013). Given this trend, it is extremely important that counselors and other health professionals have the clinical knowledge necessary to treat individuals dealing with polysubstance abuse. Yet, despite this critical need, there remains a lack of training and supervision for professionals to successfully treat this population (West & Hamm, 2012; Whitley, 2010). For example, many contemporary researchers find a need for more training and experience among practitioners providing substance and polysubstance abuse treatment. Issues related to training include (a) inadequate graduate-level training in addictions for counselors, psychologists, psychiatrists, and social workers (Bina et al., 2008; Chandler et al., 2011; Chasek, Jorgensen, & Maxon, 2012; Whitley, 2010); (b) no national training standards or uniformity between professions (Chasek et al., 2012); (c) negative attitudes of practitioners toward incorporation of evidenced-based practices (Lundgren et al., 2011); (d) lack of training or inadequate training in specific models of treatment (Najavits et al., 2011); (e) a lack of access to accredited training sites (Tontchev et al., 2011); and (f) inadequate supervision in the field of new addiction professionals (West & Hamm, 2012; Whitley, 2010).

Bina and colleagues (2008) found that a master's of social work (MSW) had a lack of training in the area of substance abuse treatment, which is often negatively correlated with the social worker's knowledge, attitudes, and effectiveness in working with individuals with substance abuse disorders. In their study, they surveyed MSW graduates regarding their perceived knowledge of a number of key content areas of substance abuse, including polysubstance abuse. These authors found that a majority of the participants had limited expertise in these areas and rated themselves as lacking in preparation to treat individuals with these concerns. Counselors and other helping professionals need to be knowledgeable about polysubstance use and how it affects the client and treatment issues. As noted earlier, these training concerns still exist for many of the professions treating addiction. According to NAADAC's (2011b) code of ethics, professionals need to strive for a better understanding of addictive disorders and seek training in areas that are beyond their area of competence.

KNOWLEDGE OF THEORY, TREATMENT, AND RECOVERY MODELS The counselor also needs to be knowledgeable about the differing theories of addiction and treatment and have a positive attitude toward training and the incorporation of new empirically validated treatments (Lundgren et al., 2011). Evidence-based or empirically based practices are interventions for which empirical validation exists to suggest that these treatment protocols improve client outcomes. Historically, there has been reluctance to adopt new treatments (Barrick & Homish, 2011).

One theory that has garnered increased empirical attention among addiction professionals over the course of the past 20 years has been Prochaska and DiClemente's (1984) Transtheoretical Model of Change (TTM). This model is one of the leading approaches for explaining and intervening across a variety of health-related behaviors, such as smoking cessation (Huber & Mahajan, 2008), alcohol abuse (Prochaska et al., 2004), dieting (Wells & Wells, 2007), and substance abuse (Barber, 1995). It has also been used to assess an addiction counselor's "readiness for change," in terms of adapting new treatment protocols, because one of the barriers to implementing evidenced-based practices is the clinician's inexperience or lack of understanding of what it takes to change attitudes and practices (Barrick & Homish, 2011; Lundgren et al., 2011; Rieckmann et al., 2011).

In terms of its theoretical underpinnings, the TTM posits four central concepts essential for client or clinician behavior change: (a) Stages of Change (e.g., Precontemplation, Contemplation, Preparation, Action, and Maintenance); (b) Processes of Change (e.g., cognitive, behavioral, and affective activities that facilitate change); (c) Self-Efficacy (e.g., client's/clinician's confidence in making changes); and (d) Decisional Balance (e.g., advantages and disadvantages of change) (Prochaska et al., 2004).

Compatible with the TTM model of change is that proposed by E. M. Rogers (as cited by Lundgren et al., 2011). Rogers's research identified five factors that accounted for most of the variance in whether practitioners would adopt a new treatment protocol or new innovation:

1. Specific properties of change and the perceived benefits of change.
2. Compatibility with the values, beliefs, past history, and current needs of individuals involved.

3. Complexity of the innovation; simple ones spread faster than complicated ones.
4. Likelihood that the change could be tried on a small scale first.
5. Observability—the ease with which observations could be made of others who had adopted the change (p. 272).

BOUNDARY VIOLATION ISSUES The relationship between the client and the counselor is vital to the recovery process; therefore, it is essential that counselors provide quality, connected, and ethical care to act in the best interest of the client in order to empower and promote positive change (ACA, 2005). According to Rogers (1961), counselors who are most effective at connecting with their clients often exhibit the following characteristics: (a) warmth, (b) dependability, (c) consistency, (d) unconditional positive regard, (e) empathy, (f) nonjudgmental understanding, and (g) a belief that individuals strive toward self-actualization. Aligning with ethical standards within the counseling profession, addiction counselors should ideally exercise conscious awareness of appropriate counselor–client boundaries and be aware of situations that may lead to boundary violations in order to avoid harm to clients (ACA, 2005).

Ethical codes and standards are in place to ensure a standardized level of practice, thus ensuring appropriate client care and interventions. Due to the complexities of the counseling relationship, counselors may be consistently faced with challenges to ethical standards and may experience boundary challenges. One example of a boundary violation may be when the counselor brings his or her personal problems with addiction into the counseling relationship (Oser, Biebel, Pullen, & Harp, 2013). Other boundary violations of which substance abuse counselors need to be conscious include becoming too emotionally invested in the client. This is particularly true for counselors in recovery. Based on their own previous experiences, these counselors may overly connect with and take on their client's problems (Doukas & Cullen, 2010). Becoming overly invested in a client may detract from effectual treatment and blur the line between counselor and client. Substance abuse counselors need to be mindful of possible transference and countertransference and overinvolvement emotionally and physically (Doukas & Cullen, 2010). It is the counselor's responsibility to maintain proper boundaries and actively exercise ethical practices, thus being mindful of potentially harmful situations and behaviors (Martin, Godfrey, Meekums, & Madill, 2011).

MULTICULTURALISM Given both social and demographic changes among African-American, Latino, Asian-Pacific Islanders, Southeast Asian, and Middle Eastern populations, addiction counselors need to be acquainted with the possible cultural differences and how these might affect the assessment and treatment of addiction disorders in culturally different clients. Counselors should also note that diversity not only includes ethnicity and race, but also encompasses sexual orientation, gender identity, age, region of origin, religion, language, and so forth. Individuals are not void of culture; therefore, culture may include a complex assignment of values, beliefs, ethnicities, race, or other distinctions between groups (Hickling, 2012; Unger, 2012). The boundaries of cultural lines have become blurred, evolving and blending into what now may be more effectually perceived as the way in which an individual understands his or her own culture (Unger, 2012). Effectual treatments necessitate the recognition of the individual's perceived cultural beliefs, and the practitioner's awareness of his or her own personal beliefs and judgments, and how the intersection of those may impact and influence treatment (Hickling, 2012). To be ethically competent, it is essential for the counselor to attend to facets beyond the substance addiction and inclusively consider language, cultural background, and treatments that include the client's perceived culture rather than the counselor's perception of culture and stereotypes (Luger, 2011).

TABLE 4.1 Boundary Crossing Decision-Making Guidelines

1. Evaluate what the positive and negative consequences would be to each person/agency involved if the boundary were crossed.
2. Check for historical and current research on the particular boundary you are considering and contemplate recommendations.
3. Consult all applicable ethics codes, laws, local legislation, and so on, for rulings on the boundary.
4. Also, consult with others in the field. Ask your colleagues their opinion on the boundary and whether crossing it could be therapeutic.
5. Monitor your emotions for any signs of uneasiness, guilt, or regret. This may be a sign to you that this is a boundary you should not have crossed.
6. Discuss the boundary with your client, preferably beforehand, and get his or her thoughts and informed consent on the possible boundary crossing.
7. Refer the client if there are any factors that might cause harm to either you or the client.
8. Document, document, document the entire process (e.g., your theoretical orientation, prescribed use of the boundary crossing, who you consulted, what the ethics code and law says about that particular boundary, etc.).

Source: Pope & Keith-Spiegel, 2008.

Based on standards of ethical practice, addiction counselors should be conscious of cultural implications as they impact the client and the challenges within the complexities of the addiction (NAADAC, 2011b). Some obstacles that might challenge substance users and may inhibit them from seeking help may be their own personal beliefs, fears of community perception, the stigma related to substance use, and their own self-perceptions and attitudes. These obstacles reinforce the necessity for addiction counselors to practice awareness to potential treatment barriers (Venner et al., 2012).

One way to identify the culture, special needs, or the diversity of the individual early in the treatment process is through the initial intake procedure where the client has the opportunity to identify his or her own cultural implications (NAADAC, 2011b). While this practice during intake is a guideline and an assessment of information, it should be noted that this should not take the place of exercising consistent, active awareness, which should be infused throughout the treatment process and counseling relationship.

There are several factors that contribute to the prevalence of substance abuse disorders. These may include low socioeconomic status, lack of education, and economical challenges (Unger, 2012). Research has found that individuals who are unemployed reported higher rates of substance abuse compared to those who had full-time employment (United States Department of Health and Human Services [USDHHS], 2013). Other findings include the differences among races in reported drug use, including American Indians (12.7%), African Americans (11.3%), Caucasians (9.2%), Hispanics (8.3%), Native Hawaiians (7.8%), and Asians (3.7%) (USDHHS, 2013). It should also be noted that age, gender, race, and economic status may have an impact on the type of substance that is abused. For example, Pilkinton and Cannatella (2012) found that there may be a connection between Caucasian males and females and higher rates of stimulant abuse compared to other races. These researchers thus recommend that counselors be actively aware of the trends of drug use associated with ethnicity, age, and gender. Ethical standards for counseling professionals mandate that counselors are to infuse active cognizance to the impact of culture and the influence that cultural values and beliefs have on the individual and group

(ACA, 2005; NAADAC, 2011b). Competent practice, treatment, and interventions should be individualized based on such influences and the distinct needs of the cultural group and the individual (ACA, 2005; NAADAC, 2011b).

EDUCATION Substance abuse and addiction continue to be a widespread problem in this country, and there are few indications that the level of severity or numbers of individuals struggling with these problems will drastically decrease in the near future (Chandler et al., 2011). As a result, there remains a critical need for competent addiction professionals. However, as previously noted, there have been some concerns about how adequately trained professionals treating addiction are in providing services for clients (Chandler et al., 2011; Miller, Scarborough, Clark, Leonard, & Keziah, 2010).

These concerns arose, because historically addiction counselors could receive certification without formal training in addiction or counseling (Rieckmann et al., 2011; Whitley, 2010), and for those who wanted training, there were a variety of ways in which that could be achieved (e.g., conferences, lectures, on-the-job training, role-playing, seminars, short courses, and workshops) (Bina et al., 2008). Currently, while there are still no national curriculum standards or credentialing and while training requirements still vary from state to state, and sometimes differ greatly even within a single state (e.g., California), some strides are being made in the education of addiction counselors (Chasek et al., 2012; Counselor License Resources, 2014; Miller et al., 2010).

For example in 2009, the Counsel for Accreditation of Counseling and Related Programs (CACREP) finalized a set of guidelines and standards for addiction counseling in relationship to knowledge, skills, and practices, as did the Center for Substance Abuse Treatment (CSAT) and the Substance Abuse and Mental Health Services Administration (SAMHSA) (Chasek et al., 2012). Further, in 2010–2011, the National Addiction Studies Accreditation Commission (NASAC) was formed to further standardize training of addiction specialists. In addition, the addiction field is striving toward a national standard (Whitley, 2010).

Other developments have included the increased consideration of the master's degree as an entry-level requirement for practice (Degree Directory, 2014; Miller et al., 2010), and currently "80% of direct care addiction treatment staff" now "hold a bachelor's degree" while "53% have a master's degree or higher" (Whitley, 2010, p. 355). However, in some states only a high school diploma or GED is required (Bureau of Labor Statistics, 2014).

There has also been the development of professional networks to further solidify the profession. For example, the addiction faculty network "INCASE" and the addiction counselor's network "NAADAC" were developed to provide a resource for addiction professionals (Myers, 2011, p. 273). Lastly, an accredited residency program has now been established to help further the training of psychiatrists specializing in addiction medicine that is managed by the American Board of Addiction Medicine (ABAM) (Myers, 2011). However, it is still the case within the United States that only psychiatrists can receive training in addiction psychiatry via accredited residencies. With few exceptions, nonpsychiatrist medical doctors can only receive nonaccredited training in addiction medicine fellowships (Tontchev et al., 2011).

However, while strides have been made to standardize the training of those who want to become addiction specialists, it has been noted that counselors who are not specializing in addiction may not receive any training beyond one course. Therefore, some professionals have called for inclusion of addiction skills, knowledge, and practices within all eight CACREP core areas of training, and call for counselor educators to include such curriculum regardless of whether CACREP mandates it, in order to provide ethical training to students (Chandler et al., 2011). (For a list of recommended best practices for the education of addiction counselors, see Table 4.2.)

TABLE 4.2 Sixteen Recommended Best Practices

1. Education and training should be competency based.
2. Continuing education should be a requirement.
3. Practice guidelines should be used as teaching tools.
4. Students should develop competency with manualized therapies.
5. Teaching methods should be evidence based.
6. Curricula should be routinely updated to address the values, knowledge, and skills essential for practice in contemporary health systems.
7. Skill development should include clinical, management, and administrative components.
8. Training should develop an understanding of all competing paradigms of service delivery and the forces that shape health care (e.g., scientific, professional, economic, and social).
9. Students should train in programs and settings in which they are likely to practice.
10. Training sites should incorporate diversity and interdisciplinary practice, and allow for student tracking of patients throughout the continuum of care.
11. The term *workforce* should be better defined and all aspects of the workforce should receive consistent training.
12. Training should be offered to culturally diverse groups.
13. Clients and family members should be engaged as teachers of the workforce in terms of understanding the experience of addiction.
14. Teachers and supervisors in the training of addiction counselors should be experienced in providing such treatment and should be currently involved in the delivery of such health care.
15. The faculty in training programs should be composed of many disciplines involved in the treatment of addiction as a diversity of approaches is needed in the delivery of behavioral health care.
16. Training programs should reward faculty for teaching excellence to promote more attention to training rather than clinical or research pursuits that have historically led to greater compensation.

Source: Hoge, Huey, & O'Connell, 2004.

COUNSELORS IN RECOVERY In the area of addiction counseling, it is not uncommon to find counselors who are previous users and are currently in recovery. Doukas and Cullen (2010) note that in the 1940s it became acceptable to utilize recovering alcoholics to assist addicts in recovery and treatment. After receiving the appropriate training, addiction counselors who are in recovery may bring a unique approach to counseling addicts. It is necessary, however, for recovering addicts to be mindful of various challenges that may yield relapse, including burnout, proximity to substances and those who use, and potential cues, which may trigger cravings (Doukas & Cullen, 2010). Leykin, Cucciare, and Weingardt (2011) reported the possibility that recovered counselors may experience lesser degrees of burnout compared to nonuser counselors, possibly because of previous exposure to the challenges in addiction recovery. Counselors in recovery provide a distinctive perspective to counseling substance users as they may be able to relate and connect on a deeper level of understanding compared to those who have not faced addiction, treatment, and recovery (Doukas & Cullen, 2010). These counselors are also more likely to view addiction through the medical model versus the moral mode and be less judgmental toward an addiction client (Davis, Sneed, & Koch, 2010). Additionally, recovered counselors may also adopt an attitude that promotes helping aspirations and the desire to help others overcome the same or similar challenges (Doukas & Cullen, 2010). On the same continuum, counselors need to be mindful not to project their own experiences into making assumptions about the client, which would lead to unethical practices (Doukas & Cullen, 2010).

There are multifaceted ethical concerns related to counselors in recovery, one in particular includes boundary issues. Perhaps as a way to mitigate this concern, the Alcoholics Anonymous (AA) Guidelines (2013) for AA members employed in the alcoholism field specifies that counselors in recovery should have at least 3–5 years of abstinence before working as an addiction counselor. Although the AA guidelines are geared toward those in recovery from alcohol, they can be extended to recovery from all mind-altering substances.

Alcoholics Anonymous

Alcoholics Anonymous (AA) is a voluntary support group located in 180 countries for individuals who wish to stop drinking alcohol. Its companion group for those who abuse other drugs is Narcotics Anonymous. AA was founded in 1935 by a New York stockbroker and an Ohio surgeon, and it is estimated there are currently over 2 million members worldwide. The only requirement for membership is the desire to stop drinking or using other substances. There are no fees or costs associated with membership, and AA is self-supporting through member donations. The philosophy behind AA is that alcoholism is an illness that cannot be cured, but can be controlled through hard work and perseverance "one day at a time." Therefore, one is always in "recovery" unless one has relapsed. The goal is to help one another through fellowship, understanding, and by working the 12 steps and 12 traditions. Each step and tradition helps the individual make changes to behaviors, beliefs, and emotions so he or she can obtain sobriety and good health.

Source: Alcoholics Anonymous, 2014.

What are the ethical implications if an addiction counselor should happen to have a relapse while engaged in counseling work? How does that affect that counselor's clients, who are struggling to maintain their own sobriety? Some counselors have sponsored their own clients for AA (Bissell & Royce, 1994). What are the ethical implications associated with that course of action?

These are not easy questions to answer and reflect the growing controversy regarding the amount of formal training acquired by current addiction counselors or other professionals providing addiction treatment (Fahy, 2007). The current AA Guidelines (2013) caution against this and suggest maintaining strict boundaries between one's clients and those one sponsors.

In terms of counselors in recovery, there are two other key issues impacting this population. These include (a) countertransference issues and (b) self-disclosure. As indicated in a previous section of this chapter, the ability of the addiction counselor to develop a strong therapeutic relationship with his or her clients is essential for behavior change. However, in developing a helping relationship with a client, a primary ethical concern, especially for counselors in recovery, is countertransference. In 1995, NAADAC conducted a survey and found that 58% of its membership was in recovery (as cited in Doyle, 2005) (*Note:* Current estimates could not be found.) Given this high percentage, what are the implications if an addiction counselor is working with someone who may be struggling with the same addiction from which the counselor, or a member of the counselor's family, is recovering? Given counselors' own history of struggle with addiction, counselors in recovery may be able to empathize with clients in rehabilitation at a higher level than those who do not have a history of addiction. However, according to White (2008), counselors with their own history of addiction may be tempted to "expect or try to cultivate in their clients the same type of rational control over alcohol and other drug (AOD) consumption that has worked successfully in the counselor's life" (p. 520). This may either help or hinder the recovery process. To minimize the potential negative effects of countertransference, counselors in recovery need to maintain regular supervision, especially when working with clients who suffer from similar addictions.

Self-disclosure in counseling should be done with consideration of ethical boundaries and appropriateness of the information shared, so as not to jeopardize the therapeutic alliance and interfere with the client's well-being (ACA, 2005). There are several reasons why a counselor may disclose his or her own struggle with an addiction. For instance, to enhance client engagement, counterresistance, minimize shame and isolation, engender hope, and illustrate a particular problem-solving strategy, a counselor may self-disclose. However, volunteering such information also comes at the risk of losing clinical focus and establishing an inappropriate level of intimacy within the therapeutic relationship (White, 2008). Therefore, when disclosing such information, it is suggested that counselors proceed with caution and be mindful of the timing, duration, and appropriateness of the disclosure.

COUNSELORS WHO HAVE NEVER BEEN USERS For some addiction professionals who have never had an AOD history, working with clients struggling with addiction can be challenging and frustrating, especially if the client's behavior continues to be self-destructive. Counselors may unconsciously stigmatize these clients by making assumptions based on media images and stereotypes. Because AOD use and addiction-related lifestyles may have the potential to conflict with the counselor's values as a member of his or her culture, it can result in possible negative feelings toward the client. This may have a deleterious consequence, such as the loss of the counselor's capacity for empathy as well as possible early client termination. Individuals working with substance abuse may benefit from examining their own values, beliefs, and self-perceived competence for treating substance abuse clients (Steenrod & van Bael, 2010). Regardless of a counselor's previous history with substance abuse, it is essential for counselors to have appropriate training, competence, and align with ethical guidelines as indicated by professional standards such as the ACA Code of Ethics and the standards of the NAADAC (Chandler et al., 2011). Aligning with ethical standards necessitates that counselors focus on doing no harm and practice active awareness and respect for the client's culture, which include values, beliefs, race, ethnicity, and all the other cultural variables noted previously in this chapter. Ultimately, the counselor must act in the best interest of the client (ACA, 2005; Linton, 2012). On the same note, it is essential for addiction counselors to be aware of their own beliefs, biases, and attitudes so as not to project personal perceptions and beliefs on the client (ACA, 2005; Linton, 2012).

SELF-CARE Another professional issue faced by addiction counselors is the issue of postsecondary trauma and self-care. It is becoming increasingly recognized in the field that substance abuse work incurs stress and trauma for those who work with this population. Addiction counselors may be faced with increased stresses, inundated by heavy workloads, experience work-setting challenges, and be tested to find a balance between role expectations and client work (Leykin et al., 2011; Wallace, Lee, & Lee, 2010). The stress involved in working with the addicted varies with the setting and the individual, but addiction counselors often endure poor working conditions due to a lack of resources, lack of support from administrators, high treatment demands from managed care and the criminal justice system, high turnover rate of employees, high chronicity of the treatment population, and lack of commitment from those being treated (Wallace et al., 2010).

Burnout may result in a lack of competence among counseling professionals; therefore, it is essential for counselors to explore effectual self-care and coping strategies (Wallace et al., 2010). While self-care is essential for any type of counselor, it is especially so for the addiction counselor. There are multiple self-care strategies that may prove to be effectual to minimize burnout, which necessitate that the counselors not utilize avoidance strategies, but rather actively and emotionally cope with work-related stresses (Wallace et al., 2010). Burnout is a serious condition that can cause detriment to both counselor and client. It is important that addiction counselors take care of themselves so they can take proper care of their clients.

CONTINUING EDUCATION Addiction counseling is a rapidly changing and growing profession. It is estimated that there will be a 27–31% increase in the number of addiction counselors between 2010 and 2020 (Bureau of Labor Statistics, 2014; Counselor License Resources, 2014). Counselors need to keep abreast of new developments and research that impact their understanding, competency, and treatment provision. This represents a significant dilemma for counselors who, while ethically responsible for knowledge of the latest research, work in an agency that does not place the same value on current knowledge in the field. Reinforcing the necessity of continuing education, the NAADAC (2011a) indicates that due to the evolution of information, cultural implications, changes, and demand of services, it is necessary for addiction counselors to keep apprised of current data in order to provide ethical and evidence-based treatments and interventions.

Continuing education aligns counselors with professional and ethical standards, as it allows counselors to stay current with new trends and information and promotes competent practice (Daughhetee, Pueleo, & Thrower, 2010). Similarly, continuing education can provide a source of motivation for counselors seeking to continue their education beyond licensure and credentialing and who have a desire to continue to grow as professionals in their field as it provides a method for skill enhancement and development (Daughhetee et al., 2010), and it is necessary for keeping credentials and licensure current (NAADAC, 2013b).

In terms of skill development, researchers have found that even a half day spent participating in a continuing education program that incorporated active learning for practicing clinicians improved the use of brief intervention and screening for alcohol and other drugs. This change was found to last as long as 5 years after the class was taken (Saitz, Sullivan, & Samet, 2000).

Continuing education or lifelong learning may take the form of coursework, workshops, mentoring, supervision, or other professional development methods. Another benefit of lifelong learning is that it may promote self-care, which then may minimize burnout (Daughhetee et al., 2010). Therefore, continuing education can be used to enhance treatment and assessment by addiction counselors and partially bridge the gap between research and practice, assuming, of course, that the continuing education program utilizes the current research.

Credentialing

Most health care professions in this country employ a combination of legal mechanisms, such as credentialing, licensure, inspections, and safety standards, to manage the organization, delivery, and quality of services provided to individuals in their care (NAADAC, 2013a). The following section will provide an overview of licensure, certification, and accreditation as it pertains to training in addiction counseling. Training, certification, and licensure requirements will vary from state to state, so those interested in this profession should start by researching what is required in their particular state (Counselor Licensure Resources, 2014). Certification for individuals and accreditation for organizations are considered the optimal industry standards, whereas licensure is often regarded as a minimal standard and is generally granted after determining that an individual or organization has met a desired criterion, generally through passing an examination.

CERTIFICATION Certification provides a professional standard and guideline, which is governed by an organization, educational requirements, and passing a standardized exam, thus establishing a common minimum competency for professionals (NAADAC, 2013b). While there are state requirements for substance abuse counseling licensure and certification guidelines, there is a lack of nationwide continuity; therefore, requirements, education, and certification may vary, contingent upon each state's standards (West & Hamm, 2012). This lack of congruence of standards between states, and the evolution of change within the addiction field, may evoke confusion and a lack of professional consistency among counselors, and may also confuse clients (Miller et al., 2010). Due to this issue, the addiction field may benefit from enabling reciprocity or a national standard, thus creating a professional foundation, which promotes consistency and an ethical framework of standards (Miller et. al., 2010).

To further demonstrate differences in addiction certification, it should be noted that not only are there statewide differences, but there are also different types of certifications offered by various agencies both domestically and internationally (El-Guebaly & Violato, 2011). For example, the International Association for Addiction and Offender Counselors (IAAOC), which is a division of the ACA, working in conjunction with the National Board of Certified Counselors (NBCC), has developed standards and a program for the certification of master's-level addiction counselors. One requirement for the MAC credential is a passing score on the Examination for Master Addiction Counselors (EMAC) (NBCC, 2014).

According to the NAADAC, the National Certification Commission for Addiction Professionals recognizes three levels of substance abuse certifications, including the National Certified Addiction Counselor (NCACI), the National Certified Addiction Counselor (NCACII), and the Master Addiction Counselor (MAC). The NAADAC will also be adding five more credentials, including the co-occurring competency and the peer-recovery support specialist credential (Brys, 2013). It also acknowledges additional specialties, such as the National Certified Adolescent Addiction Counselor and the Nicotine Dependence Specialist, among others (NAADAC, 2013b). (See the NAADAC website for more specific information.) The level of certification or licensure will dictate what an addiction counselor can do in terms of autonomy and working independently; this level can also determine status in the field. For example, an individual holding the MAC license can also obtain Substance Abuse Professional status with the federal government (Counselor Licensure Resources, 2014).

In addition, each credentialing body has different requirements for certification. These requirements vary across the different certifying agencies, and from state to state, but generally each has three broad goals in mind: (a) to define a core set of counselor job tasks, (b) to define a core knowledge base of skills that reflect the competencies expected in the addiction counseling profession, and (c) to use assessment measures of competency for individuals seeking credentialing (NCCAP, 2013a). However, many credentialing agencies and states differ in opinion regarding just how many competencies are needed. When examining the criteria for credentialing between states and certification agencies, it is evident that standards and requirements vary. One example of the core tasks and skills required for credentialing can be seen from the example of the NAADAC. Their core tasks and skills fall into the general categories of assessment, treatment planning, client orientation, case consultation, confidentiality, individual, group, and family counseling, crisis intervention, discharge planning, follow-up activities, referral, client advocacy, and personal and professional growth activities (NAADAC, 2013a).

Some credentialing organizations also have different levels of certification. For example, the International Certification Reciprocity Consortium (IC & RC), a national organization of certifying boards providing reciprocity of certification nationally and within different states, has three levels of certification: (a) Certified Addiction Counselor, (b) Certified Drug Counselor, and (c) Alcohol and Drug Counselor. Each level has different requirements in terms of training, education, and supervised experience, and the higher the level of certification, the higher the level of requirements (IC & RC, 2014). The IC & RC also acknowledges a series of addiction certifications that may be recognized internationally—thus this organization is working toward creating continuity and consistency within the profession on a global scale (IC & RC, 2014). In addition, the International Society for Addiction Medicine has now developed an international certification process for physicians (El-Guebaly & Violato, 2011).

Generally, each certifying body also requires some form of written exam applicants must pass before certification is complete. The IC & RC has a national exam used by many states. Those agencies that certify differing levels of counselors (e.g., IC & RC and NAADAC) also have different tests for each level of certification. The NAADAC exam covers the content areas of pharmacology of psychoactive substances, counseling practice, theoretical bases, and professional issues. For an overview of the MAC criteria and NAADAC exam content areas, see Tables 4.3 and 4.4, respectively.

TABLE 4.3 Master Addiction Counselor Criteria for Certification

1. The counselor must pass the National Certified Counselor (NCC) exam prior to applying for MAC certification.
2. A counselor must receive a minimum of 36 months of supervision, 24 of which must occur after date of graduation from an advanced degree in counseling.
3. Supervision must be from a master's level (or higher) professional in counseling, psychology, psychiatry, marriage and family therapy, or social work, and cannot be related to the counselor applying for certification.
4. A master's level (or higher) colleague who is not related to the counselor must also endorse the applicant seeking certification. He or she must attest that he or she believes the applicant is an ethical counselor. This colleague cannot be the counselor's supervisor and must be a professional in counseling, psychology, psychiatry, marriage and family therapy, or social work.
5. A counselor seeking MAC certification must have a minimum of 36 months of experience as an addiction counselor with at least 24 months occurring after graduation from an advanced degree. This experience must have entailed at least 20 hours per week over those 36 months.
6. To qualify for the MAC credential, a counselor must have a minimum of 12 semester (or 18 quarter) hours of graduate-level coursework in addiction counseling. These credits must include courses in drug terminology, theories of addiction, and treatment methods. These credits must be from a regionally accredited college or university. The applicant can use up to 6 semester (or 9 quarter) hours in group counseling and/or family counseling toward the total number of credits required in addiction.
7. Postgraduate counselors who wish to add the credential, but did not have addiction coursework in their graduate program, may use continuing education (CE) hours in addiction at the substitution rate of 500 CE hours per 12 semester hours (or 42 CE hours per every one semester hour).
8. Counselors must also pass the Examination for Master Addiction Counselors (EMAC). This is a 100-item, multiple-choice exam and covers the content area for assessment, treatment planning and implementation, prevention, group and family counseling, general drug terminology, specific drug information, theories of addiction, medical and psychological aspects of addiction, and treatment of addiction.

Source: National Board of Certified Counselors, 2014.

TABLE 4.4 NAADAC Exam Content Areas

Topic	Information Covered
Pharmacology of Psychoactive Substances	This area includes information on specific categories of drugs, physiological effects, psychological effects, withdrawal symptoms, drug interactions, and treatment applications.
Counseling Practice	This area includes information concerning client evaluations, treatment planning, counseling, patient care, patient management, education, continuing care, special issues, and special populations.
Theoretical Bases	This area includes information concerning behavioral, cognitive, and analytical theories of addiction, human growth and development, family, and addiction.
Professional Issues	This area includes information concerning law and regulation, professional behavior, and ethics.

Source: National Association for Alcoholism and Drug Abuse Counselors, 2013.

Realization toward a goal of a nationally accepted standard and statewide consistency is getting closer. There have been discussions for years about merging the National Certification Commission (NCC) and the IC & RC, as well as membership organizations such as the NAADAC, the Association for Addiction Professionals (AAP), and the Society of Credentialed Addiction Professionals (SCAP). These associations have agreed to seek "unification through merger," which we hope one day, will serve to standardize the credentialing of addiction counselors from state to state. However, as of 2014, this goal had not yet been achieved (Knopf, 2013).

LICENSURE Licensure is the most rigorous form of professional regulation (Miller et al., 2010). Historically, the movement to license addiction counselors was not as advanced as that of certification, but this has changed in recent years. For example, in 2003 only six states had licensure for addiction counselors, but today, most states require licensure to practice addiction counseling (Degree Directory, 2014). Unlike certification, which can be granted nationally (e.g., national certified counselor), state law establishes licensure, and each state determines the requirements for licensure. In general, to be licensed as an addiction counselor a person must pass an exam of competency and then engage in a certain number of hours of postgraduate supervised practice (Degree Directory, 2014).

The purpose of postgraduation supervised hours prior to licensure is to ensure that (a) counselors continue in their professional development; (b) the work of less experienced counselors is monitored to protect client welfare; (c) the new counselor is following the legal, ethical, and professional guidelines of the profession; and (d) applicants for licensure are practicing at the appropriate levels of competence to practice autonomously (Degree Directory, 2014).

Different states have different requirements for licensure (Miller et al., 2010). We will discuss one example from the state of Colorado. First, Colorado certifies three different levels of counselors. Those who have been certified as a level three certified addiction counselor (CAD) may be eligible for the Licensed Addiction Counselor (LAC) credential if the following requirements are met: (a) applicants must hold a current CAD III issued in the state of Colorado and be in good standing; (b) applicants must have at least a master's degree in the social sciences or an equivalent program; (c) applicants must pass either the NAADAC MAC exam or the IC & RC exam after graduating from a master's or doctoral program, and within the last 5 years prior to licensure application; and (d) as of July 1, 2004, all applicants for a certification, license, or upgrade are required by Colorado Statute to pass a mail-in Jurisprudence Examination (Code of Colorado Regulations, 2010).

ACCREDITATION Accreditation applies to the specific counselor education program within colleges and universities that educate and train addiction counselors. It does not apply to individual counselors in the way that licensure and certification does. Accreditation procedures are intended to ensure the quality and standardization of graduate education for the academic preparation of addiction counselors (Council for Accreditation of Counseling and Related Educational Programs [CACREP], 2014).

In the accreditation process, professional organizations specify standards for the training of addiction practitioners. For example, accreditation standards usually dictate student-to-faculty ratio to ensure students will get a certain degree of individualized attention. Accreditation standards also specify the critical content and experiential components of the graduate program, to ensure the knowledge base and competency of graduating students. Accrediting bodies evaluate graduate and training programs to ensure students within these programs are receiving education in line with these standards and criteria (CACREP, 2014). Programs that meet or exceed the specified standards are then accredited. These standards are constantly revised and updated to meet the needs of the profession and its clients. The CACREP standards are currently in revision to be released in 2016 (CACREP, 2014).

Different educational programs (e.g., rehabilitation vs. community counseling) will have different accreditation agencies, just as different organizations offer credentialing for addiction counselors. Examples of accrediting bodies include the CACREP for community counseling graduate programs; the Council on Rehabilitation Education (CORE) for rehabilitation counseling graduate programs (*Note:* CACREP and CORE have now become affiliated as of 2013) (CACREP, 2014); the American Psychological Association for psychology graduate programs; and the American Association for Marriage and Family Therapy (AAMFT) for family counseling graduate programs. Typical accredited master's degree programs include a minimum of 2 years of full-time study, including 600 hours of supervised clinical internship experience (Bureau of Labor Statistics, 2014).

TREATMENT AND RESEARCH ISSUES

There are many treatment issues relating to clients with addictions that could be discussed. This section will focus on topics relating to managed care and treatment funding and measuring outcomes and efficacy of treatment.

Managed Care, Treatment Funding, and Provider Reimbursement

The advent of managed care has changed the way health care provisions are administered in this country (Cohen, Marecek, & Gillham, 2006). *Managed care* refers to any type of intervention aimed at the financing of health care and focused on elimination of unnecessary and inappropriate care and reduction of costs (Beattie, McDaniel, & Bond, 2006). While the managed care system has been successful in lessening short-term costs, many consider that it has been at the price of long-term consequences for clients and practitioners (Jansson, Svikis, Velez, Fitzgerald, & Jones, 2007).

There are many ethical concerns discussed in the literature specifically regarding managed care. The core of these concerns regard cost-containment practices of setting session limits, restricting provider availability, and issues relating to conflict of interest, confidentiality, informed consent, client abandonment, pressures to breach fiduciary responsibilities, and implementing mandatory DSM diagnostic procedures (Haley & Carrier, 2010). Managed care often dictates what services and interventions will be offered. For example, there is limited reimbursement available for many evidenced-based practices, but older, less effective, and most costly treatments are still being supported, such as "opioid detoxification without aftercare" (Carroll, 2012, p. 1032).

Perhaps in recognition of addiction recovery issues, as well as other medical health concerns, the federal Patient Protection and Affordable Care Act of 2010 was passed. This act strives to ensure access to services and better coordination of care (Cousins, Antonini, & Rawson, 2012). In addition, SAMHSA has proposed what is called a "recovery-oriented system of care (ROSC)," which "advances a coordinated system of recovery that is individual-focused, provides opportunities for links between treatment and community supports, and improves individuals' quality of life (Cousins et al., 2012, p. 326). These services are not clinical in nature, but provide a range of supports for the person in recovery.

This new system of care has ushered in a determination to understand how this new model aids recovery, program performance, treatment efficacy, and client outcome. Research thus far on the ROSC has been promising; for example, some results show that individuals engaged in ROSC care have had a higher rate of abstinence and long-term recovery. Some findings show more stability for individuals in terms of housing and employment (Cousins et al., 2012).

However, a variety of issues have been noted in terms of difficulty for researchers. These are that (a) not all areas provide the same ROSC services or provide the services in the same way, (b) the individuals providing the support services can range from a volunteer to a professional, and (c) ROSC services may not be offered at the same time in each person's recovery (Cousins et al., 2012).

Another issue impacting the addiction profession is lack of parity with other health providers. Fisher and Harrison (2005) suggested addiction and other counselors advocate for substance abuse and mental health parity, and the American Society of Addiction Medicine (ASAM) has made parity its number one priority (Smith, Lee, & Davidson, 2010). Parity would mean that third-party payers (e.g., insurance companies and managed care) would be required to provide both substance abuse and mental health services, just as they offer medical services (Chi, Sterling, & Weisner, 2006). Preventive services for substance abuse and dependence would be included, just as for medical conditions. Smith et al. (2010) reported that the "Paul Wellstone and Pete Domenici Mental Health Parity and Addiction Equity Act of 2008 requires most health plans to provide benefits for addiction and mental health treatment, including financial requirements and treatment parameters, that are equivalent to those for other medical services" (p. 121). The law went into effect in January 2010; however, insurance health plans do not have to offer mental health or addiction treatment, but if they do, they are then required to provide the same type of coverage as for other illnesses (American Psychological Association, 2014).

Measuring Outcomes and Efficacy of Treatment

As noted previously, along with other counseling and medical specialties, a move toward evidence-based treatments has taken root within the addiction field (Carroll, 2012; Najavits et al., 2011). Professional associations and governmental agencies have also issued practice guidelines and treatment algorithms, which support selected treatments or levels of care for specific conditions (Daley, Baker, Donovan, Hodgkins, & Perl, 2011; Fussell, Kunkel, McCarty, & Lewy, 2011; Horvath & Yeterian, 2012). Empirically based practices are developed through clinical trials, consensus reviews, and expert opinions (Najavits et al., 2011). In the field of addiction, there are a number of scientifically based treatment approaches. These include (a) cognitive-behavioral therapy, (b) community reinforcement approaches, (c) motivational enhancement therapy, (d) the 12-step approach, (e) contingency management techniques, (f) pharmacological interventions, and (g) systems treatment (Morgenstern & McKay, 2007; Najavits et al., 2011).

While the addiction field is moving forward toward embracing evidenced-based practice, there are still a number of concerns that exist about the implementation of these practices. Some of these concerns include (a) the role of ethical values in shaping practice; (b) disagreement about the supporting evidence needed to validate some treatment protocols; (c) lack of therapist adherence to treatment protocols; (d) difficulty of implementation; (e) lack of availability of some treatment manuals; (f) lack of availability of training, consultation, technical assistance, and supervision; (g) difficulty in learning the treatment protocol; (h) cost of implementation; (i) lack of insurance reimbursements; (j) concern about how the new model impacts existing practices; and (k) how well the clients like it and will adhere to it (Carroll, 2012; Chapman, McCart, Letourneau, & Sheidow, 2013; Lundgren, 2011; Najavits et al., 2011; Rieckmann et al., 2011).

Another concern has been the issue of a disconnect between research and clinical practice. To address this concern, an alliance has been formed among researchers and addiction specialists. This alliance is called the National Drug Abuse Treatment Clinical Trials Network (CTN). The purpose of this alliance is to not only research current treatments, but also to formulate and empirically validate new ones (Rieckmann et al., 2011). For example, the CTN has recently collaborated on a large study incorporating many treatment facilities to develop, and then research the efficacy of an outpatient behavioral intervention incorporating both individual and group counseling modalities with 12-step support (Daley et al., 2011). Choices for the developed intervention sought to address some of the aforementioned concerns about empirically based practice and revolved around cost effectiveness, utility of the intervention in a treatment facility, efficacy of outcome, and empirical support (Daley et al., 2011). Another part of this research experience was that counselors were trained and supervised in the delivery of the treatment protocol to ensure standardization across the client population and support for practitioners in utilizing the new treatment (Daley et al., 2011; Fussell et al., 2011). This training has been found crucial for staff implementation of a new protocol (Lundgren et al., 2011). Therefore, a new important direction for the addiction field is the focus on "clinically significant patient outcomes" and the belief that the training and support of counselors in implementing these treatment protocols will make the adoption of evidence-based treatments more likely (Lundgren et al., 2011). It has been reported within the last couple of years that the number of practitioners using at least one evidence-based practice has increased (Carroll, 2012).

While this type of research is viewed as progress in the field, it has not been without challenges. Some of the noted difficulties with doing these kinds of multisite collaborative studies include the following: (a) not all sites are equal in resources and client population (e.g., some have insured or wealthy clients while others cater to the uninsured or mandated client); (b) the research takes massive collaboration, cooperation, and coordination among a host of professionals in different cities or states; (c) it can be difficult to get protocol standardization at each site; and (d) training on protocol implementation and data collection are often very intensive and time-consuming (Fussell et al., 2011).

Therefore, it is clear that more effective outcome research is needed to support empirically based interventions. Many organizations are moving in this direction. For example, evidence-based practice in psychology has been written into the guidelines of the American Psychological Association in 2006 to promote cultural sensitivity in service delivery, enhance communication, and advocate for best practices and benefits for clients (La Roche & Christopher, 2009).

FUTURE TRENDS

POSITIVE PSYCHOLOGY Some in the field are increasingly calling for the addiction field to forgo the labels and pathological perspective and take a wellness and positive psychology and recovery approach in treating those with addiction. Positive psychology focuses on client strengths and supports over the lifespan and embraces the notion that there is more than one way to obtain sobriety and recovery (Krentzman, 2013).

UNITY AMONG SELF-HELP GROUPS Rather than standing alone and working in parallel lines, more and more self-help groups are joining forces and pooling resources, including combining advocacy efforts, which has led to a greater public voice (Krentzman, 2013). The national advocacy group that came out of these collaborations is the Faces and Voices of Recovery and the Association of Recovery Community Organizations (Krentzman, 2013).

DISSOLUTION OF NIAA AND NIDA Amid much controversy, but at the request of the U.S. Congress, there was a proposal in 2011 to dissolve the NIAA and NIDA and create the formation of a new singular organization, the National Institute on Substance Use and Addiction Disorders. The structure of the new organization is thought to be able to optimize the strengths and minimize the weaknesses of the previous two organizations and will combine the grant-providing opportunities, research efforts, and specializations controlled by this new singular organization (Johnson et al., 2011; Roizen, 2013).

Summary and Some Final Notations

There is much involved in the ethical, legal, and competent practice of addiction counseling. The issues explored within this chapter were those related to counselor competency, certification, licensure, accreditation, managed care and treatment funding, and outcome measurement and efficacy of treatment. All of what has been discussed in this chapter are broad categories relating to the addiction profession. Students and practitioners who are interested in working with individuals with substance-abuse and addiction issues are encouraged to continue to explore these issues. The following are some useful websites that can aid in this exploration.

MyCounselingLab

Visit the MyCounselingLab site for *Foundations of Addictions Counseling,* Third Edition to enhance your understanding of concepts. You'll have the opportunity to practice your skills through video- and case-based exercises. You will find sets of questions to help you prepare for your certification exam with *Licensure Quizzes*. There is also a Video Library that provides taped counseling sessions, ethical scenarios, and interviews with helpers and clients.

Useful Websites

Alcoholics Anonymous
www.aa.org

Avoiding Exploitive Dual Relationships: A Decision-Making Model
kspope.com/dual/gottlieb.php

Commission on Rehabilitation Counselor Certification
www.crccertification.com/

Ethical Decision Making and Dual Relationships
kspope.com/dual/younggren.php

International Association for Addiction and Offender Counselors (IAAOC)
www.iaaoc.org/

International Certification Reciprocity Consortium (IC & RC)
internationalcredentialing.org/about

National Addiction Studies Accreditation Commission (NASAC)
http://nasacaccreditation.org/

Narcotics Anonymous (NA)
www.na.org

National Association of Alcoholism and Drug Abuse Counselors (NAADAC)
naadac.org/

National Board for Certified Counselors (NBCC)
www.nbcc.org/

National Institute on Alcohol Abuse and Alcoholism (NIAAA)
www.niaaa.nih.gov/

National Institute on Drug Abuse
www.nida.nih.gov/

Nonsexual Multiple Relationships: A Practical Decision-Making Model for Clinicians
kspope.com/site/multiple-relationships.php

SAMHSA's National Registry of Evidence-Based Programs and Practices (NREPP)
www.nrepp.samhsa.gov/

Substance Abuse and Mental Health Services Administration
www.samhsa.gov/index.aspx

Understanding HIPAA Privacy
www.hhs.gov/ocr/privacy/hipaa/understanding/index.html

References

Acri, M. C., Gogel, L. P., Pollock, M., & Wisdom, J. P. (2012). What adolescents need to prevent relapse after treatment for substance abuse: A comparison of youth, parent, and staff perspectives. *Journal of Child and Adolescent Substance Abuse, 21*(2), 117–129. doi:10.1080/1067828X.2012.662111

Alcoholics Anonymous. (2013). A. A. Guidelines: For A.A. members employed in the alcoholism field. Retrieved from http://aa.org/lang/en/en_pdfs/mg-10_foraamembers.pdf

Alcoholics Anonymous. (2014). Welcome to alcoholics anonymous. Retrieved from http://www.aa.org/lang/en/catalog.cfm?origpage=18&product=8

American Counseling Association. (2005). *ACA code of ethics*. Alexandria, VA: Author

American Psychiatric Association. (2013). DSM 5 development: Substance-related and addictive disorders. Retrieved from http://www.dsm5.org/Pages/Default.aspx

American Psychological Association. (2014). Mental health parity and addiction equity act. Retrieved from http://www.apa.org/news/press/releases/2014/05/mental-health-coverage.aspx

Barber, J. G. (1995). Working with resistant drug abusers. *Social Work, 40*(1), 17–23.

Barrick, C., & Homish, G. C. (2011). Readiness to change and training expectations prior to a training workshop for substance abuse clinicians. *Substance Use and Misuse, 46*, 1032–1036. doi:10.3109/10826084.2010.546821

Beattie, M., McDaniel, P., & Bond, J. (2006). Public sector managed care: A comparative evaluation of substance abuse treatment in three counties. *Addiction, 101*, 857–872.

Bina, R., Hall, D. M. H., Mollete, A., Smith-Osborne, A., Yum, J., Sowbel, L., & Jani J. (2008). Substance abuse training and perceived knowledge: Predictors of perceived preparedness to work in substance abuse. *Journal of Social Work Education, 44*(3), 7–20.

Bissell, L., & Royce, J. E. (1994). *Ethics for addiction professionals* (2nd ed.). Center City, MN: Hazelden Information and Education.

Brys, S. (2013, October 14). Live from the NAADAC: Trends for addiction professionals. *Addiction Professional.* Retrieved from http://www.addictionpro.com/blogs/shannon-brys/live-naadac-trends-addiction-professionals

Bureau of Labor Statistics. (2014). Substance abuse and behavioral disorder counselors. Retrieved from http://www.bls.gov/ooh/community-and-social-service/substance-abuse-and-behavioral-disorder-counselors.htm

Carroll, K. M. (2012). Dissemination of evidence-based practices: How far we've come, and how much further we've got to go [Editorial]. *Addiction, 107,* 1031–1033.

Chapman, J. E., McCart, M. R., Letourneau, E. J., & Sheidow, A. J. (2013). Comparison of youth, caregiver, therapist, trained, and treatment expert raters of therapist adherence to a substance abuse treatment protocol. *Journal of Consulting and Clinical Psychology, 81,* 674–680. doi:10.1037/a0033021

Chandler, N., Balkin, R. S., & Perepiczka, M. (2011). Perceived self-efficacy of licensed counselors to provide substance abuse counseling. *Journal of Addiction and Offender Counseling, 32,* 29–42.

Chasek, C. L., Jorgensen, M., & Maxson, T. (2012). Assessing counseling students' attitudes regarding substance abuse and treatment. *Journal of Addiction and Offender Counseling, 33,* 107–114.

Chi, F. W., Sterling, S., & Weisner, C. (2006). Adolescents with co-occurring substance use and mental conditions in a private managed care health plan: Prevalence, patient characteristics, and treatment initiation and engagement. *American Journal on Addiction, 15,* 67–79.

Code of Colorado Regulations. (2010). Addiction counselor certification and licensure rules. Retrieved from http://www.caap.us/images/pdf/dbh_dora/CAC%20rules%20WORD%2009-01-10.pdf

Cohen, J., Marecek, J., & Gillham, J. (2006). Is three a crowd? Clients, clinicians, and managed care. *American Journal of Orthopsychiatry, 76*(2), 251–259.

Counsel for Accreditation of Counseling and Related Educational Programs. (2014). Accreditation. Retrieved from http://www.cacrep.org/template/index.cfm

Counselor License Resources. (2014). What are addiction counselors? Retrieved from http://www.counselor-license.com/careers/addiction-counselor.html

Cousins, S. J., Antonini, V. P., & Rawson, R. A. (2012). Utilization, measurement, and funding of recovery supports and services. *Journal of Psychoactive Drugs, 44*(4), 325–333. doi:10.1080/02791072.2012.718924

Cridland, E. K., Deane, F. P., Hsu, C., & Kelly, P. J. (2012). A comparison of treatment outcomes for individuals with substance use disorder alone and individuals with probable dual diagnosis. *International Journal of Mental Health and Addiction, 10*(5), 670–683.

Daley, D. C., Baker, S., Donovan, D. M., Hodgkins, C. G., & Perl, H. (2011). A combined group and individual 12-step facilitative intervention targeting stimulant abuse in the NIDA clinical trials network: Stage-12. *Journal of Groups in Addiction and Recovery, 6,* 228–244. doi:10.1080/1556035X.2011.597196

Daughhetee, C., Puleo, S., & Thrower, E. (2010). Scaffolding of continuing competency as an essential element of professionalism. *Alabama Counseling Association Journal, 36*(1), 15–22.

Davis, S. J., Sneed, Z., B., & Koch, D. S. (2010). Counselor trainee attitudes toward alcohol and other drug use. *Rehabilitation Education, 24*(1), 35–42.

Degree Directory. (2014). What education is required to become an addiction counselor? Retrieved from http://degreedirectory.org/

Doukas, N., & Cullen, J. (2010). Recovered addicts working in the addiction field: Pitfalls to substance abuse relapse. *Drugs: Education, Prevention and Policy, 17*(3), 216–231. doi:10.3109/09687630802378864

Dow, S. J., & Kelly, J. F. (2013). Listening to youth: Adolescents' reasons for substance use as a unique predictor of treatment response and outcome. *Psychology of Addictive Behaviors, 27*(4), 1122–1131. doi:10.1037/a0031065

Doyle, K. (2005). Substance abuse counselors in recovery: Implications for the ethical issue of dual relationships. *Journal of Counseling and Development, 75,* 428–432.

El-Guebaly, N., & Violato, C. (2011). The international certification of addiction medicine: Validating clinical knowledge across borders. *Substance Abuse, 32,* 77–83. doi:10.1080/08897077.2011.555697

Fahy, A. (2007). The unbearable fatigue of compassion: Notes from a substance abuse counselor who dreams of working at Starbucks. *Clinical Social Work Journal, 35,* 19–205.

Fisher, G. L., & Harrison, T. C. (2005). *Substance abuse: Information for school counselors, social workers, therapists, and counselors* (3rd ed.). Needham Heights, MA: Allyn & Bacon.

Fussell, H. E., Kunkel, L. E., McCarty, D., & Lewy, C. S. (2011). Standardized patient walkthroughs in the National Drug Abuse Treatment Clinical Trials Network: Common challenges to protocol implementation. *The American Journal of Drug and Alcohol Abuse, 37*(5), 434–439.

Gonzales, R., Anglin, M., Beattie, R., Ong, C., & Glik, D. C. (2012). Understanding recovery barriers: Youth perceptions about substance use relapse. *American Journal* of *Health Behavior, 36*(5), 602–614. doi:10.5993/AJHB.36.5.3

Haley, M., & Carrier, J. W. (2010). Psychotherapy groups. In D. Capuzzi, D. Gross, & M. Stauffer (Eds.), *Introduction to group work* (5th ed.). Denver CO: Love Publishing Company.

Hickling, F. W. (2012). Understanding patients in multicultural settings: A personal reflection on ethnicity and culture in clinical practice. *Ethnicity and Health, 17*(1–2), 203–216. doi:10.1080/13557858.2012.655266

Hoge, M. A., Huey, L. Y., & O'Connell, M. J. (2004). Best practices in behavioral health workforce education and training. *Administration and Policy in Mental Health, 32*(2), 90–106.

Horvath, A. T., & Yeterian, J. (2012). SMART recovery: Self-empowering, science-based addiction recovery support. *Journal of Groups in Addiction and Recovery, 7*, 102–117. doi:10.1080/1556035X.2012.705651

Huber, G. L., & Mahajan, V. K. (2008). Successful smoking cessation. *Disease Management & Health Outcomes, 16*(5), 335–343.

International Certification and Reciprocity Consortium. (2014). Credentialing 101. Retrieved from http://internationalcredentialing.org/valuecred

Jansson, L. M., Svikis, D. S., Velez, M., Fitzgerald, E., & Jones, H. (2007). The impact of managed care on drug-dependent pregnant and postpartum women and their children. *Substance Use and Misuse, 42*, 961–974.

Johnson, B. A., Messing, R. O., Charness, M. E., Crabbe, J. C., Goldman, M. S., Harris, R. A., Kranzler, H. R., . . . , Thomas, J. D. (2011). Should the reorganization of addiction-related research across all the National Institutes of Health be structural?—The Devil is truly in the details. *Alcoholism: Clinical and Experimental Research, 35*(4), 572–580. doi:10.1111/j.1530-0277.2011.01493.x

Jones, K. D., Gill, C., & Ray, S. (2012). Review of the proposed DSM-5 substance use disorder. *Journal of Addiction and Offender Counseling, 33*, 115–123.

Knopf, A. (2013, April 30). NAADAC, IC&RC to collaborate for survival of the field. *Addiction Professional*. Retrieved from http://www.addictionpro.com/article/naadac-icrc-collaborate-survival-field

Krentzman, A. R. (2013). Review of the application of positive psychology to substance use, addiction, and recovery research. *Psychology of Addictive Behaviors, 27*, 151–165. doi:10.1037/a0029897

La Roche, M. J., & Christopher, S. (2009). Changing paradigms from empirically supported treatment to evidence based practice: A cultural perspective. *Professional Psychology: Research and Practice, 40*(4), 396–402.

Langås, A., Malt, U., & Opjordsmoen, S. (2011). Substance use disorders and comorbid mental disorders in first-time admitted patients from a catchment area. *European Addiction Research, 18*(1), 16–25. doi:10.1159/000332234

Leykin, Y., Cucciare, M. A., & Weingardt, K. R. (2011). Differential effects of online training on job-related burnout among substance abuse counsellors. *Journal of Substance Use, 16*(2), 127–135. doi:10.3109/14659891.2010.526168

Linton, J. M. (2012). Ethics and accreditation in addiction counselor training: Possible field placement issues for CACREP-accredited addiction counseling programs. *Journal of Addiction and Offender Counseling, 33*(1), 48–61.

Luger, L. (2011). Enhancing cultural competence in staff working with people with drug and alcohol problems—A multidimensional approach to evaluating the impact of education. *Social Work Education, 30*(2), 223–235. doi:10.1080/02615479.2011.540398

Lundgren, L., Amodeo, M., Krull, I., Chassler, D., Weidenfeld, R., de Saxe Zerden, L., Gowler, R., . . . , Beltrame, C. (2011). Addiction treatment provider attitudes on staff capacity and evidence-based clinical training: Results from a national study. *The American Journal of Addiction, 20*, 271–284. doi:10.1111/j.1521-0391.2011.00127.x

Madden, T. E., Graham, A. V., Lala, S., Strausner, A., Saunders, L. A., Schoener, E., Henry, R., . . . , Brown, R. L. (2008). Interdisciplinary benefits in project MAINSTREAM: A promising health professions educational model to address global substance abuse. *Journal of Interprofessional Care, 20*(6), 655–664.

Martin, C., Godfrey, M., Meekums, B., & Madill, A. (2011). Managing boundaries under pressure: A qualitative study of therapists' experiences of sexual attraction in therapy. *Counselling and Psychotherapy Research, 11*(4), 248–256. doi:10.1080/14733145.2010.519045

Matthews, H., Kelly, P. J., & Deane, F. P. (2011). The dual diagnosis capability of residential addiction treatment centers: Priorities and confidence to improve capability following a review process. *Drug and Alcohol Review, 30*(2), 195–199. doi:10.1111/j.1465-3362.2010.00215.x

Miller, G., Scarborough, J., Clark, C., Leonard, J. C., & Keziah, T. B. (2010). The need for national credentialing standards for addiction counselors. *Journal of Addiction and Offender Counseling, 30*, 50–57.

Morgenstern, J., & McKay, J. R. (2007). Rethinking the paradigms that inform behavioral treatment research for substance use disorders. *Addiction, 102*, 1377–1389.

Myers, P. L. (2011). Organizational breakthrough in addiction during 2011. *Journal of Ethnicity in Substance Abuse, 10*, 273–274. doi:10.1080/15332640.2011.623482

Najavits, L. M., Kivlahan, D., & Kosten, T. (2011). A national survey of clinicians' views of evidence-based therapies for PTSD and substance abuse. *Addiction Research and Theory, 19*(2), 138–147. doi:10.3109/16066350903560176

National Association for Alcoholism and Drug Abuse Counselors. (2011a). Addiction professional career ladder and scope of practice. Retrieved from http://www.addictioncareers.org/addictioncareers/resources/documents/PEP11-SCOPES.pdf

National Association for Alcoholism and Drug Abuse Counselors. (2011b). Ethical standards of alcoholism and drug abuse counselors. Retrieved from http://naadac.org/assets/1959/naadac_code_of_ethics_brochure.pdf

National Association for Alcoholism and Drug Abuse Counselors. (2013a). Certification: Guide to NCC AP credentials. Retrieved from http://www.naadac.org/certification

National Association for Alcoholism and Drug Abuse Counselors. (2013b). Re-credentialing. Retrieved from http://www.naadac.org/re-credentialing

National Association of Addiction Professionals. (2013). Code of ethics. Retrieved from http://www.naadac.org/code-of-ethics

National Board of Certified Counselors. (2014). Masters addiction counselor credential. Retrieved from http://www.nbcc.org/Specialties/MAC

National Institute on Drug Abuse. (2010). Comorbidity: Addiction and other mental illnesses. Retrieved from http://www.drugabuse.gov/sites/default/files/rrcomorbidity.pdf

Olthuis, J. V., Darredeau, C., & Barrett, S. P. (2013). Substance use initiation: The role of simultaneous polysubstance use. *Drug and Alcohol Review, 32*, 67–71. doi: 10.1111/j.1465-3362.2012.00470.x

Oser, C. B., Biebel, E. P., Pullen, E., & Harp, K. H. (2013). Causes, consequences, and prevention of burnout among substance abuse treatment counselors: A rural versus urban comparison. *Journal of Psychoactive Drugs, 45*(1), 17–27. doi:10.1080/02791072.2013.763558

Pilkinton, M., & Cannatella, A. (2012). Nonmedical use of prescription stimulants: Age, race, gender, and educational attainment patterns. *Journal of Human Behavior in the Social Environment, 22*(4), 409–420. doi:10.1080/10911359.2012.664968

Pope, K. S., & Keith-Spiegel, P. (2008). A practical approach to boundaries in psychotherapy: Making decisions, bypassing blunders, and mending fences. *Journal of Clinical Psychology: In Session, 64*(5), 638–652.

Prochaska, J. O., & DiClemente, C. C. (1984). *The transtheoretical approach: Crossing traditional boundaries of therapy.* Melbourne, FL: Krieger.

Prochaska, J. M., Prochaska, J. O., Cohen, F. C., Gomes, S. O., Laforge, R. G., & Eastwood, A. L. (2004). The transtheoretical model of change for multi-level interventions for alcohol abuse on campus. *Journal of Drug & Alcohol Education, 47,* 34–50.

Rieckmann, T., Farentinos, C., Tillotson, C. J., Kocarnik, J., & McCarty, D. (2011). The substance abuse counseling workforce: Education, preparation, and certification. *Substance Abuse, 32,* 180–190. doi:10.1080/08897077.2011.600122

Rogers, C. (1961). *On becoming a person: A therapist's view of therapy.* London, England, UK: Constable.

Roizen, R. (2013, April 13). Reflections on the Scheduled NIAAA/NIDA Merger. Retrieved from http://pointsadhsblog.wordpress.com/2012/04/13/reflections-on-the-niaaanida-merger-part-2/

Saitz, R., Sullivan, L. M., & Samet, J. H. (2000). Training community-based clinicians in screening and brief interventions for substance abuse problems: Translating evidence into practice. *Substance Abuse, 21*(1), 21–31.

Smith, D. E., Lee, D. R., & Davidson, L. D. (2010). Health care equality and parity for treatment of addictive disease. *Journal of Psychoactive Drugs, 42*(2), 121–126.

Steenrod, S. A., & van Bael, M. (2010). Substance abuse education: Perceived competence of field instructors on substance abuse. *Journal of Social Work Practice in the Addiction, 10*(4), 363–376. doi:10.1080/1533256X.2010.520624

Swendsen, J., Conway, K. P., Degenhardt, L., Glantz, M., Jin, R., Merikangas, K. R., . . . , Kessler, R. C. (2010). Mental disorders as risk factors for substance use, abuse and dependence: Results from the 10-year follow-up of the National Comorbidity Survey. *Addiction, 105*(6), 1117–1128. doi:10.1111/j.1360-0443.2010.02902.x

Tontchev, G. V., Housel, T. R., Callahan, J. F., Kunz, K. B., Miller, M. M., & Blondell, R. D. (2011). Specialized training on addiction for physicians in the United States. *Substance Abuse, 32,* 84–92. doi:10.1080/08897077.2011.555702

Unger, J. B. (2012). The most critical unresolved issues associated with race, ethnicity, culture, and substance use. *Substance Use and Misuse, 47*(4), 390–395. doi:10.3109/10826084.2011.638017

U.S. Department of Health and Human Services. (2013). National survey on drug use and health: Summary of national findings. Retrieved from http://www.samhsa.gov/data/NSDUH/2012SummNatFindDetTables/NationalFindings/NSDUHresults2012.htm

Venner, K. L., Greenfield, B. L., Vicuña, B., Muñoz, R., Bhatt, S. S., & O'Keefe, V. (2012). "I'm not one of them": Barriers to help-seeking among American Indians with alcohol dependence. *Cultural Diversity and Ethnic Minority Psychology, 18*(4), 352–362. doi:10.1037/a0029757

Wallace, S., Lee, J., & Lee, S. (2010). Job stress, coping strategies, and burnout among abuse-specific counselors. *Journal of Employment Counseling, 47*(3), 111–122.

Wells, K. M., & Wells, T. D. (2007, Spring). Preventing relapse after weight loss. *American Medical Athletic Association Journal,* 5–16.

West, P. L., & Hamm, T. (2012). A study of clinical supervision techniques and training in substance abuse treatment. *Journal of Addiction and Offender Counseling, 33,* 66–81.

White, W. L. (2008). Alcohol, tobacco, and other drug use by addictions professionals: Historical reflections and suggested guidelines. *Alcoholism Treatment Quarterly, 26*(4), 500–535.

Whitley, C. E. M. (2010). Social work clinical supervision in the addiction: Importance of understanding professional culture. *Journal of Social Work Practice in the Addiction, 10,* 343–362. doi:10.1080/1533256X.2010.521071

Chapter 5

Introduction to Assessment

Mark D. Stauffer
Walden University
David Capuzzi
Walden University, Johns Hopkins University

Kelly Aissen
Walden University

"I would like to get my life back together," Janelle told her counselor matter-of-factly. "It's been a hard two years since my divorce and I . . . I am probably drinking too much. I know I'm drinking too much . . . at least for me." Silence occurred as their eyes briefly met, and the counselor actively listened, providing a nonverbal presence. "I've just been kinda crazy . . . crying all the time . . . angry the rest. I'm just not as strong as I thought I was . . . or . . . as I normally am . . . I guess I just need some extra help." Janelle smiled uncomfortably and then said, "Don't get me wrong. I'm not really crazy." Mia, her counselor, replied in a warm and openly inquisitive tone, "Are you concerned about how I will view you as you share about your life and who you are?" Janelle hesitated before responding, "Yes." Her voice was vulnerable, yet clear. "Yes, I don't want to have to go to a meeting and say I'm a drunk for the rest of my whole life. I don't want to be put in a box . . . and . . . and . . . I don't want to be given a label like those other people. I am a strong person . . . maybe too strong! I just need to get back to myself."

Screening and assessment is a critical first step in addictions treatment. Addiction is one of the most commonly missed diagnoses in psychiatry and counseling fields, most notably due to the underreporting of drinking and drug use (both prescription and nonprescription), a less stereotypical presentation of an alcoholic/addict (hence the need to debunk myths about addiction, treatment, twelve-step programs, and who suffers from and gets addiction), and comorbid mental health issues being the focus of seeking treatment (which are exacerbated exponentially by alcohol and drug use and often mimic mental health disorders). As this opening session between Janelle and her counselor conveys, assessment, done correctly, can be a window into a person's life. Although often associated with "testing," assessment also includes clinical interviewing. If counselors are not trained in, experienced with, and competent in assessment, then clients will have unnoticed, marginalized, and thus untreated addiction. Many readers of this chapter may not be employed as addictions counselors nor planning to specialize in addictions counseling, but will still want to know what to do when a client presents with addiction, process addictions, and the ensuing addiction-related problems. This is crucial so the counselor can refer out to the appropriate counselor and/or treatment facility that can best meet the client's current needs. Just as with any other specialty clinical area (eating disorders, dual-diagnosis, sex offenders, foster care children, etc.), counselors always need to work within their scope of practice and refer when appropriate (skill level, gender-specific counselor needed, conflict of interest, etc.).

NOTE: The writers wish to thank Holly Tanigoshi for her contributions to the second edition version of this chapter.

Having a strong set of generalist counseling skills will include basic assessments for addiction, eating disorders, depression/anxiety, trauma, and other comorbid mental health disorders. Thorough assessment skills allow the counselor to make clinically appropriate and tailored referrals for current counseling and/or treatment needs, which, in turn, enhances efficacy and healing recovery rates. When clients are able to find a good fit for their treatment needs initially, the greater the chances for long-term recovery success. Learning about the knowledge and skills base one must acquire to become competent as an addictions counselor is an important first step.

This is the first of two chapters in our text that focus on assessment. As we wrote this chapter, our intent was to provide an overview of the important aspects of addictions assessment, from a holistic perspective. The holistic perspective for treatment is espoused as the most common addiction counseling and treatment practices. These practices are supported clinically, in research data, and anecdotally by counselors and treating physicians. According to Aissen (2008), it is crucial to implement the trifold approach, which addresses the physical, emotional, and spiritual components of healing when developing individual treatment plans. Effective treatment plans encompass goals for all three areas, evaluate goals, and progress at each stage of treatment. Counselors and health care professionals alike can agree that healthy humans of any kind will be open to gaining awareness about their physical, emotional, and spiritual needs for optimal health personal growth.

Janelle wanted to be viewed for who she was—to be seen and accepted. Professional helpers can keep the possibilities open when they suspend judgment. One finding of Strupp's (1993) research on the therapeutic relationship was that immediate negative evaluations of clients by therapists lead to poorer outcomes. Building rapport in the early sessions is integral to the success of any therapeutic relationship. Helpers can make assessment an art form and a dance of life when we allow our view to come from an open and nonassuming frame of mind. Some instruments related to important content matter and interviewing will be discussed in this chapter; however, a more thorough examination of specific instruments used for screening and assessment will be undertaken in Chapter 6.

PHILOSOPHICAL FOUNDATIONS OF ADDICTIONS COUNSELING

Although the history, theory, and research base that informs addictions counseling is unique and different from that of other fields—for example, developmental psychology or school counseling—we believe that addictions counselors draw on similar holistic, developmental, contextual, and multicultural approaches. Our theoretical orientation as counselors affects how we work with clients. Our actions should be informed by aspirations and guiding principles. We anecdotally present a few ideas as a philosophical foundation for the assessment of clients: (1) the client and counselor must have some level of hope; (2) assets, strengths, and well-being are as important as problems, challenges, and unpleasant realities; (3) change occurs for the whole person (i.e., intrapersonal, interpersonal, ecological, cultural systems) rather than to part of a person; (4) client change is a process that is encouraged by intrinsic motivation even when social pressure has initiated treatment; (5) a collaborative relationship between client and counselor is essential and requires the client to take responsibility for change in his or her life; (6) counselors and their clients collaborate with and use the assets of a multidisciplinary team; and (7) assessment may lead to advocacy.

Hope

Effective counselors encourage a sense of hope in clients, because hope is seen as a condition of successful psychotherapy (Babits, 2001; Moltu, Binder, & Nielsen, 2010; Shabad, 2001). It is not uncommon for a client to enter counseling lacking hope. This is diametrically true for persons seeking help for substance abuse and addiction. It can be helpful to point out to clients that the mere step of making an appointment and attending can be a sign of hope. Starting with perspective and microshifts can start the process of rapport building and give the client a reason to come back or agree to enter treatment. As we are learning, hope is vital to continued change. It is not uncommon for clients to enter counseling void of hope as this is a primary symptom of both depression and addiction disorders across the spectrum.

Would you work with a client if you felt you had no chance for success of any kind? Will clients be motivated to engage in recovery without hope? According to Bergin and Walsh (2005), there are many definitions in the literature ranging from the spiritual to the mundane. Dufault and Martocchio (1985) stated that hope is "characterized by a confident yet uncertain expectation of achieving a good future, which to the hoping person, is realistically possible and personally significant" (p. 380). With some clients, especially those with treatment refractory conditions, i.e., "nonresponders," we may have little hope for change or even maintenance of current status. Yet, an effective counselor must believe and cultivate what is possible. We must be good at suspending judgment that impedes growth. A good assessment should tap into what is most essential to the client's positive change beliefs. Understanding that addiction is a relapsing and progressive disease can help mitigate the frustration felt by clients, their families, and counselors when the identified client continues to struggle in recovery despite knowledge, support, and/or treatment experiences. Relapse is not inevitable; however, it is part of the disease cycle of addiction and speaks to the consistent need for daily maintenance practices in recovery. This understanding can help clients regain hope when long recidivism histories have prevailed. It is helpful to share with clients and their families that addiction, being a brain disease, explains the insidious behaviors but does not excuse any behavior, hurts, or consequences.

Hope can be seen in a dichotomous way: adaptive and beneficial or maladaptive and dysfunctional. Adaptive hope manifests as proper coping skills, healthy transitions, resiliency, and acceptance. In a study examining the self-identification of those with serious mental illnesses in recovery, Buckley-Walker, Crowe, and Caputi (2010) concluded that "the more meaning, hope and direction people have, the more likely they will be able to problem solve/plan and be more actively involved in managing their own recovery" (p. 224). Conversely, maladaptive hope rests on fantasies and an underlying insistence that reality should be or should have been a certain way. Maladaptive hope impinges on normal functioning and growth and prevents a person from "engaging in life as it presents itself" (Bergin & Walsh, 2005, p. 9).

Strength-Based Approaches

Strength-based approaches encourage a holistic attitude, emphasize hopeful elements, and facilitate the development of comprehensive treatment plans. Assessment includes the identification of strengths and accomplishments from the past in addition to current challenges and consequences (Lappalainen, Savolainen, Kuorelahti, & Epstein, 2009; Substance and Mental Health Services Administration [SAMHSA], 1998a). Cheon (2008) stated that, "The strengths perspective assumes that all consumers have positive capabilities and the capacity for success" (p. 769). Counselors assist clients to use assets and strengths while not avoiding difficult problems, challenges, and unpleasant realities. Helping clients to evoke a more balanced view of their strengths and challenges can lead to higher rates of treatment efficacy, sobriety, and consistent implementation of sober coping skills.

Interviewing clients is best done with a nonjudgmental orientation marked by curiosity and a matter-of-fact quality, demonstrated both verbally and nonverbally. It also should take into account the specific strengths of a client's family and social support system (McIntyre, 2004;

SAMHSA, 1998b). A new client entering counseling/treatment who lacks hope will benefit from identifying current areas of support that may already be present and/or may not be utilized. It is not uncommon for clients in early recovery to have a myopic view of their own strengths (low self-esteem), support (current family/friends), and resources available (counseling, treatment, Alcoholics Anonymous/Narcotics Anonymous [AA/NA]).

"Strength-based assessment is defined as the measurement of those emotional and behavioral skills, competencies, and characteristics that create a sense of personal accomplishment, contribute to satisfying relationships with family members, peers, and adults, enhance one's ability to deal with adversity and stress, and promote one's personal, social and academic development."

Source: Lappalainen, K., Savolainen, H., Kuorelahti, M., & Epstein, M. (2009). An international assessment of the emotional and behavioral strengths of youth. *Journal of Child & Family Studies, 18*(6), 746–747.

A Whole Person Approach

This chapter examines assessment of the "whole" person, because those who are assessed and successfully treated for an impairing addiction will most likely draw on various internal and external resources in recovery, and change aspects of lifestyle and identity seemingly unrelated to identified addictions. Aissen (2008) asserts the trifold approach is an all-encompassing approach in the treatment of mental health and addiction disorders across the diagnostic spectrum. It is essential to identifying physical, emotional, and spiritual healing needs when developing a clinically sound treatment plan regardless of presenting issue, age, gender, race, culture, or socioeconomic status (SES). Diagnostic tools and structured assessment measures have definite strengths for counselors and other health care professionals, yet client strengths and contextual factors can mistakenly be overlooked when pathology is overemphasized. Implementing a holistic approach to care, treating the tangible and intangible presenting issues, and helping rebuild client hope is the ultimate goal.

In 2013, the American Psychiatric Association (APA) published the fifth edition of the *Diagnostic and Statistical Manual of Mental Disorders* (DSM-V); the first edition of the DSM-I was published in 1960. Until recently, the DSM has been known as the gold standard for classifying mental health pathology in the United States (APA, 2000). However, there has been a push in research and practice to assess beyond the criteria sets to detail individual symptoms in context of the individual not only the pathology. The field of addictions relies heavily on the DSM's criteria sets and categorizations for addiction-related disorders, with some marked advantages. Primarily, it increases reliability in research, diagnosis, and clinical applications. Professionals across location and discipline can understand that certain terminology means roughly certain set of symptoms are occurring, to be used as markers. Individual treatment plans in addiction treatment and counseling will manifest from these baseline markers. Many less noticed benefits exist as well—for example, allowing individuals and families to normalize disorders that had been previously viewed as resulting from moral inappropriateness or character failure. Addiction is a disease and not a result of a moral failing. At the same time, that does not mean that people are free from taking responsibility for their actions, behaviors, and consequences as a result of being in their active disease of addiction. Many lay people, and even counselors and doctors not trained in addiction medicine, do not understand the mechanics of how the disease of addiction impacts the brain. The obsession-based nature of addiction manifests in the compulsive use of or compulsive behavior involving alcohol, drugs, sex, food (undereating, overeating, restricting, purging), gambling, spending, and many others. The DSM is also the best source currently available for classifying mental health disorders. Although similar, the International Classification of Diseases (ICD-10) should also be explored for its differences and because of its use in other countries. It is important for every counselor and health care professional to expand beyond commonly held ethnocentric views of society and healing. For further discussion of the history and comparative nature of DSM and ICD classification systems, see Saunders (2006).

The DSM has limitations, many of which are described in the preface to the manual itself. At the level of cautious examination, Berger and Luckman (1967), as well as Goffman (1961), reminded the profession that disorders are a social construct. Diagnostic terminology can unintentionally be turned into pejorative or misconstrued labels, leading to narrow views of individuals. When diagnoses are misused or made without a thorough assessment first, the holistic view of counseling is negatively impacted and diagnoses have the potential to become stigmatizing labels. Furthermore, the DSM categorizes disorders as specific and distinct, when actually they may exist on a continuum, as counselors and doctors qualitatively document, and share clinical experiences. While many disorders and struggles are on a continuum, counselors also need to not dismiss, deny, or ignore manifesting symptoms that arise out of fear of diagnosing/labeling. Early detection of symptoms can aid in slowing the progression of a disorder and/or stop certain symptoms all together. Therefore, acknowledging symptoms can be beneficial vs. fearing to admit problematic behaviors or experiences are occurring. Acknowledging signs and symptoms as they arise does not equate with diagnosing a mental illness, prescribing a medication, or changing any current treatment strategies. Before any diagnosis can be made, the physical, social, cultural, emotional, spiritual, and psychological factors of each client will need to be assessed.

Diagnosis using the DSM-V (APA, 2013) as a guide has a vital place in best practices for clients. Diagnostic classifications are not designed to harm clients, but to help identify and organize symptoms for counselors and doctors to tailor and treat current symptoms more directly. Diagnoses can be relieving for some clients. Many feel confused by their own experience, misunderstood by health care professionals for years, all while treating symptoms unsuccessfully. A diagnostic direction can provide an explanation for behavior, an emotional and physical acceptance tool, and a renewed energy or motivation to take action with current needs. It is not uncommon for counselors to provide education to their clients about the counseling process, the role of medicinal and nonmedicinal counseling strategies, and the utility of medication when needed. There will always be a need to learn nonmedicinal coping skills, regardless of there being a chemical component to presenting issues. As counselors, we will have frequent opportunities to debunk myths and misconceptions about counseling and who may benefit from counseling, deciphering both mental health and addiction disorders, the role of medication in conjunction with counseling, and the overall utility of mental health services.

Motivation

Counselors who are skilled at helping clients see the benefit of making changes in their lives witness the most successful outcomes when they encourage client motivation. We refer to motivation as both internal and external. Often clients enter treatment because of legal social controls, formal social controls (e.g., employer mandated), and informal social controls (e.g., friends, family, spouses) (Wild, 2006). Although the element of coercion or pressure may have brought a client to an assessment, a competent assessor will try to gauge these pressures and determine what intrinsic motivation exists. Counselors develop these skills in depth as they practice moving theory knowledge into clinical practice. In a study of 300 clients seeking substance abuse treatment, Wild, Cunningham, and Ryan (2006), found that social pressures and legal referral to enter treatment, quit, and/or cut down did not affect client treatment engagement upon entry. It is not uncommon for counselors to encounter clients entering substance abuse treatment to be lacking hope and motivation; the idea of getting sober is terrifying and unknown for many. Many clients intellectually know they need to get sober; however, that logic is not valid when the disease of addiction is present. Hence the insidiousness of addiction—it is not logical to continue participating in behaviors that cause physical, emotional, and spiritual pain. In agreement, the big book of Alcoholics Anonymous (1939), in Chapter 5, "How It Works," the disease of addiction is vividly described as "cunning, powerful, and baffling" (pp. 58–59). Many people, with and without the disease of addiction, can relate to the struggle of taking actions from theory to practice. Internal motivation may feel like pressure as well when it stems from negative self-perceptions (Tims, Leukefeld, & Platt, 2001). External pressures (i.e., saving a marriage, staying out of jail, keeping one's job) may be motivating reasons to enter treatment; however, intrinsic motivation is emphasized for greater change and what is needed for long-term recovery.

Client Collaboration in Addictions Counseling

Counselors make clear that the therapeutic process requires effort by the client for successful recovery. Ideally, clients must "work" in each counseling session and are responsible and empowered to achieve the necessary day-to-day work between sessions. Helping clients set up accountability and weekly goals can encourage and motivate client action outside of the counseling hour. Finn and Tonsager (1997) suggested a collaborative model in which counselors and clients share and explore assessment results. Whether it is a simple intake form or a more intensive assessment instrument, being on the same team is important. Many agencies will start with a self-report intake that is later followed up in person. As an example of collaboration, a counselor might open with, "Janelle, I have read over the form you filled out. I want to go over it with you so that I can hear from you directly about your life. This also helps me know that my interpretation of what you wrote is what you mean." Clients are more likely to be involved and invested in the assessment process if they are treated as collaborators and it fits with their goals. Clients involved in the assessment process are more likely to give more accurate and important information, because motivation and trust levels are higher (Sattler, 1998).

Multidisciplinary Approach

Quite often, the counselor and client work in conjunction with other helping professionals and health care providers in building comprehensive treatment plans. A client may gain the most from having his or her team of family therapist, addictions counselor, psychiatrist/medical provider, probation officer, and/or sponsor working together toward his or her desired recovery outcomes. Turning one's life around takes effort, and the best outcomes often occur when clients have access to and assistance from linked professional and community supports (SAMHSA, 1996). For example, Saitz, Horton, Larson, Winter, and Samet (2005) concluded that formally linking patients during detoxification to primary medical care services improved levels of addiction severity.

Advocacy

Assessment also provides information about areas for which clients may need an advocate (Graham, Timney, Bois, & Wedgerfield, 1995). Whether in an addictions, mental health, school, or vocational rehabilitation context, an assessment may lead to client advocacy. Lewis, Lewis, Daniels, and D'Andrea (2003) suggested that a client may need to be advocated for (direct advocacy) or on behalf of (indirect advocacy). Questions an assessor should ask are, "In what ways does my client need advocacy?" "Is my client able to advocate for himself now or once stabilized?" An assessment will often detail a variety of areas of life that may need support or changes for the client to have success in recovery long term.

THE ROLE OF AN ADDICTIONS ASSESSOR

Assessment is more successful when the relevancy of the information obtained increases. Professional helpers gather information based on the role and function of their work. Therefore, depending on the professionals' scope of practice (psychiatry, nursing, individual, couples', or family counseling, nutrition, and/or a group counseling), assessment will inquire about different areas that impede current quality of life (Sattler, 1998). SAMHSA (1998b) listed five basic objectives for the assessment of persons with substance abuse and dependence problems. See the Five Objectives for Assessment sidebar. Additionally, the role of an assessor is to create documents useful to treatment and continuity of care. *Continuity of care* refers to how treatment providers (counselor, clinic, health system) are able to assist a client over time through continued contact and involvement, by coordinating care among multiple providers, and by connecting them with community resources. This can be in the form of setting up postdetox or posttreatment care, having doctors' appointments to continue the treatment plan, and/or consulting with the client's provider about what level of care he or she is beginning next. Where counselors work and what the clinical environment is like will determine the type, availability, and frequency of collaborated care. Continuity of care among providers not only helps us as the counselor assessing and providing counseling, but aids the client with accountability across health care goals.

> ### Five Objectives for Assessment (SAMHSA, 1998b, p. 4)
>
> 1. To identify those who are experiencing problems related to substance abuse and/or have progressed to the stage of dependency
> 2. To assess the full spectrum of problems for which treatment may be needed
> 3. To plan appropriate interventions
> 4. To involve appropriate family members or significant others, as needed, in the individual's treatment
> 5. To evaluate the effectiveness of interventions implemented

POINTS TO REMEMBER ABOUT HUMAN ASSESSMENT MEASURES

Protect Client Welfare and Information

Whether an evaluation is formal or informal, there are a few points to consider to ensure an ethical and supportive experience. A client's welfare is of primary importance throughout the assessment process. Informed consent must be gained for assessment in the same way that it must be for counseling services. Counselors only release assessment results to qualified professionals in a confidential manner (Remley & Herlihy, 2010).

Be Competent to Use a Given Assessment Instrument

Counselors must know the limits of their professional competence; this includes using and interpreting results of assessment instruments. Seek proper training and exert care in the use of assessments, including circumstances where technology or testing services are employed (*ACA Code of Ethics*, American Counseling Association [ACA], 2005, E.2).

Recognize Uniqueness and Diversity

Multicultural competency is an important part of a counselor's training and ongoing practice that extends into our best practices in the realm of addiction (Arredondo et al., 1996). Knowing how culture affects assessment of addiction is important (Straussner, 2001). Principle 1 of the ethics code of the National Association of Alcohol and Drug Abuse Counselors (NAACAD) (2008) states, "I shall affirm diversity among colleagues or clients regardless of age gender, sexual orientation, ethnic/racial background, religious/spiritual beliefs, marital status, political beliefs, or mental/physical disability" (p. 1). Cultural differences may lead to variations in how an assessment is selected, administered, interpreted, and reported. For example, Cunningham (1994) contributed this clear point: "The cultural beliefs of a group of people are directly related to how alcohol and other drug problems are defined. The very definition of health differs by ethnicities and cultures. Therefore, it is of critical importance to understand how the members of an ethnic group define alcohol and other drug problems; what is considered to be a positive outcome; and what they feel are appropriate ways to prevent these problems from occurring" (p. viii). The ACA (2005) *Code of Ethics* provides this important guideline: "Counselors recognize that culture affects the manner in which clients' problems are defined" (E.5.b). For more specific ethical guidelines, refer to the Standards for Multicultural Assessment (Association for Assessment in Counseling, 2003).

WATCH OUT FOR STEREOTYPES There are a few ways one can be fooled by and encourage stereotypes and stigmas. First, a counselor can miss identifying substance and process addictions because a client's appearance or behavior does not fit into the counselor's beliefs about "addicts" (Freimuth, 2005). This is another reason that many "nonstereotypical alcoholic/drug addicts" suffer longer than others—an example would be impaired professionals as a subgroup. Second, clients often enter counseling with self-identified mental health problems and have unidentified addictions because they may be using without noticeable, current, or significant impairment externally, or they do not want to admit that their substance abuse problem is real and impairing. Third, persons should not be described by their pathology or disability. Referring to a client by saying, "Janelle is an addict" is different than saying, "Janelle's self-report of her alcohol use fits the criteria for a diagnosis of alcohol abuse." Using terms like *tendency* and *probability* as a practice may aid our suspension of judgment, allowing us to explore and experiment with the main goal of addictions counseling: to help our client who, like a mountain, may appear different depending on where one is standing.

BE TRUE TO THE INITIAL DESIGN AND PURPOSE OF THE INSTRUMENT Counselors should use screening and assessment instruments in the way they were designed to be used. For example, was the tool made to screen for addiction or measure the severity of an addiction? Knowing what a measure can or cannot indicate is imperative for the results to have meaning. For example, a severity index will not indicate level or existence of coping skills. Counselors must ascertain whether the instrument selected for assessment purposes will provide the information needed for the development of a treatment plan and the process of counseling. It is also prudent to make sure your client meets the population the assessment was developed for and to use it as only one component of the overall assessment. The combination of self-report, live interviewing, assessments, and collaboration with family or other health care providers offers the most thorough assessment when developing counseling/treatment goals.

Keep Empathic Connection Alive

Building rapport with clients supersedes any skill development or comprehension of counseling theories and techniques. It is paramount to build rapport as without it, the counselors' intelligence, education, and/or experience becomes irrelevant. Of course, that is not to say that our training, professionalism, and skill level is not integral, but it can only be utilized when rapport with the client is present. Finn and Tonsager (1997) remind counselors to "develop and maintain empathic connections with clients" when assessing (p. 378). Often initial interviews can feel mechanical, choppy, and disconnected from the client, not to mention unrelated to matters that feel most pressing. Maintain a therapeutic environment by explaining the nature of the interview process so the client can have a positive frame of reference for probing. Here is an example: "Janelle, I want to ask you some questions so that I can better get to know who you are. These questions help me understand the range of your life experience, which will make the counseling process more successful." In clinical assessment, these reassurances can help minimize client guardedness, and with hope, encourage emotional honesty.

Use Multiple Methods

Utilizing multiple sources and methods in assessment will help the counselor gather a more useful body of evidence for treatment. A detailed interview helps the counselor know what areas need further inquiry, treatment, and/or a potential referral. If too much or too little information is gathered, it may cost both the client and counselor. For example, making a diagnosis on the basis of a screening device alone will be insufficient and unethical; gathering a lot of information on nonrelevant topics may waste valuable time that could be used for treatment. To save resources and provide the best care, it is better to rely on several sources of information and utilize a multidisciplinary approach. As a short case example, Brian told his counselor he was "working hard" in treatment and maintaining his goals of "being clean." After a positive urinalysis test and further discussion with his counselor, it was clear that Brian had lapsed, but did not want to vocalize his "failure" and "disappoint" his counselor. As multiple sources of information are gathered, discrepancies may arise that help shed light on what is occurring for the client. Resolve such discrepancies in collaboration with clients (SAMHSA, 2008). Learning to ask clients similar questions from different angles may help reveal more pertinent clinical information beyond the surface presenting issues.

Continue to Assess Over Time and in Relation to Stage of Treatment

Assessment is an ongoing process. Different types of information are gathered in context at different stages of change and recovery. For example, a client who is currently intoxicated or in withdrawal may be assessed for placement into the most appropriate care to monitor detoxification and manage withdrawal (Mee-Lee, Shulman, Fishman, Gastfriend, & Griffith, 2001). In contrast, assessment of a client just leaving inpatient treatment might focus on the recovery environment and use related contextual factors (e.g., internal triggers, expectations related to use) that might help prevent relapse (Donovan & Marlatt, 2005).

Be Skilled When Communicating About Assessment Procedures and Results

Most clients have little understanding of psychological testing. Encourage client education at all stages of the assessment process and indicate that questions are welcome. Counselors interpret or "translate" in easy-to-understand terminology. Results are also interpreted in the most accurate way possible while considering a client's explicit understanding. Counselors share with clients what an assessment clearly does and does not indicate (see Sattler, 1998, Chapter 1).

Explore results that are already known and accepted by the client's worldview and reality first, especially when clients are unsure or anxious. Assessments should support a feeling and belief that clients "do know" much about their inner and outer worlds. Finn and Tonsager (1997) noted that one motive for participation in the assessment process is *self-verification*. Self-verification occurs when one's reality and concept of self is affirmed. Many clients find comfort and value in an assessment discovering or affirming their truths and experiences. Remember, a diagnosis can be a relief as it may explain signs, symptoms, and/or behaviors. It is imperative for mental health counselors to educate and explain that a mental health or addiction diagnosis does not endorse or excuse any behaviors or consequences of the untreated disorder. This is particularly important with the disease of addiction. Many members of society, families of those with addiction issues, and sadly many untrained health care professionals are lacking an understanding of the etiology of addiction. An explanation can go a long way in accepting a disorder; therefore, options become available to treat the disorder, and more clients and families are able to get the help they need and/or did not know they needed. Finally, clients may be more receptive to assessment results around addiction when it is done in conjunction with other nonaddiction-related information (e.g., health, career, family systems). So, the assessment process may be more productive when it connects to the breadth of a client's life and relates to his or her life goals, worldview, and values (Dimeff, Baer, Kivlahan, & Marlatt, 2000). To fully treat any client, it is important to assess all areas of life, regardless of their presenting issue. Many clients will report symptoms they did not realize were mitigating factors related to their current presenting issues.

FLOW OF ADDICTIONS ASSESSMENT

Assessment starts the moment a client walks through the door or contacts the office for an appointment. It is part of an ongoing process and occurs before, during, and after treatment; therefore, assessment may help with referral, diagnosis, strength identification, or therapeutic outcome evaluations at any stage of change. There are several multistage models for assessment (see Allen & Mattson, 1993; Tarter, 1990). Screening is usually the first appraisal step and may signify the need for immediate crisis intervention (see Figure 5.1). If screening does not indicate the need for crisis intervention, and indicates the need for more comprehensive assessment, then a plan for assessment is collaboratively made with the client. The multiple assessment approach is the preferred comprehensive assessment designed to create a clearer picture for best intervention practices (SAMHSA, 1998b, p. 19). The culmination of multiple findings and hypotheses can direct counseling and treatment recommendations.

The American Society of Addiction Medicine (ASAM) defines the disease of addiction as "a primary, chronic disease of brain reward, motivation, memory and related circuitry." In 2013, the addiction definition was expanded to include the "individual pathologically pursuing reward and/or relief by substance use and other behaviors" (Mee-Lee, 2013). The latter definition is more broad to include classifications for the many process addictions (e.g., sex, gambling, food, money) that have the same disease process in the brain and compulsive behavior as substance-related addictions. A thorough substance abuse assessment may include referrals to various treatment modalities: detoxification and stabilization, withdrawal management, inpatient residential treatment partial hospitalization, intensive outpatient treatment, or other outpatient community support groups (Johnson, 2003). The ASAM created a protocol, Patient Placement Criteria (PPC), Second Volume Revised (PPC-2R), that is widely used to help place clients into an appropriate addictions treatment setting by assessing their level of care needs (Mee-Lee et al., 2001). The PPC was first created by a multidisciplinary team of professionals in the 1980s. Its main goal was to develop a national set of criteria that was assessment based as well as geared toward clinical needs and outcomes-oriented continuity of care (Mee-Lee, 2005).

In October of 2014, ASAM published the newest criterion set for the Treatment of Substance-Related Disorders. Most changes hold many of the same core tenets, with minor shifts in clarity, focus, and definition. According to Mee-Lee (2014), the ASAM criteria set is currently the "most comprehensive set of guidelines for assessment, service planning, placement, continued stay and transfer/discharge of individuals with addiction and co-occurring conditions" (p. 2). Today, the ASAM criteria set is standard in over 30 states and all Department of Defense addiction programs across the world (Mee-Lee, 2014). Due to the changing climate of health care reform in the United States and abroad, criteria sets and diagnostic categories are becoming increasingly more important in order to get clients the help they need when designing individualized treatment plans.

One of the more notable changes in the 2013 ASAM criteria set was the renaming of "Detoxification" to a more accurate "Withdrawal Management" description. According to Mee-Lee (2014), the term *withdrawal management* is more inclusive; it "emphasizes the importance of using a continuum of withdrawal management services to support a person through both the physiological and psychological signs and symptoms of withdrawal" (p. 5). Withdrawal management needs go beyond the short-term medical safety detoxification that an inpatient facility can provide. Withdrawal management can last several weeks and/or months, with latent withdrawal symptoms always possible. These latent withdrawal symptoms can be managed as an outpatient and/or once the client no longer needs supervised medical detoxification services or inpatient care. Mee-Lee (2013) reiterates that the ASAM criteria are utilized clinically beyond defining specialty addiction treatment criteria sets. In Chapter 15, "Persons with Disabilities and Substance-Related and Addictive Disorders," the multidimensional assessment detailing six individual dimensions is detailed further, which provides a common language and clinical understanding across health care disciplines.

Screening

Screening is often the first step in the evaluation process. Screening may be seen as a tool for spotting "red flags," a way to indicate that a more comprehensive assessment is needed (Kaminer, 2008). *Screening* is defined as "the process through which a counselor, client and available significant others determine the most appropriate initial course of action, given the client's needs and characteristics, and the available resources within the community" (SAMHSA, 1998a, p. 29). The process of screening leads the counselor to (1) rule out addiction, (2) request a more comprehensive assessment, or (3) refer for treatment with ongoing assessment. It may also make apparent imminent crises and the need for immediate intervention. When clients are placed in the appropriate level of clinical care, recidivism rates are lessened significantly. As we have discussed earlier in the chapter, motivation and stage of change levels in early substance abuse treatment, can be tentative and not fully engaged yet. Therefore, having complications, barriers, and/or "red tape" to getting treatment or care can often derail any willingness available. Helping a client get to counseling or treatment when they are willing is key!

An immediate intervention can be crucial when the client is in need of medical detoxification services for stabilization. Many people believe they can just quit alcohol, drugs, and other medicines (over-the-counter [OTC] and/or prescribed medicines for depression, blood pressure, pain, and others) "cold turkey" and then work on recovery. Moyer (2012) warns of the dangers and even lethality depending on what alcohol, drugs, and/or other mind-altering substances are being used and/or combined. Drinking alcohol while taking benzodiazepines (sedatives) can be dangerous (even lethal); both substances are chemically similar once digested—hence the exponential impact when combined. If not properly detoxified, alcohol and sedative withdrawal can cause breathing to stop (Moyer, 2012). Assessing the amount, consistency, and longevity of a client's usage can be helpful in determining a need for a detoxification referral. Meaningful or impacting substance abuse treatment cannot truly begin until the client is physically detoxed and/or "dry" from the mind-altering chemical or obsessive behavior manifested in his or her addiction. Clients must be physically detoxified or in the process under medical supervision before any of the emotional and spiritual work of recovery can be started. Hence the many benefits of applying the multidisciplinary approach to treatment.

Crisis Intervention

An assessment may be temporarily delayed by impending crises that need to be responded to. Counselors should know what constitutes crises and what steps one should take for the most critical types of crises. Effective counselors know how to identify signs and intervene when clients are suicidal, homicidal, experience life-threatening abuse, domestic violence, psychosis, and acute physical illness. Sometimes this means seeking immediate help from other professionals (police/law enforcement, detoxification/inpatient psychiatric inpatient facilities, and/or other professionals who may already be involved in the client's care). Once you have assessed for safety and willingness to get help, the counselor may craft a more in-depth suicide intervention plan. Remley and Herlihy (2010) remind us to carefully log and record critical incidents for counselor and client safety, but also for self-reflecting on one's intervention as a counselor. These types of cases are always worth consultation with supervisors and/or professional peers.

OPERATIONALIZING ASSESSMENT INTERVIEWS

Gathering information becomes more successful as three qualities increase: reliability, validity, and relevancy. Reliability can be seen as the consistency of the assessment; a measure with high reliability will provide the same results when administered repeatedly. Validity is the correctness or accuracy of the information; a measure with high validity measures what it intends to measure (e.g., depression scale accurately measures depression and not anxiety). Lastly, relevance in assessment is about collecting information efficiently and effectively; a relevant measure obtains the most essential data.

Structured, Semistructured, and Unstructured Interviews

Assessment interviews can be placed on a continuum based on their structure. Here we will look at assessment interviews as falling into three categories: unstructured, semistructured, and structured (see Sattler, 1998). These three types have advantages and disadvantages.

Unstructured interviews allow the client to more freely share experience, which may help build initial rapport with the counselor and allow resistance to be addressed. This format also allows the clinician to divert and probe into areas that arise during the interview. Both assessor and client can initiate discussion items and questions. The level or type of language of an unstructured interview can be adjusted to meet the knowledge, skills, and development of the client. This is an essential skill for counselors who want to support clients staying in counseling and doing the emotional healing work. One is also able to examine complicated processes, meanings behind behaviors, beliefs, in-depth examples, and the "rich" narrative of a client's story related to addiction and recovery. Time efficiency, the ability to generalize, and the potential to overassess certain areas at the expense of others are limitations.

Semistructured interviews provide a framework for addictions counselors to use while still allowing a detail-oriented clinician to pursue areas of important client information and disclosure not addressed by a structured assessment tool. Often a designated list of open questions guides the interviewer. During a semistructured exam, a counselor may be able to stop the content of a session to deal with resistance or increase rapport. The finesse of working with structure and assessing independently will become more congruent the longer you are working in the field.

Structured interviews are instruments that optimize reliability and validity, with the intent of limiting assessor bias. Items are constructed with specific outcomes in mind (i.e., substance use identification), so wording of items are asked exactly as provided without interplay between counselor and client. This aids quantitative research. Language cannot be adjusted to increase clarity and comprehension. Structured interviews, in general, are time efficient, but may fall short when rapport problems or resistance arises. Structured interviews may need advanced training or certification specifically for the measure (Sattler, 1998).

Components of an Interview

A clinical interview takes into consideration many relevant components. Various protocols can be used to plan a course for information gathering. Here are ten steps that a counselor may want to follow when interviewing a client:

1. Review referral information
2. Obtain and review previous evaluations
3. Interview the client
4. Gather corroborating material (e.g., family interview)
5. Formulate hypothesis
6. Make recommendations
7. Create a report and other significant documents
8. Meet with the client over results
9. Meet with the support system of the client
10. Follow up on recommendations and referrals

Assessment Dimensions Related to Level of Care

Assessment often occurs in relationship to a client's treatment stage and level of care placement. The ASAM criteria are the most widely used and thorough set of guidelines for assessment, service planning, placement, continued stay, and discharge planning of patients with addictive disorders (Mee-Lee, 2013). Mee-Lee (2013) developed and detailed six dimensions to assess and create a holistic and bio-psycho-social assessment for assessing substance abuse clients. Each of the six dimensions is outlined in the following with corresponding questions to include in the assessment.

DIMENSION 1: ACUTE INTOXICATION AND WITHDRAWAL POTENTIAL (For example, detox and withdrawal management.) What are the current amounts and types of alcohol and/or drugs currently being taken? If any alcohol or any benzodiazepine (sedative) is reported, a thorough question about amounts and types is especially needed to assess for a medical detox referral. Many clients will need education surrounding the lethality potential from alcohol and sedative withdrawal when attempting to quit or cut down. Reminding the client that the info is needed to check for lethality and not judgment can help gain more accurate numbers. Many people with addiction are riddled with shame and fear of judgment, often prompting the under-reporting of substance abuse issues. People of any age can die from withdrawal from alcohol/sedatives if not monitored or stabilized by a medical provider.

DIMENSION 2: BIOMEDICAL CONDITIONS AND COMPLICATIONS (Physical health conditions and their impact on addiction.) What are any other medical and/or physical problems? High blood pressure? Broken leg? Asthma? Diabetes? Is the client taking any medications for any other ailments? If so, are these ailments recurring or temporary? If recurring, are they well controlled? Or in need of care? There may be a need for referrals to treat physical issues that are not stable or not being adequately treated at this time.

DIMENSION 3: EMOTIONAL, BEHAVIORAL, AND COGNITIVE CONDITIONS AND COMPLICATIONS (Co-occurring mental health disorders, cognitive/brain disorders or impairments.) Does the client have any current mental health diagnoses? If any, how long has the client had the diagnosis? How long does the client believe he or she has struggled? How long has client been on medication? If so, is the client compliant with medication? Was this mental health diagnosis made while the client was still drinking and/or using drugs regularly (or any mind-altering substance)? Many mental health disorders are mimicked when under the chemical influence of alcohol and drugs. Therefore, when sober, the same diagnosis may or may not be made. Even when comorbid depression or diagnoses remain, the level of severity is lessened exponentially when alcohol and drugs are no longer interfering with efficacy. This knowledge would be helpful and accurate for all clients taking a psychotropic medication for depression, anxiety, addiction, and/or other mental health needs.

DIMENSION 4: READINESS FOR CHANGE (ALSO READINESS FOR TREATMENT) Does the client believe he or she has an addiction problem? Does the client believe he or she needs help from outside sources? Keep in mind there is a difference between being "ready for change" and being "excited for change." Is the client experiencing repeat consequences? What does the client see as barriers to living contentedly and/or making needed changes?

DIMENSION 5: RELAPSE PREVENTION AND CONTINUED USE OR PROBLEM POTENTIAL (Contextual issues—internal and external cues, expectancy, triggers, treatment response.) How many times has the client attempted to get sober before? How many times has the client attended addiction treatment? What level of care has the client tried previously? Did the client complete treatments successfully? If so, how long was the sobriety posttreatment in the past? Does the client attend AA/NA? Questions about relationships, environment, transportation, and living environment are all areas to assess in Dimension 5.

DIMENSION 6: RECOVERY ENVIRONMENT (Family, peers, work and vocation, legal, housing, financial, culture, transportation, child care.) Where is the client living? Who also lives in the home? Do others living in the home also use alcohol and/or drugs? Are there alcohol and drugs readily available in the home? Are those living with the client supportive of the addiction recovery? Are they willing to participate in family sessions or family programming offered by the treatment center? What is their neighborhood like? Is it likely to support or hinder recovery? These questions will allow you to address these potential challenges when aftercare treatment planning. These answers may also indicate if outpatient treatment is a safe option or a setup for high relapse potential.

GATHERING BACKGROUND AND CONTEXTUAL INFORMATION

Interviews and other assessment tools allow for an understanding of client strengths and challenges, and a picture of the course, context, and current state of an addictive substance disorder. As noted in Figure 5.1, we can compartmentalize information into three categories: previously gathered assessment information, current presentation findings, and collateral information from any family member, teacher/school, hospital, or other health care provider (SAMHSA, 1998b).

In compiling a comprehensive report, one obtains a variety of information. The first type of information for an addictions assessment is basic demographics (name, address, date of birth), and other significant information. This should include essential health care contacts and insurance provider policy information. In a study of 36,081 injection drug users (IDUs), Chassler, Lundgren, and Lonsdale (2006) found that those with private health insurance were much more likely to seek more frequent treatment. The second type of information relates to client presentation and current functioning assessed through a mental status exam. A comprehensive assessment should also include information about current and past addictive behavior and contextual patterns of addiction such as internal/external triggers, expectations of what continued use will bring, and consequences experienced due to addiction, relationship demise, legal charges, financial, and various other medical complications (Johnson, 2003).

Finally, the fourth category addresses treatment specific assessment information: motivation for treatment, readiness for change, past treatment experience, treatment outcome

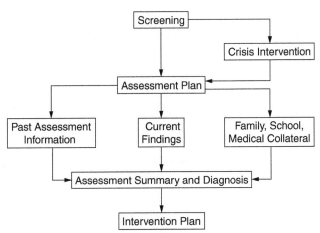

FIGURE 5.1 CSAT Treatment Improvement Protocol (TIP) 31: Screening and Assessing Adolescents for Substance Use Disorders   *Source:* SAMHSA (1998b), p. 22.

expectations, and current reasons for seeking counseling are examples of treatment specific assessment information (SAMHSA, 1998a, 1998b). Finally, an inventory of necessary and supportive information allows for a more holistic perspective. Included in this fourth category are psychosocial factors such as peer relationships, cultural contexts, family systems, and life skills (e.g., coping skills); and work, career, and spirituality.

Client Presentation and Functioning

Observing the presentation of a client provides information about overall functioning and can indicate long-term and current substance use. Presentation and functioning should be assessed on an ongoing basis. Performing a mental status exam (MSE) is one way to document client presentation and functioning. In a typical MSE, observations are made of five basic areas: sensory and cognitive function, thinking, perception, feeling and behavior, and physical appearance. Some kinds of information gathered in an MSE require only observation, while others require some form of probing dialogue and questioning. There are many derivations of a mental status exam. See Figure 5.2 for an example of MSE categories. If you are new to doing MSEs, it may be a good practice to familiarize yourself with one by filling out elements of a mental status exam sheet after each counseling session, or after role plays or counseling videos. With practice, a counselor becomes habituated to observing these attributes.

Category	Example or Subcategory
Appearance	Grooming, health, age, care/type of clothes
Behavior	Psychomotor activity, posture, gait, eye contact
Attitude (in relation to examiner)	Cooperative, aggressive, passive
Speech	Tone (melancholic), articulation, volume (loud), rate (pressured, slow), language (lisp)
Affect (displayed reaction)	Flat, labile, blunted, restricted; appropriate and inappropriate
Mood (underlying feeling state)	Sad, euphoric, angry
Attention (arousal)	Concentrated, focused, distractible
Form of thought (FOT)	Rumination, word salad, tangential, blocking
Content of thought (COT)	Fixations, irrational thought, suicidality, homicidality
Perception	Hallucinations-false sensory perception, illusions-false perception of external object
Memory	Remote memory, recent memory, immediate recall
Orientation	Person, place and time, altered orientation usually starts effects in order of time, then place, then person
Intellectual functioning	Calculation, abstraction, knowledge, construction
Insight	Emotional insight, intellectual insight
Judgment	Appropriate for a situation, reasoning
Reading and writing	Level, ability

FIGURE 5.2 Example of MSE Categories

Skilled counselors become accustomed to the physiological symptoms that are associated with addiction. How does a particular drug affect one's overall appearance (needle marks, abscesses, dilated pupils), behavior (staggered walking, overly tired), speech (pressured, fast), attention (lacks focus, clumsy)? We learn to screen for symptoms of use, withdrawal, and toxicity for different psychoactive substances which will affect functioning such as memory, attention, and executive functions (Lundqvist, 2005). This implies a familiarization with the effects of substances when used alone as well as in combination with other drugs (SAMHSA, 1998a). Inaba and Cohen's (2007) *Uppers, Downers and All Arounders: Physical and Mental Effects of Psychoactive Drugs* is an excellent text directed at drug presentation.

Examine the case about Tricia, which focuses on presentation. Use the MSE example in Figure 5.2 and your understanding of addictions to answer the following question: What elements of Tricia's mental status can you roughly determine? Which elements might you want to rule out if you were counseling this client?

Tricia, a 22-year-old woman, had become homeless in the last year. She seemed a little disoriented as she slowly walked into the lobby for her scheduled first appointment with the counselor, who had just come out. She made eye contact and gave a candid and cordial greeting. Her eyelids were drooping slightly. Her pupils were constricted to the size of pinpoints. Her eyes did not appear to dilate as she moved out of the brightly lit lobby. Her clothes were well kept and she was well groomed. She didn't smell of smoke or alcohol. Tricia was wearing a long-sleeved shirt with the logo of her favorite punk band on it. She seemed a bit tired, but commented on the hot day and how exhausted it made her feel. After making a joke about being homeless, she requested some time to get a drink and sit down for a minute, explaining that the heat had affected her. She reclined in the chair and dozed off briefly, only to revive a moment later for another sip. The counselor commented in a warm manner, "Looks like you could doze off right in that chair."

"I could use a nap," she replied. She paused, closing her eyes, and then looked at the counselor with a slight smile. "I really wanted to talk about my housing situation, but maybe I am too tired today."

CURRENT AND PAST USE AND ADDICTIVE BEHAVIORS A comprehensive assessment should include information about current and past use and addictive behaviors. Details of the last day, week, month, or 2-year period can be useful in determining addiction severity, variability, and patterns. An in-depth interview will require time to explore common substance (alcohol and all other mind-altering drugs) and process-related addictions (food, sex, money, gambling). A more comprehensive interview might inquire directly about a list of commonly used substances and their history with each. For example, the Composite International Diagnostic Interview (CIDI-Core) is used to document several types of substances used, duration, severity, amount used, methods used or route of administration (drinking, smoking, inhaling, intravenous [IV] use, transdermal), patterns of addiction (frequency, periods of abstinence, last use), preferred addiction or substance, motivation for change on each substance and process, associated beliefs and attributed meanings, as well as benefits and consequences (Robins et al., 1989). Such an interview is structured to obtain an accurate picture of the daily addiction process or substance use of the client for treatment purposes.

Sometimes a history is gathered on a single substance or addiction. For example, the Time-Line Followback for Alcohol (TFLB-Alcohol) is used for determining a current use history of alcohol (Roy et al., 2008; Sobell & Sobell, 1992). The l TFLB-Alcohol provides a picture of the severity, variability, and extent of consumption over the past week to 2 years depending on how far one wants to go back. A calendar and important dates such as holidays are used as memory aids (Sobell & Sobell, 1992). Roy et al. (2008) recommended that the Quick Drinking Screen (QDS) be used in place of the TFLB when detailed drinking data was not necessary or possible to obtain.

A counselor can also assign as homework a log to track ongoing use. The idea is for a client to track items such as the amounts, triggers, urges, circumstances, and concurrent thoughts and feelings for specific times of use. This method not only provides an excellent picture of the patterns of addiction, but allows the client to increase awareness through consistent self-monitoring. Such self-monitoring may also help to counteract the limitations of retrospective assessments. See NOVA Southeastern University's Center for Psychological Studies online resource at nova.edu/gsc/online_files.html for examples of such logs.

FIRST EXPOSURE AND SUBSEQUENT EXPOSURE   Probing into the first exposure to and subsequent pattern of addiction may reveal key information about the nature of a person's addiction. Early onset may indicate problems in a client's development (Newcomb, 1997). Did the client begin to abuse alcohol after a traumatic event at age 31, or did he or she start using at age 12 at a neighbor's home? An early age onset of the use of tobacco, alcohol, and other drugs increases significantly the risk factors for alcohol- and drug-dependence disorders as an adult. Additionally, subsequent use of other illicit drugs; high-risk and delinquent behavior; and instability of employment can become other consequences of early alcohol and drug use exposed to the brain (Jackson et al., 2002; Johnson & Mott, 2001).

THE CONTEXT OF USE AND ADDICTIVE BEHAVIOR   A contextual analysis of addictive behavior assesses the clients' current environment where the addiction is manifesting (chemically and/or behaviorally). Helping clients enhance awareness of the addictive process in both obvious and subtle ways provides information valuable for preventing lapses and relapse (Donovan & Marlatt, 2005). See the following sidebar for items considered in a contextual analysis.

What you need to know for contextual analysis of substance use:

- Expectations of use (e.g., relaxation, better social interactions, sleeping better, etc.)
- Internal triggers for use (e.g., emotions, thoughts, withdrawal, craving, etc.)
- External triggers for use (e.g., people, places, seeing needles, music, etc.)
- Immediate reinforcers (e.g., escaping or feeling relaxed or high)
- Positive aspects of use (e.g., make friends, be "cool," feel good, etc.)
- Negative aspects of use (e.g., expense, hangover, interpersonal problems, etc.)

Source: Substance and Mental Health Services Administration. (2008). Integrated dual disorders treatment workbook. *CSAT Evidenced-based Practices.* Rockville, MD: Author.

INTERNAL AND EXTERNAL TRIGGERS   Part of the contextual aspect of addiction assessment is the examination of internal and external triggers, or cues, that are connected to neurological pathways of reward, memory, motivation, and control; these triggers can induce lapses, relapses, and high-risk behavior. Triggers encourage seeking, impulsive drug use, and strong cravings. To prevent relapse, those in recovery must develop an awareness of and a fortifying response to their most salient triggers (Stippikohl et al., 2010). Next, we will discuss the manifestation of both internal and external consequences in the progressive disease of addiction.

INTERNAL CONSEQUENCES Internal consequences of addiction are defined as negative internal symptoms that are intangible, connected to internal suffering that is not known unless expressed, and any other physical, emotional, and spiritual pain that is not visible. Examples of internal consequences may include depression, anxiety, feelings of shame and guilt, stress-induced physical problems, and feelings of inadequacy. Many people in recovery from addiction may relate and connect with each other as peers in recovery through shared internal consequences. The outside content of an experience may differ, but the subsequent internal pain may be similar. Internal consequences tend to be more secretive, insidious, and particularly dangerous for persons ill-equipped with coping skills. More information is needed for substance abuse counselors to share with clients and their families as they navigate a new life in recovery.

EXTERNAL CONSEQUENCES External consequences are those that are tangible, noticeable, behavioral in nature, and unable to be hidden by choice. Examples of external consequences may include: DUI charges, being hurt physically, loss of job, health issues, car accidents, and relationships/marriages. External consequences such as car accidents, hurting oneself while under the influence, and legal charges due to alcohol and/or drugs may allow someone to get treatment sooner as problems are highlighted sooner. External consequences often increase the participation in treatment and/or counseling, attending an AA meeting (or any 12-step group or community-based support group), and/or being an active member in one's health care decisions once consequences are no longer deniable.

NEGATIVE CONSEQUENCES AND POSITIVE ASPECTS Client observation and contemplation of adverse consequences and positive aspects of use can often be the catalyst for seeking help. While consequences of addictive behaviors may coincide with the high-risk behaviors discussed later, they may also reflect less harmful but negative effects of addiction. Discrepancies between a client's goals, values, feelings, and the disadvantages of addiction provide good material for contemplation. It can be helpful to use an inventory that allows a client to place "pros and cons" side by side to contemplate choices and aid in decision making. Janis and Mann (1977) created a decisional balance sheet that is commonly used for this type of exercise. Often clients will experience physical dysfunction (blackouts, feeling ill), relationship problems (marital turmoil, divorce), intrapersonal consequences (low self-esteem, feelings of guilt or inadequacy), loss of resources (unpaid rent, debt to bookies, legal expenses, burned bridges within their support system, cost of a thousand packs of cigarettes after 3 years), unpleasant moods (lack of motivation, depression), social and legal problems (being fired/expelled, DUI charges, loss of friendships, missed opportunities), and loss of control (strong cravings, social alienation, blackouts, and other embarrassing behavior (Johnson, 2003). Client awareness of negative consequences can precipitate increased readiness for change (Shealy, Murphy, Borsari, & Correia, 2007).

EXPECTANCY Along with the consequences and positive aspects of actual addiction, a key area to explore is a client's expectations or beliefs about the outcome of use (Grotmol et al., 2010). What are some of the perceived benefits of gambling, alcohol use, or "recreational" popping of prescription drugs? Expectations related to the perceived outcomes of using and/or quitting a substance or addictive process may be part of a contextual assessment. For example, the Alcohol Expectancy Questionnaire (AEQ) examines how a client might expect to gain certain effects as a result of alcohol consumption: sexual enhancement, positive global changes in experience, social and physical pleasure, ability to be assertive, arousal/interpersonal power, and relaxation/tension reduction (Brown, Christiansen, & Goldman, 1987). Another example of an expectancy questionnaire is the Alcohol and Drug Consequences Questionnaire (ADCQ), which has two subscales related to the costs and benefits of quitting (Cunningham et al., 1997).

TREATMENT-SPECIFIC ASSESSMENT INFORMATION
Readiness for Change

Motivation has been a focal point of much research in the field of substance addiction, due to the contributions of Miller and Rollnick (2002). One factor related to motivation is readiness for change, defined as a willingness to engage with the recovery process to alter one's life (Prochaska, DiClemente, & Norcross, 1992). The Readiness to Change Questionnaire (RTCQ) is one standardized assessment tool that can be used to better understand where a client might be at in the first three stages of change (Rollnick, Heather, Gold, & Hall, 1992). De Leon (1995) notes that those who are ready to change may often want to take measures that do not include treatment; in order to distinguish the difference, the term *readiness for treatment* was integrated into clinical vocabulary. One instrument that assesses level of motivation to change is the Stages of Change Readiness and Treatment Eagerness Scales (SOCRATES) (Miller & Tonigan, 1996). Readiness for change constructs are used to help a counselor understand where a client is in the recovery process and how one might intervene at that stage. Sharing the assessment results with clients may be beneficial for those looking for tangible and/or quantitative data for goal setting. Counselors may also teach clients about the stages of change to help validate their current process and show them the stages that are available to them if they decide to give treatment a chance. Instruments and other assessment techniques serve to support counselor clinical decisions and treatment planning; they are also a helpful educational tool to use with appropriate clinical populations.

Motivation and readiness to change assessments are useful for measuring the clients' current stage of change. The clients' current stage of change can indicate the type and level of treatment and approaches most appropriate for the counselor to implement. Stage of change in adult populations can also be measured using the University of Rhode Island Change Assessment Scale (URICA). The URICA is designed as a continuous measure producing individual participant stage of change scores in precontemplation, contemplation, action, and maintenance stages; assesses attitudes toward changing problem behaviors; and indicates select treatment strategies pre and post treatment (Dozois, Westra, Collins, Fung, & Garry, 2004). The URICA has demonstrated reliability and validity in an alcoholic/addict treatment population; researchers have only begun to examine responses to this measure in other disorders (Dozois et al., 2004). According to DiClemente and Hughes (1990), URICA assessment scores measure process and outcome variables for a variety of health and addictive behaviors in adults. Assessing client URICA pre- and posttreatment scores may help counselors select the most appropriate level of care and specific treatment strategies.

Stage of Change Theory

Behavioral scientists recognized long ago that behavior was too complex to systematically and consistently respond to just one formal school of intervention (Samuelson, 1998). DiClemente (1991) and other behavioral scientists observed that the vast majority of successful self-changers unconsciously follow an unwavering sequence of activities and attitudes prior to finally extinguishing a particular negative lifestyle. These sequences of activities (stages) are formulated as the transtheoretical approach or the Stage of Change Theory; this theory has an influential perspective for understanding the process of self-change from addiction disorders (Connors, Donovan, & DiClemente, 2001).

Prochaska (1992) hypothesizes that changes occur when a person adopting a new behavior progresses through specific stages of change marked by distinct cognitive processes and behavioral indicators. This model acknowledges the importance of a developmental perspective of change rather than a theoretical approach that exclusively focuses on personality characteristics or behaviors as predictors of change. This serves to allow the "natural" dynamic tendencies regarding individual self-change to arise (Petrocelli, 2002). The Transtheoretical Model has been applied to addictions counseling and other health psychology research for decades.

Prochaska and DiClemente (1984) detail the stages of new behavior that people move through when making any life change through these four stages:

1. Pre-contemplation: The individual is not thinking about making a change. This stage is characterized by a lack of recognition of the problem.
2. Contemplation: The individual intends to make a change, but not in the immediate future. This stage is characterized by uncertainty.
3. Action: The individual actively attempts the change. The individual experiments with alternative behaviors.
4. Maintenance: The individual continues the changed behavior but it requires active or conscious effort to be sustained. A long-term reinforcement of the new healthier behaviors is needed to stabilize the change in behavior.

These stages were once considered linear; now, however, each stage is viewed as part of a cyclical process that varies for each individual (Prochaska, 1994). Prochaska et al. (1992) conceptualize the process of change according to a spiral rather than a linear model, with relapse, regression to earlier stages, and recycling through the stages as change progresses.

A similar pattern of stage development can be found in Jellinek's curve (1952), which details the progressive decline into the disease of addiction and the progressive stages into recuperative aspects of recovery (see Figure 5.3, Jellinek's curve). In addiction counseling, client needs and treatment goals will develop and vary individually as they progress living life in recovery. Markers of recovery and healing can be shown by length of sobriety, meaningful engagement in treatment and/or counseling, consistent 12-step meeting attendance and/or other recovery community peer support, and consistently integrating learned coping skills into daily living practices. As readiness, action, and acceptance stages are reached and maintained with stability, clients may then be ready for deeper work that would not have been appropriate for early treatment/recovery goals.

Prior Treatment Related to Addiction

During an interview, counselors should find out if a client has experienced counseling and addictions treatment in the past. Basic information should be gathered: dates and location of treatment, modality of treatment, length of time in treatment, reasons for exiting and effect of treatment on use, and length of time alcohol- and drug-free posttreatment. If there have been previous treatment efforts, a release of information from the client may be requested, in order to help corroborate current findings.

Counselors should also be sensitive to the feelings clients have about past therapeutic relationships. Because the therapeutic alliance rests on rapport, a counselor may have to address treatment resistance if negative associations and beliefs exist about the addiction treatment process.

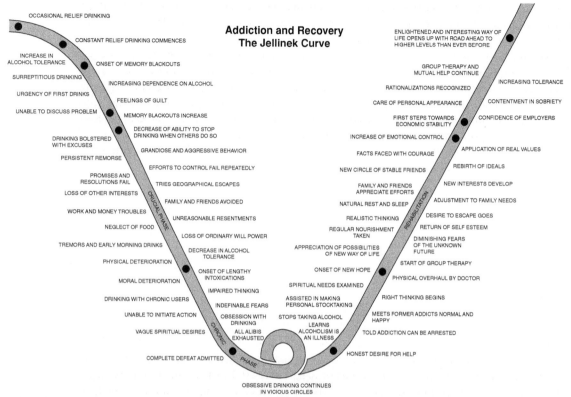

FIGURE 5.3 Jellinek's Curve

Asking about prior counseling or treatment during the assessment may unveil important information about the client's fears and hopes and what has worked for him or her in the past. Client treatment expectancy is a contributing factor in therapeutic outcomes (see Asay & Lambert, 1999). Encouraging a client in this way not only cultivates rapport, and but is fertile ground to discuss growth resulting from the interpersonal process of counseling.

Other Background Information

Understanding a client's lived experience helps to determine how distressed and impaired he or she actually is, and what treatment modalities and strengths are available. In one study of clients seeking treatment, social stability was a factor in continued abstinence after an intensive outpatient program (Bottlender & Soyka, 2005). This chapter mentions several key psychosocial components related to the recovery environment; however, there are many others that influence addiction, including the realm of psychosocial disorders.

Family Systems and Peer Relationships

According to Agrawal and Lynskey (2008), in addition to the highly genetic or heritable influences of addiction disorders, families and close peers also influence the history, use, treatment, and recovery of clients (Tobler et al., 2000; Williams, 1987). They are often a significant factor in the recovery environment and overall success in achieving sobriety. Information can be taken about the lifestyle and addictive behaviors of family members and significant others, including spouses, cohabitating partners, housemates, and close peers. A counselor may directly interview a spouse, certain family members, and/or peers to gain collateral information (Miller, 1999). Adverse childhood events (ACEs) (e.g., childhood abuse, domestic violence, household dysfunction) are risk factors for addiction (Douglas et al., 2010). Dube et al. (2003) studied a cohort of 8,613 participants and found that individuals with five or more ACEs reported greater levels of illicit drug use and addiction by 7–10 times. Inquiring in depth about client relationships may also shed light on how addiction is impacted by family roles, rituals, values, expectations, parenting styles, family grief and loss, power structures, pain and emotion management, boundaries, and communication in these relationships and relational systems. See Chapter 14 on interventions with families and couples for a more in-depth look at this topic.

Peer influence and social networks can increase risk or provide protection for a client working on living a life in recovery (Costenbader, Astone, & Latkin, 2006; Marlatt & Witkiewitz, 2009). Intimate and group relationships are often responsible for the initiation process into substance use (Draus & Carlson, 2006). Peers who use and offer drugs and engage in addictive behaviors place a person at higher risk for similar behavior. Likewise, peers that have attitudes and beliefs in opposition to substance use and addictive behaviors can be a protective factor (Chang et al., 2006). These same peer groups and intimate relationships can aid or hinder the treatment and recovery process.

HIGH-RISK BEHAVIOR High-risk behavior is often seen in conjunction with addictive behaviors (Calsyn et al., 2010; Sexton, Carlson, Leukefeld, & Booth, 2006). High-risk behaviors may include theft to procure drugs. High-risk sex may also be a factor, whether it is unprotected sex when intoxicated with a current or new partner, participating in sexual behavior not otherwise chosen when sober, or prostitution for drugs or drug money (Gilchrist, Cameron, & Scoular, 2005). IV drug use has serious associated health risks (e.g., HIV, Hepatitis B and C). Assessment explores whether IV drug use is done with clean needles, driving occurs during intoxication or sexual activity, and abuse happens as a result of intoxication or during blackouts. The assessment ascertains whether there are patterns of high-risk behavior that should be addressed by some form of harm reduction intervention.

COPING SKILLS Assessing life skills, such as coping skills, assertive communication, social skills, problem solving, and self-efficacy, may also be part of a comprehensive assessment (Bowen et al., 2009; Tobler et al., 2000). Assessing a person's ability to cope with life stressors may be useful in determining the level of care recommended as related to relapse and relapse prevention (Anderson, Ramo, & Brown, 2006). Coping strategies help those in recovery deal with the internal and external triggers and consequences described earlier in this chapter (Cleveland & Harris, 2010). Coping strategies may include behavioral and cognitive strategies directed toward problem solving to eliminate or modify problem conditions. For example, "I plan my day so that I head directly to my AA and GA meetings after work, instead of hanging out longer where I have been tempted to drink and play video poker in the past." Coping strategies that are cognitive in nature may help to perceptually control problematic experiences. Successful coping may be found in the ways that individuals frame their experience: "I experienced a lapse, but this can be part of the recovery process, and not the end of the world." The important factor is educating clients on the essential component of talking to counselors in treatment and/or peers and sponsors in recovery regularly—ideally before a lapse occurs. Other strategies may be useful in helping a person eliminate, reduce, or manage emotional consequences by, for example, reducing, avoiding, or suppressing emotional stimuli (Pearlin & Schooler, 1978).

WORK AND VOCATION A client's career and life planning and the realities of "making a living" are important in the recovery process (Graham, 2006). Employment affects treatment outcomes and may be challenged by the treatment process. Vocation is relevant to every part of treatment (SAMHSA, 1996). For example, the treatment choices available to a full-time employee who is the main income provider for a family of four can be a complicated decision. Will he or she be able to go to intensive inpatient treatment and still provide for the family? What is the cost and/or risk of not getting treatment? For many, if they stay drinking and/or using, they will eventually lose their work and the stability they are clinging on to and using for a reason why they cannot get help. Some clients need help seeing that staying in their current cycle will only serve to bring down their environment faster, not save it through denial or the illusion of being able to control their compulsion on their own someday.

The vocational component of a comprehensive assessment may look at current and past employment status, job satisfaction, employment skills, personal financial assets, employer benefits, employer programs related to addiction, client's feelings in relationship to his current employment position, how levels of treatment care affect employment needs, and employer knowledge. Other vocational information that may be important to an assessment include, but are not limited to, relapse triggers related to career and vocation, the presence of vocational resources within treatment programs, short-term goals and strategies for employment, necessary resources to make employment feasible (i.e., child care, transportation), and client knowledge of local employment and vocational services. For more specific information on the topic of vocation and addictions refer to SAMHSA's (2000) Treatment Intervention Protocol (TIP) 38 entitled *Integrating Substance Abuse Treatment and Vocational Services*.

SPIRITUALITY Considerable research has correlated spirituality to mental and physical health and overall well-being, thus meriting its inclusion into counseling (Bergin, 1988; Reinert & Bloomingdale, 1999). It has been found by millions to be important to recovery. Conner, Anglin, Annon, and Longshore (2009) found that treatment-seeking participants with high or increasing spirituality measurement scores had significantly fewer days of substance use (e.g., heroine, crack cocaine) than those with low or decreasing scores. Although this may be the case, spirituality is a factor that is often difficult to define, frequently misunderstood, and not assessed for by mental health professionals (Larson & Larson, 2003; Tisdell, 2000). Spirituality in addictions treatment may immediately bring to mind AA groups and a 12-step path to recovery. Furthermore, many clients connect their spirituality with a particular religion or traditional belief. Some clients may respond by saying "I don't attend church" when asked about spirituality. Reframing may be necessary to address the idea that spirituality has many manifestations.

There are vast differences between religion and spirituality despite the common mistake of the words being used interchangeably. These differences are important to note especially in the context of recovery from addiction. According to Aissen (2008), religion and spirituality overlap conceptually, but are different in nature. Educating clients and families that religion may include spirituality, but spirituality itself, does NOT include religion," can be exponentially helpful when debunking myths and false requirements needed for success in recovery or to "work" a 12-step recovery program. This is particularly important to share with clients who are resistant to trying 12-step meetings because they deem it a "religious program." Furthermore, many who are agnostic, atheist, Christian, Jewish, Muslim, Buddhist, Mormon, and/or many other beliefs and faiths have and continue to find their path to recovery under a 12-step model of healing. The spiritual healing begins and can stay with the power of connection, not in the semantics of a higher power entity. The AA big book warns of the dangers of "contempt prior to investigation"; to mitigate this, counselors should encourage clients to attend six to eight 12-step meetings before they decide it is not for them. The early AA big book (1939) writings suggest the alcoholic sufferer has "not only been mentally and physically ill, but spiritually sick." Furthermore, the earliest AA tenants suggest those suffering from alcoholism (or any addiction) have "an illness which only a spiritual experience can conquer." Therefore, "if the solution is spiritual in nature, the malady must too have a spiritual component" (Alcoholics Anonymous, 2001, p. 64). It is highly suggested for persons to not have "contempt prior to investigation" about their initial beliefs or views on the utility of living a 12-step way of life. As counselors, I would extrapolate that framework to any and all clients seeking counseling. Part of our work will be helping clients become more open to change and to have trust in the unknown process of counseling and recovery. Questions related to spirituality should consider that many definitions and paths exist; there is no correct path to spirituality.

Is it appropriate to refer or recommend a client to a traditional AA meeting without discussing spirituality? Consider an atheist who does not identify with a "higher power." Spirituality can be an important avenue in the recovery process and can provide additional support in educating clients and their families about the differences between religion and spirituality. The assessment can delve into how a person's religious and spiritual beliefs and practices might aid the client in treatment (even if client is feeling spiritually void at that moment or always has felt that way) (Mackinnon, 2004).

Summary and Some Final Notations

Multistage assessment is an integral part of an addictions treatment and recovery process. Initial and ongoing assessment allows a counselor to build rapport and gather vital information about a client's lived experience and relationship to addiction and substance use disorder. There are many factors that contribute to a client's ability to make positive change. Due to the complexity of circumstances and unique differences of each individual and the systems within which they exist, assessment is best done in an orderly and relevant manner that allows a client to collaborate with a team of helpers to realize a better quality of life and sense of well-being.

MyCounselingLab

Visit the MyCounselingLab site for *Foundations of Addictions Counseling,* Third Edition to enhance your understanding of concepts. You'll have the opportunity to practice your skills through video- and case-based exercises. You will find sets of questions to help you prepare for your certification exam with *Licensure Quizzes.* There is also a Video Library that provides taped counseling sessions, ethical scenarios, and interviews with helpers and clients.

Useful Websites:

12-STEP PROGRAMS IN THE COMMUNITY

Alcoholics Anonymous (AA)
www.aa.org

Narcotics Anonymous (AA)
www.na.org

Al-anon Family Groups (Al-anon)
www.alanon.org

Gamblers Anonymous (GA)
www.ga.org

Overeaters Anonymous (OA)
www.oa.org

Sex & Love Addicts Anonymous (SLAA)
www.slaafws.org/
Open to anyone who knows or thinks they have a problem with sex addiction, love addiction, romantic obsession, codependent relationships, fantasy addiction and/or sexual, social, and emotional anorexia.

American Society of Addiction Medicine (ASAM)
www.asam.org/

Association for Assessment in Counseling (AAC)
Standards for multicultural assessment link
aac.ncat.edu/resources.html

NIAAA—Information on Alcohol Measures
(i.e., Timeline Followback [TFLB], Form 90, Quantity-Frequency [QF] measures)
pubs.niaaa.nih.gov/publications/AssessingAlcohol/factsheets.htm

Substance Abuse and Mental Health Services Administration (SAMHSA)
List of free publication series:
store.samhsa.gov/facet/Treatment-Prevention-Recovery

SAMHSA Treatment, Prevention, and Recovery Publications
TIP 31 Teen Assessment, TIP 42 Co-occurring Disorders
store.samhsa.gov/product/TIP-31-Screening-and-Assessing-Adolescents-for-Substance-Use-Disorders/SMA12-4079

University of Washington
Substance Use Screening & Assessment Instruments Database
lib.adai.washington.edu/instruments/glossary.htm

References

Agrawal, A., & Lynskey, M. (2008). Are there genetic influences on addiction? Evidence from family, adoption and twin studies. *Addiction*, *103*(7), 1069–1081. doi:10.1111/j.1360-0443.2008.02213.x

Aissen, K. (2008). *Personal factors influencing impaired professionals recovery from addiction*. Unpublished doctoral dissertation. University of Florida, Gainesville, FL.

Alcoholics Anonymous. (1939). *Alcoholics Anonymous*. New York, NY: Alcoholics Anonymous World Services.

Alcoholics Anonymous (2001). *Alcoholics Anonymous* (4th ed.). New York, NY: A.A. World Services.

Allen, J. P., & Mattson, M. E. (1993). Psychometric instruments to assist in alcoholism treatment planning. *Journal of Substance Abuse Treatment*, *10*, 289–296.

American Counseling Association. (2005). *ACA code of ethics*. Alexandria, VA: Author.

American Psychiatric Association. (2000). *DSM-IV-TR: Diagnostic and statistical manual of mental disorders* (text rev.). Washington, DC: Author.

American Psychiatric Association. (2013). *Diagnostic and statistical manual of mental disorders* (5th ed.). Arlington, VA: Author.

American Society of Addiction Medicine. (2014). http://www.asam.org/

Anderson, K. G., Ramo, D. E., & Brown, S. A. (2006). Life stress, coping and comorbid youth: An examination of the stress-vulnerability model for substance relapse. *Journal of Psychoactive Drugs*, *38*(3), 255–262.

Arredondo, P., Toporek, R., Brown, S. P., Jones, J., Locke, D. C., Sanchez, J., & Stadler, H. (1996). Operationalization of the multicultural counseling competencies. *Journal of Multicultural Counseling and Development*, *24*, 42–78.

Asay, T. P., & Lambert, M. J. (1999). The empirical case for the common factors in therapy: Quantitative findings. In M. A. Hubble, B. L. Duncan, & S. D. Miller (eds.), *The heart and soul of change: What works in therapy* (pp. 33–56). Washington, DC: American Psychological Association.

Association for Assessment in Counseling. (2003). *Standards for multicultural assessment*. Alexandria, VA: American Counseling Association.

Babits, M. (2001). The phoenix juncture: Exploring the dimensions of hope in psychotherapy. *Clinical Social Work Journal*, *29*(4), 341–350.

Berger, P. L., & Luckman, T. (1967). *The social construction of reality*. New York, NY: Doubleday-Anchor.

Bergin, A. E. (1988). Three contributions of a spiritual perspective to counseling, psychotherapy, and behavior change. *Counseling and Values*, *33*, 21–31.

Bergin, L., & Walsh, S. (2005). The role of hope in psychotherapy with older adults. *Aging and Mental Health*, *9*(1), 7–15.

Bottlender, M., & Soyka, M. (2005). Efficacy of an intensive outpatient rehabilitation program in alcoholism: Predictors of outcome 6 months after treatment. *European Addiction Research*, *11*(3), 132–137.

Bowen, S., Chawla, N., Collins, S., Witkiewitz, K., Hsu, S., Grow, J., . . . , Harrop, E. (2009). Mindfulness-based relapse prevention for substance use disorders: A pilot efficacy trial. *Substance Abuse: Official Publication of the Association for Medical Education and Research in Substance Abuse, 30*(4), 295–305.

Brown, S. A., Christiansen, B. A., & Goldman, M. S. (1987). The alcohol expectancy questionnaire: An instrument for the assessment of adolescent and adult alcohol expectancies. *Journal of Studies on Alcohol, 48,* 483–491.

Buckley-Walker, K., Crowe, T., & Caputi, P. (2010). Exploring identity within the recovery process of people with serious mental illnesses. *Psychiatric Rehabilitation Journal, 33*(3), 219–227.

Calsyn, D., Cousins, S., Hatch-Maillette, M., Forcehimes, A., Mandler, R., Doyle, S., & Woody, G. (2010). Sex under the influence of drugs or alcohol: Common for men in substance abuse treatment and associated with high-risk sexual behavior. *American Journal on Addictions, 19*(2), 119–127.

Chang, F. C., Lee, C. M., Lai, H. R., Chiang, J. T., Lee, P. H., & Chen, W. J. (2006). Social influences and self-efficacy as predictors of youth smoking initiation and cessation: A 3-year longitudinal study of vocational high school students in Taiwan. *Addiction, 101*(11), 1645–1655.

Chassler, D., Lundgren, L., & Lonsdale, J. (2006). What factors are associated with high-frequency drug treatment use among a racially and ethnically diverse population of injection drug users? *American Journal on Addictions, 15*(6), 440–449.

Cheon, J. (2008). Best practices in community-based prevention for youth substance reduction: Towards strengths-based positive development policy. *Journal of Community Psychology, 36*(6), 761–779.

Cleveland, H., & Harris, K. (2010). The role of coping in moderating within-day associations between negative triggers and substance use cravings: A daily diary investigation. *Addictive Behaviors, 35*(1), 60–63.

Conner, B., Anglin, M., Annon, J., & Longshore, D. (2009). Effect of religiosity and spirituality on drug treatment outcomes. *Journal of Behavioral Health Services & Research, 36*(2), 189–198.

Connors, G. J., Donovan, D. M., & DiClemente, C. C. (2001). *Substance abuse and the stages of change. Selecting and planning interventions.* New York, NY: Guilford Press.

Costenbader, E. C., Astone, N. M., & Latkin, C. A. (2006). The dynamics of injection drug users' personal networks and HIV risk behaviors. *Addiction, 101*(7), 1003–1013.

Cunningham, J. A., Sobell, L. C., Gavin, D. R., Sobell, M. B., & Breslin, F. C. (1997). Assessing motivation for change: Preliminary development and evaluation of a scale measuring the costs and benefits of changing alcohol or drug use. *Psychology of Addictive Behaviors, 11*(2), 107–114.

Cunningham, M. S. (1994). Forward. In J. U. Gordon (Ed.), *Managing multiculturalism in substance abuse services* (p. vii–ix). Thousand Oaks, CA: Sage Publications.

De Leon, G. (1995). Therapeutic communities for addictions: A theoretical framework. *International Journal of Addictions, 30*(12), 51–63.

DiClemente, C. C. (1991). Motivational interviewing and the stages of change. In W. R. Miller & S. Rollnick (Eds.), *Motivational interviewing: Preparing people to change addictive behavior* (pp. 191–202). New York, NY: Guilford Press.

DiClemente, C., & Hughes, S. (1990). Stages of change profiles in outpatient alcoholism treatment. *Journal of Substance Abuse, 2,* 217–235.

Dimeff, L. A., Baer, J. S., Kivlahan, D. R., & Marlatt, G. A. (2000). Brief alcohol screening and intervention for college students (BASICS). *Substance Abuse, 21*(4), 283–285.

Donovan, D. M., & Marlatt, G. A. (Eds.). (2005). *Relapse prevention: Maintenance strategies in the treatment of addictive behaviors* (2nd ed.). New York, NY: Guilford Press.

Douglas, K. R., Chan, G., Gelernter, J., Arias, A. J., Anton, R. F., Weiss, R. D., . . . , Kranzler, H. R. (2010). Adverse childhood events as risk factors for substance dependence: Partial mediation by mood and anxiety disorders. *Addictive Behaviors, 35*(1), 7–13.

Dozois, D. J. A., Westra, H. A., Collins, K. A., Fung, T. S., & Garry, J. K. F. (2004). Stages of change in anxiety: Psychometric properties of the University of Rhode Island Change Assessment (URICA) Scale. *Behaviour Research and Therapy, 42,* 711–729.

Draus, P. J., & Carlson, R. G. (2006). Needles in the haystacks: The social context of initiation to heroin injection in rural Ohio. *Substance Use & Misuse, 41*(8), 1111–1124.

Dube, S. R., Felitti, V. J., Dong, M., Chapman, D. P., Giles, W. H., & Anda, R. F. (2003). Childhood abuse, neglect, and household dysfunction and the risk of illicit drug use: The adverse childhood experiences study. *Pediatrics, 111*(3), 564–572.

Dufault, K., & Martocchio, B. C. (1985). Hope: Its spheres and dimensions. *Nursing Clinics of North America, 20*(2), 379–391.

Finn, S. E., & Tonsager, M. E. (1997). Information-gathering and therapeutic models of assessment: Complementary paradigms. *Psychological Assessment, 9,* 374–385.

Freimuth, M. (2005). *Hidden addictions: Assessment practices for psychotherapists, counselors, and health care providers.* New York, NY: Jason Aronson.

Goffman, E. (1961). *Asylums: Essays on the social situation of mental patients and other inmates.* New York, NY: Anchor.

Goldfarb, L., Galanter, M., McDowell, D., Lifshutz, H., & Dermatis, H. (1996). Medical student and patient attitudes toward religions and spirituality in the recovery process. *American Journal of Drug and Alcohol Abuse, 22,* 549–561.

Graham, K., Timney, C. B., Bois, C., & Wedgerfield, K. (1995). Continuity of care in addictions treatment: The role of advocacy and coordination in case management. *American Journal of Drug & Alcohol Abuse, 21*(4), 433–451.

Graham, M. D. (2006). Addiction, the addict, and career: Considerations for the employment counselor. *Journal of Employment Counseling, 43*(4), 168–178.

Grotmol, K., Vaglum, P., Ekeberg, Ø., Gude, T., Aasland, O., & Tyssen, R. (2010). Alcohol expectancy and hazardous drinking: A 6-year longitudinal and nationwide study of medical doctors. *European Addiction Research, 16*(1), 17–22.

Inaba, D. S., & Cohen, W. E. (2007). *Uppers, downers, all arounders: Physical and mental effects of psychoactive drugs* (6th ed.). Ashland, OR: CNS Publications, Inc.

Jackson, K. M., Sher, K. J., Cooper, M. L., & Wood, P. K. (2002). Adolescent alcohol and tobacco use: Onset, persistence and trajectories of use across two samples. *Addiction, 97*(5), 517–533.

Janis, I. L., & Mann, L. (1977). *Decision making: A psychological analysis of conflict, choice, and commitment.* New York, NY: Free Press.

Jellinek, E. M. (1952). Phase of alcohol addiction. *Quarterly Journal of Studies on Alcohol, 13,* 673–684.

Johnson, S. L. (2003). *Therapist's guide to substance abuse and intervention.* San Diego, CA: Academic Press.

Johnson, T. P., & Mott, J. A. (2001). The reliability of self-reported age of onset of tobacco, alcohol and illicit drug use. *Addiction, 96*(8), 1187–1198.

Kaminer, Y. (2008). The teen addiction severity index around the globe: The Tower of Babel revisited. *Substance Abuse, 29*(3), 89–94.

Lappalainen, K., Savolainen, H., Kuorelahti, M., & Epstein, M. (2009). An international assessment of the emotional and behavioral strengths of youth. *Journal of Child & Family Studies, 18*(6), 746–753.

Larson, D. B., & Larson, S. S. (2003). Spirituality's potential relevance to physical and emotional health: A brief review of quantitative research. *Journal of Psychology & Theology, 31*(1), 37–52.

Lewis, J., Lewis, M. D., Daniels, J. A., & D'Andrea, M. A. (2003). *Community counseling: Empowerment strategies for a diverse society.* Pacific Grove, CA: Brooks/Cole.

Lundqvist, T. (2005). Cognitive consequences of cannabis use: Comparison with abuse of stimulants and heroin with regard to attention, memory and executive functions. *Pharmacology, Biochemistry & Behavior, 81*(2), 319–330.

Mackinnon, S. V. (2004). Spirituality: Its role in substance abuse, treatment and recovery. *DATA: The Brown University Digest of Addiction Theory & Application, 23*(7).

Marlatt, A., & Witkiewitz, K. (2009). Further exploring the interpersonal dynamics of relapse [Commentary]. *Addiction, 104*(8), 1291–1292.

McIntyre, J. R. (2004). Family treatment of substance abuse. In S. L. A. Straussner (Ed.), *Clinical work with substance-abusing clients* (2nd ed., pp. 237–263). New York, NY: Guilford Press.

Mee-Lee, D. (2005). ASAM's placement criteria: What's new? *Behavioral Health Management, 25*(3), 32–34.

Mee-Lee, D. (2013). *What's in it for me? The new ASAM criteria and how DSM-5 fits.* Carson City, NV: The Change Companies.

Mee-Lee, D. (2014, March). What's new in DSM-5 and the new ASAM criteria? Implications in an era of healthcare reform. *The Addiction Technology Transfer Center Network Messenger.* Retrieved from http://www.attc-network.org/find/news/attcnews/epubs/addmsg/ATTCmessengerMarch2014articleDSM5_ASAM.pdf

Mee-Lee, D., Shulman, G. D., Fishman M., Gastfriend D. R., & Griffith J. H. (Eds.). (2001). *ASAM patient placement criteria for the treatment of substance-related disorders, second edition—revised (ASAM PPC-2R).* Chevy Chase, MD: American Society of Addiction Medicine, Inc.

Miller, G. A. (1999). *Learning the language of addiction counseling.* Boston, MA: Allyn & Bacon.

Miller, W. R., & Rollnick, S. (2002). *Motivational interviewing: Preparing people for change* (2nd ed.). New York, NY: Guilford Press.

Miller, W. R., & Tonigan, J. S. (1996). Assessing drinkers' motivation for change: The stages of change readiness and treatment eagerness scales (SOCRATES). *Psychology of Addictive Behaviors, 10,* 81–89.

Moltu, C., Binder, P., & Nielsen, G. (2010). Commitment under pressure: Experienced therapists' inner work during difficult therapeutic impasses. *Psychotherapy Research, 20*(3), 309–320.

Moyer, M. (2012, February). Deadly duo: Mixing alcohol and prescription drugs can result in addiction or accidental death. *Scientific American*. Retrieved from http://www.scientificamerican.com/article/mixing-alcohol-prescription-drugs-result-addiction-accidental-death/

National Association of Alcohol and Drug Abuse Counselors. (2008). *NAADAC code of ethics*. Retrieved May 1, 2010, from www.naadac.org/resources/codeofethics

Newcomb, M. (1997). Psychosocial predictors and consequences of drug use: A developmental perspective within a prospective study. *Journal of Addictive Diseases, 16*, 51–89.

Pearlin, L., & Schooler, C. (1978). The structure of coping: Erratum. *Journal of Health & Social Behavior, 19*(2), 237.

Petrocelli, J. V. (2002, Winter). Processes stage of change: Counseling with the transtheoretical model of change. *Journal of Counseling and Development, 80*, 22–30.

Prochaska, J. O. (1992). Criticisms and concerns of the Transtheoretical Model in light of recent research. *British Journal of Addiction, 87*(6), 825–828.

Prochaska, J. O. (1994). *Changing for good: A revolutionary six-stage program for overcoming bad habits and moving your life positively forward*. New York, NY: Avon Books.

Prochaska, J. O., & DiClemente, C. C. (1984). Self-change processes, self-efficacy, and decisional balance across five stages of smoking cessation. In *Advances in Cancer Control*. New York, NY: Alan R. Liss, Inc.

Prochaska, J. O., DiClemente, C. C., & Norcross, J. C. (1992). In search of how people change: Applications to addictive behavior. *American Psychologist, 47*, 1102–1114.

Reinert, D. F., & Bloomingdale, J. R. (1999). Spiritual maturity and mental health: Implications for counselors. *Counseling & Values, 43*(3), 211–224.

Remley, T. P., & Herlihy, B. (2010). *Ethical, legal, and professional issues in counseling* (3rd ed.). Upper Saddle River, NJ: Pearson.

Robins, L. N., Wing, J., Wittchen, H. U., Helzer, J. E., Babor, T. F., Burke, J., . . . , Towle, L. H. (1989). The Composite International Diagnostic Interview: An epidemiologic instrument suitable for use in conjunction with different diagnostic systems and in different cultures. *Archives of General Psychiatry, 45*, 1069–1077.

Rollnick, S., Heather, N., Gold, R., & Hall, W. (1992). Development of the short "Readiness to Change" questionnaire for use in brief opportunistic interventions. *British Journal of Addictions, 87*, 743–754.

Roy, M., Dum, M., Sobell, L., Sobell, M., Simco, E., Manor, H., et al. (2008). Comparison of the Quick Drinking Screen and the Alcohol Timeline Followback with outpatient alcohol abusers. *Substance Use & Misuse, 43*(14), 2116–2123.

Saitz, R., Horton, N., Larson, M., Winter, M., & Samet, J. (2005). Primary medical care and reductions in addiction severity: A prospective cohort study. *Addiction, 100*(1), 70–78.

Samuelson, M. (1998). Stages of change: From theory to practice. *The National Center for Health Promotion, 2*(5), 1–8.

Sattler, J. M. (1998). *Clinical and forensic interviewing of children and families: Guidelines for the mental health, education, pediatric and child maltreatment fields*. San Diego, CA: Author.

Saunders, J. (2006). Substance dependence and non-dependence in the Diagnostic and Statistical Manual of Mental Disorders (DSM) and the International Classification of Diseases (ICD): Can an identical conceptualization be achieved? *Addiction, 101*, 48–58.

Sexton, R. L., Carlson, R. G., Leukefeld, C. G., & Booth, B. M. (2006). Methamphetamine use and adverse consequences in the rural southern United States: An ethnographic overview. *Journal of Psychoactive Drugs, 3*(38), 393–404.

Shabad, P. (2001). *Despair and the return of hope: Echoes of morning in psychotherapy*. Northvale, NJ: Jason Aronson, Inc.

Shealy, A. E., Murphy, J. G., Borsari, B., & Correia, C. J. (2007). Predictors of motivation to change alcohol use among referred college students. *Addictive Behaviors, 32*(10), 2358–2364.

Sobell, L. C., & Sobell, M. B. (1992). Timeline followback: A technique for assessing self-reported alcohol consumption. In R. Z. Litten & J. Allen (Eds.), *Measuring alcohol consumption: Psychosocial and biological methods* (pp. 41–72). New York, NY: Humana Press.

Stippekohl, B., Winkler, M., Mucha, R., Pauli, P., Walter, B., Vaitl, D., et al. (2010). Neural responses to BEGIN- and END-stimuli of the smoking ritual in nonsmokers, nondeprived smokers, and deprived smokers. *Neuropsychopharmacology: Official Publication of the American College of Neuropsychopharmacology, 35*(5), 1209–1225.

Straussner, S. L. A. (2001). *Ethnocultural factors in substance abuse treatment*. New York, NY: Guilford Press.

Strupp, H. H. (1993). Psychotherapy research: Evolution and current trends. In T. K. Fagan & G. R. VandenBos (Eds.), *Exploring applied psychology: Origins and critical analyses*. Washington, DC: American Psychological Association.

Substance and Mental Health Services Administration. (1996). *Substance abuse, disability and vocational rehabilitation*. Rockville. MD: Author.

Substance and Mental Health Services Administration. (1998a). Addiction counseling competencies: The knowledge, skills and attitudes of professional practice. *CSAT Treatment Improvement Protocol (TIP) 21*. Rockville: MD. Author.

Substance and Mental Health Services Administration. (1998b). Screening and assessing adolescents for substance use disorders. *CSAT Treatment Improvement Protocol (TIP) 31*. Rockville: MD. Author.

Substance and Mental Health Services Administration. (2000). Integrating substance abuse treatment and vocational services. *CSAT Treatment Intervention Protocol (TIP) 38*. Rockville: MD. Author.

Substance and Mental Health Services Administration. (2008). Integrated dual disorders treatment workbook. *CSAT Evidenced-based Practices*. Rockville: MD. Author.

Tarter, R. E. (1990). Evaluation and treatment of adolescent substance abuse: A decision tree model. *American Journal of Drug and Alcohol Abuse, 16*(12), 1–46.

Tims, F. M., Leukefeld, C. G., & Platt, J. J. (2001). *Relapse and recovery in addictions*. London, UK: Yale University Press.

Tisdell, E. J. (2000). Spirituality and emancipatory adult education in women adult educators for social change. *Adult Education Quarterly, 50*(4), 308–335.

Tobler, N. S., Roona, M. R., Ochshorn, P., Marshall, D. G., Streke, A. V., & Stackpole, K. M. (2000). School-based adolescent drug prevention programs: 1998 meta-analysis. *The Journal of Primary Prevention, 20*, 275–336.

Wild, T. C. (2006). Social control and coercion in addiction treatment: Towards evidence-based policy and practice. *Addiction, 101*(1), 40–49.

Wild, T. C., Cunningham, J. A., & Ryan, R. M. (2006). Social pressure, coercion, and client engagement at treatment entry: A self-determination theory perspective. *Addictive Behaviors, 31*(10), 1858–1872.

Williams, C. (1987). Child care practices in alcoholic families: Findings from a neighborhood detoxification program. *Alcohol Health and Research World, 94*, 74–77.

Chapter 6

Assessment and Diagnosis of Addictions

John M. Laux
The University of Toledo
Dilani M. Perera-Diltz
Lamar University
Stephanie A. Calmes
COMPASS Corporation for Recovery Services

Malvika Behl
The University of Toledo
Jennifer Vasquez
Cleveland State University

According to the Substance Abuse and Mental Health Services Administration (SAMHSA, 2012), approximately 7.98 million American adults meet criteria for both serious mental health and substance abuse or dependence disorders (SAMHSA, 2012). Due to the high comorbidity between substance use disorders and other serious mental health disorders, counselors, regardless of their areas of specialty, can expect to provide services to clients who have substance use disorders. For this reason, counselors should know the signs and symptoms of substance use disorders and the ways they are detected and diagnosed (Laux, Newman, & Brown, 2004). Lack of this information places counselors at risk to misdiagnose their clients' presenting problems, resulting in ill-conceived treatment plan for clients (Horrigan, Piazza, & Weinstein, 1996).

This chapter introduces the reader to many of the available screens and assessments for substance use disorders and provides the information needed to evaluate each instrument as well as the *Diagnostic and Statistical Manual* (DSM-5) (American Psychiatric Association [APA], 2013) criteria used to reach a substance-use-related diagnosis.

In this chapter, we have incorporated three case studies. The first case is about Pedro, a hypothetical person whose life circumstances could easily place him before a counselor whose task would be to help him assess the role substances play in his life. The second case is of Sara, an adult female with multiple drug use. Finally, at the end of the chapter we present to you Olivia, a teenager with an alcohol and other drug use history. We open with a review of Pedro's background and conclude the chapter with a discussion of Pedro's assessment.

Pedro is a 24-year-old single Mexican-American male and the oldest son of his first-generation American migrant farming parents. He has three younger brothers who all looked up to him while growing up. The family was proud of Pedro the day he enlisted in the U.S. Army. He had several combat engagements while in Iraq, but was spared injury until the day the Humvee he was riding in ran over a roadside improvised explosive device. The vehicle's extra armor plating protected Pedro from the flying shrapnel; however, the explosion's shock waves caused him to suffer from symptoms consistent with a closed head injury, a type of traumatic brain injury. Also, the force of the explosion ruptured his ear drums, permanently impairing his hearing. Pedro was honorably discharged following a medical examination and returned to northwest Ohio. He felt disconnected from the person he was before he left for military duty. He had difficulty falling asleep almost every night, and found himself frequently thinking about what he had seen and experienced while in combat. He felt alone and isolated from his family, who had returned to Texas for the winter. To support himself, he accepted an offer to work as a manager at a local grocery store. He quickly found it difficult to motivate himself to go to work each day. His employer, a Vietnam-era veteran, felt obliged to continue Pedro's employment out of loyalty to a fellow soldier, but made no effort to hide the fact that Pedro's work was inadequate. He liked to complain to his subordinates about catching Pedro staring off into space and how he often arrived late and left early.

As time wore on, Pedro found himself spending more time at the Veterans of Foreign Wars (VFW) post in the next town over. Initially, he would drive to the VFW after work in anticipation of the kinship he felt alongside others who had been in the service. After a while though, he noticed that his mind was focused more on the beer he drank than on those with whom he drank it. On more than one occasion, he found himself drinking until closing time. Over the course of the last month, Pedro has taken to sneaking a few bottles of beer in the storeroom before getting off work. He rationalized this behavior because he felt that he was underpaid for his services and drinking helped him to both "take the edge off" and make the drive to the VFW a little easier to tolerate. Last week, Pedro crashed his car into a parked vehicle and landed in a ditch on the drive home from the VFW at 2:00 in the morning. He was found, passed out at the wheel, by a sheriff's deputy and transported to the local hospital. Although his car was totaled, he escaped the accident uninjured. He was cited for Driving Under the Influence and for destruction of property.

Pedro retained an attorney, who advised him that it might look good in the judge's eyes if he voluntarily subjected himself to a drug and alcohol assessment at the Veterans Affairs (VA) hospital in the state capital. Pedro seriously doubted that he had an alcohol problem but, upon his attorney's advice, he called his VA hospital and set up an appointment for an assessment. He followed through with his scheduled appointment and met with a chemical dependency counselor.

Our second case example is Sara, a 36-year-old female with a history of multiple drug use. Sara reports that she first used prescription opiates at age 14 after breaking her collarbone. She states she took the medication as prescribed. She tried opiates again at age 19, when she began buying Percocet 10's off the street, and was using 2–3 pills daily. Sara reports that this pattern continued "off and on" until age 35. She denies that her use ever increased from age 19 to 35, "because I couldn't afford it." At the age of 35, Sara indicates that she began using heroin because "it was around," and started snorting "10 cc's" daily to achieve her desired effects. Within 1 month, this client was using "40 cc's" per day to achieve her desired effects, and approximately 1 year ago, Sara began injecting the drug for a more intense/faster high, which she admits took up a great deal of her time. This pattern of daily use continued until 3 months ago, when Sara was put on Suboxone at a treatment center. Client reports that she stayed sober for 1 month, but could not afford the cost of the Suboxone treatment and eventually relapsed. When she tried to stop using opiates, Sara reports that she experienced the following symptoms: muscle aches, nausea, and insomnia. Her last use of heroin was "20 cc's" injected 3 days ago.

Sara contacted a drug treatment center in her area seeking an assessment because she reports she is tired of "being sick" and always needing to use the drug in order to function. She was also convicted of drug possession last year and estimates that if she does not stop using heroin, she will be sent to jail for violating the terms of her probation. Sara is ambivalent about actually entering a treatment program, but she kept her assessment appointment and was evaluated by a counselor.

Olivia, a 17-year-old white Mennonite female, has been drinking alcohol since age 16. She drinks 4–5 beers a day plus anything else she can get her hands on. She recently began experimenting with a variety of unknown drugs. Olivia reports no consequences related to her alcohol or drug use; however, while intoxicated, she did allow inappropriate photographs of herself to be posted on the web. She says her parents are making "a big deal out of nothing." Olivia's school suspended her because of the photos as well as several alcohol-related incidents of misbehavior. In addition, she has been banned from attending her church. Both decisions please Olivia. She is verbally and physically abusive to her parents, who are deeply ashamed of her and are desperately seeking help. As you read through this chapter, think about what instrument may be appropriate for Olivia's age and reporting behavior. What are some psychometrics of the instrument you chose that may confound the results? What diagnosis does your clinical judgment indicate?

WHY USE STANDARDIZED ASSESSMENTS?

Counselors unfamiliar with assessment may believe that one's clinical judgment is all that is necessary to identify a substance use disorder. The contents of this chapter are not intended to subvert or replace clinical judgment. Rather, the benefits and limitations of standardized assessments are presented so that counselors can make informed decisions as to their implementation as a part of the clinical decision-making process.

The first benefit is that standardized assessments provide data about clients relative to a normative population. That is, the results indicate to the clinician if the client has more, less, or about the same amount of a trait as the average person in the normative population. This information is useful in many ways. Some clients who struggle with changing their substance-using behaviors compare their substance use to that of their friends or family members. Consequently, a client who argues that drinking 12 bottles of beer a day is normal in his family or his neighborhood, or is actually an amount that is less than what he saw his father drink while growing up, may truly not understand that 12 bottles of beer a day is not usual alcohol consumption within his or her demographic group. Normative data may help to broaden the client's perspective on drinking patterns.

A second benefit is that normative data in standardized assessments provide the benefit of objectivity. A client who is not ready or willing to change may claim that a counselor's professional opinion is biased and reject the counselor's diagnosis, stating that the counselor is biased or unduly motivated to recommend people into treatment. A counselor who explains that standardized assessments use the client's data, are scored in a standardized and objective method, and provide results about the person's use of substances relative to national data may not convince the client of the accuracy of the diagnosis, but may succeed in demonstrating that the argument of bias is without merit.

A common belief is that people who abuse substances deny or minimize their substance use (APA, 2013). To counter such client minimization, a third benefit is that several standardized assessments employ indirect methods of screening. Indirect methods of screening ask questions that are not overtly related to substance abuse and therefore, conceptually, cannot be answered in a way to deny or minimize one's substance use. Screens with both overt and covert scales are discussed later in this chapter.

Finally, standardized assessments aid counselors in treatment planning. Imagine four different clients' responses to a screening instrument. Client A's scores indicate that she has a severe substance use disorder. Client B scores below the substance use disorder cutoff. Client C scores higher than any client the counselor has assessed. Finally, client D's answers, while not indicative

TABLE 6.1 Client Assessment Results and Recommendations

Client	A	B	C	D
Results	At or above severe substance use cutoff level	Below cutoff level for substance use disorder	Unusually high score	Below cutoff for substance use disorder but indicates drinking more than average
Recommendation	Referral to day-treatment or IOP	No treatment recommendation	Further evaluation for medical detoxification	Referral to education on substance use

of a substance use disorder, do suggest that he drinks alcohol more than does the average person. These data provide the following treatment implications. Client A's score suggests treatment recommendations that may include referral to a day treatment program or intensive outpatient (IOP) treatment. Client B's score fails to meet DSM-5 criteria for a substance use disorder. As such, this client will not be recommended for treatment. Client C's presentation is so severe that a medical evaluation for detoxification treatment may be appropriate. Finally, client D's data suggest that educational interventions may help the client evaluate the role substance use plays in his life. This information is summarized in Table 6.1.

PHILOSOPHICAL UNDERPINNING OF INSTRUMENT CONSTRUCTION

Substance use assessments are constructed using one of two methods, or a combination of the two. These are the logical and criterion keyed methods (Cohen, Montague, Nathanson, & Swerdlik, 1988). Logically constructed instruments contain items that directly inquire about the amount, frequency, duration, and consequences of substance use. No attempt is made to hide or disguise the items' intent to assess substance use. Logically constructed instruments tend to have good internal consistency, stable construct validity across time, and content validity. However, because the items are transparent in nature, they may be subject to impression management (e.g., Barrick & Mount, 1996).

The criterion-keyed method is used to circumvent defensiveness, one of the indirect methods of gathering information indicated elsewhere. Criterion-keyed scales are constructed by selecting a target group (the criterion group) that possesses the trait of interest and statistically comparing this target group with a group of persons known to be free of the target trait. Criterion-keyed items have no direct relationship with substance use as this item can be anything that statistically differentiates the two groups. Impression management is difficult because the items are not transparent in their nature. That is, it is difficult to determine which items are keyed toward indicating a substance use disorder. While criterion-keyed scales tend to have good criterion-related validity, they sometimes suffer from poor internal consistency, multiple underlying factor structures, and poor content validity.

The decision to use a criterion-keyed screen, a logically derived screen, or a screen that combines both approaches, depends on the purpose of screening and the population of interest. Counselors concerned about detecting client concealment of use may feel more comfortable with a criterion-keyed screen. Counselors working with clients unlikely to attempt to "fake good" may opt for the logically derived method.

SCREENING, ASSESSMENT, AND DIAGNOSIS

The purpose of a screen is to determine if additional clinical attention is needed (Adger & Werner, 1994; U.S. Department of Health & Human Services, 2005). A substance use screen provides an indicator of whether a problem *may* exist. A screen does not provide a diagnosis, but may suggest that an in-depth substance use assessment may be warranted. Assessments tend to be more labor intensive than screens. The purpose of an assessment is to investigate and discover data that will either confirm or preclude clinical hypotheses. Assessments are conducted in response to referral questions (Groth-Marnat, 2009). Diagnosis is the process of determining whether a client's currently presenting symptoms are sufficient to meet standardized and prescribed criteria for diagnosis. While the training and supervision criteria necessary to perform diagnosis vary between jurisdictions, the shared lexicon of mental and emotional disorders is the DSM-5 (APA, 2013).

EVALUATING SUBSTANCE ABUSE SCREENS AND ASSESSMENTS

Piazza (2002) outlined five characteristics of a good screen. These are sensitivity, specificity, reliability, validity, and cost-efficiency. These concepts are explained here and will be used to evaluate, when applicable, each of the screens discussed later in this chapter.

Sensitivity and Specificity

Sensitivity is the ratio of persons correctly screened "positive" for having a substance use disorder to those who actually have the disorder (Altman & Bland, 1994). For example, imagine that a group of 100 persons were administered the hypothetical "Accurate Alcohol Screen-A (AASA)." Of these 100, 50 were known to have a severe substance abuse disorder and 50 were not. If 45 of the 50 persons known to have a severe substance abuse disorder tested "positive," then the AASA's sensitivity would be .90. Conversely, *specificity* refers to the proportion of people that a screen accurately identifies as *not* having a substance use disorder (Altman & Bland, 1994). If the AASA's results suggested that 25 of the 50 nondependent people in our mock sample were "negative," then the AASA's specificity would be .50. These two concepts are often inversely related. A sensitive screen may lead counselors to errantly classify nondependent persons as "positive." The frequency at which a screen makes this error is referred to as the *false positive rate*. A screen with high specificity may inaccurately classify persons as "negative" who actually have a substance use problem. Such classifications are called *false negatives*. Figure 6.1 presents the four classification categories.

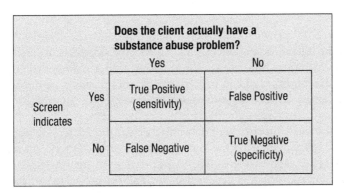

FIGURE 6.1 Sensitivity and Specificity

Ideally, a screen is able to both identify those who have the problem (high true positive) as well as rule out those who do not (high false negative). The purpose for the screening determines the acceptable sensitivity and specificity rates. A researcher may tolerate a high false positive in order to increase the sample size; an agency with limited resources needs high specificity to reduce the number of referrals resulting in false negatives.

Reliability and Validity

Reliability is the consistency of a screen's results. A screen should not vary in its measurement, provided the construct being measured does not vary. A second type of reliability is called *internal consistency*. Internal consistency is the degree to which a screen's items vary together. If a scale's items all measure facets of the same construct, then they should all be answered in a consistent manner. When an instrument's total measurement is stable over time and its items vary together, the instrument is said to be reliable. Groth-Marnat (2009) noted that reliability estimates of states, such as substance abuse or dependence, are frequently lower than those of traits, such as intelligence. Groth-Marnat suggested that clinicians evaluate a screen's reliability in the context of other screens' estimates. According to Groth-Marnat, reliability estimates of .70 or higher are optimal for trait-based screens.

High reliability is necessary but insufficient. A screen may produce consistent results across measurements but inaccurately measure the construct of interest. Validity is synonymous with accuracy. *Validity* is the degree to which a screen accurately represents the construct or criterion it was designed to measure. A screen is valid to the degree it has acceptable sensitivity and specificity. Piazza (2002) suggested that counselors consider validity estimates of .40 to be low and estimates of .90 to be high.

Cost-Efficiency

One way to evaluate a screen's cost is the direct costs associated with its purchase. Screens range in cost from several hundred dollars, when employed as part of a larger assessment battery, to those in the free domain. Less tangible are the human labor costs involved in administering, scoring, and interpreting a screen's results. Another important consideration is the implications of a screen's results. A low-cost or free screen with a high false positive rate may cause an agency to waste precious resources conducting unnecessary diagnostic assessment interviews. Conversely, a screen with poor sensitivity may cause an agency to misdiagnose persons who truly need substance abuse treatment services.

DIAGNOSIS

The DSM-5 (APA, 2013) provides general criteria for substance use disorder diagnoses and specific criteria for the following substances: alcohol, caffeine, cannabis, hallucinogens, inhalants, opioids, sedatives/hypnotics or anxiolytics, stimulants, tobacco, and other (or unknown) substances. With the exception of caffeine, the classification of substance use disorder can be applied to all other nine classes. Criteria are also provided for substance-induced conditions: intoxication, withdrawal, and substance-induced other mental conditions.

This chapter focuses on criteria of the substance use disorders. The reader is advised that while each of these substances shares the same general diagnostic criteria, the manifestations and associated behaviors of each vary greatly. It is recommended that the reader develop specific knowledge of the cultural, age, and gender features, and the prevalence of use, course, familiar pattern, and differential diagnoses associated with each substance.

Regardless of the substance, the DSM-5 specifies that a substance use disorder is characterized by a "cluster of cognitive, behavioral, and physiological symptoms indicating that the individual continues using the substance despite significant substance-related problems" (APA, 2013, p. 483). These include the following: (1) using over a longer period or more of a substance than intended; (2) express persistent desire to regulate or cut down use or have attempted to do so; (3) the exertion of significant time and effort to obtain, use, or recover from use of the substance; (4) craving or a strong desire to use the substance; (5) recurrent use that may interfere with fulfilling major role obligations; (6) persistent or recurrent social problems or interpersonal problems caused or exacerbated by substance use or effects of substance use; (7) social, occupational, or recreational activities reduced or eliminated due to the use of the substance; (8) use of substance in physically hazardous situations; (9) continued use despite knowledge of its persistent and recurrent negative physical or psychological consequences; (10) tolerance (defined as needing to consume increased amounts in order to obtain the desired effect or an experiencing of a reduction in impact while using the same amount of the substance as previously consumed); and (11) withdrawal (experienced as maladaptive behavior accompanied by physiological and cognitive manifestations due to a reduction in consumption, which cause significant distress or the continued use of a substance to avoid/relieve oneself from the same). These symptoms are categorized as pathological pattern (Criteria 1–4), social impairment (Criteria 5–7), risky use (Criteria 8–9), and pharmacological (Criteria 10–11). Substance use disorders can be diagnosed from mild to severe, dependent on the number of criteria endorsed. In general, a client who exhibits two to three of these criteria likely has a mild substance use disorder. Someone with four to five criteria has a moderate substance use disorder. And, a person with six or more criteria has a severe substance use disorder. In addition, clinicians must determine if the person meets criteria for tolerance or withdrawal. Other specifiers available are "in early remission," "in sustained remission," "on maintenance therapy," and "in a controlled environment" (APA, 2013, p. 484). View a copy of each test as you read this chapter! To aid in this endeavor, we offer the following website from the Alcohol and Substance Abuse Measurement Collection, which provides a comprehensive list of screens: utexas.edu/research/cswr/nida/instrumentListing.html

http://lib.adai.washington.edu/instruments/

Substance Use Disorder Screens

Counselors have a wide variety of substance abuse screens from which to choose in order to aid in the assessment and diagnosis of substance use disorder. The Michigan Alcoholism Screening Test (MAST) (Selzer, 1971), the CAGE (Ewing, 1984), and Substance Abuse Subtle Screening Inventory-3 (SASSI-3) (Miller, 1999) are the most often selected screening instruments (Juhnke, Vacc, Curtis, Coll, & Paredes, 2003). Other well-known and well-researched instruments include the Alcohol Use Disorders Identification Test (AUDIT) (Saunders, Aasland, Babor, de la Fuente, & Grant, 1993), the TWEAK (Russell et al., 1994), and the T-ACE (Sokol, Martier, & Ager, 1989). This chapter introduces and discusses a selected number of substance abuse screens and assessments. Self-administered screens are introduced first, followed by scales contained within the larger framework of personality assessments. The instrument section closes with discussions of a counselor-initiated comprehensive substance abuse assessment and screens used with pregnant women. We would like to caution the reader that these scales have not been tested for their psychometrics related to DSM-5 substance use disorders terminology. Therefore, you will find the previous terminology of substance use and substance dependence used when discussing assessment outcomes with these instruments.

SELF-ADMINISTERED, STAND-ALONE SCREENING INSTRUMENTS

Substance Abuse Subtle Screening Inventory-3 (SASSI-3)

First published in 1985 by G. A. Miller, the SASSI uses the criterion keying and rational approaches. The current version (SASSI-3) requires about 17 minutes to complete, score, and interpret (Lazowski, F. G. Miller, Boye, & G. A. Miller, 1998). A Spanish version is available. The first half of the SASSI has 67 true/false questions that are unrelated to substance use. These items comprise eight empirically established scales: the Symptoms (SYM), Obvious Attributes (OAT), Subtle Attributes (SAT), Defensiveness (DEF), Supplemental Addiction Measure (SAM), Family vs. Control Subjects (FAM), and Correctional (COR) scales. The Random Answering Pattern (RAP) scale provides a measure of validity. A RAP raw score of two or more raises doubt about the results' validity (G. A. Miller, Roberts, Brooks, & Lazowski, 1997). Two subscales, the 12-item Face Valid Alcohol Scale (FVA) and the 14-item Face Valid Other Drug Scale (FVOD), were rationally developed and make up the second part of the test.

The SYM scale measures causes, consequences, and correlates of substance abuse. The OAT scale assesses clients' admission of substance-abuse-related limitations. The SAT scale provides an indirect indicator of substance abuse. The DEF scale measures clients' range of openness or defensiveness. High DEF scores could represent attempts to hide substance abuse, situational defensiveness, or pervasive defensiveness. The SAM scale helps clarify whether elevated DEF scores are due to general or situational defensiveness (low SAM) or defensiveness specific to substance use (high SAM).

The SASSI-3 is interpreted by using nine decision rules (Piazza, Martin, & Dildine, 2000). Four rules are based on clients' obvious recognition of a substance use disorder. Two are designed to circumvent defensiveness and/or denial. The remaining three combine data from the obvious and subtle scales. There is a "low probability of having a substance dependence disorder" (G. A. Miller, 1999, p. 10) if no rule is endorsed. One or more rule endorsements suggest a "high probability of having a substance dependence disorder" (Miller, 1999, p. 10).

The SASSI's FAM and COR scales, experimental in nature, do not contribute to the scoring system. The FAM scale's items measure traits present in persons who focus on others' problems rather than their own and who may lack assertiveness. The COR scale contains items frequently endorsed by persons with a criminal history. FAM and COR scale interpretations should be highly tentative.

Recent survey data indicates that addictions counselors (Juhnke et al., 2003) view the SASSI-3 to be the most important and most frequently used screen. Gray (2001) reported excellent estimates of internal consistency for the face-valid scales but poor estimates for the indirect scales. Laux, Perera-Diltz, Smirnoff, and Salyers (2005) reported excellent internal consistency ($\alpha = .95$), unidimensional status, and acceptable item-to-scale correlations for the FVOD scale. Myerholtz and Rosenberg (1998) found the SASSI-3 to have acceptable temporal stability and moderate agreement with other instruments designed to assess similar constructs. Laux, Salyers, and Kotova (2005) concluded that the SASSI-3 outperformed the MAST, MacAndrew—Revised (Mac-R), and CAGE in terms of one-week test–retest reliability, internal consistency, and factor structure in a college student sample. Lazowski et al. (1998) reported that the SASSI-3 has a 95% rate of agreement with clinicians' diagnoses. Burck, Laux, Harper, and Ritchie (2010) studied the effect of faking on the SASSI-3's results. Burck et al. (2010) found that while persons who faked-good and who faked-bad could manipulate the FVA, FVOD, SYM and OAT scales, the SAT scale was not affected by attempts to fake-good and the DEF scale showed elevated scores among those who attempted to fake-good. Despite the SASSI-3's popularity among clinicians, there is some question about the subtle scales' ability to provide unique diagnostic information over and above that provided by the obvious scales (Feldstein & Miller, 2007). This concern was partially addressed by Laux, Piazza, Salyers, and Roseman (2012), who demonstrated that the subtle scales added incremental validity to the SASSI-3's results over and above that which was provided for by the face-valid scales. This finding was consistent regardless of respondents' readiness to change their substance use.

The SASSI-A2 (Miller & Lazowski, 2001), and its predecessor, the SASSI-A, is for 12- to 18-year-olds and requires a 4.4 grade reading level. The screen has 72 true–false questions and 28 face-valid questions about alcohol and other drug use and consequences. The SASSI-A2 requires approximately 15 minutes to administer and score. Counselors should use the SASSI-A2 with an 18-year-old client in high school and the SASSI-3 with an 18-year-old high school graduate. Rogers, Cashel, Johansen, Sewell, and Gonzalez (1997) reported the SASSI-A as useful for accurately identifying 75% of reporting users but as misclassifying approximately 66% of nonusers. Rogers et al. also reported a possible ethnic bias, with the SASSI-A demonstrating less efficiency in classifying Hispanic participants than in Caucasian participants. Bauman, Merta, and Steiner (1999) concluded that the SASSI-A was able to differentiate between clinical and nonclinical at-risk groups, but questioned its validity as it "classified significantly more individuals as chemically dependent than did the clinicians" (p. 68). Sweet and Saules (2003) investigated the SASSI-A's validity in a sample of 490 adolescent offenders from a Michigan juvenile court. Their results were supportive for the FVOD and FVA scales. These researchers concluded that the subtle scales had poor construct validity, and that the subtle scales were better measures of conduct problems and emotional instability than substance abuse. Stein et al. (2005) noted that SASSI-A's construct validity was somewhat supported for use with juveniles in a correctional setting whose alcohol use levels were at 3 or above, but not useful for detecting drug use behavior. More recently, Perera-Diltz and Perry (2011), using the SASSI-A2, reported that while the SASSI-A2 produced similar results between African American and European American students in a public urban high school, their data produced much lower internal consistency estimates than reported in the SASSI-A2 manual.

More information related to the SASSI and purchase information can be found at the following websites:

psychscreen.com/epiphanyWeb/FlexPage.aspx?ID=27
hsassi.com/

The Michigan Alcoholism Screening Test (MAST)

The MAST (Selzer, 1971) has 25 true–false questions about alcohol use and can be completed in 10–15 minutes (Hedlund & Vieweg, 1984). Selzer assigned weights of 0, 1, 2, or 5 based on his view of each item's indicator of alcohol abuse. Individual item scores are summed and the following schema is used to interpret the results: 0–4, not alcohol dependent; 5–6, maybe alcohol dependent; 7 or more, alcohol dependent (Hedlund & Vieweg, 1984). The MAST is considered the "gold standard" of alcohol abuse screens by many clinicians in the field (Martin, Liepman, & Young, 1990). Despite this reputation, the MAST is sometimes criticized based on the transparency of its items. Specifically, some (e.g., Friedrich & Loftsgard, 1978) suggest that MAST scores are more reflective of a willingness to self-identify as having alcohol-related problems rather than a pure measure of alcohol dependence. The MAST has been also criticized as being vulnerable to client minimization (e.g.,

Stinnett, Benton, & Whitfill, 1991). Additionally, client denial about the scope and depth of alcohol-related problems may limit the MAST's accuracy (Shedler, Mayman, & Manis, 1993).

The MAST's original standardization sample was comprised of males convicted of driving under the influence (Selzer, 1971). Men and women experience the symptoms and consequences of alcohol dependence differently (e.g., Wilke, 1994). A screen constructed based on men's experience of alcohol abuse may not apply equally to women. The practice of interpreting MAST scores based on a total score presupposes that the instrument's items are homogenous and represent a single latent variable. Some researchers suggest that the MAST consists of many different facets of alcohol use disorder (e.g., Parsons, Wallbrown, & Myers, 1994). Others, however, report that the MAST does reflect a single latent variable of alcohol dependence (e.g., Thurber & Snow, 2001). Laux et al. (2004) found that MAST scores were independent of client gender, age, education level, and income. Laux et al. (2004) also reported that the MAST was one-dimensional, and that low endorsement of certain items did not affect the screen's internal structure. However, Laux et al. found that MAST scores were susceptible to defensiveness. The MAST has a false positive rate of 33% (Jacobson, 1983) and an accuracy rate of 75% (Creager, 1989).

The MAST has been modified for use by special populations and in other languages (e.g., Turkish; Evren, Durkaya, Evren, Dalbudak, & Cetin, 2012; Okay, Sengul, Acikgoz, Ozan, & Dilbaz, 2010). A brief version, B-MAST, was published in 1972 (Pokorny, B. A. Miller, & Kaplan, 1972). The Adapted Short Michigan Alcoholism Screening Test (ASMAST) for Fathers (F-SMAST) and Mothers (M-SMAST), with 13 items each, were published in 1992 (Crews & Sher, 1992). These are used with children of alcoholics to assess the father's and mother's history of alcohol use. Counselors working with the elderly may be interested in using the MAST—Geriatric Version (MAST-G) (Blow et al., 1992), or the equally valid but briefer Short-MAST-G or Mini-MAST-G (Johnson-Greene, McCaul, & Roger, 2009).

The MAST's questions can be located at the following website:

http://www.dorris.com/objects/MichiganAlcoholScreeningTest.pdf

The CAGE

Ewing (1984) designed the CAGE for primary care physicians. Its brevity makes it easy to remember and administer (Piazza, 2002). The CAGE asks, Have you ever felt the need to **C**ut down, been **A**nnoyed by other's criticism of your drinking, felt bad or **G**uilty about drinking, or used a drink in the morning (**E**ye opener). Two or more "yes" answers are suggestive of an alcohol use disorder. The CAGE's diagnostic accuracy rates range between 40% and 95% (Sokol et al., 1989). Lifetime CAGE sensitivity rates range from 60% to 95% (O'Connor & Schottenfeld, 1998). A French version, with a cutoff score of 3 (Geneste et al., 2012), and a Norwegian version (Skogen, Overland, Knudsen, & Mykletun, 2011), have shown initial reliability and validity evidence. The CAGE screens for alcohol abuse only; however, a Dutch version of the CAGE that was modified for drug use screening, the CAGE-AID, demonstrated a sensitivity rating of .91 and a specificity rating of .98 among adolescents in a mental health setting (Couwenbergh, Van Der Gaag, Koeter, De Ruiter, & Van Den Brink, 2009). Due to its obvious nature, the CAGE is subject to manipulation. The CAGE also does not specify current or past alcohol use. As such, the CAGE could misclassify persons whose alcohol dependence is currently in remission. Fleming (1993) reported false positive rates in excess of 50%. Kitchens (1994) argued that the CAGE is useful when screening for advanced stages of alcohol dependence but lacks the sensitivity to detect early stages of alcohol abuse.

The CAGE's questions can be located at the following website: http://counsellingresource.com/quizzes/alcohol-cage/index.html

Alcohol Use Disorders Identification Test (AUDIT)

The AUDIT was developed by the World Health Organization (WHO) (Hodgson et al., 2003). Its 10 items are divided into 3 subscales: 3 questions assess the quantity and frequency of alcohol use, 3 focus on alcohol dependence, and 4 tap into the negative consequences of alcohol use (Hodgson et al., 2003). Administration and scoring requires approximately 3 minutes. Fielling, Reid, and O'Connor (2000) reviewed six AUDIT sensitivity and specificity studies. The recommended cutoff of eight points produced a sensitivity score of .61 and a specificity rating of .90. The sensitivity and specificity ratings, respectively, adjusted to .40 and .96 when the cutoff score was raised to 11 points. Fielling et al. (2000) also investigated the sensitivity and specificity of the 8-point cutoff score in groups categorized as hazardous drinkers, harmful drinkers, and at-risk drinkers. The sensitivity and specificity data for each group, respectively, was .97 and .78, .95 and .85, and .51 and .96. Using a cutoff score of 13 in a Swedish sample of suspected offenders with mental health problems, Durbeej and colleagues (2010) reported a sensitivity rating of .88 and a positive correlation with alcohol use problem severity ratings. Hallinan, McGilloway, Dempster, and Donnelly (2011) conducted a factor analysis using AUDIT data collected in Ireland and discovered two underlying factors in this sample: alcohol consumption and alcohol-related consequences. Fielling et al. (2000) concluded that the AUDIT is more useful in detecting less severe alcohol consumption than alcohol abuse or dependence. This finding was consistent with that of a study conducted among college students outside of bars where the AUDIT was found to produce good reliability and validity estimates among persons whose alcohol use was mild to moderate (Celio, Vetter-O'Hagen, Lisman, & Johansen, 2011). Contrary to these findings, Aalto, Alho, Halme, and Seppa (2010) reported that among a group of elderly Finnish persons, the AUDIT was effective at detecting heavy drinking only. Further, the AUDIT was valid for detecting severe alcohol use among anxious and depressed Dutch persons, but not abusive drinking in this population (Baschloo et al., 2010). The AUDIT has been translated into Turkish, Greek (Moussas et al., 2009), Hindi, German, Dutch, Polish, Japanese (Kawada, Inagaki, & Kuratomi, 2011), French (Geneste et al., 2012), Korean (Kim et al. 2012), Portuguese, Spanish (Santis, Garmendia, Acuna, Alvarado, & Arteaga, 2009), Danish, Flemish, Bulgarian, Chinese (Li, Babor, Hao, & Chen, 2011), Italian, and Nigerian dialects (Babor, Higgins-Biddle, Saunders, & Monteiro, 2001), but is not valid for use with the hearing impaired (Alexander, DiNitto, & Tidblom, 2005).

The AUDIT has been modified to produce three related substance abuse screens. These include the Fast Alcohol Screening Test (FAST), the AUDIT-C, and the AUDIT-3. The FAST consists of four questions (items 3, 5, 8, 10) from the original AUDIT. The FAST, administered in approximately 12 seconds, was developed for use in medical settings. The Spearman rank correlation between the AUDIT and the FAST is .79. Sensitivity and specificity of the FAST is reported to range from .89 to .95 and .84 to .90 respectively (Hodgson et al., 2003). According to Hodgson et al., the FAST compares favorably to the AUDIT across age, gender, and clinical setting. The AUDIT-C was developed to provide primary and emergency care staff with a quick alcohol screen (Bush, Kivlahan, McDonell, Fihn, & Bradley, 1998). The AUDIT-C employs the first three questions of the AUDIT. High sensitivity (.81) and specificity (.86) estimates were reported in a female veteran sample (Bradley et al., 2003). Bush et al. (1998) reported sensitivity of .95 and specificity of .60. The AUDIT-C is reported to be more efficacious for hazardous drinking patterns than for alcohol use or dependence (Bradley et al., 2003; Bush et al., 1998).

The Alcohol Use Disorders Identification Test

The AUDIT manual contains an interviewer version and a self-report version of the audit. The manual can be downloaded from the WHO at the following website:

whqlibdoc.who.int/hq/2001/WHO_MSD_MSB_01.6a.pdf

An online version of the AUDIT is available at:

testandcalc.com/etc/tests/audit.asp

Alcohol Use Inventory (AUI)

The AUI is a 228-item tool that assesses clients' perceived benefits, styles, consequences, and concerns related to alcohol use (Horn, Wanberg, & Foster, 1990). The AUI is appropriate for use with persons 16 and older who have been admitted to an alcohol use disorders treatment program. The AUI has 17 primary scales, 6 second-order scales, and a third-order general scale (Chang, Lapham, & Wanberg, 2001). Perceived benefits of alcohol use are measured by the Socialim (drinks to improve sociability), the Mentalim (drinks to improve mental functioning), the Mangmood (drinking to help manage moods), and the Maricope (drinking after having marital problems) scales. Styles of drinking are assessed by the Gregarus (social vs. solo drinking), the Compulsv (compulsive drinking), and the Sustained (sustained vs. periodic drinking) scales. The scales Lcontrol (loss of control over behavior when drinking), Rolemala (social role maladaption), Delirium (psychoperceptual withdrawal), Hangover (psychophysical withdrawal), and Mariprob (drinking causing marital problems) provide information about consequences of client drinking. Concerns about drinking are reported on the Quantity (quantity of daily use when drinking), the Guiltwor (guilt and worry associated with drinking), the Helpbefr (prior attempts to deal with drinking), the Receptiv (readiness for help), and the Awarenes (awareness of drinking problems) scales. The AUI requires approximately 35–60 minutes to complete and is constructed at a sixth-grade reading level.

Alcohol Use Inventory

Further information on the AUI is available at the following websites:

cps.nova.edu/~cpphelp/AUI.html
pubs.niaaa.nih.gov/publications/AssessingAlcohol/InstrumentPDFs/15_AUI.pdf

SUBSTANCE ABUSE SCALES FOUND ON PERSONALITY ASSESSMENT INSTRUMENTS

Many of the most reputable personality assessment instruments include substance abuse scales. This section reviews the substance abuse screens found in the Minnesota Multiphasic Personality Inventory—2 (MMPI-2; Butcher, Dahlstrom, Graham, Tellegen, & Kaemmer, 1989), the Personality Assessment Inventory (PAI; Morey, 1991), and the Millon Clinical Multiaxial Inventory-III (MCMI-III; Millon, Davis, & Millon, 1997). Note that unlike client-administered, stand-alone screening instruments, the following sections introduce only *components* of comprehensive personality assessment instruments. These scales cannot be administered independent of the entire battery of questions. The administration, scoring, and interpretation of these instruments require extensive training and credentialing. Finally, the ethical administration of a personality assessment frequently requires a clinical interview, 1–2 hours of the client's time to complete the battery, scoring time (which varies depending on the methods used), a comprehensive written report, and a feedback interview with the client. Use of the following personality assessments for the sole purpose of substance use screening is not recommended.

Minnesota Multiphasic Personality Inventory—2 (MMPI-2)

The MMPI (Butcher et al., 1989) is the most widely used personality assessment (Groth-Marnat, 2003). This tool has 567 true–false, criterion-keyed items that provide a wide range of data about an individual's overall psychological adjustment. The MMPI contains three scales designed to assess substance abuse: The MacAndrew Alcoholism Scale—Revised (MacAndrew, 1965), the Addiction Potential Scale (Weed, Butcher, McKenna, & Ben-Porath, 1992), and the Addiction Acknowledgement Scale (AAS). The following sections will address these scales in greater detail.

MMPI-2: THE MACANDREW ALCOHOLISM SCALE—REVISED (Mac-R) The Mac-R scale (MacAndrew, 1965) was constructed using the criterion-keying method. MacAndrew contrasted MMPI responses of 20 males diagnosed with alcohol dependence with those of 200 nonalcohol-dependent psychiatric patients. MacAndrew's analysis indicated that 49 nonalcohol-related items statistically differentiated these two groups. When the MMPI was revised in 1989, four of MacAndrew's original items were replaced with an equal number of items that discriminated between "alcoholic and nonalcoholic men" (*sic*) (Graham, 2000, p. 156) to form the Mac-Revised or Mac-R. Graham (2000) noted that high scores on the Mac-R "suggest the possibility of alcohol or other substance abuse problems" (p. 159).

The following rubric is generally accepted for interpreting Mac-R raw scores: 28 or more points are suggestive of substance abuse. Scores of 24–27, which are also suggestive of substance abuse, will produce false positives. Substance abusing persons are unlikely to produce scores less than 24.

The Mac-R's internal consistency estimates vary. While Butcher et al. (1989) reported alphas of .56 for men and .45 for women, Laux et al. (2004) reported an alpha of .88 for a mixed-gender outpatient sample, and Laux et al. (2005) reported an alpha of .82 in a college student sample. Estimates of the Mac-R's temporal stability have been fairly robust. For example, Laux et al. (2005), reported a 2-week stability coefficient of .97. Numerous studies (e.g., Hoffman, Loper, & Kammeier, 1974) indicate that Mac-R scores are stable over long-term treatment. Research into the Mac's factor structure (Weed, Butcher, & Ben-Porath, 1995) suggests the Mac-R measures cognitive impairment, school maladjustment, interpersonal competence, risk taking, extroversion and exhibitionism, and harmful habits.

Graham (2000) cautioned that persons with antisocial traits sometimes produce false positive Mac-R scores. Conversely, persons with schizophrenia or mood disorders who are also substance abusers may produce false negative Mac-R scores. Also, Graham (2000) reported that African Americans are sometimes overpathologized by the Mac-R. Like many screens, the Mac-R is sensitive to substance-abusing behaviors across the life span. Consequently, a person who previously abused substances but is now in recovery may produce a false positive Mac-R score.

Finally, the Mac-R reportedly screens for substance abuse in general. Therefore, clinicians whose clients produce elevated Mac-R scores will need to conduct further inquiry to determine the use of exactly which substance(s) is (are) driving the elevation. For further Mac-R information, see Craig's (2005) comprehensive review of the relevant literature.

MMPI-2: ADDICTION POTENTIAL SCALE (APS) The APS (Weed, Butcher, McKenna, & Ben-Porath, 1992), a criterion-keyed scale, was designed to subtly assess adult personality traits thought to underlie the development of an addictive disorder (e.g., extroversion, excitement seeking, risk taking, self-doubts, and self-alienation). This scale's 39 items were selected based on their ability to discriminate persons who were dependent on alcohol or another drug from persons diagnosed with a nonsubstance-use-related psychiatric disorder, and from persons with no mental health diagnosis. T-scores of 60 or more indicate the need for additional substance abuse assessment (Graham, 2000).

Weed et al. (1992) reported one-week test–retest reliability estimates in the MMPI normative sample of .69 for men and .77 for women. Internal consistency estimates are available from a college student sample ($\alpha = .48$; Svanum, McGrew, & Ehrmann, 1994), and an Introductory Psychology class ($\alpha = .47$; Clements & Heintz, 2002). Sawrie and colleagues (1996) investigated the APS's underlying factor structure in inpatient substance dependent and psychiatric samples and found five factors: dissatisfaction with self, powerlessness/lack of self-efficacy, antisocial acting out, urgency, and risk taking/recklessness. Greene, Weed, Butcher, Arredondo, and Davis (1992) examined the APS's discriminative ability and found that it successfully distinguished between psychiatric and substance abusing samples.

The research investigating the APS's utility is mixed. While Green et al. (1992) concluded that the APS was a better measure of substance abuse than the Mac-R, Svanum et al. (1994) found that the APS was weakly correlated with substance abuse classifications produced by the computerized version of the Diagnostic Interview Schedule (DIS; Robins, Helzer, Croughan, & Ratcliff, 1981). Svanum et al. concluded that the APS possesses "at least uneven if not poor ability to identify substance dependence . . ." (p. 436). Clements and Heintz (2002) reported that the APS is less useful than direct measures of substance abuse. Clements and Heintz (2002) frankly doubted whether the APS is useful for substance abuse screening at all. Rouse, Butcher, and Miller (1999) offered a potential explanation for these findings when they noted that the APS's ability to discriminate between substance abusers and non-substance abusers is compromised in samples with high rates of emotional distress.

MMPI-2: ADDICTION ACKNOWLEDGEMENT SCALE (AAS) The AAS's 13 items directly measure substance abuse. According to Weed et al. (1992), scores on the AAS represent "simple denial or acknowledgment of abuse problems" (p. 391). These scores can be interpreted as a client's direct communication about his or her substance abuse status. High scores (T-scores greater than or equal to 60) represent open acknowledgment of substance abuse (Graham, 2000). Because the items are transparent, low scores may represent an absence of substance abuse; however, low scores could reflect interest in hiding one's substance abuse. Clinicians interpreting the AAS are cautioned that scores reflect a client's willingness to report substance abuse and not necessarily the actuality of the abuse.

Weed et al. (1992) reported a coefficient alpha of .74 and a 1-week test–retest coefficient of stability of .84 for females and .89 for males. Weed et al. (1992) reported that the AAS discriminated between a sample of substance abusers who scored the highest, nonclinical participants who scored the lowest, and psychiatric patients whose scores fell between these two groups. These findings were replicated by Greene et al. (1992) in a cross-validation study. Svanum et al. (1994) reported an alpha of .55 among a sample of college students and concluded that the AAS offered a "modest ability to detect substance dependent persons" (p. 433). Svanum et al. (1994) suggested using a T-score cutoff of 59 to maximize sensitivity and minimize the false positive rate. Despite their findings of low internal consistency, Svanum et al. (1994) deemed the AAS to be the most useful of the MMPI-2 based substance abuse screens. Clements and Heintz (2002) calculated Cronbach's alpha in a college-level introductory psychology student sample and reported a value of .68. Clements and Heintz (2002) additionally compared the AAS to the APS and Mac-R, concluding that the AAS outperformed both.

Using interviewer ratings as a criterion variable, Stein, Graham, Ben-Porath, and McNulty (1990) calculated the AAS's overall hit rate, sensitivity, specificity, and positive and negative predictive powers, for men and women separately, and compared them with those of the Mac-R and the APS. They concluded that the AAS is the best of MMPI-2 substance abuse screening scales. Rouse et al. (1999) agreed and declared the AAS to be the most efficacious of the MMPI-2's substance abuse scales.

Additional information about the MMPI-2 is available at:

pearsonclinical.com/education/products/100000461/minnesota-multiphasic-personality-inventory-2-mmpi-2.html
psychscreen.com/epiphanyWeb/flexpage.aspx?ID=144

Personality Assessment Inventory (PAI)

The PAI is an adult personality and psychopathology assessment with 344 items, answered on a 4-point scale, that form 25 scales (11 clinical scales, 4 validity scales, 5 treatment scales, and 5 interpersonal style scales) (Morey, 1991). This assessment could be administered to an adult with a minimum of fourth- to sixth-grade reading level. Morey (1991) used both rational and empirical methods to assess a broad range of psychopathology, treatment-related variables, and interpersonal styles. The PAI contains one scale for assessing alcohol use (the Alcohol Problems Scale) and one for assessing drug use (the Drug Problems Scale). Siefert, Sinclair, Kehl-Fie, and Blais (2009) concluded that the theorized item–scale relationship reported in the original study of the PAI from a less symptomatic sample held true for a severely symptomatic inpatient psychiatric sample. Seifert et al. (2009) also reported that internal consistency, item divergency, and scale-level statistics for the Alcohol Problems Scale (ALC) and Drug Problems Scale (DRG) were impressive. The PAI has a short form that includes the ALC and DRG scales. The PAI—Short Form (PAI-SF) consists of the first 160 items of the PAI and includes items demonstrated to have the strongest item–scale correlations for each clinical scale. It thus is reported to have acceptable internal consistency reliability (Morey, 1991). The following sections will provide greater detail about these two PAI scales. Sinclair et al. (2010), from their research with both civil and forensic inpatients, concluded that there is a strong agreement between the PAI and PAI-SF.

PAI: ALCOHOL PROBLEMS SCALE (ALC) The ALC is a 12-item face-valid scale that measures both behaviors and experiences related to alcohol disorders (Ruiz, Dickinson, & Pincus, 2002). PAI manual reports an ALC internal consistency reliability coefficient of .93 and the test–retest reliability coefficient of .94 (Wise, Streiner, & Walfish, 2010). Schinka (1995) examined the ALC scales' reliability estimates in a sample of alcohol-dependent inpatient clients. Schinka's data produced an internal consistency alpha of .75 and a mean inter-item correlation coefficient of .21. The PAI manual (Morey, 1991) reports that the ALC correlates ($r = .89$) with the MAST (Selzer, 1971). Morey (1991) also reports that ALC scores are related to personality traits generally associated with alcohol dependence (e.g., impulsivity, psychopathology, excitement seeking, and hostility). Boone (1998) reported alpha correlates of .92 and .93 with a psychiatric and standard sample. Parker, Daleiden, and Simpson (1999) reported that ALC scores were significantly related to the Addiction Severity Index's (ASI) (McLellan, Luborsky, O'Brien, & Woody, 1980), Alcohol Composite Score ($r = .49$), and ASI Interviewer Severity Ratings ($r = .44$). Seifert et al. (2009) reported a coefficient alpha of .9, a mean item-scale correlation of .60, and a mean inter-item correlation of .42, concluding that this scale had impressive reliability. Sinclair et al. (2010) reported coefficient alpha of .84 to .89 using the PAI-SF with a civil and forensic inpatient group. For these two groups, the average item–scale correlation was .77 and .68 with a 100% item–scale convergence for both groups.

PAI: DRUG PROBLEMS SCALE (DRG) All DRG items are transparent in their nature. Schinka (1995) examined the DRG scale's reliability estimates in a sample of alcohol-dependent inpatient clients. The DRG scale was reported to have an internal consistency coefficient of .89 and a test–retest reliability coefficient of .88 in the manual (Wise et al. 2010). Schinka reported an internal consistency alpha of .92 and a mean inter-item correlation coefficient of .49. Fals-Stewart (1996) investigated the DRG and ALC scales' characteristics in a nonclinical, forensic, and drug-treatment-seeking population. Fals-Stewart's results suggested that the ALC and DRG scales were subject to response management. Further, his results indicated that 31% of the nonclinical sample produced elevated scores on these scales despite not meeting current DSM criteria for substance abuse or dependence. These findings suggest that people can "fake good" on the DRG and ALC scales. Schinka, Curtiss, and Mulloy (1994) reported that an alcohol-dependent-only group produced elevated scores on the ALC scale only, and not the DRG scale, supporting both scales' discriminative ability. A cocaine-dependent group produced elevated scores on the DRG scale only, and not the ALC scale. A third group comprised of both an alcohol- and cocaine-dependent subset and a polysubstance-dependent subset produced elevated DRG and ALC scales. Boone (1998) reported an alpha coefficient of .89 for both a psychiatric and standard sample. Seifert et al. (2009) reported the PAI DRG scale as an impressive scale with .88 coefficient alpha, .6 mean item-scale correlation, and .37 mean inter-item correlation. Sinclair et al. (2010) reported a coefficient alpha of .84–.89 for their civil and forensic inpatient groups for the PAI-SF DRG scale. For these two groups, the average item–scale correlation was .62 and .61 with a 100% item–scale convergence for both groups.

Further information about this scale is offered at the following website:

psychscreen.com/epiphanyWeb/flexpage.aspx?ID=144

Millon Clinical Multiaxial Inventory—III (MCMI-III)

The MCMI-III's (Millon, Davis, & Millon 1997) 175 items provide a wide range of information about DSM-5 (APA, 2000) related personality disorders and clinical syndromes. The MCMI-III, valid for use with adults aged 18 and older, requires approximately 25 minutes to complete and provides information on 24 scales. The MCMI-III uses one scale to measure drug dependence (T) and one to measure alcohol dependence (B). Hesse, Guldager, and Holm Linneberg (2012) reported good discriminant validity for both the drug and alcohol scales. Although a Dutch version of the MCMI-III is available, Rossi, van der Ark, and Sloore (2007) concluded that the factor structure of these two versions were different, raising concerns on validity of the construct when used across cultures.

MCMI-III: DRUG DEPENDENCE (T) According to the *MCMI-III Manual* (Millon et al., 1997), high scores on Scale T suggest that the client may have present or past problems with drug abuse, including difficulties with impulse management, acting within conventional social limits, and managing the consequences of one's behavior. Persons with high Scale T scores may have trouble organizing life's daily activities and may have difficulties with social, family, legal, and/or occupational life (Groth-Marnat, 2009). Many of Scale T's 14 items are indirect in nature. The *MCMI-III Manual* reports Scale T internal consistency and test–retest reliability estimates of .83 and .91, respectively, and a statistically significant correlation of .33 with the MAST (Selzer, 1971).

Calsyn, Saxon, and Daisy (1990) investigated Scale T's ability to discriminate between persons seeking drug treatment and psychiatric patients with no substance abuse history. Using the suggested cutoff level of 85 or higher, Scale T identified 19.7% of substance abusers. Scale T scores between 75 and 84 identified an additional 19.7% of the drug-abusing participants. Sixty percent of the drug-abusing sample did not score high enough on Scale T for the MCMI to classify them as having a drug problem. Conversely, 12% of the nonusing psychiatric sample scored high enough on Scale T to be classified as having a substance use problem. Calsyn et al. (1990) concluded that the Scale T's 39.4% true positive rate and 60.6% false negative rate should cause counselors to exercise caution when interpreting Scale T. This is in agreement with Marsh, Stile, Stoughton, and Trout-Landen's (1988) findings that only 49% of opioid-dependent persons scored higher than 74 on Scale T.

MCMI-III: ALCOHOL DEPENDENCE (B) High scores on the MCMI-III Scale B are likely indicative of persons who have a history of alcohol dependence, have attempted to overcome this issue with limited success, and/or have alcohol-related family and work complications. Scale B contains 15 items, many of which are indirect in nature. The *MCMI-III Manual* (Millon et al., 1997) reported Scale B internal consistency and stability estimates of .82 and .92, respectively, and a statistically significant correlation of .67 with the MAST (Selzer, 1971).

Further information about this scale is offered at the following website:

psychcentral.com/lib/millon-clinical-multiaxial-inventory-mcmi-iii/0006106

COUNSELOR-INITIATED COMPREHENSIVE SUBSTANCE ABUSE ASSESSMENT

Counselors interested in assessing their clients' use of alcohol or other drugs are not limited to a selection of standardized personality assessments and questionnaires. Diagnostic interviews can provide a rich source of data to help determine or clarify clients' presenting issues. While some may elect to tailor their interviews to each individual client, others prefer a more standardized approach as a way to ensure that each client receives the same degree of inquiry. One standardized interview format available for this purpose is the Addiction Severity Index (McLellan et al. 1980), addressed in the following section.

The Addiction Severity Index (ASI)

The Addiction Severity Index (ASI), now in its sixth version, is a public domain free assessment introduced in the 1980s (McLellan et al., 1980). The revised version (i.e., ASI-5) in 1992 remained essentially the same as the original version (Denis, Cacciola, & Alterman, 2013). Leonhard, Mulvey, Gastfriend, and Shwartz (2000) describe the ASI as the standard assessment tool for alcohol and other addictions. The ASI is typically administered in an oral interview within an estimated administration time of 60 minutes.

The ASI was designed to serve as a multidimensional tool with applicability across a wide variety of settings and is available in at least 17 languages. In an attempt to reduce time and cost of administering the ASI-5, a client-administered version (Butler et al., 2001), a computer-administered version (Rosen, Henson, Finney, & Moos, 2000), an Internet and automated telephone self-report version (Brodey et al., 2004), an ASI-5 "Lite" (ASI-L-VA) clinician-administered version (Cacciola, Alterman, McLellan, Lin, & Lynch, 2007), and a fifth-grade reading level teen version (T-ASI; Kaminer, Bukstein, & Tarter, 1991) are available. Pankow, Simpson, Joe, Rowan-Szal, Knight, and Meason (2012) examined the concurrent and predictive validity of the self-administered version of the Addiction Severity Index and concluded that the ASI is a reliable measure.

In addition to inquiring about demographic data, the ASI-6 investigates the same seven domains as ASI-5 (i.e., medical, employment, alcohol, drugs, family/social, legal, and psychiatric status). The lifetime and past 30-day time frames have also been retained in ASI-6, although a 6-month time frame was added for key items. Composite scores (CS) of the ASI-5 have been replaced by recent status scores (RSS).

While ASI reliability and validity investigations are generally supportive (e.g., Butler et al., 2001; Leonhard et al., 2000; Moos, Finney, Ferderman, & Suchinsky, 2000; Rosen, Henson, Finney, & Moos, 2000), Mäkelä's (2004) review of the empirical ASI literature, a total of 37 studies, led him to conclude that only three of the seven ASI composite scores demonstrated acceptable internal consistency reliability. McLellan et al. (2004), although agreeing with some of Mäkelä's (2004) points, also countered that important articles were omitted from Mäkelä's review. Comparing the RSS of ASI-6 with its ASI-5 counterpart, the CS, Denis et al. (2013) reported that the RSS better connected to its validity measures than CS. Cacciola, Alterman, Habing, and McLellan (2011) concluded that the ASI-6 scales demonstrate acceptable scalability, reliability, and concurrent validity by comparing the ASI-6 with a battery of other instruments with at least one measure responding to the seven domains of ASI-6. Similarly, Kessler and colleagues (2012) concluded that the ASI-6 version showed good reliability (i.e., correlation between ASI-6 and interviewers; correlation between ASI-6 and ASSIST; and Cronbach's alpha ranging from .64 to .95 for subscales) and concurrent validity, concluding that the instrument was good to use with the Brazilian culture.

In the ASI-6 Spanish version, Casares-Lopez et al. (2011) concluded a low discriminant-convergent validity due to low correlation between the primary and secondary scales of the ASI-6 and Clinic Global Impression score. However, they also reported statistically significant reduction in severity of Alcohol, Drug, Mental Health, and Family/Social Partner problems at six months of treatment. In a separate study, Casares-Lopez et al. (2011) concluded that the ASI-6 Spanish version had good validity as it was sensitive to therapeutic change. Similar to the conclusions of Wei, Zunyou, and Xiaoli (2010), Sun et al. (2012) concluded good internal consistency (overall $\alpha = 0.79$), acceptable 7-day test–retest reliability, and good criterion validity with Alcohol Use Disorders Identification Test (AUDIT) for the Chinese version (ASI-C-5). In the absence of ASI-6 French version psychometrics, the psychometric findings of the ASI-5 are provided here. Krenz and colleagues (2004) concluded acceptable validity and reliability (i.e., α ranging from .42 to .76) and test–retest correlation coefficients (i.e., ranging from .48 to .98) on the ASI-5 French version.

The T-ASI has been translated to Spanish, Dutch, Portuguese, Arabic, Finnish, Hebrew, Italian, and Turkish (Kaminer, 2008). Sartes, De Micheli, and Souza-Formigoni (2009) reported good internal consistency (α = .89) for substance abuse and concurrent validity with the Composite International Diagnostic Interview (CIDI) in the Brazilian Portuguese version of T-ASI. Díaz et al. (2008) reported adequate psychometric properties of the Spanish T-ASI version. Brodey et al. (2005) reported adequate to good internal consistency reliability (α > .70) for all but risky behavior domain and good convergent validity (i.e., all domains significantly correlated with all gold standard instruments), concluding the T-ASI-2 is a reliable and valid assessment tool for substance use and related behaviors.

A copy of the ASI is available at the following website:

tresearch.org/tools/download-asi-instruments-manuals/

INSTRUMENTS DESIGNED TO ASSESS ALCOHOL MISUSE DURING PREGNANCY

According to Bradley et al. (1998), lifetime rates of alcohol abuse and dependence in women seen by primary care physicians range from 23% to 25%. Although women are more susceptible to medical complications from drinking, especially if pregnant, they are less likely to be identified as having alcohol-related problems by healthcare providers (Bradley et al., 1998). Screening for women engaged in alcohol misuse during pregnancy is important due to the long-lasting impact of alcohol on children born to alcohol-misusing mothers.

Most existing alcohol screens were constructed based on male drinking patterns. Biological gender differences contribute to different effects of alcohol consumption, and knowledge on the effects of alcohol on the fetus contributes to different styles of drinking during pregnancy. Therefore, the adequacy of the currently available screens for use with pregnant women is questionable. One solution to accommodate these differences is to establish specific cutoff scores for pregnant women when using existing screens.

Because many women alter their alcohol consumption during pregnancy and deny or minimize the level of use, inquiries about alcohol use prior to pregnancy may produce more accurate information. This supposition is supported by the American College of Obstetricians and Gynecologists (ACOG) whose *Antepartum Record* (1989) presented the need for different screening methods for pregnant women. The movement to develop alcohol screening instruments for risky drinking by pregnant women has grown due to these inadequacies in the existing screening instruments. To date, the literature features two such screens: the T-ACE and the TWEAK. The following section will briefly address each.

T-ACE

The T-ACE was the first validated alcohol-risk screening instrument developed specifically for pregnant women. According to Chang (2001), the four-question T-ACE was developed based on the premise that women are less defensive when asked about tolerance to alcohol, rather than about the amount of alcohol consumed.

The T-ACE can be self-administered or administered by a counselor (Chang, 2001). The T-ACE includes one question each on tolerance (T), annoyance (A), efforts to cut down (C), and an eye-opener drink (E). The T-ACE can be administered in 1 minute and is scored on a 5-point scale by assigning 2 points for a positive "T," defined as a woman's self-report of needing more than 2 drinks to feel "high." The A, C, and E questions receive 1 point for affirmative answers. Two or more points indicate possible risk drinking during pregnancy (Chang, 2001). A Portuguese version is available with initial internal consistency ratings of .3–.56 (Moraes, Viellas, & Reichenheim, 2005).

Using cutoff points of 1, 2, and 3, T-ACE sensitivity ratings of .83, .70, and .45, and specificity estimates of .75, .85, and .97, were reported by Russell et al. (1994) among a sample of African-American women. In a diverse ethnic population, the sensitivity and specificity for risk drinking is reported as .92 and .38. When risk drinking was specified as less than 2 points, T-ACE sensitivity decreased to .74 and specificity increased to .71.

The T-ACE is available at the following website:

pubs.niaaa.nih.gov/publications/arh25-3/204-209.htm

TWEAK

The TWEAK is a 5-item instrument developed from questions from the MAST, CAGE, and T-ACE (Cherpitel, 1999). While not developed specifically to screen risk drinking in pregnant women, the TWEAK has been used almost exclusively for this purpose. The TWEAK includes one question each on Tolerance (from the T-ACE), concern (Worry) of friends and family (from the MAST), an eye-opener drink (from the CAGE), amnesia (from the MAST), and efforts to cut down (from the CAGE). The TWEAK is scored on a 7-point scale. A woman who reports consuming more than five drinks without falling asleep or passing out is awarded 2 points on the Tolerance question, as does a positive response to the Worry question. Affirmative answers to the last three questions (E, A, and K) receive 1 point each (Chang, 2001). TWEAK is also available in Portuguese (Moraes et al., 2005) with a reported internal consistency of .51 to .7. The TWEAK can be self-administered or administered by a counselor (Russell et al., 1994).

Russell et al. (1994), using cutoff points of 1, 2, and 3, reported sensitivity estimates of .87, .79, and .59, and specificity ratings of .72, .83, and .94 in a sample of African-American women. Russell et al. (1994) also reported that the TWEAK is most sensitive in screening risk drinking prior to the 15th week of pregnancy, with an overall reported sensitivity and specificity of .78 and .84, respectively, during pregnancy. At a cutoff point of 3, Cherpitel (1999) reported that the TWEAK demonstrated higher sensitivity for males and higher specificity for females. The TWEAK's specificity and sensitivity rates were best for African Americans followed by European Americans, then Hispanic Americans. Cherpitel (1999) further concluded that the TWEAK is best used in emergency and primary care service settings. Bush et al. (1998) reported low sensitivity but excellent specificity for screening alcohol abuse or dependence and for hazardous drinking. Bradley et al. (1998) reviewed the literature on alcohol screening instruments for women and concluded that the TWEAK was the optimal instrument for identifying alcohol dependence in women. Bush et al. (2003) conducted a study that resulted in findings of relatively low sensitivities (.62 and .44) but adequate specificities (.86 and .89) from a sample of 393 women. This supports the findings by Bush et al. (1998). Similarly, low sensitivities (.62 and .44) but adequate specificities (.86 and .89) at a cut point (≥1) was reported by Kristen et al. (2003).

Further information on the TWEAK, including a copy of the instrument, is available at the following website:

pubs.niaaa.nih.gov/publications/AssessingAlcohol/InstrumentPDFs/74_TWEAK.pdf

The following paragraph continues the case example presented at the beginning of this chapter. Pedro and the counselor met for approximately 2 hours, during which time he completed the MAST, SASSI-3, and the counselor-administered ASI. Pedro's responses to the MAST produced a score of 12. The SASSI-3 classified Pedro as likely substance dependent based on his elevated FVA scale score. The results of the ASI were consistent with the MAST and SASSI-3, but further suggested that Pedro receive a referral for a dual-diagnosis assessment to evaluate for additional psychological sequelae—post-traumatic stress disorder (PTSD) in particular. Pedro's counselor concluded that his presenting features supported the following DSM-IV-TR diagnoses:

303.90 (F10.20) Alcohol Use Disorder, Severe

Pedro was advised of the counselor's diagnosis and treatment recommendations. He decided to accept the recommendations to schedule an intake interview with the PTSD department and to place himself on the waiting list for inpatient treatment for alcohol use disorder. However, he felt it would be too embarrassing for him to attend AA meetings in his community.

Now that you have read through this chapter and learned about the cases of Pedro and Sara, think of the case of Olivia, the teenager who has begun to drink, drug, and exhibit inappropriate behavior. What assessment instruments would you use to support your clinical judgment? How would these instruments help you share your findings with both Olivia and her parents? Here are our thoughts for your consideration. Sara met with her assessing counselor for approximately 2 hours to complete a full diagnostic assessment. At the conclusion of the assessment, the counselor diagnosed Sara with Opioid Use Disorder, Severe. Due to the frequency and intensity of Sara's drug use, as well as her experience of multiple withdrawal symptoms, the counselor recommended that Sara promptly enter a medical detoxification program, to be followed by inpatient treatment. The counselor shared these recommendations with Sara, who was initially ambivalent about engaging in a residential level of care. However, after processing the treatment recommendations with her family, she agreed with the assessing counselor and reported to the treatment center to begin her detoxification and treatment program.

Summary and Some Final Notations

Many standardized instruments are available to aid the diagnosis of substance use disorders. The benefits of using standardized assessment instruments include allowing clinicians to compare clients against a normative group, ensuring objectivity, the opportunity to counteract the confirmation bias mind-set, and the opportunity to use objective data in clinical treatment planning and implementing of specific treatment interventions. For clarity, the benefits and limitations of the instruments discussed here are presented in Table 6.2.

TABLE 6.2 Author's Rating of Abuse Screening and Assessment Instruments

Instrument	Strengths	Limitations
ASI		Requires training. Time-consuming
AUDIT	Adequate sensitivity and specificity. Shorter versions available for quick screens	
AUI		Time-consuming
CAGE	Face valid. Cost- and time-efficient. Adequate sensitivity and specificity	Not suitable for clients who are defensive about their use
MAST	Face valid. Cost- and time-efficient	Not suitable for clients who are defensive about their use
MCMI	Adequate reliability	Requires training. Not suitable for substance abuse screening only. Costs money. Time-consuming
MMPI	Adequate reliability and validity	Requires training. Not suitable for substance abuse screening only. Costs money. Time-consuming
PAI	Adequate reliability and validity	Requires training. Not suitable for substance abuse screening only. Costs money. Time-consuming
SASSI-3	Adequate reliability and validity. Screening for adults. Includes face valid section and subtle screening for defensiveness	Requires training. Costs money
SASSI-2A	Screening for adolescents	Requires training. Costs money
T-ACE	Normed for pregnant clients. Adequate sensitivity and specificity	
TWEAK	Normed for pregnant clients. Adequate sensitivity and specificity	

Standardized assessment instruments are constructed using the logically derived method, criterion keying method, or a combination of the two. When choosing an instrument, it is important to examine the five characteristics of a good screen (i.e., sensitivity, specificity, reliability, validity, and cost-efficiency) as defined by Piazza (2002).

Screening instruments discussed in this chapter can be broadly categorized into two sections: stand-alone substance abuse screening instruments (e.g., ASI, AUI, AUDIT, CAGE, MAST, SASSI-A2, SASSI-3, T-ACE, TWEAK) and substance abuse scales found on personality assessment instruments (e.g., MMPI-2, MCMI, and PAI). Some of the stand-alone screens have different versions for special populations. For instance, MAST has a geriatric version and SASSI has an adolescent version. AUDIT and MAST have shorter versions (e.g., AUDIT C, FAST, and B-MAST) that could be administered when limited time is available for screening clients. TWEAK and T-ACE are specially used for screening for substance abuse disorders in pregnant women.

With the exception of the personality assessment instruments, most of these screening instruments could be administered and scored by clinicians without extensive training on the instrument. It is the recommendation of the authors that some of these instruments be included in the screening and assessment process of substance abuse disorders, along with clinical judgment, to provide clients with objective and accurate diagnosis.

MyCounselingLab

Visit the MyCounselingLab site for *Foundations of Addictions Counseling,* Third Edition to enhance your understanding of concepts. You'll have the opportunity to practice your skills through video- and case-based exercises. You will find sets of questions to help you prepare for your certification exam with *Licensure Quizzes.* There is also a Video Library that provides taped counseling sessions, ethical scenarios, and interviews with helpers and clients.

Useful Websites

The following websites provide additional information relating to the chapter topics:

The Addiction Research Institute of the Center for Social Work Research at the University of Texas at Austin
www.utexas.edu/research/cswr/nida/instrumentListing.html

National Institute on Alcohol Abuse and Alcoholism
www.niaaa.nih.gov/

References

Aalto, M., Alho, H., Halme, J. T., & Seppa, K. (2010). The Alcohol Use Disorders Identification Test (AUDIT) and its derivatives in screening for heavy drinking among the elderly. *International Journal of Geriatric Psychiatry, 26,* 881–885.

Adger, H., & Werner, M. J. (1994). The pediatrician. *Alcohol Health & Research World, 18,* 121–126.

Alexander, T., DiNitto, D., & Tidblom, I. (2005). Screening for alcohol and other drug use problems among the deaf. *Alcoholism Treatment Quarterly, 23,* 63–78.

Altman, D. G., & Bland, J. M. (1994). Diagnostic tests 1: Sensitivity & specificity. *British Medical Journal, 308,* 1552.

American College of Obstetricians and Gynecologists. (1989). *ACOG Antepartum Record.* Washington, DC: Author.

American Psychiatric Association. (2013). *Diagnostic and statistical manual* (5th ed.). Washington, DC: Author.

Babor, T. F., Higgins-Biddle, J. C., Saunders, J. B., & Monteiro, M. G. (2001). *The Alcohol Use Disorders Identification Test: Guidelines for use in primary care* (2nd ed.). Geneva, Switzerland: World Health Organization.

Barrick, M. R., & Mount, M. K. (1996). Effects of impression management and self-deception on the predictive validity of personality constructs. *Journal of Applied Psychology, 81,* 261–272.

Baschloo, L., Vogelzangs, N., Smit, J. H., Van Den Brink, W., Veltman, D. J., Beekman, A., & Pennix, B. (2010). The performance of the Alcohol Use Disorders Identification Test (AUDIT) in detecting alcohol abuse and dependence in a population of depressed or anxious persons. *Journal of Affective Disorders, 126,* 441–446.

Bauman, S., Merta, R., & Steiner, R. (1999). Further validation of the adolescent form of the SASSI. *Journal of Child and Adolescent Substance Abuse, 9,* 51–71.

Blow, F. C., Brower, K. J., Schulenberg, J. E., Demo-Dananberg, L. M., Young, J. P., & Beresford, T. P. (1992). The Michigan Alcoholism Screening Test–Geriatric Version (MAST-G): A new elderly-specific screening instrument. *Alcoholism: Clinical and Experimental Research, 16,* 372.

Boone, D. (1998). Internal consistency reliability of the Personality Assessment Inventory with psychiatric inpatients. *Journal of Clinical Psychology, 54,* 839–843.

Bradley, K. A., Boyd-Wickizer, J., Powell, S. H., & Burman, M. L. (1998). Alcohol screening questionnaires in women: A critical review. *Journal of the American Medical Association, 280,* 166–171.

Bradley, K. A., Bush, K. R., Epler, A. J., Dobie, D. J., Davis, T. M., Sporleder, J. L., . . . , Kivlahan, D. R. (2003). Two brief alcohol-screening tests from the alcohol use disorders identification test (AUDIT). *Archives of Internal Medicine, 163,* 821–829.

Brodey, B. B., Rosen, C. S., Brodey, I. S., Sheetz, B. G., Steinfeld, R. R., & Gastfriend, D. (2004). Validation of the Addiction Severity Index (ASI) for Internet and automated telephone self-report administration. *Journal of Substance Abuse Treatment, 26,* 253–259.

Brodey, B. B., Rosen, C. S., Winters, K. C., Brodey, I. S., Sheetz, B. G., Steinfeld, R. R., . . . , Kaminer, Y. (2005). Validation of the Teen-Addiction Severity Index (T-ASI) for Internet & automated telephone self-report administration. *Psychology of Addictive Behavior, 19,* 54–61.

Burck, A. M., Laux, J. M., Harper, H., & Ritchie, M. (2010). Detecting faking good and bad with the Substance Abuse Subtle Screening Inventory—3 in a college student sample. *Journal of College Counseling, 12,* 63–72.

Bush, K. R., Kivlahan, D. R., McDonell, M. B., Fihn, S. D., & Bradley, K. A. (1998). The AUDIT alcohol consumption questions (AUDIT-C): An effective brief screening test for problem drinking. *Archives of Internal Medicine, 158,* 1789–1795.

Butcher, J. N., Dahlstrom, W. G., Graham, J. R., Tellegen, A., & Kaemmer, B. (1989). *Minnesota Multiphasic Personality Inventory—2 (MMPI-2): Manual for administration, scoring, and interpretation, revised.* Minneapolis, MN: University of Minnesota Press.

Butler, S. F., Budman, S. H., Goldman, R. J., Newman, F. L., Beckley, K. E., Trottier, D., & Cacciola, J. S. (2001). Initial validation of a computer-administered Addiction Severity Index: The ASI-MV. *Psychology of Addictive Behaviors, 15,* 4–12.

Cacciola, J. S., Alterman, A. I., Habing, B., & McLellan, A. (2011). Recent status scores for version 6 of the Addiction Severity Index (ASI-6). *Addiction, 106*(9), 1588–1602. doi:10.1111/j.1360-0443.2011.03482.x

Cacciola, J. S., Alterman, A. I., McLellan, A., Lin, Y., & Lynch, K. G. (2007). Initial evidence for the reliability and validity of a "Lite" version of the Addiction Severity Index. *Drug & Alcohol Dependence, 87*(2/3), 297–302. doi:10.1016/j.drugalcdep.2006.09.002

Calsyn, D., Saxon, A., & Daisy, F. (1990). Validity of the MCMI Drug Abuse Scale with drug abusing and psychiatric samples. *Journal of Clinical Psychology, 46,* 244–246.

Casares-López, M., Díaz-Mesa, E., García-Portilla, P., Sáiz, P., Bobes-Bascarán, M., Fonseca-Pedrero, E., . . . , Bobes, J. (2011). Sixth version of the Addiction Severity Index: Assessing sensitivity to therapeutic change and retention predictors. *International Journal of Clinical Health & Psychology, 11*(3), 495–508.

Celio, M., Vetter-O'Hagen, C. S., Lisman, S. A., Johansen, Gerard, J. E., & Spear, L. P. (2011). Integrating field methodology and web-based data collection to assess the reliability of the Alcohol Use Disorders Identification Test (AUDIT). *Drug and Alcohol Dependence, 119,* 142–144.

Chang, G. (2001). Alcohol-screening instruments for pregnant women. *Alcohol Research and Health, 25,* 204–209.

Chang, I., Lapham, S. C., & Wanberg, K. W. (2001). Alcohol Use Inventory: Screening and assessment of first-time driving-while-impaired offenders. I. Reliability and profiles. *Alcohol and Alcoholism, 36,* 112–121.

Cherpitel, C. J. (1999). Screening for alcohol problems in the U.S. general population: A comparison of the CAGE and TWEAK by gender, ethnicity, and service utilization. *Journal of Studies on Alcohol, 60,* 705–711.

Clements, R., & Heintz, J. M. (2002). Diagnostic accuracy and factor structure of the AAS and APS scales of the MMPI-2. *Journal of Personality Assessment, 79,* 564–582.

Cohen, R. J., Montague, P., Nathanson, L. S., & Swerdlik, M. E. (1988). *Psychological testing: An introduction to tests and measurements.* Mountain View, CA: Mayfield.

Couwenbergh, C., Van Der Gaag, R., Koeter, M., De Ruiter, C., & Van Den Brink, W. (2009). Screening of substance abuse among adolescents validity of CAGE-AID in youth mental health care. *Substance Use and Misuse, 44,* 823–834.

Craig, R. J. (2005). Assessing contemporary substance abusers with the MMPI Mac Andrews Alcoholism Scale: A review. *Substance Use & Misuse, 40,* 427–450.

Creager, C. (1989). SASSI test breaks through denial. *Professional Counselor, 4,* 65.

Crews, T. M., & Sher, K. J. (1992). Using adapted short MASTs for assessing parental alcoholism: Reliability and validity. *Alcoholism: Clinical and Experimental Research, 16,* 576–584.

Denis, C. M., Cacciola, J. S., & Alterman, A. I. (2013). Addiction Severity Index (ASI) summary scores: Comparison of the Recent Status Scores of the ASI-6 and the Composite Scores of the ASI-5. *Journal of Substance Abuse Treatment, 45*(5), 444–450. doi:10.1016/j.jsat.2013.06.003

Díaz, R., Castro-Fornieles, J., Serrano, L., González, L., Calvo, R., Goti, J., & . . . Gual, A. (2008). Clinical and research utility of Spanish Teen-Addiction Severity Index (T-ASI). *Addictive Behaviors, 33*(1), 188–195. doi:10.1016/j.addbeh.2007.06.002

Durbeej, N., Berman, A. H., Gumpert, C. H., Palmstierna, T., Kristiansson, M., & Alm, C. (2010). Validation of Alcohol Use Disorders Identification Test and Drug Use Disorders Identification Test in a Swedish sample of suspected offenders with signs of mental problems: Results from the mental disorder, substance abuse and crime study. *Journal of Substance Abuse Treatment, 39,* 364–377.

Evren, C., Durkaya, M., Evren, B., Dalbudak, E., & Cetin, R. (2012). Relation of relapse with impulsivity, novelty seeking and craving in male alcohol-dependent inpatients. *Drug and Alcohol Review, 31,* 81–90.

Ewing, J. A. (1984). Detecting alcoholism: The CAGE questionnaire. *Journal of the American Medical Association, 252,* 1905–1907.

Fals-Stewart, W. (1996). The ability of individuals with psychoactive substance use disorders to escape detection by the Personality Assessment Inventory. *Psychological Assessment, 8,* 60–68.

Feldstein, S. W., & Miller, W. R. (2007). Does subtle screening for substance abuse work? A review of the Substance Abuse Subtle Screening Inventory (SASSI). *Addiction, 102,* 41–50.

Fielling, D. A., Reid, C. M., & O'Connor, P. G. (2000). Screening for alcohol problems in primary care: A systematic review. *Archives of Internal Medicine, 160,* 1977–1989.

Fleming, M. F. (1993). Screening and brief invention for alcohol disorders. *Journal of Family Practice, 37,* 231–234.

Friedrich, W. N., & Loftsgard, S. O. (1978). A comparison of the MacAndrew Alcoholism Scale and the Michigan Alcoholism Screening Test in a sample of problem drinkers. *Journal of Studies on Alcohol, 39,* 1940–1944.

Geneste, J., Pereira, B., Arnaud, B., Christol, N., Liotier, J., Blanc, O., Teissedre, F., . . . , Brousse, G. (2012). CAGE, RAPS4, RAPS4-QF and AUDIT screening tests for men and women admitted for acute alcohol intoxication to an emergency department: Are standard thresholds appropriate? *Alcohol and Alcoholism, 47,* 273–281.

Graham, J. R. (2000). *MMPI-2: Assessing personality and psychopathology* (3rd ed.). New York, NY: Oxford University Press.

Gray, B. T. (2001). A factor analytic study of the Substance Abuse Subtle Screening Inventory (SASSI). *Educational and Psychological Measurement, 61,* 102–118.

Greene, R. L., Weed, N. C., Butcher, J. N., Arredondo, R., & Davis, H. G. (1992). A cross-validation of MMPI-2 substance abuse scales. *Journal of Personality Assessment, 58,* 405–410.

Groth-Marnat, G. (2009). *Handbook of psychological assessment* (5th ed.). Hoboken, NJ: John Wiley & Sons.

Hallinan, P., McGilloway S., Dempster, M., & Donnelly, M. (2011). Factor structure and validity of the Alcohol Use Disorders Identification Test (AUDIT) in a sample of mentally disordered offenders. *The Journal of Forensic Psychiatry & Psychology, 22,* 586–602.

Hedlund, J., & Vieweg, B. (1984). The Michigan Alcoholism Screening Test (MAST): A comprehensive review. *Journal of Operational Psychiatry, 15,* 55–64.

Hesse, M., Guldager, S., & Holm Linneberg, I. (2012). Convergent validity of MCMI-III clinical syndrome scales. *British Journal of Clinical Psychology, 51*(2), 172–184. doi:10.1111/j.2044-8260.2011.02019.x

Hodgson, R. J., John, B., Abbasi, T., Hodgson, R. C., Waller, S., Thom, B., & Newcombe, R. G. (2003). Fast screening for alcohol misuse. *Addictive Behaviors, 28,* 1453–1463.

Hoffman, H., Loper, R. G., & Kammeier, M. L. (1974). Identifying future alcoholics with MMPI alcoholism scores. *Quarterly Journal of Studies on Alcohol, 35,* 490–498.

Horn, J., Wanberg, K. W., & Foster, M. (1990). *Guide to the Alcohol Use Inventory (AUI).* Minneapolis, MN: National Computer Systems, Inc.

Horrigan, T. J., Piazza, N. J., & Weinstein, L. (1996). The Substance Abuse Subtle Screening Inventory is more cost effective and has better selectivity than urine toxicology for the detection of substance abuse in pregnancy. *Journal of Perinatology, 16,* 326–330.

Jacobson, G. R. (1983). Detection, assessment and diagnosis of alcoholism: Current techniques. In M. Galenter (Ed.), *Recent developments in alcoholism* (pp. 377–413). New York, NY: Plenum Press.

Johnson-Greene, D., McCaul, M. E., & Roger, P. (2009). Screening for hazardous drinking using the Michigan Alcohol Screening Test—Geriatric Version (MAST-G) in elderly persons with acute cerebrovascular accidents. *Alcoholism: Clinical and Experimental Research, 33,* 1555–1561.

Juhnke, G. A., Vacc, N. A., Curtis, R. C., Coll, K. M., & Paredes, D. M. (2003). Assessment instruments used by addictions counselors. *Journal of Addictions and Offender Counseling, 23,* 66–72.

Kaminer, Y. (2008). The Teen Addiction Severity Index around the globe: The Tower of Babel revisited. *Substance Abuse, 29*(3), 89–94. doi:10.1080/08897070802219230

Kaminer, Y., Bukstein, O. G., & Tarter, R. L. (1991). The Teen-Addiction Severity Index: Rationale and reliability. *International Journal of Addiction, 26,* 250–254.

Kawada, T., Inagaki, H., & Kuratomi, Y. (2011). The Alcohol Use Disorders Identification Test: Reliability study of the Japanese version. *Alcohol, 45,* 205–207.

Kessler, F., Cacciola, J., Alterman, A., Faller, S., Souza-Formigoni, M., Cruz, M., & . . . Pechansky, F. (2012). Psychometric properties of the sixth version of the Addiction Severity Index (ASI-6) in Brazil. *Revista Brasileira De Psiquiatria, 34*(1), 24–33.

Kim, J. W., Lee, B. C., Lee, D. Y., Seo, C. H., Kim, S., Kang, T., & Choi, I. (2012). The 5-item Alcohol Use Disorder Identification Test (AUDIT): An effective brief screening test for problem drinking, alcohol use disorder and dependence. *Alcohol and Alcoholism, 48,* 68–73.

Kitchens, J. M. (1994). Does this patient have an alcohol problem? *Journal of the American Medical Association, 272*, 1782–1787.

Krenz, S., Dieckmann, S., Favrat, B., Spagnoli, J., Leutwyler, J., Schnyder, C., . . . , Besson, J. (2004). French version of the Addiction Severity Index (5th Edition): Validity and reliability among Swiss opiate-dependent patients. *European Addiction Research, 10*(4), 173–179. doi:10.1159/000079839

Kristen, R. B., Daniel, R. K., Tania, M. D., Dorcas, J. D., Jennifer, L. S., Amee, J. E., . . . , Katharine, A. B. (2003). The TWEAK is weak for alcohol screening among female Veterans Affairs outpatients. *Alcoholism: Clinical & Experimental Research, 27*, 1971–1978.

Laux, J. M., Newman, I., & Brown, R. (2004). The Michigan Alcoholism Screening Test (MAST): A psychometric investigation. *Measurement and Evaluation in Counseling and Development, 36*, 209–225.

Laux, J. M., Perera-Diltz, D., Smirnoff, J., & Salyers, K. M. (2005). The SASSI-3 Face-Valid Other Drug Scale: A psychometric investigation. *Journal of Addictions and Offender Counseling, 26*, 15–23.

Laux, J., Piazza, N. J., Salyers, K. M., & Roseman, C. (2012). The Substance Abuse Subtle Screening Inventory—3 and stages of change: A screening validity study. *Journal of Addiction & Offender Counseling, 33*, 82–92.

Laux, J. M., Salyers, K. M., & Kotova, E. (2005). A psychometric evaluation of the SASSI-3 in a college sample. *Journal of College Counseling, 8*, 41–51.

Lazowski, L. E., Miller, F. G., Boye, M. W., & Miller, G. A. (1998). Efficacy of the Substance Abuse Subtle Screening Inventory-3 (SASSI-3) in identifying substance dependence disorders in clinical settings. *Journal of Personality Assessment, 71*, 114–128.

Leonhard, C., Mulvey, K., Gastfriend, D. R., & Shwartz, M. (2000). Addiction Severity Index: A field study of internal consistency and validity. *Journal of Substance Abuse Treatment, 18*, 129–135.

Li, Q., Babor, T.F., Hao, W., & Chen, X. (2011). The Chinese translation of Alcohol Use Disorder Identification Test (AUDIT) in China: A systematic review. *Alcohol and Alcoholism, 46*, 416–423.

MacAndrew, C. (1965). The differentiation of male alcoholic outpatients from nonalcoholic psychiatric outpatients by means of the MMPI. *Quarterly Journal of the Study of Alcohol, 26*, 238–246.

Mäkelä, K. (2004). Studies of the reliability and validity of the Addiction Severity Index. *Addiction, 99*, 411–418.

Marsh, D. T., Stile, S. A., Stoughton, N. L., & Trout-Landen, B. L. (1988). Psychopathology of opiate addiction: Comparative data from the MMPI and MCMI. *American Journal of Drug and Alcohol Abuse, 14*, 17–27.

Martin, C. S., Liepman, M. R., & Young, C. M. (1990). The Michigan Alcoholism Screening Test: False positives in a college student population. *Alcoholism: Clinical and Experimental Research, 14*, 853–855.

McLellan, A. T., Cacciola, J. C., Alterman, A. I., Rikoon, S. H., & Carise, D. (2006). The Addiction Severity Index at 25: Origins, contributions and transitions. *The American Journal on Addictions, 15*, 113–124.

McLellan, A. T., Cacciola, J. S., Alterman, A. I., Stenius, K., Butler, S. F., Greenfield, T. K., et al. (2004). Commentaries on Mäkelä. The ASI as a still developing instrument: Response to Mäkelä. *Addiction, 99*, 411–418.

McLellan, A. T., Luborsky, L., O'Brien, C. P., & Woody, G. E. (1980). An improved diagnostic instrument for substance abuse patients, The Addiction Severity Index. *Journal of Nervous and Mental Diseases, 168*, 26–33.

Miller, F. G., & Lazowski, L. E. (2001). *The Adolescent SASSI-A2 manual: Identifying substance user disorders.* Springville, IN: The SASSI Institute.

Miller, G. A. (1985). *The Substance Abuse Subtle Screening Inventory (SASSI) manual.* Springville, IN: The SASSI Institute.

Miller, G. A. (1999). *The SASSI Manual: Substance Abuse Measures* (2nd ed.). Springville, IN: The SASSI Institute.

Miller, G. A., Roberts, J., Brooks, M. K., & Lazowski, L. E. (1997). *SASSI-3 user's guide.* Bloomington, IN: Baugh Enterprises.

Millon, T., Davis, R., & Millon, C. (1997). *Millon Clinical Multiaxial Inventory-III: MCMI-III Manual* (2nd ed.). Minneapolis, MN: NCS Pearson, Inc.

Moos, R. H., Finney, J. W., Ferderman, E. B., & Suchinsky, R. (2000). Specialty mental health care improves patients' outcomes: Findings from nationwide program to monitor the quality of care for patients with substance use disorders. *Journal of Studies on Alcohol, 61*, 704–713.

Moraes, C. L., Viellas, E. F., & Reichenheim, M. E. (2005). Assessing alcohol misuse during pregnancy: Evaluating psychometric properties of the CAGE, T-ACE and TWEAK in a Brazilian setting. *Journal of Studies on Alcohol, 66*, 165–173.

Morey, L. C. (1991). *Personality Assessment Inventory—Professional Manual.* Odessa, FL: Psychological Assessment Resources, Inc.

Moussas, G., Dadouti, G., Douzenis, A., Poulis, E., Tzelembis, A., Bratis, D., Christodoulou, C., & Lykouras, L. (2009). The Alcohol Use Disorders Identification Test (AUDIT): Reliability and validity of the Greek version. *Annals of General Psychiatry, 8*, 1–5.

Although MI began as an approach to use when working with addiction, counselors, medical professionals, social workers, and other helping professionals now use it when working with a variety of problems, such as eating disorders, community health issues, couples counseling, criminal justice situations, HIV prevention, medication compliance, sexual health, and college binge drinking (Dean, Touyz, Rieger, & Thornton, 2008; Gaume et al., 2013; Mason, 2009).

MI can be used in conjunction with a number of different counseling approaches and is not thought to be an approach to use on its own. It is not a theory of counseling, but a skill set used to engage people in counseling and the change process. Additionally, MI techniques are suitable for use through the entirety of the change process. Most important is the recognition that MI is more than merely a set of techniques. Instead, it should be conceptualized as a way of interpersonally relating to clients using collaboration, evocation, and autonomy (Miller & Rollnick, 2002).

A number of variables are considered to be important in the effective use of motivational interviewing. The counselor's individual style and use of techniques are important, as are the client's engagement, levels of resistance, intention, and experience of incongruence and discrepancy (Apodaca & Longabaugh, 2009). Clients whose counselors use MI are more likely to engage in change talk and commitment talk throughout the therapeutic process, which is predictive of better treatment outcomes (Apodaca & Longabaugh, 2009; Gaume et al., 2013).

Change talk refers to statements or affective communications from the client that indicate a desire to make a change. A counselor's job is to detect change talk when it occurs and follow through on that change talk in a positive, reinforcing manner. Counselors use *OARS* to elicit change talk from clients. The "OARS" of MI are Open-Ended Questions, Affirmations, Reflective Listening, and Summaries. Counselors are intentional about what they choose to summarize and reflect upon and are careful to ensure the change talk stemmed from the client. Coercion and pressure from the counselor should be avoided at all times.

The Primary Principles of Motivational Interviewing

There are four pillars that guide the philosophy and subsequent counseling actions of MI. These pillars inform counselors about how to relate to and act with clients engaged in any facet of the change process. The first pillar is *Expressing Empathy*. Empathy is the act of communicating to a client your understanding of his or her point of view with regard to the client's feelings, life experiences, and behaviors (Egan, 2013; Elliot, Bohart, Watson, & Greenberg, 2011). According to the principles of MI, Expressing Empathy normalizes ambivalence and demonstrates that the counselor unconditionally accepts the client.

The second pillar is *Developing Discrepancy*. This activity is directive in nature and requires active listening and reflecting from the counselor. When a client is able to experience an internal discrepancy between his or her current behaviors and his or her values, beliefs, and goals, the change process can begin. This is due in large part to the underlying principle of *cognitive dissonance*. Simply stated, when there is a discrepancy between an individual's beliefs and behaviors, the individual will seek to reduce that inconsistency (Festinger, 1957). When a client reveals incongruence between beliefs (or attitudes) and behaviors, the counselor can help amplify the incongruency, thus highlighting ambivalence. Ambivalence is considered to be the catalyst to change, with the assumption that the client will seek to reduce the stress caused by cognitive dissonance. Motivational interviewers hope to help clients find consistency by engaging in behaviors that match their cognitive beliefs about how their life should be.

The third pillar is *Rolling with Resistance*. This means that a counselor must not argue for change; instead, the counselor will view resistance as a signal that the session should go in a different direction. The counselor will allow the resistance to exist and engage in methods that best address resistance (discussed later in the chapter).

The fourth and final principle of MI is to *Support Self-Efficacy*. It is crucial for clients to believe they have personal choice and control in changing their behavior. The client's idea that change is possible and that the counselor believes in his or her ability to change will increase self-efficacy.

These four pillars highlight the collaborative nature of the helping process, in which the client makes changes in his or her life without being coerced by external factors. The client is instead internally motivated, which creates the perception of personal choice and is more likely to result in change.

Counselors should keep in mind the following guiding clinical principles when utilizing MI. First, counselors who use MI effectively increase change talk and decrease levels of client resistance more than counselors who use a confrontational or directive approach. Next, resistance talk (when clients argue against change) is inversely related to the degree of subsequent behavior change. Finally, the extent to which clients are able to verbalize commitment to change via change talk throughout the process is related to the degree of subsequent behavior change (Hettema, Steele, & Miller, 2005).

MOTIVATIONAL INTERVIEWING TECHNIQUES: EARLY IN THE CHANGE PROCESS

Five Techniques to Use Early and Often

The key book on MI (Miller & Rollnick, 2012) provides descriptors of five early methods of motivation enhancement that counselors can use beginning from initial client contact and throughout all subsequent sessions. These five methods build a foundation for the tone of therapeutic work and immediately engage the client in enhancing his or her sense of importance, responsibility, and ownership of the treatment process. Several of these techniques are learned as counselors develop initial counseling skills: *asking open-ended questions, listening reflectively,* directly *affirming* the client's personhood and efforts, and *summarizing* the client's verbal expressions and exploration. The final method, *eliciting change talk,* is especially enhanced with counselors using MI.

ASKING OPEN-ENDED QUESTIONS Counselors using MI ask *open-ended questions* and try to avoid closed questions. Open-ended questions are inquiries that cannot be answered with a one-word response such as "yes" and "no," but instead require the client to provide more lengthy and thoughtful answers. The counselor may ask a client to "tell me about the times you use alcohol to relax" as opposed to asking, "Do you ever use alcohol to relax?" Open-ended questions allow the client to explore aloud while the counselor provides encouragement and support.

In the early stages of MI, it is the counselor's task to gather information and hear the client's goals. Questions designed to elicit this information will help build trust, develop rapport, and increase collaboration and consonance in the therapeutic relationship. Ideally, the counselor will ask an open-ended question and allow the client to speak uninhibited, while the counselor responds with affirmations and encouragement so that the client may continue the verbal exploration. Counselors are cautioned against engaging in a back-and-forth question-and-answer session that may inhibit client exploration of ambivalence and intention. Counselors should also avoid closed questions that may be answered with a brief word or phrase as they provide limited options for the client, thus inhibiting exploration and sharing.

Case Study. Jane is working with a counselor named Marsha. Marsha intends to gather additional information from Jane while conveying an open and accepting stance. Marsha says to Jane, "Jane, tell me about alcohol's usefulness to you as you go about your day." Jane describes how the wine consumption helps her decompress and unwind after a hard day at work, and describes in great detail how the ritual of opening the bottle, pouring the glass, and sitting down to take the first sip make her feel. Jane says, "I know that no matter what happens, my work day ends with getting home, sitting down with a nice glass of wine, and being able to take a deep breath before I take that first sip. This is what gets me through!" Marsha responds with an empathic nod and the next prompt, "Tell me more about what happens next, after that first sip."

REFLECTIVE LISTENING Counselors using MI understand the importance of *reflective listening*, as true reflective listening will help them provide answers that help move the client's change process along. Reflective listening is simply the act of repeating back to the client the content of his or her words in an unbiased, nonjudgmental manner. For example, if a client says, "I think it's fine to use marijuana. I have no idea why I got arrested for it!," the counselor may respond with, "You're confused about why you were arrested when you feel you did nothing wrong."

Miller and Rollnick (2012) emphasize the importance of the counselor's response as crucial to the progress of the client's therapeutic work. Counselors who do not use reflective listening may respond in a manner that blocks the client's progress rather than demonstrating true listening and support. Imagine if, in the prior example, the counselor responded with, "How could you not know why you were arrested? Marijuana's illegal!" The client's exploration process would likely be stifled and the therapeutic relationship strained. This is an example of a "block" in the change process.

Counselors are cautioned against engaging in any blocking behaviors. Some of these blocks include shaming, labeling, commanding, directing, threatening, warning, persuading with logic, lecturing, disagreeing, judging, criticizing, analyzing, consoling, sympathizing, questioning (probing), withdrawing, or changing the subject (Miller & Rollnick, 2012). These responses are likely to be met with resistance or frustration, as the client may see them as attempts to change or reframe his thoughts and feelings. The counselor may use selective attention to decide which topics to reflect upon and which to pass over, yet it is essential that the client feel listened to and understood so that the client knows his or her feelings and goals will be honored throughout the change process.

Case Study. Jane's counselor, Marsha, has asked her to talk about whether she believes that the wine has become problematic in her life. Jane says, "Well, the biggest problem is that my family is harassing me endlessly about it. They don't understand how much it helps me, and the more they bug me about it, the more tense I get and the more I need help relaxing." Marsha reflects back to Jane, "Your family's comments about the wine drinking feels more stressful to you right now than the wine use itself. Their comments cause you tension and anxiety, and then you feel like you need the wine even more."

AFFIRMATION   It is important that a counselor support and *affirm* the client as exploration and sharing occurs. This may be done in a direct manner—for example, the counselor may say, "It seems that once you make a decision to change something, you give it your very best effort" or "That sounds like a great idea." The counselor is genuine and makes an effort to bring the client's strengths to the forefront. Affirmation is effective in enhancing the features and strengths that will assist the client greatly in his or her change process.

Case Study.   Jane continues to discuss the stress that she feels when others comment about her wine use. She says, "I don't want to be seen as someone who can't cope without wine. I've survived plenty in my life and I didn't need wine to get through it all." Her counselor Marsha states, "So, you have some resiliency factors that have gotten you through really tough times. You are a survivor and can make it through difficulty on your own."

SUMMARIZATION   Counselors using MI will make frequent use of *summary* statements. Summary statements recap what the client has spoken about and reinforce the content of what the client has shared thus far. Summaries are useful in ensuring the counselor understands the meaning of the client's exploration and lets that person know that the counselor has been paying close attention. Additionally, summaries give the client a chance to hear his or her own words reflected back, thus prompting a response that leads to further exploration.

Miller and Rollnick (2012) discuss three types of summary statements that are particularly helpful in MI. First, *collecting* summaries are short recaps designed to help the client maintain momentum. For example, the counselor who hears a client complain about the expense of cigarettes may respond with, "What are some additional reasons besides the expense of smoking that make you want to be a nonsmoker?"

Linking summaries use statements or ideas that the client came up with in the past (such as in prior therapeutic encounters) and relates those ideas to current information. These statements specifically address recurrent themes as presented in a series of sessions and are designed to highlight ambivalence. For example, a counselor might say, "You mentioned in our first session that you hate to be considered an addict, yet right now you would just prefer to stop caring about what people think of you rather than change the addiction. You don't want to be an addict yet you want to keep the addiction."

Transitional summaries are statements used to shift from one aspect of the therapeutic encounter to another. The counselor may use a transitional summary as a session wrap-up, or in shifting from one topic of focus to another, to be certain the prior topic is fully discussed before moving on. Transitional summaries highlight the therapeutic alliance and make certain to reflect an understanding of the client's exploration and wishes. Summaries are not lectures nor are they one-sided; instead, clients should be encouraged to correct or add information that they feel is important.

Case Study.   Jane has spent the majority of her session discussing how her family is pestering her about wine use and about how she doesn't believe she actually needs the wine to get by. Further, she has stated that she doesn't see a reason to stop entirely, but is open to cutting down a little to preserve her health and get her family off her back. Her counselor, Marsha, summarizes toward the end of the session by saying, "Jane, you have discussed cutting back on the wine consumption so that you can be relieved of the stress that your family's concern causes you, and so you don't have to worry so much about the impact the alcohol has on your health. At the same time, you are clear that you can make it through difficulty without the use of alcohol and you wish that others would remember that about you. Next, you'd like to start thinking about how much to cut back and how to make that happen. What else from today's session should be included in this summary?"

ELICITING CHANGE TALK Motivational interviewing is a process that helps clients discover and examine their own reasons to change or not change. Motivational interviewers help clients by using *change talk*—that is, talk designed to prompt change rather than reinforce the benefits of the status quo. Eliciting change talk involves collaboration with the client, not confrontation. The counselor's responsibility is to create a safe environment for the client so that the client can examine ambivalence. The client then decides upon a direction of change once the ambivalence has become uncomfortable enough to prompt change movement.

Several tools can be used to collaborate with clients and have them ask for change. One way is to ask open-ended questions. Another is the *Importance Ruler,* on which clients rate their ability to change their behavior on a scale from 1 to 10. Counselors then ask why the client chose that number rather than another one. The client's response helps reinforce the reasons to move toward change. The *Decisional Balance* can be used to help clients describe the positive and negative aspects of their behavior. During a Decisional Balance process, the counselor assists the client in fully exploring the pros and cons of change. A 2 by 2 table is often drawn, with four components: (1) the benefits of the status quo, (2) the costs of the status quo, (3) potential benefits of change, and (4) potential costs of change (Miller & Rollnick, 2009). The counselor should help the client fully explore all components here and elaborate on their answers. This can be done by simply asking the client to "tell me more about that" or "describe that in more detail, please."

Querying Extremes involves asking questions that allow clients to look at the consequences of not changing, or imagining what life may look like if they did decide to change. When trying to assist in facilitating "change talk," it could be useful to have them look back at life before their problem behavior began or look forward to what they want their life to look like.

Looking Back or *Looking Forward* are techniques that can lead to clients developing their own discrepancies between the past, present, and future. For example, imagine if Jane's counselor asks her to remember a time when she was able to get through the day without wine. The counselor may also ask her to consider what life would be like if she had the confidence to get through a day without a glass of wine. The counselor might say, "Jane, how would you think and feel about yourself if you had nonalcohol ways of relaxing and coping with life?" or "How do you imagine your daughter would feel about you once you've had 10 years sober?" Any of these ideas can help clients facilitate change talk, especially when the client is precontemplative or contemplative about change.

THE ROLE OF RESISTANCE IN THE CHANGE PROCESS

The change process inevitably involves some client resistance. Resistance can affect the therapeutic relationship either positively or negatively, depending on the counselor's attitude and behaviors when resistance occurs. *Dissonance* is when the counselor and client are struggling with one another rather than working together in a truly collaborative effort toward similar goals (Miller & Rollnick, 2012). On the converse, counselor and client may be working *consonantly*, meaning that counselor and client are allied toward common goals and ideals. Consonance is the relational state that motivational interviewers strive for, and interruptions to this state (in the form of resistance) must be skillfully restored for the sake of an optimal working relationship. When a client demonstrates apparent resistance, it is important that the counselor interpret that as a signal of strain in the relationship (dissonance) rather than a pathology or attitudinal problem within the client.

The Many Forms of Resistance

Resistance behaviors may be divided into four process categories (Miller & Rollnick, 2012). One category, *arguing*, is when the client may appear hostile and argumentative, challenging the accuracy of the helper's statements and discounting the counselor's authority or credentials.

The next category, *interrupting*, is when the client takes on a defensive manner and may talk over the counselor or cut the counselor off. This is quite intentional in nature and is different than the client's typical conversational style.

A third category, *negating*, is seen when a client appears to be unwilling to acknowledge that there is a problem and/or appears to be resistant to taking responsibility for the problems. This client will typically use excuse making or blaming as a defense or may frequently disagree with potential solutions or suggestions. This client may believe that the behavior is not putting him or her at risk for any potentially negative consequences, or may not identify as a problematic user, so will reject implications of such. The client may appear uncooperative or intensely negative, and counselors may find themselves experiencing countertransference in the form of negativity, helplessness, or anger toward these clients.

The fourth category of resistance behaviors is *ignoring*. A client may be using this form of resistance when he or she is not actively engaging in the helping conversation. The client may not be paying attention nor participating in the conversation, or not responding to prompts from the helper. The client may also be actively attempting to change the direction of the therapeutic conversation to a "safer" topic that is more amenable to the client yet off-topic and seemingly unrelated to the conversation at hand.

Counselors should be especially cautious of clients who change the subject to a "safer" topic when attempting to avoid (ignore) discussing the target behavior. Sometimes the change of subject is obvious and appears quite intentional. Other times, the change is subtle enough that a counselor may not recognize its occurrence. For instance, a client who is resistant to further discussion about decreasing heroin use may begin to discuss at length and with great emotion a troubled childhood and intense abuse. The counselor will undoubtedly feel tempted to change the course of counseling to address the childhood issues and may quickly lose sight of the initial conversation and original treatment focus.

Reducing Resistance

Counselors practicing MI will reduce client resistance to the change process by maximizing *change talk* and reducing *resistance talk*.

To maximize change talk, counselors and clients will together examine the disadvantages of the current behaviors and patterns while examining the advantages of changing the target behavior. This may be done in the form of a pros and cons list, a decisional balance form that lists advantages of change in one column and disadvantages of change in another, or a verbal exchange where these factors are examined in depth. Typically, it is helpful to discuss the client's intention to make a change and his or her feelings regarding the change (e.g., positive aspects, optimistic thoughts, and beliefs about the positive aspects of change).

At the same time, counselors will minimize resistance talk by decreasing the client's comfort with the status quo, challenging beliefs that the status quo is advantageous, and minimizing overall negativity about the change process. To accomplish this, counselors will utilize methods recommended in the practice of MI while avoiding some potential hazards such as advocacy talk.

Advocacy talk occurs when a counselor reinforces or enhances resistance talk. Advocacy talk should be reduced because of its blocking effect on the change process. Some examples of advocacy talk include arguing for the client to make a change, playing the expert (recall that MI assumes the client is the expert), blaming or criticizing the client, or being impatient or hurried during the therapeutic interaction. It is also especially concerning when the counselor puts his or her goals and ideas in the forefront, overriding the client's goals and intentions. Imagine that our client Jane has decided to reduce her drinking to one half glass of wine a day rather than two or three. Jane is not ready to eliminate her wine entirely. When Jane presents this plan to her counselor, the counselor responds with, "You really should eliminate drinking altogether rather than cut back to half a glass a day. I've seen enough clients to know that you'll probably remain an alcoholic that way." Jane's plan for positive change has been blocked and diminished through the counselor's use of advocacy talk. More specifically, the counselor used criticism and arguing for change while assuming the expert stance.

In keeping with the collaborative spirit at the core of MI, counselors should be cautious when deciding to compare their clients with other clients or situations that they are aware of. While it is appropriate for a counselor to suggest remedies tried by others (once the client is at a solution-seeking stage), it is not appropriate for a counselor to suggest that a client will have the same outcome as others who use the same drug(s) of choice or have similar circumstances. Instead, the counselor focuses on the client's unique situation and elicits change talk from the client about how his or her own circumstances might change once the target behavior is adjusted.

Resistance is usually most apparent in the precontemplation and contemplation stages of change. Although it may be tempting to confront or argue with the client, this will usually lead to an increase in resistance and defensiveness. Instead, counselors using MI will use a variety of *reflection responses* that are useful in working through resistance.

When a counselor uses reflection responses, the client does not have to become defensive and argumentative. Miller and Rollnick (2012) describe three types of reflection responses: Simple Reflection, Amplified Reflection, and Double-Sided Reflection. Consider the following examples of reflection responses to resistant statements:

Simple Reflection:

Client: I don't know why my parents are making me come here. All my friends use pot.
Counselor: It's hard to understand why your parents brought you here, when all your friends use pot.

Amplified Reflection:

Client: My boss is interfering in my life by making me come here for treatment. I don't have a problem with alcohol.
Counselor: Your boss's interference in your personal life is intolerable to you.

Double-Sided Reflection:

Client: I can't believe my wife left me over my alcohol use. I don't know what her problem is—she should be in this room talking because she is the problem, not drinking.
Interviewer: I hear you saying that you don't have a problem with drinking, but that maybe your relationship is the issue. It sounds like you care about your wife still since you are open to her coming to a session and maybe talking more about your relationship and the impact of your drinking.

Motivational interviewers will use the preceding reflections when encountering resistance. Some additional tools are also useful, include *Shifting Focus*, *Reframing*, and *Agreement with a Twist* (Miller & Rollnick, 2002).

Shifting Focus is used to talk around the feature of resistance rather than dealing with it in a straightforward manner. This is not avoiding the resistance, but instead taking a step away from the issue and refocusing on something with fewer barriers. The path to change does not need to take one giant leap over the wall, but can instead be comprised of taking on smaller walls as practice. For instance, a counselor who finds a client becoming argumentative whenever the counselor suggests reducing methamphetamine use may decide to engage the client in a conversation about his or her chronic underemployment. The client may find this a "safer" topic, but discussion about the client's repeated firings due to the aftereffects of drug binges may be an effective way to increase discomfort about the negative effects of the methamphetamine use.

Reframing entails restating what the client says, adding a new dimension to it. This may be done by adding educational information, creating or adding another meaning of the statement, or adding a different outlook. For instance, if a client says, "I've tried a hundred times to quit and each time I fail miserably," the counselor can respond with, "Yes, you are clearly determined and willing to get started in this process of change. Each attempt before has helped you get here now, to this moment, when your change process will get even further."

Combining a Reflection with a Reframe leads to the creation of another type of response, called *Agreeing with a Twist*. This is when the counselor agrees with the client's statement, then proposes a reframed outlook. For example, a counselor may say, "Yes, it may seem true that smoking cigarettes is considerably safer than your prior crack cocaine addiction. Given what you know about the dangers of smoking, do you think it's possible that cigarette smoking is more dangerous than not smoking any substances at all?"

The counselor needs to be aware of the many "traps" to avoid when encountering client resistance (Miller & Rollnick, 2002). The question/answer trap occurs when the counselor asks questions, the client provides answers, and the interview takes on the form of an interrogation or broken record rather than a thoughtful inquiry and exploration.

The confrontation/denial trap occurs when the counselor provides argument or suggestion for change, and the client responds with reasons to maintain the status quo. Counselors must remember that MI is not an attempt to coerce or convince a client to change; rather, it is intended to enhance motivation while allowing the client to make his or her own decision about the change (Miller & Rollnick, 2009).

The expert trap occurs when a counselor attempts to provide guidance or direction to a client without first laying the groundwork for such guidance. The counselor must thoroughly explore with the client his or her goals and intentions. The counselor should resist the urge to provide guidance until after the client's motivation for change is strong (Miller & Rollnick, 2012).

The labeling trap indicates that a counselor has labeled a client as "addict" or "alcoholic," likely with the intent of urging along the change process. However, this is not in keeping with the spirit of MI and should be de-emphasized.

The blaming trap occurs as clients blame others for their problems. Miller and Rollnick (2009) espouse a "no-fault" policy, which indicates that it is unnecessary to find fault or blame. It is not important to explore how the situation came to be, but only to determine the current problem, how much it bothers the client, and how to proceed in changing it.

The premature focus trap occurs when the counselor focuses too readily on a specific problem or component of a problem without careful exploration first. While MI is not a Rogerian or client-centered therapy (Miller & Rollnick, 2009), it is necessary for the counselor to follow the client's lead to fully explore problems before identifying the target behavior that may be in need of change.

GUIDING THE CHANGE PROCESS: MORE MOTIVATIONAL INTERVIEWING TECHNIQUES

Enhancing Confidence

Clients are typically resistant to change because they either are not aware there is a problem (denial) or do not have the confidence to make the change in their life. Changing any behavior can be difficult and time-consuming. It is important for counselors to remember that *enhancing confidence* is an important step in building self-efficacy, or belief in one's abilities to accomplish a given task (Bandura, 2001). While self-efficacy does not necessarily correlate with actual competence, higher self-efficacy does tend to help increase motivation to complete a task (Bandura, 2001; Greason & Cashwell, 2009).

Self-efficacy plays a vital role in helping build motivation toward change. A counselor may help a client build self-efficacy by assisting the client in finding small, manageable goals that a client can achieve in a short amount of time. These small goals help a client build self-efficacy and also lay the foundation for future change work. For instance, a client may decide that at some point in the future he would like to attend support groups and self-help meetings regularly. However, the client is not ready to attend his first meeting yet. The counselor may work with the client to create a small goal that leans in the direction of the larger goal, such as having the client look up a meeting schedule to consider the time and locations of various meetings.

Confidence is an internal process for clients and not something a counselor can create for them externally. However, there are strategies that counselors can use to enhance a client's confidence and self-efficacy. As mentioned earlier, the ruler approach could be used to first assess where the client's confidence level is at the present time. A counselor may ask, "On a scale from 1 to 10, with 10 being the most confident, what is your confidence level for changing your behavior?" Once the client has rated his or her confidence, a counselor can incorporate additional strategies to address confidence.

Some additional confidence-boosting strategies may include *reviewing past successes*, *examining personal strengths and supports*, and/or creating *hypothetical change*. *Reviewing past successes* involves counselors asking clients to discuss past successes (as determined by the client). The client then shares about the success and what he or she did to reach the goals. *Examining personal strengths and supports* involves the counselor and client together considering all of the supportive features and people that a client has access to, whether internal (e.g., sense of humor, determination) or external (e.g., supportive brother, support groups). *Creating hypothetical change* is encouraging the client to imagine what it would be like if his or her barriers were not an issue, or having the client look into the future and imagine what it would be like if he or she succeeds in change. For instance, a counselor may say, "What will your average day be like when you are drug free, employed, and living in your own home? Describe that day from start to finish. How will you feel and act?"

Strengthening Commitment

Once a client has the confidence to change, the next step is the commitment to change. Motivational interviewers use the *strengthening commitment* tool in this process. Strengthening commitment involves the counselor actively reiterating and highlighting what a client has accomplished since beginning the change process. This is a time that counselors may share advice with the client. As one of the key underlying philosophies of MI states that the client is the expert in his or her own life, so giving unwanted advice becomes counterproductive. However, when the client has made the commitment to change and asks for advice or information about the process itself, counselors may give advice with the client's permission to do so. For example, a client may ask what to do next once he or she has made the decision to stop using drugs. The counselor may reply, "Well, you have many options. You could enter residential treatment, enter outpatient treatment, continue once-a-week counseling, or attend support groups. I think that outpatient intensive treatment would be a good place for you to begin."

Another way to strengthen a client's commitment is by using a *change plan*. A change plan, most useful when clients are in the preparation or action stage of change, is a collaborative project in which client and counselor develop a written plan of change. Miller and Rollnick (2002) suggest these four components when creating a change plan: (1) set goals, (2) consider change options, (3) arrive at or negotiate a plan, and (4) elicit a commitment. Counselors should ensure that client goals are attainable and not a setup for failure. It is also important to be specific about how the goals are going to be accomplished. Counselors and clients should look at who is involved in the change process, what the change actions are, and when they will be completed. Obstacles to change may occur, and it is necessary to plan for these proactively. It is also important to know what results the client is looking for once the plan is implemented and completed.

ADVANTAGES AND DISADVANTAGES OF MOTIVATIONAL INTERVIEWING

The advantages of MI are plentiful. It allows clients, both mandated and voluntary, to discover their own reasons for making change. MI allows the impetus to change to emerge from within a client, thus honoring his or her unique circumstances and worldview.

MI has been empirically validated by numerous studies that support its use with substance abuse and dependence, as well as with a variety of other mental health and medical issues (e.g., Lundahl, Kunz, Brownell, Tollefson, & Burke, 2010).

A meta-analysis of 72 clinical trials utilizing MI describes the shorter term effects of MI use on certain populations across a wide range of problem areas (Hettema et al., 2005). Another meta-analysis of 119 studies revealed that MI contributes to counseling efforts and that delivery and various participant factors are influential variables.

However, MI may not have the same effectiveness with severely mentally ill clients as it does with other clients due to barriers inherent in the severity of the illness (Ballack & DiClemente, 1999). Ballack and DiClemente (1999) note that individuals with severe mental illness may not be motivated by the same reinforcers as most clients, thus rendering some MI techniques (e.g., affirmation) ineffective. Further, the impairment inherent in many severe mental illnesses may make the exploration process and cost-and-benefit analysis difficult at best. Imagine a client who has difficulty tracking in conversation and has flat affect, little ability to relate to others, and poor insight into his own ability to choose or not choose various behaviors. The counselor working with this client may have a difficult time practicing the early techniques for change, and may in fact not even be able to discover an adequate target behavior for change.

Additionally, it is important to note that MI may not be sufficient in reaching all of a client's goals. A client may have some goals that revolve around making a behavioral or cognitive change, but would also prefer to do work that involves merely gaining support and additional information, rather than making a change. For instance, a client who comes to therapy to learn more about healthy communication with his or her partner may be better served by a psychoeducation group than an individualized change process involving MI or other change techniques.

Summary and Some Final Notations

In this chapter, the process and stages of change were discussed as the foundation of motivational interviewing (MI). MI is not a theory of counseling; rather, it is a transtheoretical approach to the change process that encompasses both an attitude and set of techniques designed to elicit and enhance a client's internal processes with regard to change. Readers were provided the foundational pillars of MI: Expressing Empathy, Developing Discrepancy, Rolling with Resistance, and Supporting Self-Efficacy. These four pillars serve as the foundational premise for the change process.

Next, counselors learned about the MI techniques that are most effective in the early stages of engagement and retention. These techniques included asking open-ended questions, listening reflectively, affirming the client's efforts, summarizing the client's expressions, and eliciting change talk. Readers learned about client resistance and the many forms resistance can take, including arguing, interrupting, negating, and ignoring. Counselors also learned that resistance is not a client problem; instead, it is a welcome signal to the counselor that it is time to attempt a new technique rather than try harder at what is not working. In this chapter, counselors discovered a number of techniques to effectively roll with client resistance, including using Reflection, Shifting Focus, and Agreement with a Twist. Counselors also learned about the "traps" they may fall into while working with MI and were cautioned against working countertherapeutically.

Finally, readers were provided additional techniques to enhance motivation and increase momentum in the change process. Counselors learned how to strengthen and renew a client's commitment to change, and about situations in which MI may be disadvantageous and ineffective.

MyCounselingLab

Visit the MyCounselingLab site for *Foundations of Addictions Counseling,* Third Edition to enhance your understanding of concepts. You'll have the opportunity to practice your skills through video- and case-based exercises. You will find sets of questions to help you prepare for your certification exam with *Licensure Quizzes*. There is also a Video Library that provides taped counseling sessions, ethical scenarios, and interviews with helpers and clients.

Useful Websites

The following websites provide additional information relating to the chapter topics:

Motivational Interviewing Founder's Site
www.motivationalinterview.org/

Motivational Interviewing Guidelines
www.bhrm.org/guidelines/motiveint.pdf

Motivational Interviewing with a Corrections Population/Lesson Plans
www.nicic.org/Library/019791

SAMHSA Website
www.samhsa.gov/co-occurring/topics/training/motivational.aspx

Stephen Rollnick Website
www.stephenrollnick.com/

References

The American heritage dictionary of the English language. (2000). Boston, MA: Houghton Mifflin Harcourt.

Apodaca, T. R., & Longabaugh, R. (2009). Mechanisms of change in motivational interviewing: A review and preliminary evaluation of the evidence. *Addiction, 104,* 705–715.

Ballack, A. S., & DiClemente, C. C. (1999). Treating substance abuse among patients with schizophrenia. *Psychiatric Services, 50*(1), 75–80.

Bandura, A. (1993). Perceived self-efficacy in cognitive development and functioning. *Educational Psychologist, 28,* 117–148.

Bandura, A. (2001). Social cognitive theory: An agentive perspective. *Annual Review of Psychology, 52,* 1–26.

Dean, H. Y., Touyz, S. W., Rieger, E., & Thornton, C. E. (2008). Group motivational enhancement therapy as an adjunct to inpatient treatment for eating disorders: A preliminary study. *European Eating Disorders Review, 16*(4), 256–267.

Egan, G. (2013). *The skilled helper: A problem-management and opportunity-development approach to helping.* Boston, MA:Cengage Learning.

Elliott, R., Bohart, A. C., Watson, J. C., & Greenberg, L. S. (2011). Empathy. *Psychotherapy, 48*(1), 43.

Emmerling, M. E., & Whelton, W. J. (2009). Stages of change and the working alliance in psychotherapy. *Psychotherapy Research, 19*(6), 687–698.

Festinger, L. (1957). *A theory of cognitive dissonance.* Stanford, CA: Stanford University Press.

Gaume, J., Bertholet, N., Faouzi, M., Gmel, G., & Daeppen, J. B. (2013). Does change talk during brief motivational interventions with young men predict change in alcohol use? *Journal of Substance Abuse Treatment, 44*(2), 177–185.

Greason, P. B., & Cashwell, C. S. (2009). Mindfulness and counseling self-efficacy: The mediating role of attention and empathy. *Counselor Education and Supervision, 49,* 2–19.

Hettema, J., Steele, J., & Miller, W. R. (2005). Motivational Interviewing. *Annual Review of Clinical Psychology, 1,* 91–111.

Lewis, T. F., & Osborn, C. J. (2004). Solution-focused counseling and motivational interviewing: A consideration of confluence. *Journal of Counseling & Development, 82,* 38–48.

Lundahl, B. W., Kunz, C., Brownell, C., Tollefson, D., & Burke, B. L. (2010). A meta-analysis of motivational interviewing: Twenty-five years of empirical studies. *Research on Social Work Practice, 20*(2), 137–160.

Mason, M. J. (2009). Rogers redux: Relevance and outcomes of motivational interviewing across behavioral problems. *Journal of Counseling & Development, 87,* 357–362.

Miller, W. R. (1983). Motivational interviewing with problem drinkers. *Behavioural Psychotherapy, 11,* 147–172.

Miller, W. R., & Rollnick, S. (2002). *Motivational interviewing: Preparing people for change* (2nd ed.). New York, NY: Guilford Press.

Miller, W. R., & Rollnick, S. (2009). Ten things that motivational interviewing is not. *Behavioural and Cognitive Psychotherapy, 37,* 129–140.

Miller, W. R., & Rollnick, S. (2012). *Motivational interviewing: Helping people change.* New York, NY: Guilford Press.

Miller, W. R., Sovereign, R. G., & Krege, B. (1988). Motivational interviewing with problem drinkers: II. The drinker's check up as a preventive intervention. *Behavioral Psychotherapy, 16,* 251–268.

Nosen, E., & Woody, S. R. (2009). Applying lessons learned from obsessions: Metacognitive processes in smoking cessation. *Cognitive Therapy Research, 33,* 241–254.

Prochaska, J. O. (2013). Transtheoretical Model of Behavior Change. In *Encyclopedia of Behavioral Medicine* (pp. 1997–2000). New York, NY: Springer.

Prochaska, J. O., & Norcross, J. C. (2001). Stages of change. *Psychotherapy: Theory, Research, Practice, Training, 38*(4), 443.

Project MATCH Research Group. (1998). Therapist effects in three treatments for alcohol problems. *Psychotherapy Research, 8,* 455–474.

Sheeran, P., Gollwitzer, P. M., & Bargh, J. A. (2013). Nonconscious processes and health. *Health Psychology, 32*(5), 460.

Solomon, J., & Fioritti, A. (2002). Motivational intervention as applied to systems change: The case of dual diagnosis. *Substance Abuse & Misuse, 37*(14), 1833–1851.

Tucker, S., Olson, M. E., & Frusti, D. K. (2009). Validity and reliability of the evidence-based practice self-efficacy scale. *Western Journal of Nursing Research, 31*(8), 1090–1091.

West, R., & Brown, J. (2013). *Theory of addiction.* Hoboken, NJ: John Wiley & Sons.

Chapter 8

Psychotherapeutic Approaches

Cynthia J. Osborn
Kent State University

Advances in medical technology have paved the way for more sophisticated research initiatives in the areas of human genetics, neurobiology, and behavior. What has been discovered from these ongoing investigations has already had a profound impact on the addictions field. Coherent synopses of these findings are available for professionals (e.g., McCrady & Epstein, 2013) and the general public (e.g., W. R. Miller & Muñoz, 2013). Continued scientific research is shaping how problematic substance use and addiction are viewed and treated. Among professionals, this represents a challenge to longstanding and entrenched views of addiction.

COUNSELOR BELIEFS AND BEHAVIORS

It has long been known that clinician attitudes significantly influence the acceptance and implementation of new or innovative therapeutic approaches (Levenson, Speed, & Budman, 1995). In addictions treatment, this is influenced in part by clinicians' understanding of addiction in general (Ogborne, Wild, Braun, & Newton-Taylor, 1998; Shaffer & Robbins, 1991), alcoholism in particular (W. R. Miller & Hester, 2003), and the purpose and intended outcome of treatment (e.g., abstinence; Caplehorn, Lumley, & Irwig, 1998). Studies suggest that addiction ideology (e.g., medical, humanitarian or empathic, moralistic) affects the selection of specific treatment strategies (e.g., Caplehorn et al., 1998; Moyers & W R. Miller, 1993; Ogborne et al., 1998; Thombs & Osborn, 2001), as well as receptivity to evidence-based practices (McGovern, Fox, Xie, & Drake, 2004). For example, Ducharme, Knudsen, Abraham, and Roman (2010) found that substance abuse counselors' adherence to a 12-step treatment ideology was associated with their weak endorsement of offering tangible incentives for abstinence, a key strategy used in the evidence-based practice of contingency management.

Although W. R. Miller, Sorensen, Selzer, and Brigham (2006) noted a shift in how addiction is understood in the United States today, movement away from the "widespread" endorsement of substance dependence as a disease (Ogborne et al., 1998) to an understanding of addiction as a multifaceted and complex phenomenon, this shift continues to be slow. This is true in light of the disease model's history as the "dominant" model of addiction in the United States (Morgenstern, Frey, McCrady, Labouvie, & Neighbors, 1996). Definitions of addiction as a disease do vary (see Thombs & Osborn, 2013), but common elements include an acceptance of addiction (namely alcoholism) as a chronic, progressive, involuntary, irreversible, and potentially fatal illness, which has as its core criteria the loss of control over the intake of alcohol and physiological dependence. A single, standard, predetermined form of treatment is often used, without regard for individual differences among clients. Lifetime abstinence is the unquestionable goal and participation in Alcoholics Anonymous (AA) is strongly endorsed.

Many chemical dependency counselors may thus practice within the bounds of one model of addiction—likely the (ill-defined) disease model of addiction. Such a myopic perspective can have the effect of missing, ignoring, or even dismissing other and perhaps equally valid explanations for a client's addiction and that client not being able to appreciate or apply alternative treatment methods. Indeed, Tracy (2007) concluded her brief historical review of the disease concept in the United States by stating, "It may be time to embrace a more holistic view of disease and disability, to appreciate the multiplicity of factors . . . that affect what we consider 'healthy' and 'diseased'" (p. 91).

This chapter is intended to offer practitioners an array of treatment approaches in their efforts to assist a variety of clients struggling with substance use concerns. Just as there is no one "alcoholic" or "drug addict," there is no one "tried and true" treatment approach. W. R. Miller and Hester's (2003) "informed eclecticism" model guides the content of this chapter in that (a) there is no single superior approach to treatment for all individuals, (b) treatment programs and systems should be constructed with a variety of approaches that have been shown to be effective, and (c) different types of individuals respond best to different treatment approaches. In addition, W. R. Miller and Hester strongly emphasize tailoring or customizing treatment to the unique needs and strengths of each individual client, thereby increasing treatment effectiveness and efficiency. Implicit in this model is the need for all helping professionals in the addictions field to be familiar with a multiplicity of interventions so as to select from and offer the most appropriate type (or combination of types) and level of care to those needing and deserving quality services. Attention is given in this chapter to the application of research-supported counseling approaches. A list of useful websites addressing topics discussed in this chapter (namely, behavioral and cognitive-behavioral interventions, brief interventions, solution-focused counseling, and harm reduction) is provided.

EMPIRICALLY SUPPORTED TREATMENT APPROACHES

As the mental health field has been challenged with implementing evidence-based practices (see Drake, Merrens, & Lynde, 2005; Goodheart, Kazdin, & Sternberg, 2006), so too has the substance abuse counseling/chemical dependency treatment field (P. M. Miller, 2009). Recently, there has been a dramatic increase in the number of interventions for substance abuse prevention and treatment listed on the Substance Abuse and Mental Health Services Administration's (SAMHSA) National Registry of Evidence-based Programs and Practices (NREPP; nrepp.samhsa.gov). At the beginning of 2010, this number was 96. As of April 2014, 171 interventions for substance abuse prevention and treatment were listed on NREPP, a 44% increase in less than 5 years. Included are cocaine-specific coping skills training, relapse prevention therapy, motivational interviewing (MI), motivational enhancement therapy (an adaptation of MI), multisystemic therapy, contingency management, Seeking Safety (treatment for co-occurring substance abuse and trauma; seekingsafety.org), solution-focused group therapy, Twelve Step Facilitation Therapy, and several brief interventions (e.g., Brief Alcohol Screening and Intervention for College Students, BASICS). Several of the interventions are web-based applications, such as the Drinker's Check-up (drinkerscheckup.com) and the College Drinker's Check-up (collegedrinkerscheckup.com), both designed to help young adult and older adult drinkers reduce their alcohol consumption.

Despite the proven record of many addiction treatments over the past 25 years, adoption and routine implementation of these practices by facilities and practitioners providing direct service remains slow. McGovern, Saunders, and Kim (2013) estimate that only 25% of providers in addictions treatment offer evidence-based treatments. As mentioned earlier, this is due in part to the persistence of one ideology of addiction (i.e., disease) associated with certain interventions that continue to be used despite evidence that they are ineffective (e.g., confrontational counseling, group psychoeducation). Interventions with no proven track record or with a poor track record, or even those that are potentially harmful (e.g., the Drug Awareness and Resistance Education prevention program, or DARE; see Lilienfeld, 2007), are regarded as discredited treatments in the addictions field (Norcross, Koocher, Fala, & Wexler, 2010).

Other reasons for not adopting and then routinely implementing evidence-based treatments include administrative "top-down" methods used in some settings that do not consider frontline provider views and preferences, and the perceived and actual high costs of implementation, which include ongoing and quality provider training. Indeed, although the vast majority of 345 clinical directors of substance abuse treatment programs said they used at least one of four evidence-based practices in their facility (e.g., 90% reported using cognitive-behavioral therapy), very few (3%–35%) provided quality training and supervision in that evidence-based practice (Olmstead, Abraham, Martino, & Roman, 2012). This is somewhat consistent with another study (Benishek, Kirby, Dugosh, & Padovano, 2010) that found 41% of supervisors and administrators in substance abuse treatment facilities in one state believed that evidence-based practices could be implemented *without* staff training. This is unfortunate and concerning. For evidence-based practices to be used by a greater number of addiction treatment professionals, counselor training and supervision is key (Carroll & Rounsaville, 2007).

From "Trying on for Size" to Daily Wardrobe

Think of something new that you were introduced to recently—a type of clothing or fashion accessory, food, music genre, smart phone app, or leisure activity. What was your first impression of this item, experience, or behavior? You may have sampled it or "tried it on for size" and then moved on to something else. Or, you may have gone back for more, subscribing to it, and even incorporating it into your daily routine. What made the difference? If you did stick with this new item or activity, what explained your adoption or persistence? What for you made this not just a passing fad but something worth identifying with and using on a regular basis? Your answers may help to explain how innovative practices in the addictions field, such as certain evidence-based practices, are adopted and then implemented by substance abuse counselors.

Based on their extensive and exhaustive review of 363 controlled trials of 99 different alcoholism treatment modalities (involving 75,000 clients) up through the year 2000, W. R. Miller, Wilbourne, and Hettema (2003) acknowledged little overlap between modalities with strong research support and "those components often employed in U.S. alcoholism treatment programs" today (p. 41). Due to both the methodological rigor employed and the strength of treatment outcome, 18 modalities were determined to be efficacious. These included brief intervention, motivation enhancement, community reinforcement, self-change manual, behavioral self-control training, social skills training, behavioral marital therapy and family therapy, a variety of pharmacologic interventions (e.g., acamprosate, naltrexone), and cognitive therapy.

Results of W. R. Miller et al.'s (2003) review are comparable to two earlier reviews of 302 controlled clinical studies (W. R. Miller, Andrews, Wilbourne, & Bennett, 1998) and 361 controlled studies (W. R. Miller & Wilbourne, 2002) of treatments for alcohol problems through the year 1996 and 1998, respectively—that is, all treatment modalities demonstrating positive outcome in earlier reviews maintained their treatment efficacy in W. R. Miller et al.'s (2003) review. This suggests that the efficacious modalities identified over the past 15 years or so for the treatment of alcohol problems are not anomalies or "flukes," but are credible and trustworthy approaches.

This endurance also has been demonstrated in a multisite clinical trial of three different treatment conditions (alone and in combinations) for alcohol dependence (Project COMBINE; Anton et al., 2006). The combined behavioral intervention (CBI) condition provided a 20% advantage over the other two conditions (pharmacotherapy and a behavioral medical management program) at 1-year follow-up on at least two alcohol outcomes (Donovan et al., 2008). The CBI integrated certain cognitive-behavioral interventions (e.g., coping skills training) with other interventions, such as motivational interviewing, encouraging persons to sample and participate in 12-step and other support groups, and exploring client strengths and resources (see W. R. Miller, 2004). Because they have performed beneficially in a consistent fashion over the years and in different research investigations, the interventions that comprise CBI should be incorporated into routine substance abuse treatment.

BEHAVIORAL AND COGNITIVE-BEHAVIORAL ASSUMPTIONS AND PRACTICES

The behavioral and cognitive-behavioral (CB) interventions that are well represented among effective treatments for problematic alcohol use include behavioral self-control training, community reinforcement, contingency management and behavior contracting, social skills training, and behavioral couples/family counseling. Additional research suggests that these and other behavioral and CB approaches (e.g., relapse prevention) are effective in treating drug dependence (e.g., cocaine and opioids). From their meta-analysis of 34 randomized clinical/control trials, McHugh, Hearon, and Otto (2010) found that CB interventions produced an overall treatment effect size of .45, considered to be in the moderate range. Larger effect sizes were found for the treatment of cannabis, followed by cocaine and opioids, with the smallest effect sizes found for polysubstance dependence.

Clearly, there is overlap between behavioral and CB assumptions. Both are informed by basic learning principles, such as classical conditioning and operant or instrumental conditioning, and both contend that substance use behavior is shaped by these learning processes. These principles apply to humans and animals (e.g., rats) alike. A core principle specific to addictions shared by behavioral and CB theories is that substances are powerful reinforcers of behavior (McHugh et al., 2010). Unlike behavior theories, however, CB theories include cognitive principles of learning, chief among them the social learning theory of Albert Bandura. This means that CB approaches consider the role of cognitive processes such as self-efficacy, expectancies, and values in the initiation and maintenance of problematic substance use, as well as in its recovery. CB assumptions therefore pertain to humans only, focusing on internal, self-appraisal, and other cognitive functions that influence behavior. Behavioral assumptions, on the other hand, consider only observable behavior, including autonomic and other forms of physiological activity (e.g., craving), without necessarily considering the influence of cognitive activity. Approaches in this category include aversion therapy and cue exposure treatments wherein a conditioned behavior (e.g., opiate addiction) is targeted for extinction by introducing an aversive stimulus (e.g., medication that produces negative side effects) or presenting a series of drug-related cues (e.g., images or smells associated with drug use) and preventing the conditioned response (i.e., drug use).

The most effective treatments for substance use problems combine behavioral and cognitive principles, thus prioritizing CB approaches. These approaches operate according to six assumptions (Najavits, Liese, & Harned, 2005): (a) substance abuse involves complex cognitive and behavioral processes; (b) substance abuse and associated cognitive-behavioral processes are, to a large extent, learned; (c) substance abuse and associated cognitive-behavioral processes can be modified, particularly by means of CB counseling; (d) a major goal of CB counseling for substance abuse is to teach coping skills to resist substance use and to reduce problems associated with substance abuse and dependence; (e) CB counseling requires comprehensive case conceptualization that serves as the basis for selecting specific CB techniques; and (f) to be effective, CB counseling must be provided in the context of a warm, supportive, collaborative counseling relationship.

The last assumption of CB approaches dictates a practice fundamental to CB counseling: conducting a functional analysis at the start of care. This is described in this section, along with additional interventions common to CB approaches. This section concludes with a description of three CB approaches: contingency management and behavior contracting, community reinforcement, and mindfulness-based relapse prevention.

Functional Analysis

Functional analysis means understanding the function or purpose of substance use behaviors for a specific individual. It constitutes an assessment of the antecedents (or triggers) and consequences (or effects) of substance use. This is conducted at the beginning of counseling and follows an interactive and structured format, preferably using a piece of paper to record responses (triggers in one column, effects in another). Clients are first asked about the situations in which they are most likely to use, including places, people, times of day, and feeling states. Questions asked include "When are you most likely to feel like drinking or getting drunk?" and "Describe situations that for you are high risk, a place or people you're with that make it very likely that you'll smoke." Responses are recorded in the left-hand "triggers" column. Next, clients are asked what they like about using, what for them are the desired or anticipated consequences of using. Questions asked include "What does alcohol do for you that you like, that you really enjoy?" and "What for you is the attraction to smoking, what does it gives to you in return for your effort?" Client responses are recorded in the right-hand "effects" column.

Once there is a sufficient number of items recorded in each column (and counselors are encouraged to ask for elaboration after each client's response), clients are then asked to make connections between each of the entries in the triggers column with each of the entries in the effects column. The counselor demonstrates by linking two entries, for example, by saying, "It's common for people to want to drink when they're feeling highly stressed [pointing to this entry in the triggers column] so that they can experience relief or calm themselves down [pointing to the client's entry in the effects column]. Do these two go together for you?" If the client acknowledges a connection between these two entries, the counselor then draws a line between them. The client is then encouraged to make as many connections as possible between the remaining entries in the triggers column with those in the effects column, drawing a line between them so that all entries are connected.

This process of functional analysis follows the "New Roads" exercise developed by W. R. Miller and Pechacek (1987) and used in Project COMBINE (see W. R. Miller, 2004). The intended outcome is enhanced understanding—for the counselor and for the client—about the role of alcohol and other substances in the client's life. For the counselor, this is part of the important task of case conceptualization. Only by making connections between triggers and effects can "alternative paths" or "new roads" be constructed for achieving preferred outcomes (e.g., relaxation) without the use of substances. This can be done by creating a third column, entitled "alternatives," and having the client identify possible substance-free behaviors that can be linked to each entry in the "effects" column. Doing this is the start of treatment planning, allowing the counselor to formulate possible interventions, and therefore constructing this third column may be an activity saved until later in the process of counseling.

Taking Self-Inventory

Identify a behavior that you wish to change. This might be something you've considered for a long time, or may be relatively new. On a sheet of paper create two columns: the one on the left titled "Triggers," the one on the right "Effects." Under the Triggers heading, write down three or four things that contribute to this behavior happening, things that make it likely that you will engage in this behavior. On the right-hand side, under the Effects column, write down three or four effects or consequences of this behavior. In other words, what happens as a result of you engaging in this behavior? Review your two lists and connect as many of the entries on the left-hand side with those on the right-hand side. As you do so, what stands out for you about the purpose or function of this particular behavior? After engaging in this activity, how likely are you to change this behavior in the next month?

Cognitive-Behavioral Interventions that Target Triggers

Najavits et al. (2005) described specific CB interventions that address coping skills and are grouped according to five factors or types of precursors (or triggers) to addictive behaviors. Due to the multiplicity of factors that contribute to problematic substance use, interventions can and are often implemented to address more than one type of trigger. Some of the nine interventions used in the combined behavioral interventions (CBI) program of Project COMBINE (W. R. Miller, 2004) are included in these categories, such as mood management training.

Social interventions include certain lifestyle changes (e.g., exercise, meditation), enhancing one's sober social support (e.g., attending Alcoholics Anonymous/Narcotics Anonymous [AA/NA] meetings), learning and practicing effective interpersonal communication skills (e.g., differentiating between aggressive and assertive communication), and refusal skills (i.e., practicing verbal and nonverbal communication to avoid and turn down offers to use). These skills can be taught and practiced in individual and group counseling sessions, as well as with a concerned significant other (e.g., client's partner/spouse) who would be invited to one or two sessions (with client's permission) to practice communication skills.

Environmental interventions include cue exposure treatment mentioned earlier. Clients also can be advised to thoroughly clean their living space, one area or one room at a time, to reinforce their sense of control over their own personal or local environment. This practice could also symbolize a cleansing or purging of the "toxic self." Avoiding certain places (e.g., neighborhood where crack or meth house located, certain bus stops) by frequenting other, nonhigh-risk locations (e.g., community center, local museum, AA/NA meetings) could also be recommended.

Emotional interventions are designed to regulate both positive and negative emotions so that neither serves as a trigger for relapse. Through cognitive strategies, clients may be taught to stay with the feeling while reviewing to themselves (preferably verbalizing out loud) the list of things they have already accomplished to stay sober (e.g., "Mark, you are reMARKable for having said, 'Let's take a time-out of 5 minutes to cool down before we talk about this some more'"). This practice is similar to the distress tolerance skills (e.g., self-soothing) taught in dialectical behavior therapy (Linehan, 1993a, 1993b). In self-soothing, clients are taught to focus on one of the five senses at a time, pausing to fully attend to, experience, or soak in the natural or nonsubstance-induced sensation (e.g., observing the contrast of green tree leaves against a bright blue sky) in order to withstand an urge or a craving to use. In addition, certain feelings can be reframed as positive protective devices, if not acted upon in destructive ways. For example, fear and anxiety can be understood as normal responses to a brand new reality or lifestyle, and both feelings can be regarded as the client's attempts to protect what is now valuable (i.e., sobriety). One reframe that I often used with clients was: "The compulsivity of addiction is the persistence of recovery." This phrase is meant to convey that when persons with substance use problems begin and maintain recovery, they do not have to discard all behaviors associated with their addiction. Rather, they can (and perhaps need to) "channel" or redirect their frenetic energy into a "no-holds-barred" or "pull-out-all-the-stops" approach to recovery (e.g., continuing to attend AA meetings until they find their "home" fellowship).

Cognitive interventions are specifically intended to modify automatic thoughts and drug-related beliefs, as well as to modify conditional assumptions and core beliefs. Rather than automatically thinking that only marijuana can help them get to sleep, clients can be taught to catch themselves from lighting up (perhaps by telling themselves out loud, "Hold off!" or "Wait!") and reviewing the written plan constructed with their counselor detailing alternative preparations for sleep (e.g., listening to relaxing music while depressing a stress ball). A list of cognitive comebacks to urges or cravings to use can be devised so that the client has an expanding toolbox of relapse prevention strategies. Such comebacks might resemble the externalization exercise (White & Epston, 1990) used in solution-focused counseling in which the client names the problem (e.g., "restless roamer," as one heroin addict depicted his reasons and struggles in finding "peace" in his life), is able to regard the problem as an external entity (i.e., "I am not the problem . . . 'restless roamer' is the problem"), and through conversation is able to keep the problem at a distance so as to diffuse the problem's power over the client. The client can be taught to confront the problem with comebacks such as "You've led me astray!" and "I'm no longer following your twisted map!" and doing so out loud, with an amplified voice, and while standing up. Using cognitive interventions, clients can also be taught to question the evidence regarding the seemingly infinite benefits of substance use, as well as the seemingly infinite detriments or negative assumptions about sobriety. Counselors can assist in stopping any circular reasoning by interjecting "Okay, where's the evidence that this is true?" and "How do you *really* know that for sure?" Questions such as these should always be asked in a nonsarcastic, nonjudgmental manner.

Physical interventions involve activities intended to distract the person's attention away from triggers and the consequent cravings and urges to use. They also can include pharmacological intervention, such as the prescribed use of methadone or naltrexone to curb drug craving. Interventions that address physical activity and expression include engaging in physical exercise (e.g., doing chores around the house, going for a walk), talking with someone (e.g., calling one's AA sponsor), breaking out into song, or snapping a rubber band worn on the wrist. In addition, clients can be reminded of the "insanity" of their active using days, recalling "seemingly irrelevant decisions" made (see Marlatt & Donovan, 2005) and the negative physical consequences of their using. One client I worked with, a blue-collar machinist who found his employment fulfilling because "I'm able to work on things that last," made the decision one morning to no longer drink. He said he was able to uphold this decision because "I was sick and tired of being sick and tired. I didn't want to lose this job." I recall commending this client on his decision and what I heard as his desire to work not only on large truck engines that would last, but on himself as well, so that *he* would last.

Contingency Management and Behavior Contracting

Contingency management and behavior contracting are specific CB approaches that have demonstrated efficacy in treating alcohol and other drug dependence—namely, cocaine and opioid dependence—for adults and adolescents (Higgins, Silverman, & Heil, 2008; Petry, 2012). These two approaches are based in part on the theory of behavioral economics that posits behavior is chosen because of the immediate and tangible reward(s) it provides, including monetary reward. Contingency management (CM) makes use of external incentives or tangible reinforcers (namely, vouchers redeemable for goods and services, e.g., groceries, public transportation, movie theater tickets) that are contingent on the client meeting predetermined treatment goals (or target behaviors), such as submitting drug-free urine specimens and arriving to counseling on time. Reinforcing positive, nonsubstance behaviors is particularly important early in treatment and recovery. Over time, clients may be awarded with an increasing number of vouchers or opportunities to win a prize (e.g., from a raffle or drawing). This particular practice is known as prize incentives CM for substance abuse. A video demonstrating its application in actual treatment settings can be viewed online at bettertxoutcomes.org/bettertxoutcomes/PAMI.html

Despite beneficial effects in research trials, it appears that CM practices have yet to be widely adopted by practitioners due in part to the belief that substance abuse clients should not be awarded with prizes or vouchers for abstinence (Ducharme et al., 2010) and the perceived and actual costs of the program. In Olmstead et al.'s (2012) study, only 30% of substance abuse treatment program directors reported that CM was used in their facility (compared to 90% who used cognitive-behavioral therapy and 55% who used motivational interviewing). Counselors and agencies intent on offering helpful services are encouraged to pursue creative partnerships with local business representatives. These might include time-limited free access for agency clients on the local bus in exchange for free advertisement of the bus service on agency publications. In addition, local businesses could be approached to donate items (e.g., department store gift certificates) that would then be raffled off to clients who upheld their contract (Petry, Martin, Cooney, & Kranzler, 2000). In one early-intervention substance abuse program for low-income adolescents, CM implementation was found to be cost-effective ($29.40 for each participant for nine sessions total) and to significantly improve attendance (Branson, Barbuti, Clemmey, Herman, & Bhutia, 2012). Petry (2012) describes additional methods for funding a CM program.

Behavior contracting itself (apart from the use of prize incentives or vouchers) can be implemented with minimal or no cost to the counselor or agency. This practice might resemble treatment planning, but typically is not as comprehensive or expansive (i.e., the contract can focus on a specific task to accomplish in the next week) and can be done on a periodic basis. It is advised that the contracts be written (even at times on a scrap piece of paper), the intended behavior clearly described, the targeted date of task completion specified, and both the incentive and the consequence for not abiding by the contract clarified. In addition, the contract should be signed by both the counselor and client, dated, and a copy of the contract provided to the client. Incentives for upholding the contract might include meeting with the counselor outside, on the grounds of the agency; having access to the agency's basketball court following a counseling session; an extended (by 5 minutes) smoke break during group counseling; and securing from the counselor a letter of reference for a job application. Particularly in residential treatment settings, behavior contracts are routinely used to encourage greater participation and cooperation among clients. "Privileges" for upholding one's contract might include telephone access to family members, being able to receive visitors on "Family Day," and being able to skip meal preparation and cleanup or other household chores for one day.

Community Reinforcement Approach

The community reinforcement approach (CRA) is a comprehensive biopsychosocial approach to the treatment of substance use disorders based on the premise that one's environment or community plays a critical role in reinforcing one's recovery efforts. CRA enlists community reinforcers (e.g., family, recreation, employment) to support change in an individual's substance use (Meyers, Villanueva, & Smith, 2005). Two reviews (Roozen et al., 2004; Smith, Meyers, & Miller, 2001) of studies conducted with the CRA in treating problematic alcohol and other drug use attest to its efficacy, particularly when combined with contingency management (e.g., use of vouchers as incentives). Positive findings have continued in subsequent studies (Meyers, Roozen, & Smith, 2011), including for the Adolescent CRA.

Meyers et al. (2005) identified eight components of CRA, and although they conceded that each component is not necessarily used with every client, two are standard applications: functional analysis and treatment planning. After completing a functional analysis or thorough substance use assessment, including taking inventory of the client's (external and internal) motivations for substance use and its treatment, the focus of the CRA is to determine how environmental stimuli can be rearranged so that sobriety is supported and substance use is no longer tolerated or rewarded. Goals typically reflect the presence of something positive (e.g., maintaining employment, graduating from high school) rather than the absence of something negative (e.g., not drinking or drugging). Specific areas in the client's life that are considered in both assessment and treatment include social and recreational activities, employment, and family dynamics. Whenever possible, a significant other (e.g., life partner or spouse, girlfriend/boyfriend) is involved in treatment and regarded as an important ally in the construction and maintenance of a nonusing and healthy lifestyle.

The CRA can be understood as a "package"; that is, "it contains a number of procedures that may or may not be used, depending on [the] client's specific needs" (Smith, Meyers, & Milford, 2003, p. 238). Indeed, the counselor can sift through many of the CB interventions already described in this chapter and then select those strategies that are most relevant for the client's current situation. These may include job skills training, social skills training, and couples counseling to address strains in communication. Careful attention is given to the ongoing assessment of external and internal triggers for substance use. Not only are attempts made to regulate environmental stimuli; the counselor routinely inquires about the client's internal triggers (e.g., mood, beliefs, physical status). As a CB-oriented approach, the CRA is intended to equip the client with a variety of skills needed to not only effectively manage negative stimuli or triggers, but to also establish and maintain a lifestyle and an environment that support and allow one's recovery to thrive.

One adaptation and extension of CRA is Community Reinforcement and Family Training (CRAFT). CRAFT is based on the principles of CRA but it is designed for and targets the friends and family members of the person with the substance use problem, specifically the person who refuses to enter treatment (Meyers et al., 2005). Rather than working directly with the person with substance use problems, CRAFT enlists the assistance of a concerned significant other (CSO), such as a parent or a spouse, by training the CSO to interact with his or her loved one in new and more constructive ways. These would include not speaking with the family member when he or she is intoxicated (e.g., saying in a calm and measured voice, "I'll wait and talk with you about this in the morning, once you're sober") and allowing the family member to realize the natural consequences of his or her substance use (e.g., not bailing the family member out of jail). Although the goal of CRAFT is for the person with the substance use problem to enter treatment, CRAFT also is designed to help CSOs take better care of themselves and to realize a sense contentment on their own.

CRAFT has been described as "a rigorous treatment package" (Roozen, de Waart, & van der Kroft, 2010, p. 1730) and its results are impressive. A review of CRAFT studies conducted over 25 years indicates that 55%–86% of treatment-refusing family members enter treatment as a result of their CSO participating in CRAFT (Manuel et al., 2012). A video demonstrating the implementation of CRAFT with a grandmother and her grandson can be viewed online at: robertjmeyersphd.com/

Mindfulness-Based Relapse Prevention

Mindfulness practices have gained popularity in mental health care and in the addictions field in recent years. Mindfulness is understood as a centering process, a method for heightening awareness in the present moment. It is the deliberate practice of noticing, accepting, describing, and not judging one's immediate perceptual experience (Hayes, Follette, & Linehan, 2004). Essentially, it is an openness to and an attentional focus on what is taking place in the present moment, using as many senses as possible (e.g., sight, sound, smell), including attending to visceral functioning (e.g., breathing). This type of centering can serve as an antidote to impulsive behaviors, including substance use behaviors. The very act of intentional awareness of the present moment (externally and within) without responding to or acting on what is observed can delay or suspend, diminish, or erase urges to act (e.g., using a substance).

Several evidence-based approaches consider mindfulness a core skill and practice. These include dialectical behavior therapy (DBT; Linehan, 1993a) and acceptance and commitment therapy (ACT; Hayes, Strosahl, & Wilson, 2012). Although DBT and ACT are used with persons presenting with substance use problems (and a co-occurring mental health condition), there is a newer mindfulness approach that is specific to addictions: mindfulness-based relapse prevention (MBRP; Bowen, Chawla, & Marlatt, 2011). Already MBRP has demonstrated feasibility and preliminary efficacy for reducing substance use and craving during and up to 4 months after participating in an 8-week program (Bowen et al., 2009; Witkiewitz, Bowen, Douglas, & Hsu, 2013).

MBRP is intended to promote increased awareness of triggers for substance use, habitual patterns of using, and "automatic" reactions that seem to control a person's daily living. It is an aftercare program for persons who have completed out-patient or in-patient treatment for substance use disorders. It takes place in 2-hour weekly group sessions over an 8-week period. Each session offers instruction on mindfulness skills, and time is allotted for practicing these skills when urges, cravings, and other triggers to use arise. Clients enrolled in a MBRP program also are encouraged to adopt mindfulness as a recovery lifestyle. In addition to breathing exercises and body scan meditation, skills taught and practiced in MBRP (Bowen et al., 2011) include engaging in mindful movement postures (i.e., specific stretching exercises), urge surfing (i.e., staying with and "riding the wave" of an urge to use through its fluctuations in intensity; Marlatt & Gordon, 1985), and exercising SOBER breathing space. SOBER refers to the five sequential tasks of **S**topping or slowing down when experiencing a trigger to use, **O**bserving what is happening in the moment, focusing on your **B**reathing, **E**xpanding your awareness of other sensations (e.g., clammy hands, sweating), and **R**esponding (versus reacting) with awareness in a healthy, self-compassionate way.

Any of these mindfulness skills can be incorporated into substance abuse treatment and adapted for population and setting. For college students wanting to change their nicotine smoking behavior, Bowen and Marlatt (2009) instructed students to pay attention to their thoughts, sensations, or urges to smoke without trying to change or avoid them when presented with cigarette cues. The urge-surfing exercise (Marlatt & Gordon, 1985) was described, and students were encouraged to visualize their urge as a wave and to imagine riding the wave as it naturally crested and then subsided, rather than fighting the urge or giving in to it (because urges, like waves, do gradually decrease in intensity as time goes by). Compared to a control group, students in this study who completed the mindfulness exercises reported the following 7 days later: (a) they smoke significantly fewer cigarettes per day and (b) a significantly weaker connection between experiencing a negative affect (e.g., anxiety) and the urge to smoke (i.e., less reactivity).

BRIEF INTERVENTIONS

Brief interventions for problematic alcohol use have been practiced and studied for over 50 years (McCambridge, 2011). They now are part of a public health initiative known as **S**creening, **B**rief **I**ntervention, and **R**eferral for **T**reatment, or SBIRT, intended in part to integrate substance use services within primary care (McCance-Katz & Satterfield, 2012). Brief interventions are considered "a family of interventions varying in length, structure, targets of intervention, [and] personnel responsible for their delivery" (Heather, 1995, p. 287). Their common ingredients are known by the mnemonic FRAMES (W. R. Miller & Sanchez, 1994): (a) **F**eedback of personal risk or impairment, delivered in a matter-of-fact and nonjudgmental manner; (b) emphasis on personal **R**esponsibility for change, intended to be empowering for the client; (c) clear **A**dvice to change, delivered as a recommendation and, consistent with motivational interviewing, only with client permission (see Miller & Rollnick, 2013); (d) a **M**enu of alternative change options; (e) therapist **E**mpathy; and (f) facilitation of client **S**elf-efficacy or a sense of optimism and competence. These shared elements are intended to fulfill the primary purpose of brief interventions: to enhance a person's own resources for change by activating his or her own self-regulatory processes (W. R. Miller, Forcehimes, & Zweben, 2011). Hence, they often are referred to as "brief motivational interventions."

Brief interventions are, by definition, brief. It is helpful, however, to think of them as opportunistic encounters or applications, (W. R. Miller et al., 2011) or "teachable moments" that occur in a range of settings and are conducted by professionals (e.g., physicians) and nonprofessionals alike. One example is the conversation about ways to prevent high-risk drinking that a physician's assistant initiates in the emergency department prior to discharging a patient involved in an alcohol-related car accident. Another example is a local needle-exchange program volunteer who provides information about medical and counseling services in the area to a regular customer. And a third example are college students trained as "peer counselors" who offer education on "safer drinking" (including preventing alcohol poisoning) to students referred to a program because of a recent alcohol infraction. This latter intervention may be part of a BASICS program on campus (see Dimeff, Baer, Kivlahan, & Marlatt, 1999), a two-session program intended to raise awareness of drinking behaviors and to encourage a consideration of behavior change by providing feedback in a nonjudgmental manner. The BASICS program has proven effective at decreasing alcohol use and its consequences at 6-month follow-up, especially for male students, at one large university (DiFulvio, Linowski, Mazziotti, & Puleo, 2012). In addition,

Amaro et al. (2010) found that their adaptation of the BASICS program (to include screening and intervention of drinking and other drug use) reduced the quantity and frequency of substance use among college students who sought medical and mental health services at one university health center.

According to W. R. Miller et al. (2011), brief interventions may be freestanding (e.g., a single event occurring in a community setting), offered during an initial counseling session (e.g., in the hopes of retaining the client for ongoing services), or embedded within treatment focused on other issues (e.g., one or two sessions devoted to alcohol use for a client receiving mental health counseling). They may also include computerized interactive interventions, such as the one delivered on a tablet in the private hospital rooms of women who had just given birth and who had reported illicit substance use within the month prior to delivery (Ondersma, Svikis, Thacker, Beatty, & Lockhart, 2014). Regardless of the setting or the opportunity, brief interventions should always begin with an assessment of the person's readiness to change (Boyd, Harris, & Knight, 2012) and targeted to those who are low on the readiness-to-change continuum (Maisto et al., 2001). Brief interventions for problematic substance use must therefore always be an option regardless of problem severity (Sanchez-Craig, 1990), and may be used to help prepare or cultivate one's readiness for more intensive or extensive services (W. R. Miller, 1992), that is, as a precursor for treatment.

SOLUTION-FOCUSED COUNSELING

Solution-focused counseling (SFC) was conceived and developed by de Shazer and colleagues (de Shazer, 1985, 1988; de Shazer et al., 1986; Molnar & de Shazer, 1987; O'Hanlon & Weiner-Davis, 1989) at the Brief Family Therapy Center (BFTC) in Milwaukee, Wisconsin, almost 45 years ago. It emerged as a form of brief or short-term psychotherapy and therefore can be understood as a type of brief intervention. This explains the frequent reference to solution-focused brief therapy (SFBT). The emphases of SFC are pragmatism (i.e., what works) and mental health (rather than mental illness; Berg & Miller, 1992), which make SFC a radically simple approach (McKergow & Korman, 2009) and an alternative to problem-focused practices that continue to prevail in both mental health care and substance abuse treatment. SFC has its roots in the work of hypnotherapist Milton Erickson and family systems theory, and during its later years of development, in post-structural/post-modern, constructivist, or social constructionistic ideology (de Shazer & Berg, 1992).

The essence of SFC is its focus on the accomplishments, strengths, resources, and abilities of the client. Rather than prioritizing the problems and deficits that typically accompany a referral to counseling, the solution-focused practitioner solicits (from clients, family members, referral source, other treatment staff) and attends to those things in the client's life that have gone well and continue to go well. Indeed, SF counselors assume that clients want to change and that the solution, or at least part of it, is probably already taking place (Gingerich & Wabeke, 2001). This is not to say that presenting concerns are dismissed; rather, "exceptions" (de Shazer, 1988) to problem occurrence are given prominence in order to formulate with the client a solution or a series of solutions so that formal treatment is no longer necessary. Such a focus exemplifies the clinician's confidence in the client's ability to make positive changes in his or her own life by accessing and utilizing strengths and resources. Positive change is not only regarded as possible, but inevitable (Berg & Miller, 1992), characterizing SFC as the "counseling of hope" (Nunnally, 1993).

Berg and Miller (1992) are credited with being the first to apply SFC to substance abuse treatment, specifically treatment for alcohol-related problems. Since then, many others have contributed to the conversation of integrating SFC into substance abuse treatment (e.g., Berg &

Reuss, 1998; de Shazer & Isebaert, 2003; Linton, 2005; Mason, Chandler, & Grasso, 1995; Smock et al., 2008; Spilsbury, 2012). Additional contributions to the literature are needed to further support what S. D. Miller, Hubble, and Duncan (1996) described as SFC's suitability with a range of client concerns in a variety of treatment settings. SFC has not had a solid empirical research base, although there are efforts to improve the quality and quantity of investigations (see recent reviews of its research by Corcoran & Pillai, 2009; Gingerich & Peterson, 2013; Kim, 2008). It has remained a popular approach among mental health and substance abuse treatment providers. Indeed, Herbeck, Hser, and Teruya's (2008) survey of program administrators and staff members in California revealed that SFC was considered one of the more effective treatment approaches and used in more than half of the participating sites despite compelling research findings. Herbeck et al. surmised that despite compelling evidence, SFC may be intuitively appealing to treatment providers because its "techniques and tools . . . fit particularly well with the complex needs of substance-abusing populations" (p. 708). Linton (2005) also noted that SFC can be integrated well with other interventions.

Encouragement from Research

Although not a study explicitly utilizing solution-focused approaches, Iguchi, Belding, Morral, Lamb, and Husband's (1997) "shaping strategy" with 103 opioid-dependent clients (63% male, 85% White) bears resemblance to several essential aspects of SFC and offers encouraging results for the use of SFC in substance abuse treatment. Clients were randomly assigned to one of three treatment groups: (a) standard treatment (ST; individual counseling for take-home medication eligibility), (b) urinalysis-based reinforcement (UA; standard treatment plus opportunity to earn vouchers for each urine specimen testing free of unauthorized substances), and (c) treatment-plan-based reinforcement (TP). Vouchers were described to clients as "treatment assistance coupons" which could be redeemed (with appropriate receipts) only for expenses that could be tied to a specific treatment plan goal, such as clothing appropriate for a job interview and transportation to counseling sessions.

In the TP group of Iguchi et al.'s (1997) study, counselors met weekly with clients to establish the following week's behavioral tasks and "were generally free to tailor tasks to suit the needs of individual participants" (p. 423)—hence, the "shaping strategy" of TP. As opposed to the UA group, TP members earned vouchers for demonstrating their engagement in new and positive behaviors (e.g., contacting local computer training program), rather than their nonactivity in or elimination of substance use (i.e., providing a "clean" urine specimen). That is, desirable behaviors were reinforced. In addition, if the client failed to earn vouchers for these tasks (e.g., not appearing for a scheduled counseling session), the counselor would be urged to establish an easier task (e.g., participating with the counselor in an abbreviated telephone conversation). When clients succeeded in earning vouchers, counselors were directed to gradually increase the difficulty of subsequent tasks with the aim of achieving long-term treatment plan goals.

Primary results of Iguchi et al.'s (1997) study were that over the four 6-week evaluation periods, only TP clients demonstrated significant improvement in abstinence rates over time, and TP clients attended significantly more counseling sessions than clients in either of the other two groups. The authors interpreted these results to suggest that "the reinforcement of clearly defined behavioral tasks targeted toward long-term goals increases involvement in behaviors inconsistent with drug use among methadone maintenance patients" (p. 426). Overall, the TP program's encouraging outcomes indicate that a strengths-based, nonpunitive, and collaborative form of treatment—an approach consistent with SFC—is appropriate in substance abuse treatment and perhaps preferable to an approach whereby all clients receive the same type of care, are required to achieve abstinence, and are rewarded only for what they are *not* doing (i.e., using). Results such as these bode well for the continued integration of SFC in substance abuse treatment. Indeed, the design and implementation of the TP program appears to fulfill all seven of Berg and Miller's (1992) criteria of "well-formed" treatment goals: (a) saliency to the client; (b) small; (c) concrete, specific, and behavioral; (d) the presence rather than the absence of something; (e) a beginning rather than an end; (f) realistic and achievable within the context of the client's life; and (g) perceived as involving "hard work."

Related to personalized goal formulation, de Shazer and Isebaert (2003) studied nurse therapists and their patients who participated in a chemical dependency treatment program in Belgium that subscribed to a solution-focused approach. The focus of treatment was on identifying exceptions to the presenting problem and honoring clients' preferences for therapy, that is, what patients wanted from treatment. Patients were allowed to choose a treatment goal of controlled drinking or abstinence, provided in an individual, couple, or family format. Approximately 10% of the clients who initially chose controlled drinking changed their goal to abstinence.

At 4-year follow-up (former patients contacted by telephone), 50% ($n = 36$) of the former patients reported being abstinent and 32% reported success at controlled drinking. de Shazer and Isabaert (2003) reported that only 19 of the 36 former clients who claimed abstinence had originally chosen abstinence as their goal; controlled drinking had been the choice of only 12.5% ($n = 9$) of those were now claiming abstinence at follow-up. The authors stated that this result "strongly suggests that having a choice of goals and the ability to change goals makes a big difference in patients' treatment success" (p. 49). This supports the goal-setting task that Lee, Sebold, and Uken (2003) use in the first group session of SFC with domestic violence offenders. Rather than the counselor prescribing a goal (e.g., "Client will abstain from all mood- and mind-altering drugs"), solution-focused counselors elicit from the client his or her preferred outcome and honor that choice as much as possible.

de Shazer and Isabaert's (2003) study suggests that clients may actually benefit in the long run by being active participants in counseling, empowered by having had their choices heard and respected. The authors concluded that

> at least some optimism is warranted. The situation is entirely changed once a second possible remedy to the alcohol problem is introduced. With two ways to approach the goal, failure at one only means that patients should try the other approach. . . . There is a big difference between choosing to drink and believing that you have no choice but to drink. (p. 51)

It is this promotion of choice and encouraging clients to actively engage in counseling that may explain the findings of Smock et al.'s (2008) comparison of six sessions of two different forms of group therapy for persons with alcohol use problems. Members of the SFBT group were queried about their own identified goals (using the "miracle question" and scaling questions) and then encouraged to assess their progress (highlighting exceptions), whereas members of the non-SFBT control group received education about the effects of substance use on such things as mood, attitude, and grief. From pre-therapy to post-therapy, the SFBT group demonstrated significant reductions in depressive symptoms and other concerns (e.g., interpersonal relationships) compared to the control group. Smock et al. (p. 117) suggest that the "unique approach" of SFBT that encourages clients to "take ownership over" their treatment leads "to more cooperation and ultimately more successful outcomes."

Solution-Focused Integration

SFC has been used in combination with other counseling approaches, namely motivational interviewing (Lewis & Osborn, 2004), person-centered therapy (Cepeda & Davenport, 2006), existential therapy (Fernando, 2007), CB therapy and motivational interviewing (Corcoran, 2005), and creative arts therapy (Matto, Corcoran, & Fassler, 2003; Tyson & Baffour, 2004). A separate chapter of this book is devoted to motivational interviewing, and the specific practices of an integrated SFC and creative arts therapy approach appear to be particularly conducive for substance abuse counseling. Therefore, this latter combination is briefly highlighted.

Tyson and Baffour (2004) studied 108 adolescents (ranging in age from 11 to 18 years, mean age of 15.29 years; 92.6% Caucasian, 67.5% female) who participated in an SF and strengths-based group treatment program on a child and adolescent unit of an acute-care psychiatric hospital (typical length of stay was 4–7 days). Just over 10% of the participants had a primary diagnosis of substance abuse (the 4th highest among 9 primary diagnoses assigned) and 24.1% had a secondary diagnosis of substance abuse (most frequent secondary diagnosis assigned, almost twice that of any other secondary diagnosis assigned). The focus of the study was on soliciting from the young patients their positive strengths for managing stress, with the assumption being that these internal resources would be useful in accentuating exceptions to the problem. That is, patients were asked to identify crisis situations that may occur for them in the future that would not require hospitalization as a result of their implementation of positive strengths (namely, some type of expressive art that they alone identified).

Of those youth with a primary diagnosis of substance abuse, half identified "play musical instrument" as their arts-based strength (a statistically significant difference from those with a primary substance abuse diagnosis who did not identify "play a musical instrument") that would be used to "stop the problem from pushing me around." None of the youth who reported that they initially "write poetry, journals, stories" as a means of dealing with their problems had a primary diagnosis of substance abuse. Tyson and Baffour (2004) concluded that youth with a primary diagnosis of substance abuse were more likely to play a musical instrument or sing in order to deal with an impending crisis. In terms of treatment, they stated, "For these youth, it might be appropriate and personally relevant to use some form of music (e.g., play musical instrument) in the context of treatment" (p. 223).

For both adolescents and adults struggling with substance use problems, the integration of SFC and specifically art therapy may prove helpful. Matto et al. (2003) described the process of having clients draw their primary problem as being a form of externalization or detachment from the problem. They stated that such an activity "introduces fluidity to problems . . . [so that] the oppressive nature of the problem is lifted . . . " (p. 266). In addition, depending on the skill of the counselor, solutions can be constructed in the very act of drawing. That is, clients can be encouraged to modify aspects of their art work (e.g., use another color, outlining some aspect of the drawing, erasing or removing something from the art work), and this in itself conveys that solutions are constructed over time, in stages or increments (i.e., not necessarily one giant leap), and under the client's control. During this process, clients can be commended on changes made and can then be asked to draw their strengths, which can have the effect of making the strengths "more concrete and tangible [because of the] physical and emotional investment in the creative process" (p. 270).

Solution-Focused Assumptions and Practices Useful in Substance Abuse Counseling

Several solution-focused assumptions guide the practice of SFC. Although clearly not exhaustive, the solution-focused assumptions and practices presented in this section were selected in light of their feasibility to substance abuse counseling.

PRAGMATISM AND PARSIMONY Consistent with its origins as a brief or short-term therapy, SFC is known for its pragmatism and, as Berg and Miller (1992) highlight, its parsimony. This is what McKergow and Korma (2009) describe as the radically simple feature of SFBT that makes it unique. Perhaps in conducting intentional counseling that addresses directly the client's presenting concerns and preferences, one is by default keeping the work simple or parsimonious. Conversely, simplicity may engender pragmatism. Regardless of the sequence, SFC exemplifies a brief intervention in its focus on helping the client get unstuck by not dwelling on the intricacies of the problem (e.g., the "reason" for the client's substance use). In many ways this is a respectful approach in that the client's time is not wasted with gathering extensive historical data. In addition, working toward relief from pressing symptoms and concerns is prioritized.

COLLABORATION IS KEY SFC has been regarded as a means to further individualize care and to improve therapeutic partnerships with clients (Mason et al., 1995). The emphasis on or commitment to client–counselor collaboration is evident in SFC's proposition of three types of therapeutic *relationships* as opposed to three types of clients (Berg & Miller, 1992; Berg & Reuss, 1998). The *visitor-type relationship* describes the interaction that may ensue when the client believes there is not a problem and the counselor agrees, validates, or "goes along with" this perception, while at the same time offering to help the client in ways the client may be able to determine. The *complainant-type therapeutic relationship* typifies problem recognition and a shared understanding of the nature of the problem (e.g., on probation with the county municipal court for a repeated driving under the influence [DUI] charge), with the focus being on how the client can transition to seeing him- or herself as part of the solution (as opposed to looking to others for resolution, e.g., "Get my probation officer off my back"). Finally, the *customer-type relationship* involves joint construction of a solution plan or path that the client is able and willing to participate in and even take the lead on.

LANGUAGE OF HOPE Careful attention to the type of language and words used by clients is essential in the practice of counseling, as is counselor intentionality in the selection of words used with clients. This is particularly true for an SFC approach wherein words and language are thought to create reality and meaning. Given that the majority of clients in substance abuse treatment have not initiated services on their own (i.e., have been mandated by a court system or a social service agency and are thus considered "involuntary") and more than likely feel angry, demoralized, and fearful about being sent to counseling, skeptical about the need for treatment and its outcome, the specific words used by the counselor can have a significant effect on the client's amenability to and engagement in counseling. For example, use of the word *alcoholic* or *addict* to describe the counselor's assessment of the client may not initially engender cooperation and may actually further aggravate the client's frustration and reluctance to be in counseling. Gingerich and Wabeke (2001) articulated an SFC perspective on diagnostic labels by stating:

SFBT therapists eschew talk of diagnosis, disability, and pathology. Such talk, in spite of good intentions, frequently serves to confirm the client's view of himself or herself as someone who is disabled. Thus, unless there is reason to believe that diagnosing would lead to a needed medical intervention, the therapist steers conversation toward the client's desired scenario and what he or she can do to make that happen. (p. 35)

When conveying assessment results, including the preliminary diagnosis, it is recommended that the solution-focused counselor refer to the substance use disorder as a *condition*, something the client *has*, rather than someone the client *is*. A focus on the condition rather than an insinuation of the person's worth (i.e., "You are the problem") can be viewed as an effort to externalize the problem, a means for the client to exert control over the problem (i.e., client empowerment) rather than allowing the problem to continue to consume the client. This type of externalization, however, may not be considered compatible with the disease concept of addiction.

Other examples of language use in SFC that may be interpreted by the client as hopeful rather than disempowering or judgmental include the words *setbacks* rather than *relapses* (Berg & Miller, 1992), and *multiple episodes of sobriety* (Mason et al., 1995) rather than a sole or primary consideration of *multiple relapses* or reference to a client as "a chronic relapser." In addition, Berg and Reuss (1998) have made use of a "recovery checklist" (rather than a diagnostic or problem checklist) comprised of targeted positive behaviors for the client to engage in as part of his or her recovery. What may be regarded as a confrontational counseling style can be reframed as an "invitation for clarification," with the counselor beginning with, "Help me understand" (i.e., requesting clarification of two discrepant reports or stories, e.g., "I don't have a drinking problem" and a history of 3 DUIs). Overall, Lee et al. (2003) recommend that solution-focused counselors use language implying that (a) clients want to change, (b) clients are capable, (c) change has occurred or is occurring, and (d) changes are meaningful.

EXCEPTIONS FACILITATE CHANGE An example of expeditious practice in SFC is the focus on exceptions to the problem rather than on the problem itself. Exceptions refer to occasions when the problem is not a problem or times when the problem could have happened (e.g., relapse) but did not. S. D. Miller (1992) characterized exceptions as problem "irregularit[ies]" (p. 2), further illustrating the notion that exceptions are changes or alterations to what the client may have resigned him- or herself as being the "same old, same old" problem pattern. In order to help the client get unstuck from a "problem-saturated story" (White & Epston, 1990), the counselor can inquire about exceptions in one or more of four areas (Nunnally, 1993): (a) the past, (b) recent nonproblem occurrences, (c) recurrent exceptions (i.e., instances that occur periodically, often without warning), and (d) occasions in the future when the client can imagine the problem no longer existing or being influential.

Past exceptions can be detected by inquiring about life before using or occasions when the negative consequences of one's use were not prominent or even existent. "Tell me about a time before cocaine came into the picture when you felt good about something you had done, even proud of yourself" is a means of shifting the client's perspective to a nonproblem time in the past, and a time when the client experienced positive emotions that were not drug induced. If the client responds with an "I don't know," the counselor should not quickly claim defeat but should pursue with the follow-up: "Oh, take a moment to think back, maybe a time when you were in school, maybe when someone else pointed out something you had done well. Give it a shot." If the client is still not able to generate a past success story, the counselor can encourage the client to consider a hypothetical scenario, as in "If there had been a time when you felt good, even proud, of something you had done, when might that have been? What would you have hoped you would have been able to accomplish back then?"

Recent and recurrent exceptions, as with past exceptions, may not be in the client's awareness and so require the counselor's curiosity skills about recent events or experiences that can be interpreted as glimmers of a possible solution in the making. Reframing also may be necessary. This is exemplified in the following case study.

CASE STUDY
A Reframe for Exceptional Anton

"Anton" was a young and quiet African-American male who faithfully attended his counseling sessions but said he was only coming in because he "had to." "Okay, so you have to," his counselor acknowledged. "But you're here every week and on time, which is a miracle in itself compared to many other clients who come here. Tell me one thing that you've gotten out of our last few sessions that has brought you back for more." After a long pause and a brief sigh, with eyes downcast, Anton softly said, "I don't know, I guess I feel okay here, you know, like I'm not being hassled. You listen." Rather than wanting to take full credit for Anton's positive experience in counseling, his counselor followed up with, "Well, what's made it possible for you to trust this place, to trust me, a White woman, and sit and talk in here?" The intent of this question was to identify what may have very well been a new or recurrent exception to Anton's problem story (e.g., a change in thinking), an exception for which he could claim responsibility and credit, such as "I guess I need to lay off the weed so I can get through school this year. My auntie's been on me for months, but now I need to do something."

Perhaps the best known example for constructing *future exceptions* in SFC is the use of the "miracle question." de Shazer (1985) is credited with designing this creative question to encourage clients to visualize, and potentially make real, a future nonproblem period. By imagining and projecting themselves into a future situation (namely, tomorrow) in which the problem is no longer present, clients can view themselves as functioning satisfactorily (Molnar & de Shazer, 1987). The "script" for the miracle question might be worded as follows:

> "Suppose that tonight, while you are asleep, there is a miracle and the problem that brought you to counseling was solved. However, because you're asleep, you don't know that the miracle already happened. So, when you wake up tomorrow morning, what will be different that will tell you that this miracle has really taken place?"

Being the "Curious Columbos" (Selekman, 1993) and skillful inquirers that they are, solution-focused counselors will ask clients for details of their miracle morning, such as specific behaviors they will be engaging in, things that other people will notice in them, things they will be thinking about, and feelings that will be prominent to them.

"Susan," a divorced Native American in her mid-30s, struggled with visualizing her nonproblem day. Not only had she been using alcohol problematically for the past 10–15 years, she also presented with symptoms of social phobia and had been physically and sexually abused by her ex-husband. She was currently estranged from her immediate family members, including her teenage son who had decided to live with Susan's father several hours away. Rather than continuing to press Susan with a description of her miracle morning, with Susan's permission, I contacted by postal mail Susan's father and her son, requesting that they complete a questionnaire I had devised, containing specific questions that might elicit from them some "ingredients" to help Susan imagine and eventually make real at least one day that minimized or even was free of her problem.

The counseling session in which the returned and completed family questionnaires were shared with Susan remains vivid. Susan's father wrote that he was proud of his daughter's courage to finally leave her abusive husband and Susan's son wrote that he was grateful for the love and protection his mother had shown him since he was little. Her son said he was doing well in school so that she would be proud of him. Susan was tearful throughout this counseling session as she heard the "testimony" of family members dear to her, testimonials to Susan's personal strengths and qualities (exceptions!) that she had not been able to recognize in herself for a long time. Following that session, Susan was able to use what she heard from her father and her son to begin formulating her "miracle morning," one in which she awakened with courage not to consume her usual alcohol "eye opener" and to talk to her neighbor instead, doing so without experiencing panic symptoms. She said this would be her way of continuing to love her son and to make both her son and father proud of her. Rehearsing this miracle morning was something that we did over the next few sessions, knowing that miracle construction would not take place in a day, but over time, in pieces or ripples, and with practice, feedback, support, and encouragement.

NOTICE THE DIFFERENCE It is critical that SF counselors not only be on the lookout for positive differences in or exceptions to client behaviors; they must also assist their clients (and the client's family members, too) to notice when these problem irregularities occur. One Appalachian client I had the privilege to work with over several months demonstrated the importance of this. "Ricky" was in his mid-30s, married, and a father of two elementary school age daughters. He acknowledged being illiterate, experiencing discord in his marriage, consuming alcohol on a daily basis, and still grieving over the loss of his father (his "drinking buddy") 3 years earlier. Unemployed due to a physical disability, Ricky spent his time working in the garage on automobiles and motorcycles and secluding himself in a TV room he had fashioned for himself.

In one session, Ricky reported having maintained sobriety from alcohol for 4 consecutive days in the past week, a monumental effort given his long history of excessive alcohol use. After attempting to explore with Ricky how he was able to remain sober for 4 consecutive days (using solution-focused coping questions), I asked about his return to drinking after 4 days: "What happened?" His response is still haunting and tugs at my empathic heart: "No one noticed." Without his genuine efforts to initiate sobriety being recognized by those most important to him, Ricky essentially gave up, perhaps asking himself, "What's the use?" Although he may have been able to identify for himself some benefits of his 4-day sobriety, at this very early stage of his recovery, Ricky needed the positive reinforcement of others (i.e., external motivators), particularly with the co-occurrence of depressive symptoms.

If I had this client case to work with again, I would have been more intentional about including Ricky's wife periodically in counseling (consistent with outcome research indicating the efficacy of behavioral marital therapy) or at least asking her on the telephone, "What have you noticed in Ricky this past week that's different for the better?" (a question that presupposes positive change). I might have also challenged Ricky to engage in new and more positive behaviors that would be evident to his wife and daughters, things said or actions taken that would convince them that he was making strides in attaining and maintaining abstinence. A target behavior could be reviewed and even practiced in counseling (e.g., "So when the girls get home from school, what will you do instead of working in the garage?" and "What will you say differently when your wife complains about you watching too much TV? Let's practice having you say it out loud."). In addition, an assignment given such as, "When you spend time with the girls this next week, and when you say something different to your wife, notice how they respond. Be on the lookout for changes you see and hear in them. We'll talk about this next week."

COMMENDATIONS Throughout the process of counseling, solution-focused counselors are on the lookout for and notice positive differences—exceptions—in their clients. When sincere efforts or accomplishments are evident (e.g., attending one's first AA meeting), the counselor brings those to the client's attention in the form of commendations or what are referred to in motivational interviewing as "affirmations." Commendations or affirmations are not to be confused with well-intentioned, although less than substantive, "cheers" that may be regarded by the client as disingenuous. In addition, accolades that do not specify a positive behavior the client has recently implemented (e.g., "You're doing a great job!") may fail to reinforce the specific positive behavior targeted as a client goal. Consistent with the hard work criterion of well-formed treatment goals in SFC, commendations should highlight the client's hard work. For example, "Ricky" would be commended for his 4 consecutive days of sobriety ("Despite really wanting to go out to the garage and drink, you didn't. You stayed inside and watched TV with the girls. This took a lot of effort on your part."), and "Susan" would be commended for not drinking in the morning before talking with her neighbor ("You did it! How *were* you able to do that? How did you enlist your courage to actually go outside, knock on her door, and start a conversation with her? Tell me how you did all of this!").

HARM REDUCTION

Marlatt (1998), the most prominent voice of harm reduction in the addictions, described this particular ideology and its practices according to five enduring principles, assumptions, and values. Harm reduction can first be understood as a public health alternative to moral/criminal and disease models of drug use and addiction that, second, recognizes abstinence as an ideal outcome but accepts alternatives that reduce harm. This second principle implies that "prevention" is an approach intended to prevent, or at least reduce, the harmful effects of use, not use itself (Marlatt & Witkiewitz, 2002). The third principle or assumption of harm reduction is that it has emerged primarily at a local level and represents a "grass-roots" approach based on addict advocacy, rather than originating as a federal "top-down" mandate. Fourth, harm reduction promotes low-threshold access to services (i.e., meeting the individual where he or she is, respecting the individual's initial goal as a means of engaging the person in services) as an alternative to traditional, "high-threshold" approaches (e.g., requiring abstinence as the initial treatment goal). Finally, harm reduction is based on the tenets of compassionate pragmatism (i.e., focusing on managing one's daily functioning) versus moralistic idealism. This latter principle is what aligns harm reduction with palliative care. An example is the Housing First program that provides shelter (and other services) to homeless persons with severe alcohol problems, many of whom also have co-occurring mental health problems. For residents who continue to drink and may die from alcohol-related conditions, McNeil et al. (2012) describe Housing First as end-of-life care, allowing residents to die "at home" in their own bed surrounded by caring staff rather than on the street and alone.

It may be evident from this preliminary description that harm reduction reflects behavioral and cognitive-behavioral principles, embraces the FRAMES perspective of brief interventions, and bears resemblance to SFC. Indeed, as a "low-threshold" entry into addiction services, harm reduction "[accepts] the client's definition of the problem as the legitimate starting point for intervention . . . [so as] to join with that which motivates the client to seek help, meet the client's needs, and, around this motivation, facilitate a positive treatment alliance" (Tatarsky, 2003, p. 251). In addition, "Harm reduction approaches the participant as the expert of their story, respecting their solutions and pace" (Majoor & Rivera, 2003, p. 257), which echoes Walter and Peller's (2000) admonition that clinicians listen for and honor client preferences. Harm reduction thus respects the right of persons to choose how to live their lives with minimal health risks incurred by them and by others. According to Blume and Lovato (2010), it is this philosophy of empowerment that make harm reduction practices a natural fit for many racial and ethnic minority communities.

Consistent with one of the assumptions of SFC, harm reduction is a pragmatic approach to alcohol and drug use and related problems, which Kellogg (2003) described as having three purposes: staying alive, maintaining health, and/or getting better. Marlatt and Witkiewitz (2002) expanded on these in their listing of three core objectives of harm reduction: (a) reduce harmful consequences (to user, society) associated with alcohol/drug use; (b) provide alternatives to zero-tolerance approaches by incorporating using goals (abstinence or moderation) compatible with the needs of the individual; and (c) promote access to services by offering low-threshold alternatives to traditional substance use prevention and treatment. Thus, harm reduction counseling does not require abstinence as an initial treatment goal because, as W. R. Miller and Page (1991) argued, "abrupt attainment and maintenance of total abstention is the exception rather than the rule" (p. 231). In addition, as solution-focused practitioners de Shazer and Isabaert (2003) noted,

> When a problem is believed to have only one remedy, failure in an attempt at that remedy is viewed as the individual's fault. Each subsequent failure demands that the individual increase his or her efforts at applying the remedy, that is, doing more of something that is not working. (p. 50)

Other routes to abstinence are therefore often considered in harm reduction, including Miller and Page's (1991) "warm turkey" approach. This alternative includes *sobriety sampling*, whereby the client attempts to abstain for a period of time (e.g., over a weekend), on an experimental basis, is intentional about taking mental or even written inventory of the experience (e.g., completing a self-monitoring card of cravings/urges, "close calls," emotional states, and any relapses), and then reports to his or her counselor at the next session how the trial period went. Another alternative to abstinence is *tapering down* (also described as "gradualism" and "abstinence eventually"; Kellogg, 2003), wherein the amount and frequency of consumption is gradually decreased, perhaps using a weekly or monthly calendar. This practice was used with a young adult male client whose marijuana use reportedly reduced and calmed his tactile hallucinations (i.e., a sensation of bugs crawling over his body). Rather than require this client to abruptly abstain from the only "home-grown treatment" that so far had helped his co-occurring psychotic symptoms, we agreed that he would gradually reduce the number of marijuana joints he was smoking daily each week for the next month. A calendar was created on which the client was to mark the number of joints smoked each day and brought to each counseling session. This plan and practice was in place while we waited for his initial appointment with the psychiatrist for an evaluation. Similar in some ways to gradualism, a third alternative to abstinence is that of *trial moderation*, which refers to a negotiated period of time when the client is allowed to try limiting his or her intake. This takes place after a period of sobriety, with the support of a counselor or concerned significant other, and usually applies to alcohol use only.

Despite the pragmatic and humanistic philosophy of harm reduction, many addiction counselors in the United States may not eagerly embrace its practices because they seemingly contradict long-held beliefs about addiction and its treatment (e.g., abstinence as the only goal for the disease of addiction). This attitude may not have changed very much in the past 10 years.

Rosenberg and Phillips (2003) found that a majority of representatives (primarily clinical directors and program administrators) of drug and alcohol treatment agencies in the United States were receptive to implementing certain harm reduction strategies. Ten of 13 interventions listed were rated by a majority of respondents to the postal mail survey (51% return rate) as somewhat or completely acceptable, including education (63%), needle exchange (61%), and alternative therapies (e.g., acupuncture; 81%), as well as pharmacological interventions such as agents used in opiate detoxification (80%), postdetoxification (e.g., Naltrexone; 74%), and drug replacement (i.e., short-term use of methadone; 67%). Despite the rather high acceptability rates of these strategies, a majority of respondents indicated that the 13 harm reduction interventions listed were not available at their agency, primarily due an incompatibility with agency philosophy and, to a lesser extent, lack of funding and staff resources to implement such strategies. The use of nonabstinence as an intermediate treatment goal was reported by approximately one-third of respondents as available at their agencies, whereas its use as a final goal for treatment was less available.

In a more recent study, Davis and Rosenberg (2013) found that addiction counselors in their sample (15% return rate) differed in their acceptance of their clients' selection of nonabstinence as a treatment goal depending on the substance in question, its problem severity, and whether nonabstinence was an intermediate or the final treatment goal. For example, although the majority of respondents said they would accept nonabstinence as an intermediate or final treatment goal for clients diagnosed with alcohol abuse (51% and 58%, respectively), fewer were accepting of these goals when the diagnosis was drug abuse (47% and 32%, respectively). And still fewer said they would accept nonabstinence as a final treatment goal for clients with a diagnosis of either alcohol dependence (16%) or drug dependence (15%). Although these views of nonabstinence as a treatment goal are not much different from the earlier study (Rosenberg & Phillips, 2003), Davis and Rosenberg verbalize a somewhat encouraging tone to persons with substance use problems who have not accessed treatment because they are ambivalent about abstinence: Depending on your substance of choice, its problem severity, and level of treatment goal (intermediate or final), many addiction counselors will accept your wish to moderate your consumption. This tone and the overall study findings must be tempered by the low response rate. There is good reason to believe, however, that further education of staff about the legitimate benefits of harm reduction strategies (i.e., to promote a change in attitude or philosophy) is needed to help further implementation of harm reduction practices, along with parallel attitude changes in funding sources (e.g., federal government).

Similar to concerns that may be raised with implementing brief interventions in alcohol and drug treatment, harm reduction may not be deemed appropriate by some practitioners because of what might be considered its "enabling" characteristics (i.e., viewed as encouragement to continue using). However, given that the vast majority of persons in the United States today with substance use problems do not receive treatment services (SAMHSA, 2012), both brief interventions and a harm reduction approach appear well suited for reaching persons who may never obtain such services. Indeed, of the eight most frequent reasons given for not obtaining services even when a need was recognized and an initial attempt made, three would be well served by brief interventions and harm reduction: not ready to stop using (25.5%), negative opinion from community/neighbors and negative effect on job (combined 17.3%), and no transportation or inconvenient (9.5%). The remaining reasons include cost or insurance barriers (47.4%), not knowing where to go for treatment (7.3%), and not having time for treatment (7.1%).

Pragmatic and humanistic counseling practices that respect the client's initial goal for treatment, emphasize client–counselor collaboration, and address harm reduction and not just substance use elimination alone may very well benefit the 19.3 million persons in 2011 reported by SAMHSA (2012) who needed but did not receive treatment for a substance use problem. At the very least, these practices could "gently persuade" and engage persons in needed services, and in so doing, might serve as "stepping stones" to more intensive services. As Tatarsky (2003) noted,

> Harm reduction practices are one way to begin an ambitious process of change, the endpoint of which cannot be foreseen at the outset. The goal is to support the client in going as far as [he or she] possibly can toward the harm reduction ideals of optimal health, self-sufficiency, self-actualization and satisfaction in the world of relationships. (pp. 250–251)

Summary and Some Final Notations

The counseling approaches described in this chapter share several common assumptions and practices and, when each is consulted or utilized in an intentional and collective fashion (e.g., adhering to W. R. Miller & Hester's, 2003, "informed eclecticism" model), may very well form a tapestry of a strengths-based and salutary counseling posture informed by theory and empirical research. Indeed, harm reduction "suggests the need for an integrated treatment system with linkages across the spectrum of treatment modalities" (Tatarsky, 2003, p. 252), which serves as further indication of a healthy entanglement and useful behavioral and cognitive-behavioral approaches, brief interventions, solution-focused counseling, and harm reduction.

In addition to websites already included in the text of this chapter, there are additional websites that can offer further information on the topics presented and discussed in this chapter.

MyCounselingLab

Visit the MyCounselingLab site for *Foundations of Addictions Counseling*, Third Edition to enhance your understanding of concepts. You'll have the opportunity to practice your skills through video- and case-based exercises. You will find sets of questions to help you prepare for your certification exam with *Licensure Quizzes*. There is also a Video Library that provides taped counseling sessions, ethical scenarios, and interviews with helpers and clients.

Useful Websites

Center on Alcoholism, Substance Abuse, and Addictions (CASAA)
www.casaa.unm.edu
CASAA, affiliated with the University of New Mexico, is devoted to conducting and disseminating research that informs substance abuse prevention and treatment (e.g., motivational interviewing, community reinforcement approach). Numerous assessment instruments are available free of charge and downloadable from the CASAA website.

Solution-focused Brief Therapy Association
www.sfbta.org
Founded in 2002 to support the practice and research of solution-focused brief therapy. Training opportunities and products are listed.

Harm Reduction Coalition
www.harmreduction.org
The Harm Reduction Coalition is a "national advocacy and capacity-building organization that promotes the health and dignity of individuals and communities impacted by drug use."

References

Amaro, H., Reed, E., Rowe, E., Picci, J., Mantella, P., & Prado, G. (2010). Brief screening and intervention for alcohol and drug use in a college student health clinic: Feasibility, implementation, and outcomes. *Journal of American College Health, 58,* 357–364.

Anton, R. F., O'Malley, S. S., Ciraulo, D. A., Cisler, R. A., Couper, D., Donovan, D. M., . . . , for the COMBINE Study Research Group. (2006). Combined pharmacotherapies and behavioral interventions for alcohol dependence: The COMBINE study: A randomized controlled trial. *JAMA, 295,* 2003–2017.

Benishek, L. A., Kirby, K. C., Dugosh, K. L., & Padovano, A. (2010). Beliefs about the empirical support of drug abuse treatment interventions: A survey of outpatient treatment providers. *Drug and Alcohol Dependence, 107,* 202–208.

Berg, I. K., & Miller, S. D. (1992). *Working with the problem drinker: A solution-focused approach.* New York, NY: W. W. Norton.

Berg, I. K., & Reuss, N. H. (1998). *Solutions step by step: A substance abuse treatment manual.* New York, NY: W. W. Norton.

Blume, A. W., & Lovato, L. V. (2010). Empowering the disempowered: Harm reduction with racial/ethnic minority clients. *Journal of Clinical Psychology, 66,* 189–200.

Bowen, S., Chawla, N., Collins, S. E., Witkiewitz, K., Hsu, S., Grow, J., . . . Marlatt, A. (2009). Mindfulness-based relapse prevention for substance use disorders: A pilot efficacy trial. *Substance Abuse, 30,* 295–305.

Bowen, S., Chawla, N., & Marlatt, G. A. (2011). *Mindfulness-based relapse prevention for addictive behaviors: A clinician's guide.* New York, NY: Guilford Press.

Bowen, S., & Marlatt, A. (2009). Surfing the urge: Brief mindfulness-based intervention for college student smokers. *Psychology of Addictive Behaviors, 23,* 666–671.

Boyd, J. W., Harris, S. K., & Knight, J. R. (2012). Screening and brief interventions for the addiction syndrome: Considering the vulnerability of adolescence. In H. J. Shaffer (Ed.), *APA Addiction syndrome handbook, Volume 2: Recovery, prevention, and other issues* (pp. 169–194). Washington, DC: American Psychological Association.

Branson, C. E., Barbuti, A. M., Clemmey, P., Herman, L., & Bhutia, P. (2012). A pilot study of low-cost contingency management to increase attendance in an adolescent substance abuse program. *The American Journal on Addictions, 21,* 126–129.

Caplehorn, J. R. M., Lumley, T. S., & Irwig, L. (1998). Staff attitudes and retention of patients in methadone maintenance programs. *Drug and Alcohol Dependence, 52,* 57–61.

Carroll, K. M., & Rounsaville, B. J. (2007). A vision of the next generation of behavioral therapies research in the addictions. *Addiction, 102,* 850–862.

Cepeda, L. M., & Davenport, D. S. (2006). Person-centered therapy and solution-focused brief therapy: An integration of present and future awareness. *Psychotherapy: Theory, Research, Practice, Training, 43,* 1–12.

Corcoran, J. (2005). *Building strengths and skills: A collaborative approach to working with clients.* New York, NY: Oxford University Press.

Corcoran, J., & Pillai, V. (2009). A review of the research on solution-focused therapy. *British Journal of Social Work, 39,* 234–242.

Davis, A. K., & Rosenberg, H. (2013). Acceptance of nonabstinence goals by addiction professionals in the United States. *Psychology of Addictive Behaviors, 27,* 1102–1109.

de Shazer, S. (1985). *Keys to solution in brief therapy.* New York, NY: W. W. Norton.

de Shazer, S. (1988). *Clues: Investigating solutions in brief therapy.* New York, NY: W. W. Norton.

de Shazer, S., & Berg, I. K. (1992). Doing therapy: A poststructural re-vision. *Journal of Marital and Family Therapy, 18,* 71–81.

de Shazer, S., Berg, I. K., Lipchik, E., Nunnally, E., Molnar, A., Gingerich, W., & Weiner-Davis, M. (1986). Brief therapy: Focused solution development. *Family Process, 25,* 207–221.

de Shazer, S., & Isebaert, L. (2003). The Bruges Model: A solution-focused approach to problem drinking. *Journal of Family Psychotherapy, 14*(4), 43–52.

DiFulvio, G. T., Linowski, S. A., Mazziotti, J. S., & Puleo, E. (2012). Effectiveness of the Brief Alcohol Screening Intervention for College Students (BASICS) program with a mandated population. *Journal of American College Health, 60,* 269–280.

Dimeff, L. A., Baer, J. S., Kivlahan, D. R., & Marlatt, G. A. (1999). *Brief Alcohol Screening Intervention for College Students: A harm reduction approach.* New York, NY: Guilford Press.

Donovan, D. M., Anton, R. F., Miller, W. R., Longabaugh, R., Hosking, J. D., & Youngblood, M., for the COMBINE Study Research Group. (2008). Combined pharmacotherapies and behavioral interventions for alcohol dependence (The COMBINE Study): Examination of posttreatment drinking outcomes. *Journal of Studies on Alcohol and Drugs, 69,* 5–13.

Drake, R. E., Merrens, M. R., & Lynde, D. W. (Eds.). (2005). *Evidence-based mental health practice: A textbook.* New York, NY: W. W. Norton.

Ducharme, L. J., Knudsen, H. K., Abraham, A. J., & Roman, P. M. (2010). Counselor attitudes toward the use of motivational incentives in addiction treatment. *The American Journal on Addictions, 19,* 496–503.

Fernando, D. M. (2007). Existential theory and solution-focused strategies: Integration and application. *Journal of Mental Health Counseling, 29,* 226–241.

Gingerich, W. J., & Peterson, L. T. (2013). Effectiveness of solution-focused brief therapy: A systematic qualitative review of controlled outcome studies. *Research on Social Work Practice, 23,* 266–283.

Gingerich, W. J., & Wabeke, T. (2001). A solution-focused approach to mental health intervention in school settings. *Children & Schools, 23,* 33–47.

Goodheart, C. D., Kazdin, A. E., & Sternberg, R. J. (2006). *Evidence-based psychotherapy: Where practice and research meet.* Washington, DC: American Psychological Association.

Hayes, S. C., Follette, V. M., & Linehan, M. M. (Eds.). (2004). *Mindfulness and acceptance: Expanding the cognitive-behavioral tradition.* New York, NY: Guilford.

Hayes, S. C., Strosahl, K. D., & Wilson, K. G. (2012). *Acceptance and commitment therapy: The process and practice of mindful change* (2nd ed.). New York, NY: Guilford Press.

Heather, N. (1995). Brief intervention strategies. In R. K. Hester & W. R. Miller (Eds.), *Handbook of alcoholism treatment approaches: Effective alternatives* (2nd ed., pp. 105–122). Boston, MA: Allyn & Bacon.

Herbeck, D. M., Hser, Y., & Teruya, C. (2008). Empirically supported substance abuse treatment approaches: A survey of treatment providers' perspectives and practices. *Addictive Behaviors, 33,* 699–712.

Higgins, S. T., Silverman, K., & Heil, S. H. (Eds.). (2008). *Contingency management in substance abuse treatment.* New York, NY: Guilford Press.

Iguchi, M. Y., Belding, M. A., Morral, A. R., Lamb, R. J., & Husband, S. D. (1997). Reinforcing operants other than abstinence in drug abuse treatment: An effective alternative for reducing drug use. *Journal of Counseling and Clinical Psychology, 65,* 421–428.

Kellogg, S. H. (2003). On "gradualism" and the building of the harm reduction-abstinence continuum. *Journal of Substance Abuse Treatment, 25,* 241–247.

Kim, J. S. (2008). Examining the effectiveness of solution-focused brief therapy: A meta-analysis. *Research on Social Work Practice, 18,* 107–116.

Lee, M. Y., Sebold, J., & Uken, A. (2003). *Solution-focused treatment of domestic violence offenders: Accountability for change.* New York, NY: Oxford University Press.

Levenson, H., Speed, J., & Budman, S. H. (1995). Therapists' experience, training, and skill in brief therapy: A bicoastal survey. *American Journal of Psychotherapy, 49,* 95–117.

Lewis, T. F., & Osborn, C. J. (2004). Solution-focused counseling and motivational interviewing: A consideration of confluence. *Journal of Counseling & Development, 82,* 38–48.

Lilienfeld, S. O. (2007). Psychological treatments that cause harm. *Perspectives on Psychological Science, 2,* 53–70.

Linehan, M. M. (1993a). *Cognitive-behavioral treatment of borderline personality disorder.* New York, NY: Guilford.

Linehan, M. M. (1993b). *Skills training manual for treating borderline personality disorder.* New York, NY: Guilford.

Linton, J. M. (2005). Mental health counselors and substance abuse treatment: Advantages, difficulties, and practical issues to solution-focused interventions. *Journal of Mental Health Counseling, 27,* 297–310.

Maisto, S. A., Conigliaro, J., McNeil, M., Kraemer, K., Conigliaro, R. L., & Kelley, M. E. (2001). Effects of two types of brief intervention and readiness to change on alcohol use in hazardous drinkers. *Journal of Studies on Alcohol, 62,* 605–614.

Majoor, B., & Rivera, J. (2003). SACHR: An example of an integrated, harm reduction drug treatment program. *Journal of Substance Abuse Treatment, 25,* 257–262.

Manuel, J. K., Austin, J. L., Miller, W. R., McCrady, B. S., Tonigan, J. S., Meyers, R. J., . . . , Bogenschutz, M. P. (2012). Community reinforcement and family training: A pilot comparison of group and self-directed delivery. *Journal of Substance Abuse Treatment, 43,* 129–136.

Marlatt, G. A. (1998). *Harm reduction: Pragmatic strategies for managing high-risk behaviors.* New York, NY: Guilford.

Marlatt, G. A., & Donovan, D. M. (Eds.). (2005). *Relapse prevention: Maintenance strategies in the treatment of addictive behaviors* (2nd ed.). New York, NY: Guilford.

Marlatt, G. A., & Gordon, J. R. (Eds.). (1985). *Relapse prevention.* New York, NY: Guilford Press.

Marlatt, G. A., & Witkiewitz, K. (2002). Harm reduction approaches to alcohol use: Health promotion, prevention, and treatment. *Addictive Behaviors, 27,* 867–886.

Mason, W. H., Chandler, M. C., & Grasso, B. C. (1995). Solution based techniques applied to addictions: A clinic's experience in shifting paradigms. *Alcoholism Treatment Quarterly, 13*(4), 39–49.

Matto, H., Corcoran, J., & Fassler, A. (2003). Integrating solution-focused and art therapies for substance abuse treatment: Guidelines for practice. *The Arts in Psychotherapy, 30,* 265–272.

McCambridge, J. (2011). Editorial: Fifty years of brief intervention effectiveness trials for heavy drinkers. *Drug and Alcohol Review, 30,* 567–568.

McCance-Katz, E. F., & Satterfield, J. (2012). SBIRT: A key to integrate prevention and treatment of substance abuse in primary care. *The American Journal on Addictions, 21,* 176–177.

McCrady, B. S., & Epstein, E. E. (Eds.). (2013). *Addictions: A comprehensive guidebook* (2nd ed.). New York, NY: Oxford University Press.

McGovern, M. P., Fox, T. S., Xie, H., & Drake, R. E. (2004). A survey of clinical practices and readiness to adopt evidence-based practices: Dissemination research in an addiction treatment system. *Journal of Substance Abuse Treatment, 26,* 305–312.

McGovern, M. P., Saunders, E. C., & Kim, E. (2013). Editorial: Substance abuse treatment implementation research. *Journal of Substance Abuse Treatment, 44,* 1–3.

McHugh, R. K., Hearon, G. A., & Otto, M. W. (2010). Cognitive-behavioral therapy for substance use behaviors. *Psychiatric Clinics of North America, 33,* 511–525.

McKergow, M., & Korman, H. (2009). In between—Neither inside nor outside: The radical simplicity of solution-focused brief therapy. *Journal of Systemic Therapies, 28*(2), 34–49.

McNeil, R., Guirguis-Younger, M., Dilley, L. B., Aubry, T. D., Turnbull, J., & Hwang, S. W. (2012). Harm reduction services as a point-of-entry to and source of end-of-life care and support for homeless and marginally housed persons who use alcohol and/or illicit drugs: A qualitative analysis. *BMC Public Health, 12,* 312/1–9. Retrieved from http://www.biomedcentral.com/1471-2458/12/312

Meyers, R. J., Roozen, H. G., & Smith, J. E. (2011). The community reinforcement approach: An update of the evidence. *Alcohol Research & Health, 33,* 380–388.

Meyers, R. J., Villanueva, M., & Smith, J. E. (2005). The community reinforcement approach: History and new directions. *Journal of Cognitive Psychotherapy, 19,* 247–260.

Miller, P. M. (Ed.). (2009). *Evidence-based addiction treatment.* New York, NY: Academic Press/Elsevier.

Miller, S. D. (1992). The symptoms of solution. *Journal of Strategic and Systemic Therapies, 11,* 1–11.

Miller, S. D., Hubble, M. A., & Duncan, B. L. (Eds.). (1996). *Handbook of solution-focused brief therapy.* San Francisco, CA: Jossey-Bass.

Miller, W. R. (1992). The effectiveness of treatment for substance abuse: Reasons for optimism. *Journal of Substance Abuse Treatment, 9,* 93–102.

Miller, W. R. (Ed.). (2004). *COMBINE Monograph Series, Volume 1. Combined Behavioral Intervention Manual: A clinical research guide for therapists treating people with alcohol abuse and dependence.* Bethesda, MD: National Institute on Alcohol Abuse and Alcoholism.

Miller, W. R., Andrews, N. R., Wilbourne, P., & Bennett, M. E. (1998). A wealth of alternatives: Effective treatments for alcohol problems. In W. R. Miller & N. Heather (Eds.), *Treating addictive behaviors* (2nd ed., pp. 203–216). New York, NY: Plenum.

Miller, W. R., Forcehimes, A. A., & Zweben, A. (2011). *Treating addiction: A guide for professionals.* New York, NY: Guilford Press.

Miller, W. R., & Hester, R. K. (2003). Treating alcohol problems: Toward an informed eclecticism. In R. K. Hester & W. R. Miller (Eds.), *Handbook of alcoholism treatment approaches: Effective alternatives* (3rd ed., pp. 1–12). Boston, MA: Allyn & Bacon.

Miller, W. R., & Muñoz, R. F. (2013). *Controlling your drinking: Tools to make moderation work for you* (2nd ed.). New York, NY: Guilford Press.

Miller, W. R., & Page, A. C. (1991). Warm turkey: Other routes to abstinence. *Journal of Substance Abuse Treatment, 8,* 227–232.

Miller, W. R., & Pechacek, T. F. (1987). New roads: Assessing and treating psychological dependence. *Journal of Substance Abuse Treatment, 4,* 73–77.

Miller, W. R., & Rollnick, S. (2013). *Motivational interviewing: Helping people change* (3rd ed.). New York, NY: Guilford Press.

Miller, W. R., & Sanchez, V. C. (1994). Motivating young adults for treatment and lifestyle change. In G. S. Howard & P. E. Nathan (Eds.), *Alcohol use and misuse by young adults* (pp. 55–81). Notre Dame, IN: University of Notre Dame Press.

Miller, W. R., Sorensen, J. L., Selzer, J. A., & Brigham, G. S. (2006). Disseminating evidence-based practices in substance abuse treatment: A review with suggestions. *Journal of Substance Abuse Treatment, 31,* 25–39.

Miller, W. R., & Wilbourne, P. L. (2002). Mesa Grande: A methodological analysis of clinical trials of treatments for alcohol use disorders. *Addiction, 97,* 265–277.

Miller, W. R., Wilbourne, P. L., & Hettema, J. E. (2003). What works? A summary of alcohol treatment outcome research. In R. K. Hester & W. R. Miller (Eds.), *Handbook of alcoholism treatment approaches: Effective alternatives* (3rd ed., pp. 13–63). Boston, MA: Allyn & Bacon.

Molnar, A., & de Shazer, S. (1987). Solution-focused therapy: Toward the identification of therapeutic tasks. *Journal of Marital and Family Therapy, 13,* 349–358.

Morgenstern, J., Frey, R. M., McCrady, B. S., Labouvie, E., & Neighbors, C. J. (1996). Examining mediators of change in traditional chemical dependency treatment. *Journal of Studies on Alcohol, 57,* 53–64.

Moyers, T. B., & Miller, W. R. (1993). Therapists' conceptualizations of alcoholism: Measurement and implications for treatment decisions. *Psychology of Addictive Behaviors, 7,* 238–245.

Najavits, L. M., Liese, B. S., & Harned, M. S. (2005). Cognitive and behavioral therapies. In J. H. Lowinson, P. Ruiz, R. B. Millman, & J. G. Langrod (Eds.), *Substance abuse:*

A comprehensive textbook (4th ed., pp. 723–732). Philadelphia, PA: Lippincott Williams & Wilkins.

Norcross, J. C., Koocher, G. P., Fala, N. C., & Wexler, H. K. (2010). What does not work? Expert consensus on discredited treatments in the addictions. *Journal of Addiction Medicine, 4,* 174–180.

Nunnally, E. (1993). Solution focused therapy. In R. A. Wells & V. J. Giannetti (Eds.), *Casebook of the brief psychotherapies* (pp. 271–286). New York, NY: Plenum.

Ogborne, A. C., Wild, T. C., Braun, K., & Newton-Taylor, B. (1998). Measuring treatment process beliefs among staff of specialized addiction treatment services. *Journal of Substance Abuse Treatment, 15,* 301–312.

O'Hanlon, W., & Weiner-Davis, M. (1989). *In search of solutions: A new direction in psychotherapy.* New York, NY: W. W. Norton.

Olmstead, T. A., Abraham, A. J., Martino, S., & Roman, P. M. (2012). Counselor training in several evidence-based psychosocial addiction treatments in private US substance abuse treatment centers. *Drug and Alcohol Dependence, 120,* 149–154.

Ondersma, S. J., Svikis, D. S., Thacker, L. R., Beatty, J. R., & Lockhart, N. (2014). Computer-delivered screening and brief intervention (e-SBI) for postpartum drug use: A randomized trial. *Journal of Substance Abuse Treatment, 46,* 52–59.

Petry, N. M. (2012). *Contingency management for substance abuse treatment: A guide to implanting this evidence-based practice.* New York, NY: Routledge/Taylor & Francis.

Petry, N. M., Martin, B., Cooney, J. L., & Kranzler, H. R. (2000). Give them prizes, and they will come: Contingency management for treatment of alcohol dependence. *Journal of Consulting and Clinical Psychology, 68,* 250–257.

Roozen, H. G., Boulogne, J. J., van Tulder, M. W., van den Brink, W., De Jong, C. A. J., & Kerkhof, A. J. F. M. (2004). A systematic review of the effectiveness of the community reinforcement approach in alcohol, cocaine, and opioid addiction. *Drug and Alcohol Dependence, 74,* 1–13.

Roozen, H. G., de Waart, R., & van der Kroft, P. (2010). Community reinforcement and family training: An effective option to engage treatment-resistant substance-abusing individuals in treatment. *Addiction, 105,* 1729–1738.

Rosenberg, H., & Phillips, K. T. (2003). Acceptability and availability of harm-reduction interventions for drug abuse in American substance abuse treatment agencies. *Psychology of Addictive Behaviors, 17,* 203–210.

Sanchez-Craig, M. (1990). Brief didactic treatment for alcohol and drug-related problems: An approach based on client choice. *British Journal of Addiction, 85,* 169–177.

Selekman, M. D. (1993). *Pathways to change: Brief therapy solutions with difficult adolescents.* New York, NY: Guilford.

Shaffer, H. J., & Robbins, M. (1991). Manufacturing multiple meanings of addiction: Time-limited realities. *Contemporary Family Therapy, 13,* 387–404.

Smith, J. E., Meyers, R. J., & Milford, J. L. (2003). Community reinforcement approach and community reinforcement and family training. In R. K. Hester & W. R. Miller (Eds.), *Handbook of alcoholism treatment approaches: Effective alternatives* (3rd ed., pp. 237–258). Boston, MA: Allyn & Bacon.

Smith, J. E., Meyers, R. J., & Miller, W. R. (2001). The community reinforcement approach to the treatment of substance use disorders. *The American Journal on Addictions, 10*(Suppl.), 51–59.

Smock, S. A., Trepper, T. S., Wetchler, J. L., McCollum, E. E., Ray, R., & Pierce, K. (2008). Solution-focused group therapy for level 1 substance abusers. *Journal of Marital and Family Therapy, 34,* 107–120.

Spilsbury, G. (2012). Solution-focused brief therapy for depression and alcohol dependence: A case study. *Clinical Case Studies, 11,* 263–275.

Substance Abuse and Mental Health Services Administration. (2012). *Results from the 2011 National Survey on Drug Use and Health: Summary of national findings* (NSDUH Series H-44, HHS Publication No. [SMA] 12-4713). Rockville, MD: Author.

Tatarsky, A. (2003). Harm reduction psychotherapy: Extending the reach of traditional substance use treatment. *Journal of Substance Abuse Treatment, 25,* 249–256.

Thombs, D. L., & Osborn, C. J. (2001). A cluster analytic study of clinical orientations among chemical dependency counselors. *Journal of Counseling & Development, 79,* 450–458.

Thombs, D. L., & Osborn, C. J. (2013). *Introduction to addictive behaviors* (4th ed.). New York, NY: Guilford Press.

Tracy, S. W. (2007). Medicalizing alcoholism one hundred years ago. *Harvard Review of Psychiatry, 15,* 86–91.

Tyson, E. H., & Baffour, T. D. (2004). Arts-based strengths: A solution-focused intervention with adolescents in an acute-care psychiatric facility. *The Arts in Psychotherapy, 31,* 213–227.

Walter, J. L., & Peller, J. E. (2000). *Recreating brief therapy: Preferences and possibilities.* New York, NY: W. W. Norton.

White, M., & Epston, D. (1990). *Narrative means to therapeutic ends.* New York, NY: W. W. Norton.

Witkiewitz, K., Bowen, S., Douglas, H., & Hsu, S. H. (2013). Mindfulness-based relapse prevention for substance craving. *Addictive Behaviors, 38,* 1563–1571.

Chapter 9

Treatment of Comorbid Disorders

Scott E. Gillig
St. Thomas University

Pamela A. Cingel
St. Thomas University

It appears that the comorbidity of substance use disorders and other mental health disorders is extensive and highly correlated (Brems & Namyniuk, 1999; Johnson, Brems, Wells, Theno, & Fisher, 2003; Schneider, 2005; Substance Abuse and Mental Health Services Administration [SAMHSA], 2013). This chapter addresses the history of how mental health systems have adapted to meet the needs of clients with multiple disorders.

The prevalence of comorbidity is examined in this chapter. With the publication of the *Diagnostic Statistical Manual* (5th ed., DSM-5; American Psychiatric Association [APA], 2013), the previous term of *co-occurring* (which replaced the earlier term *dual diagnosis*) has itself been replaced with the term of *comorbid* in describing clinical situations involving both substance use disorders and other mental health disorders. Therefore, the term comorbid rather than the more dated terms of dual-diagnosis or co-occurring will be used in this chapter. Additionally, the DSM-5 has dropped the terms abuse and dependence and replaced them with the phrase *substance use disorders*. Therefore, the phrase *substance use disorders* will be used here to signify "abuse" of substances and "dependence" on substances. Substance use disorder is further defined by the specifiers of *mild*, *moderate*, or *severe* in the DSM-5 depending on the number of symptoms (APA, 2013).

Issues related to assessment, diagnosis, treatment, and care needs are addressed. Suggestions for a multidisciplinary team approach to treatment will be covered. The components of the counseling process will be reviewed and a case example showing comorbid disorder (comorbid) assessment, diagnosis, and treatment planning will be presented.

HISTORY OF HOW MENTAL HEALTH SYSTEMS HAVE ADAPTED TO MEET THE NEEDS OF CLIENTS WITH MULTIPLE DISORDERS

Grella (2003) reported that those with comorbid psychiatric problems usually have shorter stays in treatment, poorer treatment outcomes, and higher treatment costs than those with only one disorder. Because dually diagnosed patients have diverse needs, their care requires flexible and integrated treatment methods and services. However, integrative treatment has historically been the exception rather than the rule. Most dually diagnosed individuals have traditionally received either mental health treatment or substance use disorders treatment, rather than both simultaneously. Researchers have found that those working in substance use disorders and mental health settings hold conflicting views about which treatment approaches work best for the dually diagnosed (Grella, 2003). While both substance use disorders and mental health professionals attributed the psychiatric symptoms of substance users to an underlying cause, it appears that substance use disorders professionals more strongly supported strict policies on the necessity of abstinence, discharge criteria, confrontational, and self-help methods than did mental health professionals (Grella, 2003).

According to Sciacca (1997), confrontation was traditionally used to break down the defense system and denial of substance abusing clients. On the other hand, mental health clients were treated in a supportive, nonthreatening way to help them maintain their already unstable defenses. Prior to 1984, there were few, if any, treatments available to serve those clients who entered the mental health system presenting with substance use disorders issues that they denied and who were thus unmotivated for substance use disorders treatment. Sciacca (1997) reports that dual-diagnosis treatment programs had their beginning in 1984 at a New York State outpatient psychiatric facility and that in the following year, such joint treatment programs were applied across multiple program sites in New York and throughout the country.

In 1984, Sciacca (1997) developed a nonconfrontational approach with the aim of providing nonjudgmental acceptance of clients' symptoms and experiences related to both mental illness and substance disorders. Her method involves engaging clients in phase-by-phase interventions that move clients from denial to abstinence. The components of her approach include development of trust, exploring symptoms, exploring interaction effects that stem from substance use disorders and mental health symptoms, working on client motivation, collaborating with the client to ameliorate symptoms, achievement of partial or full remission, and participation in an individualized maintenance routine for relapse prevention.

Helping professionals became progressively more aware of the link between substance use disorders and mental disorders in the late 1970s and early 1980s. During the 1980s and 1990s, studies found that 50–75% of substance use disorders clients had some type of comorbid mental disorder while 20–50% of mental health clients had a comorbid substance use disorder (SAMHSA, 2013). Besides its relationship to mental illness, substance use disorder was found to drastically complicate treatment outcomes for those with mental illness. Those with mental illness coupled with substance use disorders spent twice as many days in the hospital, had higher rates of HIV infection, more relapse, and higher suicide rates than those with mental illness alone (SAMHSA, 2013). Brems and Namyniuk (1999) emphasize the high financial and social costs associated with comorbid disorders. Such costs include loss of productivity, difficulty keeping jobs, increased health care and hospitalization costs, less satisfying family relationships, poorer treatment outcomes, increased criminal and suicidal behavior, poor medication compliance, and faster relapse. Although substance use disorders appeared to complicate mental health treatment, it was also found that treatment of clients with comorbid mental illness and substance use disorders can be effective (SAMHSA, 2013).

PREVALENCE OF COMORBIDITY

New counselors working in the field of substance use disorders treatment may wrongly assume that treating someone with a substance use disorder is a straightforward process and that the identified disorder will be the sole focus of treatment. In practice, however, for a client to present with a single substance use disorder, without a coexisting substance use disorder(s), or without a coexisting psychiatric disorder(s), would be the exception rather than the rule. According to Johnson et al. (2003) and Schneider (2005), comorbidity involves mental and emotional disorders that coincide with substance use disorders within an individual.

According to Von Steen, Vacc, and Strickland (2002), substance use treatment usually takes place in either specialized substance use treatment facilities or in community mental health centers. They report that about 25–30% of alcoholics experience depression and anxiety, respectively, while approximately 25% of all suicides are committed by individuals with chronic alcohol use disorders. They also report that counselor training programs need to offer increased coursework to prepare counselors to work in comorbid settings. Based on their findings, they suggest that counselors in community and mental health counseling programs receive specific training in substance use disorders assessment, 12-step work, family counseling for substance-abusing clients, relapse prevention, and treatment planning for clients with substance use disorders.

"Rates of regular heavy drinking (five or more drinks for men or four or more for women in a single day, on 12 or more days during the past year) were also found to be high for respondents who had a past year major depression (9%) or specific phobia (8.3%). Respondents with lifetime antisocial, obsessive-compulsive, and paranoid personality disorders also showed regular heavy drinking patterns (8.7%, 8.9%, and 7%, respectively). In general, the national estimates for those adults with a comorbid SUD and a mental disorder range from 5.2 million to 6.6 million."

Source: Substance Abuse and Mental Health Services Administration, 2009.

It is also important for counselors to keep in mind that clients with comorbid disorders often have cognitive limitations. Some of these limitations, which include difficulty concentrating, may improve during the initial weeks of treatment but some may become more obvious as part of a specific disorder (e.g., schizophrenia, attention deficit disorder). Strategies to address these limitations can include being more concrete in communicating, using simpler concepts, repeating concepts, and using multiple formats. Role-playing may be a useful technique and can be used for anything from practicing making a phone call to a sponsor to appropriate sharing in a group situation.

Since abstinence requires the development and utilization of a new set of recovery skills, clients with mental disorders and cognitive limitations usually have a harder time learning these new skills. That is why repetition and practice is especially important for these clients (SAMHSA, 2013).

The following case study provides an example of the use of repetition and skill building with a comorbid client:

In individual counseling sessions with Susan H., a 34-year-old Caucasian woman with bipolar disorder and alcohol use disorder, the counselor observes that often she is forgetful about details of her recent past, including what has been said and agreed to in therapy. Conclusions the counselor thought were clear in one session seem to be fuzzy by the next. The counselor begins to start sessions with a brief review of the last session. He also allows time at the end of each session to review what has just happened. As Susan H. is having difficulty remembering appointment times and other responsibilities, he helps her devise a system of reminders in big letters on her refrigerator. (SAMHSA, 2013)

While Susan's case illustrates a client with comorbid diagnoses, it is not uncommon to have a client with multiple diagnoses such as the following case of Matt G. This case involved a complex web of treatment issues: marital issues, family issues, sexual preference issues, religious orientation issues, early childhood abuse issues, clergy abuse issues, multiple physical illnesses, multiple substance use disorders, multiple psychiatric and personality disorder issues (e.g., those commonly found with comorbid disorders such as major depression, borderline personality disorder, and compulsive behaviors). According to APA (2013), major categories of mental disorders for comorbid schizophrenia and other psychotic disorders include anxiety disorders, mood disorders, somatoform disorders, dissociative disorders, eating disorders, sleep disorders, impulse-control disorders, sexual and gender identity disorders, and personality disorders. The Substance Abuse and Mental Health Services Administration (SAMHSA, 2009) has some excellent fact sheets related to comorbid disorders. Links can be found at the end of the chapter.

CASE STUDY

Matt, a 30-year-old, contacted Dr. Reid for individual counseling. During the intake session, he reported that issues from his family of origin were affecting his marriage. Matt additionally complained that he had been feeling angry, anxious, bored, confused, depressed, fearful, and tense. He identified other problems as important also: family, sexual orientation, marriage, religion, procrastination, lack of motivation, and physical health. Matt presented with a history of drug/alcohol use, impulsivity around sex, a pattern of unstable relationships, affective instability, feelings of boredom, and intense fear of abandonment. He complained that his in-laws are opposed to his being married to their daughter, especially in light of their discovery of his gay lifestyle. He also indicated his brother is currently in prison for rape. Matt stated he was abused both emotionally and physically as a child by this older brother. Of importance is that Matt initially experienced a conflict between the religion that he grew up with (Lutheran) and that to which he converted to please his wife (Jehovah Witness). His wife's religious support system was highly opposed to his gay experiences.

Matt began dating at 18 years of age. He indicated he has had difficulty trusting women. He is currently married to Nancy, 32, for 2 years and has been separated for approximately 1 year. He reported that he told her of his homosexual orientation prior to marriage. Matt initially expressed ambivalence about wanting to separate from his spouse until he resolved his family of origin issues. Matt stated that he and his wife had previously been in therapy with Dr. Buford in a private practice off and on with apparent limited investment.

Matt initially reported past use of marijuana for 14 years, cocaine use for 3 years, and alcohol use for 15 years. He also initially reported that he rarely uses alcohol and does not use any other mind-altering chemicals except for Zantac prescribed by his family doctor, Dr. Espino. Over the course of several sessions with Dr. Reid, it became evident that Matt had lost control over his drinking on numerous occasions. It was also observed that when he is in a relationship, he tends to put on weight and discontinues having anonymous sex with partners he meets in bars, and limits his drinking and drugging (cocaine and marijuana). When he is not in a committed relationship, he loses weight and resumes drinking, drugging, and sexual acting out.

Dr. Reid met with Matt and his wife for several couples counseling sessions. While Matt initially lived with his wife and her two children at the onset of his counseling, as counseling went on, Matt was very certain about both his gay identity and his desire to be separated and/or divorced from his wife. After becoming divorced, his ex-wife and children moved to another part of the state and maintained a separate residence there.

As part of his counseling treatment with Dr. Reid, Matt was referred to an Adults Molested as Children program to help him address his child abuse issues. He did not follow through with this except for an initial visit. Then Matt attempted several times to establish a gay support system on his own. Unfortunately, two of the individuals whom he sought for support, attempted to seduce Matt. One was a paraprofessional and his actions were reported to the State Counseling Board. It was hypothesized that while Matt was a victim, he was reenacting the childhood dynamic of when his brother sexually molested him and his father failed to protect him. Matt appeared to put Dr. Reid in the role of his father. He agreed with this interpretation put forth by Dr. Reid and seemed to move forward in his counseling as a result of this insight. He refused to attend Alcoholics Anonymous (AA) meetings, but his counseling sessions with Dr. Reid involved attempts to help Matt stop drinking and drugging. On a positive note, while in treatment with Dr. Reid, Matt did follow through with his sessions and attended regularly. He reported at the time that he felt more comfortable interacting with males as a result of his counseling with Dr. Reid. He reported himself not to be currently suicidal. Dr. Reid was planning to continue long-term counseling with this client, who seemed to have the resources to improve himself. Unfortunately, Matt impulsively self-terminated counseling without notifying Dr. Reid and moved out of state.

After moving out of state, Matt contacted Dr. Reid by phone asking him for a referral. From his report, Matt had entered an inpatient chemical dependency treatment program that offered him no aftercare plan or referrals. He had suffered two drug overdoses before entering chemical dependency treatment. He reported that while in this inpatient chemical dependency treatment for chemical dependency, he was found to be infected with Hepatitis B.

Dr. Reid gave Matt several referral options in his new location. According to reports by his new counselor, Dr. Brown, Matt developed a severe clinical depression, as indicated by a score of 36 on the Beck Depression Inventory, and attempted suicide while in counseling there. He was referred to a psychiatrist, Dr. Germaine, entered a treatment center for comorbid disorders, and was put on Prozac. Matt responded quite well initially, but then showed hypomanic behavior and lost therapeutic motivation. He began to drink and frequent gay bars more often.

Dr. Reid was contacted by phone at a later date by Matt, who indicated he was moving to another location to live with his sister. Matt indicated he had appointments with both therapist and a psychiatrist there.

A DSM-5 diagnosis of the client is as follows:

309.81—Post-traumatic Stress Disorder, With Delayed Expression

305.00—Alcohol Use Disorder, Mild

305.60—Cocaine Use Disorders, Mild

305.20—Cannabis Use Disorder, Mild

307.79—Other Specified Sexual Dysfunction

301.83—Borderline Personality Disorder

V61.03 Disruption of Family by Separation or Divorce

Treatment recommendations include having the client receive weekly individual counseling sessions; attend AA, Drug Addicts Anonymous, Overeaters Anonymous, and Sex Addicts Anonymous meetings (as many as possible weekly); engage in a gay support system; continue with routine psychiatric treatment; obtain employment; continue to explore family of origin issues (i.e., sexual abuse, physical abuse); and be monitored for suicidal ideation on an ongoing basis.

Some of the innovations in treatment of comorbid disorders include the following: the development of new models that stress the importance of knowledge of both mental health and substance use disorders treatment when working with clients for whom both issues are present; the provision of a classification of treatment settings to assist in systematic planning, consultations, collaborations, and integration; and a reduction in the double stigma associated with both disorders through increased acceptance of substance use disorders and mental health concerns as a standard part of health care assessment (Substance Abuse and Mental Health Services Administration, 2013).

ASSESSMENT

According to APA (2013), all substance and behavioral use disorders have the following behaviors in common: compulsive use without control, continued use despite negative consequences, obsession with using or obtaining the drug or behavior, and a craving or a strong desire or urge to use a substance. Drug and alcohol use disorders, combined with mental health issues, can create a very complex clinical picture. The use of standardized testing instruments can be helpful to gain clinical clarity with assessment of comorbid issues.

Juhnke, Vacc, Curtis, Coll, and Paredes (2003) surveyed master's-level addictions counselors (MACs) who hold the National Certified Counselor (NCC) credential and additionally specialize in treating substance use disorders. They found that five assessment instruments were seen both as most important to use and most often used by substance use disorders counselors. These instruments include the Substance Abuse Subtle Screening Inventory (SASSI) (both the SASSI-3 and the SASSI Adolescent versions), the Beck Depression Inventory (BDI), the Minnesota Multiphasic Personality Inventory—2 (MMPI-2), the Addictions Severity Index (ASI), and the Michigan Alcoholism Screening Test (MAST). Interestingly, two of the five instruments, the BDI and the MMPI-2, are primarily used to detect mental and emotional disorders, not substance use disorders per se.

Junhke et al. (2003) also found that while MACs mostly agree on the importance and relative frequency of use of these assessment instruments, counselors who specialize in substance use disorders treatment use these instruments infrequently. Possible reasons cited for why counselors are not using assessment instruments more often include the following: the belief held by counselors that they can arrive at accurate diagnoses without the use of standardized assessment instruments, or that the use of such instruments could promote a pathology rather than a wellness focus, and that counselors believe they lack substance use disorders-specific training in use of assessment instruments. Juhnke et al. (2003) have suggested that use of such assessment instruments could do much to enhance counselors' ability to assess clients with substance use disorders issues.

Johnson et al. (2003) studied use of the Brief Symptom Inventory as a screening tool and found that 64% of 700 participants met the criteria for having comorbid substance use disorders and other psychiatric symptoms. Comorbid individuals were more apt to be homeless, unemployed, and Caucasian; have a higher past arrest rate, more severe drug use disorders, and lower age of first drug use; and were more likely to have used various drugs more frequently than those without comorbidity (Johnson et al., 2003).

During the assessment process, counselors might ask, "Which came first, the substance use disorder or the psychiatric problem?" It appears that either can be the case. According to Schneider (2005), use of addictive substances can initiate, exacerbate, mask, or mimic psychiatric problems. Similarly, psychiatric problems can make one more susceptible to substance use disorders. Given alcohol's depressing and disinhibiting effects, many alcoholics are depressed and many have been diagnosed with antisocial personality disorder (Schneider, 2005). On the other hand, people who are depressed may self-medicate and get a temporary lift from drinking alcohol. A depressed person may also turn to cocaine or an amphetamine to get a lift since these are stimulants. However, withdrawal from these substances can result in increased depression and lack of energy. While children with attention deficit hyperactivity disorder (ADHD) are at higher risk of later substance use disorders, treatment with stimulants, such as Ritalin, make substance use disorders less likely to occur in the future (Schneider, 2005). The reason for this may be that these children were more closely monitored by their family physicians, which may of help in prevention of later substance use disorders (Schneider, 2005). So the role of early intervention coupled with stimulant treatment for ADHD may have accounted for the decrease in later substance use disorders.

If a client has both a substance use disorder and a psychiatric disorder, there are several questions that a counselor should consider in addition to "Which one came first?" Examples would be "Which one is primary?" and "Which one should be treated first?" Typically, symptoms like aggression and depression that stem from substance use disorders decrease once the person stops using the addicting substance. If this does not happen, it is likely that the psychiatric problem was first. Such an assumption can be strengthened by taking a thorough client history. When assessing a client with both a mental health problem and a substance use disorder, the one that came first is usually primary and is important to address for relapse prevention. However, in either case, the substance use disorder is typically dealt with first through detoxification and/or other medical intervention (Schneider, 2005).

To illustrate the importance of determining primacy and treatment importance, consider the assessment of a drug-dependent gang member. If it were determined that this gang member also met diagnostic criteria for conduct disorder or antisocial personality disorder, it would be important to determine whether drug use disorders and/or criminal activity started first, and if either or both started before or after joining the gang. According to Duffy and Gillig (2004), gang members use drugs more often and at higher levels than do nongang members. It appears that being involved in gangs encourages involvement in drug use, drug trafficking, gun carrying, violence, and drug sales. It also appears that substance use opens the door to increased crime and violence. Substance use requires a steady stream of drugs, and many addicted young gang members increase their criminal activities in order to obtain the drugs needed to support their habits. This is the vicious cycle of drug use—it leads to more crime and increased drug use (Duffy & Gillig, 2004). If joining a gang opened the doorway for drug use, then exploring issues around gang membership should be considered very important for relapse prevention.

During assessment, effective comorbid counselors will also pay attention to compulsive behavioral patterns. Compulsive behaviors can interfere with treatment and can lead to relapse. This author recalls working with a 30-year-old male client who would drink alcohol excessively, overeat, and would isolate himself and stay home when depressed. When his depression lifted, he would begin to lose weight, use cocaine, visit the bars and nightclubs, and have compulsive sex with multiple anonymous partners. So, the substance use disorders, behavioral compulsions, and the mood disorder all needed to be addressed in order to assist this client. Some of the areas to assess for behavioral compulsions include sex, work, shopping, relationships, eating, exercise, and gambling.

Cultural Issues Related to Assessment

The culture of the client is an important issue to address during the assessment phase. The number of minority, racial, and ethnic groups in the United States is on the rise (SAMHSA, 2013). Each geographic region has its own cultural blend, and counselors are advised to learn as much as possible about the cultures within their treatment populations. Especially during assessment, it is important that counselors understand the background of clients in addition to methods of communication, healing, and understanding of both mental disorders and substance use disorders. Culturally effective counselors study the interpersonal interactions and expectations of family. For instance, in some groups, people may be inclined to somaticize symptoms of mental disorders, and clients from such cultures may assume the clinician will work to relieve their physical complaints. The same client may be insulted by too many probing, personal questions asked during assessment early in treatment and will prematurely self-terminate. Likewise, understanding the client's role in the family and its cultural impact is important (e.g., expectations of a daughter's responsibilities to her parents, protectiveness of the family toward the youngest child, and grandfather as patriarch) (SAMHSA, 2013).

Although counselors need to be attuned to the impact of culture on clients, overgeneralizing their views about clients based on culture is not helpful. It is possible that the level of acculturation and the particular experiences of an individual may result in that person identifying with the dominant culture, or even other cultures. For example, a person from China adopted by American parents at an early age may know little about the cultural norms in her country of origin. For such clients, it is still important to acknowledge the birth country and discover what this connection means to the client (SAMHSA, 2013).

Mericle, Ta Park, Holck, and Arria (2012) examined racial and ethnic differences in comorbid disorders. They found that rates of comorbidity vary significantly among differing racial and ethnic groups. More of the Whites (8.2%) received comorbid diagnoses than did racial and ethnic minorities. For example, only 5.4% of Blacks, 5.8% of Latinos, and 2.1% of Asians received comorbid diagnoses. Such findings come with the caution that racial and ethnic minorities tend to face more barriers to getting accurate diagnoses and care.

Mental health issues can create perceived cultural constraints within clients. Brems and Namyniuk (1999) indicate that treating clients diagnosed with comorbid disorders tends to be more difficult, as these clients can be inclined to perceive more treatment barriers than noncomorbid clients. The authors point to the importance of attending to comorbidity issues to increase client retention in treatment. They cited a study of 500 drug-abusing or -dependent patients by Ross, Glaser, and Germanson, who found that 68% had current and 84% had a past or current comorbid psychiatric diagnosis. It was found that 73% had a current personality disorder, with 53% of patients having Cluster B diagnoses, 28% with Cluster A diagnoses, and 24% with Cluster C diagnoses.

According to SAMSHA (2013), it is important that counselors be aware of cultural and ethnic bias in diagnosis. For example, there has been a tendency to overdiagnose African Americans as having paranoid personality disorders and women as being histrionic. Native Americans with spiritual visions have been misdiagnosed as delusional. Culturally sensitive counselors would refrain from overdiagnosing Germans with obsessive-compulsive disorder or Latino/Hispanic people with histrionic disorder. In addition, it has been reported that African-American, Latino/Hispanic, and Asian-American clients are more inclined to self-report a lower level of functioning, and to be seen by clinical staff as experiencing more serious and enduring symptomatology and as showing poorer psychosocial development (SAMSHA, 2013).

Researchers have also found that non-White clients tend to have less community resources available to them than White clients, and that clinicians have more difficulty linking them with needed services. The diagnostic criteria should be modulated by sensitivity to cultural differences in behavior and emotional expression and by an awareness of the clinician's own prejudice and stereotyping (SAMSHA, 2013).

In researching 192 ethnically diverse and substance-using pregnant women, Brems and Namyniuk (1999) found that more than 70% of the subjects had at least one *Diagnostic Statistical Manual* (4th ed.) (1994) diagnosis in addition to substance use disorder. Many clients had more than one such other diagnosis. Regarding psychiatric disorders, 24% had affective disorders, 15% anxiety disorders, 4% adjustment disorders, 3% psychotic disorders, 2% impulse control disorders, 2% eating disorders, 2% developmental disorders, and 2% had other disorders. Personality disorders were recorded for 24% of clients. Brems and Namyniuk (1999) found that comorbid clients had more pathology, higher suicide risk, and more drug usage that noncomorbid clients. They stress the importance of routinely assessing clients for comorbidity at all chemical treatment centers.

It is strongly recommended that culturally sensitive methods be used with clients with a comorbid diagnosis. Culturally sensitive counselors pay attention to cultural aspects of clients' lives while doing assessment, diagnosis, and treatment planning with people from diverse cultures. They respect culture and language as client strengths to be utilized in helping clients. Such counselors make their helping models fit the culture of clients rather than expecting clients to change cultural values to fit their models. Culturally responsible counselors work to educate themselves about clients' cultures while working to reduce their own biases (SAMSHA, 2013).

TREATMENT AND CARE NEEDS

Certain comorbid treatment program elements appear to be essential according to experts who design such treatment. To be qualified to treat comorbid conditions, these best practices should be present in both residential and outpatient programs: screening, assessment, referral, physical and mental health consultation, the presence of a prescribing on-site psychiatrist, availability of medication and medication oversight, psych educational classes that focus on mental health and substance use disorders including relapse prevention, on-site mental health and substance use disorders groups, off-site dual-recovery mutual self-help groups tailored to the special needs of a variety of people with comorbid disorders, and family education and treatment (SAMSHA, 2013).

According to Johnson et al. (2003), those providing counseling services to clients with comorbidity must apply specialized techniques to deal with an increased probability of high-risk behaviors (e.g., sharing needles, unprotected sex, prostitution). Comorbid clients often have inadequate social support and recovery support systems, unstable relationships, insufficient housing, are at higher risk for sexually transmitted diseases, and may be unemployed. Individuals presenting with comorbidity require careful treatment planning that addresses both substance use disorders and mental health issues. Such treatment includes psych educational interventions and relapse prevention that address the role of their high-risk behaviors in maintaining their substance use disorders.

"Double Trouble in Recovery is a twelve-step fellowship of men and women who share their experience, strength and hope with each other so that they may solve their common problems and help others to recover from their particular addiction(s) and manage their mental disorder(s). DTR is designed to meet the needs of the dually-diagnosed, and is clearly for those having addictive substance problems as well as having been diagnosed with a psychiatric disorders." (Double Trouble in Recovery, 2009).

Chartas and Culbreth (2001) indicate that while there is a positive correlation between substance use disorders and domestic violence, no cause-and-effect relationship has been demonstrated. They further indicate that those counselors involved primarily with substance use disorders treatment differ in their case conceptualizations from those who specialize in working with domestic violence alone. Domestic violence counselors tend to hold the view that intoxication may lead to loss of control of hostile impulses or may serve as an excuse to attack rather than provide a reason for attack. On the other hand, substance use disorders counselors often view battering as a symptom of substance use disorders (Chartas & Culbreth, 2001).

This philosophical schism between substance use disorders counselors and domestic violence counselors could impede the helping of clients when the two issues co-occur. For example, Chartas and Culbreth (2001) state that domestic violence counselors tend to be parental in their approach with substance users domestic violence perpetrators and assume that batterers are using their substance use disorders to justify their battering. Therefore, these counselors tend to utilize reinforcement and punishment as therapeutic techniques. On the other hand, substance use counselors would be more likely to see substance use disorders as a disease, with domestic violence as a consequence or symptom of that disease, and treat the perpetrators accordingly. Similarly, substance use disorder victims of domestic violence tend to be perceived and treated differently by domestic violence counselors and substance use disorders professionals. Such paradigm inconsistencies, especially when they manifest within multidisciplinary treatment teams or between professionals who work with the same clients, can lead to mixed messages that contribute to client confusion and reduction of treatment effectiveness.

An effort to eliminate client confusion regarding comorbid treatment is the recent creation of a policy called the "No Wrong Door Policy." The goal of this policy is that individuals can be treated for all their problems at the same time whether they are initially seeking treatment for a mental health problem or a substance use disorder. Without such a policy, if an individual initiated treatment for his or her substance use disorder at a treatment center exclusively for substance use disorders, the mental health problem might not be addressed. This policy emphasizes the necessity for multiple agencies to coordinate services (mental health and substance use disorders) and serve clients through a one-entry process that is overseen by one agency. Such a policy also helps eliminate duplication of services and ensures that clients get the support they need (Armor-Garb, 2004).

Most recently, confrontation as a therapeutic technique has been found to be ineffective in working with clients diagnosed with substance use disorders in studies using both control and treatment groups. Several studies have found damaging effects of confrontation, such as higher relapse and dropout rates (Miller & White, 2008).

Coexisting psychiatric disorders such as major depression can interfere with a client's ability to pay attention or concentrate sufficiently to benefit from substance use disorders treatment (Schneider, 2005). It has been one of the present co-author's (Gillig's) experience that it is often necessary to coach a substance use disorder client on how to use AA effectively.

CASE STUDY

The following case study demonstrates how counselors could coach and prep a comorbid disorder client for an AA meeting.

> Juan is a 35-year-old person with schizophrenia who talks about seeing pink elephants in therapy and tends to speak of this among family and friends. However, his counselor anticipates that in the room at AA meetings, Juan may be ridiculed by other members and scapegoated by the group, and thus not benefit from the healing effects of the group. Essentially, Juan with schizophrenia is part of a unique culture that is not common to the AA group in general. Juan's therapist has advised him to talk about the pink elephants in individual therapy but to be silent about them in AA meetings. Juan continues to make progress with both his mental health and substance use disorders, but with different therapeutic modalities for each.

An individual such as Juan, who has not been coached by his counselor ahead of time to keep quiet about the hallucinations during the AA meeting, runs the risk of being ostracized by the group. Such an incident is unfortunate and avoidable with proper preparation for the AA group participation. Helping a recovering alcoholic, including one with schizophrenia, to stay in an AA group will allow that person to address the problem of alcoholism as well as to benefit from the curative factor that Yalom (in Corey, 2001) refers to as *universality*, even though the group itself does not address the schizophrenia. The schizophrenia issues can be dealt with in another format, such as individual therapy or another group specifically geared to these issues.

COMORBID TREATMENT MODELS

When teaching a class on substance use disorders and treatment in counseling, Gillig (co-author) spends considerable time with the students addressing the question "Is a substance abuse disorder a disease?" While such a discussion is beyond the scope of this chapter, it does have considerable bearing on the type of model a new counselor will develop and what methods that counselor will choose to assist comorbid clients. If a counselor adheres to a "disease concept" model, then working in conjunction with 12-step groups that see substance use disorders as a disease is a more natural fit. Such counselors would likely be more comfortable with a goal of abstinence for clients. On the other hand, if the disease concept does not fit with a particular counselor's worldview, then some of the alternative models may be better fits. In our opinion, there is plenty of room for both disease concept and alternative models in the treatment of comorbid clients, and either or both may be appropriate for a given client. For clients who have more numerous and more severe symptoms, perhaps a disease concept model makes most sense. These clients may be best served with a goal of abstaining from substance use altogether. Clients who have fewer or less severe symptoms may be better served by an alternative treatment modality and may be better candidates to learn to drink responsibly, for example. In either case, there is no definitive answer, and such a discussion is beyond the scope of this chapter.

Disease Concept Model

For those counselors who are comfortable working from a disease concept model with a comorbid client, using 12-step groups as a treatment adjunct makes sense. In our experience, matching such clients to the proper community resources including the location of nearby 12-step meetings is essential for comorbid clients. Familiarity with the culture of the meetings is important in that some meetings may have more of a religious focus and be more suited to some clients than others. Also, some meetings may be more supportive and provide a more healing environment for comorbid clients than others.

It is helpful for mental health counselors who work with comorbid clients on an outpatient basis to understand the culture and language of the 12-step recovery programs their clients may attend. A few of these programs are Alcoholics Anonymous, Cocaine Anonymous, Al-Anon, and Overeaters Anonymous. In some communities, alternatives to 12-step groups are available, such as Secular Organizations for Sobriety. It is especially important for the counselor to be aware of which 12-step groups are known for accepting of, or specifically designed for, clients with comorbidity.

One way a counselor can learn about AA, for example, is to read AA literature such as the Big Book (1939) or the *Twelve Steps and Twelve Traditions* (1952), visit groups, or discuss groups with colleagues. The counselor can also watch the movie *My Name is Bill W.*, based on the true story of Bill W., a thriving stockbroker whose life crumbled after the stock market crash in the

1920s and how he coped with alcoholism. Together with a fellow alcoholic, he formed a support group that would ultimately become Alcoholics Anonymous (Amador, 1989).

After the counselor and comorbid client eventually choose a group, the counselor should ensure that the client take small steps that are self-reinforcing. These could include trying out several meetings before deciding which is the best group, getting a phone number of someone from a meeting, calling that person, getting a temporary sponsor, or getting a permanent sponsor. Helping the client find a sponsor who understands comorbidity would be ideal, but may be difficult. Knowing that he or she has a sponsor who understands the nature of two disorders may bring a certain sense of relief to the client.

When working with a comorbid client who is involved with a 12-step recovery program, it is important to prepare the client for how to participate in the group. The group process can be particularly stressful for clients with a high level of anxiety or serious mental illness. The counselor should be aware of the difficulties that a client may have in participating in a group. For instance, the counselor may need to help the client rehearse certain group activities like holding hands or reciting prayers. In some cases, the client may need additional help working out how he or she can actually attend the meeting. The counselor may need to write down very detailed instructions, such as how to physically get to the meeting by noting the bus schedule and the walking route to the building (SAMHSA, 2013).

According to SAMHSA (2013), the debriefing after the first 12-step meeting may be the turning point in recovery. The counselor must help the client overcome any initial obstacles after attending the first group. This may include a discussion of the client's reaction to the group and how he or she can prepare for future attendance. It may also include the importance of finding an appropriate sponsor.

CASE STUDY

The following case study describes how the counselor helps the client find a sponsor.

> Linda C. had attended her 12-Step group for about 3 months, and although she knew she should ask someone to sponsor her, she was shy and afraid of rejection. She had identified a few women who might be good sponsors, but each week in therapy she stated that she was afraid to reach out, and no one had approached her, although the group members seemed "friendly enough." The therapist suggested that Linda C. "share" at a meeting, simply stating that she'd like a sponsor but was feeling shy and didn't want to be rejected. The therapist and Linda C. role-played together in a session, and the therapist reminded Linda C. that it was okay to feel afraid. If she couldn't share at the next meeting, they would talk about what stopped her. After the next meeting, Linda C. related that she almost "shared" but got scared at the last minute, and was feeling bad that she had missed an opportunity. They talked about getting it over with, and Linda C. resolved to reach out, starting her sharing statement with, "It's hard for me to talk in public, but I want to work this program, so I'm going to tell you all that I know it's time to get a sponsor." This therapy work helped Linda C. to put her need out to the group, and the response from group members was helpful to Linda C., with several women offering to meet with her to talk about sponsorship. This experience also helped Linda C. to become more attached to the group and to learn a new skill for seeking help. While Linda C. was helped by counseling strategies alone, others with a "social phobia" also may need antidepressant medications in addition to counseling (SAMHSA, 2013).

A new treatment option uses a combination of an antidepressant and opioid antagonist for the treatment of comorbid substance use and bipolar and major depressive disorders. A total of 170 patients with major depression and alcohol use disorder participated in a 14-week double-blind, placebo-controlled trial. It was found that the patients treated with a combination of sertraline and naltrexone fared better than those receiving just sertraline or the naltrexone alone. Combination patients were less likely to be depressed at the end of treatment and achieved more abstinence from alcohol use disorders (Pettinati, O'Brien, & Dundon, 2013).

Weiss, Griffin, and Kolodziej (in Tolliver & Hartwell, 2012) suggest that patients with bipolar and substance use disorder be considered to have one multifaceted disorder or bipolar substance use disorders rather than two distinct disorders. Their study had two patient groups that received group drug counseling. However, one group was encouraged to take responsibility for their treatment and recovery, while the other group, serving as the control group, received group drug counseling only. It was reported that the combined approach reduced alcohol and other drug use compared with the treatment group receiving drug counseling only.

Alternative Models

Osborn (2001) argues against the disease concept model and states that those with alcohol use disorders can be best served by matching treatment to individual client needs and that brief interventions that target specific symptoms are just as effective as more intensive and long-term treatment. Osborn (2001) also indicates that perhaps those with alcohol use disorders should be treated differently than those who have problems with alcohol consumption but are not dependent.

An alternative model to the disease concept model is presented by Whittinghill, Whittinghill, and Loesch (2000), who suggest that substance use disorders are not all at the same level of severity as some substance use disorders counselors believe, but rather, that severity falls on within continuum, with sporadic detrimental use on one end and relentless addiction on the other. They see it as unfortunate that most users are forced into a one-size-fits-all approach that includes abstinence and the working of the AA 12 steps even when the severity of their problem is minimal. They indicate that such an approach is doomed to failure with those who are abusing but not addicted.

Marlatt, Baer, and Quigley (1994) proposed a self-efficacy model that matches treatment focus with level of substance use disorder severity that ranges from pre-use to severe addiction. The authors describe five types of self-efficacy that assist in substance use disorder treatment. First, *resistance self-efficacy* is preventative and helps individuals learn to refuse pressure by others to begin using substances. Second, *harm reduction self-efficacy* is used to help substance users lessen problematic use by reducing frequency and amount of the substance used. Third, *action self-efficacy* is used to help addicted persons quit using by assisting them to see themselves as able to quit. Fourth, *coping self-efficacy* is used to help prevent relapse in those who are newly sober by learning and practicing refusing a substance. Fifth, *recovery self-efficacy* helps addicts to interpret relapses as learning experiences rather than failures so they can return to abstinence.

Kim-Berg and Miller (1992) challenged domination of the disease concept and the components of the 12 steps in treatment of alcoholism. The authors confront what they perceive to be a circular argument by proponents of the traditional model of alcoholism that discredits positive outcomes to alternative treatments. Kim-Berg and Miller (1992) indicate that clients who respond favorably to briefer and alternative treatments are dismissed as not having been real alcoholics to begin with. In utilizing a solution-focused approach, Kim-Berg and Miller (1992) emphasize client successes, strengths, and resources rather than their illness or failures. They also stress the importance of accepting and working "within the client's frame of reference . . . assuming an atheoretical, nonnormative, client-determined posture toward alcohol problems . . ." (Kim-Berg & Miller, 1992, p. 7). This means keeping solutions simple rather than complex, and paying attention to changes that happen naturally, using those changes to find a solution, focus on the present and future, and collaborate and cooperate with clients in finding and implementing solutions.

"No single theory has been adequate to address the diversity of needs of individuals who are most accurately characterized as chemically dependent. No single theory has demonstrated a clear advantage in terms of efficacy over any other theoretical approach including the philosophy of Alcoholics Anonymous . . ." (Loos, 2002, p. 2). Loos's model of assisting chemically dependent clients is based on humanistic-existential theoretical models and encompasses other approaches, based on the needs of clients. After doing a client assessment including a thorough biopsychosocial history, clients are oriented to the therapeutic process and educated about the counselor's theoretical orientation. Clients are also educated about six basic feeling states: sad, happy, scared, hurt, angry, and embarrassed. They are additionally educated about owning their thoughts and feelings, choosing behaviors, expressing feeling behaviorally, making meaning through beliefs and values, attaching feelings to beliefs and values, and behaving morally and ethically. During counseling, cognitive-behavioral, cognitive-affective, and affective-behavioral interventions are used. This model borrows techniques from Ellis, Bandura, and Meichenbaum, such as confronting clients' thinking through guided imagery; changing maladaptive thinking, beliefs, and behaviors; role-play; assertiveness training; desensitization; homework assignments; and problem solving. Clients are also taught how to recognize and scale their emotions on a 1–10 scale, with 1 being absence of the emotion, and 10 being the highest expression of the emotion (Loos, 2002).

OTHER TREATMENT ISSUES

When a substance use disorder or comorbid client questions a particular counselor or staff member about whether he or she is in recovery from a substance use disorder, especially in front of other clients, this has the potential to create a we–they situation if not handled effectively. Whether the counselor states that he or she is or is not in recovery, either of these responses opens the door for the client to split staff. If the counselor answers in the affirmative that he or she is in recovery, such a statement can create the perception that since he or she is an addict in recovery, then that counselor is better able to empathize with the client who is also an addict. That makes this counselor the "good guy" and those staff members not in recovery the "bad guys," as they could not possibly possess the same level of empathy because they have not struggled with a substance use disorder.

In the present authors' opinions, it is best to redirect such questioning by asking, "How will knowing about my recovery be of help to you in your recovery?" or "How is your concern with my issues taking your focus off of your own recovery?" Other responses can be effective, such as "Staff have a policy to refrain from disclosing such information because we have found that such discussions do little to help clients focus on their own issues" or "Does a doctor have to have diabetes in order to treat a patient with diabetes? What is important is our ability to work together to accomplish your goals."

MULTIDISCIPLINARY TREATMENT TEAM

Multidisciplinary treatment teams are often beneficial to a client's recovery because each team member offers a unique perspective to diagnosis and treatment. Multidisciplinary teams typically include mental health counselors and substance use disorder treatment counselors, case managers, nursing staff, and psychiatric consultants. While team members may play different roles, all are familiar with every client on the caseload, and all should be cross-trained in other disciplines. The team typically includes case managers who can provide useful assistance in life management (e.g., housing, income, and transportation) and some direct counseling or other forms of treatment. It is recommended that treatment programs that serve comorbid clients have mental health specialists—such as mental health counselors with an understanding of substance use disorders and mental disorders—on staff to assist with assessment and diagnosis. In addition to provision of direct client services, such professionals could function as consultants to the rest of the team on matters related to mental disorders.

Having an on-site prescribing psychiatrist is crucial to sustaining recovery and stable functioning for people with comorbid disorders and has been shown to improve treatment retention and decrease substance use (SAMHSA, 2013). The on-site psychiatrist brings diagnostic, medication, and psychiatric services to clients for the major part of their treatment. Such use of an on-site psychiatrist can be an effective way to overcome impediments presented by off-site referral, such as distance and travel limitations, and the inconvenience and discomfort of starting services in another agency that is separate from the primary treatment unit. The psychiatrist should have expertise in working with substance use disorders that can include certification by the American Academy of Addiction Psychiatry, the American Society of Addiction Medicine, or the American Osteopathic Association (SAMHSA, 2013).

It is recommended that each member of a comorbid treatment team have extensive competency in both the substance use disorders and mental health fields, including training in the following 10 areas:

1. Identifying and understanding the symptoms of the various mental disorders
2. Comprehending the relationships among different mental symptoms, drugs of choice, and treatment history
3. Specifying and altering approaches to meet the needs of particular clients and achieve treatment goals
4. Obtaining services from multiple systems and collaborating on integrated treatment plans
5. Understanding the differing perspectives regarding the characteristics of the person with comorbid diagnoses
6. Understanding the nature of substance use disorders
7. Becoming aware of the nature of mental disability
8. Understanding the impact of the conduct of treatment and staff roles in the treatment process
9. Comprehending the interactive effects of both conditions on the person and his or her outcomes
10. Dealing with staff burnout (SAMHSA, 2013)

A BRIEF DESCRIPTION OF THE COUNSELING PROCESS THAT LEADS TO TREATMENT PLANNING

Diagnosis and treatment with comorbid clients requires that helping professionals have the ability to diagnose and treat mental and emotional disorders, including substance use disorders. While counselor training is based on a wellness perspective, mental health counselors, additionally, have training in assessment, diagnosis, and treatment of psychopathology. Such training gives mental health counselors a unique and ideal combination of capabilities. Mental health counselors can look at clients through a wellness lens that encompasses their strengths and capabilities and are able to examine clients for mental and emotional disorders, including substance disorders. Consequently, mental health counselors can examine from both a wellness and a psychopathology lens simultaneously.

A nonpathological method of assessment would involve helping clients identify their treatment issues as a part of the diagnostic process. With a wellness lens, counselors can assess and render a diagnosis based on the identified issues alone, including asking clients about their strengths and resources, as well as what has been working in their lives and what they have used in the past to solve similar issues. At the same time, a wellness focus would not preclude mental health counselors from forming a well-thought-out DSM-5 diagnosis based on diagnostic evidence from the client. Having both an issues-based and a DSM-5–based diagnosis can be helpful in developing a collaborative treatment plan with comorbid clients.

However, before treatment planning can begin, it is important that counselors help clients identify their treatment issues that are behavioral and measurable. By being specific, behavioral, and measurable, an identified issue can serve as a baseline or a pretest, which will help in evaluating treatment progress. For instance, instead of saying that a client has a checking compulsion, it would be more beneficial to say that the client reports that she has a checking compulsion as evidenced by stopping her car to check to see if she hit someone for an average of 10 minutes a day, 5 days a week on the way to work, but not on the ride home. Of course, we would want to investigate the other situations in which the client does compulsive checking as well.

Setting measurable and meaningful objectives is the most difficult, but perhaps most important, part of the treatment planning process. Once we have identified a specific, behavioral, and measurable issue, we can set treatment objectives that are specific, behavioral, and measurable as well. In working with a client's issues, we could set lofty objectives (e.g., the elimination of checking behavior) or moderate objectives (e.g., reduction of stopping her car to check to see if she hit someone for an average of 2 minutes, 3 days a week) depending on whether the client is allowed to see the counselor for two sessions or ten sessions. In other words, the objectives also need to be relevant and achievable given the setting and the client's resources.

Treatment planning is also the portion of the therapeutic process in which we help the client to select the specific counseling strategies and techniques, as well as setting timelines. Homework assignments can be used as the steps to fulfilling the treatment objective(s). Once we create such a treatment plan in collaboration with the client, we can rather easily evaluate treatment "products" both formatively (during and after each session) and summatively (at termination of treatment and follow-up).

In addition to a balanced use of the nondirective counseling skills (i.e., attending, clarifying, supporting, and silence), use of formative evaluation during and after each session, and especially early in the counseling relationship, has the potential to facilitate the therapeutic alliance. Formative evaluation can be both process (i.e., evaluating the counseling process) and product (i.e., evaluating the progress toward issue resolution and obtainment of treatment objectives). After a session, a counselor could inquire about how well the client thought the counselor understood the client's concerns. In doing so, the counselor would be using formative process evaluation. A counselor could also self-evaluate by asking herself the same question and comparing her answer to her client's answer. Following a session, a counselor could ask the client about how much progress the client has made toward identified treatment objectives. By doing this, the client is using formative product evaluation. Once again, the counselor could compare her self-evaluation with that of the client.

Just as formative evaluation can be both process and product, summative evaluation, which occurs at the end of treatment and at follow-up, can be both process (i.e., by summarizing how much a counselor was empathic and caring toward a client throughout treatment) and product (i.e., with a client self-rating how strongly she agrees that she has better insight into and understanding of her concerns at termination and follow-up).

Counselors should be aware of how their role and the healing process are seen by persons who are of different cultures. Wherever appropriate, healing practices meaningful to these clients should be incorporated into treatment. An example would be the medically supervised use of traditional herbal tobacco with certain Native American tribes to establish rapport and promote emotional balance, or use of herbal tea to calm a Chinese client or help control cravings (SAMHSA, 2013).

CASE STUDY

A Case Study of Dwayne

For illustrative purposes, a case of a client with a comorbid diagnosis will be presented. This case will demonstrate assessment, diagnosis, and treatment planning with a client with a comorbid diagnosis. First, we will present an assessment of the client. Next, we will present both psychopathology-based and issues-based diagnostic summaries. Taken together, these diagnostic summaries will form the basis for development of the treatment plan.

Referral

Dwayne, a 16-year-old African-American high school junior was referred for assessment and outpatient therapy by the family physician due to a progression of school suspensions for fighting and drinking leading to Dwayne's current expulsion from school. In the final incident, the client pulled a knife on a female student in the classroom, before class. He denied this when later caught and confronted. From reports, it appears that he experienced a blackout during this incident that was witnessed by students and a teacher. While speaking with the high school principal, the evaluator was told that the client would be allowed to return to school after completing three counseling sessions. Several weeks later after completing the sessions, Dwayne was permitted to return to school only to be expelled again for giving alcohol to a classmate.

Assessment Methods Used

Assessment methods to evaluate Dwayne included: clinical interview and observation during which time both biopsychosocial history and mental status information were gathered (with and without mom present; other family members and extended family members were unable and/or unwilling to be present); MAST; Drug Abuse Screening Test (DAST); MMPI-2; School Behavior Checklist; a review of school records including IQ scores on the Wechsler Intelligence Scale for Children (WISC-III); review of court records; review of medical records; and phone conversations with both the school principal and the family doctor.

Records Review

According to school records, Dwayne has passed all grades thus far, but his grade point average (GPA) has dropped from 3.1 in junior high school to his current GPA of 1.8. His best subjects are math and science, in which he usually gets Bs. He does poorly in English and spelling, typically getting Ds and Fs in these subjects. He has Wechsler Intelligence Scale for Children (WISC-III) verbal, performance, and full scale scores of 120, 115, and 118, respectively, which are above average, and a GPA of only 1.8, which is below average. By other school reports and observation, it appears as if the client is above average intelligence.

From court, hospital, and school records, 5 years ago the client was charged with assault and battery after badly beating another boy in a fight at school. The school filed and later dropped charges. He was charged with stealing and purse snatching prior to 5 years ago, but these charges were dropped as well. Three years ago, the client was charged with assault with a weapon, convicted, and put on probation. Since he was drinking two to three beers weekly and smoking two marijuana cigarettes weekly when the incident occurred, his probation officer along with his mother had him admitted to Savanna Hospital for inpatient chemical dependency treatment. He is currently off probation. The school is considering filing charges for the latest knife-pulling incident. Also, during the course of counseling, the client was accused of raping a 17-year-old girl, which he denied. Charges are pending.

Biopsychosocial History from Interview and Sessions

The client is an African-American male currently expelled from a predominantly white, middle-class, rural high school. He does not feel that he fits in and holds different values from his classmates. He attended an inner-city grade school, but his mother decided to move the family to a location where the client could have a chance not to be labeled and avoid following in his older brother's footsteps.

During the initial session, the client admitted to using both alcohol and marijuana in the past and admitted to current alcohol usage. According to his self-report, he drinks only two beers twice a week and has not used marijuana for more than a year. His mother, Mrs. Blake, also in attendance, reported that her son "drinks a little now and then." She believed he currently drinks about a six-pack of beer a week and concurred that he has not smoked marijuana for more than a year. Dwayne denied other drug use/experimentation. The school principal stated that students and teachers reported smelling alcohol on Dwayne's breath a couple of times.

After several sessions, Dwayne admitted to drinking four to six beers on most nights. Sometimes he would skip a night or two if he knew in advance that his drinking would be questioned. In addition, he would drink up to a pint of vodka if it were available, which was the case about once a week. Dwayne also admitted to smoking four to five marijuana cigarettes weekly. While Dwayne reported that he began drinking at age 11 and smoking marijuana at age 13, he did so, at first, only occasionally and for "kicks." He admitted he became violent the first time he drank (he consumed approximately a pint of whiskey) and began throwing furniture around at a friend's house.

By the mother's and principal's report, the client becomes hostile, abusive, violent, and fights (using weapons) when intoxicated. The client reports that prior to beginning to drink, he had gotten into more than 100 fights. Even prior to his beginning to drink, school and court records indicate a history of stealing, running away from home on at least five occasions, constant truancy, starting fights, and purse-snatching. During the course of counseling, the client was accused of raping a 17-year-old girl, which he denied.

Dwayne reports himself to be single and unemployed. He held a job as a dishwasher in a local restaurant 1½ years ago for 3 months. However, the client was fired for drinking house wine with an older employee during his work time. The client was a good junior high athlete in both track and football. After playing varsity football as a freshman, he was kicked off the football team his sophomore year for drinking at school.

The client has not formally dated but brags that he has had sex with as many as 10 girls beginning at age 10. He does not currently have a girlfriend. He reports he picks his lovers up at parties and takes them out. According to his report, he strongly identifies with his father and feels that "women were put here to make me feel good."

During the course of treatment, when his mother's boyfriend offered to give him his car if he brought up his grades, the client maintained a 3.0 for one 6-week period. However, after getting the car, his grades slipped back again. This provides evidence for his need for external, monetary rewards to do well in school. That he has an IQ of 118, which is above average, and a GPA of only 1.8, which is below average, is an indication that he is not working up to his potential scholastically.

Both client and his mother report that the client is in good health physically, and medical records confirm this. He has a scar on the right forearm as a result of being stabbed there 2 years ago in a fight. He is currently not taking any prescription medications. He reports no known allergies (in addition to alcohol and possibly marijuana). His father was a heavy drinker and the client's paternal grandfather and father's brother also had drinking problems, according to his mother.

Dwayne was admitted as an inpatient to the adolescent unit at Savanna Hospital 3 years ago for a 28-day treatment. He completed inpatient treatment for alcohol use disorders, but failed to attend aftercare as mom worked and could not bring him. He apparently attended several Alcoholics Anonymous meetings during treatment and after discharge, but quit going after the first 2 weeks after discharge. The client denies having received other mental health and/or drug/alcohol treatment.

His parents are Esther, age 50, and Donald, age 53. They were married 22 years ago and have been divorced for the past 10 years. The client has not seen his father for 10 years and currently lives with his mom. Client reports that his parents fought frequently when married and that dad was the disciplinarian. Mom would undermine dad's efforts to discipline the children. Mom currently has a 46-year-old boyfriend, Hal, whom the client dislikes.

Family functioning is typified by rigid boundaries and narrow definitions of what it is to be a man or a woman in society. Mom went to nursing school and got an LPN degree. She brought in a second (and sometimes primary) income for the last 5 years of the marriage. Dad was a heavy drinker and a womanizer, according to mom. He received two DUIs during the marriage. The client's sister, Kathy, was daddy's girl and his enabler.

Client is the youngest of three children. He has one brother, Andy, age 21, and one sister, Kathy, age 19. Kathy is a single parent with a 6-month-old baby. She works full time and lives alone with the baby in an apartment. Andy was the family scapegoat who was constantly in trouble. He was a gang member in California and has been in prison for armed robbery. The client identifies with his brother. The client served as the mascot and tried to lessen family tensions by being funny. Kathy was good at making the client and his brother look bad.

The client reports having been physically beaten by his father's fist and belt. He reports his brother was likewise beaten, but denies that his sister was. Dad was verbally/emotionally abusive, often putting mom and the kids down. From observation in session, mom is subtly abusive and has labeled Dwayne a bad boy with no chance to redeem himself. The client and mom both denied sexual abuse within the family. Mom indicates that Children's Services investigated dad's abuse of the children years ago.

Mental Status Evaluation

This 16-year-old African-American youth appeared about 2–3 years older than his stated age as evidence for early physical maturation. He appeared well nourished, was about 6 feet tall, and weighed about 180 pounds. He had a very athletic physique. He was well groomed and neat.

He maintained good eye contact throughout the session. The client was alert with no evidence of problems with psychomotor behavior. He did not appear to be intoxicated at the time of the initial session nor at subsequent sessions (with the exception of the last session). Neither did he smell of alcohol or marijuana. He later stated that he usually drank and/or smoked marijuana only at night and our sessions were during the daytime.

He was attentive and showed no evidence of speech or thinking disturbance. He was oriented to person, day of the week, day of the month, time, month, and year. While his long-term, remote memory appeared intact, when asked to recall what he had eaten for breakfast, he reported that he had eggs and toast. His mother reported that he had eaten only cereal that morning. He appeared to have confabulated to compensate for his problem with recent memory. This problem was later found to be just a motivational deficit as he could remember recent events when he wanted to. His short-term memory appeared intact as his ability to repeat digits forward and backward was within the normal range for his age.

The client had a flat affect as demonstrated by a monotone voice, lack of facial gestures while talking, and posture. While the client reported himself to be depressed, he denied almost all of the relevant symptoms reported in DSM-5 for depression. Mom confirmed that he is usually quieter earlier in the day and picks up his mood when it is time to go out with friends.

No evidence was shown for delusions or hallucinations. He gave no hint of obsessions, compulsions, or anxiety. The client was neither depressed nor suicidal. He denied any intention to commit homicide, but indicated that he was never one to walk away from a fight. He admitted to a tendency to be impulsive in his conduct and experienced little fear or autonomic nervous system arousal when confronted to fight. Neither did he experience guilt when he badly hurt classmates while fighting at school.

His insight into his drinking/smoking problems is limited as he denies that he has a real problem and states that he can quit at any time. He does admit, however, that he gets into more trouble and fights, and realizes that he feels invincible when drinking. He demonstrates poor judgment by his response to the question, "What would you do if a younger, smaller boy tried to start a fight with you?" He responded, "I'd kick the hell out of him." He demonstrated good abstract thinking when asked about the meaning of proverbs.

Psychological Testing

Although Dwayne was given both the Michigan Alcohol Screening Test (MAST) and the Drug Abuse Screening Test (DAST) as a part of the initial interview, both failed to detect evidence of either alcohol or drug use disorders. However, his high score on the MacAndrew Alcoholism Scale of the MMPI-2 is suggestive of alcohol or other substance use disorders. The interviewer used caution in drawing definitive conclusions as it has been shown that African-American adolescent nonabusers sometimes have high scores on the MacAndrew Alcoholism Scale, making it appear as if they are abusers when they are really not. He has WISC-III verbal, performance, and full-scale scores of 120, 115, and 118, respectively, which are above average, and a GPA of only 1.8, which is below average.

In using the MacAndrew Alcoholism Scale-R of the MMPI-2, raw scores equal to or greater than 28 suggest substance abuse problems while raw scores less than 24 suggest unlikely substance abuse problems. Interpretation should be made with knowledge of the specific norm group representing the client. (Graham, 1999)

Psychopathology-Based Diagnostic Summary

Alcohol Use Disorder, Severe

It appears as if Dwayne's primary substance is alcohol. Dwayne continues to drink despite numerous blackouts and fighting while drinking, reports unsuccessful attempts to quit, drives while intoxicated, and has gotten kicked out of school and off the football team (which he enjoyed) for missing practice while drinking. He has demonstrated an increase in tolerance as he reports that he needs to drink at least a six-pack to get high. Dwayne admitted that at times when he plans not to drink or to have only one or two, he drinks until he is intoxicated. He has had failed attempts to control usage. He also stated that he has quit before on his own several times but always starts back up. He also admits to missing school repeatedly due to being hungover. He now states that when he doesn't drink, he becomes anxious and depressed.

Marijuana Use Disorder, Mild

Dwayne did admit to smoking four to five marijuana cigarettes. He admits he spends his dating money on marijuana and drives while getting high. One time he rode past a police car with his window open, smoking a joint. This has continued for more than a year. He does not feel bad when he runs out of marijuana, but merely increases his alcohol intake.

Conduct Disorder, Adolescent Onset Type

Finally, using DSM-5 criteria, Dwayne was found to have a conduct disorder, as evidenced by the following history, which predated both his drinking and marijuana smoking: getting into more than 100 fights, stealing, running away from home on at least five occasions, constant truancy, fighting (using weapons), and purse-snatching. These occurred prior to the client's first drink and extended over at least 5 years' time. This type of behavior continued and intensified after he began drinking and smoking marijuana. During the course of counseling, the client was also accused of raping a 17-year-old girl, which he denied. Since he didn't start any of this behavior until age 10, he was diagnosed with the adolescent onset type. Most of his acting out was done alone and is therefore a solitary aggressive type and apparently severe.

ISSUES-BASED DIAGNOSTIC SUMMARY
CLIENT STRENGTHS

1. Above-average intelligence as evidenced by AEB: having WISC-3 verbal, performance, and full-scale scores of 120, 115, and 118, respectively, which are above average.
2. A history of doing well in math and science AEB: getting mostly B's in these courses up to now.
3. Superior athletic ability in track and football AEB: client's and mother's self-report.
4. Generally good physical health AEB: family physician's medical summary.

CLIENT ISSUES

1. Alcohol/marijuana issues AEB: increased tolerance, blackouts, continued use despite negative consequences (i.e., fighting, kicked out of school, threat of having probation restated, getting kicked off football team for drinking), failed attempts to control usage, frequent withdrawal such that he misses school, frequent intoxication, driving while drunk.
2. Conduct issues AEB: kicked off football team, school suspensions, pending rape charge, believes women were put here to make him feel good, fighting with and without weapons, stealing, running away, constant truancy, purse-snatching.

3. Decreased grades AEB: significant grade drop from 3.1 to 1.8 GPA since junior high.
4. Family history of abuse AEB: client and brother beaten by dad's fist and belt, dad's verbal and emotional abuse, mom's verbal abuse.
5. Client lacks an effective male role model AEB: father had history of family violence, older brother is in prison for armed robbery and assault, client dislikes mom's current boyfriend.
6. As an African American, client reports he feels he is a misfit in his predominantly white, middle-class, rural high school.
7. Mom requests help with parenting skills AEB: observation during sessions and her self-report that she cannot control client.

TREATMENT PLAN: PRIORITY GOALS (OTHER GOALS ARE PUT ON THE BACK BURNER FOR THE TIME BEING)
1. Abstinence from mood-altering substances.
2. Elimination of antisocial behavior.

SPECIFIC ISSUES
1. Client drinks at least a six-pack of beer each night and a pint of vodka once a week at night, smokes four to five marijuana cigarettes a week. Three years ago, he drank two to three beers twice a week and smoked two marijuana cigarettes a week. He drinks and smokes marijuana with two friends usually at a local park between 10:00 P.M. and 1:00 A.M. nightly, and later on weekends.
2. The client gets into a fight on the average of once a week and every other fight is with a weapon. Approximately half of the fights take place at school and the other half occur after school, usually on the way home from school.

TREATMENT OBJECTIVES
1. Short term (within 1 month): Reduce relapse into drinking every other day instead of every day, and three instead of six beers with no vodka; marijuana to one cigarette twice a week.
2. Long term (within 3 months): Complete abstinence from all mood-altering chemicals.
3. Short term (within 1 month): Reduce fighting to once a week with no weapons.
4. Long term (within 3 months): Eliminate fighting.

TREATMENT STRATEGIES
1. Structural and strategic family therapy.
2. Individual cognitive-behavioral therapy for client and mom.
3. Brief solution-focused therapy.

TREATMENT TECHNIQUES (Give as assignments and use timelines here as well.)
1. Involve a school representative and probation officer in family sessions.
2. Help to empower mom to assume parental responsibility within the family.
3. Get client involved in a Big Brother program through which he is paired with an African-American adult role model who can help him to work on feeling proud of his heritage and culture.
4. Get client involved in a sports activity every night after school.
5. Work with client on understanding the consequences of his use and how his life has been unmanageable.

6. Work with mom and client to get him in the house on school nights by 10:00 P.M., weekends by 11:00 P.M.
7. Reinforce client using token economy each week he refrains from fighting.
8. Have mom pay attention to client when he is behaving prosocially.
9. Find out what client does when he is successful in avoiding a fight.

Summary and Final Notations

In summary, it appears to be the rule rather than the exception that mental health disorders and substance use disorders co-occur. Because those clients with comorbid disorders have varied needs, their care requires flexible and integrated treatment methods and services. In assessing a client who presents with both a substance use disorder and a psychiatric disorder, counselors need to discover which came first and which is primary, and decide which one to begin treating first. Such discovery should be based on a thorough biopsychosocial history and records review. The culture of the client is also an important issue to address. Culturally effective counselors study the client's interpersonal interactions and familial expectations.

It appears that those with alcohol use disorders can be best served by matching treatment to individual client needs and that both traditional and alternative interventions can be effective given specific client characteristics. It is advisable that interdisciplinary team members working with clients with comorbid disorders be trained in both mental health and substance use disorders disciplines. Both psychopathology-based and issues-based diagnostic summaries can be helpful in forming the basis for an effective, comprehensive, and collaborative treatment plan with objectives that are specific, behavioral, measurable, and meaningful.

MyCounselingLab

Visit the MyCounselingLab site for *Foundations of Addictions Counseling,* Third Edition to enhance your understanding of concepts. You'll have the opportunity to practice your skills through video- and case-based exercises. You will find sets of questions to help you prepare for your certification exam with *Licensure Quizzes.* There is also a Video Library that provides taped counseling sessions, ethical scenarios, and interviews with helpers and clients.

Useful Websites

The following websites provide additional information relating to the chapter topics:

Addiction Treatment Forum
www.atforum.com/

Centers for Disease Control and Prevention: Information About Intimate Partner Violence and Treatment

National Institute on Alcohol Abuse and Alcoholism (NIAAA)
www.niaaa.nih.gov/

National Institute on Drug Abuse (NIDA)
www.nida.nih.gov/

National Institute on Drug Abuse (NIDA): Patients and Families
www.drugabuse.gov/patients-families

Resources for Comorbid Addiction and Personality Disorders

Substance Abuse and Mental Health Services Administration (SAMHSA)
www.samhsa.gov/

Substance Abuse and Mental Health Services Administration (SAMHSA) Fact Sheets
http://coce.samhsa.gov/searchresults.aspx?obj=85&key=fact%20sheet
http://coce.samhsa.gov/comorbid_resources/PDF/AlcoholQuickFacts.pdf
http://coce.samhsa.gov/comorbid_resources/PDF/ElderlyQuickFacts.pdf
http://coce.samhsa.gov/comorbid_resources/PDF/GamblingQuickFacts.pdf
http://findtreatment.samhsa.gov/
http://store.samhsa.gov/product/Substance-Abuse-Treatment-for-Persons-With-Co-Occurring-Disorders/SMA07-4034
http://store.samhsa.gov/product/Substance-Abuse-Treatment-for-Persons-With-Co-Occurring-Disorders/SMA12-4035
http://store.samhsa.gov/product/Substance-Abuse-Treatment-for-Persons-With-Co-Occurring-Disorders/SMA08-4036
http://store.samhsa.gov/product/TIP-42-Substance-Abuse-Treatment-for-Persons-With-Co-Occurring-Disorders/SMA13-3992
store.samhsa.gov/product/A-Practitioner-s-Resource-Guide-Helping-Families-to-Support-Their-LGBT-Children/PEP14-LGBTKIDS
store.samhsa.gov/product/A-Provider-s-Introduction-to-Substance-Abuse-Treatment-for-Lesbian-Gay-Bisexual-and-Transgender-Individuals/SMA12-4104
store.samhsa.gov/product/American-Indian-and-Alaska-Native-Culture-Card/SMA08-4354
store.samhsa.gov/product/Addressing-the-Needs-of-Women-and-Girls-Core-Competencies-for-Mental-Health-and-Substance-Abuse-Service-Professionals/SMA11-4657
http://store.samhsa.gov/product/Considerations-for-the-Provision-of-E-Therapy/SMA09-4450
http://store.samhsa.gov/product/Differences-in-Substance-Abuse-Treatment-Admissions-between-Mexican-American-Males-and-Females/TEDS10-0505

Double Trouble in Recovery: A Recovery Group for the Dually Diagnosed
nrepp.samhsa.gov/ViewIntervention.aspx?id=13

References

Alcoholics Anonymous. (1939). *Alcoholics Anonymous*. New York, NY: Alcoholics Anonymous World Services.

Alcoholics Anonymous. (1952). *Twelve Steps and Twelve Traditions*. New York, NY: Alcoholics Anonymous World Services.

American Psychiatric Association. (1994). *Diagnostic and statistical manual of mental disorders* (4th ed.). Washington, DC: Author.

American Psychiatric Association. (2013). *Diagnostic and statistical manual of mental disorders* (5th ed.). Washington, DC: Author.

Amador, H. (1989). [Review of the movie *My Name Is Bill W.*] Earth's Biggest Movie Database on the Web. Retrieved November 9, 2006, from http://www.imdb.com/title/tt0097939/plotsummary

Armor-Garb, A. (2004). *Point of entry systems for long-term care: State case studies*. Prepared for the New York City Department of Aging.

Brems, C., & Namyniuk, L. L. (1999). Comorbidity and related factors among ethnically diverse substance using pregnant women. *Journal of Addictions & Offender Counseling, 19*, 2.

Chartas, N. D., & Culbreth, J. R. (2001). Counselor treatment of coexisting domestic violence and substance abuse: A qualitative study. *Journal of Addictions & Offender Counseling, 22*, 1.

Corey, G. (2001). *Theory and practice of counseling and psychotherapy* (6th ed.). Belmont, CA: Brooks-Cole of Wadsworth/Thompson Learning.

Double trouble in recovery. (n.d.). Retrieved September 6, 2009, from http://www.doubletroubleinrecovery.org/

Duffy, H., & Gillig, S. E. (Eds.). (2004). *Teen gangs: A global view*. Westport, CT: Greenwood Press.

Graham, J. (1999). *MMPI-2: Assessing personality and psychopathology: Second edition*. New York, NY: Oxford University Press.

Grella, C. (2003). Contrasting the views of substance abuse and mental health treatment providers on treating the dually diagnosed. *Substance Use & Misuse, 38*(10), 1433–1446.

Johnson, M., Brems, C., Wells, R., Theno, S., & Fisher, D. (2003). Comorbidity and risk behaviors among drug users not in treatment. *Journal of Addictions & Offender Counseling, 23*, 108–118.

Juhnke, G., Vacc, N., Curtis, R., Coll, K., & Paredes, D. (2003). Assessment instruments used by addictions counselors. *Journal of Addictions & Offender Counseling, 23,* 66–72.

Kim-Berg, I., & Miller, S. (1992). *Working with the problem drinker.* New York, NY: W.W. Norton & Company.

Loos, M. D. (2002). Counseling the chemically dependent: An integrative approach. *Journal of Addictions & Offender Counseling, 23,* 2–14.

Marlatt, G. A., Baer, J. S., & Quigley, L. A. (1994). Self-efficacy and addictive behavior. In A. Bandura (Ed.), *Self-efficacy in changing societies.* Marbach, Germany: Johann Jacobs Foundation.

Mericle, A., Ta Park, V., Holck, P., & Arria, A. (2012). Prevalence, patterns, and correlates of co-occurring substance use and mental disorders in the United States: Variations by race/ethnicity. *Comprehensive Psychiatry, 53,* 657–665.

Miller, W. R., & White, W. (2008). *Confrontation in addiction treatment.* Retrieved November 9, 2006, from http://www.addictioninfo.org/articles/2276/1/Confrontation-in-Addiction-Treatment/Page1.html

Osborn, C. (2001). Brief interventions in the treatment of alcohol use disorders: Definition and overview. *Journal of Addictions & Offender Counseling, 21*(2), 76–84.

Pettinati, H., O'Brien, C., & Dundon, W. (2013). Current status of co-occurring mood and substance use disorders: A new therapeutic target. *American Journal of Psychiatry, 170,* 23–30.

Schneider, J. P. (2005). Coexisting disorders. In R. H. Coombs (Ed.), *Addiction counseling review: Preparing for comprehensive, certification and licensing examinations* (pp. 293–316). Mahway, NJ: Lawrence Erlbaum Associates.

Sciacca, K. (1997). Removing barriers: Dual diagnosis and motivational interviewing. *Professional Counselor, 12*(1), 41–46.

Substance Abuse and Mental Health Services Administration. (2009). *SAMHSA's Comorbid Center for Excellence, fact sheets.* Retrieved September 6, 2009, from http://coce.samhsa.gov/searchresults.aspx?obj=85&key=fact%20sheet

Substance Abuse and Mental Health Services Administration. (2013). *Substance abuse treatment for persons with cooccurring disorders* [Treatment Improvement Protocol (TIP) Series, No. 42. HHS Publication No. (SMA) 133992]. Rockville, MD: Author.

Tolliver, B., & Hartwell, K. (2012). Implications and strategies for clinical management of co-occurring substance use in bipolar disorder. *Psychiatric Annals, 42*(5), 190–197.

Von Steen, P., Vacc, N., & Strickland, I. (2002). The treatment of substance-abusing clients in multiservice mental health agencies: A practice analysis. *Journal of Addictions & Offender Counseling, 22,* 61–71.

Whittinghill, D., Whittinghill, L., & Loesch, L. (2000). The benefits of a self-efficacy approach to substance abuse counseling in the era of managed care. *Journal of Addictions & Offender Counseling, 20*(2), 64–74.

Chapter 10

Group Therapy for Treatment of Addictions

Laura R. Haddock
Walden University

Donna S. Sheperis
Lamar University

One very common treatment modality for substance use disorders is group counseling. Within the last decade, studies have indicated approximately 94% of treatment facilities within the United States utilize group counseling for treatment of substance abuse (Weiss, Jaffee, de Menil, & Cogley, 2004), and it has replaced individual counseling as the treatment approach of choice (Johnson, 2004; Ruis & Strain, 2011). In addition to the low cost of group counseling, the popularity of this approach has evolved from peer-based self-help groups such as Alcoholics Anonymous (AA) and Narcotics Anonymous (NA) to include psychoeducational and psychotherapeutic approaches (Behavioral Health Treatment, 1997; Center for Substance Abuse Treatment, 2005a).

Groups have a number of important functions in substance abuse treatment, including education, therapy, and support. This chapter will address the theory behind utilizing a group counseling approach as well as examine common types of groups employed for treatment of addictions. Additionally, ethical and legal issues, managing diversity in group settings, and group therapy with family members will be discussed.

THEORY BEHIND GROUP WORK

The research supporting the use of group work in the treatment of a variety of concerns is well established. Essentially, group counseling is an interpersonal treatment approach that emphasizes an expression of thoughts and feelings geared toward insight and behavioral change. Yalom and Lesczc (2005) proposed that groups offer a number of advantages over individual or other counseling methods including creating a sense of universality or the understanding that clients are not alone in their struggles. The empathy and support provided through group work creates the necessary atmosphere for the counseling process. Participants can explore relationship styles, try on new behaviors, and participate in rehearsal for change using the medium of the group (Corey, 2011). Ideally, through interpersonal learning and group cohesiveness, members develop a greater understanding of themselves and can capitalize on this insight by making necessary changes in the way they live their lives (Yalom & Lesczc, 2005).

Group counseling can be used for many purposes, both preventative and remedial in nature (Corey, 2011).

Preventative groups are those that members participate in to *avoid using substances*. They take place in schools, agencies, and communities. *Remedial groups* address *unhealthy behaviors that currently exist* and have resulted in negative consequences for the client. In addictions counseling, *aftercare groups* that offer treatment in an outpatient setting following an inpatient treatment stay would be considered remedial.

The content of the group may be preset or determined by the membership (Corey, 2011). Advantages of group counseling include using a collective mind-set to gain perspective on an individual counseling issue. Concepts related to interpersonal skills and trust are inherently worked through in a group environment. However, group counseling is not for everyone. The dynamics and interpersonal risks involved may prove to be too overwhelming for some clients, and some counseling issues are not best treated through the group process.

GROUP TREATMENT OF ADDICTION

When treating addiction, there are specific dynamics that make group counseling the approach of choice. Although the design of a group may vary, there are certain benefits that contribute to the behavior change process. While many evidence-based interventions are individualized, addictions counselors disproportionately conduct treatment clients in groups (Sanders & Mayeda, 2009).

The influence of group members who have similar experiences is helpful in breaking down the denial frequently associated with addiction (Sadler, 2003; Washton & Zweben, 2008). Because individuals who participate in long-term substance abuse typically exhibit poor communication skills and the inability to perpetuate healthy interpersonal relationships, group therapy affords an opportunity to interact with others, promoting effective social skills and self-disclosure; explore new behaviors in a safe environment; and emotionally invest in others and in education about addiction (Campbell & Page, 1993; Johnson, 2004).

Joan has been a problem drinker for a number of years. She and her husband, Michael, have experienced a decline in their relationship over the last 5 years. Michael says he cannot talk to Joan, that she shuts him out, and that all she does is blame him for their troubles. How might group treatment for Joan's alcohol abuse facilitate a different style of communication in her marriage? Is Joan's behavior in group related to how she interacts with her husband, or are these unrelated concepts? What impact might feedback from other group members have on Joan? Is it possible she might be able to hear the observations of other group members or a group facilitator in spite of the fact that she rejects her husband's observations or perceptions about her relating style?

Group therapy also offers an opportunity for positive interpersonal exchange to replace isolated self-involvement. Group members presented with an opportunity to identify and relay needs and emotions may result in their identifying and confronting maladaptive patterns of behavior (Weiss et al., 2004). According to Campbell and Page (1993), "Any effective therapeutic intervention must target not only drug use, but also a means by which meaningful communication can occur" (p. 34). Additionally, many individuals with addictions have blind spots for their own defenses but not necessarily those of others. Thus, the members may assist one another in confronting defense mechanisms and blind spots, resulting in accomplishment of treatment goals. Finally, group treatment uses peer influence and motivation to enhance individual commitment to recovery (Johnson, 2004).

AN OVERVIEW OF TYPES OF GROUPS

The general purposes of a therapeutic group are to assist members in determining the issues they are most interested in addressing while increasing members' awareness and understanding of themselves and others in their lives, and providing participants with the support needed to make these changes (Corey, Corey, & Corey, 2013). Essentially, members get an opportunity to "try on" new behaviors in a setting that is safe and receive honest feedback from others concerning these behaviors. Often it is the first time individuals have an opportunity to learn how others perceive them.

The Association for Specialists in Group Work (ASGW, 2000) developed a four-category system for classifying types of group work. ASGW standards identify standards of competence for the leaders and identifies particular areas of group work, including (1) task groups, (2) psychoeducational groups, (3) counseling groups, and (4) psychotherapy groups. As counseling groups are not aimed at major personality changes and not concerned with the treatment of severe behavioral disorders, they are not frequently implemented for addictions work.

Psychoeducational Groups

A variety of issues common to recovery from addiction require specific planned treatment interventions. Because the focus of treatment combines educating members with fostering self-understanding through the dynamics of the group, these groups are sometimes referred to as psychoeducational treatment groups. Psychoeducational groups are an increasingly popular and important source of help for many clients. Perhaps their greatest asset is that they provide a planned framework that can be replicated, modified, and/or adapted to fit different types of client groups.

In structured psychoeducational groups, it is not unusual for the agenda to be established before the group session. Compared to less structured, process-centered approaches, structured group approaches give the counselor greater responsibility for group goals and the way the group conducts its work. Although in psychotherapeutic approaches members are encouraged to take informal leadership roles and develop their own goals, agendas, and contracts, in psychoeducational groups the members' input is generally limited to modifying goals, agendas, and contracts the counselor has already developed. The interventions are planned and focus on specific learning outcomes. Integrating behavioral therapies with experiential learning is common practice. The group can aim to help members translate what they learn into specific action.

There are a variety of time-limited, structured groups that focus on transferring information about drugs and the consequences of use. Meetings usually contain a combination of educational material, exercises, role-play, and simulations to help members process discussion of the material and the problems they are experiencing outside the group.

It is not uncommon for school counselors to implement time-limited structured groups that are preventative in nature. For example, elementary school counselors might utilize programming that examines the reasons that children use drugs and offer alternatives to drug use. Parents may also be included in the process through the use of homework.

In a series of studies on the efficacy of group work, members of groups with specific purposes, homogeneous concerns, clear agendas, and structured group meetings demonstrated greater success with treatment outcome than members of groups with less structure (Martin, Giannandrea, Rogers, & Johnson, 1996; Toseland & Rivas, 2001). Members report that they appreciate the leader providing specific information and effective strategies to help with their concerns. Thus, in a group program for individuals recovering from substance abuse, the leader can provide information about addiction, communication skills, assertiveness/social skills training, and other topics deemed appropriate. Studies have shown that even spiritual concerns can be successfully addressed within this format, allowing participants to examine beliefs and gain increased understanding of their feelings, problems, and questions within this domain (Phillips, Lakin, & Pargament, 2002). Psychoeducational designs also provide members with an opportunity to discuss specific concerns and learn stress reduction and other coping techniques.

Leaders of psychoeducational groups vary depending on the topics to be covered; they may be licensed professional counselors or paraprofessionals trained in the treatment of addictions.

Group leaders should keep in mind that members' concerns and needs are not always served by a time-limited, structured-group approach. A flexible structure maximizing member input has been found to be more effective in helping members to vent their concerns and give and receive help from fellow group members (Toseland & Rivas, 2001). Group counselors should be savvy enough to determine the goals and specific agendas that will best meet the needs of members.

There are also psychoeducational groups designed to assist in the *prevention* of addiction. Drug Abuse Resistance Education (D.A.R.E.) and similar programs are based on the theory that teaching children about the harmful effects of alcohol and drugs while helping them build self-esteem will deter the desire to abuse chemicals later in life (Doweiko, 2010). The D.A.R.E. program is typically conducted by local law enforcement and taught within a classroom setting. There is a great deal of testimonial support for these programs, but very little empirical evidence that they are effective in reducing substance abuse among children or adolescents (Doweiko, 2010; Gorman, 2003).

Psychotherapeutic Groups

Psychotherapeutic groups are commonly utilized in addictions treatment. Because group members have serious impairments in functioning as a result of their substance abuse, these types of groups explore the foundation of current behaviors, seeking to build insight and replace dysfunctional coping patterns with healthy ones.

Group psychotherapy offers a number of advantages over individual counseling. Group members can learn from and offer feedback to each other and provide behavioral models for each other; this is useful for clients who do not trust the counselor. The group format provides an opportunity for clients to work on many of the interpersonal deficits that contribute to their own addiction within the safety of the group setting.

Counselors sometimes utilize experiential activities with members. For example, genograms, or family maps, help counselors and clients see a family more clearly. A *genogram* is a visual representation of a person's family tree, created with lines, words, and geometric figures (Gladding, 2010). For addictions treatment, the genogram may reveal patterns of addiction, codependence, or other problem behaviors in the client's family system.

Finally, because of the nature of group therapy, each individual might find other members who provide a reflection of his or her family of origin, allowing the individual to work through problems from earlier stages of growth.

Individuals may participate in group counseling as part of an inpatient treatment regimen or as an adjunct to individual counseling in an outpatient setting. The majority of substance abuse rehabilitation programs use counseling groups as the primary method of working with clients (Doweiko, 2010; Weiss et al., 2004). For clients receiving inpatient treatment as a result of involuntary commitment, a common difficulty is resistance to group work. Many members begin with attitudes of resentment, blaming others, and operating under the conviction that they do not need counseling. Techniques and strategies must be employed to address resistance.

Individuals who experience chronic substance dependence or usage exhibit behavioral characteristics that can interfere with the ability to develop effective communication and to sustain healthy interpersonal relationships. As use of substances persists, social, personal, and work-related activities are negatively affected (Campbell & Page, 1993). Social and psychological problems develop or are exacerbated by the prominence of drugs in the user's lifestyle. Psychosocial aspects of the individual's life become so impaired that interpersonal interactions develop with maladaptive behavioral patterns (American Psychiatric Association, 2013). In attempting to treat these issues, a variety of methods may be employed, including methods intended to prompt reversion to past experiences, approaches to work with unconscious dynamics, and techniques designed to assist members in processing traumatic circumstances so that catharsis can occur (Corey et al., 2013).

While psychotherapeutic groups typically do not have specific agendas for each session, the group counselor may choose to offer specific topic areas for a session, encouraging the participants to explore pertinent life issues. If group topics address real-life issues of the group members, they can generate meaningful discussion (Corey et al., 2013). The topics chosen should reflect the purpose of the group. When working with participants suffering from addiction, topics could include identifying and dealing with family-of-origin issues, painful affective states that may contribute to the urge to use chemicals, and shame-based issues. Additionally, grief issues are a common focus of process groups as newly sober members attempt to cope with loss of friends, loss of coping mechanisms, and in general, loss of a way of life.

Inpatient treatment providers frequently encounter grief issues. Group members may struggle to say goodbye to a drug or behavior of choice, loss of power or money, or the social relationships associated with their addiction (Bradley, Whiting, Hendricks, Parr, & Jones, 2008). Group leaders may suggest writing letters to say goodbye, designing eulogies, or even holding an actual funeral service for the issue.

It has been posited that up to 50% of individuals receiving treatment for addiction also have co-occurring disorders (James & Gilliland, 2005). Group counseling helps dually diagnosed clients develop the insight they need to sustain recovery from chemical dependence while maintaining psychiatric stability (Center for Substance Abuse Treatment, 2005b). The group process offers members the opportunity to share experiences involving addiction and mental illness in an atmosphere of acceptance and support while learning how their addictions influence their mental illness and how their mental illness affects their addiction. The group format allows clients to challenge one another in a climate that reinforces the reality and acceptance of both the addiction and the mental illness.

A skilled counselor knowledgeable in both addictions and group therapy treatment is recommended to facilitate group psychotherapy of addicted clients. The counselor should be educated about mental illness and well versed in the jargon of self-help groups, such as AA, as clients may use self-help language as a defense to keep them from getting into deeper issues. A skilled group counselor will be able to balance the need to attend to substance abuse issues, while maintaining awareness about mental illness, resistance, and behavior destructive to the group therapy process. The group counselor must also be sensitive to the fact that not all addicted clients are compatible with group counseling. Individuals with severe pathology may not be capable of making the affective connection necessary to facilitate recovery (Behavioral Health Treatment, 1997).

Unfortunately, there is limited evidence that group psychotherapy approaches are effective in the treatment of substance disorders (Doweiko, 2010). However, treatment approaches that incorporate a larger proportion of group counseling to individual counseling are positively associated with increased likelihood of treatment success (Panas, Caspi, Fournier, & McCarty, 2003). Additionally, studies indicate that substance-addicted clients participating in group counseling as part of a treatment regimen improved significantly on depression, suicide risk, and trauma symptoms (Hunter, Witkiewitz, Watkins, Paddock, & Hepner, 2012; Sunich, 2013).

Self-Help Groups

Instead of seeking help from a mental health professional, many individuals seek assistance from self-help, or mutual-help, groups. These voluntary groups have members that share a common problem and meet for the purpose of exchanging social support. Most are self-governing, with members rather than experts or mental health professionals determining activities. They also tend to stress the importance of treating all members fairly and giving everyone an opportunity to express their viewpoints. The members face common problems so they benefit from the universality of the other members' concerns. These groups stress the importance of reciprocal helping, because members are expected to both give help to others and receive help from others. Self-help groups usually charge little in the way of fees. AA is an example of a self-help or mutual-help group. AA is the "most frequently consulted source of help for drinking problems" (Doweiko, 2010, p. 446). In the years since its development, AA has grown to an association of more than 114,000 groups with over 2 million members in 150 countries (AA Services, 2013). There is an enormous variety of self-help groups.

Why are AA and NA *not* considered group therapy? The primary difference is the *role of the leader*. Recall that psychotherapeutic groups are led by counselors who facilitate the group. This person is trained in group roles and dynamics and typically has experience in providing group counseling. The group facilitator may or may not have personal experience in the topic under discussion. In other words, a psychotherapeutic group counselor facilitating an addiction recovery group may NOT be an addict him- or herself. Regardless of personal history, the group counselor in a psychotherapeutic group is not a participant, but is exclusively a facilitator. AA and NA were developed as self-help or mutual-help groups. As such, they are led by individuals with history and experience in the topic under discussion. That is, *the leader of an AA or NA group is in addiction recovery* and functions in both a leadership and member role within the group.

Many groups based on the 12 steps of AA have emerged, including NA for the treatment of drug addiction and Gamblers Anonymous (GA) for the treatment of compulsive gambling. Other groups based on the 12-step model have also emerged in response to the needs of family members requiring support, including Adult Children of Alcoholics (ACOA), Al-Anon, and Nar-Anon. These groups are covered in more detail in Chapter 12.

TABLE 10.1 Comparison of Types of Groups Commonly Used in Addictions Counseling

Type	Basic Goal	Leader	Examples
Psychoeducational Group	Educating members on specific areas while providing emotional support	Both licensed mental health professionals and trained paraprofessionals	Addiction education group, anger management group, communication skills group
Psychotherapeutic Group	Improve psychological functioning and adjustment of individual members	Mental health professional, psychologist, clinical social worker, or certified alcohol and drug counselor	Interpersonal or cognitive-behavioral group counseling, psychodrama groups, interpersonal groups
Self-Help Group	Help members cope with or overcome specific problems while providing support to one another	Typically led by a volunteer participant and may not include a leadership position	Alcoholics Anonymous, Narcotics Anonymous, Al-Anon, SMART Recovery

While the most prominent self-help groups are based on the 12-step model, SMART Recovery® (n.d.) is a group based on a cognitive behavioral model. It assists persons with substance or behavioral addictions through a four-point program. This four-point program includes enhancing and maintaining motivation to abstain, coping with urges, problem solving, and lifestyle balance (smartrecovery.org). SMART Recovery® states on its website that its purpose is offering assistance to persons choosing to abstain or considering abstinence from addictive behaviors by instruction in making changes in self-defeating cognitions, affect, or behaviors, and working toward satisfaction with life circumstances.

SMART Recovery® offers face-to-face meetings, online meetings, and an online message board for members to offer support to one another. Meetings are educational in nature and involve open discussions and treatment based on scientific knowledge, including the use of psychotropic medication and psychological treatment. Topics include teaching self-empowerment and self-reliance, teaching tools and techniques for self-directive change, and advocating for the appropriate use of medications (smartrecovery.org).

When determining the most appropriate group treatment method for clients, consideration of the group format, general goals, and types of leadership is critical. Table 10.1 provides a visual comparison of typical group types and lists examples of each.

ETHICAL AND LEGAL ISSUES WITH GROUPS

The efficacy of group work within the field of addictions is well established. Addictions counselors face additional considerations when they undertake group treatment methods. The ethical and legal aspects of conducting group counseling are numerous. Counselors are best served by having a thorough understanding of how the *ACA Code of Ethics* (American Counseling Association [ACA], 2005) as well as state and federal laws affect the services they provide. While many of the ethical and legal aspects of addictions work was covered in Chapter 4, the following section provides a view of group work in the field of addictions through the lens of the inherent legal and ethical components.

Competence of the Leader

Addictions groups may be facilitated by leaders who vary in formal training and personal experience with the recovery model. For example, addictions groups may be run by academically trained counselors in recovery, formally educated counselors with no personal history of addiction, or individuals in recovery with no formal academic training but much experience in the arena of recovery. For the purposes of this chapter, we will focus on counselors who have pursued formal academic training in counseling. Despite having a master's degree or higher, counselors may lead groups with limited training in the theory and techniques specific to group counseling (Gazda, Ginter, & Horne, 2001). Counselors who lead groups are called to practice within the scope of competence. The *ACA Code of Ethics* (2005) states that counselors may only practice within areas in which they have received the necessary education, training, experience, and supervision. The ethical code further indicates a need for counselors to commit to ongoing education and training in any field of practice (ACA, 2005). While the code explicitly addresses competence, it remains somewhat vague and open to interpretation as to what constitutes necessary and sufficient education, training, experience, and supervision. Consequently, group counselors would do well to consult the ASGW "Professional Standards for the Training of Group Workers" (2000) for further clarification regarding leader competence.

The ASGW outlines the specific minimum training guidelines recommended by leading psychoeducational and psychotherapeutic groups. In addition to one graduate course in group counseling and 10 or more hours of group experience, the ASGW recommends specific advanced coursework and 45–60 clock hours of supervised experience in order to specialize in group psychoeducation, counseling, or psychotherapy (ASGW, 1998). Demonstration and evaluation of core competencies are required, and the ASGW (1998) recommends practica and internship experiences that correspond with the Council for Accreditation of Counseling and Related Educational Programs (CACREP). It is important to note that the competencies set forth by both ASGW and CACREP require the future group leader to participate in a personal group experience, the rationale being that such participation enhances the leader's understanding of the practical application of group theory.

Does meeting minimum standards ensure competence? Ethical group leaders do more than meet minimal requirements for training and experience. Being a competent and ethical group practitioner "[i]mplies functioning at a level of consciousness geared toward doing whatever it takes to function at the highest level, both personally and professionally" (Corey, Williams, & Moline, 1995, pp. 161–162). The group counselor is, after all, a human being prone to the same mishaps and errors of judgments as his or her clients. Group practitioners bring their personal lives to the profession of counseling, and their experiences, characteristics, and values play a part in the efficacy of their leadership style (Corey et al., 2013). Consistent and persistent evaluation of the effectiveness of counseling activities is the responsibility of all group leaders desirous of maintaining ethical standards and competence.

Screening of Participant

Group therapy is often the treatment of choice in addictions work. Whether agency structure, managed care influences, or treatment efficacy is behind the decision, many clients find themselves participating in groups. Group counselors are skilled at managing a diverse dynamic in a group setting and have an ethical responsibility to both the individual client and the group as a whole. In Section A.8.a., the *ACA Code of Ethics* (2005) specifically calls counselors to screen members for compatibility with group goals and membership. Ultimately, it is the group counselor's responsibility to maximize treatment outcome and minimize any adverse effects on individual clients throughout group treatment while maintaining the integrity of the group process. Once properly screened and determined to be suitable for placement in a group, the client is entitled to the process of informed consent.

Informed Consent

Group leaders educate and engage clients through the use of informed consent, which communicates basic rights and responsibilities to the prospective group member. Because clients have the right to choose whether or not to enter into a particular counseling relationship (ACA, 2005), a thorough informed consent is part of the screening process to ensure that client and group treatment method are a good fit. The informed consent should cover what the client should know before joining the group, as well as his or her rights and responsibilities during the group process (Corey et al., 2013). Ethically, group counselors inform prospective clients of the nature of the group process; benefits and limitations to such counseling; education training and credentials of the group counselor; expectations of the client within the group; the right to terminate the counseling relationship; and other concerns relevant to receiving services in a group environment (Corey et al., 2013). Finally, because of the nature of addiction, specifically illegal drug use, it is important for informed consent to address potential legal ramifications of disclosures made throughout the group counseling process.

Confidentiality

Confidentiality is of primary concern in the group treatment of addictions. Several decades ago, Congress took interest in the fact that addicts and alcoholics were avoiding treatment because of confidentiality concerns. To address this stigma, the federal government enacted a law commonly referred to as 42CFR Part 2 that defines limits of confidentiality for substance abuse programs in the United States (Substance Abuse and Mental Health Services Administration, 2010). Because of 42 CFR Part 2, a client's mere presence in a chemical dependency facility is considered a diagnosis and cannot be revealed without a written consent, nor can it be denied if someone inquires. However, in addition to confidentiality at the facility level, the group counselor is responsible for establishing the limits of confidentiality within the treatment group.

Informed consent is critical in conveying information and expectations regarding confidentiality of the group counselor and the group members. The *ACA Code of Ethics* (2005) makes this clear, stating, "In group work, counselors clearly explain the importance and parameters of confidentiality for the specific group being entered" (p. 8). However, because only the counselor solicits consent from the client, confidentiality cannot be guaranteed as an absolute. That is, the group counselor cannot guarantee that breaches will not occur as this type of counseling includes, by its very nature, persons other than the client and the counselor. It has been the experience of these authors, as well as the reported experience of noted group experts Irwin Yalom (Yalom & Leszcz, 2005) and Gerald Corey (2012), that breaches in group confidentiality are rare. Careful planning and presentation of expectations and limitations is paramount to creating the climate for confidentiality. After all, it is only within a climate of confidentiality that groups will enter into a productive, working stage.

Many group counselors find that involving the group in the process of establishing rules related to confidentiality is the most ethically responsible approach. As you might expect, members involved in establishing rules are often more responsive to those rules. Initial informed consent sets the stage for confidentiality expectations, but periodic reminders during group meetings are suggested to minimize risk (Corey, 2011). In addition to the right to confidentiality enjoyed by group members, group counselors must also explain the exceptions to confidentiality. Similar to exceptions to confidentiality in any counseling setting, the group counselor must discuss the ethical code that requires counselors to breach confidentiality when needed "to protect clients or identified others from serious and foreseeable harm or when legal requirements demand that confidential information must be revealed" (ACA, 2005, p. 7). Additionally, group counselors may need to breach confidentiality when a high risk of contracting a contagious, life-threatening disease exists (ACA, 2005). Finally, issues of confidentiality related to the group members and the group counselor encountering each other outside of the group session should be discussed. Many addictions group counselors practice their own recovery programs and could encounter group members in community 12-step groups. Establishing the ground rules for these boundary crossings should be part of the initial discussion of confidentiality. While these discussions are crucial, written agreements provide the clearest method of meeting the ethical and professional requirements related to confidentiality.

Voluntary Versus Involuntary Participation

Group counselors are often challenged with providing services to clients placed in the setting involuntarily. Examples include court-ordered treatment, groups conducted in correctional facilities, or even inpatient treatment facilities to which clients have been committed. Specific counseling and ethical concerns arise when faced with involuntary group participants. The counselor must work diligently to engage and encourage involuntary members to cooperate to avoid undermining the efficacy of the treatment (Corey, 2012). Because consequences are often built into the placement of clients in involuntary treatment, the counselor faces an enormous challenge to engage clients authentically. Clients may elect to attend, but not fully participate in the process, diminishing the treatment results.

In the experience of the authors, it is common practice for city and county judges to refer individuals arrested for public intoxication to the local mental health center for addiction education classes. Members are court ordered and required to complete classes as a portion of their legal consequences. At the conclusion of classes, participants are provided evidence of completion, which they submit to the courts. Members who do not complete classes as ordered often face jail time. The classes are psychoeducational in nature, and facilitators are often challenged to deal with a variety of issues, including resistance, denial, minimizing, and even overt resentment. Thus, having leaders who are trained and prepared to deal with court-ordered or involuntary group members is critical for the success of the group.

When involuntary clients are placed into a voluntary setting, the group counselor faces additional practical and ethical challenges. Because involuntary members might have different objectives for participating in the group than voluntary members (i.e., to remove or avoid a legal consequence), any behaviors that would undermine another member's ability to receive quality treatment would need to be assessed by the group counselor. The ethical code tells us that we must protect clients from any harm or trauma and must screen participants to ensure that the needs and goals of members are compatible with the group (ACA, 2005).

GROUP CONFLICT

The group therapy setting offers ample opportunity for resistance and conflict. Group therapy can be quite stimulating emotionally for members and the power differential between the leader and the members can also facilitate anxiety. While individual therapy offers a clearly defined authority figure, group therapy may be less formal, depending on the leader's style and the type of group. Additionally, because members receive feedback from a variety of people, this can lead to powerful reactions from members (Kelch & Piazza, 2011).

When conducting group therapy, it is important for the counselor to consider the implications for resistance and conflict on a macro and micro level. Members may be resistant to or have conflict toward the whole group. In other cases, a member may be resistant to or have conflict with specific members or the leader. Authors have offered lists of individual intragroup resistance behaviors and it includes such things as arguing, interrupting, and ignoring (Corey et al., 2013; Gladding, 2011). These behaviors can have implications for the group process, and counselors should be prepared to address them. Group counselors may need to educate group members on the counterproductive nature of these behaviors while recognizing that these behaviors are often representative of reluctance to participate in the process. Ultimately, group leaders should be prepared to explore the hesitations and anxieties the members are experiencing.

Occasionally, group conflict escalates into hostile behavior. Overtly hostile behavior such as direct caustic remarks is easy to recognize, although more passive aggressive behavior such as sarcasm or jokes may be more subtle and hard to identify. Leaders are charged to realize that group members detest making themselves susceptible to being mocked or degraded. Leaders might choose to invite the members to offer feedback on how they are affected by the hostile member. Overall, the key is for leaders to remain fully aware of both overt and covert conflict behaviors and be prepared to confront the behaviors and educate group members.

MANAGING DIVERSITY IN GROUP SETTINGS

Competent counselors understand the value of attending to diversity needs within all counseling environments, particularly within the group setting. Because no group is comprised of truly homogeneous members, the responsibility for attending to the diverse needs of the members lies with the counselor who facilitates the group, whether it is psychoeducational or psychotherapeutic in nature. Seminal research by Arredondo (1991), and further supported in the literature (e.g., Reese & Vera, 2007), proposed that groups are best addressed from a cultural perspective when three distinct dimensions are considered. The first includes classic issues of age, culture, ethnicity, gender, sexual orientation, and social class. Second, the counselor is challenged to address concepts such as educational background, geographic region, relationship status, and spiritual belief systems. Finally, Arredondo (1991) proposed that counseling is only truly culturally sensitive when it accounts for the historical era and context of the current societal climate. Addiction treatment providers also suggest that the "best way to address racial and cross-cultural tension, as a group facilitator, is directly" (Sanders & Mayeda, 2009, p. 24). Talking about issues openly in group can minimize the effects they have on the group process. For the purposes of this chapter, we will focus on the profound impact that issues of ethnicity, gender, sexuality, and type of addiction have on group counseling and its benefits.

Ethnicity

Counselors leading groups for clients who have addictions will naturally experience the impact and benefit that diverse ethnic backgrounds bring to the treatment approach. People of all ethnic backgrounds experience the ravages of addiction regardless of cultural approval or disapproval of the use of the substance (Frances & Miller, 2005). However, African-American and Hispanic clients are three times as likely to seek treatment for substance abuse than Caucasian clients (Dowd & Rugle, 1999). As previously discussed, group counseling interventions are likely to be part of that treatment.

Arredondo (1991) indicates that all group counseling is cross-cultural, affected by societal biases and norms, and challenging to the leader regardless of the leader's ethnicity. Group counselors facilitate a balance of power or status among the members. Race carries inherent status cues that can alter the balance initially (Napier & Gershenfeld, 2003), requiring the counselor to continually assess the impact ethnicity has on the overall group alliance. The effective group counselor will be aware of personal values, the worldview of the client, and subsequently develop culturally appropriate interventions and group approaches (Arredondo, 1991).

Gender

Within residential treatment facilities, clients are routinely housed in all-male or all-female environments. The rationale behind this approach is to increase the safety of the clients as they work on extremely difficult life concerns. There are some drawbacks to this approach as heterogeneous group experiences afford participants the opportunity to work through family-of-origin and cross-gender relational issues while addressing addiction. However, distractions inherent in heterosexual relationships between men and women are minimized within gender-specific environments.

Gender plays a role in the group counseling process. Some men find the practice of group counseling unmasculine. The process of group therapy is a more stereotypically feminine method of dealing with interpersonal issues, with its heavy reliance on talking through conflicts and providing verbal supportive feedback (Gazda et al., 2001). As such, males often respond better to male-only groups where all are participating in what might be considered a feminine activity.

Men are typically conditioned to be independent and self-reflective. Group therapy by definition requires interdependence and a reliance on the thoughts and assistance of others. The "process" element of the group experience is frequently counterintuitive to the male experience, but the practicality and efficacy of that element often appeals to men and has become perhaps the most beneficial method in facilitating the therapeutic experience of men. Gazda et al. (2001) indicate that counselors leading men's groups "should be sensitive and do work around shame, guilt, abandonment, grief, fear, dependency, and anger, but not be afraid of any of these emotional states" (p. 71). Because these are often difficult emotions to address, counselors must be aware of their own fears about challenging men, resulting from some of the same gender stereotyping that challenges the group members. Men have the ability to create a nurturing and supportive environment and generally grow through the process of sharing their own stories (Gazda et al., 2001). The counselor sensitive to the needs and challenges of an all-male group experience can assist members in the creation of an environment where work on the addiction can occur.

In contrast, many groups dealing with varied counseling concerns are *de facto* women's groups because women are more naturally drawn to the sharing climate that defines the group experience. As with groups of any gender, working with women requires the counselor to facilitate interaction that encourages insight leading to behavioral change, and to maintain the sensitivity and range of clinical skills necessary to address concerns specific to this population. Women's groups led by women counselors may, in fact, be the most powerful, given that female counselors may be more in tune than their male counterparts with the underlying emotions that need to be addressed (Gazda et al., 2001). All-female groups are more likely to focus on feelings related to the effects the addiction has had on parenting, and on the guilt and shame that may be present as a result. An additional component that supports the efficacy of all-women groups is the increased likelihood of women survivors of sexual abuse participating in the treatment (NeSmith, Wilcoxon, & Satcher, 2000). This probability adds pressure to an already difficult dynamic as women struggle to overcome their addictions. However, other research has indicated that the negative elements predicted in male-led groups for women may not be a reality and that women respond favorably to male leadership in the group environment (NeSmith et al., 2000).

While there is strong research on the efficacy of the all-female group, some results indicate that a mixed-gender experience may be even more powerful for women clients. In fact, some evidence suggests that the mixed experience allows women the opportunity to participate in healthy relationships with men in a safe, controlled environment, which better prepares them for the realities of working in community-based 12-step groups and participating in a mixed-gender society overall (NeSmith et al., 2000). In spite of such benefits, the idea of mixed-gender treatment is helpful only when the sexes are equally represented in the group. Research indicates that women who are in the minority in groups tend to fall prey to exaggerated sex role stereotypes and may lack the assertiveness needed to be honest and have their needs met within the group structure (Gazda et al., 2001). Women are often dominated by men in group experiences in general, which may reduce the efficacy of such an approach (NeSmith et al., 2000). The challenge again falls to the counselor, who must remain sensitive to both the needs of the group as an entity and the needs of each individual member. An understanding of gender from a developmental and cultural perspective, as well as an awareness of the implications inherent in that perspective, is a critical attribute of the group counselor working with addictions.

Sexuality

Sexual minorities, such as gay, lesbian, and bisexual clients, are indicated to have two to three times the risk for addiction than their heterosexual counterparts (Cochran, Ackerman, Mays, & Ross, 2004). As such, group leaders may have the opportunity to run groups comprised of sexual minorities or may find themselves facilitating groups containing both heterosexual and lesbian, gay, bisexual, transgendered, and questioning members.

Ben has been admitted to an inpatient facility for treatment of addiction to opioid pain medication. He reveals in group that when he is high, he engages in random sexual encounters. Although he considers himself heterosexual, he will go home with men or women when under the influence of narcotics. Group members insist he is bisexual, but he does not agree. Would the group process benefit from having Ben choose a label? How can this exchange be productive to the process and not a distraction?

Group counselors will then face the challenge of negotiating sexual identity stereotypes within the group environment, much like the gender stereotypes discussed previously.

Perhaps more than any other minority group, integrating sexual minorities into a largely heterosexual experience requires sensitivity and planning on the part of the group counselor to provide for member safety. Objective and unbiased treatment of sexual identity issues can challenge heterosexual facilitators and members, who may have a hard time setting aside their own beliefs for the greater good of the group experience. It falls upon the group counselor to both teach and model respect and to keep the focus on the recovery process. The skilled group counselor, aware of personal values and sensitive to the needs of the client as an individual and the group as a whole, is best suited to facilitating a climate for change.

Type of Addiction

There is an interesting phenomenon in the field of addictions, specifically alcohol and drug counseling, which may present a challenge to the group counselor. While group counseling is effective as a treatment intervention for a variety of substances, there are some dynamics between substance users that make group cohesion difficult.

> Dre is a 21-year-old African-American male with an addiction to crack cocaine. Harold is a 67-year-old Caucasian male with a fifth-a-day vodka habit. What impact might the cultural differences between these two members have on their willingness to participate? In spite of the obvious differences, what similarities might these members share?

Group counselors working in addictions find that differences in how members perceive the various types of substance use may create distance between members. These counselors find that individuals who have problems with alcohol may prefer treatment groups comprised of other alcoholics. Conversely, clients who are drug abusing or dependent are more open to treatment groups that address multiple substances.

In group settings, it is natural for defense mechanisms to emerge (James & Gilliland, 2005). The mind-set of "well, alcohol is legal" and "at least I'm not a crackhead" creates challenges for the counselor working with a group comprised of members with diverse types of addictions. While NA acknowledges alcohol as a drug (World Service Office, 1993), the reverse is not true for AA (AA Services, 2002). Drug-abusing or dependent clients may experience this division in local AA meetings, and this way of thinking may carry over into the psychoeducational or psychotherapeutic group realm. Experienced group counselors often have to navigate some tricky waters integrating these members into a working group setting.

GROUP COUNSELING FOR FAMILY MEMBERS OF ADDICTS

Because the spouses and children of addicts experience their own personal problems arising from the addiction, it is not difficult to understand the need for treatment opportunities to offer these family members. Additionally, the "attitudes, structure and function of the family system have been shown to be perhaps the most important variables in the outcome of treatment" for addicts (James & Gilliland, 2005). Thus, if the family system changes, it may assist the addict in sustaining progress and change.

The rationale for the treatment of the family member is clear. While the client receives treatment for addiction, the family members may require opportunities to learn new ways of coping and assistance in modifying stereotyped, repetitive, and maladaptive attitudes and responses to their family member's behavior. For example, family members often fail to recognize and admit that the symptoms of addiction have been present for some time; or they tolerate chronic addictive behavior, then reject the addict for displaying the behavior. Just as the addict rationalizes and makes excuses for using substances, addicts' family members often make excuses to themselves and to friends for the behavior instead of accepting that the individual is ill and needs treatment.

To aid an addict in recovery, family members must identify their own thoughts and attitudes, modify reactive behavior, and be educated about addiction and recovery (Rowe, 2012). This assists the family in learning how to stop centering their lives around the addict and detach from the substance abuse, while learning to allow the addict to solve his or her own problem and to start to live life fully.

Many groups exist exclusively to offer support to family members of addicts. One such self-help group is Al-Anon. The book *Al-Anon's Twelve Steps and Twelve Traditions* (AA Services, 2002) offers a short history of its inception. According to this account, the wives of alcoholics attending AA began talking among themselves about the problems associated with living with an addict. Eventually, the wives designed their own set of 12 steps based on the AA steps, and Al-Anon became an official group. Many groups now exist, including Alateen for teenage family members of alcoholics, Nar-Anon for family members of drug addicts, and Adult Children of Alcoholics (ACOA) for adults realizing they have problems as a result of growing up in an alcoholic family system.

Regardless of the group format, family members of addicts should be provided an opportunity to come together to share their experiences, discuss problems, provide encouragement to each other, and learn to cope more effectively with various concerns. Through these groups, family members are afforded an opportunity to detach emotionally from the alcoholic's behavior while still loving the individual. Group therapy can also assist family members in understanding they did not cause the alcoholic to drink and to realize they can build a rewarding life in spite of the continued substance abuse or dependence.

CASE STUDIES

The following case studies illustrate two examples of group therapy for the treatment of substance abuse. One is psychoeducational in nature and the second is an open focus approach. Each contains examples of topics that are frequently included in substance abuse treatment.

Case Study I: Development of a Six-Session Alcohol and Drug Education Group

Group Dynamics

David, a substance abuse counselor, is organizing a psychoeducational group to offer addiction education to both addicts and families of addicts. The group members will be both self-referred and court ordered. Some members will be seeking information on addiction; some will be fulfilling the requirements of a judgment following a driving under the influence (DUI) arrest, or management referrals after a positive drug screen at work. Still others will be seeking to educate themselves about the behavior of a family member. The group will be ongoing and cyclical in nature so members may begin at any time and simply continue until they have completed all six sessions. Each session will have a specific agenda and cover subject matter pertinent to gaining general understanding of the process of addiction and related topics. Attendance will vary from week to week, and the sessions are scheduled to meet for 60 minutes.

Questions for Consideration

1. How might the combination of both individuals addicted to substances and family members of those addicted to substances as group members affect the topic selection from week to week?
2. What types of conflict could arise with a mixed enrollment of court-ordered and voluntary participants?
3. What legal and ethical issues are pertinent to this group?
4. What special considerations must be made to accommodate the proposed cyclical nature of the group?

David's Response

After consideration of the types of members making up the groups, David designs the following model:

Session I: Addiction: What Is It?

This session will explore the biological, psychological, and sociological aspects of addiction. It will examine the chemicals and behaviors associated with addiction, as well as co-occurring disorders. It will examine causes of addiction, including genetics, brain chemistry, and societal influence. It will offer perspective on addiction including the disease model and addiction as a complex maladaptive behavior.

Session II: Codependency and Enabling

This session will explore the reciprocal and complementary nature of dependency based on the chemical dependent's need for care to survive and the caretaker's need to control the addict's behavior. It examines the differences between the behavior toward an addict (enabling) and one's relationship with an addict (codependency).

Session III: Life Skills Enhancement

During this session, members will be introduced to stress-management techniques, examine personal problem-solving skills, and practice assertiveness training. It will emphasize the importance of communication and utilizing positive leisure and recreation alternatives. It will teach tools and techniques for self-directed change and promote recovery and the importance of living a satisfying life. It will offer suggestions on maintaining motivation and thinking rationally.

Session IV: Recovering Lifestyle

Group members will explore the various components and benefits of therapeutic intervention for the treatment of addiction, including individual therapy, group therapy, and self-help programs. The session will address the concept of addiction as a complex maladaptive behavior with possible physiological factors and examine approaches to relapse prevention. This may include advocating the use of prescribed medications and psychological treatments.

Session V: What to Do and What Not to Do After Achieving Sobriety

This session includes review of important aspects of maintaining sobriety, including removing alcohol and/or drugs from the environment, buying over-the-counter medications, and promoting positive mind states and attitudes. This may include teaching HALT (hungry, angry, lonely, tired) as stress-producing states to avoid. Emphasis will be placed on coping with cravings and leading a balanced lifestyle.

Session VI: Self-Awareness/Spirituality

This session is devoted to endorsing the mind–body-spirit connection. It will focus on the importance of self-acceptance and spiritual cultivation to promote a sense of connectedness with self, others, and the universe. This session reiterates the link between negative emotions and thoughts and self-medicating with substances.

Discussion

Obviously, David must be well versed in addictions and addictions treatment. Maintaining structure in the group will help ensure that the limited time is used most effectively. Yet, the structure must be malleable, as processing of information may be necessary to ensure it is being received and understood. Structure through activities might offer concrete examples that will allow members to understand the implications for their own lives. David should be prepared to answer questions, provide additional information or resources, and make referrals.

David will have a number of diversity issues to address, in addition to the potential for conflict and resistance. As the chapter explores, gender and socioeconomic differences present inherent challenges. Specific to the needs of this group membership, David will need to be sensitive to the different perspectives of the identified addict and the family members present. Family members may resent being placed in a group setting with addicts and may lash out at their family member who is the impetus for their being in the group, or may displace that anger onto other clients. In addition, there could be conflict or resistance among and between the members that are voluntary and involuntary.

Because this is a revolving, open group, David will have additional challenges. Informed consent becomes critical in this type of environment. Membership in the group implies that the client has an addiction or that the group client is a family member of someone with an addiction. Because confidentiality is impossible for David to guarantee, as he can only control his own disclosures, he will need to conduct a thorough prescreening of members and carefully explain the limits of confidentiality at each meeting. Continually revisiting informed consent will assist David as he manages group members who are each at a different place in the group cycle of topics.

Case Study II: Psychotherapeutic Group, Open Focus

Group Dynamics

Nikki is a counselor for an inpatient alcohol and drug treatment facility. The treatment approach is based on the 12-step model of recovery. Each day, she facilitates a process-oriented therapy group for clients receiving treatment for addiction. The group is made up of adult males and females of various racial, ethnic, and socioeconomic backgrounds. Some members were voluntarily admitted to treatment and others were involuntarily committed to treatment. The group members have a variety of issues including chemical and behavioral addictions. Members will begin participation in the group upon admission to the program and continue until discharge. The size of the group could vary daily, but is typically between 8 and 16 members. Additionally, some members may be diagnosed with a co-occurring disorder.

Questions for Consideration

1. What are common issues for clients seeking treatment for addiction?
2. How might the variation of gender affect the interpersonal dynamics of the groups? Race? Socioeconomic status? Number of treatment attempts? Voluntary versus involuntary participation?
3. How should the facilitator address the issue of having a group made up of members at varying stages of relapse or recovery?
4. What legal and ethical considerations are pertinent to this group?

Nikki's Response

After consultation, Nikki realizes there are many issues for consideration. She recognizes the need to be educated and prepared to process the following issues:

Assertiveness Training

The group therapy format facilitates learning the difference between aggressive behavior and assertive behavior by offering ample opportunity for verbal exchange about sensitive subjects. Members learn to interact with one another and the leader in an honest, open way. Members are taught that aggression can take place passively, with remarks such as "You're right, I wouldn't know about hangovers, I only smoke marijuana" or overtly, with remarks such as "You're a whore that traded her body for drugs."

Character Defects

There are many characteristics of dysfunctional coping styles that show up through inappropriate interpersonal communication. Working with group members on self-pity, arrogance, lack of humility, overconfidence, and grandiosity are typical. The addict's defenses are "primitive and regressive" and may "personify the addict as self-centered and dependent" (James & Gilliland, 2005, p. 279). Such comments as "Why should I listen to you when your brain is fried?" facilitates members learning to recognize that grandiose behavior is overcompensation for feeling low. This lays the groundwork for successfully interacting with humility and teaches clients to respect others and avoid making generalizations.

Denial

A persistent and pervasive personal defense system, denial is the emotional refusal to acknowledge a person, situation, condition, or event the way it actually is (James & Gilliland, 2005). It is commonplace for substance abusers to deny they are "addicted" to their chemical or behavior of choice. While denial is a normal adaptive process for self-protection, within the addict it becomes an ongoing form of self-deception. Many addicts begin the process of recovery with remarks such as "I can stop any time I want to."

Grief

The process of recovery often promotes an overwhelming sense of grief. Group members express sentiments such as "I feel like I have lost my best friend." Group leaders may elect to teach members symptoms of grief, utilizing such resources as the Kubler-Ross Model (1969) of the cycle of grief to explain that the myriad of feelings being experienced is typical, and emphasize the importance of learning healthy coping alternatives.

Minimization

Statements such as "I only drink beer" or "I didn't inhale" are commonplace among chemically dependent individuals. "Clients often minimize the extent of their use in an attempt to convince themselves and others that they can continue to use" (Johnson, 2004, p. 116). In fact, minimization is so prevalent that many substance abuse professionals routinely assume that the amount of alcohol or drug use reported is only a small percentage of what is actually used. Family members of clients may also minimize reports of use as part of their own denial of the extent of the problem.

Modeling of New and Healthier Coping Strategies

Many inpatient treatment facilities allow their clients to gain privileges through the course of treatment, allowing the client to leave the facility to go home or visit friends and family. Upon returning, clients are afforded an opportunity to process their thoughts and feelings about being in the community, encountering friends or situations that challenge them, and reviewing what has and has not been working to cope with these circumstances.

Rationalization

Considered a characteristic of denial, rationalization is the chronic use of excuses to support both addiction and the feelings of inadequacy that lead to destructive acting and behaving. Addressing these excuses may be difficult for group leaders and family members because there may be elements of truth included in the "reasons" for using. For example, some addicts did have abusive childhoods or are involved in dysfunctional relationships. Even such comments as "After the accident I couldn't sleep at night" are not uncommon. However, the goal of rationalizing is to convince others that the user is justified and should not be confronted (Johnson, 2004).

Relapse and Aftercare Concerns

Exploration of the concepts of triggers and coping mechanisms for dealing with triggers including how to handle craving are common topics for group members. There is a great deal of fear involved in considering what the future holds, including the ability to cope with high-risk situations and the motivation to change behavior or return to past behavior. Research suggests a strong association between negative affective states and relapse, so the exploration of negative feelings is critical (Doweiko, 2010).

Resentment/Blame

It is not unusual for some clients to be resentful of being in treatment. Some may demonstrate hostility toward a family or staff member. A client might make statements such as "My wife is such a nag, she makes me drink." Exploration of the displacement of these feelings and attempts to move clients toward personal responsibility are primary themes for building a foundation of sobriety.

Spiritual Cultivation

A major component of many chemical dependency programs is the careful analysis of clients' spiritual resources (James & Gilliland, 2005). This investigation has little to do with religion and instead focuses on the despair and hopelessness addicts feel and the emptiness in their lives they attempt to fill through their addiction. Being prepared to explore these feelings is critical.

Testing Behaviors

Clients often test the limits to determine consistency in the counselor's treatment approach by disobeying rules. As a result, breaking the ground rules should immediately be confronted by the group counselor. For example, if a member is late for a group and makes an excuse such as "I forgot the time," the group leader may use this as an opportunity to address the excuse and explore whether the client has used this excuse to perpetuate the use of substances.

Discussion

In addition to addressing the issues just outlined, Nikki will have a number of diversity challenges in her setting. Issues of gender play out in inpatient facilities that, as previously indicated, often results in same-sex group meetings. Since Nikki will be managing a group whose composition will fluctuate regularly, she will need to manage any power differentials inherent in gender bias. Additionally, ethnic diversity carries its own set of social and cultural biases, and Nikki will need to continuously evaluate that impact on the dynamic of the group to generate a climate most conducive to change. Because some clients will be there under an involuntary order, or after multiple treatment attempts, Nikki will be challenged with the impact resistance, anger, denial, and rationalization have on the group process. The stage set for the group in this case study is especially dynamic given its ongoing structural changes and challenges, creating a rich opportunity for the skilled group counselor to actively facilitate a multifaceted treatment approach.

Because the group is set within a larger treatment model provided by the institution, legal and ethical concerns may be first addressed within the overarching structure of the treatment facility. Informed consent for all components of treatment, including this group approach, will initially be addressed upon admission with a thorough informed consent. As previously indicated, confidentiality cannot be guaranteed when in a group setting, but federal law protects clients in inpatient alcohol and drug treatment from having information shared outside of the facility by the employees of that facility. Following her own code of ethics as a counselor, it will be important for her to address confidentiality in the screening of group members, as well as with the overall group each session. Nikki's code of ethics as a counselor guides her to provide for the welfare of the client first and foremost. Because some members may be diagnosed with a co-occurring disorder, the impact this would have on the group dynamic would need to be evaluated. She will have to make decisions about group inclusion that may require her to offer alternative treatment to clients who would not benefit from—or might even be detrimental to—the group setting.

Nikki must learn, understand, and know how to use the group process to involve clients in positive change (Johnson, 2004). It takes skill and practice to engage members in talking to others while promoting safety to talk about self. Knowledge of a number of theories and models is recommended. Nikki must remember that essentially, in entering the program, members have admitted they have been unable to change on their own. As such, she must utilize the strongest interpersonal skills she possesses to help them change. She must always be cognizant that the alliance that evolves between herself and clients is one important factor in a positive outcome of the treatment process. Research indicates that empathy combined with a "supportive-reflective" style of therapy seems to be most effective (Doweiko, 2010).

STRATEGIES FOR EFFECTIVE GROUP TREATMENT

Clearly one very important factor for addiction treatment providers is retaining clients in treatment. Studies indicate that clients who complete treatment have higher recovery rates than those who drop out (Sanders & Mayeda, 2009). Thus, consideration of factors that can minimize conflict and prevent dropout are of critical significance. Sanders and Mayeda (2009) suggest the following strategies to increase group cohesion and address group conflict:

- Address outbursts directly and quickly to promote members feeling safe.
- Encourage members to maintain a normal tone of voice and avoid loud voices or yelling.
- Create contracts with members to address behaviors that require practice. For example, if a member has a tendency to lash out verbally when faced with conflict, when the group member demonstrates distress, address this history and request permission to address the issue in group in an effort to find appropriate ways to express feelings.
- If group members demonstrate emotions that seem linked to resentment related to giving up alcohol or drugs, address the issue openly to facilitate an opportunity to discuss this anger.
- Ask members to repeat back what they hear other members say when tension creates interference with hearing one another.
- If members seem to be relating strongly to another member, consider that members often have conflict with other members that are much like them. Ask those who are at odds to identify similarities between themselves.
- Facilitators must pay attention to and promptly take apart subgroups.
- Deal with members who monopolize group time in a straightforward and open manner.
- Allowing opportunities to shift between emotion and thoughts can be calming and allow room for growth.

Summary and Some Final Notations

This chapter reviewed group therapy, one of the primary treatment models for addiction within the United States. Psychotherapeutic, psychoeducational, and self-help groups were examined in detail, including proposed topic areas, considerations for facilitators, and diversity issues. Various legal and ethical issues related to the use of group therapy with addicted populations were examined. A review of the potential effectiveness of group therapy with family members of addicts was also provided. Comprehensive case studies were presented to assist students in understanding issues that must be considered when designing and facilitating a therapy group to treat addiction.

MyCounselingLab

Visit the MyCounselingLab site for *Foundations of Addictions Counseling,* Third Edition to enhance your understanding of concepts. You'll have the opportunity to practice your skills through video- and case-based exercises. You will find sets of questions to help you prepare for your certification exam with *Licensure Quizzes*. There is also a Video Library that provides taped counseling sessions, ethical scenarios, and interviews with helpers and clients.

Useful Websites

The following websites provide additional information relating to the chapter topics:

The Addiction Recovery Guide
www.addictionrecoveryguide.org/treatment/online.html
Offers a variety of online treatment resources for alcohol and drug treatment by trained experts via the Internet.

American Counseling Association Code of Ethics
www.counseling.org/knowledge-center/ethics
Allows counselors to access the *ACA Code of Ethics* pertaining to group counseling.

Association for Specialists in Group Work
www.asgw.org/
A division of ACA founded to promote quality in group work, training practice, and research.

National Institute on Drug Abuse: Drug Counseling for Cocaine Addicts
www.nida.nih.gov/TXManuals/DCCA/DCCA5.html
Provides an overview of group treatment for cocaine addiction, including outlines for psychoeducational and problem-solving groups.

SMART Recovery®
smartrecovery.org
SMART Recovery® is a nationwide, nonprofit organization that offers free support groups to individuals who desire to gain independence from any type of addictive behavior. SMART Recovery® also offers a free Internet message board discussion group, and sells publications and offers multiple free resources related to recovery from addictive behavior.

Sober Recovery
www.soberrecovery.com/
Online resource guide to 12-step and 12-step-alternative programs. Includes information about addiction and recovery and provides support information for families and friends, with lists of, and links to, inpatient and outpatient recovery programs for adults and teens.

References

AA Services. (2002). *Al-Anon's twelve steps and twelve traditions.* New York, NY: Al-Anon Family Group Headquarters, Inc.

AA Services. (2013). *Alcoholics Anonymous big book* (5th ed.). New York, NY: Alcoholics Anonymous World Services, Inc.

AA Services. (2013) *A.A. at a glance.* New York, NY: AA Worldwide Services Inc., Retrieved August 29, 2014, http://www.aa.org/assets/en_US/f-1_AAataGlance.pdf

Alcoholics Anonymous World Services. (2013). Estimate of AA groups and members as of January 1, 2013. Retrieved from http://www.aa.org/en_pdfs/smf-53_en.pdf

American Counseling Association. (2005). *ACA code of ethics.* Alexandria, VA: Author.

American Psychiatric Association. (2013). *Diagnostic and statistical manual of mental disorders* (5th ed.). Washington, DC: Author.

Arredondo, P. (1991). Multicultural counseling competencies as tools to address oppression and racism. *Journal of Counseling and Development, 77*(1), 102–109.

Association for Specialists in Group Work. (1998). Best practice guidelines. *Journal for Specialists in Group Work, 23*(3), 237–244.

Association for Specialists in Group Work. (2000). Professional standards for the training of group workers. *Journal for Specialists in Group Work, 29*(3), 1–10.

Behavioral Health Treatment. (1997). Group therapy works well for addiction [Electronic version]. *Behavioral Health Treatment, 2*(1), 1–3.

Bradley, L., Whiting, P., Hendricks, B., Parr, G., & Jones, E. (2008). The use of expressive techniques in counseling. *Journal of Creativity in Mental Health, 3*(1), 44–59. doi:10.1080/15401380802023605

Campbell, L., & Page, R. (1993). The therapeutic effects of group process on the behavioral patterns of a drug addicted group [Electronic version]. *Journal of Addictions & Offender Counseling, 13*(2), 34–46.

Center for Substance Abuse Treatment. (2005a). *Substance abuse treatment: Group therapy* (Treatment Improvement Protocol [TIP] Series, No. 41: 1 Groups and Substance Abuse Treatment). Rockville, MD: Substance Abuse and Mental Health Services Administration. Retrieved from http://www.ncbi.nlm.nih.gov/books/NBK64223/

Center for Substance Abuse Treatment. (2005b). *Substance abuse treatment for persons with co-occurring disorders* (Treatment Improvement Protocol [TIP] Series, No. 42: 5 Strategies for Working With Clients With Co-Occurring Disorders). Rockville, MD: Substance Abuse and Mental Health Services Administration. Retrieved from http://www.ncbi.nlm.nih.gov/books/NBK64179/

Cochran, S. D., Ackerman, D., Mays, V. M., & Ross, M. W. (2004). Prevalence of non-medical drug use and dependence among homosexually active men and women in the US population. *Addiction, 99*(8), 989–999.

Corey, G. (2011). *Theory and practice of group counseling* (8th ed.). Belmont, CA: Brooks Cole Learning.

Corey, G. (2012). *Theory and practice of counseling & psychotherapy* (9th ed.). Pacific Grove, CA: Brooks/Cole.

Corey, G., Williams, G. T., & Moline, M. E. (1995). Ethical and legal issues in group counseling. *Ethics & Behavior, 5*(2), 161–183.

Corey, M. S., Corey, G., & Corey, C. (2013). *Groups: Process and practice* (9th ed.). Pacific Grove, CA: Brooks/Cole.

Dowd, E. T., & Rugle, L. (Eds.). (1999). *Comparative treatments of substance abuse.* New York, NY: Springer.

Doweiko, H. E. (2010). *Concepts of chemical dependency* (7th ed.). Belmont, CA: Thomson Cengage Learning.

Frances, R. J., & Miller, S. I. (2005). *Clinical textbook of addictive disorders* (3rd ed.). New York, NY: Guilford Press.

Gazda, G. M., Ginter, E. J., & Horne, A. M. (2001). *Group counseling and group psychotherapy: Theory and application.* Boston, MA: Allyn & Bacon.

Gladding, S.T. (2010). *Family therapy: History, theory and practice* (5th ed.). Upper Saddle River, NJ: Pearson Education, Inc.

Gladding, S. T. (2011). *Groups: A counseling specialty* (6th ed.). Upper Saddle River, NJ: Pearson Education, Inc.

Gorman, D. (2003). The best of practices, the worst of practices: The making of science-based primary intervention programs. *Psychiatric Services, 54,* 1087–1089.

Hunter, S. B., Witkiewitz, K., Watkins, K. E., Paddock, S. M., & Hepner, K. A. (2012). The moderating effects of group cognitive–behavioral therapy for depression among substance users. *Psychology Of Addictive Behaviors, 26*(4), 906–916. doi:10.1037/a0028158

James, R. K., & Gilliland, B. E. (2005). *Crisis intervention strategies* (5th ed.). Belmont, CA: Thomson Brooks/Cole.

Johnson, J. L. (2004). *Fundamentals of substance abuse practice.* Belmont, CA: Brooks/Cole-Thomson Learning.

Kelch, B. P., & Piazza, N. J. (2011). Medication-assisted treatment: Overcoming individual resistance among members in groups whose membership consists of both users and nonusers of MAT: A clinical review. *Journal of Groups In Addiction & Recovery, 6,* 307–318. doi:10.1080/1556035X.2011.614522

Kubler-Ross, E. (1969). *On death and dying.* New York, NY: McMillan Publishing.

Martin, M. K., Giannandrea, P., Rogers, B., & Johnson, J. (1996). Beginning steps to recovery: A challenge to the "come back when you're ready" approach. *Alcoholism Treatment Quarterly, 13*(2), 45–58.

Napier, R. W., & Gershenfeld, M. K. (2003). *Groups: Theory and experience* (7th ed.). Boston, MA: Houghton Mifflin.

NeSmith, C. L., Wilcoxon, S. A., & Satcher, J. F. (2000). Male leadership in an addicted women's group: An empirical approach. *Journal of Addictions and Offender Counseling, 20*(2), 75–84.

Panas, L., Caspi, Y., Fournier, E., & McCarty, D. (2003). Performance measures for outpatient substance abuse services: Group versus individual counseling. *Journal of Substance Abuse Treatment, 25*(4), 271–279.

Phillips, R. E., Lakin, R., & Pargament, K. I. (2002). Development and implementation of a spiritual issues psychoeducational group for those with serious mental illness. *Community Mental Health Journal, 38*(6), 487–496.

Reese, L. E., & Vera, E. M. (2007). Culturally relevant prevention programs: Scientific and practical considerations. *The Counseling Psychologist, 35,* 763–778. doi:10.1177/0011000007304588

Rowe, C. L. (2012). Family therapy for drug abuse: Review and updates 2003–2010. *Journal of Marital & Family Therapy, 38*(1), 59–81. doi:10.1111/j.1752-0606.2011.00280.x

Ruiz, P., & Strain, R. (Eds.). (2011). *Lowinson and Ruiz's substance abuse: A comprehensive textbook* (5th ed.). Philadelphia, PA: Lippencott Williams & Wilkins.

Sadler, M. J. (2003). The convergence of group psychotherapy and the Twelve Steps of AA. *Journal of Addictive Disorders.* Retrieved from http://www.breininginstitute.com/TheJOURNAL2003.htm

Sanders, M., & Mayeda, S. (2009, November/December). Decrease conflicts in groups. *Addiction Professional,* pp. 21–25.

SMART Recovery: Self-Management and Recovery Training. (n.d.). Retrieved February 21, 2014, from http://www.smartrecovery.org/resources/pdfs/faq.pdf

Substance Abuse and Mental Health Services Administration. (2010). *Frequently asked questions applying the substance abuse confidentiality regulations to health information exchange (HIE).* Retrieved from http://www.samhsa.gov/healthprivacy/docs/ehr-faqs.pdf

Sunich, M. F. (2013). Cognitive group addiction treatment: A fresh perspective. *Psyccritiques, 58*(28). doi:10.1037/a0033213

Toseland, R. W., & Rivas, R. F. (2001). *An introduction to group work* (4th ed.). Needham Heights, MA: Allyn & Bacon.

Washton, A. M., & Zweben, J. E. (2008). *Treating alcohol and drug problems in psychotherapy practice: Doing what works.* New York, NY: Guilford Press.

Weiss, R. D., Jaffee, W. B., de Menil, V. P., & Cogley, C. B. (2004). Group therapy for substance use disorders: What do we know? *Harvard Review of Psychiatry, 12*(6), 339–351.

World Service Office. (1993). *It works: How and why: The Twelve Steps and Twelve Traditions of Narcotics Anonymous.* Van Nuys, CA: World Service Office.

Yalom, I. D., & Leszcz, M. (2005). *The theory and practice of group psychotherapy* (5th ed.). New York, NY: Basic Books.

Chapter 11

Addiction Pharmacotherapy

Cass Dykeman
Oregon State University

RATIONALE FOR A CHAPTER ON PHARMACOTHERAPY OF ADDICTION

Why should a professional counselor read a chapter on the pharmacotherapy of addiction? Isn't it strange to use a drug to defeat an addiction to another drug? Also, isn't pharmacotherapy the sole domain of physicians? In the course of this chapter, I hope to orient you to the increasing role of pharmacotherapy in addiction treatment. With this knowledge, you will be in the best position to help your clients take full advantage of the myriad of treatment options that exist.

The pharmacotherapy approaches discussed in this chapter are not without controversy in the addictions treatment community. Many subscribe to the adage "you can't treat a drug with a drug" (O'Brien, 2005). Others disparage medication as a "crutch" and press clients to remain "drug free" (O'Brien, 2005). Indeed, a government report listed the "antimedication" bias in the addiction treatment community as a critical barrier to the development of addiction pharmacotherapy in the United States (Goodman et al., 1997). As a professional counselor, you are under an ethical obligation to provide your clients treatment based not upon bias but upon scientific evidence of effectiveness. Thus, attention to addiction pharmacotherapy is an ethical mandate no matter what prejudices you encounter at your worksite.

Personal reflection and integration: How do you really feel?

1. On a scale from 1 (*very low*) to 10 (*very high*), how would you rate the useful of medication to treat addiction?
2. Why did you pick that number?
3. What personal and/or professional experiences served as the background for the number that you picked?

This chapter has four parts. In the first, we will focus on the specialized terms and concepts used in pharmacotherapy. These can be intimidating to professional counselors without an extensive background in the biological sciences. Yet, understanding these terms and concepts is essential to understanding the specific pharmacotherapies used in the addiction field. The figures that appear in the first section were inspired by Shiloh, Stryjer, Weizman, and Nutt's amazing *Atlas of Psychiatric Pharmacotherapy* (2006). The professional counselor desiring further knowledge about mental health pharmacotherapy is directed to consult this work first. In the second part, I will offer an explication of the biology of craving. Next, I will address the professional counselor's role in addiction pharmacotherapy. In the final part, we will look at how psychopharmacology is applied through the lens of one substance abuse disorder.

TERMS AND CONCEPTS

Key Pharmacotherapy Terms

As with learning foreign languages and statistics, terms are the foundation to knowledge acquisition. What follows are the key pharmacotherapy terms any professional counselor should know because they will be encountered frequently in your professional practice and reading. Other pharmacotherapy-specific terms I will use appear in a glossary at the end of this chapter.

ADDICTION (FROM A PSYCHOPHARMACOLOGICAL PERSPECTIVE) A chemical or behavior used to produce pleasure and to reduce painful affects, employed in a pattern characterized by two key features: (1) recurrent failure to control the behavior; and (2) continuation of the behavior despite significant harmful consequences (Goodman, 2008). Several neurotransmitters (e.g., glutamate) and hormones (e.g., insulin) are core factors in this desire to produce pleasure and reduce painful affects (Leggio, 2009).

AGONIST A ligand (i.e., molecule) that activates a receptor (Preston, O'Neal, & Talaga, 2013).

ANTAGONIST A ligand that blocks other ligands from activating a receptor (Preston et al., 2013).

NEUROTRANSMITTER Chemicals released by nerve cells at synapses that influence the activity of other cells. Neurotransmitters may excite, inhibit, or otherwise influence the activity of cells (National Institute of Neurological Disorders and Stroke, 2007). In reference to addiction pharmacotherapy, the main neurotransmitters of interest include acetylcholine (ACH), glutamate (GLU), γ-aminobutyric acid (GABA), serotonin (5HT), norepinephrine (NA), opioid (OP), and dopamine (DA).

RECEPTOR The location at which ligands bind to the nervous system to exert their effects (i.e., chemical signaling between and within cells) (Julien, 2010; Neubig, Spedding, Kenakin, & Christopoulis, 2003).

REUPTAKE Reabsorption of a neurotransmitter by way of a reuptake transporter pump embedded in a cell membrane (Preston et al., 2013).

KEY CONCEPTS OF NEUROLOGY IN PHARMACOTHERAPY

While fascinating, a comprehensive examination of pharmacotherapy neurology lies beyond the scope and goals of this chapter. Thus, we will focus on one key part of this neurology—the neurology of the synapse. A synapse has three parts: (1) a minute space between, (2) a presynaptic membrane of one neuron, and (3) a postsynaptic membrane of a receiving neuron (Julien, 2010). This minute space is known as the synaptic cleft. The presynaptic membrane is located at the axon terminal of a neuron (i.e., terminal bouton). The postsynaptic membrane is located on a dendrite of a neuron. See Figure 11.1 for a graphical overview of this neurology.

The presynaptic side of this neurology controls neurotransmitter release (Shiloh, Stryjer, Weizman, & Nutt, 2006). Generally, most neurons release only one transmitter (Shiloh et al., 2006). In the presynaptic axon terminal, there are three parts to note: (1) reuptake transmitter pumps, (2) receptors, and (3) intracellular vesicles containing the neurotransmitter. Please note that there are receptors that can stimulate neurotransmitters and receptors that can inhibit such release. See Figure 11.2 for a graphical representation of the presynaptic side.

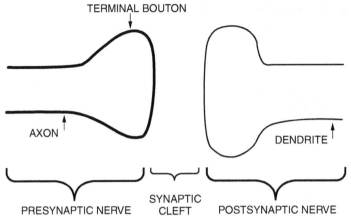

FIGURE 11.1 The Neurology of the Synapse

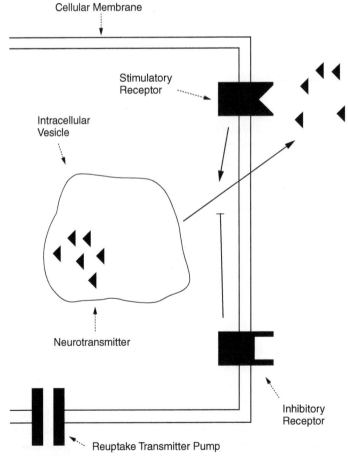

FIGURE 11.2 Presynaptic Neurology

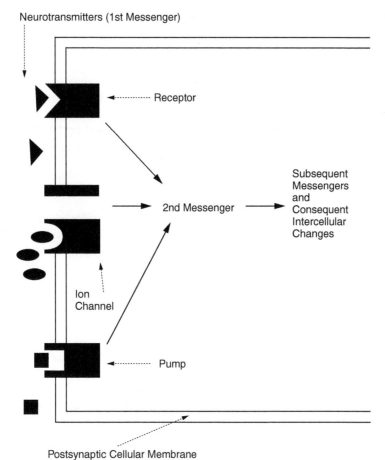

FIGURE 11.3 Postsynaptic Neurology

The postsynaptic side of this neurology facilitates intracellular response (Shiloh et al., 2006). The postsynaptic nerve has three parts of note: (1) ion channels, (2) receptors, and (3) pumps. All three parts can either enhance or suppress the permeability of the postsynaptic membrane (Shiloh et al., 2006). See Figure 11.3 for a graphical representation of the postsynaptic side.

In thinking about neurology of intracellular change, it may be helpful to employ the metaphor of "messengers" (Shiloh et al., 2006). Neurotransmitters can be thought of as "first messengers." These messengers interact with the postsynaptic nerve to induce consequent intracellular changes (Shiloh et al., 2006). Within the postsynaptic nerve, the first messengers set off a cascade of messenger changes including second, third, and fourth messengers. The nature and function of the final three messengers lies beyond the scope of this chapter.

DIVERSITY AND PHARMACOTHERAPY

There are considerable cross-ethnic variations in drug effects (Lin & Poland, 2000). An example is drugs that impact pupil dilation. When the same amount of this type of medication was applied, Blacks were the least responsive, Asians in the middle, and Caucasians at the other extreme (Lin & Poland, 2000). In their major work in ethnic psychopharmacology, Lin and Poland (2000) concluded,

Clinically, the importance of culture and ethnicity has been significantly intensified because of the rapid and accelerating population shifts occurring in all metropolitan areas of the world. Furthermore, because of the rapid pace of intercontinental transportation and large-scale migration, most psychiatrists no longer have the luxury of practicing their trades in culturally or ethnically homogeneous settings. Patients seeking help enter the clinic with divergent beliefs, expectations, dietary practices, and genetic constitution. These all have the potential of significantly affecting the outcome of psychopharmacotherapy and should not be ignored. (p. 1917)

Another example concerns ethnic variations of the presence of an enzyme (CYP 2D6) that strongly impacts drug metabolism (*n.b.*, PM = Poor Metabolizer). Concerning CYP 2D6, Chaudhry, Neelam, Duddu, and Husain (2008) reported that:

The frequency of CYP2D6 PMs ranges from >3% in the Cuna Amerindians, Middle Easterners, Mexican Americans and Asians to 10% in Caucasians in Europe and North America. ... Among black Africans, there is a wide range of frequencies with 0–8% of Saharan Africans, 4% of Venda in South Africa, 1.9% of African-Americans and 19% of Sans Bushmen being classified as PMs. ... (p. 676)

Chaudhry et al. (2008) noted that these ethnic variations result from a complex interchange of genetic factors with ethnically based variables such as culture, diet, and societal attitudes. Figure 11.4 presents a provisional causal chain based on the research reviews on ethnic psychopharmacology (Campinha-Bacote, 2007; Chaudhry et al., 2008; Chen, Chen, & Lin, 2008).

Given the existence of wide ethnic variations in the impact of medications, consideration of the interplay between ethnicity and pharmacotherapy represents best practice for the professional counselor. However, all the reviewers cautioned that *intra*-ethnic differences in psychopharmacology can be as large as *inter*-ethnic differences. As such, it is the wise clinician who avoids applying even well-researched ethnic distinctions indiscriminate of the history of each individual client. Hunt and Kreiner (2013) warned that this type of indiscriminate application can be "carte blanche for practicing racialized medicine" (p. 232).

Personal reflection and integration: Respecting diversity or practicing racialized medicine?

1. Can the cultural patterns you learned about in your training program devolve into stereotyping? If so, how?
2. Think of a colleague who indiscriminately applied some global cultural patterns to a specific client and then answer the following questions:
   a. What was the outcome of that counseling?
   b. What were the counselor's motivations for this indiscriminate application?
   c. In your own clinical work, how do you account for *intra*-cultural variation?

Sex is another factor in the effects of a drug. In a major review of studies on sex differences in drug abuse, Lynch, Roth, and Carroll (2002) concluded,

It is apparent that sex influences the behaviors induced by drugs, as well as pharmacological responses to drugs. Further research examining the factors that underlie sex differences may allow for the development of safe and effective sex-specific behavioral and pharmacological therapies for drug abuse. (p. 133)

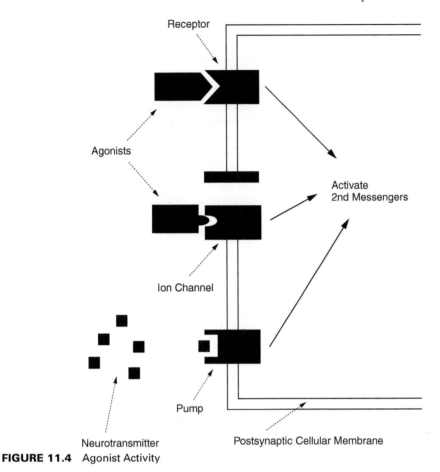
FIGURE 11.4 Agonist Activity

As with ethnicity, consideration of the interplay between sex and pharmacotherapy represents best practice for the professional counselor.

PHARMACOTHERAPY CASE STUDY I

Generalized Anxiety Disorder (DSM 5 300.02), Alcohol Use Disorder (DSM 5 303.90 Severe), and Sedative, Hypnotic, or Anxiolytic Dependence Use Disorder (DSM 5 304.10 Moderate)

Michael Williams is a single, 32-year-old multiracial (African-American and Haitian) resident of Los Altos, California. He is the chief financial officer of an Internet startup company. Michael has suffered from anxiety as long as he can remember. About 2 years ago, he started to hear rumors of his company's demise. Also, his father was diagnosed with prostate cancer. Michael found that he could not shut his mind off from thinking about potential disasters in all parts of his life.

To cope with both his high state and trait anxiety, Michael started to drink heavily. His drinking led both to a breakup with his long-time partner and to chronic insomnia. About a year ago, he was arrested for driving under the influence (DUI) while driving home from a party. Michael has always had a strong self-image as a law-abiding person, so his arrest disturbed him greatly. Thus, Michael went to see his family doctor for help with both his drinking and anxiety.

Michael's family physician, Dr. Chen, diagnosed Michael with both Generalized Anxiety Disorder and Alcohol Use Disorder and suggested a trial with an SSRI for anxiety and oxazepam (Serax) to manage any alcohol withdrawal symptoms. Michael declined use of an SSRI because he had heard about the potential sexual side effects of this class of medication. As an alternative, Dr. Chen referred Michael to a local cognitive-behavioral (CBT) counselor skilled in working with alcoholism and anxiety comorbidity. Michael did quit drinking; however, he continued his use of oxazepam beyond the 5-day outpatient alcohol detoxification protocol Dr. Chen was following (see Prater, Miller, & Zylstra, 1999). He found it easy to obtain ample amounts of oxazepam from friends and co-workers who had been prescribed the medication for anxiety. Over the next 6 months, Michael's use of oxazepam steadily increased due to tolerance.

At Michael's annual physical, Dr. Chen ran a drug and alcohol screen as part of Michael's blood work. This screen revealed Michael's oxazepam use. Dr. Chen confronted Michael about his continuing oxazepam use, at which point Michael broke down and admitted this use, as well as having not gone to counseling. Dr. Chen agreed to help Michael get off oxazepam if he agreed to (1) go to counseling, and (2) sign release of information agreements so that Dr. Chen and the counselor could communicate. Michael readily agreed.

After listening to Michael, Dr. Chen diagnosed him with Sedative, Hypnotic, or Anxiolytic Use Disorder. To ease the withdrawal symptoms while quitting, Dr. Chen opted for a slow withdrawal substitution strategy—specifically, substituting the long half-life benzodiazepine diazepam (Valium) for oxazepam, and slowly lowering the dosage over 14 weeks (see Ashton, 2002, for an example schedule). At a 14-week check-in, Michael reported that he had quit the diazepam at Week 13 without a problem. Also during this time period, he completed a 10-session course of CBT. At discharge from counseling, Michael's score of 10 on the Hamilton Anxiety Scale was well below the cut-off point for GAD. In addition, he happily reported that his long-time partner had reentered his life.

KEY CONCEPTS OF NEUROTRANSMITTERS IN PHARMACOTHERAPY

There are a number of endogenous chemicals that serve as neurotransmitters. The three with most relevance to addiction pharmacotherapy are serotonin (5HT), dopamine (DA), and norepinephrine (NA). Reiness (2009) describes the life cycle of neurotransmitters as follows:

> It is often convenient to divide up the "life cycle" of a neurotransmitter into particular stages. Usually these include: (1) synthesis of the transmitter; (2) packaging and storage in synaptic vesicles; (3) if necessary, transport from the site of synthesis to the site of release from the nerve terminal; (4) release in response to an action potential; (5) binding to postsynaptic receptor proteins; and (6) termination of action by diffusion, destruction, or reuptake into cells. (p. 1)

Blocking reuptake is a major mechanism of the medications that we will discuss later in this chapter.

KEY CONCEPTS OF PHARMACOKINETICS IN PHARMACOTHERAPY

In discussing the four pharmacokinetic processes, Julien (2010) used a drug most readers of this chapter should be well familiar with: aspirin. In reference to aspirin, these processes can be described as follows:

1. *Absorption* of the aspirin into the body from the swallowed tablet.
2. *Distribution* of the aspirin throughout the body.
3. *Biotransformation* of the aspirin into by-products (i.e., metabolites).
4. *Elimination* of the waste by-products (Julien, 2010; Preston et al., 2013).

It is important to note that every drug will exhibit a unique kinetic profile (like a fingerprint) composed of these four processes (Preston et al., 2013).

The most important pharmacokinetic concept is half-life. The half-life of a drug is used to determine dosage amounts and time intervals (Preston et al., 2013). Knowledge of a drug's half-life is also important because it tells one how long a drug will remain in the body (Julien, 2010). For, instance it takes approximately 4 half-lives for 94% of a drug to clear the body (Julien, 2010). Significantly, even individual medications of the same type (i.e., benzodiazepines) can have very different half-lives.

KEY CONCEPTS OF PHARMACODYNAMICS IN PHARMACOTHERAPY

In the previous section, we addressed how the body affects drugs. Now we turn our attention to how drugs affect the body. To produce an effect, a drug must bind to and interact with a receptor (Julien, 2010). Generally, it will do this in one of two ways: as an agonist or antagonist.

First, let us consider drugs as agonists. Once it binds to a receptor, an agonist activates or enhances cellular activity in a similar way to endogenous transmitters (Shiloh, Nutt, & Weizman, 2001). This activity sets off the complex cascade of intracellular messengers mentioned earlier. See Figure 11.5 for a graphical representation of this process.

Now let us discuss drugs as antagonists. Antagonists bind to a receptor but do not activate the receptor (Stolerman, 2010). However, its presence at a receptor blocks the binding of agonists

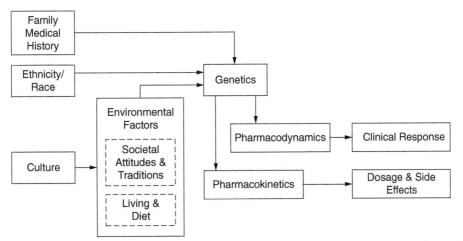

FIGURE 11.5 Provisional Casual Chain Concerning Ethnic Psychopharmacology *Nota bene:* this figure is an adaptation of a figure that appeared in Chen, Chen, and Lin (2008) and integrates the work of Campinha-Bacote (2007), Chaudhry et al. (2008), and Hunt and Kreiner (2013).

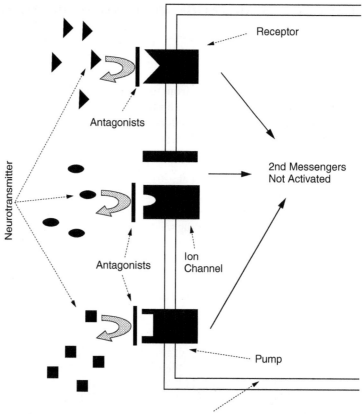

FIGURE 11.6 Antagonist Activity

or neurotransmitters to the receptor (Stolerman, 2010). See Figure 11.6 for a graphical representation of this process.

Finally, let us consider receptors. The receptor is a membrane-spanning protein molecule (Julien, 2010). The life of a receptor is from 12 to 24 hours, after which time it wears out or is reabsorbed into the cell (Julien, 2010). The processes of downregulation and upregulation refer to the decrease or increase in the total number of receptors.

Good job, reader! You have made it through the basic science part of this chapter. We have examined the terms *neurology, diversity issues, pharmacokinetics,* and *pharmacodynamics*—terms necessary to understanding addiction pharmacotherapy. Before we examine treatment of specific addictions, let us turn our attention to the emerging biological theory of *craving* that underpins many pharmacotherapy strategies.

A BIOLOGICAL THEORY OF CRAVING

Why care about the biology of craving? The reason is that the development of craving plays a crucial role in (1) the transition from substance use to dependence, (2) the mechanisms underlying relapse, and (3) treatment (Verheul, Brink, & Geerlings, 1999). In addiction, there is not one type of craving, but multiple types. These types are psychological readouts of dysregulation in different neurotransmitter systems.

As an illustration, let us examine these types in reference to alcohol addiction. Dutch addiction scholar Roel Verheul posited three types of craving for alcohol: (1) reward, (2) relief (stress-reduction), and (3) obsessive (disinhibition) (Caputo et al., 2014; Verheul & Brink, 2005). There is excellent research backing for his theory (Martinotti et al., 2013). Verheul et al. (1999) described *reward-sensitivity*-based craving as the desire for the rewarding, stimulating, and enhancing effects of alcohol consumption. They presented evidence that such a craving is the result of dysregulation of the opioidergic/dopaminergic (OP/DA) neurotransmitter systems. Specifically, this form of craving arises out of a deficiency in the base levels of endogenous opioids and/or dopamine.

Verheul and Brink (2005) described *stress-reduction*-based craving as the desire for the reduction of tension or arousal. They presented evidence that such a craving is the result of dysregulation of the GABAergic/glutametergic (GABA/GLU) neurotransmitter systems. Specifically, this form of craving arises out of anxiety resulting from a deficiency in the base level of GABA (an inhibitory neurotransmitter) and excess in the base level of GLU (an excitatory neurotransmitter).

Verheul et al. (1999) described *disinhibition*-based craving as the desire emerging from a lack of control. This lack can be either cognitive/attentional (i.e., obsessive) or behavioral, or both. They presented evidence that such a craving is the result of dysregulation of the 5HT neurotransmitter system. Specifically, this craving arises out of a deficiency in the base level of 5HT. The obsessive disinhibition form of craving can be defined as a loss of control in which obsessions flood in and overwhelm perception (Addolorato, Abenavoli, Leggio, & Gasbarrini, 2005). This craving is similar to obsessive-compulsive disorder except that the obsession centers on alcohol (Anton, 2000). The behavioral disinhibition form of craving can be defined as a loss of control over impulsiveness, harm avoidance, and deviant behavior (Verheul & Brink, 2005).

A research team at the Catholic University of Rome has been focusing on the role of hormones in alcohol craving (Addolorato, Mirijello, & Leggio, 2013). In particular, they have preliminary evidence that polymorphisms (DNA variations) within the following lead to deregulation in alcohol craving: (a) appetite-stimulating hormones such as ghrelin, (b) appetite-suppressing hormones such as leptin, and (c) volume-regulating hormones such as vasopressin. The team hopes to identify how these hormone polymorphisms can be modified in order to limit their effect on alcohol craving.

This research team described the addiction-treatment situation aptly:

> Before the discovery of anti-craving drugs, the administration of disulfiram and surveillance by relatives and/or therapeutic groups, waiting for spontaneous craving exhaustion, were the only treatment strategies to control craving. (Addolorato et al., 2005, p. 59)

In the final part of this chapter, I will examine specific addiction pharmacotherapies, with an emphasis on current anticraving medications. I will start with chemical addictions (e.g., alcohol), moving on to behavioral addictions (e.g., gambling). However, before examining specific medications, let us first address the professional counselor's role in addiction pharmacotherapy.

Personal reflection and integration: The Craving Types: (a) reward craving, (b) relief (stress-reduction) craving, and (c) obsessive (disinhibition) craving.

1. Which craving type have you encountered most in your clinical work?
2. Which craving type has presented you with the most clinical challenges?

3. According to Verhuel's theory, relief craving emerges from a GABA/GLU dysregulation. How does this biologically based theory inform or disrupt your understanding about what causes addiction?
4. According to Verhuel's theory, the obsessive (disinhibition) craving type occurs because of a dysregulation in the 5HT neurotransmitter system. What clinical signs would you anticipate seeing in a client with this craving type?

THE PROFESSIONAL COUNSELOR'S ROLE IN ADDICTION PHARMACOTHERAPY

While you may find the information presented thus far interesting and even important, you may be wondering what role you, as a professional counselor, have to play in addiction pharmacotherapy. The answer is: a critical role. The prescribing physician works on a 15-minute billing cycle and unfortunately has little time for patient education. Also, many clients feel intimidated by physicians and do not voice their questions or concerns. This situation is problematic, because client attitudes toward the pharmacotherapy they are receiving predicts treatment adherence (Pettinati et al., 2005). For example, the questionnaire item "Sometimes, the medical profession makes me feel uncomfortable" was predictive of attendance in an alcohol dependence pharmacotherapy study (Pettinati, Monterosso, Lipkin, & Volpicelli, 2003). Indeed, research has shown that psychological interventions aimed at pharmacotherapy adherence improve addiction treatment outcomes (Reid, Teesson, Sannibale, Matsuda, & Haber, 2005).

Professional counselors differ from prescribing physicians in having (a) more contact with their clients, and (b) more in-depth knowledge on how to form a strong working alliance. Thus, the professional counselor is in a better position to address the knowledge and attitudinal barriers to client-treatment adherence.

Addiction clients often balk at a physician's recommendation of pharmacotherapy. In a study of the mental illness treatment preferences of the lay public, less than 15% chose pharmacotherapy as the first treatment option (Riedel-Heller, Matschinger, & Angermeyer, 2005). Prominent reasons for psychiatric medication noncompliance include sexual dysfunction (Kennedy et al., 2006), weight gain (Kalinichev et al., 2005), and medication interfering with personal strategies for treatment (Deegan, 2005). Youth prefer expert-led guidance about addiction (Dykeman & Nelson, 1996).

There has been some fear that the total abstinence philosophy of Alcoholics Anonymous (AA) may lead to noncompliance with addiction pharmacotherapy. However, in a study comparing AA participants and nonparticipants, no difference was found in attitudes toward the use of medication to treat alcoholism. Overall, 15% agreed it was all right, 29% disagreed that it was all right, and 56% stated that they did not know (Tonigan & Kelly, 2006). Interestingly, a large study of addictions counselors found that those clinicians who held a 12-step treatment philosophy were significantly less likely to support a pharmacotherapy intervention even when they had been provided evidence as to pharmacotherapy's effectiveness (Knudsen, Ducharme, Roman, & Link, 2005). At this point, the impact of counselor treatment prejudices on client noncompliance with addiction pharmacotherapy is unknown.

What can a clinician do to promote medication compliance in their clients? Weiden and Rao (2005) gave the following sage advice: (1) ask for—and listen to—the client's beliefs and attitudes about the prescribed medication, (2) work to understand the client's perspective rather than trying to contradict or correct this perspective, (3) understand that it is the client's subjective beliefs, rather than objective medical reality that influences client compliance, (4) withhold responding until the client has discussed all major arguments for and against a medication, and (5) ground any discussion of compliance concerns within the client's point of view.

I would like to end with one recommendation in terms of client knowledge barriers to pharmacotherapy adherence. I think it is important for every professional counselor to have a psychopharmacological reference guide on hand when the need for client education arises. Both Stahl (2013) and Preston et al. (2013) are clear and concise references and contain excellent suggestions for client education.

Now let us move on to application. The length restrictions for this chapter do not permit an in-depth discussion of pharmacotherapies for all addictions. However, it is not the role of the professional counselor to have in-depth pharmacotherapy knowledge for all addictions. What professional counselors must possess is a generic sense of how pharmacotherapy is conducted with addiction. To build this sense, we will examine pharmacotherapy through the prism of the most prevalent addiction: Alcohol Use Disorder (AUD).

APPLICATION EXAMPLE: PHARMACOTHERAPY OF ALCOHOL USE DISORDER

The γ-aminobutyric acid (GABA), glutametergic (GLU), opioidergic (OP), dopaminergic (DA), cholinergic (ACH), and serotonergic (5HT) systems all play a role in the neurochemical basis of alcohol dependence (Kiefer & Mann, 2010). As such, a variety of medications impacting these various systems have been developed to help conquer this addiction. In fact, in the last 50 years more than 150 medications have been used to treat various aspects of alcohol dependence (Schik et al., 2005). The rest of this section will examine the three main alcohol addiction pharmacotherapy subareas: (a) aversion treatment, (b) alcohol withdrawal treatment, and (c) anticraving treatment.

Aversion Treatment, First-Line: Disulfiram (Antabuse)

This medication was the first pharmacotherapy available for alcohol addiction. Upon use of alcohol, this medication creates a very unpleasant intoxication with the goal of developing an aversion to alcohol (Kiefer & Mann, 2010). In the professional addiction literature, the reports of disulfiram efficacy are mixed (Kiefer & Mann, 2010). The effectiveness of this medicine seems to be limited to three client groups: (1) adherent clients, (2) specific high-risk clients, and (3) clients with whom administration can be supervised (Garbutt, 2009).

Alcohol Withdrawal Treatment

Alcohol Withdrawal Syndrome is a common event in addiction treatment (McKeon, Frye, & Delanty, 2008). This syndrome has been described as follows:

> Symptoms of alcohol withdrawal result from the lack of opposition to sympathetic nervous system activity in the brain once the central nervous system (CNS) depressant (alcohol) is stopped. Symptoms of uncomplicated withdrawal include tremor, tachycardia, increased blood pressure, increased body temperature, diaphoresis, insomnia, anxiety, and gastrointestinal upset. . . . Ten percent of alcoholics experience severe symptoms such as seizures and delirium tremens. In delirium tremens, or alcohol withdrawal delirium, the patient suffers from confusion, disorientation, illusions, and visual, tactile, and auditory hallucinations. (Prince & Turpin, 2008, p. 1039)

Now let us turn to an examination of the treatments for Alcohol Withdrawal Syndrome.

First-Line: Diazepam (Valium) and the Other Longer Half-Life Benzodiazepines

These medications belong to the anxiolytic class of pharmacotherapies. There is a long-standing history on the use of benzodiazepines to alleviate alcohol withdrawal. A Cochrane Library review on such use of benzodiazepines reported this type of medication effective against alcohol withdrawal symptoms when compared to placebo (Ntais, Pakos, Kyzas, & Ioannidis, 2005). The American Society of Addiction Medicine's (2003) practice guideline for alcohol withdrawal suggests the use of longer half-life (hl) benzodiazepines such as lorazepam (Ativan, 12-hour hl), diazepam (Valium, 20-hour hl), and chlordiazepoxide (Librium, 30-hour hl). While effective, benzodiazepines increase sedation, memory deficits, respiratory depression, and addiction (Leggio, Kenna, & Swift, 2008). These side effects highlight the importance of nonbenzodiazepine treatments for alcohol withdrawal such as baclofen, carbamazepine, and gabapentin.

PHARMACOTHERAPY CASE STUDY II

Alcohol Withdrawal (DSM 5 291.81) and Alcohol Use Disorder (DSM 5 303.90 Severe) in a Pregnant Patient (ICD-10-CM O99.3)

Dr. Cathy Smith is an obstetrician in private practice in Spokane, Washington. Last December 12, she was the on-call obstetrician at Deaconess Medical Center in the same city. At 3 A.M., she was called to Deaconess's emergency room to see a pregnant patient. This patient was Camila Rodriguez, a Mexican-American aged 22. On December 9, her obstetrician told her she was pregnant and about 20 weeks along. Camila presented at the emergency room (ER) complaining of nausea, abdominal pain, anxiety, insomnia, and "seeing things." When Dr. Smith arrived at the ER, she met Camila and engaged in *plática* (a chat) to put Camila at ease and build rapport. Dr. Smith then took a complete medical history, examined Camila and found the following: a pulse rate of 117 beats per minute (bpm), hand tremors, and various forms of psychomotor agitation. Camila reported to Dr. Smith that as soon as she discovered that she was pregnant that she had gone "cold turkey" with drinking to protect her baby.

Dr. Smith commended Camila for her desire for a healthy baby, but advised her that hospitalization was indicated for treating her delirium tremors. Camila asked Dr. Smith if she could just go home. The doctor warned Camila that the delirium tremors were threatening the health of both her and her fetus. She then told Camila that she was sending her upstairs to the Labor and Delivery unit for blood work to assess fluids and electrolyte status. In addition, Dr. Smith told Camila that she would be getting intravenous (IV) fluid for dehydration. To treat the delirium tremors, Camila was given diazepam (Valium). Camila asked how long she was going to be in the hospital. Dr. Smith estimated 3 days. Camila's eyes filled with tears, and Dr. Smith asked what was wrong. Camila reported fears about what impact her alcohol consumption has had upon her baby. Dr. Smith addressed her concerns about fetal alcohol syndrome. The doctor told Camila she was going to refer her to Perinatology later that day for counseling and an ultrasound assessment. She also referred Camila to the Deaconess's social services department so she could become aware of community resources that could help her abstain from alcohol.

Second-Line: Baclofen (Lioresal)

This medication belongs to the anticonvulsant class of pharmacotherapies. Baclofen is a GABA agonist. Baclofen monotherapy was able to suppress alcohol withdrawal symptoms (Leggio, 2009). In addition, baclofen lowered alcohol intake and alcohol craving (Caputo et al., 2014).

Second-Line: Carbamazepine (Tegretol)

This medication belongs to the anticonvulsant class of pharmacotherapies. It works by both blocking voltage-sensitive sodium ion channels and inhibiting GLU release (Stahl, 2013). It has some advantages over the traditional use of benzodiazepine for alcohol withdrawal, including lack of (a) addictive potential, (b) interaction with alcohol, (c) a greater than benzodiazepine side effect profile, and (d) sedatory effects (Leggio, 2009; Schik et al., 2005). A recent study found that oxcarbazepine (Trileptal), a second-generation analogue of carbamazepine, was equally effective with alcohol withdrawal (Schik et al., 2005) and had the advantage of possessing some anticraving properties as well (Schik et al., 2005).

Anticraving Treatment: Overview

There are two first-line treatments of alcohol craving—acamprosate and naltrexone. Building on the work of Verheul, it has been hypothesized that the "relief drinker/craver" is associated with glutametergic dysfunction and responds to acamprosate, while the "reward drinker/craver" is associated with dopaminergic and opioidergic dysfunction and responds to naltrexone (Mann et al., 2009). Now let us examine these two first-line treatments in detail.

Anticraving Treatment: First-Line: Acamprosate (Campral)

This medication belongs to the anticraving class of pharmacotherapies. Acamprosate is a GLU antagonist. It modulates overactive GLU brain activity that occurs after stopping chronic heavy alcohol use (Robinson, Meek, & Geniza, 2014). In addition, this medication can lessen the glutametergically driven reinforcing properties of alcohol consumption (Olive, 2005). The purpose of this medication is to maintain abstinence from alcohol (Verheul, Lehert, Geerlings, Koeter, & Brink, 2005). Comprehensive reviews of high-quality studies found that acamprosate effectively maintained complete abstinence in detoxified alcohol-dependent clients (Kranzler & Gage, 2008; Ross & Peselow, 2009). I do need to note that major U.S. and German government studies did *not* find acamprosate efficacious in the treatment of alcohol dependence (Mann et al., 2013). Despite U.S. Food and Drug Administration (FDA) approval, it is clear that further research on acamprosate is needed.

Anticraving Treatment: First-Line: Naltrexone (ReVia, Depade)

This medication belongs to the anticraving class of pharmacotherapies. Garbutt (2009) describes it as follows:

> Naltrexone, by blocking endogenous opioids, reduces the rewarding properties of alcohol . . . thereby counteracting this important component of the behavioral response to alcohol. In fact, in the initial human studies of naltrexone for alcohol dependence, it was reported that patients who consumed alcohol and who were taking naltrexone were significantly less likely to experience their usual "high" or level of intoxication. . . . In addition, naltrexone has been reported to reduce alcohol craving in a number of clinical trials. (p. S17)

There exists excellent evidence of naltrexone's efficacy with alcohol dependence (Donovan et al., 2008; Ross & Peselow, 2009). Interestingly, a recent study reported naltrexone's efficacy with Type A alcoholics but not Type B (Bogenschutz, Tonigan, & Pettinati, 2009). In contrast to a Type B alcoholic, a Type A can be described as having (a) later onset of disease, (b) fewer childhood risk factors, (c) less severe symptoms of substance abuse disorders, (d) less alcohol-related social and physical consequences, (e) less psychopathology, (f) less stress, and (g) less chance of prior treatment (Leggio, Kenna, Fenton, Bonenfant, & Swift, 2009). The reason for these differences is unclear.

Alcohol Withdrawal and Anticraving Treatment: Second-Line: Sodium Oxybate-SMO (Xyrem)

This medication belongs to both the antiwithdrawal and anticraving classes of pharmacotherapies. The information is this subsection is drawn from an excellent review conducted by the top researchers on SMO (Skala et al., 2014). SMO interacts in a complex manner with both GABA and γ-hydroxybutyric acid (GBH) receptors. This complexity leads to SMO having multiple beneficial effects. First, it has sedative and anxiolytic effects similar to benzodiazepines and thus can treat alcohol withdrawal symptoms. Second, it has an alcohol-mimicking effect that lowers craving for that substance and hence decreases the likelihood of relapse. The benefit to using SMO is that its side-effects profile is lower than the first line medications for both alcohol withdrawal and relapse prevention. Case Study #3 contains a description of an off-label use of SMO with a patient for both alcohol withdrawal and relapse prevention.

PHARMACOTHERAPHY CASE STUDY III

Alcohol Use Disorder (DSM 5 305.00 Mild) and Major Depressive Disorder—Moderate (DSM 5 296.22)

Daniel Tourneur is a 37-year-old White male who graduated with a baccalaureate in agriculture from the University of California—Davis. After college, Daniel moved to Fresno to work at a local farm implement dealership and eventually rose to his present position as sales manager. He has been married for 12 years and has 2 sons aged 10 and 8.

In the last 6 months, Daniel has lost pleasure in activities he previously enjoyed. He quit his recreational indoor soccer team and no longer goes to watch his sons play soccer. Daniel's sleep is fitful and in the last 2 months he has averaged missing one workday out of every five since he "didn't have it in him." Since he has been married, Daniel has maintained a weight of 150 lbs and a body mass index (BMI) of 21.5. However, in the last 6 months his weight has dropped to 126 lbs and his BMI to 18.1. Also in the past 6 months, his two beers at day drinking habit has increased to three or more a day. At his wife's request, Daniel tried to cut back to a beer a day but found that his ruminating about alcohol had just increased as a result. During the past week, Daniel missed three out of five days at work. On those days he felt he didn't even have enough energy to get out of bed.

Daniel's wife has become increasingly concerned about her husband's behavior. When he couldn't get out of bed for work for three straight days she made an appointment for Daniel with their family doctor, Dr. Garcia. On the day of the appointment, Daniel's wife drove him to

Dr. Garcia's office and attended the consultation between Daniel and the doctor. Dr. Garcia inquired about changes in Daniel's activity level, weight, and drinking. The doctor found Daniel listless. Daniel scored a 3 on the CAGE. Daniel's score on the Beck Depression Inventory (BDI), filled out prior to the appointment, was 24 (Moderate Depression). When Daniel's wife reported her perceptions on changes in Daniel's activity level and drinking, Daniel appeared visibly surprised. It was at this point that Daniel broke into tears and stated that he needed help. Dr. Garcia gave him a dual diagnosis of Major Depression and Alcohol Use Disorder. Given the presence of this dual diagnosis, the doctor prescribed two medications. First, Dr. Garcia prescribed fluoxetine (Prozac) for depression. Second, Dr. Garcia had considered prescribing lorazepam (Ativan) for withdrawal symptoms, but instead prescribed off-label sodium oxybate (Xyrem) for both the withdrawal symptoms and relapse prevention. Dr. Garcia had Daniel and his wife schedule an appointment for 6 weeks later to check on his progress. At the 6-week check-in, Daniel's score was 10 on the BDI (Minimal Depression). He reported greater energy and a perfect work attendance over the previous 3 weeks.

Anticraving Treatment: Second-Line: Lamotrigine (Lamictal)

This medication belongs to the anticonvulsant class of pharmacotherapies. It works by both blocking voltage-sensitive sodium ion channels and inhibiting the release of excitatory neurotransmitters (e.g., GLU) (Stahl, 2013). How can lowering GLU levels reduce craving? Gass and Olive (2008) reported the following:

> Pharmacological agents that attenuate glutamatergic signaling, either by receptor antagonism, release inhibition, or enhancement of cellular uptake, tend to reduce the reinforcing and rewarding effects of most drugs of abuse, and can also attenuate the reinstatement of drug-seeking behavior. . . . Given that glutamate transmission is one of the primary neurochemical substrates of synaptic plasticity, and the overwhelming evidence reviewed here that all drugs of abuse interact with glutamate transmission, it is not surprising that drugs of abuse can cause long-lasting neuroadaptions of glutamate systems in the brain. These adaptations somehow lead to compulsive drug use, loss of volitional control over drug intake, and hypersalience of drug-associated environmental cues or contexts, all of which are characteristic of addiction. (p. 240)

This medication has also been found to ameliorate both bipolar and unipolar depression (Parker & Fletcher, 2014; Zavodnick & Ali, 2012). Lamotrigine is efficacious in reducing alcohol consumption and craving in treating schizophrenic clients with alcohol dependence (a common comorbidity) (Kalyoncu et al., 2005). Given the efficacy of lamotrigine with different types of mental illnesses, this medication may be a useful tool in the treatment of alcohol/mental illness comorbidity.

Anticraving Treatment: Alternative Medications

Finally, it is important to note that a variety of alternative medications have been investigated for use with AUD. These medications include kudzu (Tang, Hao, & Leggio, 2012), ayahuasca (Thomas, Lucas, Capler, Tupper, & Martin, 2013), classic hallucinogens (Bogenschutz & Pommy, 2013), and ibogaine (Koenig, et al., 2013).

GLOSSARY OF PHARMACOTHERAPY TERMS

ACETYLCHOLINE A neurotransmitter. In this chapter it will be referred to by the abbreviation ACH. *Nota bene*: the adjective form is "cholinergic." There are two types of ACH receptors. The ones that respond to nicotine are known as nicotinic acetylcholine receptors (nACH).

AGONIST SUBSTITUTION PHARMACOTHERAPY The administration of a medication pharmacologically related to the one producing dependence. Agents suitable for this pharmacotherapy are those that have the capacity to prevent the emergence of withdrawal symptoms and reduce craving. In general, it is desirable for substitution medicines to have a longer duration of action than the drug they are replacing, so as to delay the emergence of withdrawal symptoms and reduce the frequency of administration. This results in less disruption of normal life activities by the need to obtain the abused substance. Equivalent terms: substitution therapy, agonist pharmacotherapy, agonist replacement therapy, substitution maintenance therapy, and agonist-assisted therapy (World Health Organization, 2004).

ALPHA 2 RECEPTOR A receptor located on the NA presynaptic terminal that, when stimulated, inhibits the release of NA (Shiloh et al., 2001).

ANTICONVULSANTS A class of medication used to treat seizures (Stahl, 2013).

ANXIOLYTICS A class of medication used to treat anxiety (Ingersoll & Rak, 2006).

AXON Long nerve cell fibers that conduct electrical impulses. Axons contact other nerve, muscle, and gland cells at synapses and release neurotransmitters that influence those cells (National Institute of Neurological Disorders and Stroke, 2007).

BEHAVIORAL SENSITIZATION A neuroadaptation (resulting from repeated exposure to an addictive drug) that leads to a progressive increase of behavioral responses to that drug (Faria et al., 2008). Put another way, an addictive drug usurps the normal learning mechanisms and thereby "cements" behavioral responses related to drug-seeking behavior; this can progress to a form of habit-based learning so strong that it persists even in the face of tremendous adverse personal consequences (Wolf, 2002).

BRAND NAME Medicines may have one or more brand names. These names are chosen by the company that makes them. Several companies may make the same medicine, each with its own brand name (Patient UK, 2006). In this chapter, the generic name will be used first, followed in parentheses by the most common brand names.

CANNABINOIDS Both (1) the bioactive constituents of the marijuana plant, and (2) endogenous lipids with cannabinoid-like activity (Begg et al., 2005). In this chapter, cannabinoids will be referred to by the abbreviation: CB.

CHEMICAL ADDICTION An addiction to various chemicals such as alcohol (Grant, 2008).

CYCLOOXYGENASE (COX) An enzyme that is part of the inflammatory pathway (Silasi & Kolb, 2007).

DENDRITES The treelike branches from nerve cell bodies that receive signals from other nerve cells at synapses (National Institute of Neurological Disorders and Stroke, 2007).

DOPAMINE A neurotransmitter. In this chapter it will be referred to by its common abbreviation, DA. *Nota bene*: the adjective form is "dopaminergic."

DOWNREGULATION A decrease in the number of receptors, making the cells less sensitive to a drug (Ingersoll & Rak, 2006).

ENDOGENOUS A term meaning "produced by the body."

ETHNIC PSYCHOPHARMACOLOGY The study of differences in drug response and disposition among ethnic groups (Mendoza, Smith, Poland, Lin, & Strickland, 1991).

EXCITOTOXICITY Neuronal damage as the result of excessive glutamate exposure (De Witte, Littleton, Parot, & Koob, 2005).

FIRST-LINE AGENT A proven medication typically given first to a patient.

GABA (γ-aminobutyric acid) A neurotransmitter. In this chapter, it will be referred to by the abbreviation, GABA. *Nota bene*: the adjective form is "GABAergic."

GENERIC NAME Each medicine has an approved name called the *generic name* (Patient UK, 2006). In this chapter, the generic name will be used first, followed by the most common brand names in parentheses.

GLUTAMATE A neurotransmitter. In this chapter, it will be referred to by the abbreviation, GLU. *Nota bene*: the adjective form is "glutametergic."

HALF-LIFE The time for the plasma level of a drug to fall by 50% (Julien, 2010). In this chapter, it will be referred to by the abbreviation "hl."

HORMONES Extracellular signaling molecules secreted by specialized cells that are released into the blood to exert specific biochemical actions on target cells located at distant sites (Chedrese, 2009).

IMMUNOTHERAPY The use of drug antibodies to prevent drugs of abuse from entering the central nervous system. How does immunotherapy work? The leading expert in addiction immunotherapy describes this therapy as follows: "Drugs of abuse are small molecules that can readily cross the blood brain barrier, while antibodies are larger molecules that cannot get into the brain" (Kosten, 2005, p. 177). Thus, he notes that any drug bound to an antibody also cannot cross the blood–brain barrier and cannot enter the brain. The primary uses in addiction treatment are (1) overdose treatment and (2) relapse prevention (Kosten & Owens, 2005).

ION CHANNELS Ion channels are membrane proteins that form a pore to allow the passage of specific ions. The opening and closing of ion channels are controlled by various means, including voltage (Jentsch, Hübner, & Fuhrmann, 2004).

MONOTHERAPY AND POLYTHERAPY Monotherapy is the use of one medication in treatment. Polytherapy is the use of multiple medications in treatment.

NEURON   A type of cell that is the basic component of the central nervous system (Julien, 2010). *Nota bene*: the adjective form is "neuronal."

N METHYL D ASPARTATE (NMDA)   One type of glutamate receptor. Antagonists to this type of receptor include the drugs of abuse ketamine and phencyclidine (PCP).

NOREPINEPHRINE   A neurotransmitter. In this chapter, it will be referred to by the abbreviation, NA. *Nota bene*: the adjective form is "noradrenergic."

OPIOID   Any agent that binds to opioid receptors. These agents include natural and synthetic narcotics as well as endogenous opioid peptides (National Institute of Drug Abuse, 2000). In this chapter, it will be referred to by the abbreviation, OP. *Nota bene*: the adjective form is "opioidergic."

PARTIAL AGONIST   An agonist that produces a submaximal response as well as antagonizing full (i.e., system maximal) agonists (Nature, 2009).

PHARMACODYNAMICS   A drug's impact on the body (Preston et al., 2013).

PHARMACOKINETICS   The body's impact upon a drug (Preston et al., 2013).

SECOND-LINE AGENT   A proven medication typically given to a patient when a first-line agent: (1) does not work, (2) has too many side effects, or (3) stops working.

SENSITIZATION   The repeated exposure to psychostimulants that results in increased behavioral responses to the same dose of drug (Torres-Reverón & Dow-Edwards, 2005). Cross-sensitization to other drugs is possible.

SEROTONIN   A neurotransmitter. In this chapter, it will be referred to by the abbreviation, 5HT (Shiloh et al., 2006). *Nota bene*: the adjective form is "serotonergic."

UPREGULATION   An increase in the number of receptors making the cells more sensitive to a drug (Ingersoll & Rak, 2006).

Summary and Some Final Notations

In this chapter, we first examined the scientific foundations of addiction pharmacotherapy. Next we explored the emerging biological theory of craving. Then we discussed the professional counselor's role in addiction pharmacotherapy. Finally, the pharmacotherapy for AUD was detailed.

MyCounselingLab

Visit the MyCounselingLab site for *Foundations of Addictions Counseling,* Third Edition to enhance your understanding of concepts. You'll have the opportunity to practice your skills through video- and case-based exercises. You will find sets of questions to help you prepare for your certification exam with *Licensure Quizzes*. There is also a Video Library that provides taped counseling sessions, ethical scenarios, and interviews with helpers and clients.

Useful Websites

The following websites provide additional information relating to the chapter topics:

American College of Neuropsychopharmacology
www.acnp.org

American Psychiatric Nurses Association (APNA)
www.apna.org/

Society for Neuroscience
www.sfn.org

References

Addolorato, G., Abenavoli, L., Leggio, L., & Gasbarrini, G. (2005). How many cravings? Pharmacological aspects of craving treatment in alcohol addiction: A review. *Neuropsychobiology, 51,* 59–66. doi:10.1159/000084161

Addolorato, G., Mirijello, A., & Leggio, L. (2013). Alcohol addiction: toward a patient-oriented pharmacological treatment. *Expert Opinion on Pharmacotherapy, 14,* 2157–2160. doi:10.1517/14656566.2013.834047

American Society of Addiction Medicine. (2003). *Pharmacological management of alcohol withdrawal: A meta-analysis and evidence-based practice guideline.* Chevy Chase, MD: Author.

Anton, R. F. (2000). Obsessive-compulsive aspects of craving: Development of the Obsessive Compulsive Drinking Scale. *Addiction, 95*(Suppl. 2), S211–S217. doi:10.1046/j.1360-0443.95.8s2.9.x

Ashton, H. (2002). *Benzodiazepines: How they work and how to withdraw.* Newcastle upon Tyne, UK: The Royal Victoria Infirmary.

Begg, M., Pacher, P., Bátkai, S., Osei-Hyiaman, D., Offertáler, L., Mo, F. M., . . ., Kunos, G. (2005). Evidence for novel cannabinoid receptors. *Pharmacology & Therapeutics, 106*(2), 133–145. doi:10.1016/j.pharmthera.2004.11.005

Bogenschutz, M. P., & Pommy, J. M. (2012). Therapeutic mechanisms of classic hallucinogens in the treatment of addictions: From indirect evidence to testable hypotheses. *Drug Testing and Analysis, 4*(7-8), 543–555. doi:10.1002/dta.1376

Bogenschutz, M., Tonigan, J. S., & Pettinati, H. (2009). Effects of alcoholism typology on response to naltrexone in the COMBINE Study. *Alcoholism: Clinical & Experimental Research, 33,* 10–18. doi:10.1111/j.1530-0277.2008.00804.x

Campinha-Bacote, J. (2007). Becoming culturally competent in ethnic psychopharmacology. *Journal of Psychosocial Nursing and Mental Health Services, 45,* 27–33.

Caputo, F., Vignoli, T., Grignaschi, A., Cibin, M., Addolorato, G., & Bernardi, M. (2014). Pharmacological management of alcohol dependence: From mono-therapy to pharmacogenetics and beyond. *European Neuropsychopharmacology, 24,* 181–191. doi:10.1016/j.euroneuro.2013.10.004

Chaudhry, C., Neelam, K., Duddu, V., & Husain, N. (2008). Ethnicity and psychopharmacology. *Journal of Psychopharmacology, 22,* 673–681. doi:10.1177/0269881107082105

Chedrese, P. J. (2009). *Reproductive endocrinology: A molecular approach.* New York, NY: Springer.

Chen, C., Chen, C., & Lin, K. (2008). Ethnopsychopharmacology. *International Review of Psychiatry, 20,* 452–459. doi:10.1080/09540260802515997

Deegan, P. E. (2005). The importance of personal medicine: A qualitative study of resilience in people with psychiatric disabilities. *Scandinavian Journal of Public Health, 66,* 29–35.

De Witte, P., Littleton, J., Parot, P., & Koob, G. (2005). Neuroprotective and abstinence-promoting effects of acamprosate: Elucidating the mechanism of action. *CNS Drugs, 19,* 517–537. doi:10.2165/00023210-200519060-00004

Donovan, D., Anton, R., Miller, W., Longabaugh, R., Hosking, J., & Youngblood, M. (2008). Combined Pharmacotherapies and Behavioral Interventions for Alcohol Dependence (The COMBINE Study): Examination of posttreatment drinking outcomes. *Journal of Studies on Alcohol & Drugs, 69,* 5–13.

Dykeman, C., & Nelson, J. R. (1996). Students' evaluation of the effectiveness of substance abuse education: The impact of different delivery modes. *Journal of Child & Adolescent Substance Abuse, 5*(2), 43–61. doi:10.1300/J029v05n02_03

Faria, R. R., Lima Rueda, A. V., Sayuri, C., Soares, S. L., Malta, M. B., Carrara-Nascimento, P. F., . . ., Camarini, R. (2008). Environmental modulation of ethanol-induced locomotor activity: Correlation with neuronal activity in distinct brain regions of adolescent and adult Swiss mice. *Brain Research, 1239,* 127–140. doi:10.1016/j.brainres.2008.08.056

Garbutt, J. (2009). The state of pharmacotherapy for the treatment of alcohol dependence. *Journal of Substance Abuse Treatment, 36* (Suppl. 1), S15–S23.

Gass, J., & Olive, M. (2008). Glutamatergic substrates of drug addiction and alcoholism. *Biochemical Pharmacology, 75,* 218–265. doi:10.1016/j.bcp.2007.06.039

Goodman, A. (2008). Neurobiology of addiction: An integrative review. *Biochemical Pharmacology, 75,* 266–322. doi:10.1016/j.bcp.2007.07.030

Goodman, C., Ahn, R., Harwood, R., Ringel, D., Savage, K., & Mendelson, D. (1997). *Market barriers to the development of pharmacotherapies for the treatment of cocaine abuse and addiction: Final report.* Washington, DC: Department of Health and Human Services.

Grant, J. (2008). *Impulse control disorders: A clinician's guide to understanding and treating behavioral addictions.* New York, NY: W. W. Norton.

Hunt, L. M., & Kreiner, M. J. (2013). Pharmacogenetics in primary care: The promise of personalized medicine and the reality of racial profiling. *Culture, Medicine, and Psychiatry,* pp. 1–10. doi:10.1007/s11013-012-9303-x

Ingersoll, R. E., & Rak, C. F. (2006). *Psychopharmacology for helping professionals.* Belmont, CA: Thompson.

Jentsch, T. J., Hübner, C. A., & Fuhrmann, J. C. (2004). Ion channels: Function unravelled by dysfunction. *Nature Cell Biology, 6,* 1039–1047. doi:10.1038/ncb1104-1039

Julien, R. M. (2010). *A primer of drug action.* New York, NY: Worth.

Kalinichev, M., Rourke, C., Daniels, A. J., Grizzle, M. K., Britt, C. S., Ignar, D. M., & Jones, D. N. (2005). Characterisation of olanzapine-induced weight gain and effect of aripiprazole vs olanzapine on body weight and prolactin secretion in female rats. *Psychopharmacology, 182*(2), 220–231. doi:10.1007/s00213-005-0081-9

Kalyoncu, A., Mirsal, H., Pektas, O., Unsalan, N., Tan, D., & Beyazyurek, M. (2005). Use of lamotrigine to augment clozapine in patients with resistant schizophrenia and comorbid alcohol dependence: A potent anti-craving effect? *Journal of Psychopharmacology, 19,* 301–305. doi:10.1177/0269881105051542

Kennedy, S., Fulton, K., Bagby, R. M., Greene, A., Cohen, N., & Rafi-Tari, S. (2006). Sexual function during bupropion or paroxetine treatment of major depressive disorder. *Canadian Journal of Psychiatry, 51,* 234–242.

Kiefer, F., & Mann, K. (2010). Alcohol abuse and dependence. In I. P. Stolerman (Ed.), *Encyclopedia of psychopharmacology* (pp. 56–60). Berlin, Germany: Springer-Verlag.

Knudsen, H. K., Ducharme, L. J., Roman, P. M., & Link, T. (2005). Buprenorphine diffusion: The attitudes of substance abuse treatment counselors. *Journal of Substance Abuse Treatment, 29,* 95–106.

Koenig, X., Kovar, M., Rubi, L., Mike, A. K., Lukacs, P., Gawali, V. S., . . ., & Sandtner, W. (2013). Anti-addiction drug ibogaine inhibits voltage-gated ionic currents: A study to assess the drug's cardiac ion channel profile. *Toxicology and Applied Pharmacology, 273,* 259–268. doi:10.1016/j.taap.2013.05.012

Kosten, T., & Owens, S. M. (2005). Immunotherapy for the treatment of drug abuse. *Pharmacological Therapies, 108,* 76–85. doi:10.1016/j.pharmthera.2005.06.009

Kosten, T. R. (2005). Future of anti-addiction vaccines. *Studies in Health Technology and Informatics, 118,* 177–185.

Kranzler, H., & Gage, A. (2008). Acamprosate efficacy in alcohol-dependent patients: Summary of results from three pivotal trials. *American Journal on Addictions, 17,* 70–76. doi:10.1080/10550490701756120

Leggio, L. (2009). Understanding and treating alcohol craving and dependence: Recent pharmacological and neuroendocrinological findings. *Alcohol and Alcoholism, 44,* 341–352. doi:10.1093/alcalc/agp026

Leggio, L., Kenna, G., Fenton, M., Bonenfant, E., & Swift, R. (2009). Typologies of alcohol dependence. From Jellinek to genetics and beyond. *Neuropsychology Review, 19,* 115–129. doi:10.1007/s11065-008-9080-z

Leggio, L., Kenna, G. A., & Swift, R. M. (2008). New developments for the pharmacological treatment of alcohol withdrawal syndrome. A focus on non-benzodiazepine GABAergic medications. *Progress in Neuro-Psychopharmacology and Biological Psychiatry, 32*(5), 1106–1117. doi:10.1016/j.pnpbp.2007.09.021

Lin, K. M., & Poland, R. E. (2000). Ethnicity, culture, and psychopharmacology. In F. E. Bloom & D. J. Kupfer (Eds.), *Psychopharmacology: The fourth generation of progress* (pp. 1907–1917). New York, NY: Raven Press. Retrieved from http://www.acnp.org/g4/GN401000184/Default.htm

Lynch, W. J., Roth, M. E., & Carroll, M. E. (2002). Biological basis of sex differences in drug abuse: Preclinical and clinical studies. *Psychopharmacology, 164,* 121–137. doi:10.1007/s00213-002-1183-2

Mann, K., Kiefer, F., Smolka, M., Gann, H., Wellek, S., & Heinz, A. (2009). Searching for responders to acamprosate and naltrexone in alcoholism treatment: Rationale and design of the predict study. *Alcoholism: Clinical & Experimental Research, 33*(4), 674–683. doi:10.1111/j.1530-0277.2008.00884.x

Mann, K., Lemenager, T., Hoffmann, S., Reinhard, I., Hermann, D., Batra, A., . . ., Anton, R. F. (2013). Results of a double-blind, placebo-controlled pharmacotherapy trial in alcoholism conducted in Germany and comparison with the US COMBINE study. *Addiction Biology, 18*(6), 937–946. doi:10.1111/adb.12012

Martinotti, G., Di Nicola, M., Tedeschi, D., Callea, A., Di Giannantonio, M., & Janiri, L. (2013). Craving Typology Questionnaire (CTQ): A scale for alcohol craving in normal controls and alcoholics. *Comprehensive Psychiatry, 54*(7), 925–932. doi:10.1016/j.comppsych.2013.03.023

McKeon, A., Frye, M. A., & Delanty, N. (2008). The alcohol withdrawal syndrome. *Journal of Neurology, Neurosurgery & Psychiatry, 79*, 854–862. doi:10.1136/jnnp.2007.128322

Mendoza, R., Smith, M. W., Poland, R. E., Lin, K. M., & Strickland, T. L. (1991). Ethnic psychopharmacology: The Hispanic and Native American perspective. *Psychopharmacological Bulletin, 27*, 449–461.

National Institute of Drug Abuse. (2000). *The brain: Understanding neurobiology through the study of addiction* (NIH Publication No. 00-4871). Washington, DC: National Institutes of Health.

National Institute of Drug Abuse. (2001). *Nicotine addiction* (NIDA Research Report—Nicotine Addiction: NIH Publication No. 01-4342). Washington, DC: National Institutes of Health.

National Institute of Neurological Disorders and Stroke. (2007). *Spinal cord injury: Emerging concepts*. Retrieved from http://www.ninds.nih.gov/news_and_events/proceedings/sci_report.htm#Summary

Nature. (2009). Glossary terms. *Nature Reviews Drug Discovery*. New York, NY: NPG. Retrieved from http://www.nature.com/nrd/journal/v6/n9/glossary/nrd2361.html

Neubig, R. R., Spedding, M., Kenakin, T., & Christopoulos, A. (2003). International Union of Pharmacology Committee on Receptor Nomenclature and Drug Classification. XXXVIII. Update on terms and symbols in quantitative pharmacology. *Pharmacological Review, 55*, 597–606. doi:10.1124/pr.55.4.4

Ntais, C., Pakos, E., Kyzas, P., & Ioannidis, J. P. A. (2005). Benzodiazepines for alcohol withdrawal. *The Cochrane Database of Systematic Reviews, 3*. Art. No.: CD005063.

O'Brien, C. P. (2005). Anticraving medications for relapse prevention: A possible new class of psychoactive medications. *American Journal of Psychiatry, 162*, 1423–1431. doi:10.1176/appi.ajp.162.8.1423

Olive, M. F. (2005). mGlu5 receptors: Neuroanatomy, pharmacology, and role in drug addiction. *Current Psychiatry Reviews, 1*, 197–214. doi:10.2174/1573400054065578

Parker, G., & Fletcher, K. (2014). Differentiating bipolar I and II disorders and the likely contribution of DSM-5 classification to their cleavage. *Journal of Affective Disorders, 152*, 57–64. doi:10.1016/j.jad.2013.10.006

Patient UK. (2006). *Generic vs. brand names for medicines*. Retrieved from http://www.patient.co.uk/showdoc/23069074/

Pettinati, H. M., Monterosso, J., Lipkin, C., & Volpicelli, J. R. (2003). Patient attitudes toward treatment predict attendance in clinical pharmacotherapy trials of alcohol and drug treatment. *The American Journal on Addictions, 12*, 324–335. doi:10.1111/j.1521-0391.2003.tb00547.x

Pettinati, H. M., Weiss, R. D., Dundon, W., Miller, W. R., Donovan, D., Ernst, D. B., & Rounsaville, B. J. (2005). A structured approach to medical management: A psychosocial intervention to support pharmacotherapy in the treatment of alcohol dependence. *Journal of Studies on Alcohol and Drugs, 15*(Supplement), 170–178.

Prater, C., Miller, K., & Zylstra, R. (1999). Outpatient detoxification of the addicted or alcoholic patient. *American Family Physician, 60*, 1175–1183.

Preston, J. D., O'Neal, J. H., & Talaga, M. C. (2013). *Handbook of psychopharmacology for therapists*. Oakland, CA: New Harbinger.

Prince, V., & Turpin, K. (2008). Treatment of alcohol withdrawal syndrome with carbamazepine, gabapentin, and nitrous oxide. *American Journal of Health-System Pharmacy, 65*, 1039–1047. doi:10.2146/ajhp070284

Reid, S., Teesson, M., Sannibale, C., Matsuda, M., & Haber, P. S. (2005). The efficacy of compliance therapy in pharmacotherapy for alcohol dependence: A randomized controlled trial. *Journal of Studies on Alcohol, 66*, 833–841.

Reiness, G. (2009). *Neurotransmitters*. Portland, OR: Lewis & Clark College. Retrieved January 3, 2010, from http://legacy.lclark.edu/~reiness/neurobiology/Lectures/Neurotransmitters.pdf

Riedel-Heller, S. G., Matschinger, H., & Angermeyer, M. C. (2005). Mental disorders—who and what might help? Help-seeking and treatment preferences of the lay public. *Social Psychiatry and Psychiatric Epidemiology, 40*, 167–174. doi:10.1007/s00127-005-0863-8

Robinson, S., Meeks, T. W., & Geniza, C. (2014). Evidence-Based Reviews Medication for alcohol use disorder: Which agents work best? *Current Psychiatry, 13*(1), 22–29.

Ross, S., & Peselow, E. (2009). Pharmacotherapy of addictive disorders. *Clinical Neuropharmacology, 32*, 277–289. doi:10.1097/WNF.0b013e3181a91655

Schik, G., Wedegaertner, F., Liersch, J., Hoy, L., Emrich, H., & Schneider, U. (2005). Oxcarbazepine versus carbamazepine in the treatment of alcohol withdrawal. *Addiction Biology, 10,* 283–288. doi:10.1080/13556210500224015

Shiloh, R., Nutt, D., & Weizman, A. (2001). *Essentials in clinical psychiatric pharmacotherapy.* Boca Raton, FL: CRC Press.

Shiloh, R., Stryjer, R., Weizman, A., & Nutt, D. (2006). *Atlas of psychiatric pharmacotherapy.* Boca Raton, FL: CRC Press.

Silasi, G., & Kolb, B. (2007). Chronic inhibition of cyclo-oxygenase-2 induces dendritic hypertrophy and limited functional improvement following motor cortex stroke. *Neuroscience, 144,* 1160–1168. doi:10.1016/j.neuroscience.2006.10.030

Skala, K., Caputo, F., Mirijello, A., Vassallo, G., Antonelli, M., Ferrulli, A., Walter, H., Lesch, O., & Addolorato, G. (2014). Sodium oxybate in the treatment of alcohol dependence: From the alcohol withdrawal syndrome to the alcohol relapse prevention. *Expert Opinion in Pharmacotherapy, 15*(2), 245–257. doi:10.1517/14656566.2014.863278

Stahl, S. M. (2013). *Essential psychopharmacology.* Cambridge, UK: Cambridge University Press.

Stolerman, I. P. (2010). Antagonists. In I. P. Stolerman (Ed.), *Encyclopedia of psychopharmacology* (p. 90). Berlin, Germany: Springer-Verlag.

Tang, Y. L., Hao, W., & Leggio, L. (2012). Treatments for alcohol-related disorders in China: A developing story. *Alcohol and Alcoholism, 47*(5), 563–570. doi:10.1093/alcalc/ags066

Thomas, G., Lucas, P., Capler, N. R., Tupper, K. W., & Martin, G. (2013). Ayahuasca-assisted therapy for addiction: Results from a preliminary observational study in Canada. *Current Drug Abuse Reviews, 6,* 1–13.

Tonigan, J. S., & Kelly, J. F. (2003). AA-exposure and attitudes of 12-step proscriptions about medications. Retrieved from http://www.j-satresources.com/Library/Article/4171-AA-Exposure-and-Attitudes-of-12-Step-Proscriptions-About-Medications

Torres-Reverón, A., & Dow-Edwards, D. L. (2005). Repeated administration of methylphenidate in young, adolescent, and mature rats affects the response to cocaine later in adulthood. *Psychopharmacology, 181,* 38–47.

Verheul, R., & Brink, W. V. D. (2005). Causal pathways between substance use disorders and personality pathology. *Australian Psychologist, 40,* 127–136. doi:10.1080/00050060500094613

Verheul, R., Brink, W. V. D., & Geerlings, P. (1999). A three-pathway psychobiological model of craving for alcohol. *Alcohol and Alcohol Dependence, 34,* 197–222.

Verheul, R., Lehert, P., Geerlings, P. J., Koeter, M. W. J., & Brink, V. D. W. (2005). Predictors of acamprosate efficacy: Results from a pooled analysis of seven European trials. *Psychopharmacology, 178,* 167–173. doi:10.1007/s00213-004-1991-7

Weiden, P. J., & Rao, N. (2005). Teaching medication compliance to psychiatric residents: Placing an orphan topic into a training curriculum. *Academic Psychiatry, 29,* 203–210. doi:10.1176/appi.ap.29.2.203

Wolf, M. E. (2002). Addiction: Making the connection between behavioral changes and neuronal plasticity in specific pathways. *Molecular Interventions, 2,* 146–157. doi:10.1124/mi.2.3.146

World Health Organization. (2004). *Substitution maintenance therapy in the management of opioid dependence and HIV/AIDS prevention: Position paper.* Geneva, Switzerland: Author.

Zavodnick, A. D., & Ali, R. (2012). Lamotrigine in the treatment of unipolar depression with and without comorbidities: A literature review. *Psychiatric Quarterly, 83*(3), 371–383. doi:10.1007/s11126-012-9208-4

Chapter 12

12-Step Facilitation of Treatment

Adrianne L. Johnson
Wright State University

Groups are a highly effective modality for the treatment of addictions and have a long and successful history in the field of chemical dependency. Twelve-step groups are sometimes referred to as "self-help groups" because not all self-help groups have exactly 12 steps. The terms will be used interchangeably throughout this chapter.

The primary focus of self-help groups is to provide emotional and practical support and an exchange of information. Such groups use participatory processes to allow people to share knowledge, common experiences, and problems. Through their participation, members help themselves and others by gaining knowledge and information, and by obtaining and providing emotional and practical support. Traditionally, self-help groups have been in-person meetings, but more recently, Internet self-help groups have become popular.

One of the most widely recognized groups for the treatment of addictions is Alcoholics Anonymous (AA). Miller and McCrady (1993) note that AA is the "most frequently consulted source of help for drinking problems" (p. 3). In fact, approximately 1 in every 10 adults in the United States has attended an AA meeting at least once (Doweiko, 1999; Miller & McCrady, 1993; Zweben, 1995). Concurrently, affiliation with 12-step groups has been consistently linked to the achievement of abstinence among persons experiencing alcohol and other drug problems (Laudet & White, 2005). It is highly recommended that counselors, even if they do not regularly incorporate these groups into their counseling practice, should at least be familiar with them. The goal of this chapter, then, is to help counselors meet the following objectives:

1. To have a basic understanding of the foundation, history, and development of the 12-step model of treatment for addictions;
2. To gain a basic knowledge of the advantages and disadvantages of these groups, and how to use this knowledge to make appropriate referrals; and
3. To understand how to incorporate 12-step groups into culturally sensitive and client-appropriate addiction treatment for the most effective outcome.

HISTORY: DEVELOPMENT OF 12-STEP GROUPS

Alcoholics Anonymous

As will be discussed later, AA is one of the most widely recognized 12-step groups, and has been an instrumental force in the establishment of other groups using its model. AA was founded on June 10, 1935, when Dr. Robert Holbrook Smith, an alcoholic physician, had his last drink (Doweiko, 1999).

His cofounder, Bill Wilson, a failed Wall Street stockbroker, had previously been affiliated with the New York Oxford Group, a nondenominational group of Christians committed to overcoming a common drinking problem. The two men met coincidentally in Ohio while Wilson was seeking support to stay sober during a business trip (Miller, 2005). The plan for the group was devised by the two men, with a shared aim to spread the supportive message of sobriety to other alcoholics.

During its early years, AA worked to find a method that would support its members in their struggle to both achieve and maintain sobriety. Within 3 years of its founding, three AA groups were in existence, yet "it was hard to find two score of sure recoveries" (*Twelve Steps and Twelve Traditions*, 1981, p. 17). The then-new organization was unable to establish exactly *how* and *why* the message of the group worked for some members, but not for all. Since then, several dynamics have been identified that will be discussed later in this chapter. The new organization continued to grow to approximately 100 members in isolated groups by its fourth year (Doweiko, 1999). The early members decided to write about their struggle to achieve sobriety in order to share their discoveries with others, leading to the principles of the now well-established foundation. In the half century since its founding, AA has grown to a fellowship of 87,000 groups, including chapters in 150 countries, with a total membership estimated at more than 2 million (Doweiko, 1999; Humphreys & Moos, 1996). The first edition of *Alcoholics Anonymous* was published in 1939, detailing the well-known Steps and Traditions that now serve as the established guide to addictions recovery and maintenance among group members. The organization took its name from the title of the book, which has since come to be known as the "Big Book" of AA (*Twelve Steps and Twelve Traditions*, 1981).

Twelve Steps

1. We admitted we were powerless over alcohol—that our lives had become unmanageable;
2. Came to believe that a Power greater than ourselves could restore us to sanity;
3. Made a decision to turn our will and our lives over to the care of God as we understood Him;
4. Made a searching and fearless moral inventory of ourselves;
5. Admitted to God, to ourselves and to another human being the exact nature of our wrongs;
6. Were entirely ready to have God remove all these defects of character;
7. Humbly asked Him to remove our shortcomings;
8. Made a list of all persons we had harmed, and became willing to make amends to them all;
9. Made direct amends to such people wherever possible, except when to do so would injure them or others;
10. Continued to take personal inventory and when we were wrong promptly admitted it;
11. Sought through prayer and meditation to improve our conscious contact with God, as we understood Him, praying only for knowledge of His will for us and the power to carry that out; and
12. Having had a spiritual awakening as the result of these steps, we tried to carry this message to alcoholics, and to practice these principles in all our affairs.

Twelve Traditions

1. Our common welfare should come first; personal recovery depends upon A.A. unity.
2. For our group purpose there is but one ultimate authority—a loving God as He may express Himself in our group conscience. Our leaders are but trusted servants; they do not govern.
3. The only requirement for A.A. membership is a desire to stop drinking.
4. Each group should be autonomous except in matters affecting other groups or A.A. as a whole.
5. Each group has but one primary purpose—to carry its message to the alcoholics who still suffer.
6. An A.A. group ought never endorse, finance, or lend the A.A. name to any related facility or outside enterprise, lest problems of money, property, and prestige divert us from our primary purpose.

7. Every A.A. group ought to be fully self-supporting, declining outside contributions.
8. Alcoholics Anonymous should remain forever non-professional, but our service centers may employ special works.
9. A.A., as such, ought never be organized; but we may create service boards or committees directly responsible to those they serve.
10. Alcoholics Anonymous has no opinion on outside issues; hence the A.A. name ought never be drawn into public controversy.
11. Our public relations policy is based on attraction rather than promotion; we need always maintain personal anonymity at the level of press, radio, and films.
12. Anonymity is the spiritual foundation of all our traditions, ever reminding us to place principles before personalities.

Al-Anon

According to *Al-Anon's Twelve Steps and Twelve Traditions* (1985), wives would often wait while their husbands were at the early AA meetings. While they waited, they would talk about their problems and struggles. At some point, they decided to try applying the same 12 Steps that their husbands had found so helpful to their own lives, and the group known as Al-Anon was born (*Al-Anon's Twelve Steps and Twelve Traditions*, 1985; Doweiko, 1999). In the beginning, each isolated group made whatever changes it felt necessary in the Twelve Steps. By 1948, however, the wife of one of the cofounders of AA became involved in the growing organization, and in time, a uniform family support program emerged. This program, known as the Al-Anon Family Group, borrowed and modified the AA Twelve Steps and Twelve Traditions to make them applicable to the needs of families of alcoholics (Doweiko, 1999).

Co-Dependents Anonymous

Co-Dependents Anonymous (CoDA) was founded in 1986 in Phoenix, Arizona, and is a 12-step program that strives for healthy relationships, from the point of departure of codependence on someone with an addiction. CoDA adheres to 12 steps and traditions similar to those of AA. Each group is allowed to function autonomously to meet its own needs, as long as it has no other affiliation except CoDA and does not affect other groups of CoDA as a whole ("What Happened?," n.d.). There are approximately 1,200 CoDA groups in the United States, and it is active in more than 40 countries.

Narcotics Anonymous

In 1953, a self-help group patterned after AA was founded, and called itself Narcotics Anonymous (NA). Although this group honors its debt to AA, the members of NA feel that:

> We follow the same path with only a single exception. Our identification as addicts is all-inclusive in respect to any mood-changing, mind-altering substance. "Alcoholism" is too limited a term for us; our problem is not a specific substance, it is a disease called "addiction." (Narcotics Anonymous, 1982, p. x)

To the members of NA, it is not the specific chemical that is the problem, but the common disease of addiction. There is an important distinction to be made between AA and NA: The language of AA speaks of alcoholism, whereas NA speaks of "addiction" or "chemicals." Each offers the same program, with minor variations, to help the addicted person achieve sobriety (Doweiko, 1999).

Alateen

By 1957, in response to the recognition that teenagers presented special needs and concerns, Alateen was established after modifications to Al-Anon. These members follow the same 12 Steps outlined in the Al-Anon program, but the goal of the program is to provide teenagers the opportunity to share experiences, discuss current problems, learn how to cope more effectively, and offer encouragement to each other (*Facts about Alateen*, 1969).

Other Support Groups

Rational Recovery (RR) was founded in 1986 by Jack Trimpey, a California licensed clinical social worker, and is a source of counseling, guidance, and direct instruction on self-recovery from addiction to alcohol and other drugs through planned, permanent abstinence. This concept is designed as an alternative to AA and other 12-step programs ("Groups Offer Self-Help," 1991). The program closely follows the cognitive-behavioral school of counseling, and views alcoholism as reflecting negative, self-defeating thought patterns (Ouimette, Finney, & Moos, 1997). While RR and AA promote abstinence, the programs use different strategies. There are approximately 600 RR groups in the United States (Doweiko, 1999; McCrady & Delaney, 1995).

Rational Recovery (RR) specifically adheres to the following tenets:

- RR does not regard alcoholism as a disease, but rather a voluntary behavior;
- RR discourages adoption of the forever "recovering" drunk persona;
- There are no RR recovery groups;
- Great emphasis is placed on self-efficacy;
- There are no discrete steps and no consideration of religious matters.

Secular Organizations of Sobriety (SOS) was also founded in 1986; Dorsman (1996) estimates that approximately 1,200 SOS groups meet each week in the United States. SOS emerged as a reaction to the heavy emphasis on spirituality found in AA and NA (Doweiko, 1999; "Groups Offer Self-Help," 1991); the guiding philosophy of SOS stresses personal responsibility and the role of critical thinking in recovery (Doweiko, 1999).

Women for Sobriety (WFS) was founded in 1975 ("Groups Offer Self-Help," 1991), and McCrady and Delaney (1995) estimate that approximately 325 WFS groups meet in the United States. Doweiko (1999) states that this organization is specifically designed for and comprised of women, and is founded on the theory that the AA program fails to address the very real differences between the meaning of alcoholism for men and women. For this group, however, there are 13 statements, not 12.

Women for Sobriety (WFS) is specifically designed for and comprised of women, and is founded on the theory that the AA program fails to address the differences of the meaning of alcoholism between men and women (Lewis, 1994). Additionally, WFS focuses on negative thought patterns, tendencies of guilt, relationships, and spiritual and personal growth. These points are delineated in the Thirteen Statements of Acceptance (Kirkpatrick, 1990; Miller, 2005):

1. I have a life-threatening problem that once had me.
2. Negative thoughts destroy only myself.
3. Happiness is a habit I will develop.
4. Problems bother me only to the degree I permit them to.

5. I am what I think.
6. Life can be ordinary or it can be great.
7. Love can change the course of my world.
8. The fundamental object of life is emotional and spiritual growth.
9. The past is gone forever.
10. All love given returns.
11. Enthusiasm is my daily exercise.
12. I am a competent woman and have much to give life.
13. I am responsible for myself and my actions.

Alcoholics Anonymous for Atheists and Agnostics (Quad A) tends to draw heavily from the traditional Alcoholics Anonymous (Rand, 1995), but with one important distinction: Quad A tends to downplay the emphasis on religion inherent in the traditional AA foundation. In fact, this organization tends to remove the power given to a higher force than the members themselves, instead stressing the forces in the individual's life that support recovery (Doweiko, 1999).

Moderation Management (MM) was established in 1994 as a free-of-charge, nonprofit support group that welcomes those concerned about their drinking, regardless of level of consumption. The founder, Shirley Kishline, states that the goal of MM is to "provide a supportive environment in which people who have made the decision to reduce their drinking can come together and to help each other change" (Kishline, 1996, p. 55). MM is a controversial group because moderation is the goal, not abstinence (Kishline, 1996). MM emphasizes that individuals will be most successful at attaining their goals with alcohol when these goals are chosen by the individual, and proposes that individuals should be responsible for their behavior and can change lifetime habits with a program of support.

National Association for Children of Alcoholics (NACoA) was formed in February 1983 in California, after two groups of professionals from across the country met twice during 1982 to share their concerns, knowledge, and experiences regarding children of alcoholics. One group included clinicians concerned with the needs of adults whose mental health problems stemmed from a childhood in an alcoholic family. The other group included counselors and social workers who primarily worked with young children experiencing a broad range of problems in families with parental alcoholism. The 22 physicians, psychologists, social workers, and educators who attended these meetings concluded that a national membership organization was needed to identify and address the unique problems of children of alcoholics and to provide them with a means through which to voice their concerns (Wenger, 1997). NACoA provides support and information through its confidential telephone, letter, and email helplines, and via its website.

THE GROUP PROCESS: HOW 12-STEP GROUPS WORK

Goals

As with other counseling groups, 12-step addictions groups have established goals for members to work toward, which help them in their main goal of achieving addiction recovery. In a survey of outpatient drug abuse programs (Mejta, Naylor, & Maslar, 1994; Price et al., 1991), the following treatment goals that share similarities with other treatment modalities were identified:

- Abstinence from alcohol and other drugs;
- Steady employment;
- Stable social relationships;

- Positive physical and emotional health;
- Improved spiritual strength; and
- Adherence to legal mandates/requirements as applicable.

It is reasonable to assume that most 12-step groups incorporate these general goals into their general treatment foundation (a noted exception being Moderation Management, as discussed in the previous section), although individual groups differ in membership composition, individual aims and goals, and foundational beliefs. For example, the primary purpose of AA is twofold. Members strive to "carry the message to the addict who still suffers" (The Group, 1976, p. 1), and the organization seeks to provide for its members a program for living without chemicals. Doweiko (1999) notes that this is accomplished by presenting the individual with a simple, truthful, realistic picture of the disease of addiction; and by sharing their life stories, public confession of lies, distortions, self-deceptions, and denial that supported his/her own chemical use (p. 477).

The Twelve Steps and Twelve Traditions

AA pioneered the 12-step model from which most other 12-step groups now operate. Each group of AA is self-supporting, not-for-profit, and "in cooperation with but not affiliated with" the professional community (Alcoholics Anonymous World Services, 1991). All AA groups are guided by the Twelve Steps and Twelve Traditions, which serve as a basis for many other groups as well.

AA is not officially associated with any particular religious denomination, political affiliation, or organization, and notes that it "does not discriminate against any prospective member" (Alcoholics Anonymous World Services, 1991, p. 1), including those with addictions other than alcohol. It thus welcomes nonalcoholics to open meetings. AA does explicitly state, however, that while some professionals refer to alcoholism and drug addiction more generally as substance abuse or chemical dependency, the group makes the clear distinction that only those with alcohol problems are allowed to attend closed meetings (Alcoholics Anonymous World Services, 1991). There are six noted types of 12-step meetings (Miller, 2005); the counselor should be familiar with all types, and should invest time in attending some to gain a better understanding of the powerful dynamics at work:

1. Open meetings generally involve one recovering person speaking to the group about his/her addiction and recovery story. Nonaddicts are invited to attend and listen, and these meetings are generally helpful for those who want to learn more about addiction.
2. Closed meetings involve addicted individuals only.
3. Discussion meetings typically focus on a topic discussed by those addicts in attendance. Note that these meetings are called "participation meetings" in California.
4. In speaker meetings, one addicted person speaks to the audience about his or her addiction and recovery story, and the meeting may be open or closed.
5. In step meetings, the topic for discussion is one of the 12 steps, and these meetings are typically for addicted individuals only.
6. In Big Book meetings, a chapter from *Alcoholics Anonymous* is read and discussed.

It is important to note that, while the aforementioned Steps and Traditions have been the foundation for many other self-help groups, other groups have diverged due to differences in individual needs or in the belief systems of group members. More attention will be given to this later in the chapter.

Group Dynamics as Applied to 12-Step Groups

There are many different types of groups, as well as many different theoretical approaches to groups. Among the many varieties of group counseling, there is an enormous diversity in format, goals, and roles of the leader (McKay & Paleg, 1992). There are also many ways to select the members of a group. For example, they may be homogeneous by type or by age. There are advantages and disadvantages to every combination (Lawson, Lawson, & Rivers, 2001), and those aspects of diversity, composition, theoretical orientation, base, and foundation all play enormous roles in the outcome of the groups' efficacy. In their exploration of why certain self-help groups are so effective, Roots and Aanes (1992) identified eight characteristics that seem to contribute to a group's success:

1. Members have shared experience, in this case their inability to control their drug/alcohol use;
2. Education is the primary goal of AA membership;
3. Self-help groups are self-governing;
4. The group places emphasis on accepting responsibility for one's behavior;
5. There is but a single purpose to the group;
6. Membership is voluntary;
7. The individual member must make a commitment to personal change; and
8. The group places emphasis on anonymity and confidentiality.

As will be discussed later in this chapter, clinicians often choose to include groups as part of the treatment plan, and make that decision based on the assessed needs of the client and his or her fit with the potential group. Although most treatment programs include both group and individual counseling, Lawson et al. (2001) found that often it is in a group that the client makes the most progress toward significant therapeutic movement and suggests that as social beings, we are influenced more by a group of people than by just one person for any number of contextual, environmental, or personal reasons.

Twelve-step groups such as AA, Cocaine Anonymous (CA), and NA consider that helping others makes recovery possible. This helping component relies on the exchange of dialogue, reinforcing behavior, and encouraging messages of recovery through efforts modeled by the leader, which then filter throughout the group, often resulting in a successful outcome. Some studies suggest that AA and similar groups help individuals recover through common process mechanisms associated with enhancing self-efficacy, coping skills, and motivation; and by facilitating adaptive social network changes (Kelly, Magill, & Stout, 2009).

THE ROLE OF SPONSORS IN RECOVERY

Sponsorship reflects the structure of AA and functions on two levels. A sponsor is a more experienced person in recovery who guides the less-experienced "sponsee" through the program (Alcoholics Anonymous World Services, 1991). Level I Sponsorship is concerned with sobriety; the sponsor helps the sponsee to become or to stay sober. With Level II Sponsorship, the sponsor counsels the sponsee through the Twelve Steps so that recovery can be achieved (Brown, 1995).

The personal nature of the behavioral issues that lead to seeking help in 12-step fellowships results in a strong relationship between sponsee and sponsor. As the relationship is based on spiritual principles, it is unique and not generally characterized as a "friendship." Fundamentally, the sponsor has the single purpose of helping the sponsee recover from the behavioral problem that brought the sufferer into 12-step work, which reflexively helps the sponsor recover (*Twelve Steps and Twelve Traditions*, 1981).

The focus of the relationship, for both sponsor and sponsee, is on the Twelve Steps, with the sponsor serving as a guide and facilitator of the recovery process. The AA model encourages a gradual transition from primary dependence on the sponsor to a focus on the process itself. This shift demonstrates increased confidence and courage in the recovering addict working through the Steps, and allows for progress to be qualitatively evaluated by both the sponsor and the sponsee (Brown, 1995; Knack, 2009).

DO 12-STEP PROGRAMS REALLY WORK?

As already stated, 12-step groups have a long and successful history in the field of chemical dependency treatment. Lawson (2003) found that participation in 12-step groups during and after formal treatment has been associated with positive outcomes among substance users; and Donovan and Wells (2007) found that involvement in 12-step self-help groups, through both attending meetings and engaging in 12-step activities, is associated with reduced substance use and improved outcomes among alcohol- and cocaine-dependent individuals. Not surprisingly, a higher intensity of involvement has been associated with better drinking outcomes (Emrick et al., 1993; Zemore, Zaskutas, & Ammon, 2004). For example, individuals who are heavier substance users and have more substance-related problems are more likely to affiliate with 12-step self-help groups and less likely to drop out after treatment than less impaired clients (Connors, Tonigan, & Miller, 2001; Tonigan, Bogenschutz, & Miller, 2006). Research also suggests that early 12-step attendance might help to maintain better long-term alcohol abstinence for adolescents aged 13–15 years. Sterling, Chi, Campbell, and Weisner (2009) found that adolescents who attended 10–20 meetings within a period of 6 months had alcohol and drug abstinence rates significantly higher than adolescents who attended fewer meetings.

The benefits of 12-step participation observed among adult samples extend to adolescent outpatients. Community 12-step fellowships appear to provide a useful sobriety-supportive social context for youths seeking recovery, but evidence-based youth-specific 12-step facilitation strategies are needed to enhance outpatient attendance rates.

Source: Kelly, J. F., & Urbanoski, K. (2012). Youth recovery contexts: The incremental effects of 12-Step attendance and involvement on adolescent outpatient outcomes. *Alcoholism: Clinical and Experimental Research, 36*(7), 1219–1229.

Other findings have consistently concluded that 12-step participation can enhance treatment outcomes among problem drinkers (Emrick et al., 1993; McIntire 2000; Tonigan, Toscova, & Miller, 1996; Zemore et al., 2004); and scientific reviews of available data indicate that AA and related 12-step treatments such as NA are at least as helpful as other intervention approaches. Likewise, research on NA typically supports the efficacy of this approach (Alford, Koehler, & Leonard, 1991; Christo & Franey 1995; Johnsen & Herringer, 1993; Kelly et al., 2009; Toumbourou, Hamilton, U'Ren, Steven-Jones, & Storey, 2002; Zemore et al., 2004).

If this is the case, why run any other type of group? While specific advantages and disadvantages will be discussed later, some of the challenges of self-help groups are addressed here. First, it is unclear just how many people respond to self-help groups. Laudet (2003) suggests that the effectiveness of 12-step groups may be limited by high attrition rates and low participation. It may be safe to assume that some members who attend one or more of these groups do not attend consistently, do not reach group or therapeutic goals, or do not maintain sobriety. By the same measure, it may also be safe to assume that some members of these groups are sober, yet not happy or fully functioning. It is also important to remember that self-help groups are self-selective; because of this, membership consists of people who want to be members and who are willing to follow the guidelines of the group. This may explain the high degree of success reported among members (Lawson et al., 2001).

Although AA has been a social force in the United States for more than half a century, there has been surprisingly little empirical research into what elements of this and other 12-step programs are effective (Emrick et al., 1993), or for what types of people the 12-step model might be most useful (Galanter, Castaneda, & Franco, 1991; George & Tucker, 1996; McCaul & Furst, 1994; Tonigan & Hiller-Sturmhofel, 1994). Laudet, Magura, Cleland, Vogel, and Knight (2003) found that the following characteristics among group members are associated with the greatest long-term group retention, often leading to successful recovery: older age; more lifetime arrests; more psychiatric symptoms but not taking psychiatric medication; being more troubled by substance abuse than by mental health; having a greater level of self-efficacy for recovery; residing in supported housing; and being enrolled in outpatient treatment at follow-up. And while a study of sponsorship as practiced in AA and NA found that providing direction and support to other alcoholics and addicts correlates with sustained abstinence for the sponsor, the study also found that there were few short-term benefits for the sponsee (Crape, Latkin, Laris, & Knownlton, 2002).

SPECIFIC ADVANTAGES AND DISADVANTAGES OF 12-STEP GROUPS

Advantages

There are many advantages to incorporating 12-step groups into treatment. First, as discussed earlier, certain dynamics that can facilitate personal growth are more likely to exist in groups than in individual counseling. Kelly et al. (2009) suggest that AA-related changes occur via intrapersonal, behavioral, and social processes. The group setting offers support for new interaction dynamics, and encourages experimentation and behavioral rehearsal that is useful in generalizing to the world beyond the group. Additionally, they suggest that participants are able to explore their style of relating to others and to learn more effective social skills (Corey & Corey, 1992). AA provides a social outlet for its members. The 12-step group offers a safe, predictable, chemical-free place in which members can learn or relearn important social skills while experiencing a shared sense of purpose and belonging.

Predictability, consistency, universality, the opportunity to build social skills without chemical dependence, and the learning of coping skills are all factors present in self-help groups that lead to effective outcomes. There is a re-creation of the everyday world in some groups, particularly if the membership is diverse (Corey & Corey, 1992). The 12-step group allows its members to recognize that their problems are not unique, and members have the opportunity to learn about themselves through the experience of others; to experience emotional closeness and caring that encourage meaningful disclosure of the self; and to identify with the struggles of other members. This universality normalizes the recovery experience.

Another primary strength may lie in a group's ability to provide free, long-term, easy access and exposure to recovery-related common therapeutic elements (Kelly et al., 2009). Lawson et al. (2001) suggests that economically, groups are a logical choice because a counselor can see approximately three times the number of clients in groups than in individual counseling. For counselors, this is an important point; incorporating self-help groups into treatment helps clients build skill that would be fundamentally lacking in individual sessions, and counselors who engage themselves in the self-help group process as leaders (if the group allows this) have the opportunity to reach a greater number of clients in single sessions.

For many addicted clients, economic concerns far outweigh the potential benefits of treatment, especially among culturally diverse, minority, and marginalized populations. Self-help groups offer a free opportunity to achieve treatment goals; Tonigan et al. (1996) found that affiliation with 12-step groups such as AA and NA, both during and after treatment, was identified both as a cost-effective and useful approach to promoting abstinence among persons experiencing alcohol- and other drug-related problems. Additionally, meetings are often held at multiple locations and times in order to reach a wider client base, so clients have frequent, regular opportunities to attend meetings between individual counseling sessions.

Disadvantages

While there are numerous advantages to self-help groups, there are significant disadvantages as well. Laudet and White (2005) point counselors to a lack of consistent empirical support for their effectiveness, as well as a general lack of trained professionalism (e.g., groups that are not led by counselors); the risk that members may become overly dependent on the group; that members may, and sometimes do, get bad advice from other group members; and that the usefulness of these groups is limited in time (i.e., only needed in early recovery) or in scope (i.e., deals with only one substance while some clients have multiple issues). Certainly, the boundaries of any group are dependent upon the amount of structure present, and that structure is dependent upon the ability of members to provide the necessary motivation and commitment to keep the group operating. Without appropriate modeling from a trained professional, there is the risk that boundaries will be violated and structure will be lacking, and harm or attrition may result. Further, addictions are often superficial, albeit damaging, problems. Clients with addictions may engage in replacing one problem symptom for another, without ever confronting or challenging the real issue(s) beyond the group process.

Lawson et al. (2001) also suggest that there is often a subtle pressure to conform to group norms, values, and expectations. Participants sometimes unquestioningly substitute a group's values and norms for those they had unquestioningly acquired in the first place. In other words, members may be susceptible to replacing detrimental values, norms, and even behaviors with equally detrimental ones exhibited and observed in the group. This is especially salient when referring clients with possible Axis II disorders; clients may choose to abandon the chemical for a similar dependence on an observed behavior, an adopted value, or even another individual.

Hence, not all people are suited to all groups. The screening process for self-help groups is limited, and in most cases, especially in open groups, nonexistent. Some individuals are inappropriate for groups (e.g., too suspicious, too hostile, or too fragile) and do not benefit from a group experience. As a result, some individuals are psychologically damaged by attending certain groups. Inevitably, some make the group a place to ventilate their miseries and be rewarded for their engagement in the catharsis process. Others use groups as vehicles for expressing their woes, in the hope that they will be understood and totally accepted, and make no attempt to actually effect substantial change in their lives (Lawson et al., 2001). Before an individual is referred to a group, all these factors need to be carefully weighed by both the counselor and the client, to increase the likelihood that the person will benefit from the self-help group experience.

An even stronger point of resistance to the incorporation of self-help groups into treatment by counselors is based on the fact that many groups operate from a foundation of Christianity. The 12-step literature explicitly encourages helping as part of the recovery process, a point reinforced dramatically by AA's twelfth step: "having had a spiritual awakening as a result of these steps, we tried to carry this message to other alcoholics, and to practice these principles in all our affairs" (Alcoholics Anonymous World Services (1991), as cited in Zemore et al., 2004). Twelve-step groups have been historically controversial for this very reason, and several aspects of the recovery program have been identified as potential stumbling blocks for both substance users and clinicians (Chappel & DuPont, 1999; Laudet, 2000). This is due to a multiplicity of factors, and a main criticism includes the lack of cultural sensitivity inherent in the foundation of many groups. Further, Davis and Jansen (1998) suggest that the [twelve-step model's] emphasis on spirituality, surrender, and powerlessness contradicts contemporary dominant western cultural norms of self-reliance and widespread secularism.

It is important for counselors to be culturally sensitive and aware of the predominantly white, middle-strata, male-defined view of addictions upon which most 12-step programs are founded. Effective counselors are aware of their own biases and assumptions about human behavior, and must acquire knowledge of the particular groups they are working with; they must be able to use culturally appropriate intervention strategies in working with diverse groups (Sue & Sue, 2013).

Heyward (1992) suggests that for women in particular, it is difficult to listen to religious language, which may be interpreted as sexist from a dominant cultural standpoint. Further studies suggest that women are often more likely to participate in AA (i.e., number of meetings and duration of attendance) than men, and they benefit more than do men from long-term involvement in terms of drinking-related outcomes (Witbrodt & Delucchi, 2011). There is also additional clinical evidence suggesting that men who are less religiously oriented and those with social networks supportive of drinking are less likely to attend (Witbrodt & Delucchi, 2011). Subsequently, clinicians working with clients, especially male clients who are averse to AA's spiritual focus, may need to provide other alternatives. Treatment programs with a 12-step orientation might also consider facilitating engagement in AA in a way that clients do not feel coerced into accepting certain beliefs (Kaskutas, Subbaraman, Witbrodt, & Zemore, 2009).

The reliance on external support, and particularly on spiritual support as one of the cornerstones of the 12-step program, has been identified as a potential point of resistance to these organizations from certain ethnic groups (Laudet, 2003; Peteet, 1993; Smith, Buxton, Bilal, & Seymour, 1993). Often, African-American clients, as well as people in other nondominant cultures, tend to see addiction issues as secondary to such problems as illiteracy, racism, and poverty (Bell, 1993). The reliance on the spiritual component of the group, therefore, may not be as relevant—and not as helpful—when considering the hierarchy of immediate needs of nondominant groups.

However, it should be noted at this point that the spiritual component of the 12-step group must be addressed on an individual basis with the client. Many clients from minority backgrounds (e.g., African Americans) have values shaped by cultural factors, which must be taken into consideration by the counselor before deciding to incorporate group participation into treatment. For example, note that African Americans tend to be more group centered and sensitive to interpersonal matters, to have strong kinship bonds, to be work and education oriented, and to have a strong commitment to religious values and church participation (McCollum, 1997; Sue & Sue, 1999). Thus, a 12-step group may in fact be an advantageous tool for the counselor because of the group's focus and emphasis on spirituality.

Case Study. Nick identifies himself as an atheist, and tells his counselor that after serving as a combat soldier in Iraq, he no longer believes in a higher power. He appears committed to recovery, but resistant to suggestions of attending a 12-step group because of his personal views toward religious issues. He tells the counselor that he has lost many friends due to his beliefs and his continued alcohol use, and drinks daily to forget his combat experiences and fight the loneliness. The counselor inquires about prior treatment history, and Nick confides, "My last counselor referred me to AA for support, but I never went." The counselor believes that a group referral may be beneficial in assisting Nick toward recovery. What considerations should the counselor include in the decision to make a referral?

USING THE 12-STEP GROUP AS PART OF TREATMENT

While disadvantages and notable challenges exist with the 12-step model of addictions treatment, self-help groups that follow this model are still frequently used in the treatment of chemical abuse because of the advantages already discussed, and because aftercare support posttreatment is underfunded by both the public and private sectors (Subbaraman & Kaskutas, 2012).

Of the 20.6 million persons aged 12 or older in 2012 who were classified as needing substance use treatment but did not receive treatment at a specialty facility in the past year, 1.1 million persons (5.4%) reported that they felt they needed treatment for their illicit drug or alcohol use problem. Of these 1.1 million persons who felt they needed treatment, 347,000 (31.3%) reported that they made an effort to get treatment. Based on combined 2009–2012 data, the primary reason for not receiving treatment among this group of persons was a lack of insurance coverage and inability to pay the cost (38.2%) (Substance Abuse and Mental Health Services Administration, 2013).

Currently, 12-step groups are combined with other treatment modalities to maximize the potential for a successful outcome. Del Toro, Thom, Beam, and Horst (1996) suggest that 12-step programs, in addition to supportive medical follow-up visits and appropriate use of medications if needed, may greatly increase the probability of success and sustained recovery for addicts. A large number of studies have examined community AA group participation in relation to long-term outcomes following a variety of treatment approaches. These studies have found AA attendance over follow-up to be associated with enhanced abstinence outcomes and remission rates among different patient subgroups, including women, youth, dually diagnosed individuals, and various populations of diverse ethnic backgrounds (Kelly, Magill, & Stout, 2009).

For clients with substance dependence and major depressive disorder, attendance at 12-step meetings is associated with mental health benefits that extend beyond substance use, and reduced depression could be a key mechanism whereby 12-step meetings reduce future drinking in this population.

Source: Worley, M. J., Tate, S. R., & Brown, S. A. (2012). Mediational relations between 12-Step attendance, depression and substance use in patients with comorbid substance dependence and major depression. *Addiction, 107*(11), 1974–1983.

Traditional intervention strategies used in chemical dependency programs frequently include a combination of individual and group counseling, educational lectures on drug abuse, 12-step assignments, and self-help groups (Mejta, Naylor, & Maslar, 1994). Roman and Blum (1998) found in a representative sample of 450 private substance-user treatment centers, 90% of the facilities based their treatment on 12-step principles or variations of this model, with nearly one-half of the remaining 10% incorporating 12-step principles in combination with other approaches, including encouraged attendance at 12-step meetings.

Each counseling approach to the treatment process provides its own rationale for using groups as a therapeutic technique (Lawson et al., 2001). The reason a counselor chooses to use 12-step groups as part of that treatment plan should be congruent with the type of group chosen and the motivation of the client. Generally, self-help groups may work well with addicted clients in providing support for recovery, reducing a sense of isolation, and helping the client develop a sense of self-regulation (Khantzian & Mack, 1994; Miller, 2005). In addition, these groups provide overall support to counseling itself (Bristow-Braitman, 1995; Johnson & Phelps, 1991; Miller, 2005; Riordan & Walsh, 1994).

Counselors have a uniquely important role in helping clients process and reflect on their group experiences in individual sessions, helping them to generalize the new skills and values to situations and contexts beyond both individual counseling and the group. Since participation in 12-step meetings is typically voluntary, especially post-treatment, the decision of whether to incorporate self-help groups into long-term treatment or maintenance of recovery rests with both counselor and client, but primarily with the client.

The Role of the Counselor

An effective addictions counselor has a willingness to work with clients who suffer from addiction, is able to make appropriate referrals for a diverse client population at any time, and has an intimate knowledge of the workings of 12-step groups and how these and similar groups may enhance the counseling process and potential outcome when used in conjunction with counseling (Miller, 2005). Because the role of the addictions counselor is comprehensive and multifaceted, counselors have long been recognized as having a key role in substance users' treatment outcomes (Najavits, 2002). Counselors not only have significant influence on clients' attitudes toward 12-step groups, but it may also be concluded that clinicians' practices are critical to client outcomes (e.g., Luborsky, McLellan, Diguer, Woody, & Seligman, 1997; Najavitz, Crits-Christoph, & Dierberger, 2000; Project MATCH Research Group, 1998). 12-step referral practices are likely to be particularly important for clients' post-treatment recovery as well (Laudet & White, 2005).

Despite the wide incorporation of 12-step programs into substance abuse treatment, many clients fail to engage them. The lack of engagement might arise for multiple reasons, but the attitudes referring substance abuse professionals have toward 12-step culture are generally a strong contributing factor.

Source: Dennis, C. B., & Earleywine, M. (2013). Assessing the attitudes substance abuse professionals have toward 12-step culture: Preliminary results. *Journal of Social Work Practice in the Addictions*, 13(4), 373–392.

For example, Laudet and White (2005) found that referrals to 12-step groups were effective at increasing meeting attendance irrespective of clients' religious backgrounds, and all clients experienced significantly better substance abuse outcomes when they participated in these groups. In fact, McCaul and Furst (1994) suggest that many substance abuse rehabilitation counselors view AA as being the single most important component of a person's recovery program. At least one study found that AA participation was the only significant predictor of long-term recovery (McCaul & First, 1994).

Norcross (2003) and Miller (2005) suggest that self-help groups can include client education, motivation, empowerment, reinforcement, and social support, and strongly encourage counselors to incorporate the concept of self-help groups from the beginning of counseling. Counselors have an important role in educating clients about self-help groups, including addressing their misconceptions and concerns, suggesting particular group meeting formats (e.g., meetings for newcomers or specialized meetings for women; gay, lesbian, bisexual, transsexual, questioning [GLBTQ]; or veterans), and reviewing different 12-step fellowships (e.g., AA, NA, CA) and alternative recovery support structures (e.g., Women for Sobriety, Secular Organization for Sobriety, church-based recovery ministries) (Laudet & White, 2005).

Counselors should also have a comprehensive understanding of the types of addictions and their associated groups. For example, addictions are not limited to the use of alcohol and illegal drugs, but include process addictions as well. Similar to a substance addiction, in which an individual is dependent upon alcohol or a drug, a process addiction is a series of activities or interactions on which a person becomes dependent. Process addictions include but are not limited to work, shopping, sex, money, exercising, eating, gambling, religion, and relationships.

Research suggests that Gamblers Anonymous (GA) or other peer-led self-help groups for gambling could play a primary role in gambling recovery. Counselors would benefit from establishing relationships with the local GA members who would be willing to meet with gamblers new to recovery and to provide support after hours when counselors are unavailable (Nower, 2013).

Groups that fall into the process addiction category include: Online Gamers Anonymous (OLGA); Overeaters Anonymous (OA); Gamblers Anonymous (GA); Marijuana Anonymous (MA); Pagans in Recovery (PIR); and Workaholics Anonymous (WA). Sussman, Lisha, and Griffiths (2011) estimated prevalence rates for gambling addiction (2%), Internet addiction (2%), sex addiction (3%), exercise addiction (2%), and eating addiction (2%) among the general American population. The diagnostic criteria of process addictions are similar to those of substance addiction, and are based on five criteria (Asanjo & Wells, 2006):

1. Loss of willpower;
2. Harmful consequences;
3. Unmanageable lifestyle;
4. Tolerance or escalation of use;
5. Withdrawal symptoms upon quitting.

As already discussed, it is difficult to assess clients' views of 12-step programs in the addictions services field, but available findings suggest that they are generally amenable to participating in 12-step groups (Freimuth, 1996; Laudet, 2003), especially if their clinician has made an informed referral. Literature suggests that clinicians refer most of their substance-using clients to 12-step groups, and Humphreys (1997) found that, in a large survey of treatment programs within the Veteran's Administration system, 79% of clients were referred to AA, 45% to NA, and 24% to CA. Counselors making referrals to these groups should be aware of their role as perceived experts in this area, and make referrals appropriately after conducting a thorough assessment of the fit between the client and the group, engaging the client in the decision-making process if possible.

However, while clinicians are generally favorable toward the incorporation of 12-step groups into treatment plans for clients, and although most treatment programs recommend that clients attend 12-step groups, many clients still drop out of post-treatment. Laudet (2003) found that clients frequently cite convenience and scheduling issues as possible obstacles to attending 12-step groups. Laudet (2003) asserts the importance of fostering motivation for change, the need to assess clients' beliefs about and experiences with 12-step groups on a case-by-case basis, and to find a good fit between clients' needs and inclinations on the one hand and the tools and support available within 12-step groups on the other.

It is important for counselors to understand how powerful culture, gender, and ethnicity are as salient factors in service accessibility (Lewis, 1994). It is critical for counselors to incorporate multicultural considerations into their referrals to 12-step groups. While working with a diverse client population, counselors must have an awareness of the dynamics of the cultural system in which a client functions, and how the comprehensive treatment plan will best meet the client's needs. For example, when making referrals to self-help groups, counselors should consider a client's worldview, feelings of powerlessness, and history of oppression. Just like other treatment modalities, not all 12-step groups meet the needs of all clients. And just as counselors need to be aware of the individual needs of the client, they have an ethical obligation to be aware of all cultural components and competencies in counseling clients with chemical addictions, especially taking into account the specific circumstances which affect client worldview.

These differences in worldview can lead to mismatches between helping approaches and client expectations. As Sue, Arredondo, and McDavis (1992) point out, "helping styles and approaches may be culturally bound" (p. 483). And as stated previously, some of the methods used routinely in addictions treatment, including those in 12-step groups, are based on a worldview perceived as "mainstream" but that actually reflects the values of the dominant white male American culture.

Counselors need to make appropriate referrals to groups compatible for their clients and to be especially sensitive to the impact of such factors as racism, gender socialization, inequality, discrimination, and victimization on their clients' ability to benefit from groups (Lewis, 1994). Women clients, specifically, need the opportunity to focus on the cultural context of their addictions, and should be actively encouraged to explore issues related to gender and oppression because their substance abuse is often rooted in the gender socialization process. In many cases, an appropriate supportive group can be a safe place to learn and build social skills, and can provide the outlet needed to work through these issues with other members who share similar experiences.

Case Study. Rochelle, a 39-year-old African-American woman in an urban community, has sought the assistance of a counselor at the insistence of her husband for what he describes as "excessive alcohol use." She tells the counselor that she has been drinking daily for 3 years since the death of a close friend and that her family is concerned about her. She complains that she doesn't feel supported by the community, and that her husband, whom she identifies as Caucasian, doesn't understand her. She appears resistant to counseling and tells the counselor that she has tried it before and doesn't feel that the counselor "gets what she's saying." The counselor is considering a referral to a group. What considerations should the counselor include in the decision to make a referral?

SUGGESTIONS FOR COUNSELORS PROVIDING CARE Actively integrating 12-step approaches into the treatment process provides low- or no-cost options for members and increases the capacity for providing treatment (Donovan & Wells, 2007). When making a referral to a self-help group or determining whether to incorporate a group into treatment, the counselor needs a list of all available self-help groups in the client's community. This information should be shared and discussed with the client to assess how the client's needs may best be served by the group. It is important for counselor and client to consider all groups that fit within the scope of meeting the goals of the treatment plan, but to choose those in which the client will feel the most comfortable and accepting to maximize the potential of a successful outcome.

To address a client's initial resistance to groups, "Making Alcoholics Anonymous Easier" (MAAEZ) was developed to equip clients to deal with some of the experiences they are likely to encounter in an AA meeting, so that they will not immediately reject AA as a potential source of help (Kaskutas & Oberste, 2002). MAAEZ is a manualized group-format intervention designed to help formal treatment centers introduce participants to the 12-step culture. MAAEZ aims to overcome resistance to 12-step groups by changing participants' attitudes toward the people in AA/NA/CA, addressing the perceived social desirability of becoming involved in AA/NA/CA, and increasing participants' ability to control and manage their experiences with 12-step meetings, their choice of people with whom they become involved, and their interpretation of the 12-step philosophy.

MAAEZ consists of six weekly 90-minute group-format sessions run by counselors who are themselves active 12-step members. Each session is outlined on a laminated two-sided sheet that indicates lecture points, issues for discussion, recommended length of time to spend on the issue, take-home messages, and homework assignments for the week. To implement the intervention, two MAAEZ sessions are conducted weekly: the introductory session (for new clients and clients who have completed the core sessions), and one of the four core sessions ("Spirituality," "Sponsorship," "Principles Not Personalities," and "Living Sober" for continuing clients).

A trial of "Making Alcoholics Anonymous Easier" (MAAEZ), a *group*-format *12-step* facilitation program, showed significantly higher odds of past 30-day abstinence after 12 months among those who had been treated in MAAEZ compared to usual care, especially for clients with high prior AA/NA/CA meeting attendance.

Source: Subbaraman, M. S., & Kaskutas, L. A. (2012). Social support and comfort in AA as mediators of "Making AA Easier" (MAAEZ), a 12-Step step facilitation intervention. *Psychology of Addictive Behaviors, 26*(4), 759–765.

When evaluating which group is most appropriate for the needs of the client and whether the client is appropriate for a group, counselors should note the following information:

- Does the client have a desire to stop the addiction? What type of addiction is it, or does the problem fall into more than one category?
- What is the gender of the client? To what extent may the addiction be conceptualized in terms of gender-role socialization?
- What is the cultural background of the client? What is his or her ethnicity? What cultural/ethnic background does he or she most identify with?
- What is the client's belief system? Is the client spiritual? Does the client adhere to a rigid religious structure? Is the client affiliated with any particular religious denomination?
- What is the client's affect like? Is he or she: Angry? Proud? Tearful? Manipulative? Mistrustful? Defensive? Guilty? Full of shame?
- Does the client demonstrate any personality traits or features that may affect adjustment to the group, and vice versa?

As pointed out earlier, accessibility may be an issue for some clients. If clients are being treated in one location and live in another, it is important that they attend groups in an area convenient both during and after addictions treatment (Miller, 2005). However, the counselor should take note if the client objects to attending groups near his or her home for anonymity reasons, in which case it is the counselor's responsibility to provide alternative group options for that client. Additionally, counselors need to make clients aware that while members of self-help groups make a commitment to not divulge specific information about meetings or identities of members in attendance to encourage free sharing in the group, there is no guarantee of anonymity. Acquiring this and other information at the outset of counseling will help the counselor determine if the client is appropriate for a group, and which group(s) he or she is appropriate for. This information will serve as a guide for the counselor in forthcoming sessions while processing the content of the group toward the aims and goals of treatment.

HOW CAN I LEARN MORE ABOUT GROUPS?

Consult. Colleagues are a valuable resource for addictions and process information, and can provide case conceptualizations; personal experiences; mistakes and errors as well as successful outcomes; additional community resources; and collaborative opportunities for training and advocacy. Counselors should also seek supervision while providing client care; consistent supervision for practitioners is essential for competent, ethical practice. As the addictions counselor provides guidance, support, and education on the addictions process to the client, so does the supervisor provide the same for the addictions counselor.

Research. Staying current on relevant research in the areas of addictions and associated treatment groups broadens the counselor's conceptualization of methods, models, and approaches to the treatment of addictions. Journal articles, texts, and educational resources provide a broad spectrum of information that helps expand the counselor's skill and knowledge base in this area. Counselors are cautioned to approach Internet resources skeptically; the Internet has generated a seemingly unlimited amount of useful articles and resources on the treatment of addictions and on process groups. However, there is a high potential for false information, which may be harmful to the client and the recovery process. Suggested websites with recent and accurate information about specific groups are provided at the end of this chapter.

Get involved. The effective addictions counselor has an intimate working knowledge of how 12-step/self-help groups work and how to incorporate them into treatment. Counselors should contact organizations and request literature on groups, and should attend various groups to familiarize themselves with the tenets, the process, membership requirements (if any), and the aims/goals of various groups to help in the client referral process. Maintaining professional networks within the addiction counseling field is also strongly recommended to increase and maintain a current working knowledge of treatment trends, continued educational opportunities, and a collegial support system for the counselor.

Summary and Some Final Notations

Counselors can contribute to the Institute of Medicine's (1990) goal of broadening the base of treatment for substance-use-related problems within their community (Caldwell, 1999). Twelve-step groups are often incorporated into treatment and combined with other treatment modalities to maximize the potential for a successful outcome. Group assignments and tenets are increasingly being integrated into formal services; and the attitudes, beliefs, and knowledge base of counselors regarding the role of 12-step groups in addictions treatment are greatly influential in clients' decision to participate.

Prior to a referral or the inclusion of a group into treatment, counselors need to become thoroughly familiar with the different types of 12-step groups and with their processes and procedures; how to engage the client in selecting the best match between his or her needs and treatment goals, and the foundations, aims, and structure of the group; and any cultural factors that may play a part in the efficacy of the outcome. Further, counselors have an essential role in incorporating diversity into referrals to 12-step groups. The addictions counselor needs to be aware of the client's worldview and the cultural circumstances that affect the client's willingness to participate in a group. It is imperative that the counselor closely consider the multicultural implications of the inclusion of a group into treatment, and all considerations should be made from a position of awareness, sensitivity, and advocacy.

A few of the 12-step and affiliated groups discussed in this chapter include Alcoholics Anonymous, Al-Anon, Narcotics Anonymous, Alateen, Rational Recovery, Secular Organizations of Sobriety, Women for Sobriety, Alcoholics Anonymous for Atheists and Agnostics, and Moderation Management. Many groups have been established to address the multitude of needs and differing belief systems of group members, and all groups have their own guidelines to which they adhere. Effective addictions counselors will have lists of, and information on, all self-help groups in the client's community, including descriptions, meeting times, education materials, literature, brochures, and videos if available. The referral process should be a collaborative one between counselor and client, and the counselor should make a thorough determination of whether the client will benefit from a group experience while working toward treatment goals, as not all clients are appropriate for all groups.

Benefits of groups include the power dynamics of universality, a supportive environment for the practicing of new behaviors and skills, and the opportunity for clients to learn about themselves through the sharing of experiences that serve to facilitate personal growth. Conversely, disadvantages include a foundation of spirituality that may not be inclusive of all cultures, members working issues out inappropriately in the group setting, and the lack of professional training among group leaders. The 12-step/self-help groups are voluntary and nonprofit, but counselors often cite accessibility and cultural insensitivity as reasons for noninclusion in treatment.

The importance of counselor inclusion of 12-step/self-help groups into addictions treatment has been acknowledged by several professional organizations (Laudet, 2003). Laudet and White (2005) suggest that counselors are expressing a growing interest in the potential role of groups in addictions treatment and are currently seeking further information about how to best incorporate them into their practice. They suggest that, because counselors play an important role in fostering 12-step participation, the insights they develop through their research and practice can greatly contribute to the field of addictions counseling (Laudet, 2003).

MyCounselingLab

Visit the MyCounselingLab site for *Foundations of Addictions Counseling,* Third Edition to enhance your understanding of concepts. You'll have the opportunity to practice your skills through video- and case-based exercises. You will find sets of questions to help you prepare for your certification exam with *Licensure Quizzes.* There is also a Video Library that provides taped counseling sessions, ethical scenarios, and interviews with helpers and clients.

Useful Websites

The following websites provide additional information relating to the chapter topic:

Al-Anon
www.al-anon.org

Alateen
www.al-anon.alateen.org

Alcoholics Anonymous
www.aa.org

Cocaine Anonymous (CA)
www.ca.org/

Co-Dependents Anonymous (CoDA)
www.codependents.org/

Crystal Meth Anonymous (CMA)
www.crystalmeth.org/

Debtors Anonymous (DA)
www.debtorsanonymous.org/

Drug and Alcohol Registry of Treatment
www.dart.on.ca/

Drug Rehab and Drug Rehabilitation Treatment Centers
www.drug-rehab.com/index.htm

Emotional Health Anonymous (EHA)
www.emotionsanonymous.org/

Gamblers Anonymous (GA)
www.gamblersanonymous.org/

Marijuana Anonymous (MA)
www.marijuana-anonymous.org/

Moderation Management (MM)
moderation.org/

Nar-Anon
nar-anon.org/

Narcotics Anonymous
www.na.org

National Association for Children of Alcoholics (NACoA)
nacoa.org/

National Center on Addiction and Substance Abuse at Columbia University
www.casacolumbia.org

National Institute on Alcohol Abuse and Alcoholism
www.niaaa.nih.gov

Nicotine Anonymous (NicA)
www.nicotine-anonymous.org/

Online Gamers Anonymous (OLGA)
www.olganon.org/

Overeaters Anonymous (OA)
www.oa.org/

Pagans in Recovery (PIR)
pagansinrecovery.com/

Rational Recovery
www.rational.org/recovery

Secular Organizations for Sobriety
www.sossobriety.org

Sexaholics Anonymous (SA)
www.sa.org/

SMART Recovery
www.smartrecovery.org/

Substance Abuse and Mental Health Services Administration
www.health.org

Women for Sobriety, Inc.
www.womenforsobriety.org

Workaholics Anonymous (WA)
www.workaholics-anonymous.org/page.php?page=home

References

Al-Anon's Twelve Steps & Twelve Traditions. (1985). New York, NY: Al-Anon Family Group Headquarters.

Twelve Steps and Twelve Traditions. (1991). New York, NY: Alcoholics Anonymous World Services.

Alford, G. S., Koehler, R. A., & Leonard, J. (1991). Alcoholics Anonymous–Narcotics Anonymous model inpatient treatment of chemically dependent adolescents: A 2-year outcome study. *Journal of Studies on Alcohol, 52*, 118–126.

Asanjo, B., & Wells, K. (2006). Addiction. In *Gale Encyclopedia of Children's Health: Infancy through Adolescence*. Retrieved August 1, 2014 from Encyclopedia.com: http://www.encyclopedia.com/doc/1G2-3447200018.html

Bell, P. (1993, July). *Chemical dependency and the African-American*. Presentation to the annual conference of the National Association of Drug and Alcohol Counselors, Chicago, IL.

Bristow-Braitman, A. (1995). Addiction recovery: 12-Step programs and cognitive behavioral psychology. *Journal of Counseling and Development, 73*, 414–418.

Brown, S. (1995). *Treating alcoholism*. San Francisco, CA: Jossey-Bass.

Caldwell, P. E. (1999). Fostering client connections with Alcoholics Anonymous: A framework for social workers in various practice settings. *Social Work in Health Care, 28*(4), 45–61.

Chappel, J., & DuPont, R. (1999). Twelve-step and mutual-help programs for addictive disorders. *Addictive Disorders, 22*(2), 425–446.

Christo, G., & Franey, C. (1995). Drug user's spiritual beliefs, locus of control and the disease concept in relation to narcotics anonymous attendance and six-month outcomes. *Drug and Alcohol Dependence, 38,* 51–56.

Connors, G. J., Tonigan, J. S., & Miller, W. R. (2001). A longitudinal model of intake symptomatology, AA participation and outcome: Retrospective study of the Project MATCH outpatient and aftercare samples. *Journal of Studies on Alcohol and Drugs, 62,* 817–825.

Corey, G., & Corey, M. S. (1992). *Group process and practice* (4th ed.). Pacific Grove, CA: Brooks/Cole Publishing Co.

Crape, B. L., Latkin, C. A., Laris, A. S., & Knowlton, A. R. (2002). The effects of sponsorship in 12-step treatment of injection drug users. *Drug and Alcohol Dependence, 6*(3), 291–301.

Davis, D. R., & Jansen, G. G. (1998). Making meaning of Alcoholics Anonymous for social workers: Myths, metaphors, and realities. *Social Work, 43*(2), 169–182.

Del Toro, I. M., Thom, D. J., Beam, H. P., & Horst, T. (1996). Chemical dependent patients in recovery: Roles for the family physician. *American Family Physician, 53*(5), 1667–1681.

Dennis, C. B., & Earleywine, M. (2013). Assessing the attitudes substance abuse professionals have toward 12-step culture: Preliminary results. *Journal of Social Work Practice in the Addictions, 13*(4), 373–392.

Donovan, D. M., & Wells, E. A. (2007). Tweaking 12-Step: The potential role of 12-step self-help group involvement in methamphetamine recovery. *Addiction, 102,* 121–129.

Dorsman, J. (1996). Improving alcoholism treatment: An overview. *Behavioral Health Management, 16*(1), 26–29.

Doweiko, H. (1999). *Concepts of chemical dependency* (4th ed.). Pacific Grove, CA: Brooks/Cole Publishing Company.

Emrick, C. D., Tonigan, J. S., Montgomery, H., & Little, L. (1993). Alcoholics Anonymous: What is currently known? In B. S. McCrady & W. R. Miller, (Eds.), *Research on Alcoholics Anonymous: Opportunities and alternatives* (pp. 41–78). New Brunswick, NJ: Rutgers Center of Alcohol Studies.

Facts about Alateen. (1969). New York, NY: Al-Anon Family Group Headquarters.

Freimuth, M. (1996). Psychotherapists' beliefs about the benefits of 12-step groups. *Alcoholism Treatment, 14,* 95–102.

Galanter, M., Castaneda, R., & Franco, H. (1991). Group therapy and self-help groups. In R. J. Frances & S. I. Miller (Eds.), *Clinical textbook of addictive disorders.* New York, NY: Guilford Press.

George, A. A., & Tucker, J. A. (1996). Help-seeking for alcohol-related problems: Social contexts surrounding entry into alcoholism treatment or Alcoholics Anonymous. *Journal of Studies on Alcohol, 57,* 449–457.

Group, The. (1976). Narcotics Anonymous World Service Office, Inc.

Groups offer self-help: Alternatives to AA. (1991). *Alcoholism & Drug Abuse Week, 3*(37), 6.

Heyward, C. (1992). Healing addiction and homophobia: Reflections on empowerment and liberation. *Journal of Chemical Dependency Treatment, 5*(1), 5–18.

Humphreys, K. (1997). Clinicians' referral and matching of substance abuse patients to self-help groups after treatment. *Psychiatric Services, 48,* 1445–1449.

Humphreys, K., & Moos, R. H. (1996). Reduced substance-abuse-related health care costs among voluntary participants in Alcoholics Anonymous. *Psychiatric Services, 47,* 709–713.

Institute of Medicine. (1990). *Broadening the base of treatment for alcohol problems.* Washington, DC: National Academy Press.

Johnsen, E., & Herringer, L. G. (1993). A note on the utilization of common support activities and relapse following substance abuse treatment. *Journal of Psychology, 127,* 73–78.

Johnson, P. N., & Phelps, G. L. (1991). Effectiveness in self-help groups: Alcoholics Anonymous as a prototype. *Family and Community Health, 14,* 22–27.

Kaskutas, L. A., & Oberste, E. A. (2002). *MAAEZ. Making Alcoholics Anonymous easier.* Berkeley, CA: Alcohol Research Group, Public Health Institute.

Kaskutas, L. A., Subbaraman, M. S., Witbrodt, J., & Zemore, S. E. (2009). Effectiveness of Making Alcoholics Anonymous Easier (MAAEZ), a group format 12-step facilitation approach. *Journal of Substance Abuse Treatment, 37,* 228–239.

Kelly, J. F., Magill, M., & Stout, R. L. (2009). How do people recover from alcohol dependence? A systematic review of the research on mechanisms of behavior change in Alcoholics Anonymous. *Addiction Research & Theory, 17*(3), 236–259.

Kelly, J. F., & Urbanoski, K. (2012). Youth recovery contexts: The incremental effects of 12-Step attendance and involvement on adolescent outpatient outcomes. *Alcoholism: Clinical and Experimental Research, 36*(7), 1219–1229.

Khantzian, E. J., & Mack, J. E. (1994). How AA works and why it's important for clinicians to understand. *Journal of Substance Abuse Treatment, 11,* 77–92.

Kirkpatrick, J. (1990). *Stages of the "new life" program.* Quakertown, PA: Women for Sobriety.

Kishline, A. (1996). A toast to moderation. *Psychology Today, 29*(1), 53–56.

Knack, W. A. (2009). Psychotherapy and Alcoholics Anonymous: An integrated approach. *Journal of Psychotherapy Integration, 19*(1), 86–109.

Laudet, A. (2000). Substance abuse treatment providers' referral to self-help: Review and future empirical directions. *International Journal of Self-Help & Self-care, 1*(3), 195–207.

Laudet, A. (2003). Attitudes and beliefs about 12-step groups among addiction treatment clients and clinicians: Toward identifying obstacles to participation. *Substance Use and Misuse, 38*(14), 2017–2047.

Laudet, A. B., Magura, S., Cleland, C. M., Vogel, H. S., & Knight, E. L. (2003). Predictors of retention in dual-focus self-help groups. *Community Mental Health Journal, 39*(4), 281–297.

Laudet, A. B., & White, W. L. (2005). An exploratory investigation of the association between clinicians' attitudes toward twelve-step groups and referral rates. *Alcoholism Treatment Quarterly, 23*(1), 31–45.

Lawson, G. W., Lawson, A. W., & Rivers, P. C. (2001). *Essentials of chemical dependency counseling* (3rd ed.). Gaithersburg, MD: Aspen Publishers, Inc.

Lawson, S. (2003). Surrendering the night: The seduction of victim blaming in drug and alcohol facilitated sexual prevention strategies. *Women Against Violence, 13,* 33–38.

Lewis, J. A. (1994). Issues of gender and culture in substance abuse treatment. In J. A. Lewis (Ed.), *Addictions: Concepts and strategies for treatment* (pp. 37–40). Gaithersburg, MD: Aspen Publishers, Inc.

Luborsky, L., McLellan, A. T., Diguer, L., Woody, G., & Seligman, D. (1997). The psychotherapist matters: Comparison of outcomes across twenty-two therapists and seven patient samples. *Clinical Psychology: Science and Practice, 4,* 53–65.

McCaul, M. D., & Furst, J. (1994). Alcoholism treatment in the United States. *Alcohol Health & Research World, 18,* 253–260.

McCollum, V. J. C. (1997). Evolution of the African American family personality: Considerations for family therapy. *Journal of Multicultural Counseling and Development, 25,* 219–229.

McCrady, B. S., & Delaney, S. I. (1995). Self-help groups. In R. K. Hester & W. R. Miller (Eds.), *Handbook of alcoholism treatment approaches* (2nd ed.). New York, NY: Allyn & Bacon.

McIntire, D. (2000). How well does AA work? An analysis of published AA surveys (1968–96) and related analyses/comments. *Alcoholism Treatment Quarterly, 18,* 1–18.

McKay, M., & Paleg, K. (Eds.). (1992). *Focal group psychotherapy.* Oakland, CA: New Harbinger Publications.

Mejta, C. L., Naylor, C. L., & Maslar, E. M. (1994). Drug abuse treatment: Approaches and effectiveness. In J. A. Lewis (Ed.), *Addictions: Concepts and strategies for treatment* (pp. 59–77). Gaithersburg, MD: Aspen Publishers, Inc.

Miller, G. (2005). *Learning the language of addiction counseling* (2nd ed.). Hoboken, NJ: John Wiley & Sons, Inc.

Miller, W. R., & McCrady, B. S. (1993). The importance of research on Alcoholics Anonymous. In B. S. McCrady & W. R. Miller (Eds.), *Research on Alcoholics Anonymous.* New Brunswick, NJ: Rutgers Center of Alcohol Studies.

Najavitz, L. M., Crits-Christoph, P., & Dierberger, A. (2000). Clinicians' impact on the quality of substance use disorder treatment. *Substance Use Misuse, 35* (12–14), 2161–2190.

Narcotics Anonymous. (1982). Van Nuys, CA: Narcotics Anonymous World Service Office.

Norcross, J. C. (2003, August). *Integrating self-help into psychotherapy: A revolution in mental health practice* [Invited address]. Rosalee G. Weiss lecture on psychotherapy at the American Psychological Association, Toronto, Ontario, Canada.

Nower, L. (2013). Research directions and unanswered questions in the treatment of disordered gambling: Results of an empirical study. In D. C. S. Richard, A. Blaszczynski, & L. Nower (Eds.), *The Wiley-Blackwell handbook of disordered gambling.* West Sussex, UK: John Wiley & Sons.

Ouimette, P. C., Finney, J. W., & Moos, R. H. (1997). Twelve-step and cognitive-behavioral treatment for substance abuse: A comparison of treatment effectiveness. *Journal of Consulting and Clinical Psychology, 65,* 230–240.

Peteet, J. (1993). A closer look at the role of a spiritual approach in addictions treatment. *Journal of Substance Abuse Treatment, 10*(3), 263–267.

Price, R. H., Burke, A. C., D'Aunno, T. A., Klingel, D. M., McCaughain, W. C., Rafferty, J. A., & Vaughn, T. E. (1991). Outpatient drug abuse treatment services, 1988. Results of a national survey. In R. Pickens, C. G. Leukefeld, & C. Schuster (Eds.), *Improving drug abuse treatment* (pp. 63–91). Rockville, MD: National Institute on Drug Abuse. [(ADM) 91–1754]

Project MATCH Research Group. (1998). Matching alcoholism treatments to client heterogeneity: Project MATCH three-year drinking outcomes. *Alcoholism: Clinical & Experimental Research, 22,* 1300–1311.

Rand, L. (1995). A different road. *Chicago Tribune, 148*(53), Tempo Sect., 1, 7.

Riordan, R. J., & Walsh, L. (1994). Guidelines for professionals. Referral to Alcoholics Anonymous and other twelve step groups. *Journal of Counseling and Development, 72,* 351–355.

Roman, P. M., & Blum, T. C. (1998). National Treatment Center Study. *Summary Report (No. 3): Second Wave On-Site Results.* Unpublished manuscript, University of Georgia.

Roots, L. E., & Aanes, D. L. (1992). A conceptual framework for understanding self help groups. *Hospital and Community Psychiatry, 43,* 379–381.

Smith, D., Buxton, M., Bilal, R., & Seymour, R. (1993). Cultural points of resistance to the 12-step recovery process. *Journal of Psychoactive Drugs, 25*(1), 97–108.

Sterling, S., Chi, F., Campbell, C., & Weisner, C. (2009). Three-year chemical dependency and mental health treatment outcomes among adolescents: The role of continuing care. *Alcoholism: Clinical & Experimental Research, 33*(8), 1417–1429.

Subbaraman, M. S., & Kaskutas, L. A. (2012). Social support and comfort in AA as mediators of "Making AA Easier" (MAAEZ), a 12-step facilitation intervention. *Psychology of Addictive Behaviors, 26*(4), 759–765.

Substance Abuse and Mental Health Services Administration. (2013). *Results from the 2012 National Survey on Drug Use and Health: Summary of national findings* [Publication No. (SMA) 13-4795]. Rockville, MD: Office of Applied Studies. Retrieved March 2014 from http://www.samhsa.gov/data/NSDUH/2012SummNatFindDetTables/NationalFindings/NSDUHresults2012.htm

Sue, D. W., Arredondo, P., & McDavis, R. J. (1992). Multicultural counseling competencies and standards: A call to the profession. *Journal of Counseling & Development, 70,* 477–486.

Sue, D. W., & Sue, D. (1999). *Counseling the culturally different: Theory and practice* (3rd ed.). New York, NY: John Wiley & Sons, Inc.

Sue, D. W., & Sue, D. (2013). *Counseling the culturally different: Theory and practice* (6th ed.). New York, NY: John Wiley & Sons, Inc.

Sussman, S., Lisha, N., & Griffiths, M. (2011). Prevalence of the addictions: A problem of the majority or the minority? *Evaluation & the Health Professions, 34*(1), 3–56.

Tonigan, J. S., Bogenschutz, M. P., & Miller, W. R. (2006). Is alcoholism typology a predictor of both Alcoholics Anonymous affiliation and disaffiliation after treatment? *Journal of Substance Abuse Treatment, 30,* 323–330.

Tonigan, J. S., & Hiller-Sturmhofel, S. (1994). Alcoholics Anonymous: Who benefits? *Alcohol Health & Research World, 18,* 308–310.

Tonigan, J. S., Toscova, R., & Miller, W. R. (1996). Meta-analysis of the literature on Alcoholics Anonymous: Sample and study characteristics moderate findings. *Journal of Studies on Alcohol, 57*(1), 65–72.

Toumbourou, J. W., Hamilton, M., U'Ren, A., Steven-Jones, P., & Storey, G. (2002). Narcotics Anonymous participation and changes in substance use and social support. *Journal of Substance Abuse Treatment, 23*(1), 61–67.

Twelve Steps and Twelve Traditions. (1981). New York, NY: Alcoholics Anonymous World Services.

Wenger, S. (1997). National association for children of alcoholics. *Alcohol Health & Research World, 21*(3), 267–270.

What happened? (n.d.). Retrieved September 5, 2014, from Co-Dependents Anonymous: http://coda.org/index.cfm/whathappened/

Witbrodt, J., & Delucchi, K. (2011). Do women differ from men on Alcoholics Anonymous participation and abstinence? A multi-wave analysis of treatment seekers. *Alcoholism: Clinical and Experimental Research, 35*(12), 2231–2241.

Worley, M. J., Tate, S. R., & Brown, S. A. (2012). Mediational relations between 12-Step attendance, depression and substance use in patients with comorbid substance dependence and major depression. *Addiction, 107*(11), 1974–1983.

Zemore, S. E., Zaskutas, L. A., & Ammon, L. N. (2004). In 12-step groups, helping helps the helper. *Addiction, 99*(8), 1015–1023.

Zweben, J. E. (1995). Integrating psychotherapy and 12-step approaches. In A. M. Washton (Ed.), *Psychotherapy and substance abuse.* New York, NY: Guilford Press.

Chapter 13

Maintenance and Relapse Prevention

Rochelle Moss
Henderson State University

Christopher C. H. Cook
Durham University

INTRODUCTION

After the client has completed the initial stages of treatment, the focus of the counseling process should be on establishing a firm foundation in a maintenance program for the prevention of a relapse. Although client relapse often occurs, this setback can be reframed as a learning experience in the growing awareness of one's limitations and weaknesses. The initial portion of this chapter delves into relapse prevention for addictive behavior, identifies high-risk situations, and examines by case study how seemingly irrelevant decisions play a part in a relapse. We also discuss the abstinence violation effect. The latter portion describes relapse prevention with specific daily maintenance practices as applied within a case study. In conclusion, some of the most recent findings in the field of substance abuse will be summarized to help us better understand the dynamic, complex issues of relapse and maintenance.

RELAPSE PREVENTION FOR ADDICTIVE BEHAVIORS

A *relapse* is often defined as a return to drug use after a period of abstention. Attempting to determine rates of relapse can be challenging due to many variables. Relapse rates are different depending on the drug, severity of the addiction, length of treatment, and how relapse is defined. Several studies have indicated a relapse as high as 90% for alcoholics (Doweiko, 1990; Orford & Edwards, 1977). A recent government study compared the relapse rates of drug addiction to other chronic illnesses (National Institute on Drug Abuse, n.d.). This study estimated the percentage of people with drug addictions who relapsed as 40–60% compared to Type 1 diabetes at 30–50%, and both asthma and hypertension at 50–70%. Regardless of the many factors involved, both practitioners and researchers agree that most individuals who attempt any significant behavior change will experience lapses and/or relapses.

Alcoholism is a relapsing condition that is found to be no different than other addictive behaviors (Polich, Amour, & Braiker, 1981). What do we mean by "relapsing condition"? In the broader context of medicine, *relapse* might be defined as a return of disease after an apparently full or partial recovery. However, the term is used even more broadly, in everyday life, to refer to falling back into a pattern of habitual (usually negative) behavior. In addiction treatment it can be used in either or both of these senses, but it might best be understood here to refer specifically to a return to a pattern of addictive behavior that had (for a shorter or longer period of time) apparently abated.

Relapse can occur following apparently spontaneous cessation of addictive behavior, self-motivated and deliberate attempts to overcome an addiction, involvement with a self-help (or mutual-help) program of recovery, or following involvement with a formal medical or psychological treatment program. However, for the present purposes, it is perhaps best to think of *relapse* as something that occurs following an intervention or treatment intended to control or eliminate the behavior in question. Thus, a single drink taken by an alcoholic who had been completely abstinent for some months, as a result of engagement in a program of recovery supported by attendance at Alcoholics Anonymous (AA) or Rational Recovery (RR), would count as a relapse. The basic philosophy of such groups is that a relapse is a normal part of the addiction process and it is *not* a part of recovery. Similarly, a return to heavy drinking, by a client seeing a substance abuse counselor who had been assisting her in moderating her alcohol use, would also be a relapse. But a single drink taken by the latter client might not be understood as a relapse at all, as it might have been well within the limits agreed to with her counselor. This distinction immediately raises a series of important considerations.

First, *relapse* can mean different things for different clients engaged in different therapeutic programs. This is not only a question of degree. For example, most 12-step programs aim at abstinence from all mood-altering substances. Thus, consumption of one glass of wine might count as a relapse for a formerly opioid-dependent client attending Narcotics Anonymous, but be considered quite immaterial by the counselor of the same client engaged in a purely psychological program of cognitive-behavior therapy focused on illicit drug use. Similarly, an alcoholic client who remains completely abstinent from alcohol might begin using tranquilizers in an addictive fashion and thus have relapsed—even though the counselor neglected to tell the client not to use tranquilizers. Such action by the client is referred to within AA circles as the "trading of one addiction in for another."

Second, it will sometimes be necessary to distinguish a "lapse" from a "relapse" (Marlatt & George, 1984), as a single glass of wine has a different significance for the client enrolled in a controlled drinking program, as compared with a member of AA. Thus, a single glass of wine consumed by one aiming at complete abstinence (whatever program of treatment one is engaged in as a means of achieving that goal) might well constitute a relapse when it is denied, leads to further drinking, or constitutes a breach of terms of employment in a safety-sensitive workplace. However, for another client, where the same behavior leads immediately to a meeting with a sponsor or counselor, and thus to a helpful discussion about how it could be avoided in the future, it might be referred to merely as a *lapse*. A *lapse* is thus a technical or modest breach of agreed treatment goals, which allows for learning and therefore eventual achievement of the ultimate aims and objectives of treatment. A relapse is a more serious violation of treatment goals, or a more minor violation in which such learning is not evident.

Third, relapse prevention is an approach to treatment compatible with other treatment models of widely varying philosophy. Multimodal therapies in conjunction with a supportive 12-step program offer the greatest promise for long-term abstinence. But this in turn raises another important question. What is *relapse prevention* in its pure form?

Relapse prevention is difficult to define because it constitutes a range of therapeutic methods applicable to a range of very different addictive behaviors, as well as to habits or behaviors that might not normally be considered "addictive" at all. In each case, the aim is to prevent relapse, but like *relapse* the word *prevention* can mean different things. Thus, for example, a program of relapse prevention might be considered successful in the short term if it results in a reduction of the severity or frequency of relapse, even if it does not result in complete elimination of addictive behavior. On the other hand, another program of treatment might achieve complete abstinence in a larger proportion of clients but no reduction at all in those who are not abstinent.

Relapse prevention usually involves training clients in techniques that they will find useful in preventing or eliminating relapse. It is thus, in a sense, a form of "self-help" or self-regulation. However, it is not limited specifically to the realm of addictive behavior. There is reason to believe that overall lifestyle has an important part to play in the maintenance or elimination of addictive behavior; and so relapse prevention can legitimately address itself to matters such as spirituality, diet, exercise, and recreation, as well as to specific issues narrowly concerned with the addictive behavior itself. Furthermore, relapse prevention might involve prescription of pharmacological agents such as acamprosate or naltrexone, which can play a role in supporting or augmenting psychological treatments by reducing the urge or craving to use (Franck & Jayaram-Lindstrom, 2013).

Relapse prevention might, ideally, completely remove the underlying causes of addictive behavior. However, in practice it is focused specifically upon the addictive behavior itself. A good outcome is thus defined purely in terms of an observed change in addictive behavior, and not on the basis of hypothesized or actual underlying factors. This is not to say that such considerations are unimportant, but simply that they are not an essential or distinctive component of this approach to treatment. Relapse prevention is sometimes employed in treatment settings where attention to such factors is considered vital; in other cases, it is employed as part of a purely behavioral approach, where observable behavior alone is the criterion of success.

While we are mindful of all these various meanings of the term *relapse prevention*, we will use it here to refer primarily to approaches to the recovery from addictive disorders, which may be taught or learned, with the objective of reducing the frequency and/or severity of relapse. The best possible outcome, of course, is that relapse prevention leads to a total elimination of relapse. However, no treatment for addictive disorders results in a 100% improvement for all clients. Relapse prevention allows the possibility of a degree of success even where there is not total success. More importantly, it allows the possibility that at least some failures (notably "lapses") can be learning experiences that predict a better outcome in the longer term.

RELAPSE PREVENTION MODEL

The Relapse Prevention (RP) model (Marlatt & Gordon, 1985; Hendershot, Witkiewitz, George, & Marlatt, 2011; Donovan & Witkiewitz, 2012) is one of the most well-known models used to prevent or manage relapse. It is an approach based upon cognitive-behavioral theory and includes aspects of social learning theory. This model has evolved over time, and its proponents describe the relapse process as a complex, multidimensional system (Witkiewitz & Marlatt, 2004).

Counselors using the RP model are interested in understanding the factors that influence an individual to remain abstinent or to relapse. These include both intrapersonal and interpersonal factors. Intrapersonal factors include self-efficacy, outcome expectancies, craving, level of motivation, coping ability, and emotional states. Interpersonal factors involve social support, or the amount of emotional support available to the individual in treatment (Witkiewitz & Marlatt, 2004).

Self-Efficacy

Self-efficacy is defined as the degree to which a person feels capable and competent of being successful in a specific situation (Bandura, 1977). This belief in one's ability is context specific and often derived from past successes in a similar situation. Self-efficacy level and rate of relapse are strongly related. If clients experience a lapse, their self-efficacy begins to fluctuate, and they have an increased risk of a full-blown relapse (Shiffman et al., 2000). However, if individuals maintain abstinence (e.g., success in smoking cessation), their self-efficacy increases (Gwaltney, Metrik, Kahler, & Shiffman, 2009).

Melanie was beginning a smoking cessation program. This was her third attempt to quit smoking. She expressed a high level of self-efficacy when discussing her ability to abstain from smoking while she was at work. She knew strategies that helped her resist the urge to smoke on her job, and had successfully used these strategies during the first two attempts. However, she had not been successful in refraining from smoking while out with friends. In this circumstance, she expressed a low level of self-efficacy. What strategies could the counselor use to help Melanie increase self-efficacy for not smoking while out with friends?

Outcome Expectancies

Outcome expectancy refers to the client's beliefs or thoughts about what is going to happen after using a substance. A positive outcome expectancy is associated with increased relapse rates because the individual anticipates positive consequences from the drug use.

Tyler is a college freshman receiving counseling for anxiety and drug abuse. He believes that drinking a couple of six packs of beer will result in him being more popular at the fraternity party because he will have less anxiety. This positive outcome expectancy results in Tyler's lapse. The counselor is hoping to assist Tyler in developing a negative outcome expectancy to increase the likelihood of him remaining abstinent. How could the counselor use cognitive behavioral therapy in this process?

Have you experienced the urge to smoke while trying on a bathing suit? These two events have actually been linked! Because body dissatisfaction leads to negative feelings, young women have the urge to smoke. These women believe that they will lose weight if they smoke and therefore feel better about themselves in a bathing suit (a positive outcome expectancy), which increases the likelihood of relapse (Lopez, Drobes, Thompson, & Brandon, 2008).

Craving

Cravings refer to physiological responses that prepare the individual for the effect of a substance. When an addict is deprived of the substance (during abstinence) and is subject to cue exposure (e.g., seeing a beer advertisement), the individual will experience a craving and this may lead to relapse (Schneekloth et al., 2012). If the person believes that the beer is readily available, this increases the craving (Wertz & Sayette, 2001). However, high self-efficacy and effective coping strategies can be the "braking mechanism" to prevent relapse (Niaura, 2000).

Coping

Coping skills refer to strategies that help individuals to effectively manage their behavior, especially in high-risk situations. Many types of coping strategies are used in the field of substance abuse counseling. Behavioral approaches, such as meditation and deep breathing exercises, and cognitive coping strategies, such as mindfulness and self-talk, have proven to be effective in lowering relapse rates for substance abuse.

One of your best coping strategies is your ability to self-regulate. But can your self-regulation "muscle" get tired (Baumeister, Heatherton, & Tice, 1994)? If you've been under a lot of stress, resulting in overuse of self-control resources, your self-regulation muscle may become exhausted. This fatigue leads to using more ineffective coping strategies, such as drinking more.

Motivation

The level of motivation a person has to change a behavior is one of the most important factors in the efficacy of treatment. The transtheoretical model of motivation (Prochaska & DiClemente, 1984; Norcross, Krebs, & Prochaska 2011) described five stages of readiness to change: Precontemplation, Contemplation, Preparation, Action, and Maintenance. Each stage represents an increase in motivation and readiness to follow through with the change process. Although this model describes a linear progression, there are usually many backward slides as well as forward movement. Levels of motivation depend upon positive and negative reinforcement and can be influenced by situations, life events, moods, social pressure, and numerous other variables.

Think of a time when you've tried to change a behavior. Maybe you're attempting to eliminate junk food from your diet. Did you experience a linear movement from early motivation to reaching your goal? Probably not! Most of us are affected by daily moods, unexpected life events, and changes in our confidence level. So you may have carried out your plan and had no junk food for a few days—then you had a conflict with your boss. After a few days of chips and candy, you re-evaluate and go back to the planning stage!

Emotional States

Both positive and negative feelings have been identified as major reasons for drug use, but negative feelings are thought to be the primary motive. An individual's abstinence self-efficacy, or the confidence in oneself to remain sober, is lowest when the person is experiencing emotions such as sadness, anger, anxiety, or regret. Most clients will experience shame and remorse, which are triggers for relapse. Negative affect has been specifically linked with lapses in alcohol use (Witkiewitz & Villarroel, 2009).

It seems as though traumatic events and disasters are linked to early relapse rates. Following the September 11 tragedy, early relapse rates were reported among smokers attempting to quit. The use of other substances increased also. Similar behaviors were found after the Oklahoma City bombing. The increased levels of smoking were associated to higher stress levels, worry about safety, and post-traumatic grief (Forman-Hoffman, Riley, & Pici, 2005).

Social Support

In substance abuse counseling, the importance of social support for abstinence cannot be downplayed. Social support can be both positive and negative. Families, spouses, and friends can provide a positive, supportive system that can improve the client's level of self-efficacy and negative mood.

However, it is often difficult for a client's family and friends to stay supportive through numerous relapses and subsequent pain and distress. When clients are successful in minimizing negative support, they are more likely to maintain sobriety (Lawhon, Humfleet, Hall, Reus, & Munoz, 2009).

The Value of One—It Can Go Either Way!

The importance of a supportive social network cannot be emphasized enough! Being involved with others and receiving high levels of support from even **one** person prior to treatment leads to better outcomes. But drinkers' social networks include many other drinkers, and having even **one** person in the social network who drinks increases the risk of relapse (Havassy, Hall, & Wasserman, 1991).

Substance abuse counselors have found that clients are more likely to lapse or relapse immediately following treatment. But over time, the recovering individuals have a tendency to relapse less as they learn coping strategies and increase their self-efficacy. To help a client stabilize and maintain sobriety, counselors need to be familiar with some common issues. Three of these essential elements in the RP model are (1) high-risk situations, (2) seemingly irrelevant decisions, and (3) the abstinence violation effect.

HIGH-RISK SITUATIONS

At the heart of relapse prevention therapy is the observation that for every addict certain identifiable sets of circumstances present a high risk of relapse. These high-risk situations (HRSs) are key events in relapse, which may pose a threat to one's level of confidence about exercising self-control (Marlatt & Gordon, 1985). The better able a client is to identify his or her own HRSs and to prepare in advance a repertoire of coping strategies designed to manage them without relapse, the more likely he or she is to achieve a good outcome. Marlatt and Gordon (1980) report that most relapses were associated with three kinds of HRS: (1) frustration and anger, (2) interpersonal temptation, and (3) social pressure.

Clients often recognize that they are more likely to drink when feeling negative emotions—anxiety, depression, etc.—but often overlook the fact that emotional highs can also be a problem. One of the coauthors of this chapter (CCHC), engaged in a research follow-up of clients from a 12-step treatment program some years ago, encountered the case of an alcoholic who had been abstinent for a year or more but who died from acute alcoholic poisoning on the night of his first and only relapse of drinking. The relapse was precipitated by his desire to celebrate success in clinching an important business deal. This idea seems to echo the words of Dr. William Silkworth, author of "The Doctor's Opinion" in *Alcoholics Anonymous*. "I have had many men who had, for example, worked a period of months on some . . . business deal which was to be settled on a certain date, favorably to them. They took a drink a day or so prior to the date, and then the phenomenon of craving at once became paramount to all other interests so that the important appointment was not met. These men were not drinking to escape; they were drinking to overcome a craving beyond their mental control" (*Alcoholics Anonymous*, 2001, pp. xxvii–xxviii).

Counselors who work with teens may think that an increase in substance abuse is due to conflict with adults or peers, or strong negative emotions. However, a recent study has shown that over two-thirds of adolescents relapse when they are trying to enhance a positive emotional state. In other words, teens use drugs and alcohol in an attempt to increase an already elated mood (Ramo & Brown, 2008).

Interpersonal temptation due to conflict is often recognized as preceding relapse but is easily used by addicts as a way of blaming others for their plight. In relapse prevention therapy, this is understood as being an HRS, in which the client is responsible for putting into effect previously planned coping strategies as ways to manage anger, rejection, or conflict without relapse.

Social pressures to drink are often subtle and are pervasive in Western society. However, within given subcultures there are countless pressures to use other drugs, to engage in gambling, overeating, spending beyond personal means, and a variety of other potentially addictive behaviors. Once these pressures are recognized for what they are, it is possible to plan in advance how they will be managed. Many relapses occur simply because addicts do not plan ahead but allow themselves to be caught unawares. As most of us are not able to think up a convincing alternative plan of action at a moment's notice, a long-reinforced and familiar pattern of addictive behavior becomes the inevitable outcome for anyone being pressured to conform to social pressure to drink or use drugs or to engage in other patterns of addictive behavior. This is especially true where friends, family, or respected authority figures exert the social pressure.

Rachel had successfully abstained from drinking for 3 months but was now dreading going home for the holidays. She explained to the counselor that alcohol was at the center of much of her family's celebration. During counseling sessions, she detailed all of the situations in which she might feel pressured to drink. She and the counselor brainstormed refusal skills and rehearsed behavioral strategies, such as always having a drink (soft drink) in her hand. What other behavioral strategies could the counselor use with Rachel to help her maintain sobriety?

Relapse prevention therapy begins by assisting a client to identify his or her own HRSs. Keeping a diary of emotional states, social interactions, cravings, and lapses/relapses can assist in this process. A variety of questionnaires are also available to help with this process, such as the Inventory of Drinking Situations (Annis, 1982). Having identified the HRSs that are most difficult for a particular individual to manage, it is then important to consider what the habitual coping strategies for handling these situations might be. Clearly, addictive behavior (drinking, drug use, etc.) is likely to be the predominant pretreatment response. However, other coping strategies a client has used may be ineffective and thus unlikely to help prevent relapse.

Specific coping strategies must then be considered, planned, and implemented. This process begins with brainstorming—either individually or as part of a group—about what kinds of strategies might be possible for each HRS. After generating a list of as many possible coping strategies as can be imagined, the counselor should assist the client in the process of refining, modifying, combining, and improving upon a selected number of coping strategies. Ideally, these are then rehearsed. For example, there is much to be gained from encouraging alcoholics to role-play drink-refusal skills. The benefit is even greater if the role-plays are videotaped and played back, with discussion of how the client managed the situation. Alcoholics also benefit from recognizing the ploys that have been used by others to persuade them to join in with "social" drinking. Helpful suggestions in preparing for HRSs include the following:

1. Be aware of intrapersonal triggers (thought patterns and related emotions) that lead one to substance abuse (e.g., expectations, anger, fear, resentment, irritation, frustration, disappointment, shame, etc.).
2. Use mnemonic devices to remember countermeasures in a plan of action.

3. Acquire a system of markers (emotional barometers) that will engage the memory to prompt the recall of an action plan.
4. Develop a back-up plan to diffuse emotions, utilizing resources, people, and activities.
5. Use multiple methods of stress relief; specifically, nonaddictive, healthy alternatives such as developing hobbies, meditation, relaxation, and physical exercise.

Have you surfed recently? A group of college students interested in decreasing their smoking habits were encouraged to do some "urge-surfing." If you want to try this, first think of specific urges you experience for an unwanted habit or behavior. Then picture the urges as waves, and imagine riding these waves as they naturally ebb and flow, rather than fighting the urge or giving in to it (Bowen & Marlatt, 2009).

Annis and Davis (1991) offered one of the more comprehensive relapse prevention models. This model, which is designed to initiate and maintain changes in drinking behavior, focuses on building confidence in one's ability and promoting self-efficacy. Procedures for this model include:

1. Develop a hierarchy of substance-abuse risk situations.
2. Identify strengths and resources in the environment and cope with affective, behavioral, and cognitive issues.
3. Design homework assignments by which the client is able to (a) monitor thoughts and feelings in specific situations, (b) anticipate problematic situations, (c) rehearse alternative responses to drinking, (d) practice new behaviors within the more difficult situations, and (e) reflect on personal progress and increased levels of competence.

Counselors need to keep in mind specific risk factors that can influence whether or not a person will be successful in maintaining sobriety in the face of HRSs. These factors include stressful life events, the loss of family/social support, acute psychological distress, situational threats to self-efficacy, and both positive and negative emotions. Also, some clients have a greater potential for relapse due to a family history of alcoholism or drug addiction, the nature and severity of the addiction, and comorbid psychiatric and substance abuse diagnoses (Donovan, 1996; Shiffman, 1989).

SEEMINGLY IRRELEVANT DECISIONS (SIDs)

High-risk situations are not simply circumstances imposed by other people or the social environment. Sometimes they are the result of an individual's thought processes. These thought processes are varied and diverse, and a comprehensive account is not possible here. Where thinking errors and psychological "traps" appear to be a prominent cause of relapse, there may be benefit in gaining specialist help in the form of cognitive therapy. On the other hand, there is much wisdom as to how such processes operate within the world of 12-step groups such as AA. Research in maintenance and relapse prevention indicates that multimodal treatment, along with attendance in a 12-step program, offers the best chance for long-term recovery and abstinence (Inaba & Cohen, 2000). Quite often the 12-step groups will prove to be more accessible and, as they come with the voice of personal experience, advice given there will be listened to more seriously than that offered by the professional counselor with no personal experience.

"Seemingly irrelevant decisions," or SIDs (also known as "set-ups"), are decisions an individual makes that may seem irrelevant at the time, but very often can lead to a relapse. SIDs are perhaps best illustrated by way of an example.

It was a fine day, and John had finished work early after receiving a highly positive annual appraisal from his boss. He decided to walk home from work. He varied his usual route so as to stroll through the local park, enjoying the warm sun, the trees in blossom, and the sounds of children playing ball. He felt good about life, and his days of alcoholic drinking seemed far away. As he walked out of the park he passed a bar where he used to drink. Knowing that he did not want to drink anymore, but remembering that his old friends would be wondering what had happened to him, he went in to see how they all were "just for old time's sake." Once there, they ignored his pleas that he no longer drank alcohol and bought him a "proper man's drink." Telling him they were angry he hadn't called on them for weeks, they said that they'd let bygones be bygones if only he joined them for "just one drink." Telling himself that there was nothing else he could do under the circumstances, John gave in. Within only a few hours the barman refused to serve him any more on grounds of his obviously drunken behavior. When he got home, his wife was also angry, so he knew that he had "no choice" but to go to the home of another of his drinking friends, where he spent the night consuming yet more alcohol.

Decisions to walk home rather than take a bus, or to choose one route rather than another, are "seemingly irrelevant" to the mental processes of alcoholism. However, with hindsight, such decisions can set in motion an inexorable process of movement toward a relapse due to environmental triggers. Such relapses are often later viewed as "unavoidable." After all, what could John do once he was back in the bar, with all his old friends insisting that he drank alcohol?

Much of what has been said earlier is relevant to this example. John could have been aware that his feelings of well-being and success were as much an HRS as any disappointment in life. Had he also rehearsed a range of realistic strategies with which to resist pressures from his drinking friends, he might have been more likely to emerge from the bar without having had a drink. More importantly, he might have recognized that simply going into the bar was an extremely bad idea in the first place. However, the overall problem here was that an unconscious chain of decisions was being forged that made relapse almost inevitable. Because the decisions were seemingly irrelevant, and because their true purpose was partly or completely unconscious, John was able to argue that events had caught him off guard. However, having once recognized such patterns of decision making (and most addicts are readily able to think of examples), it becomes extremely difficult to continue engaging in them without making conscious decisions. Once the process has become conscious, SIDs lose much of their power and the client can bring relapse prevention strategies into play.

THE ABSTINENCE VIOLATION EFFECT

One more psychological trap is worthy of mention here, if only because of the controversy it engenders among counselors and clients alike. The basis of this trap is that once human beings have set themselves a rule there seems to be an irresistible temptation to break the rule. Quite apart from the spiritual implications of this, and the responses to it offered by the world's major faith traditions, this observation has important psychological implications for the addictive process. This process is known as the *abstinence violation effect* (Marlatt & George, 1984).

The trap can present itself in various ways. The most common, and simplest, is that minor infringements of the rule are taken as a justifiable basis for major infringements. Thus, if Jenny has decided to stick to a diet in which she will not eat cake or candy, and if she finds herself forgetfully accepting a slice of birthday cake at a friend's celebration, she will then decide to go home and binge on cake and candy, because she has already failed. The rule has been broken, so she may as well enjoy breaking it to the full. Of course, in reality, if this is the first piece of cake that Jenny has had for a month she has not failed at all—she is doing enormously well. But, psychologically, she feels as though she has failed and so there is no longer any point in trying to adhere to the rule.

There are many more subtle manifestations of this psychological trap, but the general feature seems to be the transition from seeing the rule as being set by oneself for one's own good, to seeing it as imposed externally in some way and for its own sake (or for someone else's benefit). Circumstances are thus engineered whereby breaking the rule appears to be permissible, or breaking the rule a lot is seen to be no worse than breaking it a little.

From the perspective of relapse prevention, the important consideration is that small violations of the rule ("lapses") need not inevitably progress to major violations ("relapses"). Coping strategies can be learned that prevent this progression, and over a period of time, make the behavior manageable. But herein lies the problem: other approaches to addiction therapy emphasize the unmanageability of addictive behavior. Step 1 of the 12 steps of AA states, "We admitted we were powerless over alcohol—that our lives had become unmanageable." (Members of AA are often reminded that "one drink makes one drunk.") The reinforcement of this message of powerlessness is thus criticized by some counselors as making relapse after only a single drink an inevitability, for alcoholics no longer have any reason at all to control their behavior, or any grounds for believing that they might be able to control their drinking if they tried. Alcoholism is a lack of ability to control drinking, and therefore one drink will lead immediately, inevitably, and inexorably back to alcoholic drinking.

It is not possible to review the merits and demerits of these two positions here in full detail. However, some observations are important. First, if clients are involved in relapse prevention therapy based on a model of the psychology of learned behavior, as well as being engaged in a self-help program of recovery, it is better to talk about these apparent conflicts rather than pretend they do not exist. Second, there is not necessarily as much of a conflict as might first appear. Many members of AA, having had a relatively minor "slip," have gone to an AA meeting, or have sought help from their sponsor, and have found help that has prevented the "inevitable" relapse. Equally, a "slip" or "lapse," perhaps following a series of SIDs, can itself present an HRS that was better avoided in the first place—even according to relapse prevention theory. There is much wisdom in both traditions. Third, and finally, when planning relapse prevention therapy counselors should remember that people are all different. What might be possible for one might not be possible for another. However, admitting the impossibility of a certain set of circumstances inevitably presents the risk that when those circumstances are encountered no effort will be made to overcome them.

LIFESTYLE CHANGE

A key issue for many people with addictive disorders is that of imbalance in lifestyle. The dependence syndrome is characterized by salience—a phenomenon that involves the object of addiction assuming greater significance, and occupying more time in life, than it should. This has sometimes devastating consequences. Relationships, work, ethical standards, leisure activities, diet, sleep, health, values, spirituality, and other aspects of life may suffer. However, one way or another, the use of time and energy become seriously distorted, with more attention being given to engaging in (and defending) addictive behavior and less time being given to other things and people than is conducive to well-being.

Sometimes the lifestyle imbalance may result from the addiction. Sometimes it may contribute to it. Unemployment, for example, may be a consequence of drinking at work, or of the impaired ability to fulfill obligations at work as a consequence of drinking at other times. However, unemployment may also be one of the contributory stresses around which heavier drinking develops, or may simply allow more time for drinking. Teasing out these cause and effect relationships is rarely productive in practice. What is clear is that a more balanced lifestyle will require less time drinking and more time devoted to constructive activity (such as job seeking or volunteer work if paid employment is not an option). Practical measures to evaluate and change use of time may therefore be very important as a part of an overall relapse prevention strategy.

A useful exercise can sometimes be the exploration of how an addicted person approaches the "shoulds" and "wants" of life. Often it will be found that much time is devoted to one at the expense of the other. Thus, obligations are prioritized, with relentless disregard for leisure time and personal well-being, until the point is reached at which a relapse is inevitable (because drinking is the only habitual coping strategy employed to deal with the stress that this imbalance generates). Or else, a self-indulgent lifestyle is pursued with equally relentless disregard for relationships or social obligations. Within such a lifestyle, drinking (or other addictive behavior) usually features prominently. If it does not, it soon emerges as a consequence of the lack of structure and discipline that such a lifestyle entails.

A 60-year-old male, Stanley, sought counseling after he was forced to take early retirement from a powerful state position. He was currently spending his days idle, remembering the importance of his life only a short time ago. He described his life after retirement as lonely and boring, and he felt useless and depressed. He realized he had a drinking problem when he "washed down breakfast with a beer" soon after his wife left for work each morning and spent his time finding "creative hiding places" for his liquor. He began attending a 12-step program and did well in the beginning (the meetings gave him a new focus) but relapsed after 6 months of sobriety. What lifestyle changes may have affected Stanley's initial drinking and relapse? What changes do you think would benefit him?

Exploration of lifestyle issues usually gets to the heart of what matters to people. How they spend their time, and what they devote their energy to, is usually a reflection of important desires and priorities in life. Once identified, these can provide motivational levers to enable change. For example, a desire to maintain custody of a child may provide motivation to comply with a court-mandated addiction treatment program. However, they also point to core beliefs and priorities that, explicitly or implicitly, are spiritual and/or religious. Identification of these core beliefs and priorities can help in regaining perspective and in identifying a treatment approach that will address the spiritual, as well as the psychological, social, and physical aspects of the addictive disorder. This may entail a 12-step treatment program (see Chapter 12) or a religious program, or it may be a reconnection with religious roots that occurs alongside engagement with a secular treatment program of some kind (Cook, 2009, 2010), or it might involve adoption of a spiritual practice such as mindfulness to support relapse prevention (Mason-John & Groves, 2013; Witkiewitz, Bowen, Douglas, & Hsu, 2013; Witkiewitz, Lustyk, & Bowen, 2013). It is therefore important that counselors are able to facilitate discussion of spiritual and religious matters in an affirming manner, without either proselytizing or undermining healthy religious beliefs that may be different than their own. On the other hand, some kinds of "pathological" spirituality (e.g., associated with extreme cults or with an addictive pattern of religious behavior) may need gentle challenging (Crowley & Jenkinson, 2009). The balance requires wisdom and a nonjudgmental willingness to explore spirituality from the perspective of what may be in the client's best interests.

DEVELOPING A MANAGEMENT PLAN

There are various ways in which relapse prevention might be incorporated into an overall management plan. Among these, the 9-step approach utilized by Terence Gorski (2003) is helpful:

1. **Stabilization:** Following detoxification, at least a few days of sobriety are wise, and it is important not to rush in too quickly with much new material that patients will not be able to retain in the immediate postdetoxification period.
2. **Assessment:** This will be a full assessment of psychological, social, physical, and spiritual issues pertinent to treatment and recovery, according to usual professional practice. However, Gorski especially emphasizes the need for a life history of alcohol/drug use, including the history of past episodes of recovery and relapse.
3. **Relapse Education:** This is the point at which information about the nature of lapse and relapse is provided. Gorski recommends involving family and friends, as well as 12-step sponsors, at this stage.
4. **Identify Warning Signs:** Relapse is often preceded by warning signs that can be identified and that can thus allow early intervention and relapse prevention. These signs will be closely related to understanding the nature and identity of HRSs for each client.
5. **Identify Problem Solving Strategies:** Each identifiable warning sign or HRS should be the focus for identifying a range of coping strategies that will enable coping without alcohol/drug use.
6. **Recovery Planning:** A plan for recovery can now be identified that will include appropriate support groups, professional help, workplace support, engagement with 12-step programs and all other resources that can reinforce and support relapse prevention.
7. **Inventory Training:** It can be helpful for the client/patient to have a regular time each morning and/or evening in which to identify and plan for management of HRSs that have emerged, or might emerge, during a 24-hour period.
8. **Family Involvement:** Family can be involved in relapse prevention in various ways, but this might be a point at which to encourage involvement in Al-Anon, Families Anonymous, or other 12-step fellowships for families.
9. **Follow-up:** Gorski recommends regular review and updating of the treatment plan: monthly for 3 months, quarterly for 2 years, and annually thereafter.

CASE STUDY OF RELAPSE PREVENTION

The latter section of this chapter presents a case study utilizing principles of maintenance and relapse prevention. Both the biopsychosocial model (disease model) and the cognitive-social learning model are used to provide interventions from a multimodal perspective. Although some strategies are associated to a larger extent with a particular model, the necessary strategies for relapse prevention are very similar. These models take into consideration the biological, psychological, and social aspects of substance abuse and use a wide range of counseling techniques to minimize the possibility of relapse. The interventions rely heavily on techniques from behavioral, cognitive, and social learning theories, as well as addressing the client's physical health and well-being (Chiauzzi, 1991).

The client for this case study is Thomas, a 27-year-old male currently employed as a salesman, who is married and the father of a 2-year-old daughter. Thomas enters counseling when he realizes his life is out of control. His wife has threatened to leave him, he cannot keep a job for longer than a few months, and his angry outbursts have become more frequent. He has had a couple of anxiety attacks in recent months and has begun to consider suicide, thinking that life is not worth living.

Thomas reports that he has been consuming alcohol since high school. He reports drinking approximately a case of beer daily, the amount depending on his stress level. He often switches to bourbon and spends many weekends with his friends in a drunken state. His dependency on alcohol consumption has become more self-evident as the consequences of his drinking have become increasingly serious.

Thomas's initial treatment to stabilize his condition included several visits to his physician to regulate antianxiety and antidepressant medications. During therapy, he is taught the importance of remaining on these medications and following the prescribed dosage. With Thomas's previous history of anxiety and depression, maintaining sobriety may be partially dependent upon his consistent use of these medications.

In the recovery phase, after withdrawal and stabilization, the relapse prevention counselor has several treatment goals. First of all, Thomas needs to be able to identify HRSs; he must then develop strategies to cope with these situations. Also, the counselor must help Thomas identify (and possibly establish) support systems. These may include positive social support networks such as AA, church, supportive friends, and family members. Additional goals include learning about the nature of addictions, and identifying and managing warning signs of relapse. Finally, goals must include exploration of multisystemic issues related to Thomas's life—his relationships, environment, health, recreation, and family—and an evaluation of where positive change is needed.

Self-Assessment of HRSs

Initially, Thomas is taught to self-monitor HRSs. He is instructed to keep track of when, where, and why he wants to use alcohol. Thomas is given a chart on which he can track the risky situations, his thoughts and feelings at the time he has urges, and the coping strategies he uses to avoid substance use or to limit the amount consumed. Because substance use becomes habitualized after years of use and seems to be an automatic response, the self-monitoring strategy forces him to be consciously aware of his actions (Marlatt & Gordon, 1985).

When Thomas meets with his counselor, they use the chart as both an assessment tool and an intervention strategy. After examining the chart together, the counselor helps Thomas to see that the cues are centered mostly on stressful events, such as pressure to meet a quota on his sales job or a difficult argument with his wife. Thomas believes he deserves a reward (in the form of a drink) for making it through the situation, or that he must have a drink to relieve the stress. He is experiencing severe anxiety regarding his wife's threats to leave him and thinks a drink will help relieve his stress and give him more courage. His feelings often include nervousness, anger, or disappointment.

Self-Monitoring Chart

Date	Time	Situation	Thought(s)	Feeling(s)	Action
June 1	8:30 AM	Late for work; boss seems agitated	I'm probably going to get fired; he always seems down on me. I need a drink.	Anxiety and disappointment in self	Get prepared for first client.
June 1	5:30 PM	Driving for 1½ hours in traffic	I am so mad at those stupid drivers. I deserve a drink when I get home. What a day!	Anger, frustration	Listen to upbeat music.
June 6	7:30 PM	Confrontation with wife	I don't know what I'll do if she leaves me. I won't be able to go on. If I could only have a drink, I would have more confidence to convince her to stay.	Sadness, desperation	Go outside, walk around, and prepare what to say.

Coping Strategies

The self-monitoring chart also helps Thomas become aware of the critical times when he makes a decision to drink and the alternative responses that help him resist. Thomas and his counselor brainstorm alternative behaviors for different HRSs and together determine several effective coping strategies for each. During future sessions, the counselor sets up a variety of situations and has Thomas rehearse these strategies.

For example, Thomas becomes aware that the stress of driving in rush-hour traffic usually results in an overwhelming urge to have a drink. After brainstorming alternatives, Thomas realizes that he could use this time to unwind after his work by listening to music that produces a good mood. In addition, his counselor helps him to recognize his dysfunctional thinking during this situation. He has a tendency to blame the other drivers ("He cut me off on purpose. These stupid drivers need to get out of my way"), which increases his stress. He is helped to change to a healthier, less stress-inducing way of thinking, such as "All the drivers are trying to get home just like me. They didn't single me out to cut off." Thomas practices these strategies during counseling sessions by visualizing driving in traffic, listening to upbeat music, and thinking the more rational thoughts. This process teaches him to recognize his triggers, develop coping strategies, and use cognitive-behavioral techniques to change his dysfunctional thinking to minimize relapse (Gorski, 1993).

Lapse and Relapse Prevention Techniques

Also during the initial stage, the counselor teaches Thomas about lapses (single episode of use) and relapses (return to uncontrolled use). Although told that lapses and relapses are common, he is encouraged to use the knowledge gained from lapses to identify precipitating events and better coping strategies. In this way, lapses are reframed as learning experiences that can help prevent relapses. This view reduces the guilt, anxiety, and doubt that are often felt after a lapse and eliminates any moral injunctions against the client (Lewis, Dana, & Blevins, 1994).

The reframing of lapses as a learning experience can also help Thomas to dispute the "all or nothing" belief. Many times people with addictive behaviors have the irrational belief that if they slip one time then their situation is hopeless and they might as well give up, which leads to a total relapse. This was referred to previously as the abstinence violation effect (AVE), where the client believes that absolute abstinence and complete loss of control are the only options. When viewing lapses as a normal part of the recovery process from which he can learn, Thomas realizes that he can regain control. This sense of control then leads to self-efficacy, enabling him to believe that he can have control in similar future situations.

At this time, the counselor provides several strategies to help in reducing lapses. Thomas is given a therapeutic contract to sign, which states that he agrees to leave the situation when a lapse occurs (Marlatt, 1985). This gives him a "time out" and limits the extent of alcohol use at the time of the lapse. Also, the counselor and Thomas work together to construct reminder cards of specific steps to take, as well as a list of support people to call (including their phone numbers). The cards may also include positive statements, such as "Remember, you are in control," "This slip is not a catastrophe. You can stop now if you choose," and "Visualize yourself in control." Thomas commits to using these strategies immediately following a lapse.

A counseling session soon follows, during which Thomas reports a lapse and describes the situation. He describes his week as having been extremely difficult, with problems at work as well as a major argument with his wife. He left his house Saturday morning, still angry after the disagreement on Friday evening, and decided to visit one of his friends. Thomas admits knowing this was a dangerous thing to do as the friend was one of his "drinking buddies." He states that his feelings of anger and frustration were overwhelming and "it just didn't matter." After a few beers, while Thomas was alone in the restroom, he remembered the card. He read the positive reminders and remembered the long-term versus the short-term consequences of drinking. He thought about the consequence of possibly losing his wife if he continued to drink and remembered the contract he had signed to leave immediately after the lapse. Thomas then told his friend one of his rehearsed excuses and made a quick exit. At the end of the session, the counselor helps Thomas to explore what he learned from this event and encourages feelings of self-efficacy.

Afterward, the counselor examines the situation for treatment gaps. She realizes that Thomas needs more work in handling negative emotions. During subsequent sessions, they return to the brainstorming stage so that he can learn (or be reminded of) coping strategies to use when he is angry, agitated, or depressed. Also, his support system is re-examined to determine the best person or group to go to for help when he is experiencing intense emotions.

Support Systems and Lifestyle Changes

Thomas and his counselor further examine his support system. Thomas has attended a 12-step program for several months, and although these meetings have provided him with a way to meet nonusing people, it is essential that he have a system of support outside the meetings. With a system of nonusing friends and family, the possibility of relapse is much less likely.

Thomas's wife has been supportive of him since he entered treatment and has attended a family treatment program independent of Thomas's program. Although emotionally disengaged in the beginning, she has made gains in reconnecting with Thomas, as she sees him showing a commitment to maintaining sobriety. Also, because Thomas reported that communication was a major problem in his marriage, he and his counselor have worked on developing skills and role-playing communication between him and his wife.

(It is important to mention here that although the involvement of the family is critical in relapse prevention, the process is not simple. The principle of family homeostasis must be considered when working with close family members. Central to this principle is the idea that when one member of the family experiences change, the other members will be affected and adjust in some manner [Jackson, 1957]. Boundaries, roles, and rules will need to be reorganized to establish a new sense of balance.)

Thomas's wife had taken on the role of main provider and was seen as the strong person in the family. Emotional roles were present, also, with Thomas being the angry one and his wife being the sullen, stoic one. Rules revolved around communication and sexual activity. Since Thomas's wife had become emotionally disengaged, she limited both communication and sex with him so as to avoid any sense of intimacy. As Thomas practiced sobriety and the will to be committed to his program, his wife was able to gradually become somewhat more open to both communication and sexual activity. However, the fear of being hurt again continues to cause her to withhold herself to some extent.

The issue of having a system of nonusing friends is important to Thomas not only for support but for companionship in recreational activities. Because Thomas's drinking has taken precedence the past few years, his only friends have been his drinking friends, and he has cultivated little interest in any activities outside of work. The counselor helps Thomas to establish a list of activities he thinks he would enjoy and would like to pursue. At the top of his list is working out at the gym. Since he and his wife have a family membership, he is able to begin right away and finds that working out actually produces a feeling of accomplishment and well-being. He establishes a friendship with a trainer who works at the gym, as well a couple of men who attend the gym at the same time.

These friendships provide social modeling for Thomas, who sees their interest in health and fitness as something he wishes to emulate. Social modeling can often be a strong motivator in changing individual behavior. Thomas perceives these individuals as having positive traits he wishes to acquire, and their personal encouragement helps him to develop an improved self-concept.

Along with the need to acquire healthy relationships and activities is the need to change old friends and unhealthy environments. This becomes an important focus during treatment. Thomas has several friends he refers to as his "drinking buddies" who often call and attempt to persuade him to meet them at their favorite bar. After an outing to the bar results in a 2-month relapse, Thomas realizes that he can no longer keep these friends and stay sober. During counseling, refusal skills are rehearsed, and Thomas and his counselor role-play different situations that Thomas previously encountered with his friends.

In addition, the counselor helps him explore other environments in which external cues prompt cravings and urges. He learns that being exposed to these cues often leads to a feeling of deprivation and an urge to use. Thomas is instructed by his counselor to determine which cues he can avoid, as well as which ones are more difficult or impossible to avoid. Social outings where others are drinking prove to be a major trigger, or cue, for Thomas. He learns that taking care of himself and maintaining his sobriety is his current priority and that he can decline these invitations without feeling guilty. The counselor also instructs him to remove as many cues as possible from his daily environment to decrease the frequency of his urges and cravings. One such change was as simple as taking a different route home from work so that he did not have to pass his favorite bar.

For unavoidable situations, Thomas is taught other strategies, including body awareness cues and mnemonic devices. Through body awareness techniques, he is able to identify the onset of physical urges to drink. The counselor has Thomas visualize a time when he feels a craving to drink and to give a detailed description of what is occurring in his body. He reports that he first feels his heart rate increase, then his hands start trembling and his mind begins to race. The counselor instructs Thomas to use the onset of these physical signs as a cue to identify an HRS.

At that time, the counselor explains the use of a mnemonic device, or memory aid, to help Thomas recall what he needs to do. An acrostic is given, using the word *STOP*. His instructions are to use each letter to evoke a reminder of his plan. *S* stands for *situation*—be aware of the high-risk situation; *T* stands for *think*—think about what I need to do; *O* is for *options*—recall the different options or strategies I've rehearsed for this situation; *P* is for *plan*—proceed with plan.

Other Lifestyle Changes

All areas in a client's life that could possibly lead to relapse need to be approached eventually during therapy. From the beginning, Thomas indicates that his job as a salesman is a major stressor. The pressure of having to reach a quota is often a cue for him to have a drink, and he thinks of himself as unsuccessful and inadequate. He and his counselor explore his options, and Thomas decides he needs to find work where he experiences less pressure. He finds an assistant manager position with a different company and, though he takes a salary cut, is relieved that he does not have the stress of meeting a quota.

Because of his employment record and past spending habits, Thomas has financial problems, leading to a huge amount of stress. For once in his life he is attempting to be responsible and remain sober, but creditors are harassing him and he has no money to pay for a broken furnace. Without financial assistance, the likelihood of a relapse is high. Thomas seeks help from his local bank; by consolidating his debt and getting a small loan, he feels capable of getting out from under his financial difficulties.

THE REALITY OF RELAPSE PREVENTION

When reading about the multitude of strategies and interventions involved in treatment of substance abuse, maintaining abstinence and preventing relapse may appear to be an overwhelming task. This chapter condenses a case study so that the interventions appear to be introduced at a rapid pace, but in actuality the case extends over many months. Although the counselor had a long list of the lifestyle changes needed to prevent relapse, these changes were prioritized and broken down into small, achievable steps.

To prevent clients from feeling overwhelmed, counselors must present the interventions at a pace at which clients can experience success and build self-efficacy. Realistic goals must be established, and the counselor has to be aware of the danger of having too many "shoulds" on the client's plate (Fisher & Harrison, 2000). Starting out slowly and finding a balance is important. The stress of clients trying to build their lives too quickly and taking on too much can lead to relapse. The "shoulds" need to be balanced with fun and pleasure. Feelings of resentment and shame are slowly replaced with gratitude and forgiveness (C. Wildroot, personal communication, January 12, 2010).

Counselors and therapists also need to recognize the challenges and complexities of working in this field and should be prepared for responding appropriately to the transference and countertransference issues that will arise. Sometimes, feelings of anger, frustration, inability to help, or even despair can be indicators of psychological issues projected by the client, and may provide important clues to how others close to the client (family, friends, colleagues) are also feeling. The best advice is always to have good supervisory support, whether as a treatment team or on a one-to-one basis, so that the counselor/therapist has space in which to reflect on these issues and respond constructively to them.

Summary and Some Final Notations

Relapse prevention and maintenance are complex and dynamic processes. All clients have their own individual risk factors. Multiple influences contribute to high-risk situations (HRSs)—years of dependence, family history, social support, comorbid psychopathology, and physiological states (physical withdrawal). Cognitive factors also affect the risk of relapse, including the abstinence violation effect, level of motivation, self-efficacy, and outcome expectancies. When a person relapses, there is probably not one single distinct cause but rather a multitude of internal and external factors (Marlatt & Gordon, 1985).

In the Relapse Prevention model, cognitive behavioral strategies are taught and practiced. Counselors help clients identify more effective coping strategies to use during HRSs. Relaxation skills and mindfulness meditation (Marlatt, 2002) are practiced, and lifestyle changes encouraged. A supportive social network is stressed.

When an individual relapses, the goal of relapse prevention is to lessen the length and severity of the relapse and to decrease the amount of time it takes for the client to stabilize and return to maintenance. An integrated, multifaceted approach (Knack, 2009) provides the tools for the most effective treatment in preventing relapse—including medication, 12-step programs, and cognitive-behavioral models. Although there is a high rate of relapse, the good news is that the longer clients maintain sobriety, the less likely they are to relapse.

MyCounselingLab

Visit the MyCounselingLab site for *Foundations of Addictions Counseling,* Third Edition to enhance your understanding of concepts. You'll have the opportunity to practice your skills through video- and case-based exercises. You will find sets of questions to help you prepare for your certification exam with *Licensure Quizzes.* There is also a Video Library that provides taped counseling sessions, ethical scenarios, and interviews with helpers and clients.

Useful Websites

The following websites provide additional information relating to chapter topics:

About.com: Alcoholism & Substance Abuse
alcoholism.about.com/od/relapse/Relapse_Prevention.htm

Dual Recovery Anonymous
www.draonline.org/relapse.html

Information for Individuals and Families
www.addictionsandrecovery.org

Website of Terence Gorski
www.tgorski.com/

References

Alcoholics Anonymous. (2001). New York, NY: Alcoholics Anonymous World Services, Inc.

Annis, H. (1982). *Inventory of drinking situations (IDS-TOO).* Toronto, Canada: Addiction Research Foundation of Ontario.

Annis, H., & Davis, C. (1991). Relapse prevention. *Alcohol Health & Research World, 15*(3), 204–212.

Bandura, A. (1977). Self-efficacy: Toward a unifying theory of behavioral change. *Psychological Review, 84,* 191–215.

Baumeister, R. F., Heatherton, T. F., & Tice, D. M. (1994). *Losing control: How and why people fail at self-regulation.* San Diego, CA: Academic Press.

Bowen, S., & Marlatt, A. (2009). Surfing the urge: Brief mindfulness-based intervention for college student smokers. *Psychology of Addictive Behaviors, 23*(4), 666–671.

Chiauzzi, E. J. (1991). *Preventing relapse in the addictions: A biopsychosocial approach.* New York, NY: Pergamon Press.

Cook, C. C. H. (2009). Substance misuse. In C. Cook, A. Powell, & A. Sims (Eds.), *Spirituality and psychiatry* (pp. 139–168). London, UK: Royal College of Psychiatrists Press.

Cook, C. (2010). Spiritual and religious issues in treatment. In E. J. Marshall, K. Humphreys, & D. M. Ball, (Eds.), *The treatment of drinking problems* (5th ed., pp. 227–235). Cambridge, UK: Cambridge University Press.

Crowley, N., & Jenkinson, G. (2009). Pathological spirituality. In C. Cook, A. Powell, & A. Sims (Eds.), *Spirituality & psychiatry* (pp. 254–272). London, UK: Royal College of Psychiatrists Press.

Donovan, D. M. (1996). Marlatt's classification of relapse precipitants: Is the emperor still wearing clothes? *Addiction, 91* (Suppl.), 131–137.

Donovan, D., & Witkiewitz, K. (2012). Relapse prevention: From radical idea to common practice. *Addiction Research & Theory, 20*, 204–217.

Doweiko, H. E. (1990). *Concepts of chemical dependency.* Pacific Grove, CA: Brooks/Cole.

Fisher, G. L., & Harrison, G. L. (2000). *Substance abuse: Information for school counselors, social workers, therapists, and counselors* (2nd ed.). Needham Heights, MA: Allyn & Bacon.

Forman-Hoffman, V., Riley, W., & Pici, M. (2005). Acute impact of the September 11 tragedy on smoking and early relapse rates among smokers attempting to quit. *Psychology of Addictive Behaviors, 19*(3), 277–283.

Franck, J., & Jayaram-Lindstrom, N. (2013). Pharmacotherapy for alcohol dependence: Status of current treatments. *Current Opinions in Neurobiology, 23*, 692–699.

Gorski, T. T. (1993). Relapse prevention: A state of the art overview. *Addiction & Recovery,* March/April, 25–27.

Gorski, T. T. (2003, May 28). How to develop a RP plan. Retrieved September 22, 2014, from http://www.tgorski.com/gorski_articles/developing_a_relapse_prevention_plan.htm

Gwaltney, C. J., Metrik, J., Kahler, C. W., & Shiffman, S. (2009). Self-efficacy and smoking cessation: A meta-analysis. *Psychology of Addictive Behaviors, 23*(1), 56–66.

Havassy, B. E., Hall, S. M., & Wasserman, D. A. (1991). Social support and relapse: Commonalities among alcoholics, opiate users, and cigarette smokers. *Addictive Behaviors, 16*, 235–246.

Hendershot, C. S., Witkiewitz, K., George, W. H., & Marlatt, G. A. (2011). Relapse prevention for addictive behaviors. *Substance Abuse Treatment, Prevention, and Policy, 6*, 17.

Inaba, D., & Cohen, W. (2000). *Uppers, downers, all arounders.* Ashland, OR: CNS Publications.

Jackson, D. D. (1957). The question of family homeostasis. *Psychiatric Quarterly Supplement, 31*, 79–90.

Knack, W. A. (2009). Psychotherapy and Alcoholics Anonymous: An integrated approach. *Journal of Psychotherapy Integration, 19*(1), 86–109.

Lawhon, D., Humfleet, G. L., Hall, S. M., Reus, V. I., & Munoz, R. F. (2009). Longitudinal analysis of abstinence-specific social support and smoking cessation. *Health Psychology, 28*(4), 465–472.

Lewis, J. A., Dana, R. Q., & Blevins, G. A. (1994). *Substance abuse counseling: An individualized approach* (2nd ed.). Pacific Grove, CA: Brooks/Cole Publishing.

Lopez, E. N., Drobes, D. J., Thompson, J. K., & Brandon, T. H. (2008). Effects of a body image challenge on smoking motivation among college females. *Health Psychology, 27*(Suppl. 3), 243–251.

Marlatt, G. A. (1985). Relapse prevention: Theoretical rationale and overview of the model. In G. A. Marlatt & J. R. Gordon (Eds.), *Relapse prevention: Maintenance strategies in the treatment of addictive behaviors* (pp. 3–70). New York, NY: Guilford Press.

Marlatt, G. A. (2002). Buddhist psychology and the treatment of addictive behavior. *Cognitive and Behavioral Practice, 9*, 44–49.

Marlatt, G., & George, W. (1984). Relapse prevention: Introduction and overview of the model. *British Journal of Addiction, 79*, 261–275.

Marlatt, G. A., & Gordon, J. R. (1980). Determinants of relapse: Implications of the maintenance of behavior change. In P. O. Davidson & S. M. Davidson (Eds.), *Behavioral medicine: Changing health lifestyle* (pp. 410–452). New York, NY: Brunner/Mazel.

Marlatt, G., & Gordon, J. (1985). *Relapse prevention.* New York, NY: Guilford Press.

Mason-John, V., & Groves, P. (2013). *Eight step recovery: Using the Buddha's teachings to overcome addiction.* Cambridge, UK: Windhorse.

National Institute on Drug Abuse. (n.d.). *Addiction science: From molecules to managed care* [Data file]. Available from National Institutes on Drug Abuse site, *http://www.drugabuse.gov/pubs/teaching/Teaching6/Teaching9.html*

Niaura, R. (2000). Cognitive social learning and related perspectives on drug craving. *Addiction, 95,* 155–164.

Norcross, J. C., Krebs, P. M., & Prochaska, J. O. (2011). Stages of change. *Journal of Clinical Psychology, 67,* 143–154.

Orford, J., & Edwards, G. (1977). *Alcoholism*. Oxford, UK: Oxford University Press.

Polich, J. M., Amour, D. J., & Braiker, H. B. (1981). *The course of alcoholism: Four years after treatment.* Report prepared for the National Institute on Alcohol Abuse and Alcoholism, U.S. Department of Health, Education, and Welfare. Santa Monica, CA: Rand Corporation.

Prochaska, J. O., & DiClemente, C. C. (1984). *The transtheoretical approach: Crossing the traditional boundaries of therapy.* Malabar, FL: Krieger.

Ramo, D. E., & Brown, S. A. (2008). Classes of substance abuse relapse situations: A comparison of adolescents and adults. *Psychology of Addictive Behaviors, 22*(3), 372–379.

Schneekloth, T. D., Biernacka, J. M., Hall-Flavin, D. K., Karpyak, V. M., Frye, M. A., Loukianova, L. L., Stevens, S. R., ..., Mrazek, D. A. (2012). Alcohol craving as a predictor of relapse. *American Journal of Addiction, 21*(Suppl 1), S20–S26.

Shiffman, S. (1989). Conceptual issues in the study of relapse. In M. Gossop (Ed.), *Relapse and addictive behavior* (pp. 149–179). London, UK: Routledge.

Shiffman, S., Balabanis, M., Paty, J., Engberg, J., Gwaltney, C., Liu, K., ..., Paton, S. M. (2000). Dynamic effects of self-efficacy on smoking lapse and relapse. *Health Psychology, 19,* 315–323.

Wertz, J. M., & Sayette, M. A. (2001). A review of the effects of perceived drug use opportunity on self-reported urge. *Experimental and Clinical Psychopharmacology, 9,* 3–13.

Witkiewitz, K., Bowen, S., Douglas, H., & Hsu, S. H. (2013). Mindfulness-based relapse prevention for substance craving. *Addictive Behaviors, 38,* 1563–1571.

Witkiewitz, K., Lustyk, M. K., & Bowen, S. (2013). Retraining the addicted brain: A review of hypothesized neurobiological mechanisms of mindfulness-based relapse prevention. *Psychology of Addictive Behaviors, 27,* 351–365.

Witkiewitz, K., & Marlatt, G. (2004). Relapse prevention for alcohol and drug problems: That was Zen, This is TAO. *American Psychologist, 59*(4), 224–235.

Witkiewitz, K., & Villarroel, N. A. (2009). Dynamic association between negative affect and alcohol lapses following alcohol treatment. *Journal of Consulting and Clinical Psychology, 77*(4), 633–644.

Chapter 14

Alcohol Addiction and Families

Misty K. Hook
Institute for Healthy Relationships

The United States has long had a love–hate relationship with alcohol and other types of drugs. Although the government has employed various efforts to eliminate or curtail drug and alcohol use (e.g., Prohibition, the War on Drugs), prescription drugs are used liberally, illicit drugs are easily obtained, and the presence of alcohol in our culture remains strong. Happy hours are a staple of corporate life and becoming of legal drinking age is something many young adults eagerly anticipate. However, despite the largely favorable role drugs and alcohol play in our culture, addiction can have serious consequences—and nowhere is this more evident than in families who have one or more addicted members. Addiction has a long-term and devastating effect on the family, disrupting healthy family dynamics, and increasing the likelihood that family members will suffer negative physical and psychological harm.

Although the impact of addiction may not be widely discussed, it is quite pervasive. In a 2012 report, the annual National Survey on Drug Use and Health (NSDUH) revealed that approximately 22.2 million Americans aged 12 years or older were dependent on either alcohol or illicit drugs (Office of Applied Studies, Substance Abuse and Mental Health Statistics, 2012). On an even broader scale, McIntyre (2004) estimates that 11% of the U.S. population abuses or is addicted to substances. During 2009, 4.3 million people were treated for alcohol or drug abuse in the United States (Substance Abuse and Mental Health Services Administration [SAMHSA], 2010).

In addition, for every person who is addicted to drugs or alcohol, it is believed that there are at least four to six other people, especially parents, partners, and children, who are equally affected. Using these percentages, we estimate that the number of people affected by alcohol or illicit drug abuse increases to approximately 45–68% of the U.S. population. Addiction also affects future generations. Estimates from NSDUH concluded that 5.9% of U.S. women giving birth used illicit drugs sometime during their pregnancy and 11.5% drank at some time during pregnancy.

When focusing just on alcohol, the number of children of alcoholics (COAs) appears to be rising. Black (2010) estimated that the number of COAs in the United States under the age of 18 was approximately 27.8 million. However, the numbers are most likely even higher given the tendency of families with alcoholic members to be closed systems that hide their "secret" of addiction (Edwards, 2003). Consequently, due to the frequency of alcohol and drug abuse in American society, counselors and other health care professionals will almost certainly encounter families suffering from addiction (Miller, Forcehimes, & Zweben, 2011). In order to offer the best treatment possible, counselors need to know how addiction affects the family and how best to treat it.

Public schools are beginning to acknowledge the adverse impact of an alcoholic member in the family. School counselors are being advised that almost 40% of their students may be being raised by an alcoholic caregiver. Given the negative academic outcomes for these students, the vast majority of school counselors agree there is a strong need for counseling and preventative services. However, the accrediting bodies have yet to make substance abuse coursework and training mandatory.

Before delving into the literature on families and addictions, it is important to note that it contains some serious gaps. Most studies examining the conceptualization and treatment of addicted family systems deal almost exclusively with Caucasian, heterosexual, intact families in which the male partner is addicted to a single substance. Studies involving addictions in women, people of color, same-sex couples, divorced parents, or individuals with comorbid drug problems and/or psychopathology are virtually absent (Roberts & Linney, 2000). The lack of attention to psychological difficulties is particularly problematic, as a large number of addicted people exhibit comorbid psychopathology. One study found that close to 60% of substance abuse patients had a dual diagnosis personality disorder, usually from Cluster B (Antisocial, Borderline, Histrionic, or Narcissistic) (Rounsaville et al., 1998). It seems evident that people with dual disorders are suffering from immense psychic pain given their much higher rates of suicide and suicide attempts than the general population (Drake, Wallach, Alverson, & Muesser, 2002; Grawe, Hage, Espeland, & Mueser, 2007). Since understanding the motivations behind the substance abuse are an important part of treatment, more needs to be known about the role psychopathology plays in addiction.

It is also important to note the primary role of alcohol in the addictions literature. Although addiction to legal and illicit drugs, gambling, and sexual addictions have equally damaging effects on families as alcohol abuse, few studies focus solely on these other dependencies. Some of the reasons behind the almost singular emphasis on alcohol may include the fact that it is legal, widely available, and accepted; alcohol addiction plays a larger role in our culture than do other drug addictions; alcohol abuse affects larger numbers of people than gambling or sexual addictions; and sexual addiction is an emerging trend, particularly with the increasingly widespread use of the Internet (Schneider, 2002). Thus, although the effects on the family from any kind of addiction are similar, this chapter will focus primarily on alcohol addiction.

Although drug-based definitions of addiction are still predominant in the field, a growing number of professionals are looking at other behaviors that are potentially addictive. These behaviors include gambling, computer game playing, shopping, exercise, eating, sex, and Internet use. All of these activities can and are done in moderation. However, the difference between a fun activity and an addiction is that healthy activities enhance life while addictions detract from it (Griffiths, 2005).

ADDICTION AND THE FAMILY

Family Counseling

In the early days of addictions counseling, counselors used to work only with the addict and family members were excluded. However, it quickly became clear that family members were influential in motivating the addict to get sober or in preventing the addict from making serious changes

(Liddle, Rowe, Dakof, Henderson, & Greenbaum, 2009; Steinberg, Epstein, McCrady, & Hirsch, 1997). Consequently, including family members in counseling sessions became an integral part of treatment. Systems theorists strongly believe in the concept of *homeostasis*, the tendency of systems like families to balance themselves in response to change. Whenever there is a disruption in one family member, other members react to return the overall family dynamics to something that resembles normal functioning. Family counselors pay close attention to several aspects of family dynamics, including the structure of the family (boundaries, roles), family rules, and generational interactions.

In terms of structure, the family is viewed as an organism surrounded by a semipermeable boundary, a set of rules determining how people interact with those both inside and outside the family. Within each family, members occupy one or more roles that determine how they act and how others react to them. A healthy family structure is one that requires clear boundaries and flexible roles. Family rules govern the range of behavior a family system can tolerate. Positive rules take into account the needs of everyone in the family. Finally, generational interactions are the ways in which communication is conducted between the various subsystems (e.g., parental, sibling, partner). Healthy generational interactions are ones in which there is a clear hierarchy, flexible roles, and open communication.

Case Study.   Joanna and Leroy Williams have been married for 15 years. They have two children, Shoshana, age 12, and James, age 9. While Leroy always drank, it has only been a problem for the last 6 years. He will come home from work and drink the rest of the evening. Leroy refuses to help with any of the household chores or child care responsibilities. He is verbally and emotionally abusive to Joanna and the children when he's been drinking and avoidant and withdrawn during the weekend days when he is sober. Joanna and Leroy attempted counseling once and Leroy did attend rehab, but quickly relapsed after 3–4 months. He refuses to return to counseling and does not want Joanna to go either.

Question: What are some of the roles and rules in the Williams family?

ADDICTED FAMILY DYNAMICS: HOMEOSTASIS   In addicted families, the substance abuse initially threatens family homeostasis. People who become addicted to substances start to demonstrate clear patterns of behavior: They socialize with other users, family or friends who do not use are excluded, denial is frequent, and family relationships become strained. Leroy's drinking definitely causes a strain on the family. He either goes out with his friends to drink or drinks alone at home. In both situations, he does not interact with other family members while he is drinking. He is asked to help out with the kids and do chores around the house, but refuses, frequently leading to arguments with Joanna. Leroy also does not attend school or athletic functions for the kids. They are angry with him because of his absence in their lives but are afraid to say anything for fear he will start yelling. No one, especially Leroy, mentions that his refusal to participate in family life is because of his drinking.

Once homeostasis is broken, other family members adapt to the substance use behavior in an effort to return balance to the family. They deny the addiction, change their behavior to cover up the substance abuse, and often sacrifice their needs for the sake of protecting the addict and the family system. Family members start to hide their true feelings and distort reality (Kinney, 2003). As Leroy's drinking started becoming a regular nightly event, Joanna kept denying there was a problem. At first she repeatedly asked him to participate with the kids and the household routine but, eventually, she quit asking. She now does everything herself. On days when she cannot drive the kids where they need to go, she enlists the help of neighbors and other adults. In addition to holding down a full-time job and attending school part time, she takes care of everything around the house. She also has sex with Leroy whenever he wants, even if it's late and she's tired. She believes it's easier to give in than to risk a confrontation. Joanna ignores her own anger and exhaustion and seeks individual counseling to help her cope better. Shoshana and James also participate in household chores and try to ease Joanna's burden. They avoid Leroy whenever possible. Thus, in attempting to maintain homeostasis, the Williams's family dynamics maintain the substance use (Lawson & Lawson, 2005; Meyers, Apodaca, Flicker, & Slesnick, 2002). Leroy has no domestic responsibilities and other family members avoid upsetting him, so he is free to drink whenever he is home. He pays no overt price for his addiction. As such, his drinking is now so insidious that it is the primary organizing factor around which the Williams family preserves its structure and stability (Chamberlain & Jew, 2003).

ADDICTED FAMILY DYNAMICS: BOUNDARIES Boundaries delineate the ways in which people relate to each other. They govern the rules surrounding how close family members can get to one another, how the family connects with the larger society, and how conflict is tolerated. In general, addictive family systems tend to have rigid, disengaged boundaries. Family members exhibit poor communication, higher levels of negativity and conflict, inadequate problem-solving skills, low cohesion, and an overall lack of organization and consistency (Fals-Stewart, Kelley, Cooke, & Golden, 2003; Lorber et al., 2007). Given the unpleasantness of interpersonal encounters, they eventually become isolated from one another. Moreover, due to the secrecy surrounding the addiction, they also become isolated from the community. Consequently, emotional intimacy tends to be low in addicted family systems. However, the alcohol itself can be used as a way for the family to gain artificial closeness or as a tool to defuse conflict (Lawson & Lawson, 2005). Some studies have found that positive family interactions (e.g., avoiding conflict, achieving closeness, fun times) tend to occur only when the addicted family member is intoxicated (Roberts & Linney, 2000). In this way, the addiction is even further maintained by the family system.

In the Williams family, conversation tends to be at a minimum. Joanna talks with Shoshana and James about their school and extracurricular activities, but discussion about the family rarely, if ever, occurs. The kids do not ask about Leroy and Joanna does not mention him. Whenever Leroy gets upset, he yells and says hurtful things. There have been times when he has pushed or poked one of the children. Consequently, Joanna and the kids have learned to give Leroy what he wants or stay out of his way when he is upset. Joanna tries to negotiate household tasks with Leroy but quickly gives up when he decides he is not going to do them. Thus, Shoshana and James have no positive role models for how to negotiate relationship difficulties. When there is a problem between Joanna and one of the kids or between Shoshana and James, nothing gets solved. The kids also do not have the opportunity to see positive role models for relationships in the community. While they both attend school and play sports, they have minimal interaction with community members beyond these events. People are never invited over to the house for fear of what they will see.

Addicted family systems miss some key ingredients of healthy families. These include willingness to spend time together, effective communication patterns, the ability to deal positively with crises, encouragement of individuals, clear roles, and a growth-producing structure.

ADDICTED FAMILY DYNAMICS: ROLES In families, as in other systems, people like to know how they are supposed to act and how they should respond to others. As such, they tend to take on roles, or specific ways of behaving. Everyone then knows what they are supposed to do and how they are expected to respond to the roles others play. In healthy family systems, roles can range from general (e.g., youngest child) to specific (e.g., the funny one), but will ultimately differ based on gender, culture, and the individual family.

While there are role variations in addicted family systems, Claudia Black (1981, 1992) described the four main roles children occupy. The first is that of the family hero. These children are extremely successful, self-reliant, and responsible. They give self-worth and validation to the family through their achievements. They often take care of everyone in the family and are sometimes labeled as parentified. As is befitting her gender and status as the oldest child, Shoshana is the William family hero. She gets good grades, helps around the house, and is a star on her soccer team. Whenever Joanna's exhaustion is too much to handle, Shoshana steps in and takes care of cooking dinner and helping James with his homework. Joanna is relieved that Shoshana can take care of herself and is pleased that she is so responsible. She does not see that Shoshana's self-reliance is covering up her depression and anxiety.

The second role is the scapegoat. This child acts out and is blamed for all of the family's problems. By acting out, the scapegoat takes the focus off the family's problems. The third role is that of the lost child or the adjuster (Black, 1981, 1992). These children follow directions, adjust to family dynamics, and offer relief by not needing attention. The last role is the mascot. These children are funny and outgoing. Everyone in the family tends to like them as they provide distraction by entertaining everyone around them (Fields, 2004; van Wormer & Davis, 2003). In the Williams family, James occupies the role of mascot. He does acceptable academic work, and his teachers talk about how funny and lively he is in class. At home, James makes Joanna, Shoshana, and even Leroy laugh with his funny stories and fantastic impressions. James is rarely serious and seems unable to identify or express emotions like anger, sadness, or fear.

In healthy families, roles remain flexible, but in addicted family systems, they become rigid, particularly during times of stress. Thus, in the Williams family, as Leroy's drinking becomes more disruptive, Shoshana becomes more serious and responsible, and James becomes more playful. If the children do not receive help, they are likely to play these roles throughout their lives. However, while the roles described earlier are helpful in understanding family dynamics, it must be noted that they are generalizations. They should not be used to stereotype people nor are they exclusive to only families with addiction issues; families who do not have alcohol-abuse problems may display these roles as well (Alford, 1998; van Wormer & Davis, 2003).

ADDICTED FAMILY DYNAMICS: RULES All families have rules that help organize family life. Some rules are overt, such as the exact time of curfew or not talking with one's mouth full. Other rules are covert. These are the unspoken rules that govern interpersonal behavior. Examples of covert rules in healthy families include ignoring Grandma's memory problems or giving large displays of affection when people come and go. In healthy families, both overt and covert rules tend to be present, logical, consistent, and designed to promote growth. In contrast, rules in addicted family systems tend to be arbitrary, illogical, inconsistent, and/or punitive (Brooks & Rice, 1997). Family members may use shaming to enforce rules or there may be a lack of consequences for breaking rules. The children in the family may feel out of control or anxious because they do not know or understand what they are supposed to do.

Typical rules in alcoholic families involve how best to deal with the addict and how to keep the addiction secret in order to protect and preserve the family (Lawson & Lawson, 2005).

Wegscheider (1981) outlined the three major rules that characterize an addicted family system. The first and most important rule is that the addict's drug use is the most important thing in the family's life. The household routine, family outings, finances, holidays, and how family members interact with one another all depend on the substance abuse. For the Williams's family, everyone has to work around Leroy. If he joins them for dinner, they are not to say anything that will upset him. Even when money is tight, great care is taken to make sure there is always beer available. No one wants Leroy to drive while intoxicated to get more beer. Extended family get-togethers are planned well in advance and sometimes have to be cancelled (without complaint by anyone else) if Leroy says he is not up to making the trip.

The second rule is that the addict is not responsible for her or his behavior, and the drug is not the cause of the family's problems. Excuses are made for how the addicted person responds. Joanna explains that Leroy's tiredness after a long day at work and his difficulty dealing with stress are reasons why he drinks. However, it is not the alcohol that is the problem. Instead, their problems stem from never having enough money, the fact that Leroy's parents did not teach him how to handle adversity, or that his friends are bad influences.

The third rule is that the status quo must be maintained at all times. Family members are extremely careful not to upset the routine. The Williams family cannot expect anything from Leroy nor can they tell other people, even extended family members, about his drinking.

In addition to these rules, Black (1981) listed three other rules for people living in an addicted family system: don't talk, don't trust, don't feel. Family members are not allowed to talk about the addiction. As talking does not promote emotional intimacy and frequently leads to conflict, it is not encouraged. The reality of the addiction is distorted (Brooks & Rice, 1997) such that no one acknowledges the elephant in the room. As a result, children in particular learn that they cannot trust their inner experiences. They also learn that they cannot trust others. The addicted family system is one in which people are not there for each other; they often do not nurture one another. Consequently, trusting both self and others becomes dangerous and something to be avoided. Finally, addicted family systems do not honor the feelings of anyone other than the addict. Other family members are encouraged to hide their feelings in order to preserve the family system. Feelings that threaten the status quo will be discouraged and/or ignored.

Stages in Addicted Family Systems

Washousky, Levy-Stern, and Muchowski (1993) have delineated four stages in the family system of the addict. The first stage is denial. The family begins to hide the abuse from each other and everyone else, offering other explanations for the addict's behavior and isolating themselves from people who may suspect the addiction. The second stage involves home treatment—attempts by family members to get the addict to stop using, usually by controlling her or his behavior. Family roles may undergo significant shifts as children try to care for parents, coalitions are formed, and other members' problems are neglected in order to keep the emphasis on the addict.

The third stage is chaos. The addiction is now so out of control that it can no longer be hidden. Other family members spin out of control, conflicts and confrontations escalate without resolution, and consequences for family members become more pronounced. This is the stage in which partners and/or children may experience serious emotional or physical problems, and threats of divorce or separation are made but not completed. The last stage is control. Other family members identify the problem as an addiction, and control is often attempted through divorce, separation, or total emotional isolation. The family then becomes ensnared in a cycle of helplessness and futile attempts to control the addict's behavior.

In counseling, the success of the treatment is frequently dependent upon which stage the family is currently experiencing (DiClemente & Velasquez, 2002). Many families in treatment are still in the denial stage and are not ready to change. In these instances, all counselors can do is plant seeds of change in family members (McIntyre, 2004) and wait for the family to cycle to another stage. To help counselors know where they should concentrate their energy, Miller and Tonigan (1996) have created an assessment instrument—The Stages of Change Readiness and Treatment Eagerness Scales, or SOCRATES—that determines the level of motivation to change.

Parenting in an Addicted Family System

The role of parent is one that brings a lot of stress. This is especially true in the United States, where unrealistic expectations set standards that most parents cannot meet. American culture perpetuates the myths that one or two people at most can adequately parent a child and that all people, especially women, know instinctively how to care for their children (Barnett & Rivers, 2004). Without sufficient information, ample time, energy, and assistance, good parenting skills are hard to achieve. Given these difficulties, it is hardly surprising that, for both women and men, becoming a parent can lead to decreased enjoyment in other social roles and subsequent abuse of alcohol (Richman, Rospenda, & Kelley, 1994).

While there are gender differences, research shows that gender is less important than we think it is. Women are not better at parenting than men simply by virtue of their gender. Instead, parenting behavior—good or bad—is determined more by the situation than by your sex.

Alcohol and other substance abuse make good parenting difficult, if not impossible. Alcoholic parents are less likely to display positive affect toward their children (Fals-Stewart, Kelley, Fincham, Golden, & Logsdon, 2004; Fitzgerald, Zucker, & Yang, 1995), be less satisfied with being a parent (Watkins, O'Farrell, Suvak, Murphy, & Taft, 2009), experience higher stress related to parenting, frequently engage in more punitive behavior, and may be less responsive to their infants (Schuler & Nair, 2001). Moreover, substance-abusing mothers in particular are at high risk of experiencing multiple problems that weaken their capacity to care for their children, including depression, increased exposure to parental and partner violence, sexual abuse, psychiatric disorders, violent behavior, and criminal behavior (Nair, Schuler, Black, Kettinger, & Harrington, 2003).

However, parents, especially the nonabusing parent, can have a buffering effect on children living in an addicted family system. Research has demonstrated that when at least one parent (usually the mother) can provide consistency and stability, positive outcomes can be achieved (McCord, 1988). For example, in an oft-cited study, Wolin, Bennett, and Noonan (1979) found that families who were able to maintain family rituals did not transmit alcoholism to their offspring. In contrast, families whose rituals were disrupted were more likely to produce alcoholic children. The authors concluded that regular and daily rituals serve to structure family life, increase connection, and provide a stable family identity. Similarly, Berlin and Davis (1989) demonstrated the critical nature of the mother's support and nurturance as a factor leading to a nonalcoholic outcome in adulthood. Yet another study found that children of alcoholic fathers have more stable homes and are better cared for than those with two alcoholic parents or an alcoholic mother (Kelley & Fals-Stewart, 2002; Williams, 1987). Thus, having the mother as the nonaddicted parent was an important factor in positive outcomes. However, other studies have not reported a gender difference. Consequently, it seems clear that as long as one parent can provide this stability, children have a better chance of good psychological outcomes.

ADDICTION AND THE COUPLE

Although the couple relationship in addicted family systems is of great importance, it has often been overlooked. As Fals-Stewart, Birchler, and Ellis (1999) pointed out over a decade ago, almost all of the empirical family studies with drug-abusing patients have ignored the partner subsystem in order to concentrate on the family of origin. While more research on couples in an addicted system have emerged, the ways in which the addiction affects partner interactions and serves as a tool for the relationship are still largely shrouded in mystery. Moreover, just like research on addicted family systems in general, research on relationship functioning among alcoholics has not been completed with varied populations. Instead, it has focused primarily on married, middle class, Caucasian male problem drinkers with no comorbid psychopathology. Consequently, our knowledge about how addiction affects partner relationships is limited at best.

The Impact of Alcohol on Couple Relationships

Research has demonstrated that alcohol abuse has a strong detrimental effect on romantic relationships. Alcohol abuse contributes to sexual inadequacy (O'Farrell, 1990), marital discord (Joutsenniemi et al., 2011; Marshal, 2003), higher rates of psychological and physical problems among nondrinking spouses (Copello et al., 2009), as well as higher rates of marital aggression, separation, and divorce (Schumm, O'Farrell, Murphy, & Fals-Stewart, 2009). Moreover, alcohol hinders the development of intimacy (Collins, Ellickson, & Klein, 2007) because the addiction serves as a substitute for real-life experiences within a relationship (Miller et al., 2001).

The quality of the partnership is also correlated with the presence of a drinking problem. However, the research in this area is mixed. Some studies have shown that partners report more satisfying relationships during periods of abstinence (Homish, Leonard, Kozlowski, & Cornelius, 2009) and that when the addict is in recovery, couple functioning appears to improve (Moos, Finney, & Cronkite, 1990). Other studies observed that couples who drink together are more satisfied (Homish & Leonard, 2007; Navarra, 2007) while others discovered that because of the function of substance abuse within a relationship, intimate partners may not experience negative fallout (Fals-Stewart, Lam, & Kelley, 2009; Howells & Orford, 2006). For example, the drinking can provide a welcome facilitation of emotional expression or allow for caretaking and affection that might otherwise be witheld or refused.

Alcohol also appears to play a major role in interpersonal violence (McKinney, Caetano, Harris, & Ebama, 2009; Schafer, Caetano, & Cunradi, 2004; Wekerle & Wall, 2002). Some studies place estimates of male violence against women at 24% and female violence against men at 37% (e.g., Wiersma, Cleveland, Herrera, & Fischer, 2010). Clinical samples from substance-abusing couples put the prevalence of partner violence at 50% (e.g., Chermack, Fuller, & Blow, 2000). While the exact reasons for this are unclear, the presence of alcohol is a major risk factor for female partners in particular (Cox, Ketner, & Blow, 2013). Statistics from a National Institute of Justice (2000) report show that 1.3 million women are assaulted by an intimate partner annually.

Studies of addiction treatment groups also yielded startlingly high numbers of domestic violence offenders. In two separate studies, O'Farrell and Fals-Stewart (2000) discovered that approximately 60% of alcoholics had been violent toward their female partner in the year prior to treatment. Other studies found that the prevalence of domestic violence was at least twice as high in addiction treatment groups than in the general population (Fals-Stewart, Kashdan, O'Farrell, & Birchler, 2002; Schumm et al., 2009). Moreover, male physical aggression toward their female partner was more than eight times higher on days when they drank. There also appears to be a link between violence and sexual functioning in alcoholic couples (Epstein & McCrady, 1998).

In addition to the human toll, domestic violence is quite expensive. The Centers for Disease Control and Prevention (2013) recently reported that batterers' abuse costs over $5.8 billion per year nationally for their victims' health care and lost productivity. This amount does not include money spent by law enforcement agencies or other branches of the civil and criminal legal system.

Alcohol can have a major influence on the dissolution of the relationship. In longitudinal prospective studies of both older and younger couples, frequent substance abuse was predictive of subsequent divorce (Collins et al., 2007), while Amato and Previti (2003) found that substance use is the third highest reason for divorce. For heterosexual couples, there is some question about whether the gender of the addicted partner makes a difference in the termination of the romantic relationship. The evidence for the impact of gender is confusing. Some studies (Leonard & Roberts, 1998; Roberts & Linney, 1998) have found that the husband's drinking, but not the wife's, predicted instability, while others found the exact opposite (Cranford, Floyd, Schulenberg, & Zucker, 2011). Still others revealed that problem drinking was linked to lower marital quality regardless of who was doing the drinking (Grzywacz & Marks, 1999). Whatever the influence of gender, it is apparent that alcohol can significantly contribute to the end of a relationship.

Case Study. Michelle and Billy met in a bar. Although Michelle is generally a shy person, the alcohol made her friendly and she responded to Billy's flirting. The two have been married now for 10 years. They have no children. While both of them enjoy drinking after work, Michelle has really struggled to avoid abusing alcohol. A few years ago, she attended Alcoholics Anonymous (AA) at Billy's request but stopped after only a few months. Michelle accepts the limitations Billy puts on her drinking when he is at home; however, she will occasionally drink until she is intoxicated. Her drinking is the source of many heated arguments, and Billy periodically threatens to leave the marriage.

Question: How much of a role has alcohol played in Michelle and Billy's relationship?

THE IMPACT OF COUPLES ON ALCOHOL ABUSE While alcohol clearly affects the relationship, in true systemic fashion, some researchers are trying to determine if the relationship itself influences the drinking behavior. For example, Cox et al. (2013) found that problematic marital interactions can stimulate drinking or even bring about renewed drinking. Moreover, alcohol can have a short-term positive effect on interpersonal interactions (Roberts & Linney, 2000). When people have difficulty obtaining intimacy or want to avoid conflict, they frequently draw a third person or object into their interaction. In this way, they are no longer forced to deal only with each other and can instead concentrate on the additional person or object. In such cases, alcohol can serve as the third point in the triangle. Thus, when the alcohol is removed, relationships can suffer.

Studies have demonstrated that drug-abusing couples have significant difficulties in multiple areas, including communication (Morrissette, 2010), lack of emotional support (Collins et al., 2007), abusiveness, lack of problem-solving skills, and high attribution of blame

(Johnson, Noel, & Sutter-Hernandez, 2000). However, as causality has not been determined, it is difficult to know if these couples had these problems before the addiction or if the addiction instigated them.

Alcohol definitely served as a way to help Michelle and Billy interact. Michelle freely admits that she probably would have ignored Billy had she not been intoxicated when they first met. Moreover, given her high level of anxiety and low self-confidence, Michelle has used alcohol to enhance their sex life. Although Billy gets angry about Michelle's excessive drinking, he too uses alcohol to help the two of them feel closer to one another. They rarely have deep conversations without alcohol present. However, their communication in general is superficial and problems are rarely, if ever, truly solved. Instead, they both blame one another for any conflicts that arise and avoid talking about anything even remotely controversial.

ENABLING AND CODEPENDENCE In the early days of addictions treatment, researchers and counselors alike began wondering why the partner, usually female, stayed with the alcohol abuser. One theory that arose was the codependent personality. Codependency is excessive dependence upon a loved one by a person who looks to external sources for fulfillment. It is exemplified by inadequate or lost identity, neglect of self, and low self-esteem. Codependent people rescue others at the expense of their own needs and use control as a way of distracting attention from these needs. They are obsessed with the loved person and often believe that survival, theirs or their partner's, depends on maintaining the relationship. Codependency quickly became a popular theory for why (primarily) women stayed in horrible relationships, especially those characterized by addiction. However, there has been severe criticism of this theory. Rotunda and Doman (2001) pointed out that the construct of codependence has not been empirically defined. Dear and Roberts (2002) argued that codependency is merely a way to pathologize society's socialization of women to connect in any way possible. Moreover, society's ideal of true love—a relationship in which two people are fused into one entity (the couple)—actually promotes codependency (Zelvin, 2004).

Like codependency, enabling is another theory that explains the actions of the nonaddicted partner. Enabling is the manner in which the partner inadvertently maintains the drug or alcohol use. For example, one type of enabling behavior is the attempt to control both the addicted person's behavior as well as the surrounding environment. This allows some partners to appear to be in control of their lives and to be labeled overresponsible (Marks, Blore, Hine, & Dear, 2012) when, in reality, they are attempting to prevent their world from falling apart. Such controlling behavior can engender defiance in the substance abuser, allow her or him to project responsibility for the consequences onto the enabler, and reinforce the mistaken belief that the addiction can be controlled. Thus, it becomes quite easy to blame the enabler for her/his role in the addiction instead of looking at how enabling is the result of living with a loved one's addiction and other dysfunctional family behaviors (Zelvin, 2004). As is true with codependency, enabling has not been empirically validated as a pathological personality trait (Rotunda, Scherer, & Imm, 1995). Despite this, codependency support groups are still used widely for support around change.

While Billy does not exhibit codependent traits, he demonstrates enabling behavior. When Michelle was in AA, he would drink alcohol in front of her. When confronted with this, he stated that she needed to learn self-discipline. Billy also enables Michelle's drinking by keeping alcohol around the house and by trying to strictly regulate her alcoholic intake. He measures out the exact amount of alcohol he has deemed acceptable for Michelle to drink each night. If she goes over that amount, he gets very upset. For her part, Michelle gets angry with his attempts to control her drinking and, when he goes out of town, drinks more to spite him.

PARTNERS AS RESOURCES Partners can serve as important motivators for their significant others to change their addictive behavior and can be of great assistance in counseling. Research has shown that improving partner relationships can be a major factor in getting addicted people to stop drinking (Powers, Vedel, & Emmelkamp, 2008). For example, one study discovered that 53% of male alcoholics were motivated by their spouses or family to seek treatment (Steinberg et al., 1997). Similarly, partners can be valuable allies in counseling sessions. Nonalcoholic partners may provide essential information, give constructive feedback and support to the clients (Kelley & Fals-Stewart, 2003), and help the addicted partner identify high-risk situations (Stanton, 2005). Moreover, treating the relationship problems of drug-abusing couples has been shown to result in improved relationship variables (O'Farrell, Murphy, Stephan, Fals-Stewart, & Murphy, 2004).

However, while partners can be indispensable in treatment, there may be challenges. Sobriety or even a reduction in substance use can increase tension in the couple's relationship after the honeymoon period ends (Stanton, 2005). One major reason for increased tension is the need for forgiveness. To restore trust to the relationship, the nonaddicted partner frequently wants the addicted partner to understand how painful their addiction was and to apologize for the hurt. Once the forgiveness process has been negotiated, couples work can begin. Targets of intervention for couples include power (the couple needs to negotiate a workable power structure and increase tolerance for conflict), intimacy (both partners need to allow themselves to be vulnerable and learn how to negotiate for getting their needs met), boundaries, and determining the function of the drug abuse (Kelley & Fals-Stewart, 2002).

Billy was of great assistance in the counseling sessions with Michelle. She admitted that she wanted to stop drinking because it was the only way to save her marriage. Michelle was much more willing to listen to Billy's suggestions for ways to engage in abstinence than she was her counselor's. When counseling first started and their relationship started to change, both initially questioned whether it was worth it to maintain the marriage. However, once they began to see the positive results of increased communication and intimacy, both agreed to continue with counseling.

ADDICTION AND THE CHILDREN

Although addiction significantly affects the entire family, children are most affected. Despite this truth, early addictions literature focused almost solely on the addict and ignored the other people in the system. However, with the advent of the Adult Children of Alcoholics (ACOA) movement, attention shifted to include the outcomes of children living in an addicted family environment. While much of the literature base is focused on adult children living out of, but still affected by, the dysfunctional family system, it seems as though the outcomes for children both in and out of the family environment are roughly the same. Consequently, this chapter will use the terms COAs and ACOAs interchangeably.

The problems associated with living in an alcoholic family are much greater than we may realize. Research estimates that there are 26.8 million COAs in the United States with over 11 million under the age of 18. Moreover, 76 million Americans, roughly 43% of the adult population, have been exposed to alcoholism in the family.

Of all family members, children have the least control over what happens and rarely have the freedom to leave. Moreover, the ways addiction affects children can begin before birth. First, there seems to be a genetic component to alcoholism and other types of addictions. Family studies, twin studies, adoption studies, half-sibling studies, and animal studies have all shown a tendency for addiction to run in families (Erickson, 2007). Thus, children of alcoholics tend to have an elevated risk for developing alcoholism themselves (Brook et al., 2003).

Second, children of addicted parents are at risk for prenatal exposure to drugs and alcohol (Carmichael Olson, O'Connor, & Fitzgerald, 2001), which can lead to a host of cognitive, physiological, and psychosocial difficulties (Fields, 2004). Children suffering from fetal alcohol syndrome show effects in morphological anomalies, growth retardation, and central nervous system deficits (Chasnoff, Wells, Telford, Schmidt, & Messer, 2010). Other negative effects can occur with lower levels of prenatal alcohol exposure.

A third way children are affected by alcohol addiction is by growing up in an addicted family system characterized by chaos, uncertainty, and an ever-changing reality (Ranganathan, 2004). There is an overall lack of structure (e.g., distorted hierarchies, triangulation, parentification, rigid or nonexistent boundaries), and there may be inconsistencies in parenting or a lack of parenting altogether (Lawson & Lawson, 2005). Inconsistencies in discipline make it hard for children to learn cause-and-effect connections. Family rules are often arbitrary, unclear, and contradictory (Juhnke & Hagedorn, 2006) and can change depending on whether the addict is in a wet (active intoxication) or dry cycle (Lawson & Lawson, 2005). Emotional and physical neglect, high levels of conflict, partner instability, disorganization, violence, and/or physical and sexual abuse are all common. Instead of a place of safety and love, the family environment consists of tension, fear, and shame and a basic lack of safety, all of which play into the child's sense of self. Children in addicted family systems are forced to adapt to the ongoing trauma (Kinney, 2003) and are deprived of the opportunity to attend to their own development.

Violence is yet another way children can be affected by addiction. In fact, the presence and risk of violence in addicted family systems cannot be understated. The link between alcohol use and interpersonal violence has been widely documented (Nicholas, & Rasmussen, 2006). Parental substance abuse is a risk factor for child abuse (Schafer, Caetano, & Cunradi, 2004; Wekerle & Wall, 2002). Children of drug abusers are at greater risk for abuse, neglect, and disruption in primary caregiving (Werner & Johnson, 2004). This is especially true when the addict is the mother. Grant and her colleagues (2011) found that maternal substance abuse increases the likelihood that children will be removed from the home.

Physical abuse is not the only type of violence that can occur to children in an addicted family system. Sexual abuse is also frequent, but for different reasons. While addicted parents can and do sexually abuse their children, research has found that sexual abuse among children of alcoholics was more likely to have been perpetrated by "friends" of the family (Steinglass, Bennett, Wolin, & Reiss, 1987) rather than family members themselves. A main reason for this rests with the nonexistent boundaries found in some addicted family systems. Some families dealing with addiction rigidly control their children's access to the community (children are taught to view the world outside the family as dangerous and are punished for talking to people outside the home), while others leave their children completely unattended. Consequently, friends of the parents and other adults can have unsupervised access to children and frequently molest them (Windle & Tubman, 1999).

Although substance abuse has a significant and usually detrimental effect on the children of addicted family systems, they do not all demonstrate negative outcomes. Many research studies have shown that children of alcoholics do not have physical or psychological outcomes that differ significantly from those who have not lived in an addicted family system (Langeland, Draijer, & van den Brink, 2004). The diathesis-stress model may be one answer to the question of why many COAs go on to live relatively normal lives. According to this model, the variation between personality characteristics (e.g., coping styles) and stressful life events (Belsky & Pluess, 2009) can make a difference. More positive personality traits coupled with less stressful life events can lead some COAs toward resilience while others, with different personality/stress pairings, spiral downward. The presence of psychiatric disorders within the family may be another reason why some COAs have better outcomes than others. Nicholas and Rasmussen (2006) found that psychosocial outcomes among COAs vary depending on the existence of paternal comorbid antisocial behavior. Consequently, it appears as though there are many factors other than the presence of substance abuse that impact COAs' lives.

Behavioral Outcomes

Although many COAs and ACOAs go on to lead normal lives, it is important to know about the negative outcomes that can appear in both groups. Children living in an addicted family system can experience significant damaging effects as a result of the dysfunction. Many studies have documented the severe physiological consequences of living in an addicted environment. These include lower cognitive performance (Fitzgerald et al., 1995; Carmichael Olson, et al., 2001), attentional deficits (Díaz, Gual, García, Arnau, & Pascual, 2008), and poorer neurological functioning (Poon, Ellis, Fitzgerald, & Zucker, 2000).

The link between COAs and negative behavioral outcomes is also well established. Children of alcoholics have elevated rates of impulsivity, conduct disorders (Fitzgerald et al., 1993), alexithymia, depression, and anxiety (Díaz et al., 2008). They also exhibit lower academic achievement (Poon et al., 2000) and a more external locus of control (Mun, Fitzgerald, Puttler, Zucker, & Von Eye, 2000), which makes them further affected by a negative environment.

Finally, COAs are at elevated risk for alcoholism. Brook et al. (2003) found that COAs are 1.5 to 9 times more likely to develop an alcohol disorder in adulthood. This is especially true if the addicted family is extremely enmeshed and reactive to the alcohol abuser. Research has demonstrated that the lower the levels of differentiation in the family (i.e., being able to separate oneself from others), the higher the chance of transmitting addictive behaviors from one generation to the next (Lawson & Lawson, 2005).

Psychosocial Outcomes

Psychosocial outcomes of COAs also are affected as a result of an addicted family environment. Children's development of self can be severely disrupted. Because the reality of life in an addicted family system is constantly distorted, children quickly learn that they cannot trust their internal emotions and, as such, cannot trust themselves (Brooks & Rice, 1997; Fields, 2004; Kinney, 2003). Moreover, their home environment is one in which they have no control. COAs may have no opportunity to develop and internalize feelings of mastery or power because of the chaos. Consequently, they try to gain some kind of control, often by believing that they are the cause of the problem and if they can work hard enough at fixing themselves, the family can be healed (Lawson & Lawson, 2005).

THE COA SELF Brown (1992) hypothesized that, in response to trauma, COAs develop a defensive self, one that decreases their vulnerability. A defensive self includes denial, perceptual and cognitive distortions, fear of losing control, black and white thinking, overresponsibility, and a negation of self. Unfortunately, while the creation of a defensive self can be an adaptive coping mechanism while in the addicted family system, it ultimately can lead to unremitting distrust of others, inhibition of curiosity, distrust of one's own senses, and feelings of unreality. Other characteristics of COAs that are supported by the literature (Rubin, 2001) can be found in Table 14.1.

TABLE 14.1 Functions and Characteristics of COAs

Characteristic	Function of the Characteristic
Dependence	Child's own needs are less important than supporting the family system; independence is a threat to parental authority
Difficulty expressing emotions	Disclosure is unwelcome and would risk exposure of faults, thereby causing anger in adults
Difficulty relaxing	Fear of being thought lazy; evolved from lack of opportunity to relax and play independently
Excessive loyalty	Terrified of abandonment; loyalty ensures the child's belief as deserving of approval
Overly responsible	Method of maintaining control; may be their role in the system
Fear of losing control	If others do not need them, it conveys the feeling that they are incapable, incompetent, and have shortcomings
Fear of conflict	Try to avoid at all costs due to fear of painful interactions and a lack of problem-solving skills
Overly self-critical	Internalized messages from others that they cannot do anything right and are responsible for the family's problems
Sensation seeking	Evolved from the childhood abuse that robbed them of their natural impulsivity, playfulness, and creativity

COAS' RELATIONSHIPS WITH OTHERS Living in an addicted family system necessarily affects the COA's relationships with others. As discussed previously, the distortion of reality makes it difficult for COAs to trust either themselves or others. This is especially true when considering the issues surrounding attachment (Rubin, 2001). Alcoholic parents are unpredictable and often abusive. They frequently discourage normal processes of development, including autonomy, desire for affection, and creation of critical thinking skills. Instead, children are encouraged to be dependent and compliant and not ask for too much lest they be considered needy. Attachment to such a parent lends itself to "splitting," or black and white thinking. In an effort to accept their conflicted feelings about addicted caregivers, children blame themselves for the abusive behavior and see themselves as deficient and unworthy of respect and care. In this fashion, they can avoid placing the blame on the "good" caregiver. As a result of splitting behavior, other people tend to be seen as either good or bad, with nothing in between (Brooks & Rice, 1997). This way of looking at people generalizes to other relationships, including romantic partners (Olmstead, Crowell, & Waters, 2003), and to the COA's relationship with his or her own children (Rubin, 2001). Moreover, in an alcoholic environment, it becomes difficult to develop good relationship skills. Consequently, COAs often fail to develop appropriate prosocial skills and find it difficult to have positive friendships (Kearns-Bodkin & Leonard, 2008; Windle & Tubman, 1999). Similarly, COAs are at increased risk for maladaptive relationship outcomes, including partner conflict and dissatisfaction, disrupted family environments, and ineffective or inefficient parenting practices (Fields, 2004; Kinney, 2003).

Case Study. Betty and Leo are both children of drug-addicted fathers. They have been married for 15 years, but are unable to have children. They have entered counseling due to Leo's extramarital affair and dependency on prescription drugs. Betty is clearly overresponsible, as she is the primary breadwinner and takes care of the household and the couple's relationships with others. Leo complains that she rarely has time for him. While both Betty and Leo are always busy, their activities vary. Betty is usually occupied with some household task while Leo constantly seeks excitement. Neither one appears able to discuss emotions or handle conflict appropriately. Whenever problems arise, they either yell at each other or wait for the problem to go away. Leo mentions that Betty is very hard on herself while Betty complains that Leo has minimal self-discipline.

Question: How would you help this couple with their distortions of reality?

COUNSELING ADDICTED FAMILY SYSTEMS

Efficacy of Couples and Family Counseling

The emphasis in addictions treatment has shifted from an almost sole focus on the addict to at least minimal inclusion of other family members. Research has consistently found that couples and family counseling have among the best outcomes for recovery from addiction. In the early 1990s, the National Institute of Drug Abuse funded several treatment outcome studies to evaluate the usefulness of family counseling with adolescent substance abusers. Most found family counseling to be superior to other modalities (Friedman, Tomko, & Utada, 1991; Joanning, Quinn, Thomas, & Mullen, 1992; Liddle & Diamond, 1991). More recent meta-analyses have shown that couples and family therapies are among the top five treatments for substance abuse and were superior to individually oriented treatment modalities (Baldwin, Christian, Berkeljon, Shadish, & Bean, 2012), peer group counseling, and various forms of treatment as usual (Shadish & Baldwin, 2003). Family counseling has been found to be particularly effective at engagement and retention of problem drinkers (O'Farrell & Fals-Stewart, 2003) as well as adolescent substance abusers (Rowe & Liddle, 2003).

One possible reason for the efficacy of couples and family counseling may be due to the lack of empirically validated treatments. By its very multidimensional nature, couples and family counseling cannot be manualized (there are too many variables present) and can thus provide the flexibility needed to increase therapeutic outcome. Thus, the task of counselors is to conceptualize behavior problems within a multidimensional framework and direct intervention strategies toward the systems targeted for change (Baldwin, Christian, Berkeljon, Shadish, & Bean, 2012).

Assessment of Addicted Family Systems

In deciding whether family counseling is appropriate for a family in which substance abuse is present, some researchers have suggested examining the impact of alcohol in the family. Thus, counselors should determine whether the family is indeed an alcoholic family or a family with an alcoholic member (Steinglass et al., 1987). This assessment will assist in determining which subsystems should be targeted for interventions specific to alcoholic families (Walitzer, 1999). Counselors need to be aware that alcoholic families contain three diagnostic tracks—the environment, the family system, and the individual—all of which respond differently to the supremacy of the alcoholism (Brown & Schmid, 1999). For example, the cultural milieu (the environment) can often determine how someone will respond to the development of an addiction. In a study examining gender differences in role expectations, the authors found that men may consider the development of addictions to be a natural part of participating in male culture, while women frequently are both more remorseful and more aware of the harmful impact of their behavior on their relationships (Strassner & Zelvin, 1997). Counselors must therefore take care to include questions about each diagnostic track in their initial assessment.

Although many practitioners advocate the use of formal assessment instruments during initial sessions, others maintain that the structured clinical interview is best, as long as honest disclosure is obtained (Chamberlain & Jew, 2003). In addition to helping the family feel more comfortable, the clinical interview allows for development of a solid therapeutic alliance and the counselor's observance of the family's nonverbal interactions. One assessment technique that is quite useful is the genogram. A *genogram* is a graphic, symbolic representation of generational family relationships. Because of its breadth and complexity, it can be used to pinpoint patterns of behavior and the psychological factors that disrupt relationships. Thus, this is a good therapeutic tool allowing for a more systemic focus and providing counselors with vital information the family may attempt to hide. For example, a special emphasis on the health status of family members (i.e., prominent histories of heart disease and other cardiovascular problems, liver disease, depression, suicide, miscarriages, mental retardation, or learning disabilities that may be linked to fetal alcohol syndrome), as well as close attention to legal problems, frequently can signify a substance abuse problem the family denies.

Ideally, assessment should include all adult members and school-age children who live in the family system. Including as many family members as possible allows for the utilization of many different sources of information, and serves to minimize distortions and inaccuracies (Chamberlain & Jew, 2003). All members must come to the session sober and agree that the counseling emphasis will be on the addiction as a family problem. Moreover, everyone must consent to the exploration of basic safety considerations during every session, especially if there is a history of domestic violence or child abuse.

As with every assessment, counselors should conduct the session in a supportive, caring, and nonjudgmental manner. The supportive and nonjudgmental nature of the questions and interpersonal interactions is especially important for a family struggling with addiction, however, as they already feel guilty, responsible, and shamed by the situation (Rafferty & Hartley, 2006). The counselor's sensitivity and lack of blame will help encourage self-disclosure and motivate family members toward change. Specific assessment questions should focus on the function and severity of the addiction for each individual and the family as a whole, the presence of emotional and behavioral problems for each person, and the existence of strengths, capabilities, and resilience they have developed in response to chemical dependency (McIntyre, 2004). Counselors also should be alert to the social problems common in an addict's life, such as excessive job loss, drug arrests, domestic violence, break-up of important relationships, frequent moves, and lack of interest in activities that once were important to the person (Chamberlain & Jew, 2003). In addition to the necessary questions, assessment should include validation of family stories and a demonstration of how family problems are directly connected to the addiction (Hartel & Glantz, 1999). Counselors also need to assess for the psychological, attitudinal, and behavioral skills the family will need to develop in order to support their substance-free existence (McIntyre, 2004).

Treatment Strategies for Addicted Family Systems

Within the addictions treatment community, there is debate about how much attention counselors should pay to having the addicted person achieve full sobriety. While many counselors believe that little work can be done without abstinence (Hartel & Glantz, 1999; Stanton & Heath, 1995; Steinglass et al., 1987), others maintain that it is not the counselor's job to monitor the sobriety of an addicted individual (Pascoe, 1999; Rotunda et al., 1995). Instead, they should pay close attention to how family dynamics maintain the alcohol consumption and work to change those. In this way, abstinence is not the primary foundation upon which the effectiveness of the counseling rests. Some counselors operate from a harm reduction model (i.e., accepting the person wherever she or he is in the stages of change and assisting that person through the process) so that when relapse occurs (as it will, since recovery is a process), everything is not lost.

As with assessment, treatment should be conducted through the three areas of interest: the environment, the system, and the individual. While working on the environment and the family system can occur in two separate phases, individual work can be accomplished throughout. In treating the environment, counselors must accomplish two primary tasks (Chamberlain & Jew, 2003). First, the family must create safety from external threats and the internalized family, or the family of origin. Toward this end, counselors should be nonblaming and noncontrolling (Stanton & Heath, 1995) and use consistency and predictability in interacting with the family.

Second, each family member must tell the story of the trauma. This is an important part of treatment because it helps eliminate the compartmentalizing, denial, and repression characterized by alcoholic families (van der Kolk & Kadish, 1987) and allows everyone to hear each family member's perspective. To accomplish this huge task, counselors must strive to make the counseling session an extremely safe place. While not a primary task in this area of treatment, an analysis of social-relational changes and how best to help at-risk individuals manage these transitions can be helpful in preventing future relapses (Richman et al., 1994).

The family system is the arena in which most work will take place. Counselors must be extremely active during this period of work, repairing the distortions of reality by educating about alcoholism, inferring the family rules and the punishments for breaking them, and challenging the rationalizations that supported the rules (Chamberlain & Jew, 2003; Hartel & Glantz, 1999). During this period, families may experience what is known as the "emotional desert." This is when family processes are upset and the members become uncomfortable. Many family members may feel depressed and detached, and may feel the desire to return to the "wet" patterns of behavior (Steinglass et al., 1987). Counselors can help them through this difficult time by normalizing and validating their experiences and working through the issues eroding their desire for change (Stanton & Heath, 1995).

McIntyre (2004) also suggests some experiential exercises to help the family regain their desire for healing. For example, he encourages families to remain distrustful of the change process as a way of respecting their fear and previous experiences. He recommends an intervention known as "distrust days." Family members are asked to actively distrust each other on certain specified days while building trust the rest of the time. They are then asked to decide which they like better. In this way, nonaddicted family members start becoming less reactive to the substance abuser and can begin working on their own emotional processes. Family members are also told that they are expected to only do a little bit right and are sure to make mistakes (McIntyre, 2004). This lowers expectations of treatment and allows for small successes.

Another strategy for crossing the emotional desert is to use a criticism journal, in which family members keep track of every critical and fearful thought they have about the addict and the process of recovery. Family members can keep the journal until the end of counseling, at which time they can look back and see what changed.

Another intervention is to have family members write heartfelt letters to each other (McIntyre, 2004). All of these experiential treatment strategies give family members things to do while validating their experiences.

This period of work can allow time to focus on the couple subsystem. In matching the treatment to fit the family, counselors may want to change strategies and focus more on behavioral interventions. These can be more technical, with counselors teaching the nonabusing partner how to terminate the reinforcement contingencies that promote drinking and increase behaviors that support abstinence (Roberts & Linney, 2000). Other interventions can be more general, such as teaching problem-solving and communication skills (McCrady & Epstein, 1995). Developing increased cooperation and empathic understanding through communication exercises also can be beneficial (Rotunda et al., 1995).

Once the majority of the recovery work is done, counseling needs to focus on restabilizing the family so that they develop more healthy patterns of relating (Steinglass et al., 1987). During this period, counselors must identify strengths, help families create alternate coping strategies, and develop interactions that do not focus on the substance abuse (Hartel & Glantz, 1999; Stanton & Heath, 1995). They should address relapse prevention and teach families how to positively manage the effects of conflict (Rotunda et al., 1995). Once families believe they are firmly in recovery, the process of termination can begin.

Summary and Some Final Notations

Addiction affects not only the addicted person. It affects whole families, particularly the partners and children of substance abusers. Family members respond as best they can to addiction but frequently end up maintaining, instead of eliminating, the addiction. Addicted family systems tend to be characterized by unhealthy interactions and can result in most family members experiencing negative physical and emotional outcomes. Consequently, in order to provide the most effective service delivery, counselors must include the entire family in addictions treatment. In sessions, family counselors focus on the role family dynamics play in maintaining the addiction and concentrate interventions toward changing the ways family members relate to one another.

MyCounselingLab

Visit the MyCounselingLab site for *Foundations of Addictions Counseling,* Third Edition to enhance your understanding of concepts. You'll have the opportunity to practice your skills through video- and case-based exercises. You will find sets of questions to help you prepare for your certification exam with *Licensure Quizzes.* There is also a Video Library that provides taped counseling sessions, ethical scenarios, and interviews with helpers and clients.

Useful Websites

The following websites provide additional information relating to the chapter topics:

American Psychological Association's Division on Psychopharmacology and Substance Abuse
www.apa.org/divisions/div28/

American Psychological Association's Division on Family Psychology
www.apa.org/divisions/div43/

International Association of Addiction and Offender Counselors
www.iaaoc.org/

National Association of Alcoholism and Drug Abuse Counselors
/naadac.org/

National Institute on Drug Abuse
www.nida.nih.gov/

References

Alford, K. M. (1998). Family roles, alcoholism, and family dysfunction. *Journal of Mental Health Counseling, 20*, 250–261.

Amato, P. R., & Previti, D. (2003). People's reasons for divorcing: Gender, social class, the life course, and adjustment. *Journal of Family Issues, 24*(5), 602–626.

Baldwin, S. A., Christian, S., Berkeljon, A., Shadish, W. R., & Bean, R. (2012). The effects of family therapies for adolescent delinquency and substance abuse: A meta-analysis. *Journal of Marital and Family Therapy, 38*(1), 281–304.

Barnett, R., & Rivers, C. (2004). *Same difference: How gender myths are hurting our relationships, our children, and our jobs.* New York, NY: Basic Books.

Belsky, J., & Pluess, M. (2009). Beyond diathesis stress: Differential susceptibility to environmental influences. *Psychological Bulletin, 135*, 885–908.

Berlin, R., & Davis, R. B. (1989). Children from alcoholic families: Vulnerability and resilience. In T. F. Dugan & R. Coles (Eds.), *The child in our times* (pp. 107–123). New York, NY: Brunner/Mazel.

Black, C. (1981). *It will never happen to me.* Denver, CA: M. A. C. Publishers.

Black, C. (1992). Effects of family alcoholism. In S. Saitoh, P. Steinglass, & M. A. Schuckit (Eds.), *Alcoholism and the family* (pp. 272–281). Philadelphia, PA: Brunner/Mazel.

Black, C. (2010). The many faces of addiction: The journey to healing and recovery. *Psychology Today.* Retrieved from http://www.psychologytoday.com/blog/the-many-faces-addiction/201002/children-addiction

Brook, D. W., Brook, J. S., Rubenstone, E., Zhang, C., Singer, M., & Duke, M. R. (2003). Alcohol use in adolescents whose fathers abuse drugs. *Journal of Addictive Disease, 2*, 11–43.

Brooks, C. S., & Rice, K. F. (1997). *Families in recovery: Coming full circle.* Baltimore, MD: Paul H. Brookes Publishing Co.

Brown, S. (1992). *Safe passage: Recovery for adult children of alcoholics.* New York, NY: Wiley.

Brown, S., & Schmid, J. (1999). Adult children of alcoholics. In P. J. Ott, R. E. Tarter, & R. T. Ammerman (Eds.), *Sourcebook on substance abuse: Etiology, epidemiology, assessment, and treatment* (pp. 416–429). Needham Heights, MA: Allyn & Bacon.

Carmichael Olson, H., O'Connor, M. J., & Fitzgerald, H. E. (2001). Lessons learned from study of the developmental impact of parental alcohol use. *Infant Mental Health Journal, 22*(3), 271–290.

Centers for Disease Control and Prevention. (2013). *Intimate partner violence: Consequences.* Retrieved from http://www.cdc.gov/violenceprevention/intimatepartnerviolence/consequences.html

Chamberlain, L., & Jew, C. L. (2003). Family assessment of drug and alcohol problems. In K. Jordan (Ed.), *Handbook of couple and family assessment* (pp. 221–239). Hauppauge, NY: Nova Science Publishers.

Chasnoff, I. J., Wells, A. M., Telford, E., Schmidt, C., & Messer, G. (2010). Neurodevelopmental functioning in children with FAS, pFAS and ARND. *Journal of Developmental and Behavioral Pediatrics, 31*(3), 192–201.

Chermack, S. T., Fuller, B. E., & Blow, F. C. (2000). Predictors of expressed partner and non-partner violence among patients in substance abuse treatment. *Drug and Alcohol Dependence, 58*, 43–54.

Collins, R. L., Ellickson, P. L., & Klein, D. J. (2007). The role of substance use in young adult divorce. *Addiction, 102*(5), 786–794.

Copello, A., Templeton, L., Orford, J., Velleman, R., Patel, A., Moore, L., & Godfrey, C. (2009). The relative efficacy of two levels of a primary care intervention for family members affected by the addiction problem of a close relative: A randomized trial. *Addiction, 104*, 49–58.

Cox, R. B., Ketner, J. S., & Blow, A. J. (2013). Working with couples and substance abuse: Recommendations for clinical practice. *American Journal of Family Therapy, 41*(2), 160–172.

Cranford, J. A., Floyd, F. J., Schulenberg, J. E., & Zucker, R. A. (2011). Husbands' and wives' alcohol use disorders and marital interactions as longitudinal predictors of marital adjustment. *Journal of Abnormal Psychology, 120*(1), 210–222.

Dear, G. E., & Roberts, C. M. (2002). The relationships between codependency and femininity and masculinity. *Sex Roles, 46*(5–6), 159–165.

Díaz, R., Gual, A., García, M., Arnau, J., Pascual, F., et al. (2008). Children of alcoholics in Spain: From risk to pathology: Results from the ALFIL program. *Social Psychiatry and Psychiatric Epidemiology, 43*(1), 1–10.

DiClemente, C. C., & Velasquez, M. M. (2002). Motivational interviewing and the stages of change. In W. R. Miller & S. Rollnick (Eds.), *Motivational interviewing* (2nd ed., pp. 201–216). New York, NY: Guilford Press.

Drake, R. E., Wallach, M. A., Alverson, H. S., & Mueser, K. T. (2002). Psychosocial aspects of substance abuse by clients with severe mental illness. *Journal of Nervous and Mental Disease, 190*(2), 100–106.

Edwards, J. T. (2003). *Working with families: Guidelines and techniques* (6th ed.). Durham, NC: Foundation Place Publishing.

Epstein, E. E., & McCrady, B. S. (1998). Behavioral couples treatment of alcohol and drug use disorders: Current status and innovations. *Clinical Psychology Review, 18,* 689–711.

Erickson, C. K. (2007). *The science of addiction.* New York, NY: W. W. Norton & Company.

Fals-Stewart, W., Birchler, G. R., & Ellis, L. (1999). Procedures for evaluating the dyadic adjustment of drug-abusing patients and their intimate partners. *Journal of Substance Abuse Treatment, 16,* 5–16.

Fals-Stewart, W., Kashdan, T. B., O'Farrell, T. J., & Birchler, G. R. (2002). Behavioral couples therapy for drug-abusing patients: Effects on partner violence. *Journal of Substance Abuse Treatment, 22,* 87–96.

Fals-Stewart, W., Kelley, M. L., Cooke, C. G., & Golden, J. C. (2003). Predictors of the psychosocial adjustment of children living in households of parents in which fathers abuse drugs: The effects of postnatal parental exposure. *Addictive Behavior, 28,* 1013–1031.

Fals-Stewart, W., Kelley, M. L., Fincham, F. D., Golden, J., & Logsdon, T. (2004). Emotional and behavioral problems of children living with drug-abusing fathers: Comparisons with children living with alcohol-abusing and non-substance-abusing fathers. *Journal of Family Psychology, 18*(2), 319–330.

Fals-Stewart, W., Lam, K., & Kelley, M. (2009). Learning sobriety together: Behavioral couples therapy for alcoholism and drug abuse. *Journal of Family Therapy, 31,* 115–125.

Fields, R. (2004). *Drugs in perspective: A personalized look at substance use and abuse* (5th ed.). New York, NY: McGraw-Hill.

Fitzgerald, H. E., Zucker, R. A., & Yang, H. (1995). Developmental systems theory and alcoholism: Analyzing patterns of variation in high-risk families. *Psychology of Addictive Behaviors, 9*(1), 8–22.

Friedman, A. S., Tomko, I. A., & Utada, A. (1991). Client and family characteristics that predict better family therapy outcome for adolescent drug abusers. *Family Dynamics of Addiction Quarterly, 1*(1), 77–93.

Grant, T., Huggins, J., Graham, J. C., Ernst, C., Whitney, N., & Wilson, D. (2011). Maternal substance abuse and disrupted parenting: Distinguishing mothers who keep their children from those who do not. *Children and Youth Services Review, 33*(11), 2176–2185.

Grawe, R. W., Hage, R., Espeland, B., & Mueser, K. T. (2007). The better life program: Effects of group skills training for persons with severe mental illness and substance use disorders. *Journal of Mental Health, 16*(5), 625–634.

Griffiths, M. D. (2005). A "components" model of addiction within a biopsychosocial framework. *Journal of Substance Use, 10,* 191–197.

Grzywacz, J. G., & Marks, N. F. (1999). Family solidarity and health behaviors: Evidence from the National Survey of Midlife Development in the United States (MIDUS). *Journal of Family Issues, 20,* 243–268.

Hartel, C. R., & Glantz, M. D. (1999). The treatment of drug abuse: Changing the paths. In M. D. Glantz & C. R. Hartel (Eds.), *Drug abuse: Origins and interventions* (pp. 243–284). Washington, DC: American Psychological Association.

Homish, G. G., & Leonard, K. E. (2008). The social network and alcohol use. *Journal of Studies on Alcohol and Drugs, 69*(6), 906–914.

Homish, G. G., Leonard, K. E., Kozlowski, L. T., & Cornelius, J. R. (2009). The longitudinal association between multiple substance use discrepancies and marital satisfaction. *Addiction, 104,* 1201–1209.

Howells, E., & Orford, J. (2006). Coping with a problem drinker: A therapeutic intervention for the partners of problem drinkers, in their own right. *Journal of Substance Use, 11,* 53–71.

Joanning, H., Quinn, W., Thomas, F., & Mullen, R. (1992). Treating adolescent drug use: A comparison of family systems therapy, group therapy, and family drug education. *Journal of Marital and Family Therapy, 18*(4), 345–356.

Johnson, J. D., Noel, N. E., & Sutter-Hernandez, J. (2000). Alcohol and male acceptance of sexual aggression: The role of perceptual ambiguity. *Journal of Applied Social Psychology, 30*(6), 1186–1200.

Joutsenniemi, K., Moustgaard, H., Koskinen, S., Ripatti, S., & Martikainen, P. (2011). Psychiatric comorbidity in couples: A longitudinal study of 202,959 married and cohabiting individuals. *Social Psychiatry and Psychiatric Epidemiology, 46*(7), 623–633.

Juhnke, G. A., & Hagedorn, W. B. (2006). *Counseling addicted families: An integrated assessment and treatment model.* New York, NY: Routledge/Taylor & Francis Group.

Kearns-Bodkin, J. N., & Leonard, K. E. (2008). Relationship functioning among adult children of alcoholics. *Journal of Studies on Alcohol & Drugs, 69,* 941–950.

Kelley, M. L., & Fals-Stewart, W. (2002). Couples- versus individual-based therapy for alcohol and drug abuse: Effects on children's psychosocial functioning. *Journal of Consulting and Clinical Psychology, 70*(2), 417–427.

Kinney, J. (2003). *Loosening the grip: A handbook of alcohol information.* New York, NY: McGraw-Hill.

Langeland, W., Draijer, N., & van den Brink, W. (2004). Psychiatric comorbidity in treatment-seeking alcoholics: The role of childhood trauma and perceived parental dysfunction. *Alcoholism: Clinical and Experimental Research, 28*(3), 441–447.

Lawson, A. W., & Lawson, G. W. (2005). Families and drugs. In R. H. Coombs (Ed.), *Addiction counseling review: Preparing for comprehensive, certification, and licensing examinations* (pp. 175–199). Mahwah, NJ: Lawrence Erlbaum Associates.

Leonard, K. E., & Roberts, L. J. (1998). Marital aggression, quality, and stability in the first year of marriage: Findings from the Buffalo Newlywed Study. In T. N. Bradbury (Ed.), *The developmental course of marital dysfunction* (pp. 44–73). New York, NY: Cambridge University Press.

Liddle, H., & Diamond, G. (1991). Adolescent substance abusers in family therapy: The critical initial phase of treatment. *Family Dynamics of Addiction Quarterly, 1*(1), 55–68.

Liddle, H. A., Rowe, C. L., Dakof, G. A., Henderson, C. E., & Greenbaum, P. E. (2009). Multidimensional family therapy for young adolescent substance abuse: Twelve-month outcomes of a randomized controlled trial. *Journal of Consulting and Clinical Psychology, 77*(1), 12–25.

Lorber, W., Morgan, D. Y., Eisen, M. L., Barak, T., Perez, C., & Crosbie-Burnett, M. (2007). Patterns of cohesion in the families of offspring of addicted parents: Examining a nonclinical sample of college students. *Psychological Reports, 101*(3), 881–895.

Marks, A. D. G., Blore, R. L., Hine, D. W., & Dear, G. E. (2012). Development and validation of a revised measure of codependency. *Australian Journal of Psychology, 64*(3), 119–127.

Marshal, M. P. (2003). For better or worse? The effect of alcohol use on marital functioning. *Clinical Psychology Review, 23*(7), 959–997.

McCord, J. (1988). Identifying developmental paradigms leading to alcoholism. *Journal of Studies on Alcohol, 49,* 357–362.

McCrady, B. S., & Epstein, E. E. (1995). Directions for research on alcoholic relationships: Marital and individual-based models of heterogeneity. *Psychology of Addictive Behaviors, 9,* 157–166.

McIntyre, J. R. (2004). Family treatment of substance abuse. In S. L. A. Straussner (Ed.), *Clinical work with substance-abusing clients* (2nd ed., pp. 237–263). New York, NY: Guilford Press.

McKinney, C. M., Caetano, R., Harris, T. R., & Ebama, M. S. (2009). Alcohol availability and intimate partner violence among US couples. *Alcoholism: Clinical & Experimental Research, 33,* 169–176.

Meyers, R. J., Apodaca, T. R., Flicker, S. M., & Slesnick, N. (2002). Evidence-based approaches for the treatment of substance abusers by involving family members. *The Family Journal: Counseling and Therapy for Couples and Families, 10*(3), 281–288.

Miller, T., Bilyeu, J., Veltkamp, L., Clayton, R., Welsh, R., & Elzie, N. (2001). Intimacy in addicted couples: Clinical issues and case studies. In Barbara Jo Brothers (Ed.), *Couples, intimacy issues, and addiction* (pp. 51–63). New York, NY: Haworth Press.

Miller, W. R., Forcehimes, A. A., & Zweben, A. (2011). *Treating addiction: A guide for professionals.* New York, NY: Guilford Press.

Miller, W. R., & Tonigan, J. S. (1996). Assessing drinkers' motivation for change: The Stages of Change Readiness and Treatment Eagerness Scales (SOCRATES). *Psychology of Addictive Behaviors, 10,* 81–89.

Moos, R. H., Finney, J. W., & Cronkite, R. C. (1990). *Alcoholism treatment: Context, process and outcome.* New York, NY: Oxford University Press.

Morrissette, P. J. (2010). Couples at the crossroads: Substance abuse and intimate relationship deliberation. *The Family Journal, 18*(2), 146–153.

Mun, E.-Y., Fitzgerald, H. E., Puttler, I. I., Zucker, R. A., & Von Eye, A. (2000). Temperamental characteristics as predictors of externalizing and internalizing behavior problems in the contexts of high and low parental psychopathology. *Infant Mental Health Journal, 22,* 393–415.

Nair, P., Schuler, M. E., Black, M. M., Kettinger, L., & Harrington, D. (2003). Cumulative environmental risk in substance abusing women: Early intervention, parenting stress, child abuse potential and child development. *Child Abuse & Neglect, 27,* 997–1017.

National Institute of Justice. (2000). *Full report of the prevalence, incidence, and consequences of violence against women: Findings from the National Violence Against Women Survey Research Report* (NCJ 183781). Washington, DC, and Atlanta, GA: U.S. Department of Justice, National Institute of Justice, and U.S. Department of Health and Human Services, Centers for Disease Control and Prevention. Retrieved from http://www.nij.gov/topics/crime/intimate-partner-violence/Pages/extent.aspx

Navarra, R. (2007). Family response to adults and alcohol. *Alcoholism Treatment Quarterly, 25*(1/2), 85–104.

Nicholas, K., & Rasmussen, E. (2006). Childhood abusive and supportive experiences, inter-parental violence, and parental alcohol use: Prediction of young adult depressive symptoms and aggression. *Journal of Family Violence, 21,* 43–61.

O'Farrell, T. (1990). Sexual functioning of male alcoholics. In R. L. Collins, K. E. Leonard, B. H. Miller, & J. S. Searles (Eds.), *Alcohol and the family: Research and clinical perspectives* (pp. 244–271). New York, NY: Guilford Press.

O'Farrell, T. J., & Fals-Stewart, W. (2000). Behavioral couples therapy for alcoholism and drug abuse. *Behavior Therapist, 23*(3), 49–54.

O'Farrell, T. J., & Fals-Stewart, W. (2003). Alcohol abuse. *Journal of Marital and Family Therapy, 29*(1), 121–146.

O'Farrell, T. J., Murphy, C. M., Stephan, S. H., Fals-Stewart, W., & Murphy, M. (2004). Partner violence before and after couples-based alcoholism treatment for male alcoholic patients: The role of treatment involvement and abstinence. *Journal of Consulting and Clinical Psychology, 72,* 202–217.

Office of Applied Studies, Substance Abuse and Mental Health Statistics. (2012). *Results from the 2012 National Survey on Drug Use and Health: Summary of National Findings.* Retrieved from http://www.samhsa.gov/data/NSDUH/2012SummNatFindDetTables/NationalFindings/NSDUHresults2012.htm#ch2.3

Olmstead, M. E., Crowell, J. A., & Waters, E. (2003). Assortative mating among adult children of alcoholics and alcoholics. *Family Relations, 52*(1), 64–71.

Pascoe, W. (1999). Enhancing the creative process in couple therapy. *Journal of Couples Therapy, 8*(1), 5–10.

Poon, E., Ellis, D. A., Fitzgerald, H. A., & Zucker, R. A. (2000). Intellectual, cognitive and academic performance among sons of alcoholics during the early elementary school years: Differences related to subtypes of familial alcoholism. *Alcoholism: Clinical and Experimental Research, 24,* 1020–1027.

Powers, M. B., Vedel, E., & Emmelkamp, P. M. G. (2008). Behavioral couples therapy (BCT) for alcohol and drug use disorders: A meta-analysis. *Clinical Psychology Review, 28*(6), 952–962.

Rafferty, P., & Hartley, P. (2006). Shame about the children: A legacy of distress for adults who have grown up with parental problem drinking and family disharmony? *Journal of Substance Use, 11*(2), 115–127.

Ranganathan, S. (2004). Families in transition: Victims of alcoholism and new challenges ahead. *International Journal for the Advancement of Counselling, 26*(4), 399–405.

Richman, J. A., Rospenda, K. M., & Kelley, M. A. (1994). Gender roles and alcohol abuse across the transition to parenthood. *Journal of Studies on Alcohol, 56,* 553–557.

Roberts, L. J., & Linney, K. D. (1998, November). *Alcohol use, marital functioning and the family life cycle.* Paper presented at the annual meeting of the National Council on Family Relations, Milwaukee, WI.

Roberts, L. J., & Linney, K. D. (2000). Alcohol problems and couples: Drinking in an intimate relational context. In K. B. Schmaling & T. G. Sher (Eds.), *The psychology of couples and illness: Theory, research, & practice* (pp. 269–310). Washington, DC: American Psychological Association.

Rotunda, R., & Doman, K. (2001). Partner enabling of alcoholics: Critical review and future directions. *The American Journal of Family Therapy, 29*(4), 257–270.

Rotunda, R. J., Scherer, D. G., & Imm, P. S. (1995). Family systems and alcohol misuse: Research on the effects of alcoholism on family functioning and effective family interventions. *Professional Psychology: Research and Practice, 26,* 95–104.

Rounsaville, B. J., Kranzler, H. R., Ball, S., Tennen, H., Poling, J., & Trifflman, E. (1998). Personality disorders in substance abusers: Relation to substance abuse. *Journal of Nervous and Mental Diseases, 186,* 78–95.

Rowe, C. L., & Liddle, H. A. (2003). Substance abuse. *Journal of Marital and Family Therapy, 29*(1), 97–120.

Rubin, D. H. (2001). *Treating adult children of alcoholics: A behavioral approach.* New York, NY: Academic Press.

Schafer, J., Caetano, R., & Cunradi, C. B. (2004). A path model of risk factors for intimate partner violence among couples in the United States. *Journal of Interpersonal Violence, 19*(2), 127–142.

Schneider, J. P. (2002). The new "elephant in the living room": Effects of compulsive cybersex behaviors on the spouse. In A. Cooper (Ed.), *Sex and the Internet: A guide book for clinicians* (pp. 169–186). New York, NY: Brunner-Routledge.

Schuler, M. E., & Nair, P. (2001). Witnessing violence among inner-city children of substance abusing and non-substance abusing women. *Archives of Pediatrics & Adolescent Medicine, 155,* 342–346.

Schumm, J. A., O'Farrell, T. J., Murphy, C. M., & Fals-Stewart, W. (2009). Partner violence before and after couples-based alcoholism treatment for female alcoholic patients. *Journal of Consulting and Clinical Psychology, 77,* 1136–1146.

Shadish, W. R., & Baldwin, S. A. (2003). Meta-analysis of MFT interventions. *Journal of Marital and Family Therapy, 29,* 547–570.

Stanton, M. (2005). Couples and addiction. In M. Harway (Ed.), *Handbook of couples therapy* (pp. 313–336). Hoboken, NJ: John Wiley & Sons.

Stanton, M. D., & Heath, A. W. (1995). Family treatment of alcohol and drug abuse. In R. H. Mikesell, D.-D. Lusterman, & S. H. McDaniel (Eds.), *Integrating family therapy: Handbook of family psychology and systems theory* (pp. 529–541). Washington, DC: American Psychological Association.

Steinberg, M. L., Epstein, E. E., McCrady, B. S., & Hirsch, L. S. (1997). Sources of motivation in a couples outpatient alcoholism treatment program. *American Journal of Drug and Alcohol Abuse, 23,* 191–205.

Steinglass, P., Bennett, L. A., Wolin, S. J., & Reiss, D. (1987). *The alcoholic family.* New York, NY: Basic Books.

Strassner, S. L. A., & Zelvin, E. (1997). *Gender and addictions: Men and women in treatment.* Northvale, NJ: Aronson.

Substance Abuse and Mental Health Services Administration. (2010). *Results from the 2009 National Survey on Drug Use and Health: Volume I. Summary of findings* (Office of Applied Studies, NSDUH Series H-38A, HHS Publication No. SMA 10-4586 Findings). Rockville, MD.

van der Kolk, B. A., & Kadish, W. (1987). Amnesia, dissociation, and the return of the repressed. In B. A. van der Kolk (Ed.), *Psychological trauma.* Washington, DC: American Psychiatric Press.

van Wormer, K., & Davis, D. R. (2003). *Addiction treatment: A strengths perspective.* Pacific Grove, CA: Brooks/Cole Thomson Learning.

Walitzer, K. S. (1999). Family therapy. In P. J. Ott, R. E. Tarter, & R. T. Ammerman (Eds.), *Sourcebook on substance abuse: Etiology, epidemiology, assessment, and treatment* (pp. 337–349). Needham Heights, MA: Allyn & Bacon.

Washousky, R., Levy-Stern, D., & Muchowski, P. (1993). The stages of family alcoholism. *EAP Digest,* 38–42.

Watkins, L. E., O'Farrell, T. J., Suvak, M. K., Murphy, C. M., & Taft, C. T. (2009). Parenting satisfaction among fathers with alcoholism. *Addictive Behaviors, 34,* 610–612.

Wegscheider, S. (1981). *Another chance: Hope and help for the alcoholic family.* Palo Alto, CA: Science & Behavior Books.

Wekerle, C., & Wall, A. (2002). Introduction: The overlap between relationship violence and substance abuse. In C. Wekerle & A. Wall (Eds.), *The violence and addiction equation: Theoretical and clinical issues in substance abuse and relationship violence* (pp. 1–21). New York, NY: Brunner-Routledge.

Werner, E. E., & Johnson, J. (2004). The role of caring adults in the lives of children of alcoholics. *Substance Use and Misuse, 39,* 699–720.

Wiersma, J. D., Cleveland, H. H., Herrera, V. M., & Fischer, J. L. (2010). Intimate partner violence in dating, cohabitating, and married drinking partnerships. *Journal of Marriage and Family, 72,* 360–374.

Williams, C. (1987). Child care practices in alcoholic families: Findings from a neighborhood detoxification program. *Alcohol Health and Research World, 94,* 74–77.

Windle, M., & Tubman, J. G. (1999). Children of alcoholics. In W. K. Silverman & T. H. Ollendick (Eds.), *Developmental issues in the clinical treatment of children* (pp. 393–414). Boston, MA: Allyn & Bacon.

Wolin, S., Bennett, L., & Noonan, D. (1979). Family rituals and the recurrence of alcoholism over generations. *American Journal of Psychiatry, 136,* 589–593.

Zelvin, E. (2004). Treating the partners of substance abusers. In S. L. A. Straussner (Ed.), *Clinical work with substance-abusing clients* (2nd ed., pp. 264–283). New York, NY: Guilford Press.

Chapter 15

Persons with Disabilities and Substance-Related and Addictive Disorders

Debra A. Harley
Malachy Bishop

Lebogang Tiro
University of Kentucky

INTRODUCTION

Substance-related and addictive disorders are significant public health issues, leading to effects detrimental to the individual's physical, social, and psychological health, vocational prospects, and employment outcomes, and the welfare of family members, significant others, and coworkers. While it is difficult to determine the exact number of people who are substance abusers, in 2012 an estimated 22.2 million individuals were classified as having a diagnosis of alcohol abuse or addiction, compared to 20.6 million in 2011 (Substance Abuse and Mental Health Services Administration [SAMHSA], 2013a) based on criteria specified in the *Diagnostic and Statistical Manual of Mental Disorders*-5 (DSM-5) (American Psychological Association [APA], 2013). Many of these are individuals with coexisting disabilities. In the United States there are approximately 58 million people with disabilities (PWDs) (Erickson, Lee, & von Schrader, 2012). Of these, 2.8 million were classified with dependence or abuse of both alcohol and illicit drugs, 4.5 million had dependence or abuse of illicit drugs but not alcohol, and 14.9 million had dependence or abuse of alcohol but not illicit drugs. Alcohol is the most used substance and marijuana is the most commonly used illicit drug (SAMHSA, 2013a). See Table 15.1 for a summary of substance use by Americans. One of the substances that is often omitted from or overlooked in the estimation of people with addictions is caffeine, which is recognized as a personal and public health issue in all first-world countries (Kole & Barnhill, 2013; Meredith, Juliano, Hughes, & Griffiths, 2013). In the United States, about 7% of the population may experience five or more symptoms, along with functional impairment consistent with DSM-5 diagnosis of caffeine intoxication. Substance use affects multiple brain circuits, including those involved in reward and motivation, learning and memory, and inhibitory control over behavior. Over time, the effects of prolonged exposure on brain functioning compromise the ability to make decisions and exercise control. Some individuals are more vulnerable than others to becoming addicted, depending on the interplay between genetic makeup, health status, and other environmental influences (National Institute on Drug Abuse [NIDA], 2012).

The presence and/or history of substance-related and addictive disorders are considered both a substance abuse disorder and a disability with chronic, relapsing condition (Glenn, Huber, Keferl, Wright-bell, & Lane, n.d.). The prevalence of substance abuse disorders is thought to be at least twice as high in adults with disabilities as in the general population (Office on Disability, 2013).

TABLE 15.1 Substance Abuse by Americans

Substance	Number	Current Percent
Alcohol	14.9 million	6.8
Tobacco	69.5 million	26.7
Marijuana	4.3 million	1.7
Pain Relievers	2.1 million	0.8
Cocaine	1.1 million	0.4
Heroin	467,000	0.2
Hallucinogens	331,000	—

Source: Based on information provided in SAMHSA (2013a). Data are based on Americans aged 12 or older.

Approximately 25% of persons with disabilities who participate in public vocational rehabilitation programs also experience a significant secondary issue with substance abuse (Weiss, 2013). Individuals with disabilities are disproportionately at greater risk of substance abuse due to multiple risk factors such as health problems, medication, societal enabling, lack of identification of potential problems, and lack of appropriate and accessible prevention and treatment services. Those with traumatic brain injury (TBI), spinal cord injury (SCI), mental illness (MI), deafness, arthritis, multiple sclerosis, orthopedic disabilities, vision impairment, and amputation are especially at risk, at a rate of 40–50% compared to 10% of the general population (Bombardier et al., 2004; Office on Disability, 2013), and persons with developmental disabilities (e.g., mental retardation, autism) are so at a rate of about 14% (Winkel, 2011). For people with disabilities and/or those who participate in vocational rehabilitation services, prevalence rates are greater than for members of the general population (Ebener & Smedema, 2011; Krahn, Deck, Gabriel, & Farrell, 2007; Hollar, McAweeny, & More, 2008; McAweeney, Keferl, Moore, & Wagner, 2008; National Rehabilitation Information Center, 2011).

Substance abuse cuts across the age spectrum among persons with disabilities, with younger adults reported to use more illicit drugs and older adults more likely to abuse prescription medication (Bachman, Drainoni, & Tobias, 2004; Brucker, 2008). In addition, substance abuse disorders are the most frequently occurring comorbid disability among persons with mental health diagnoses (Ostacher, 2011; SAMHSA, 2009a), at a rate of 8.9 million persons, and approximately 25% (2.8 million) of those with a serious mental illness also have a co-occurring substance use disorder (SAMHSA, 2012). Research has documented a high rate of co-occurring substance abuse disorders among Supplemental Security Income (SSI) beneficiaries with mental health disorders (Bachman et al., 2004; Slayter, 2010). For individuals with mental disorders, the relationship between the disorder and substance abuse is complex and potentially interactive, in that dependency can be masked by the symptoms of psychiatric disorders such as depression, anxiety, post-traumatic stress disorder (PTSD), or bipolar disorder (Kinney, 2011; Ostacher, 2011). There are distinct risk factors for substance-related disorders by race and ethnicity. Substance misuse by ethnic minority populations have risk factors associated with socioeconomic status/poverty, criminal history and criminal activity in the community, and neighborhood disorganization (Le Cook & Alegria, 2011; Tragesser, Beauvais, Swain, Edwards, & Oetting, 2007). Harrell and Broman (2009) found that being younger, having less education, as well as alcohol use, marijuana use, inhalant use, and delinquent behavior during adolescence, were associated with prescription drug misuse, and there are unique racial/ethnic profiles for substance use risk behaviors for this age.

TABLE 15.2 Barriers to Treatment for Persons with Disabilities

Health promotion materials may be written at too high a reading level for persons with an intellectual disability.

Materials may be unavailable in formats accessible to persons with visual impairments.

Educational and prevention literature and materials primarily show images of persons without disabilities, sending the inaccurate message that PWDs are not at risk.

Treatment centers are often inaccessible to those with physical disabilities.

Effective communication may be hampered as a result of limited availability of assistive supports or interpreters for persons who are deaf or hard of hearing.

Cultural insensitivity by service providers may prevent persons with disabilities from seeking education, risk management, and treatment for substance abuse.

Transportation issues and sheer distance complicate access to specialized treatment centers for PWDs.

Lack of staff with an understanding of disabilities.

Inadequate management of psychiatric concerns for persons with dual diagnoses.

Limited family support or having competing needs for family time and resources.

Cost prohibitive because PWDs are unable to qualify for publicly funded services.

Belief that the stigma of having a disability impedes treatment success.

Perceived stigmatization and victimization by substance abuse treatment system.

Mistrust of the treatment system.

Source: Based on information provided in Krahn, Farrell, Gabriel, and Deck (2006) and Office on Disability (2013).

A significant number of people currently seeking treatment for substance abuse disorders also have a physical, cognitive, sensory, psychiatric, or affective disability. Many PWDs are unable to access treatment they desperately need because of the double stigma of having a substance abuse disorder and a coexisting disability. Barriers to treatment for PWDs are presented in Table 15.2. In addition, persons with both disabilities and substance abuse disorders are less likely to enter or complete treatment because physical, attitudinal, or communication barriers limit their treatment options or else render their treatment experiences unsatisfactory (West, Graham, & Cifu, 2009a). Disparities in access to substance abuse treatment are greatest for individuals with comorbidity of intellectual disabilities (ID), substance abuse (SA), and serious mental illness (SMI). Slayter (2010) found that factors associated with initiation of treatment among those with ID/SA/SMI included being nonwhite, living in a rural area, and not being dually eligible for Medicare; factors associated with engagement of treatment included all of these and having a fee-for-service plan, a chronic SA-related disorder, or both. Another factor attributed to the low treatment participation of PWDs could be the failure of physicians to identity and refer these individuals to treatment (West, Luck, et al., 2009).

As one of the largest and most diverse minority groups in the United States, PWDs are disproportionately represented among those with substance abuse disorders. As specified in the DSM-5, substance abuse is a disability, and not a symptom of another disabling condition (APA, 2013). Although it is possible that a reciprocal causal relation exists between substance abuse and disability, most recent research supports the hypothesis that the presence of a disability significantly increases the risk for alcohol and illicit drug use and prescription abuse (Brucker, 2007; Ebener & Smedema, 2011; Office on Disability, 2013). Individuals with mental illness who participate in treatment are significantly more likely to abuse prescription drugs and opiates, persons with developmental disabilities are significantly less likely to do so, and those with and without disabilities who have primary problems with alcohol, cocaine, and marijuana are at significantly decreased risk of having a secondary problem of opiate abuse (Brucker, 2008). One of the major issues in the diagnosis of substance abuse and addictions in persons with disabilities is that abuse and addiction are frequently either seen as occurring secondary to another disability, and thus receive limited clinical attention, or else they are not recognized at all (West, Luck et al., 2009).

The purpose of this chapter is to discuss issues that affect persons with disabilities in regard to substance-related and addictive disorders. The chapter presents material on how issues of substance abuse and addiction can be specifically addressed in rehabilitation counseling settings. In addition, an overview of the characteristics and status of persons with disabilities and addictions is presented, including racial disparities in substance abuse and disability, risk factors for persons with disabilities, treatment utilization and outcomes, and intervention strategies in rehabilitation settings. Case studies are integrated throughout the chapter.

Workers in a majority of inpatient rehabilitation training programs have expressed concern about alcohol and drug problems among their patients (Basford, Rohe, Barnes, & DePompolo, 2002; Goodwin, 2009). Rehabilitation counselors tend to have a positive attitude toward working with individuals with substance use disorders (Rodgers-Bonaccorsy, 2010). Rehabilitation counselors, other counselors, and human and social service providers need to understand addiction as it relates to persons with disabilities. Given recent developments in service provision and legislative mandates, rehabilitation counselors and other human and social service providers must also be aware of new trends regarding culturally diverse populations, immigrants, veterans, offender populations, and persons with AIDS among PWDs and substance-related and addiction disorders.

As a framework for this chapter, several issues are presented to provide clarity to the reader. First, it should be noted that any type of substance-related or addictive disorder is characterized by a pattern of continued pathological use of a substance or participation in a behavior, which results in repeated adverse personal and social consequences related to use or behavior. According to Crozier and Sligar (2010), behavioral addiction includes a multitude of symptoms in which individuals engage compulsively or uncontrollably in certain behaviors. "Substance use disorders occur in a broad range of severity, from mild to severe, with severity based on the number of symptom criteria endorsed" (APA, 2013, p. 484). Second, although this chapter addresses substance-related and addictive disorders, other addictions—such as eating disorders, gambling compulsion, Internet and technology addiction, workaholism, and sexual addictions—are becoming increasingly prevalent in society, with a common core of behaviors (Ciaccio, 2010; Fisher & Harrison, 2013; Hawley, Glenn, & Diaz, 2012; Hawley, Glenn, & Keferl, 2011; Kole & Barnhill, 2013). Croizer and Sligar (2010) concur with Peele (1985) that the current concept of addiction has moved beyond a focus on drug use to a broader, more holistic construct. Third, increasingly individuals are polysubstance users or have multiple or cross addictions. This can enhance the effects of the drugs and help manage the side effects of coming down or withdrawing from one drug (Doweiko, 2015). Fourth, several case studies are presented to highlight a number of important considerations that will be revisited and discussed throughout the chapter. You are invited to review the information in these case studies as a counselor, and to consider the concept of addiction in light of the potential risk factors, intervention strategies, and treatment recommendations that will enhance the client's ability to gain and maintain sobriety. Particular attention should be given to sociocultural issues, age, gender, sexuality, recreational habits, employment status, and the existence of multiple addictions.

Finally, throughout this chapter we use the terms *substance abuse, substance use disorder, alcohol dependence,* and *addiction* interchangeably. However, we acknowledge that the *Diagnostic and Statistical Manual of Mental Disorders* (5th ed., DSM-5) (APA, 2013) provides specific diagnostic criteria for alcohol and/or substance use disorders. The reader should refer to the DMS-5 for additional information.

CHARACTERISTICS AND STATUS OF PEOPLE WITH DISABILITIES AND ADDICTIONS

People with disabilities in the United States are often classified by categories (e.g., type of disability: cognitive, mental, physical, sensory, etc.) and by their need for assistance based on functional limitations (e.g., activities of daily living; ability to perform work-related tasks). In addition, an individual may be categorized based on the severity of his or her disability (Brault, 2012). Across these categories, PWDs' employment rate is also impacted, and there is divergence in the employment rate trends across gender and ethnicity/race (Beveridge & Fabian, 2007; Dutta, Gervey, Chan, Chou, & Ditchman, 2008; Jung & Bellini, 2011). According to Brault (2012), of the 303.9 million people in the civilian noninstitutionalized population, 56.7 million (18.7.0%) had a disability in 2010, of which 38.3 million (12.6%) had a severe disability. Of those aged 21–64 with a disability, 41.1% were employed; of those with severe disability, 27.5% were employed compared to 71.2% of people with a nonsevere disability and 79.1% with no disability. Further examination of the data by gender and race/ethnicity reveals even more startling statistics for those with severe disabilities. That is, for all races and genders, 14.8% of those with disabilities had severe disabilities, non-Hispanic White accounted for 17.4%, African American (including Black) 22.3%, Asian 14.4%, and Hispanic (any race) 17.8%. As of 2010, the employment rate of PWDs has shown a consistently lower rate for those with severe disabilities and those of ethnic minority groups (Barnow, 2008; Brault, 2012). Additional information on employment and earnings of PWDs can be obtained from the U.S. Census Bureau in *Americans with Disabilities: 2010 Household Economic Studies* (Brault, 2012).

Employment rates and income earnings are only two of the indicators that describe the status of PWDs. Another distinguishing factor is the occurrence of substance abuse and addiction among this population. People with disabilities and substance-related and addictive disorders have the lowest successful closure rates in vocational rehabilitation agencies (Hollar, McAweeney, & Moore, 2008; McAweeny, Keferl, Moore, & Wagner, 2008). The Office on Disability (2013) reported that approximately 25% of PWDs in vocational rehabilitation programs experience a significant secondary problem with substance abuse. Interestingly, with the Contract with America Advancement Act of 1996 (P.L. 104-121), which mandated that individuals no longer qualify for SSI solely because they were disabled as a result of substance abuse, higher rates of drug use have been found among people receiving rehabilitation services for all major drug categories (Bachman et al., 2004). In addition, under the Americans with Disabilities Act (ADA) a person who is a "current" drug user is not covered as a "qualified individual with a disability."

Other studies have shown that substance abuse disorders affect PWDs more than other mental disorders. For example, Bombardier et al. (2004) found that 14% of persons with multiple sclerosis (MS) in their sample screened positive for possible alcohol abuse or dependence, and 7.4% reported misusing illicit drugs or prescription medications. The authors of this study reported that substance abuse may be present in up to 19% of the sample and contributes to high rates of depression. In addition, there may be greater risk of harm due to substance abuse in people with MS because of the potential magnification of motor and cognitive impairment.

The Americans with Disabilities Act (ADA)

A person who is a current substance abuser does not qualify as having a disability as defined by the ADA. "Qualified individuals" under the ADA include those who:

- Have been successfully rehabilitated and who are no longer engaged in the illegal use of drugs
- Are currently participating in a rehabilitation program and are no longer engaging in the illegal use of drugs
- Are regarded, erroneously, as illegally using drugs

A former drug addict may be protected under the ADA because the addiction may be considered a substantially limiting impairment. However, according to the Equal Employment Opportunity Commission (EEOC, 1994) *Technical Assistance Manual on the Employment Provisions (Title I) of the Americans with Disabilities Act*, a former *casual* drug user is not protected:

> A person who casually used drugs illegally in the past, but did not become addicted is not an individual with a disability based on the past drug use. In order for a person to be "substantially limited" because of drug use, she or her must be addicted to the drug.

Source: 42 U.S.C. § 12114(b) (1994). *EEOC Technical Assistance Manual on the Employment Provisions (Title I) of the Americans with Disabilities Act*, 8.5.

In a study of individuals with brain injury and spinal cord injury, Kolakowsky-Hayner et al. (2002) found that persons with SCI were more likely to drink on a daily basis post-injury, and persons with TBI were more inclined to use illicit drugs post-injury. Both SCI and TBI were associated with a higher rate of post-injury versus pre-injury drug use. Yet other research has identified rates of pre- and post-injury substance abuse among TBI and SCI groups equating to substantial numbers of individuals in need of substance abuse treatment (Langlois, Rutland-Brown, & Thomas, 2004; National Spinal Cord Injury [SCI] Statistical Center, 2008). Basford et al. (2002) found that individuals with nervous system injuries are more likely to report substance abuse. Brucker (2008) reported that persons with developmental disabilities are significantly less likely to use prescription drugs and opiates than others in treatment. Other studies suggest that among persons with developmental disabilities, such as intellectual disability and autism, rates of abuse have been estimated to be as high as 14% (Burgard, Donohue, Azrin, & Teichner, 2000; McGillicuddy, 2006). Overall, people with disabilities who have substance-related and addictive disorders tend to abuse substances at a higher rate than people without disabilities, have a higher rate of isolation and reduced socialization, and have increased risk for abusing alcohol and other drug (AOD) abuse. Further, PWDs with specific types of disabilities abuse substances at a higher rate; similar for women without disabilities, gender bias exists about alcohol and drug use for women with disabilities who abuse substances; and attitudes about substance abuse for PWDs are more negative than for people without disabilities (Brault, 2012; SAMHSA, 2013a).

A look at PWDs by race/ethnicity who abuse substances reveals that Hispanics have the lowest rates of polydrug use disorder and Whites have the highest rates of lifetime alcohol and anxiety disorders (NIDA, 2003; Perron et al., 2009). Perron et al. also found that for those who had at least one lifetime drug use disorder, Whites exhibited the highest rate of abuse, followed by African Americans/Blacks, and Latinos/Hispanics. In a follow-up to the *Surgeon General's Report on Mental Health of 1999*, Sherer (2002) indicated that the overall prevalence of mental health problems among Asian Americans and Pacific Islanders (AA/PIs) does not significantly differ from that of other Americans, but AA/PIs have the lowest utilization rates of mental health services among ethnic groups. Mexican Americans (MAs) born outside the United States have lower prevalence rates of lifetime disorders than MAs born in the United States, and 25% of Mexican-born immigrants show signs of mental illness or substance abuse, compared with 48% of U.S.-born MAs. African Americans are twice as likely to have somatic symptoms than White Americans (WAs). American Indians (AIs) are five times more likely to die of alcohol-related causes than WAs (Sherer, 2002).

Taken together, the evidence suggest that ethnic minorities are overrepresented among the nation's vulnerable and have, relative to Whites, disproportionately higher disabilities resulting from unmet mental health needs. However, one must be aware that wide differences exist within minority groups and lumping them together in statistical analyses does not distinguish between the 561 tribes and some 200 languages of AIs; diverse cultures of Hispanic groups; the 43 separate ethnic groups of AA/PI groups from countries ranging from India to Indonesia; and geographical diversity of African Americans (Sherer, 2002). Harley (2005) reported that while African Americans' alcohol use is less than that of Whites, they tend to use more in response to stressors, their use rests in historical patterns and influences, and alcohol and other drug use frequently results in more adverse outcomes with regard to severity and devastation in their lives, families, and communities. Although substance-related and addiction disorders disproportionately affect minority populations, it is important to note that high rates of abstinence also occur among African Americans, American Indians, and Latino populations (National Survey of Substance Abuse Treatment Services [N-SSATS], 2009; SAMHSA, 2013a). This is often overlooked because a gross examination of drinking prevalence appears to support the idea that these populations have a higher alcohol consumption rate than other ethnic groups or subgroups in the United States (Fisher & Harrison, 2013).

CASE STUDY

The Case of Rita

Rita is a 33-year-old Latino-American female. Rita sustained injuries in an automobile accident resulting in paraplegia, partial hearing loss, and loss of vision in one eye. Subsequently, she was diagnosed with PTSD, substance abuse, chronic pain, and seizure disorder. She was discharged from the rehabilitation hospital after 3 months of therapy. She is a single mother of two boys, ages 10 and 7. Rita attended 9 months of technical college with a major in nursing. After dropping out of college, she worked in several entry-level jobs as a cook, cashier, and telemarketer. Prior to her injuries, she considered herself to be a social drinker and liked to party with her friends (e.g., drinking, gambling, and hanging out together). Since her injury, Rita spends most of her time at home, alone. She indicates that now she does not spend much time with her friends and family because they think she is "broken" and do not want to be around her. Her children have moved in with her mother, but no legal guardianship has been established.

Rita receives SSDI, food stamps, and subsidized housing. She has a care attendant to come and care for her and to prepare meals. About 2 months ago, at Rita's request, the care attendant moved in. Six months later, Rita is facing eviction for nonpayment of rent. Rita tells her mother that the reason she is behind in her rent payments is because her medication is too expensive, and she has had to start using alternative drugs for her pain. In an effort to help Rita, her mother offers to help pay the rent, but demands that the caretaker (who has progressed to being her boyfriend) move out. Her mother tells her that after what has happened to her as a result of the accident, she deserves to use whatever she can to help ease her pain.

A social worker has been asked to make a home visit to investigate and identify what type of assistance Rita needs. At the time of the home visit, the social worker discovers that Rita has been using heroin, supplied by her care attendant. Rita rationalizes that her drug use helps to reduce her pain and makes her feel more confident about handling her problems.

RISK FACTORS FOR PERSONS WITH DISABILITIES

Risk factors are those issues that can contribute to the person engaging in alcohol and other drugs (AOD). Although persons with disabilities abuse substances for many of the same reasons (e.g., stress reduction, experimentation, compensation for feelings of guilt, shyness, or low self-esteem) as people without disabilities, their usage is linked to specific reasons as well. Other reasons include but are not limited to isolation, depression, employment and financial issues, as a coping mechanism for adjustment to disability, and as a means to self-medicate. Persons with disabilities may be vulnerable and are often targets for others to take advantage of financially, sexually, and emotionally. To further complicate matters, many family members believe that PWDs are entitled to use recreational chemicals because of their disability (Doweiko, 2015). Moreover, the high rates of occurrence of alcohol and substance abuse disorders co-occurring with mental disorders further complicate risk factors (SAMHSA, 2013a). Additional research confirms that PWDs have more frequent interactions with the medical community than nondisabled persons and may receive more prescriptions, especially for opiates, stimulants, and depressants, thus increasing the opportunity for abuse (Brucker, 2008).

Another risk factor for PWDs is societal and attitudinal. Attitudes about disability influence the ways nondisabled people react to persons with disabilities, which can affect the latter's treatment outcomes. In addition, stereotypes and expectations of others influence the ways people think about their own disabilities. Some examples of attitudinal and societal risks/barriers are beliefs that (a) PWDs do not abuse substances; (b) PWDs should receive exactly the same treatment protocol as everyone else, so that they are not singled out as being different—the assumption is that being mainstreamed into society means that you should do exactly the same things as everyone else; (c) serving people with disabilities requires going to the extremes; (d) people with cognitive disabilities are not capable of learning how to stay sober; and (e) PWDs deserve pity, so they should be allowed more latitude to indulge in substance use (Bachman et al., 2004; Brucker, 2007). Many of these attitudes include the perception that PWDs are not normal, or are helpless, fragile, and sick. Many of these beliefs are common among counselors and other professionals. Counselors (and other helping professionals) who hold these beliefs may screen out those who would benefit from their programs, deny clients appropriate accommodation for their disability, or unwittingly enable clients to use their disabilities to avoid treatment (West et al., 2009a). Persons with disabilities often end up with labels of social deviance, which render them as double outcasts when identified as having AOD abuse (Kinney, 2011). Clearly, counselor perception may be a significant barrier to overcome for persons with disabilities in accessing treatment for addictions.

There are a number of reasons directly related to the disability which might contribute to the increased risk of AOD abuse among persons with disabilities. These risk factors can be divided into five categories: health and medical, psychological, social, economic and employment, and access (Brucker, 2007; West, Graham, & Cifu, 2009b). Each is discussed in the following sections.

Health and Medical Risk Factors

People with disabilities often use medications over extended periods of time. Some disability-related conditions require multiple concurrently prescribed medications. Individuals using prescribed medications require specific information on how these drugs influence behavior or interact with other drugs such as alcohol and over-the-counter medication. Disabilities such as arthritis, bipolar disorder, diabetes, epilepsy, and cystic fibrosis may place a person at risk for problems related to medication use. For example, in the case of a person who has polytrauma and a diagnosis of PTSD and bipolar disorder, for which he or she takes medication, and he or she drinks alcohol, the use of alcohol may interact dangerously with his medication. When the person is aware of the potential dangers of using alcohol with medication, he or she may knowingly stop taking the medication so that he or she can use alcohol. As a result of discontinuing medication, the person may have a psychiatric episode. Thus, the risk may result as a function of alcohol use and as one of discontinuing to take medication in order to use alcohol. In either case, the individual is at an increased risk of health and medical complications.

Other medical conditions (e.g., hypoglycemia, HIV/AIDS, ulcers, hematological diseases, cardiovascular diseases) (Kinney, 2011) associated with some disabilities can decrease a person's tolerance for AOD. This decreased tolerance can lead to dangerous levels of intoxication, especially when medications are combined with alcohol. In addition, individuals who experience chronic pain or discomfort can become dependent on prescribed medications or use other drugs such as alcohol to attempt to achieve temporary relief (SAMSHA, 2013a). Awareness of such considerations is critical for counselors. It is also important that counselors help their clients to be aware that the presence of a disability or chronic illness may create an increased risk of accidents from AOD misuse due to issues of coordination and balance, slow response time, poor decision making, mobility, or vision impairments.

Psychological Risk Factors

Psychological risk factors include enabling behavior, increased stress on family life, and the stress associated with adjustment to disability. Frequently, family, friends, and professionals may inadvertently encourage individuals with disabilities to use AOD inappropriately. Enabling behavior (making it easy for someone to engage in a behavior) may be motivated by misplaced feelings of sympathy, guilt, frustration, or camaraderie. Clearly, in Rita's case, her mother encourages her to use drugs as a way of coping with pain and as a way to express her feelings.

With the onset of a disability, a family may experience additional expenses, difficult adjustments to daily routines, and reduced income due to loss of a job. Such factors significantly increase the stress that can lead to unhealthy AOD-related behaviors. Initial reactions to the onset of a disability or illness can include shock, denial, anger, anxiety, depression, withdrawal, resentment, guilt, and embarrassment (Taormina-Weiss, 2012). In a study of psychosocial factors and adjustment to chronic pain in persons with SCI, acquired amputation, cerebral palsy (CP), multiple sclerosis (MS), and muscular dystrophy (MD), Jensen, Moore, Bockow, Ehde, and Engel (2011) found that psychosocial factors were significantly associated with pain and dysfunction in all disability groups. The psychosocial factors most closely associated with pain and dysfunction included catastrophizing conditions; task persistence, guarding, and resisting coping responses; and perceived social support and solicitous responding social factors. An unhealthy coping strategy for any of these reactions could be the use and/or abuse of alcohol and other drugs.

Interpersonal and Social Risk Factors

Social factors include peer group differences, reduced levels of social support, and isolation. Individuals with disabilities, especially those who acquired the disability before adulthood, may have less opportunity for association with peer groups (West et al., 2009b). These social limitations can result in gravitation to peer groups that tolerate abuse of alcohol and other drugs, and other aberrant behavior. In addition, this could mean that persons with disabilities may be vulnerable to AOD abuse through peer pressure due to a lack of social experience or a need for acceptance. Rita turns to her caretaker/boyfriend to provide her with the social opportunity to engage in drug use. In addition, her caretaker/boyfriend may not have effective coping skills and therefore may reinforce her use of drugs.

Individuals with disabilities tend to have fewer social outlets and have related problems with excess free time. Both of these situations contribute to risk of AOD abuse. A person with fewer social options can have difficulty finding new friends in order to avoid negative influences. Isolation further exacerbates this problem. Individuals with disabilities are frequently isolated due to a lack of transportation, recreational, or social opportunities. This can lead to depression and low self-esteem, both of which can contribute to substance abuse and addiction (Taormina-Weiss, 2012). In addition, persons with disabilities may experience negative outcomes that include the increased likelihood of being the victims of crime. Persons age 12 or older who had disabilities experienced on average 923,000 nonfatal violent crimes during 2011. The rate of violence for males with disabilities was 42 per 1000 in 2011, compared to 22 per 1000 for males without disabilities. For females with disabilities, the rate of violence was 53 per 1000, compared to 17 per 1000 for females without disabilities (Harrell, 2012).

Economic and Employment Risk Factors

Individuals with disabilities have a disproportionate amount of bills associated with medical treatment, assistive technology, transportation, and related costs, which create financial anxieties and stress. Likewise, as a group, they experience higher rates of underemployment or unemployment. Unemployment is one of the most profound issues facing the disability community. Only 41.1% of Americans with disabilities aged 21–64 are working compared to 71.1% of people in this age group without disabilities. In 2010 only 27.5% of persons with severe disabilities were employed compared to 71.2% of adults with nonsevere disabilities (Brault, 2012). In 2012, an estimated 16.9% of unemployed adults were classified with dependence or abuse, while 9.1% of full-time employed adults and 10.3% of those employed part-time were classified as such. Of the 20.7 million adults classified with dependence or abuse, 10.7 million (51.9%) were employed full time. Approximately 9.0% of persons with severe disabilities receiving Medicare, Social Security, or SSI reported employment (SAMHSA, 2013a).

Type of disability is associated with various employment status and work limitations. For example, persons with communicative disabilities only were more likely to be employed (73.4%) than those with disabilities in any other domain or combinations thereof. Persons with physical disabilities only were employed at a rate of 40.8%, those with mental disabilities only at 51.9%, and persons with the combination of disabilities in the physical and mental domains have a decreased likelihood of employment (Brault, 2012). In a review of literature from 1990 to 2010 on unemployment and substance use, Henkel (2011) found the following main results: (a) risky alcohol consumption (e.g., hazardous, binge, heavy drinking) is more prevalent among the unemployed, (b) problematic substance use increases the likelihood of unemployment and decreases the chance of finding and holding down a job, (c) unemployment is a significant risk factor for substance use and the subsequent development of substance use disorders, and (d) unemployment increases the risk of relapse after alcohol and drug addiction treatment. In addition, the unemployed are more likely to be smokers, to use illicit and prescription drugs, and to have alcohol and drug disorders (e.g., abuse and dependence). Although no direct cause and effect connection is made between unemployment and substance abuse, one can glean that high unemployment rates among persons with disabilities may also put them at risk for substance-related and addiction disorders.

Access Risk Factors

Individuals with disabilities frequently encounter limited access to substance abuse materials or programs that are responsive to their needs. This has been found to be especially true among those who experienced traumatic injuries, SCI, and mobility limitations (West et al., 2009b). As mentioned earlier, many of the issues of access to treatment programs are due to physical accessibility of the facility. For individuals with disabilities whose primary language is other than English, communication barriers may also be a factor. For a number of reasons, therefore, the individual with a disability should be referred, when possible, to an AOD agency or program in his or her community. Consideration must also be given to different learning styles and cognitive or sensory limitations. If local treatment in the community is not possible, steps should be taken to ensure that access to programs is appropriate and equitable.

Specialized treatment is often necessary for people with certain types of disabilities. For example, many members of the Deaf community benefit from specialized services, which are better equipped to handle specific cultural, language, and community issues that may arise. Many individuals who are D/deaf will prefer to be served by programs that specifically address their needs and whose staff is fluent in sign language. Unlike many other people with disabilities, people who are Deaf often do not identify with a medical model of disability and instead embrace a cultural model that emphasizes their abilities within the Deaf community and their own language and values (Kvam, Leob, & Tambs, 2007). (The reader should note that the use of *D* refers to those who are Deaf and identify with Deaf culture, whereas the use of *d* refers to those who are deaf or hard of hearing [HOH] who do not identify with Deaf culture.) Because the D/deaf population is considered "low incidence" (less than 1% of the population), and because there are so few professionals trained to assess individuals for substance-related and addiction disorders, successful community-based treatment may be unrealistic. In addition, because a substantial amount of treatment occurs outside the formal group and individual counseling settings, D/deaf clients have less opportunity to converse with their peers in treatment (Guthmann & Graham, n.d.). Realistically, most programs are unable to provide such specialized and/or segregated services for clients who are D/deaf. A reasonable alternative may therefore be the arrangement of an accommodation, such as a sign language interpreter, the use of pencil and paper, or technology/assistive devices (e.g., Computer Assisted Realtime Transcription [CART] services) for communication. Other accommodations may include signed or captioned video, extended time to complete assignments, and the opportunity to complete activities other than in written English (Guthmann & Graham, n.d.).

American Sign Language (ASL) is one of the primary languages used for communication within the Deaf community. ASL is a visual language, which encompasses gestures, body movements, facial expression, and finger spelling. It has its own grammar, syntax, and vocabulary, and is shaped by the culture of the Deaf community. In tandem with a lack of qualified professionals trained in ASL, these are two major reasons that information about substance-related and

The D/deaf and Substance Abuse

D/deaf people are disproportionately affected by substance abuse.
Not all D/deaf people use the same communication method.
The use of a third party/interpreter to an interview will change the dynamics and may impact the validity of the assessment.
D/deaf people experience greater levels of isolation than other groups with disabilities.
Substance use is one of the major coping strategies employed by D/deaf people.
Accessibility to treatment programs is difficult for D/deaf people.
The use of sign language in treatment programs is highly preferred by D/deaf people.
ALS is the first language for D/deaf people and English language learning is secondary.
The Deaf community is a small close-knit one with a communication network for sharing information on a national level.
D/deaf people are more likely to encounter other clients or staff that they have knowledge of because of familiarity within the Deaf community, which can limit their treatment options.
D/deaf people are referred to as having a hidden disability because the disability does not become evident until the person begins to communicate.

addiction disorders has not been well communicated in the Deaf community (Guthmann & Graham, n.d.). Accommodation does not mean giving special preferences; it does mean reducing barriers to equal participation in the program. It is likely that, on occasion, there will be only one deaf client in a program. Kvam et al. (2007) stressed that there is a need for focusing more attention on the mental health of D/deaf people, and society must be made aware of the special risks that they encounter with respect to mental health. In the case of Abram, his mental health status can be exacerbated by his alcohol abuse and his cultural isolation. His ability to communicate effectively as a participant in a treatment program is further hampered by his limited English skills and rudimentary use of ASL. Clearly, Abram has physical access to a treatment program; however, his opportunity to benefit from services is restricted because full inclusion is less likely to occur.

CASE STUDY

The Case of Abram

Abram is a 30-year-old Russian immigrant to the United States. He has lived in the United States for 18 months and has a limited comprehension of English. Abram is Deaf and has diagnoses of bipolar disorder and alcohol dependence. While living in Russia, he had a history of institutionalization in psychiatric hospitals. He has had one such hospitalization in the United States and subsequently was referred for substance abuse treatment. Abram has no family in the United States and is being sponsored by a local church. Due to his deafness, limited comprehension of English, and rudimentary use of American Sign Language (ASL), Abram found himself isolated from his culture, unable to communicate effectively with both hearing and deaf persons, and experiencing a great deal of boredom. He had a limited work history in Russia as a ticket taker at a movie theater and has no work history in the United States. Abram was referred to vocational rehabilitation for services.

Sociocultural Factors

Although substance-related and addiction disorders are significant public health problems for all racial and ethnic groups, it is becoming increasingly important to understand their impact on ethnic minority groups, and to do so from four cultural perspectives—sociocultural, physiological, psychological, and developmental. *Sociocultural* risk factors refer to the ways a person perceives who he or she is within larger social and cultural contexts (Sue & Sue, 2013). For example, American Indians and Alaska Natives use substances to cope with mourning, as a result of historical consequences, and as a result of modeling. Concepts that are inherent to the cultural context, identity, adaptability, and perseverance of American Indians/Alaska Natives include a holistic approach to life, a desire to promote the well-being of the collective, an enduring spirit, and a respect for all ways of healing (Beals et al., 2005), which influences self-perception, must also be considered in working with these populations. *Physiological* risk factors predispose a group to a particular condition or disorder because of medical or health situations (e.g., metabolic disorders). Research examining the physiological theory of substance dependence and addiction is inconclusive.

Psychological risk factors refer to one's locus of control (internal vs. external). Many Latinos, for example, have an external locus of control related to health barrier perceptions (Valentine, Godkin, & Doughty, 2008). According to Fisher and Harrison (2013), language deficiencies can severely limit one's sense of personal autonomy and perceived control, reinforcing how one sees opportunities for economic, social, or educational improvement. The shame associated with such deprivation can exacerbate lowered feelings of self-worth and put Latino individuals at psychological risk for substance abuse and addiction. *Developmental* risk factors are related to attaining satisfactory life and work aspirations. Failure to achieve one's goals can frequently be expressed in depression and dependency. For example, high unemployment among African-American men has a deleterious effect upon drinking behavior and is correlated with increased risk of alcohol problems (Bonhomme, Stephens, & Braithwaite, 2006). Substance-related and addiction disorders among ethnic minorities is also a function of rate of acculturation and assimilation, and self-control characteristics (Buchanan & Smokowski, 2009; Fosados et al., 2007; Myers et al., 2009; Pokhrel, Herzog, Sun, Rohrbach, & Sussman, 2013; Valentine et al., 2008). Thus, in working with clients who are members of racial and ethnic minority groups, gaining a sense of their cultural orientation and becoming familiar with their values, practices, and worldview is important. Each of these cultural factors and risk factors has implications for the treatment process.

Cultural variables play a significant role in contributing to a person's identity, personality, beliefs, and behavior, as well as define a group's cultural uniqueness. In addition, cultural variables influence understanding of substance abuse and addiction and offer some insight as to possible approaches to treatment engagement and therapeutic options. Thus, service plans should focus on social-environmental concerns as well as substance abuse issues in a cultural context (Upsher, 2008). Similarly, historical trauma, which Muid (2008) defined as "the collective emotional and psychological injury both over the life span and across generations, resulting from a cataclysmic history of genocide" (p. 11), is another cultural avenue through which to understand persons with substance-related and addiction disorders. Historical trauma often leads to negative consequences that manifest in succeeding generations, frequently leads to a sense of powerlessness, and can create a subculture that is in stark contrast to authentic culture that is supportive and nurturing (Brave Heart, 2003; Leary, 2005; Muid, 2008).

TREATMENT UTILIZATION AND OUTCOMES

Given that substance abuse and addiction have numerous dimensions and disrupt many aspects of an individual's life, treatment is complex and is even more complicated for PWDs (NIDA, 2012). Treatment processes differ according to treatment program. Typically, counselors help guide persons with substance abuse problems or addictions through three stages of care: detoxification, rehabilitation, and aftercare (Doweiko, 2015). At times, medical intervention may be required, depending on an individual's general health, either before or concurrently with treatment. For example, an individual may need vitamin treatment, dental care, and other basic health care due to malnutrition and poor hygiene. Substance abuse and addictions treatment is provided in a number of venues—such as inpatient, outpatient, or partial hospitalization (i.e., day care)—and through an array of techniques and modalities—such as medical intervention (e.g., antabuse, chemotherapy), individual counseling, group work, working with families, self-help, pharmacotherapy, spiritual counseling, meditation, activity therapy, self-help programs, or behavioral approaches (Doweiko, 2015; Kinney, 2011). Treatment programs should be integrated and inclusive. Most people with disabilities do not want or need separate programs, which often limit opportunities and perpetuate segregation and the misperception of what it means to be different. However, service components can and should be individualized. Since the 1970s, scientific research has shown that treatment can help individuals addicted to AOD stop using, avoid relapse, and successfully recover their lives. Based on this research, key principles have emerged that should form the basis for any effective treatment program. Although many of these principles (e.g., remaining in treatment for an adequate period of time, treatment does not need to be voluntary to be effective, treatment attends to multiple needs of individuals across cultural, psychosocial, personality) are effective across various populations, additional elements are needed to address PWDs with substance-related and addiction disorders (see Table 15.3).

Treatment for substance-related and addiction disorders can be inpatient/residential (minimum of 4 weeks up to 6 months), outpatient (an unspecified period of time), or partial hospitalization (often runs 5 or more hours a day, 5 days a week, for 4–6 weeks) (Nugent & Jones, 2009). Treatment for substance abuse and addiction disorders occurs most frequently in outpatient settings. Clients with less serious and more stabilized mental and substance abuse problems, for the most part, receive outpatient treatment (Forman & Nagy, 2006). Residential

TABLE 15.3 Key Principles of Effective Treatment Programs for PWDs

Accessibility of facilities
Appropriate accommodations
Integrated/comprehensive services
Employ culturally appropriate methods
Manage countertransference
Increase structure and support
Counselor responds consistently in a nurturing and nonjudgmental manner
Differentiate between medication side effects and substance-induced changes
Counselors/staff understand special sensitivities and specific accommodations of the person
Differentiate among mood and anxiety disorders; commonplace expressions of anxiety and depression; and anxiety and depression associated with more serious mental illness or medical conditions

treatment programs can be extremely effective, especially for those with more severe problems. The type of setting selected for treatment depends on the needs of the client. For example, a client with medical complications may benefit from inpatient or partial hospitalization, whereas a client who is employed and needs to continue working may find outpatient care more feasible. Although standard treatment models have been adapted to meet the needs of people with disabilities, more work must be done (Quintero, 2011). However, there are specific guidelines for determining the type of treatment an individual may require. The American Society of Addiction Medicine (ASAM) has developed patient placement criteria to guide decisions about the appropriate treatment setting. Six dimensions have been identified as germane to determining the type of treatment required. These dimensions are presented as follows:

1. Dimension 1: Acute intoxication and/or withdrawal potential.
2. Dimension 2: Biomedical conditions and complications.
3. Dimension 3: Emotional, behavioral, or cognitive conditions and complications.
4. Dimension 4: Readiness to change.
5. Dimension 5: Relapse, continued use, or continued problem potential.
6. Dimension 6: Recovery/living environment.

Taking into account assessment results in these domains, a continuum of care has been identified within five broad levels ranging from 0.5 to 4.0. These levels specify the kind of care required, given the client's status and include the following:

1. Level 0.5: Early intervention.
2. Level 1: Outpatient services.
3. Level 2: Intensive outpatient (2.1) and partial hospitalization (2.5) services.
4. Level 3: Residential/inpatient services, which includes clinically managed low-intensity residential services (3.1), clinically managed population-specific high-intensity residential services (3.3–3.5), and medically monitored intensive inpatient services (3.7).
5. Level 4: Medically managed intensive inpatient services. (Mee-Lee, 2013)

For persons with physical and psychiatric disabilities, these criteria for treatment services are crucial, because such persons may have multiple medical problems and chronic conditions, which further complicate treatment. To better facilitate positive outcome rates in treatment, clients with disabilities must be assessed in a more culturally specific, flexible, and holistic way (West et al., 2009b). However, matching studies suggest that little improvement in outcomes has resulted from matching (Ouimette, Finney, Gima, & Moos, 1999a, 1999b). In fact, "the least

TABLE 15.4 Advantages and Disadvantages of Treatment Programs

	Inpatient	**Outpatient**	**Self-help**
Advantages	Intensive education	Cost	Free
	Intensive counseling	Continue to work	Convenient
	New friends	Life with support	Open to everyone
	Protected setting		History of success
Disadvantages	Cost	Lack of insurance	Biases
	Protected from real life	Limited spaces available	May not be for everyone
		Less structured	
		Increased relapse	

restrictive environment for treatment should be used unless the severity of the substance use disorder and related medical, psychiatric, and social problems is such that structured or medically monitored treatment is needed" (Daley & Marlatt, 2006, p. 39). The advantages and disadvantages of types of treatment programs are presented in Table 15.4. Specific intervention strategies in rehabilitation settings are discussed next.

INTERVENTION STRATEGIES IN REHABILITATION SETTINGS

Rehabilitation settings for substance-related and addiction disorders treatment and recovery include such settings as halfway or transition houses, VA hospitals, general hospitals and clinical settings, programs for the homeless, prisons and jails, and substance abuse programs. These settings may or may not offer treatment that is gender specific, designed for lesbian, gay, bisexual, and transgender populations, or emphasize cultural components. One setting in which individuals with disabilities and addiction disorders are increasing is in the criminal justice system (discussed in detail later in this chapter). Counselors working in substance abuse or rehabilitation settings are likely to face complex clinical decisions when determining eligibility for services—for example, deciding whether treatment will commence despite continued use of substances, or whether abstinence from all drugs (i.e., medications) should be required for services (Toriello & Leierer, 2005). Counselors can deliver intervention from a traditional (i.e., medical/disease) model, a contemporary clinical orientation (i.e., client-centered approaches), or somewhere along the continuum (Goodwin, 2009).

Treatment and intervention for persons with disabilities in rehabilitation settings must include a continuum of care, starting with assessment, moving to individualized intervention, and ending with aftercare (or continuing care) services. Given the chronic nature of addictions, before proceeding further several statements about rehabilitation expectations should be made. First, recovery takes time because addictions encroach upon every aspect of one's life and thus must be diffused systematically. Second, progress is not constant in the recovery process. There is occasional backsliding, and plateaus are common. Third, as is possible in any chronic illness, relapse is part of recovery. Finally, addiction is behavioral, neurobiological, and genetic (Mee-Lee, 2013). Witkiewitz and Masyn (2008) found that substance disorder relapse and noncompliance rates are similar to other chronic conditions. Regardless of the substance of choice and population, research studies consistently find that a substantial percentage of people who receive treatment for AOD problems use again after leaving treatment, typically within the first 3 years (Doweiko, 2012; Fisher & Harrison, 2013).

For people with a coexisting disability, their ability to function effectively in a post-treatment setting may be influenced by several factors, including the severity, duration, or specific functional limitations of the disability; societal reaction to and expectations of the person; and the developmental stage at time of the disability's onset (Cardoso, Wolf, & West, 2009; White, 2012). Some of those individuals are knowledgeable of what types of intervention their disabilities require, and others are not. Typically, people with both a substance-related disorder and a coexisting disability have life problems (previously discussed in this chapter) that make treatment more complex and heighten the possibility of relapse. Those individuals may need assistance and individualized accommodations in order to

1. Learn activities of daily living (ADL) such as basic grooming, dressing appropriately, using public transportation, and cooking.
2. Develop prevocational skills.
3. Learn social skills that may be lacking because of both substance use disorders and disability-related problems.

4. Learn to engage in healthy recreation.
5. Obtain financial benefits for which they are eligible.
6. Parenting and child care skills.
7. Simplifying language for those with developmental disabilities or translating 12 steps into sign language for the deaf.
8. Build new peer networks. (Zubenko, 2006)

In addition, research indicated that persons with AOD problems and disabilities encounter procedural and other obstacles when they attempt to rectify such problems. For example, if a client has been sober for 6 months or more (even though such a requirement is counterproductive and can act to maintain a vicious cycle between a lack of vocational skills and substance use disorders), he or she may be declared ineligible for some vocational rehabilitation programs (Bachman et al., 2004; Brucker, 2008; Krahn et al., 2007; National Rehabilitation Information Center, 2011).

One subgroup of individuals with disabilities that is increasing and deserving of discussion is the offender population. Those who are incarcerated, in diversion treatment programs, or pretrial programs present a constellation of challenges for rehabilitation professionals in the provision of services. SAMHSA (2013b) identified several barriers of criminal justice settings to the delivery of substance abuse treatment. Some of the barriers are specific to the setting and the availability of treatment, and others to the offender's attitudes and behaviors and whether criminogenic personality features will impede involvement in treatment. Other barriers include the following: treatment may not be offered to those in need because the methods for screening participants may not be comprehensive, and services are not always responsive to the offender's psychological, social, medical, and mental health needs. The jail setting has some additional challenges, including time constraints because of the duration of jail incarceration is usually short, some offenders have special needs that are too complex to be addressed fully in short-term treatment, and the ability to ensure confidentiality. In jails, especially in small, rural areas, offenders with substance use disorders are well known, and offenders and officers often know each other. Counselors working with offenders with substance-related disorders and disabilities in criminal justice settings should be cognizant of the intensity level of treatment required because of the individual's type and severity of disability, the influence of factors on motivation to participate in treatment (e.g., sanctions, rewards), and the level of community supervision and monitoring needed upon reintegration.

In whatever setting one is counseling persons with addiction problems and disabilities, counselors must have a clear understanding of the client's psychosocial history and presenting problems. This should include an individual's work history; educational background; family; marital history; employment status; military history; mental health history; functional limitations; criminal history; history of substance use and treatment; involvement in vocational, physical, or social rehabilitation; and past history of abuse (since many people with disabilities have been victims of physical, emotional, and/or sexual abuse) (Goodwin, 2009). Let us take the case of Rita for illustrative purposes. The counselor should ask her some basic questions, such as the following:

1. Do you feel you have a disability, or has anyone ever told you that you have one?
2. Have you ever had to stay in a hospital overnight, or gone to an emergency room for any reason?
3. Have you ever seen a doctor for a long period of time, more frequently than just one visit or for routine check-ups?
4. Do you take any kind of medication (prescription and over-the-counter)? (Expand with questions regarding compliance with medications.)

5. Were you ever diagnosed with a disability? (Consider asking this question in regard to specific types of disabilities.)
6. Have you ever incurred any type of injury? If so, what type? What were the outcomes?
7. How many jobs have you had in the past 3 years? What was the longest job that you held?
8. What hobbies do you have?
9. What is your family life like? (Ask a series of questions about family life and relationships.)

Other questions should focus on cultural needs, cross-addictions, and medical needs. The result of these questions and the interview is to help identify areas in which Rita may have disabilities, impairments, and functional limitations. Assessment of her responses will help the counselor determine how these limitations will affect her participation in the program and identify additional information needed to make sure she can get the maximum benefit from treatment. Given that females with disabilities have often been victimized by family members and caregivers, and have been victims of crimes (Renzetti, Edleson, & Bergen, 2011; ncjrs.gov/ovc_archives/factsheet/disable.ht;victimsofcrimes.org/library/crime-information-and-statistics/crimes-against-people-with-disabilities), gender-specific questions should also be asked. Based on affirmative responses, a broad range of interconnected services that address problems related to trauma, mental health, and substance abuse should be implemented.

For treatment to succeed, counselors should consider how settings can impact clients' strengths and limitations. In general, people have a number of skills that strengthen their ability to cope with the stresses and transitions that occur throughout their lifetime, and learning these skills is a critical part of human development (Kail & Cavanaugh, 2010). A strength-based approach to treatment is especially important for people with disabilities because they have so frequently been viewed in terms of what they cannot or should not attempt. As a result, PWDs may have learned to define themselves in terms of their limitations and inabilities. According to Koppelman and Goodhart (2008), PWDs are often viewed as incapable of possessing certain skills of self-determination. However, this is not to say that persons with disabilities should not understand their functional limitations, especially in relation to their risk for relapse (Fisher & Harrison, 2013). For continuity of care for PWDs, the following are suggestions in rehabilitation settings:

1. Incorporate opportunities to strengthen resiliency skills as part of the rehabilitation program. Address those factors that place a person at risk for problems related to substance abuse and addictions; assist clients by providing for their development in all areas: psychosocial, emotional, mental, and physical (Center for Substance Abuse Treatment [CSAT], 2005).
2. Locate or establish peer-support prevention counseling programs. Positive role models are important for people with disabilities who are confronting life challenges. Too often, establishing effective peer support programs for PWDs is a challenge, especially for those with hidden disabilities and for ethnic minorities (Perron et al., 2009; Velez, Campos-Holland, & Arndt, 2008).
3. Promote healthy lifestyle changes and skills training through multidisciplinary and interdisciplinary support groups (Fallot & Harris, 2004).
4. Establish educational and decision-making sessions on coping, assertiveness training, stress management, healthy living, modification skills, and substance abuse (Zubenko, 2006).
5. Organize 12-step meetings in independent living centers (ILCs) and other disability service agencies that are accessible to and used by people with disabilities; and encourage the development of accessible recovery support groups in other 12-step programs for the individual and family members (Krahn et al., 2007).

In addition, Galanter and Kleber (2008) recommended that counselors in substance abuse treatment and recovery programs who are not skilled in disability-related issues should refer clients to ILCs. Unavailability of, or limited access to, specialized substance abuse and addictions programs for persons with disabilities may necessitate collaborative and coordinated efforts across agencies and programs, or the creation of alternatives. Alternatives are typically required because neither the mental health nor substance abuse treatment systems provide sufficient resources for treatment of co-occurring addictions and disabilities (i.e., clients are treated for their disabilities in one facility and their addictions in another) (Yalisove, 2004). Other treatment programs promote sequential treatment in which one condition (usually a psychiatric disorder) is treated before the addiction disorder. The belief is that the client must be mentally stable to benefit from substance abuse treatment. Yet, some programs offer parallel treatment in which the client is simultaneously involved in addiction and mental health treatment. For persons with disabilities, an integrated treatment approach in which both mental health and addiction treatment are combined into a unified and comprehensive program involving counselors and clinicians cross-trained in both approaches is best (Galanter & Kleber, 2008; Kinney, 2011).

As a means to increase access to treatment, PWDs should be screened for substance abuse and related mental health issues. Treatment programs in rehabilitation settings should contain certain guidelines (see Table 15.5). Counselors in rehabilitation settings will need to select appropriate and effective strategies from various models to apply to persons with disabilities. Most importantly, intervention must match the client's clinical severity, biopsychosocial, cultural, and social needs. Uniform client placement criteria to determine appropriate levels of care may not be possible for persons with disabilities and addictions. Nevertheless, counselors will need to rely on multiple program resources and on multidimensional and integrated program planning and service delivery to meet the needs of persons with disabilities and addictions. The counselor should work with the client to set up incremental goals, rather than expecting major changes all at once (SAMHSA, 2009b; Stevens & Smith, 2009).

TABLE 15.5 Guidelines for Treatment Programs

- *Assessment:* Include a medical examination, drug use history, psychosocial evaluation, and when warranted, a psychiatric evaluation and a review of socioeconomic factors; and eligibility for public health, public assistance, employment, and educational and vocational assistance programs.
- *Same-day intake:* To retain the client's involvement and interest in treatment.
- *Documenting findings and treatment:* To enhance clinical case supervision.
- *Preventive and primary medical care:* Provided on site if possible.
- *Testing for infectious diseases:* At intake and at intervals throughout treatment, for infectious diseases such as hepatitis, retrovirus, tuberculosis, HIV and AIDS, syphilis, gonorrhea, and other sexually transmitted diseases.
- *Weekly random drug testing:* To ensure abstinence and compliance with treatment.
- *Pharamacotherapeutic interventions:* By qualified medical practitioners, as appropriate for those patients having mental health disorders, those addicted to opiates, and HIV-positive individuals and AIDS patients.
- *Group counseling interventions:* To address unique emotional, physical, and social problems.
- *Basic substance abuse counseling:* Including individual, family, or collateral counseling, trained and certified when possible. Staff training and education are integral to successful treatment.

- *Practical life skills counseling:* Including vocational and educational counseling and training. These can be provided through linkages with community programs.
- *General health education:* Including nutrition, sex, and family planning, with an emphasis on contraception counseling for adolescents and women.
- *Peer support groups:* Particularly useful for those with disabilities to provide role models.
- *Liaison services:* With immigration, legal aid, and criminal justice system authorities.
- *Social activities:* To establish or restore clients' perceptions of social interaction.
- *Alternative housing:* For homeless clients or for those whose living situations are conducive to maintaining the addict lifestyle.
- *Relapse prevention:* Which combines aftercare and support programs such as 12-step programs within an individualized plan to identify, stabilize, and control the stressors that trigger and promote relapse to substance abuse.
- *Outcome evaluation:* To enable refinement and improvement of service delivery.

Source: Based on information in Kleber (1994).

Summary and Some Final Notations

Persons with disabilities are more likely to have substance-related and addictive disorders and less likely to get effective treatment for these problems than those without a coexisting disability. Too often, people with disabilities are enabled by family members and professionals to use substances because of misperceptions and stereotypes. In addition to having the same risk factors as those without disabilities, persons with disabilities are at increased risk because of societal attitudes; for social and economic reasons; and due to higher rates of depression or anxiety, health and medical issues, and greater isolation. The presence of a disability increases the risk for substance abuse.

People with disabilities come to rehabilitation settings with issues that require a great deal of understanding on the part of counselors and other service providers. These clients need a thorough psychosocial and cultural assessment, and individualized treatment plans to meet their needs. Treatment programs must address not only the substance abuse problem but the disability and any medical conditions as well. Any effort to address addictions without addressing disabilities usually yields limited outcomes for the client. In addition, attention must be paid to the requirements of the specific setting, and settings are expanding to include atypical ones such as jails and prisons.

Clients bring assets to the treatment process, which must be incorporated into the treatment process. Clients with addictions and disabilities may benefit from an integrated, multidisciplinary approach to treatment. Counselors should select an intervention approach that meets the individualized needs of clients.

Summary of Key Points of People with Disabilities

- Are disproportionately affected by substance abuse.
- Have higher rates of isolation and unemployment.
- Usually have multiple interrelated issues leading to substance abuse.
- In addition to substance abuse, treatment programs must address the disability and medical problems.
- Clients bring assets to their treatment.

MyCounselingLab

Visit the MyCounselingLab site for *Foundations of Addictions Counseling*, Third Edition to enhance your understanding of concepts. You'll have the opportunity to practice your skills through video- and case-based exercises. You will find sets of questions to help you prepare for your certification exam with *Licensure Quizzes*. There is also a Video Library that provides taped counseling sessions, ethical scenarios, and interviews with helpers and clients.

Useful Websites

The following websites provide additional information relating to the chapter topic, substance-related and addictive disorders for people with disabilities:

American Academy of Addiction Psychiatry (AAAP)
www.aaap.org

American Medical Association (AMA)
www.ama-assn.org

Disability.gov: Health: Substance Abuse
www.disability.gov

DRM Webwatcher: Substance Abuse and People with Disabilities
www.disabilityresources.org/SUBSTANCE-ABUSE.html

National Institute on Alcohol Abuse and Alcoholism
www.niaaa.nih.gov/

National Institute on Drug Abuse
www.drugabuse.gov/

Substance Abuse and Mental Health Services Administration (SAMHSA)
www.samhsa.gov/

Substance Abuse Resources and Disability Issues (SARDI)
www.med.wright.edu/citar/sardi/

U.S. Department of Health and Human Services Office on Disability
www.hhs.gov/od

References

American Psychiatric Association. (2013). *Diagnostic and statistical manual of mental disorders* (5th ed.). Washington, DC: Author.

Bachman, S. S., Drainoni, M., & Tobias, C. (2004). Medicaid managed care, substance abuse treatment, and people with disabilities: Review of the literature. *Health and Social Work, 29*, 189–196.

Barnow, B. S. (2008, November). The employment rate of people with disabilities. *Monthly Labor Review*, pp. 44–50.

Basford, J. R., Rohe, D. E., Barnes, C. P., & DePompolo, R. W. (2002). Substance abuse attitudes and policies in U.S. rehabilitation training programs: A comparison of 1985 and 2000. *Archives of Physical Medicine and Rehabilitation, 83*, 517–522.

Beals, J., Manson, S. M., Whitesell, N. R., Spicer, P., Novins, D. K., & Mitchell, C. M. (2005). Prevalence of DSM-IV disorders and attendant help-seeking in 2 American Indian reservation populations. *Archives of General Psychiatry, 62*(1), 99–108.

Beveridge, S., & Fabian, E. (2007). Vocational rehabilitation outcomes: Relationship between individualized plan for employment goals and employment outcomes. *Rehabilitation Counseling Bulletin, 50*(4), 238–246.

Bombardier, C. H., Blake, K. D., Ehde, D. M., Gibbons, L. E., Moore, D., & Kraft, G. H. (2004). Alcohol and drug abuse among persons with multiple sclerosis. *Multiple Sclerosis, 10*, 35–40.

Bonhomme, J., Stephens, T., & Braithwaite, R. (2006). African-American males in the United States prison system: Impact on family and community. *The Journal of Men's Health & Gender, 3*, 223–226.

Brault, M. W. (2012, July). *Americans with disabilities: 2010 Household economic studies*. Washington, DC: U.S. Department of Commerce.

Brave Heart, M. (2003). Historical trauma response and substance abuse. *Journal of Psychoactive Drugs, 35*(1), 11–13.

Brucker, D. (2007). Estimating the prevalence of substance use, abuse, and dependence among Social Security disability benefit recipients. *Journal of Disability Policy Studies, 18*, 148–159.

Brucker, D. L. (2008). Prescription drug abuse among persons with disabilities. *Journal of Vocational Rehabilitation, 29,* 105–115.

Buchanan, R. L., & Smokowski, P. R. (2009). Pathways from acculturation stress to substance use among Latino adolescents. *Substance Use and Misuse, 44*(5), 740–762.

Burgard, J. F., Donohue, B., Azrin, N. H., & Teichner, G. (2000). Prevalence and treatment of substance abuse in the mentally retarded population: An empirical review. *Journal of Psychoactive Drugs, 32,* 293–298.

Cardoso, E., Wolf, A. W., & West, S. L. (2009). Substance abuse models, assessments, and interventions. In F. Chan, E. Cardoso, & J. A. Chronister (Eds.), *Understanding psychosocial adjustment to chronic illness and disability: A handbook for evidence-based practitioners in rehabilitation* (pp. 399–441). New York, NY: Springer.

Center for Substance Abuse Treatment. (2005). *A strength-based approach toward addiction treatment for women.* Rockville, MD: U.S. Department of Health and Human Services.

Ciaccio, C. P. (2010). IV. Cyber law: A notes: Internet gambling: Recent developments and state of the law. *Berkeley Technology Law Journal Annual Review, 25,* 529–553.

Crozier, M. K., & Sligar, S. R. (2010). Behavioral addictions screening during the vocational evaluation process. *Vocational Evaluation Work Adjustment Association Journal, 37*(1), 45–57.

Daley, D. C., & Marlatt, G. A. (2006). *Overcoming your alcohol or drug problem: Effective recovery strategies. Therapist guide* (2nd ed.). New York, NY: Oxford University Press.

Doweiko, H. E. (2015). *Concepts of chemical dependency* (9th ed.). Stamford, CT: Cengage Learning.

Dutta, A., Gervey, R., Chan, F., Chou, C. C., & Ditchman, N. (2008). Vocational rehabilitation services and employment outcomes for people with disabilities: A United States study. *Journal of Occupational Rehabilitation.* doi:10.1007/s10926-008-9154-z

Ebener, D. J., & Smedema, S. M. (2011). Physical disability and substance use disorders: A convergence of adaptation and recovery. *Rehabilitation Counseling Bulletin, 54*(3), 131–141.

Equal Employment Opportunity Commission. (1994). *A technical assistance manual on the Employment Provisions (Title I) of the Americans with Disabilities Act 42 U.S.C. § 12114(b), 8.5.* Washington, DC: Author.

Erickson, W., Lee, C., & von Schrader, S. (2012). *2011 Disability Status Report: United States.* Ithaca, NY: Cornell University Employment and Disability Institute. Retrieved from http://www.disabilitystatistics.org/StatusReports/2011-PDF/2011-StatusReport_US.pdf

Fallot, R. D., & Harris, M. (2004). Integrated trauma services team for women survivors with alcohol and other drug problems and co-occurring mental disorders. In B. W. Veysey & C. Clark (Eds.), *Responding to physical and sexual abuse in women with alcohol and other drug and mental disorders: Program building* (pp. 181–199). Binghamton, NY: Haworth Press.

Fisher, G. L., & Harrison, T. C. (2013). *Substance abuse: Information for school counselors, social workers, therapists, and counselors* (5th ed.). Boston, MA: Pearson.

Forman, R. F., & Nagy, P. D. (2006). *Substance abuse: Clinical issues in intensive outpatient treatment: A treatment improvement protocol—TIP 47.* Rockville, MD: Substance Abuse and Mental Health Services Administration.

Fosados, R., McClain, A., Ritt-Olson, A., Sussman, S., Soto, D., Baezconde-Garbanati, L., & Unger, J. B. (2007). The influence of acculturation on drug and alcohol use in a sample of adolescents. *Addictive Behaviors, 32*(12), 2990–3004.

Galanter, M., & Kleber, H. D. (Eds.). (2008). *The American Psychiatric Publishing textbook of substance abuse treatment* (4th ed.). Arlington, VA: American Psychiatric Publishing.

Glenn, M. K., Huber, M. J., Keferl, J., Wright-Bell, A., & Lane, T. (n.d.). Substance use disorders and vocational rehabilitation: VR counselor's desk reference. Rehabilitation Research and Training Center on Substance Abuse, Disability and Employment. Retrieved November 21, 2013, from http://www.med.wright.edu/sites/default/files/citar/.../VR_Desk_Reference.pdf

Goodwin, L. R. (2009). Treatment for substance use disorders. In I. Marini & M. A. Stebnicki (Eds.), *The professional counselor's desk reference* (pp. 703–723). New York, NY: Springer.

Guthmann, D., & Graham, V. (n.d.). Substance abuse: A hidden problem within the D/deaf and hard of hearing communities. Retrieved November 13, 2013, from http://www.mncddeaf.org/articles/hidden_ad.htm

Harley, D. A. (2005). African Americans and substance abuse. In D. A. Harley & J. M. Dillard (Eds.), *Contemporary mental health issues among African Americans* (pp. 119–131). Alexandria, VA: American Counseling Association.

Harrell, E. (2012). Crime against persons with disabilities, 2009–2011. Retrieved November 11, 2013 from http://www.bjs.gov/index.cfm?ty=pbdetail&iid=4574

Harrell, Z. A. T., & Broman, C. L. (2009). Racial/ethnic differences in correlates of prescription drug misuse among young adults. *Drug and Alcohol Dependence, 104,* 268–271.

Hawley, C. E., Glenn, M., & Diaz, S. (2012). Vocational evaluation issues germane to individuals with gambling related problems. *Vocational Evaluation and Work Adjustment Association Journal, 39*(1), 2–11.

Hawley, C. E., Glenn, M., & Keferl, J. (2011). Understanding connections between problem gambling and disability: Implications for vocational evaluators. *Vocational Evaluation and Work Adjustment Association Journal, 38*(1), 2–8.

Henkel, D. (2011). Unemployment and substance use disorder: A review of the literature (1990–2010). *Current Drug Abuse Review, 4*(1), 4–27.

Hollar, D., McAweeney, M., & Moore, D. (2008). The relationship between substance use disorders and unsuccessful case closures in vocational rehabilitation agencies. *Journal of Applied Rehabilitation Counseling, 39,* 48–52.

Jensen, M. P., Moore, M. R., Bockow, T. B., Ehde, D. M., & Engel, J. M. (2011). Psychosocial factors and adjustment to chronic pain in persons with physical disabilities: A systematic review. *Archives of Physical Medicine and Rehabilitation, 92*(1), 146–160.

Jung, Y., & Bellini, J. L. (2011). Predictors of employment outcomes for vocational rehabilitation consumers with HIV/AIDS: 2002–2007. *Rehabilitation Counseling Bulletin, 54*(3), 142–153.

Kail, R. V., & Cavanaugh, J. C. (2010). *Human development: A lifespan view* (5th ed.). Belmont, CA: Wadsworth.

Kinney, J. (2011). *Loosening the grip: A handbook of alcohol information* (10th ed.). Boston, MA: McGraw-Hill.

Kleber, H. D. (1994). *Assessment and treatment of cocaine-abusing methadone-maintained patients.* Treatment Improvement Protocol Series (No. 10, NIH Pub. No. 94-3003). Rockville, MD: U.S. Department of Health and Human Services.

Kolakowsky-Hayner, S. A., Gourley, E. V., Kreutzer, J. S., Marwitz, J. H., Meade, M. A., & Cifu, D. X. (2002). Post-injury substance abuse among persons with brain injury and persons with spinal cord injury. *Brain Injury, 16,* 583–592.

Kole, J., & Barnhill, A. (2013). Caffeine content labeling: A missed opportunity for promoting personal and public health. *Journal of Caffeine Research, 3*(3), 108–113.

Koppelman, K. L., & Goodhart, R. L. (2008). *Understanding human differences: Multicultural education for diverse America.* Boston, MA: Pearson.

Krahn, G., Deck, D., Gabriel, R., & Farrell, N. (2007). A population-based study on substance abuse treatment for adults with disabilities: Access, utilization, and treatment outcomes. *The American Journal of Drug and Alcohol Abuse, 33,* 791–798.

Kvam, M. H., Loeb, M., & Tambs, K. (2007). Mental health in deaf adults: Symptoms of anxiety and depression among hearing and Deaf individuals. *Journal of Deaf Studies and Deaf Education, 12*(1), 1–7.

Langlois, J. A., Rutland-Brown, W., & Thomas, K. E. (2004). *Traumatic brain injury in the United States: Emergency department visits, hospitalizations, and deaths.* Atlanta, GA: Centers for Disease Control and Prevention, National Center for Injury Prevention and Control.

Leary, J. D. (2005). *Post-traumatic slave syndrome: America's legacy of enduring injury and healing.* Portland, OR: Uptone Press.

Le Cook, B. & Alegria, M. (2011). Racial-ethnic disparities in substance abuse treatment: The role of criminal history and socioeconomic status. *Psychiatric Services, 62*(11), 1273–1281.

McAweeney, M., Keferl, J., Moore, D., & Wagner, J. (2008). Predictors of successful closure in the state-federal vocational rehabilitation system: Findings from a sample of persons with disability and substance use disorders. *Journal of Applied Rehabilitation Counseling, 39*(2), 30–36.

McGillicuddy, N. B. (2006). A review of substance use research among those with mental retardation. *Mental Retardation and Developmental Disabilities Research Reviews, 12,* 41–47.

Mee-Lee, D. (2013). The *ASAM Criteria: Treatment for addictive, substance-related, and co-occurring conditions.* Chevy Chase, MD: American Society of Addiction Medicine.

Meredith, S. E., Juliano, L. M., Hughes, J. R., & Griffiths, R. R. (2013). Caffeine use disorder: A comprehensive review and research agenda. *Journal of Caffeine Research, 3*(3), 114–130.

Muid, O. (2008). Seeing through the lens of historical trauma. *Resource Links, 7*(2), 11–12.

Myers, R., Chou, C. P., Sussman, S., Baezconde-Garbanti, L., Pachon, H., & Valente, T. W. (2009). Acculturation and substance use: Social influence as a mediator among Hispanic alternative high school youth. *Journal of Health and Social Behavior, 50*(2), 164–179.

National Institute on Drug Abuse. (2003). *Drug use among racial/ethnic minorities* (NIH Publication No. 03-3888). Bethesda, MD: Author.

National Institute on Drug Abuse. (2012). *Principles of drug addiction treatment: A research-based guide* (3rd ed.) (NIH Publication No. 12-4180). Washington, DC: U.S. Department of Health and Human Services.

National Rehabilitation Information Center. (2011, January). Substance abuse & individuals with disabilities. Retrieved February 15, 2014, from http://www.naric.com/?=en/publications/volume-6-number-1-january-2011-substance-abuse-individuals-disabilities

National Spinal Cord Injury Statistical Center. (2008, January). Spinal cord injury facts and figures at a glance. Washington, DC: National Institute on Disability and Rehabilitation Research. Retrieved December 16, 2009, from http://www.spinalcord.uab.edu

Nugent, F. A., & Jones, K. D. (2009). *Introduction to the profession of counseling* (5th ed.). Upper Saddle River, NJ: Pearson.

Office on Disability. (2013). Substance abuse and disability. Retrieved October 16, 2013, from http://www.hhs.gov/od/about/fact_sheet/substanceabuse.html

Ostacher, M. (2011). Bipolar and substance use disorder comorbidity: Diagnostic and treatment considerations. *FOCUS: The Journal of Lifelong Learning in Psychiatry, 9*(4), 428–434.

Ouimette, P. C., Finney, J. W., Gima, K., & Moos, R. H. (1999a). A comparative evaluation of substance abuse treatment III. Examining mechanisms underlying patient-treatment matching hypotheses for 12-step and cognitive-behavioral treatments for substance abuse. *Alcoholism: Clinical and Experimental Research, 23,* 545–551.

Ouimette, P. C., Finney, J. W., Gima, K., & Moos, R. H. (1999b). A comparative evaluation of substance abuse treatment IV. The effect of comorbid psychiatric diagnoses on amount of treatment, continuing care, and 1-year outcomes. *Alcoholism: Clinical and Experimental Research, 23,* 552–557.

Peele, S. (1985). *The meaning of addiction: Compulsive experience and its interpretation.* New York, NY: Lexington Books.

Perron, B. E., Mowbray, O. P., Glass, J. E., Delva, J., Vaughn, M. G., & Howard, M. O. (2009). Differences in service utilization and barriers among Blacks, Hispanics, and Whites with drug use disorders. *Substance Abuse Treatment, Prevention, and Policy, 4.* Available online at http://www.substanceabusepolicy.com/content/4/1/3

Pokhrel, P., Herzog, T. A., Sun, P., Rohrbach, L. A., & Sussman, S. (2013). Acculturation, social self-control, and substance use among Hispanic adolescents. *Psychology of Addictive Behaviors, 27*(3), 674–686.

Quintero, M. (2011). Substance abuse in people with intellectual disabilities. *Social Work Today, 11*(4), 26–30.

Renzetti, C. M., Edleson, J. L., & Bergen, R. K. (2011). *Sourcebook on violence against women* (2nd ed.). Thousand Oaks, CA: Sage.

Rodgers-Bonaccorsy, R. A. (2010). Rehabilitation counselor attitudes toward counseling individuals with substance use disorders. *Rehabilitation Education, 24*(3-4), 135–148.

Sherer, R. A. (2002, March). Mental health problems among minorities: Follow-up to Surgeon General's report on mental health. *Psychiatric Times, 19*(3), 1–4.

Slayter, E. M. (2010). Disparities in access to substance abuse treatment among people with intellectual disabilities and serious mental illness. *Health & Social Work, 35*(1), 49–59.

Stevens, P., & Smith, R. L. (2009). *Substance abuse counseling: Theory and practice* (4th ed.). Upper Saddle River, NJ: Merrill.

Substance Abuse and Mental Health Administration. (2009a). *Rates of co-occurring mental and substance use disorders.* Retrieved October 16, 2013, from http://www.samhsa.gov/co-occurring/topics/data/disorders.aspx

Substance Abuse and Mental Health Services Administration. (2009b). *Results from the 2009 National Survey on Drug Use and Health: Mental health findings* (Center for Behavioral Health Statistics and Quality, NSDUH Series H-39, HHS Publication No. SMA 10-4609). Rockville, MD: Author.

Substance Abuse and Mental Health Services Administration. (2012). *Results from the 2010 National Survey on Drug Use and Health: Mental health findings* (NSDUH Series H-42. HHS Publication No. [SMA] 11-4667). Rockville, MD: Author.

Substance Abuse and Mental Health Services Administration. (2013a). *Results from the 2012 National Survey on Drug Use and Health* (NSDUH Series H-46, HHS Publication No. [SMA] 13-4795). Rockville, MD: Author.

Substance Abuse and Mental Health Services Administration. (2013b). *Substance abuse treatment for adults in the criminal justice system: A treatment improvement protocol TIP 44* (HHS Publication No. [SMA] 13-4056). Rockville, MD: Author.

Sue, D. W., & Sue, D. (2008). *Counseling the culturally diverse: Theory and practice* (5th ed.). Hoboken, NJ: Wiley & Sons.

Taormina-Weiss, W. (2012, August 14). Psychological and social aspects of disability. *Disabled World.* Retrieved November 11, 2013, from http://www.disabled-world.com/disability/social-aspects.php

Toriello, P. J., & Leierer, S. J. (2005). The relationship between the clinical orientation of substance abuse professionals and their clinical decisions. *Rehabilitation Counseling Bulletin, 48,* 75–88.

Tragesser, S. L., Beauvais, F., Swaim, R. C., Edwards, R. W., & Oetting, E. R. (2007). Parental monitoring, peer drug involvement and marijuana use across three ethnicities. *Journal of Cross Cultural Psychology, 38,* 670–694.

Upsher, C. (2008). Cultural competency and its impact on addiction treatment and recovery. *Resource Links, 7*(2), 1–5.

Valentine, S. R., Godkin, J., & Doughty, G. P. (2008). Hispanics' locus of control, acculturation, and wellness attitudes. *Social Work Public Health, 23*(5), 73–92.

Velez, M. B., Campos-Holland, A. L., & Arndt, S. (2008). City's racial composition shapes treatment center characteristics and services. *Journal of Ethnicity in Substance Abuse, 7,* 188–199.

Weiss, T. C. (2013, July 22). Substance abuse and persons with disabilities. *Disabled World.* Retrieved November 11, 2013, from http://www.disabled-world.com/medical/pharmaceutical/addiction

West, S. L., Graham, C. W., & Cifu, D. X. (2009a). Rates of alcohol/other drug treatment denials to persons with physical disabilities: Accessibility concerns. *Alcoholism Treatment Quarterly, 27,* 305–316.

West, S. L., Graham, C. W., & Cifu, D. X. (2009b). Prevalence of persons with disabilities in alcohol/other drug treatment in the United States. *Alcoholism Treatment Quarterly, 27,* 242–252.

West, S. L., Luck, R. S., Capps, C. F., Cifu, D. X., Graham, C. W., & Hurley, J. E. (2009). Alcohol/other drug problems screening and intervention by rehabilitation physicians. *Alcoholism Treatment Quarterly, 27,* 280–293.

White, W. L. (2012). *Recovery/remission from substance use disorders: An analysis of reported outcomes in 415 scientific reports, 1868–2011.* Rockville, MD: U.S. Department of Health and Human Services, Center for Substance Abuse Treatment.

Winkel, B. (2011). *Autism and substance abuse.* Treatment Solutions Network. Retrieved November 1, 2013, from http://www.treatmentsolutionsnetwork.com/blog/

Witkiewitz, K., & Masyn, K. E. (2008). Drinking trajectories following an initial lapse. *Psychology of Addictive Behaviors, 22*(2), 157–167.

Yalisove, D. (2004). *Introduction to alcohol research: Implications for treatment, prevention, and policy.* Boston, MA: Pearson.

Zubenko, N. (2006). Substance abuse treatment for disabled persons. *Counselor, 7,* 62–67.

Chapter 16

Substance Abuse Prevention Programs Across the Life Span

Abbé Finn
Florida Gulf Coast University

THE NEED FOR PREVENTION PROGRAMS ACROSS THE LIFE SPAN

The National Center for Chronic Disease Prevention and Health Promotion (NCCDPHP) has identified alcohol, tobacco, and drug abuse as leading causes of serious health problems, disability, and premature death (2002). People are exposed to drugs and alcohol along every stage of development across the life span. People can suffer addiction from womb to tomb.

Many people are exposed to dangerous intoxicating substances before they are born. These are the youngest and most innocent victims. Even though these substances have been used for many, many years, the study of their impact on a developing fetus is comparatively recent. The impact of cigarette smoking on the fetus has only been studied since the 1960s (Becker, Little, & King, 1968), alcohol and opiates since the 1970s (Finnegan, 1978; Jones & Smith, 1973), and other illicit substances since the 1980s (Chasnoff, Burns, Schnoll, & Burns, 1985). In spite of massive education regarding the risks of prenatal exposure to alcohol, tobacco, and other drugs, findings from the National Survey on Drug Use and Health indicate that approximately 4.5–5% of pregnant women continue to use these substances. There is a disturbing finding that pregnant teenagers are even more likely to use drugs than their nonpregnant counterparts (22% vs. 13.4%) (Substance Abuse and Mental Health Services Administration [SAMHSA], 2013a). Prenatal exposure to these substances can have the immediate effect of premature delivery with the long-term complications pertaining to health, growth, and neurological development, and the long-term effect of congenital defects, learning difficulties, impaired learning and language development, and neurological defects with learning and behavioral implications (Behnke, Smith, & Committee on Substance Abuse and Committee on Fetus and Newborn, 2013). Prevention programs that target pregnant women have the added value of intervening in the mother and the child's health and welfare. They even have an impact on the development of future children. It is truly the gift that keeps on giving because treatment for the mother reduces the need for care and special services for the future children.

In 2012, approximately 23.9 million Americans from 12 years of age and older had used illicit drugs within the past 30 days. This represents 9.2% of the population aged 12 or older, with the greatest use among 18- to 20-year-olds at 19.9% using illicit drugs within that 30-day time period. This is roughly the same population as people living in the state of Michigan. (See Figure 16.1.) In 2012, an estimated 22.2 million persons aged 12 or older met the criteria for substance dependence or abuse in the past year. This comes to 8.5% of the U.S. population. Individuals numbering 2.8 million were classified with dependence on or abuse of both alcohol and illicit drugs. Another 4.5 million were diagnosed with

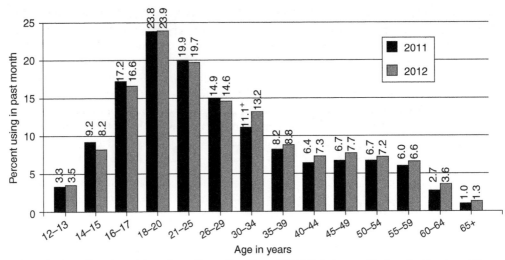

FIGURE 16.1 Number of Americans Reporting Use of Illicit Substances During the Previous 30 Days *Source:* Substance Abuse and Mental Health Services Administration. (2013). *Results from the 2012 National Survey on Drug Use and Health: Summary of national findings* (NSDUH Series H-46, HHS Publication No. [SMA] 13-4795). Rockville, MD: Author.

dependence on or abuse of illicit drugs (other than alcohol), and 14.9 million were dependent on alcohol but not illicit drugs (Centers for Disease Control and Prevention [CDC], 2012).

Substance abusers usually initiate use during childhood or adolescence, negatively impacting the rest of their lives. The peak ages for alcohol abuse are between 18 and 29 years old. For 65%, the initial drug used was cannabis, with 25% starting with medications prescribed to someone else (SAMHSA, 2013b). Full-time enrolled college students show higher rates of alcohol use and abuse than their noncollege peers, 60.3% versus 40.1% (Dawson, Grant, Stinson, & Chou, 2004; Johnston, O'Malley, & Bachman, 2003; Slutske et al., 2004; Slutske, 2005; SAMHSA, 2013a). Twenty percent of college students meet the diagnostic criteria for alcohol abuse—twice the rate of the average population (Dawson et al., 2004; Knight et al., 2002; National Center on Addiction and Substance

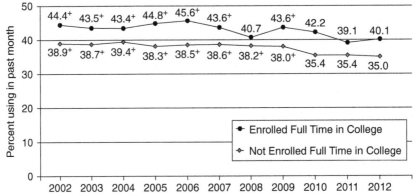

FIGURE 16.2 Binge Alcohol Use Among Adults Aged 18 – 22, by College Enrollment: 2002–2012 *Source:* Substance Abuse and Mental Health Services Administration. (2013). *Results from the 2012 National Survey on Drug Use and Health: Summary of national findings* (NSDUH Series H-46, HHS Publication No. [SMA] 13-4795). Rockville, MD: Author.

Abuse at Columbia University [CASA], 2007; SAMSHA, 2013a; Slutske, 2005). (See Figure 16.2.). College students who are members of fraternities and sororities have the highest rate of binge alcohol abuse and are most likely to be diagnosed with alcohol addiction (Knight et al., 2002). During a 10-year period, the proportion of students abusing controlled prescription drugs has increased exponentially. For example, the abuse of pain killers (Percocet, Vicodin, and OxyContin) has increased by more than 300%; stimulants (Ritalin and Adderall) by 90%; and daily marijuana use by 110% (CASA, 2007). The CASA (2007) report concluded that the rate of combined alcohol and substance abuse by American college students threatens the well-being of the current generation and the capacity of the United States to maintain its lead in a global economy.

Approximately 20% of college students meet the diagnostic criteria for alcohol abuse—twice the rate of the average population. Alcohol and drug abuse are also predictive of high-risk sexual behaviors, which may lead to HIV. Almost 80% of juveniles in the American criminal justice system were under the influence of a psychoactive substance when they committed their first crime.

In addition, alcohol and drug abuse are also predictive of high-risk sexual behaviors, which may lead to HIV, a major killer of young adults (NCCDPHP, 2002; CASA, 2007). However, effective drug prevention programs can reduce the risk for all three behaviors (LaBrie, Lewis, Atkins, Neighbors, Zheng et al., 2013; McCoy, Lai, Metsch, Messiah, & Zhao, 2004) and increase the health, productivity, and life expectancy of adolescents and young adults.

The variety of abused substances is increasing as new drugs are invented. Some young people abuse chemicals such as gasoline or spray paint rather than drugs. These chemicals and products, which were never intended for human consumption, are intentionally inhaled for the purpose of intoxication. In 2012, 500,000 people older than 12 years of age admitted that they had used inhalants (SAMSHA, 2013a). In the vernacular, this is a process known as "huffing." These substances are potentially lethal, carcinogenic, and toxic to the liver. There can be irreversible brain damage or death from a single use. It is difficult to monitor the use of these substances, since many are found in products available in every home, market, or school.

Among the young adult and adult population, alcohol, prescription drug abuse, and tobacco use for active military and recently discharged veterans is much higher than the civilian population. Twenty-seven percent of recently discharged combat veterans meet the criteria for substance abuse (Institute of Medicine [IOM], 2013). These addictions become life-long social, medical, and legal concerns. The report indicates that 1,000 troops were hospitalized for drug overdoses in 2010.

In the United States, the problem of substance abuse is enormous, with dire consequences for the quality of life of millions of people. For example, almost 80% of juveniles in the American criminal justice system were under the influence of a psychoactive substance when they committed their crime (CASA, 2004).

In 2007 (the most recent date for these estimates), the composite projected cost for the manufacturing industry, social service organizations, the criminal justice system, and the health care industry from substance abuse in the United States was estimated to be more than $193 billion (National Drug Intelligence Center, 2011). These figures are computed by estimating the cost to manufacturing industry due to the loss of productivity caused by on-the-job injuries, accidents, and increased health benefit costs of substance-abusing employees; expenses caused by absenteeism; and damages caused by impaired workers on the job. Health care cost estimates include the expense of treating patients suffering physical consequences of substance abuse, such as increased rates of liver disease, or medical treatment of traumatic injury incurred while under the influence of intoxicants.

As expensive as these numbers appear, the greatest toll cannot be assigned a monetary value. It is the cost borne by those who love and depend on the substance abuser. Long before drugs take the life of the addict, they damage lives and destroy the addict's relationships with others (van Wormer & Davis, 2003). These consequences include partner violence, sexual violence, property crimes, child abuse and neglect, loss of life (Executive Office of the President, 2001), and destruction of relationships with employers, family, and friends.

In addition, the younger the onset of drug abuse, the greater the negative consequences to the person's cognitive, interpersonal, and educational development. There is evidence that children and adolescents are particularly vulnerable to physical problems associated with exposure to alcohol, drugs, and tobacco products. There is additional evidence that drug and alcohol use during adolescence, when the brain is continuing to develop, causes irreversible damage to the brain's higher order cortical function (Volkow & Li, 2005; Wuetrich, 2001). The incomplete development of the prefrontal cortex increases susceptibility to high-risk behavior because this part of the brain is responsible for judgment, decision making, and emotional control (Gogtay et al., 2004).

The younger the onset of drug abuse, the greater the negative consequences to the person's cognitive, interpersonal, and educational development. In 10 years, the number of emergency room admissions due to complications from recreational use of prescription narcotics (oxycodone or hydrocodone) increased by 352%. In the past 12 years, the rate of opioid and benzodiazepine prescription drug abuse has risen 344% and 450%, respectively. Over the last 5 years, the number of people who used heroin doubled from 373,000 in 2007 to 669,000 people in 2012 (SAMSHA 2013a).

While use of some illicit substances by young people has recently been declining, the illegal use of prescription drugs, such as benzodiazepines and narcotic pain killers, and the use of medical and nonmedical inhalants have shown a sharp increase (Johnston, O'Malley, Bachman, & Schulenberg, 2005; Kurtzman, Otsuka, & Wahl, 2001; Sung, Richter, Vaughan, Johnson, & Thom, 2005). The rates of illicit drug and alcohol use by adolescents and young adults are on the rise, with the percentage increasing from 27% in 1992 to 40% in 1996 (Johnston, O'Malley, & Bachman, 1996). Specifically, use of opioids has risen to 9.4% of high school seniors illegally using narcotics during the past year (Johnston et al., 2003). In 10 years, the number of emergency room admissions due to complications from recreational use of prescription narcotics (oxycodone or hydrocodone) increased by 352%. Sung et al. (2005) describe typical adolescent opioid abusers as poor Black females with drug-abusing environmental role models. On the other hand, McCabe, Boyd, and Teter (2005) describe typical adolescent opioid abusers as White male cigarette and marijuana smokers who drink alcohol. The accurate profile of young opioid users is hazy, but it is clear that opioid abuse by adolescents is becoming a new epidemic in need of effective prevention programs (Compton & Volkow, 2006; McCabe et al., 2005; Sung et al., 2005). A new media campaign warns parents and grandparents of the increased risk of prescription drug abuse by their children or grandchildren, through theft of their prescription medications, and trains adults in the safe disposal of unneeded prescription medications (Compton & Volkow, 2006; McCabe et al., 2005; Office of National Drug Control Policy, 2002; Sung et al., 2005).

On college campuses, the rate of substance use and abuse has been growing at an alarming rate. For example, between 1995 and 2007 the abuse of prescription opioid pain medications increased by 344%. During that same period, there was a 450% increase in abuse of a class of depressants known as benzodiazepines, including drugs commonly known as Valium and Ativan. There is an increased health risk because college students are combining these medications with alcohol, leading to rapid intoxication and overdoses, some of which lead to premature death (CASA, 2007).

In addition to the risks of addiction due to substance abuse, half of newly diagnosed HIV patients are under the age of 25, indicating that they contracted the virus while adolescents or young adults. One-third of people infected with HIV contracted the disease through intravenous drug use (IDU) (CDC, 2005). Drug users who do not use intravenous drugs also show a much higher rate of HIV infection than nondrug users (McCoy et al., 2004), because substance use increases the likelihood of other high-risk behaviors such as unsafe sexual practices with multiple partners while it inhibits the likelihood of protected sex (CDC, 2005). Therefore, preventing drug use has the added value of decreasing the risk of contracting HIV/AIDS, other sexually transmitted infections, unplanned pregnancies (CASA, 2007), and reducing the likelihood of fetal drug and alcohol exposure.

The extent of the problem of drug abuse among the elderly is unknown because there have been very few studies conducted targeting this population. Wu and Blazer (2011) reviewed the literature from 1990 to 2010 and found that people from 50 to 64 years old were more likely to abuse illicit and prescription drugs than did people older than 65. However, the rate for abuse is expected to rise as this cohort ages (Simoni-Wastila & Yang, 2006). However, older adults are much less likely to seek treatment and have little insight regarding the seriousness of their problem. Unfortunately, none of the screening instruments are validated for use with the elderly (Culberson & Ziska, 2008). Simoni-Wastila and Yang (2006) found that illicit drug use among the elderly is increasing and that it contributes to the loss of cognitive functioning, social isolation, and reduction in the level of functioning. The National Survey on Drug Use and Health indicates that the use of illicit drugs and the abuse of prescription medications increased from 5.1% in 2002 to 9.2% in 2007 for adults older than 50 years old. Han, Gfroerer, Colliver, and Penne (2009) projected that substance abuse among senior adults will double from 2.8 million (annual average) in 2002–2006 to 5.7 million in 2020. Culberson and Ziska (2008) found that a fourth of prescription medications are used by the elderly. Of these, it is predicted that 11% of the elderly abuse substances. Given this information, it is surprising that there is so little research on this topic and there is no information regarding prevention programs designed directly for older adults. The only prevention programs found for older adults are aimed at medical practitioners and health care professionals.

PUBLIC HEALTH PREVENTION PROGRAM MODEL

According to the public health model of disease prevention, substance abuse prevention programs fall into three general types: primary, secondary, and tertiary. Some programs are designed to include all youth; others are designed to focus on targeted vulnerable groups (James & Gilliland, 2001).

Primary Prevention Programs

Primary prevention programs target problem behaviors before symptoms occur. Participants are selected because they fall into an at-risk category. The purpose of these programs is to stop the problem before it begins. An example of this type of prevention program would be one that targets elementary school children for education regarding the risks involved with tobacco use. This is a reasonable target group because research shows that most people who become addicted to tobacco began use during middle or high school; and because tobacco products are so highly addictive, experimentation can easily lead to addiction (McDonald, Roberts, & Descheemaeker, 2000).

Primary prevention programs target problem behaviors before symptoms occur. Secondary prevention programs are designed for people who have already demonstrated problematic behaviors. The goal of a tertiary prevention program is to reduce the risk of further harm.

Secondary Prevention Programs

Secondary prevention programs are designed for people who have already demonstrated problematic behaviors. The goal is to stop the behavior before it escalates to a serious problem with dangerous consequences. Some secondary prevention programs can be described as a harm reduction model. For example, when it comes to alcohol, some programs focus on responsible drinking rather than abstinence (Marlatt & Witkiewitz, 2002; van Wormer & Davis, 2003).

Tertiary Prevention Programs

Juvenile Drug Court (JDC) diversionary programs are examples of tertiary prevention programs. Their goal is to divert drug offenders to treatment and recovery programs rather than jail, thus breaking the cycle of addiction and recidivism within the criminal justice system. Other examples include the mandated counseling programs for students convicted of violating alcohol and drug use policies on campus (Carey, Henson, Carey, & Maisto, 2009) and the relapse prevention program that is part of most drug-abuse recovery programs (Compton et al., 2005).

EVIDENCED-BASED PREVENTION PROGRAMS

Effective substance use and drug prevention programs share the following five elements. These are: identification of and addressing both risk and protective factors of particular populations. In order to accomplish this, needs assessments must be conducted to measure levels of risk, protective factors, and substances of abuse in this population. All levels of risk are prioritized and addressed as appropriate. The target population within the needs assessment must be defined by discreet factors such as age, grade, rank, socioeconomic status, education, location, workplace, and school.

The interventions have research data to substantiate the effectiveness. These programs do the following: (1) reduce either the supply or demand for substances of abuse, (2) strengthen the norms or attitudes toward healthy living, (3) strengthen healthy life skills and drug refusal skills, (4) strengthen functioning of the family or unit, and (5) make certain that the intervention is culturally appropriate.

These interventions must be implemented when developmentally appropriate and are timely responses to needs and events. The program curriculum and activities are delivered in appropriate settings in an efficient manner. These programs are initiated early in the problem behavior to reduce harm, and the curriculum is planned so that there are repeated exposures to "boost" the impact of the curriculum (Office of National Drug Control Policy, 2001). For a prevention program to be effective, it must be designed especially to address the community needs. It is better to prevent people from becoming addicted than to try to treat them after the problem has emerged. To stop drug abuse in adults, it is important to prevent the experimentation and use by adolescents of identified gateway drugs.

Program Needs Assessment

For a prevention program to be effective, it must be designed especially to address community needs. These assessments identify the types of drugs being abused or likely to be abused in the future, community services that are already in place or need to be developed, community and institutional goals, and resources necessary for the implementation of a proposed substance abuse prevention program. The four types of needs indicators are "drug use indicators, problem-behavior indicators, psychological or developmental characteristics, and social or economic conditions" (Sales, 2004, p. 82). Drug use indicators identify the types of drugs, prevalence rate of use, and the number of people secondarily impacted. Drug use indicators are comprised of arrest records, survey responses, incarceration rates, school disciplinary actions, and treatment data. Problem-behavior indicators are behaviors associated with and caused by addictions. These could include children in foster care due to parental substance abuse, neglect, or parental drug-related incarceration; school dropout rates; and positive HIV secondary to drug use. Psychological and developmental vulnerabilities also contribute to the risk factors. These include many correlated factors such as age-related developmental factors; family structures and interaction styles; and individual characteristics such as a history of physical and/or sexual abuse, low self-esteem, homelessness, and/or mental or psychiatric disorders. Social, economic, and environmental factors include poverty, high crime rates, community tolerance for violence and drug distribution and use, substandard housing, blighted communities resources, and disadvantages associated with discrimination (Sales, 2004).

Some of this data is available through community and governmental agencies, or can be collected from surveys and/or interviews. The National Association on Substance Abuse has several instruments that can be modified or used in their original forms for needs assessment.

The most effective substance abuse treatment programs target previously identified problems through needs assessments; apply scientifically proven intervention methods for reducing substance abuse risk actors; enhance resistance and resiliency factors; and monitor the impact of the programs (Arthur & Blitz, 2000).

TYPES OF SUBSTANCE ABUSE PREVENTION PROGRAMS

Clearly, preventing people from becoming addicted in the first place is better than trying to treat them after the problem has emerged. The question is: What programs are best at preventing addictions? Many types of programs have been tried. These programs have used scare tactics, social skills and peer pressure resistance training, education regarding drug abuse facts, and parent and family training regarding behavior management and communication skills (Catalano & Hawkins, 1996; Dwyer, Nicholson, Battistutta, & Oldenburg, 2005; Hawkins, Catalano, & Arthur, 2002).

Prevention Program Strategies

Prevention programs can be categorized along nine different strategies—each will be reviewed:

1. School/college-based prevention programs focusing on education, peer mediation, and reduction of negative peer pressure
2. Mass media campaigns reporting risks and consequences of drug use, and restriction of media campaigns that glamorize the use of harmful substances
3. Early diagnosis and treatment of emotional problems
4. Improvement of personal and interpersonal skills

5. Harm reduction programs
6. Campaigns to reduce the access to drugs
7. JDC, drug court, and other diversionary programs
8. Approaches focusing on improving the family, improving parenting skills, and reduction of child abuse
9. Multimodal programs using some features from all of the previous eight

PREVENTION PROGRAMS TARGETING ALL AGE GROUPS

Restriction of Access to Drugs

Amid a great deal of political fanfare, in 1971 President Nixon declared a "war on drugs." Congress pledged that the country would be drug free by 1995. Obviously, that pledge has not been fulfilled. There has been an attempt to control the recreational and nonmedical use of prescription drugs and to restrict the flow of drugs into the country. However, 13–18 metric tons of heroin is consumed yearly in the United States (Department of Health and Human Services [DHHS], 2004). In 2005, the U.S. government budgeted $6.63 billion for U.S. government agencies directly concerned with restricting illicit drug use. The U.S. government has attempted to restrict importation by strengthening the borders and interdicting illegal substances before they enter the United States and has also attempted to reduce importation from the supply side. It also uses foreign aid to pressure drug-producing countries to stop cultivating, producing, and processing illegal substances. Some of the foreign aid is tied to judicial reforms, antidrug programs, and agricultural subsidies to grow legal produce (DHHS, 2004).

In an attempt to reduce drug supplies, the government has incarcerated drug suppliers. Legislators have authorized strict enforcement of mandatory sentences resulting in a great increase in prison populations. As a result, the arrest rate of juveniles for drug-related crimes has doubled in the past 10 years, while arrest rates for other crimes have declined by 13%. A small minority of these offenders (2 out of every 1,000) will be offered JDC diversionary programs as an option to prison sentences (CASA, 2004).

The arrest rate of juveniles for drug-related crimes has doubled in the past 10 years while arrest rates for other crimes have declined by 13%. Eighty percent of adjudicated youth are in jail due to drug crimes. JDC programs are cost beneficial: Incarceration for each of the 122,696 drug-offending juveniles in prison costs $43,000 per year. Because of the differing needs of children compared with adults, prevention programs are usually designed with specific age groups in mind. Many of these will be explored in this chapter.

SUBSTANCE ABUSE PREVENTION PROGRAMS FOR CHILDREN AND ADOLESCENTS AND YOUNG ADULTS

Early Diagnosis and Treatment of Emotional Problems

Practitioners working in psychiatric treatment facilities have long noticed a co-occurrence of substance abuse and psychiatric problems (Fals-Stewart & Lucente, 1994). These include depression, suicidal behavior, conduct disorder, attention-deficit hyperactivity disorder, eating disorders, psychosis (Zeitlin, 1999), and post-traumatic stress disorder. Seventy-five percent of adolescents in treatment for substance abuse have a co-occurring psychiatric disorder (Biederman, Faraone, Wozniak, & Monteaux, 2000; Hser, Grella, Collins, & Teruya, 2003). Usually the symptoms of the psychiatric disorders are present before the emergence of experimentation and use of intoxicating and addictive substances. Therefore, it is recommended that adolescents in treatment for psychiatric disorders should receive drug abuse prevention as part of their psychiatric treatment plan (Hser et al., 2003; Zeitlin, 1999).

Seventy-five percent of adolescents in treatment for substance abuse have a co-occurring psychiatric disorder.

High schools and colleges are ideal platforms for launching drug abuse prevention programs because they provide convenient access to target populations, and offer opportunities to administer program curriculum, practice the activities, and evaluate the outcome. The earliest school/college-based programs focused on providing the facts regarding the dangers of drug use and encouraging healthy alternatives and healthy expression of emotions (Botvin, 2000). Other programs have taught students the social skills thought necessary for drug avoidance. Because the temptation to use drugs is omnipresent, social skills such as the ability to refuse drugs are considered essential if adolescents and young adults are to successfully avoid the consequences of drug abuse (Botvin et al., 2000).

Juvenile Drug Court Diversionary Programs

Once a young person enters the juvenile court system, it is very likely that they have fallen into the abyss of a lifetime within the prison system (National Institute of Justice [NIJ], 2000). JDC diversionary programs provide supervision through weekly or biweekly hearings. The JDC team may consist of a judge, prosecutor, defense attorney, probation officer, substance abuse treatment provider, law enforcement officials, the juvenile and his or her family, social workers, counselors and vocational counselors, and educators (CASA, 2004). The team decides on a case-by-case basis which drug-offending juveniles are most likely to benefit from the program. Participants are selected from a pool of convicted, drug-abusing juvenile delinquents. The first JCD began in Las Vegas, Nevada, in 1994. As of November 2003, there were 294 JCDs in 46 states with 4,500 participants and 4,000 completers (CASA, 2004).

Juveniles in the JCD program receive close supervision by a parole officer and periodic drug testing. If they fail to follow all the provisions of the treatment plan or test positive for substances during the designated period of supervision, they are rearrested and sent to jail, to serve out their sentence.

Eighty percent of adjudicated youth are in jail due to drug crimes. These include possession of illegal substances, driving while under the influence; crimes committed to acquire substances or support the expensive drug habit, and crimes such as assaults and murder committed to control their competitors and maintain the drug business (NIJ, 2000).

Of the 80% of youth incarcerated for crimes involving drugs and alcohol, 44% meet the clinical diagnosis for substance abuse or dependence. Once in jail, however, only 1.6% receive any treatment for addictions (McAuliffe, Woodwarth, Zhang, & Dunn, 2002; CASA, 2004). JDC diversionary programs have the added benefit of providing an opportunity for diagnosis and treatment of coexisting psychiatric disorders among juvenile offenders. It is estimated that 64–71% of adjudicated youth have a diagnosable mental disorder, with 20% having conditions in the serious range (Teplin, Abram, McClelland, Dulcan, & Mericle, 2002).

In addition to being more humane than incarceration, JDC programs are also cost beneficial. For example, the cost of incarceration for each of the 122,696 drug-offending juveniles in prison is $43,000 per year; JDC diversionary programs cost $5,000 per year—saving federal, state, and local governments $4,662,448,000 (CASA, 2004). Even if many failed the treatment, there would still be very large savings, even without computing the cost benefit of children maturing to lead productive lives rather than lives of crime, incarceration, addiction, and premature disability or death (CASA, 2004).

School-Based Substance Abuse Prevention Programs

Lynskey et al. (2003) hypothesize that if effective school-based substance abuse prevention programs were implemented nationwide, the onset of substance use in children and young adults would be delayed by an average of 2 years and substance use would decline for 1.5 million. Effective prevention programs can be expected to result in a reduction by 8% of youth aged 13–15 in binge drinking. Also, 11.5% fewer youth would not have used marijuana, 45.8% fewer youth would have used cocaine, and 10.7% fewer youth would become addicted to tobacco. Miller and Hendry (2009) estimated that for every dollar spent on substance use prevention, 18 dollars is saved.

In researching drug addiction, some common characteristics have emerged and have been identified as risk factors. These characteristics precede the onset of substance use (Hser, Grella, Collins, & Teruya, 2003). They cluster into five categories. The first consists of individual characteristics such as mental illness, school failure, antisocial behavior, drug experimentation at a young age, and criminal activity. The second cluster includes attitudes such as distrust of authority figures, anger toward adults, and a fascination with deviant behaviors. The third cluster includes psychosocial characteristics such as low self-esteem, poor social skills, desire to fit in with peers, poor peer-pressure refusal skills, and lack of self-advocacy skills. The fourth cluster consists of family characteristics such as family history of drug use or dependence, family antisocial behavior, and parents with ineffective behavior management skills. The fifth and final category includes environmental characteristics such as poverty; lack of support services; community tolerance of drug use, violence, and criminal behavior; easy access to drugs and alcohol; and family and friends who use drugs (Goldberg, 2006). The presence of the risk factor does not presume a cause–effect relationship. All people presenting with these characteristics will not automatically become substance abusers. It is assumed that the greater number of factors present, the more vulnerable the young person is to the threat of addiction (Callas, Flynn, & Worden, 2004).

Program administrators utilize the risk factor approach in several ways. Some use the information to profile students and identify which ones should be included in the primary prevention program (Bousman et al., 2005; Ellickson & Morton, 1999; Griffin, Botvin, Nichols, & Doyle, 2003). Others utilize risk factors so that, when a risk factor is identified, addiction prevention can be included with intervention for the other identified problem; for example, post-traumatic stress disorder (Beiderman, Faraone, Wozniak, & Monteaux, 2000; Zeitlin, 1999). Vulnerabilities and other factors are further explored in Chapter 19 in this text.

Most adolescent drug abuse prevention programs focus on keeping students from experimenting with tobacco, alcohol, and marijuana, which have been identified as "gateway drugs." When surveyed, most substance abusers in treatment identify these as the first drugs they experimented with and used. These drugs were viewed as landmarks for the port of entry into drug abuse. That is why so many of the early prevention programs focused on abstinence. Any use of substances was understood to be the first step on a slippery slope leading to drug abuse and addictions. According to this assumption, in order to stop drug abuse in adults, it is important to prevent the experimentation and use by adolescents of these identified gateway drugs. However, there is controversy regarding the assumption of inevitable progression from the experimental use of a drug such as tobacco to addiction or abuse of the most dangerous drugs (Golub & Johnson, 2002).

D.A.R.E.

The most well-known school-based drug abuse prevention program is Drug Abuse Awareness and Resistance Education (D.A.R.E.). It is the most widely implemented and well-funded alcohol and drug abuse prevention program to date, with $750 million in funding in 1991 (Clayton, Cattarello, & Johnstone, 1996); 80% of school districts in America used some form of the program in 2001 (Birkeland, Murphy-Graham, & Weiss, 2005). Developed in 1983 by the Los Angeles Unified School District in cooperation with the Los Angeles Police Department, it originally targeted children making the transition from elementary to middle school, an age thought to be most vulnerable to poor decisions due to the stress encountered at developmental turning points and to consequences from bad choices. However, in some school districts, D.A.R.E. was expanded to include children from kindergarten to third grade, middle school, and high school.

D.A.R.E.'s core curriculum advocates strict abstinence from any drug use. It provides information about the effects of drugs and promotes skills and techniques that help students refuse drugs, resist peer pressure, avoid drug use related to gang involvement, and enhance self-esteem and self-advocacy. The program calls for 1 hour of education and training each week for 17 consecutive weeks, using a copyrighted curriculum taught by uniformed police officers. (The officers take 80 hours of classes covering instruction techniques and information regarding the dangers of drug use.) The program is delivered in lecture and interactive format. In 1991, the D.A.R.E. program was touted as the cure for the child and adolescent drug abuse epidemic (Department of Justice, 1991).

Evaluative Reviews of D.A.R.E.

Initial efficacy studies showed some positive impact from the D.A.R.E. program. For example, a study of seventh-grade students indicated that program participants were better at refusing drugs and used at a lower rate than did the comparison group of nonparticipants (DeJong, 1987). Other outcome studies demonstrated changes in students' attitudes toward drug use, finding them to have a more negative attitude toward drugs and finding their use to be less attractive (Harmon, 1993; Ringwalt, Ennett, & Holt, 1991). In research evaluating the long-term impact of D.A.R.E. on the drug use patterns of high school seniors, utilizing qualitative and quantitative methods of enquiry, researchers found that the D.A.R.E. training had a minimal effect on the prevention of drug use in adolescents and its initial positive effects decayed over time (Griffin et al., 2003; Clayton et al., 1996; Lynam et al., 1999; Rosenbaum & Hanson, 1998; Wysong & Wright, 1995). After a 7-year follow-up study utilizing quantitative and qualitative methods, Wysong and Wright (1995) concluded that there was no positive long-term impact from the D.A.R.E. curriculum. Focus groups conducted with graduates who had been student role models for the younger participants revealed their doubts at having made any substantial impact on the lives of the participants. In a 7-year follow-up study with at-risk students, the findings were even more pessimistic. Study subjects recalled the D.A.R.E. experience in negative terms, stating that the curriculum was "boring" and the situations were "phony" (Wysong & Wright, 1995, p. 296).

Researchers found that the D.A.R.E. training had minimal effect on the prevention of drug use in adolescents and the initial positive effects following the training decayed over time.

In spite of the lack of evidence demonstrating the effectiveness of D.A.R.E., many school districts continue to utilize the program. Administrators continue the program for many reasons. Some say they disbelieve the evidence, in light of anecdotal data that they have collected. Others ignore the data because the program evaluators only measured the outcome of the officially stated goals. For example, some educators continue to value D.A.R.E. because of the improved relationship between law enforcement officers and the school community. In a community in which this relationship is historically strained, this is a highly valued, but unmeasured, outcome. In addition, community stakeholders may have very different reasons for valuing the D.A.R.E. curriculum. For example, they may perceive an increased rate of community involvement in education as a result of the D.A.R.E. community outreach (Birkeland et al., 2005).

There may be a high rate of measurement error with these program evaluations. For example, Fendrich and Rosenbaum (2003) did follow-up surveys with high school students who had participated in D.A.R.E. during the seventh grade. They found that over the course of their middle through high school years, from 41% to 81% of survey respondents recanted their stories regarding the amount and variety of their substance use. The highest level of recanting occurred regarding the use of cocaine and methamphetamines. It is hypothesized that since the D.A.R.E. program uses uniformed officers to communicate the curriculum and collect the data, as students mature they may distrust whether the information is truly confidential. It cannot be overlooked that this high rate of inconsistency among survey responses over time decreases the reliability of the research findings.

D.A.R.E. is not the only prevention program showing little or no long-term impact. To test the efficacy of a social skills training drug prevention program, Botvin et al. (2000) randomly assigned students to a treatment or a control group. During the seventh grade, the treatment group received training and education regarding peer pressure resistance, the influence of advertising on behavior, and the influence of modeling by parents, friends, and media personalities on behavior (Botvin, 2000). The students had reinforcing education in the eighth and ninth grades. Six and a half years later, both groups of students were surveyed again to measure the efficacy of the prevention program. The data indicated that students who had received the life skills training were significantly less likely to use illicit drugs during their high school years than those who had not (Botvin et al., 2000).

Early Action Against Teen Drug Use

Another school drug prevention program—Early Action Against Teen Drug Use: Teens as Communicators to Their Peers—is designed for high school students. It combines drug awareness education, problem-solving skills training, interactive role plays, communication skills training, critical thinking skills language arts, and recognition of positive peer influences. The product of a collaboration between the Office of National Drug Policy and the *New York Times* in Education Program (*New York Times* Knowledge Network, 2003), this program is an integrated curriculum designed to meet national educational content standards in language arts, health, life skills, visual arts, mathematics, and behavioral studies. An integrated curriculum is very important in order to justify the classroom time spent on prevention programs, because educators are encouraged to demonstrate that they are meeting their state educational standards while teaching these programs. In the era of high-stakes testing, administrators will not approve lessons that do not reinforce the state grade standards. Counselors and educators are driven by the pressure to demonstrate that their activities improve student learning. These programs have the longer range goal of preventing drug use in the future while meeting state educational standards.

The lesson plans for Early Action Against Teen Drug Use: Teens as Communicators to Their Peers are available on the web free of charge to educators: nytimes.com/learning/teachers/NIE/earlyaction/. There are 14 learning modules available integrating newspaper articles, current research findings, and resources that guide students and teachers in the fight against substance abuse. The lesson plans include activities such as lists of topics for role-plays of drug resistance strategies, and an imaginary letter from a friend describing his or her new friends who are encouraging her to smoke cigarettes. The students must respond to the friend's request for help, developing strategies to avoid exposure to marijuana use. In addition, the *New York Times* links current articles that cover timely topics about the risks of substance use to classes registered with them online. At this time, there are no evaluations of this program.

In-School Drug Testing

Some school-based programs attempt to limit drug use by identifying drug users through drug testing (Naylor, Gardner, & Zaichkowsky, 2001). Those who test positive are either sanctioned in some way or required to enter treatment programs. Schools justify drug testing because of the belief that it will reduce drug use among students and increase student learning and school performance. The test sample can come from sweat, saliva, hair, breath, or urine.

According to a 2008 study from the National Drug Abuse Institute, about 14% of schools had drug testing policies. The study found that of the districts with drug testing policies, almost all tested athletes, and 65% targeted all students in extracurricular activities. Further, more than one-quarter of those schools drug tested all students, which is outside of the court's recommendations. The 2011 University of Pennsylvania study—which used a limited student sample—pegged the number at 27% (James-Burdumy, Goesling, Deke, & Einspruch, 2010).

Schools that use drug testing must develop the testing protocols in a scientific and systematic manner so that reliability, validity, and confidentiality are guaranteed. Also, before initiating a drug testing policy, the school must get legal advice and make certain that there is informed consent from the parents, faculty, and students. Without community support, the program is doomed to failure (Office of National Drug Control Policy, 2002). Most schools that enact drug testing policies select students participating in extracurricular activities (James-Burdumy et al., 2010). When parents challenged the right of school personnel to drug test students, the U.S. Supreme Court (*Vermonia School District 47* v. *Acton*, 1995) supported the constitutionality of these procedures for students participating in competitive extracurricular sports.

STUDENT TESTING USING RANDOM NOTIFICATION (SATURN) In another study, known as SATURN (Student Testing Using Random Notification), drug use patterns of students from two different schools were compared. In the drug testing school (DT), athletes were tested during the preseason. In the control school (C), they were not tested. Students at both schools completed confidential drug use questionnaires. In the DT school, if students tested positive to substances, their parents were notified and the student was referred to counseling. However, no disciplinary actions were taken. At the end of the school year, evaluation of the data indicated that this was a highly successful program. The drug-tested athletes had significantly lower rates of illicit drug use (including steroids) while the untested group increased their use. In the DT group, 75% fewer athletes used illicit drugs than the C group (Goldberg et al., 2003).

When people think of drug testing, they often think of screenings for performance-enhancing drugs. Anabolic steroid abuse is not a problem confined to adults. Approximately half of male and female high school students participate in some type of organized sports. There is a tremendous amount of pressure for these young people to excel in their sports. The external pressure and internal desire to win can drive many athletes to resort to unhealthy, extreme measures. These can play out in the form of eating disorders and use of performance-enhancing drugs (Mayo Clinic, 2007). Unfortunately, most high school athletes are not deterred from drug use by random drug screens because most are not tested for drugs (Naylor et al., 2001), and those who are tested are only under scrutiny during their competitive season. The students who said they did not use because of the testing also reported that they planned to use in the future when the testing was over (James-Burdumy et al., 2010). It is therefore unknown if this intervention has had any lasting impact.

ATHLETES TARGETING HEALTHY EXERCISE AND NUTRITION ALTERNATIVES (ATHENA) In an effort to address these concerns, Elliott, Goldberg, Moe, DeFrancesco, and Durham (2004), from the Department of Medicine at Oregon Health & Science University, designed and developed a program targeting female athletes, known as ATHENA (Athletes Targeting Healthy Exercise and Nutrition Alternatives). The ATHENA program utilizes a team-centered approach capitalizing on the potential for positive peer influences. The ATHENA program requires team members to participate in eight 45-minute classroom sessions during the season. Each team is divided into squads consisting of six members, with one identified as the squad leader. A coach supervises the squads and a squad leader, and a member of the coaching staff leads the sessions. Each squad leader participates in a 90-minute video training session and follows a script during the sessions; participants follow workbook activities. The sessions focus on providing accurate nutritional information; information about the dangers of amphetamines and other performance-enhancing drugs; social skills training, including drug-refusal skills; and information regarding the influence of media campaigns on the perpetuation of unrealistic physical standards of beauty. The squads become a support group encouraging healthy eating habits and maintenance of healthy exercise and dietary norms. The participants have nutritional guides as resources and complete journals recording nutritional intake, physical activities, and emotions. These activities were included because female athletes, compared with their age mates, are at an increased risk for eating disorders (Elliot et al., 2004).

The ATHENA program utilizes a team-centered approach capitalizing on the potential for positive peer influences. The responsibility for preventing drug abuse on campus is shared by all members of the academic community.

Multimodal Programs

Multimodal programs address addictions prevention from several perspectives simultaneously. Some are launched in prekindergarten through Grade 12 schools or higher education institutions, providing services to students, families, and educators. Others focus on changing the community and the environment. This type of program is based upon the Ecological Systems Theory (Santrock, 2009), which posits that behavior is influenced by socioeconomic, environmental, and cultural factors; family relations; parental behaviors; and parenting competency. Epidemiological research on addiction and abuse has supported these findings. These characteristics can have a protective or compromising influence on a young person's ability to avoid drug, alcohol, or tobacco use (Volkow & Li, 2005). Therefore, it is logical to train a wide range of influential members in the person's environment—parents, classmates, and educators—on ways to improve communication, teach effective behavior management skills, and increase knowledge regarding the impact of family dynamics on adolescent drug abuse (Dishion & Kavanagh, 2000). Parents participate because, although their children push them away in their quest for freedom and self-actualization, they continue to exert a powerful influence on their children. Peers and classmates participate because, during this developmental period, teens increasingly turn to friends for information and look to them as role models for normative behavior. Teachers also participate because, since most adolescents are in school, they have opportunities to observe them and provide immediate feedback on their behavior.

Ecological Systems Theory posits that behavior is influenced by socioeconomic, environmental, and cultural factors.

The Adolescent Transition Program (ATP) is an example of this type of program. The project is funded by a grant by the National Institute on Drug Abuse and run by the staff and administration of the schools. The program calls for a Family Resource Room that contains a library and counseling offices. ATP provides prevention services and counseling to middle school students, their families, teachers, and classmates. Counseling services are available to students and their families in the school and in home visits. Parents are given access to parenting and family management training, and education regarding drug use and abuse (Dishion & Kavanagh, 2000). These services are available throughout the school year, with home visits during the summer.

Another example of a school-centered multimodal approach is the SHAPe Curriculum (Success, Health, and Peace), a 6-week health education training during which students are given homework assignments to complete with their parents. The goals of these assignments are to improve the parent and child relationship, as well as increase school success, healthy choices, self-advocacy, self-respect, emotional maturity, and peaceful problem-solving skills (Dishion & Kavanagh, 2000). Weekly newsletters and programs on public access television provide additional information.

INSTITUTIONS OF HIGHER EDUCATION (IHE) SUBSTANCE ABUSE INTERVENTION PROGRAMS College students have two major tasks when they leave home: to assimilate into a new culture and to achieve academically. These tasks are, paradoxically, at cross purposes because, when students spend too much time making new friends their grades suffer, and when they focus solely on studying, they are often socially isolated. Many freshman use alcohol and drugs to reduce their social anxiety, to fit in socially, and for a major part of their recreational activities (Vaughan, Corbin, & Fromme, 2009). When college students enter the Greek system of fraternities and sororities, their rate of alcohol abuse increases dramatically (Capone, Wood, Borsari, & Laird, 2007; Iwamoto, Corbin, Lejuez, & MacPherson, 2014; Park, Sher, Wood, & Krull, 2009). College and university health centers provide counseling services and implement programs to combat these and other psychological problems (Cooper 1999; Gallaghar, 2009; Minami et al., 2009), and 93.4% report an increase of students with severe psychological problems (Gallagher, 2009). Iwamoto et al. (2014) found that college men are more likely that their female counterparts to exhibit behaviors that are high risk and health compromising, including binge drinking. This leads to alcohol-related problems, including criminal activity and violence.

This was especially true if they identified with the "Playboy" archetype. However, when the college men associated masculinity with self-control and responsibility, they were less likely to fall into negative behaviors. With this information, character education would either be excluded or included in the curriculum. This finding underscored the need to know the dispositional attributes of the target population.

It is estimated that 20% of students on college campuses meet the *Diagnostic Statistical Manual* (4th ed., text rev.) (DSM IV-TR) criteria for alcohol substance abuse, and 8.2% of students had abused prescription drugs in the past month (CASA 2007; Grant et al., 2004). Beyond the ethical imperative to address substance abuse problems on campus, there are also compelling financial reasons, since IHEs are open to liability for failing to prevent foreseeable threats to students' health and safety. For example, Massachusetts Institute of Technology and the University of Miami paid court-ordered awards of 6 million and 14 million dollars respectively for substance-related student deaths (CASA, 2007). The responsibility for preventing drug abuse on campus is shared by all members of the academic community. It is recommended that IHEs develop comprehensive programs focusing on a culture change in collaboration with alumni, student organizations, community members, National Collegiate Athletic Association (NCAA), faculty, parents, and students.

CASA (2007) made some specific recommendations for administrators. For example, IHEs should have clear policies banning drug use on campus and in dormitories. In addition, CASA suggests banning smoking on campus. There should also be comprehensive health and counseling/psychological services on campus, with no negative consequences for utilizing these resources. Recreational activities, including sporting events, should be alcohol and drug free. Offers for endorsements from alcohol and tobacco companies should be refused. Further, the CASA (2007) report recommends scheduling classes and examinations on Fridays and Saturdays to counteract the increasing trend of beginning the weekend on Thursday evenings. Where appropriate, substance abuse prevention information should be included in the curriculum.

Administrators are asked to commit the appropriate financial resources to combat substance abuse on campus. These include sufficient funding to support student health and psychological/counseling services. In addition, student health and wellness programs should be implemented, focusing on changing campus attitudes toward drug use, identifying students at highest risk for abuse, and providing assessments and intervention services when appropriate (CASA, 2007). There will be many students whose level of addiction and other mental health issues require interventions beyond the scope of the university health and wellness programs. Therefore, students' health insurance policies should provide mental health and addiction coverage.

Harm Reduction Programs

Proponents of harm reduction programs characterize their philosophy as more realistic and pragmatic (Marlatt & Witkiewitz, 2002). They recognize that thrill-seeking adolescents and college students view prohibitions as a challenge, resulting in their doing the opposite of what they are told. In addition, when society reserves the use of alcohol solely for adults, it becomes forbidden fruit. As a result of this prohibition, it has become a cultural expectation that some young adults drink to intoxication on their 21st birthday, flaunting their new legal status. Because of the rise in deaths due to alcohol poisoning, bars in some places are forbidding birthday celebrants from having "21 in 21" parties, where the person celebrating his birthday drinks 21 shots of distilled spirits within 21minutes (MSNBC, 2005). Promoters of the harm reduction model believe that fewer people would die from alcohol poisoning if responsible drinking were publicly promoted, rather than the unrealistic demand of abstinence until 21 years of age (Toumbourou et al., 2007).

The proponents of harm reduction programs characterize their philosophy as more realistic and pragmatic, recognizing that thrill-seeking adolescents and college students view prohibitions as a challenge, resulting in their doing the opposite of what they are told. An example of a harm reduction program is the media campaign "Friends Don't Let Friends Drive Drunk."

There is international support for this approach. The World Health Organization (WHO) recommends the utilization of a wide range of programs, including harm reduction approaches. The organization suggests exposing all citizens to accurate information about moderate use of alcohol as a primary prevention, for example, with early identification and intervention for people who show signs of abuse (WHO, 2001). WHO suggests focusing on informing young people about the dangers of binge drinking, which is viewed as an international problem (Marlatt & Witkiewitz, 2002). Binge drinking is defined as six or more drinks by a man or five or more drinks by a woman in one sitting within five hours (Wechsler, Lee, Kuo, & Lee, 2000).

Brief Alcohol Screening and Intervention for College Students (BASICS)

The Brief Alcohol Screening and Intervention for College Students (BASICS) program is another example of a harm reduction program. It is based on the premise that most college students will experiment with alcohol and substance use but most will emerge into adulthood without an addiction problem. The goal of this program is to reduce the likelihood of the development of drug dependence. The goal is to teach college students, presumed to be new to alcohol, how to drinks alcohol more safely. The first step is to conduct a brief alcohol use assessment of patterns of use, attitudes about use, and readiness for change. This is followed by a 50-minute training session. In this session, participants are given general information about the effects of alcohol, techniques for moderating use and effects, and most importantly computer printouts about their specific patterns of use, attitudes, and risk factors for future abuse. They also receive training on cognitive behavioral strategies for self-efficacy and motivation for change. Students who are severely alcoholic, or have medical conditions where any alcohol use is contraindicated, are not considered candidates for this program (Dimeff, Baer, Kivlahan, & Marlatt, 1999).

Another example is the campaign "Friends Don't Let Friends Drive Drunk." This campaign was funded by the liquor industry to improve its public image and to reduce the number of casualties caused by drunk driving.

Mass Media Campaigns Aimed at Young Adult Population

Mass media is an effective means for transmitting information to the public. Specific groups can be effectively reached through targeting print journalism, television, and other programs watched by teens. Targeted media includes magazines such as *Sports Illustrated*, sports programs, MTV, and other network programming. The goals of using mass media are to communicate information to enable young people to refuse drug use, to prevent young people from experimentation, and to encourage occasional users to stop (National Institute on Drug Abuse, 2003). In the past, government-funded advertising campaigns attempted to protect young people from the ravages of drug abuse through scare tactics and exaggerations regarding the risks of drug use. One infamous commercial showed an egg frying in a very hot pan. The voice over said, "This is your brain on drugs." The simplistic message became material for comedy routines, but did little to educate youths regarding the real risks of experimentation, use, and abuse of substances. Although scare tactics may frighten some people away from use, they are not effective with the most vulnerable individuals, who tend to be both thrill seeking and impulsive. There is evidence that the frightening messages attract rather than deter them from experimentation (van Wormer & Davis, 2003).

More recently, antidrug media messages have focused on refusal skills and on the power of parents as "the antidrug." The purpose of the message is to empower parents to intervene in their children's lives and to get involved. The sophisticated public service commercials give direct information to parents and offer web addresses for more information and advice (theantidrug.com). Unfortunately, these messages may be less than effective. When asked, adolescents report having been exposed to the commercials and remembering the message, but said they had little impact on their behavior. However, there is evidence to show that the commercials are very effective with parents. Research indicates that parents experience a change in attitudes regarding the dangers of drugs such as marijuana. Research also shows that, as a result of the media campaign, more parents are having substantive discussions with their children regarding the dangers of substance use and increasing their monitoring of their children's activities (Hornik, Maklan, Cadell, Barmada, & Jacobsohn, 2003). Media campaigns are an important part of comprehensive drug abuse prevention programs (Sanders, 2000).

Risk Reduction and Protective Programs

The public health model of epidemiology assumes that the natural history of diseases can be studied to gain a better understanding of contributing factors so that disease can be prevented or controlled. Risks as well as risk reduction factors are analyzed and isolated. The more risk factors present, the greater the likelihood that the disease will emerge (Ellickson & Morton, 1999). In theory, if risk/precursor factors are controlled and resiliency/protective factors increased, the risk for developing the disease will decline (Hawkins et al., 2002). Risk and protective factors vary among communities. Therefore, after a disease or disorder has been identified, the risk and protective factors should be isolated for that population and targeted for intervention (Dishion, Capaldi, & Yoerger, 1999).

When risk factors are controlled and resiliency factors increased, the rate of disease declines.

Risk and protective factors fall into the following categories: personal, family, community, school, peer groups, and demographic. They often interact in an additive way, creating a synergistic effect. Many substance abuse prevention programs begin by assessing the presence of risk factors, then targeting groups in which they are highest. Personal risk factors include a history of mental illness, thrill-seeking behavior, and impulsivity. Family risk factors include heightened levels of family discord, dysfunctional communication styles, parent and family drug use, lack of parental supervision (Kilpatrick et al., 2000), and divorce (Morgan, 2005). Some programs focus on strengthening family interactions and parenting skills. For example, in the addiction recovery program for addicted mothers, all participants received traditional treatment for addiction, but half of the participants additionally received child development training, and attachment and parenting skills education (Suchman et al., 2004). Others focus on the behavior of adolescents to improve healthy decision making (Poulin & Nicholson, 2005).

The university setting is a village with its own culture, community members, standards of behavior, and goals, predominantly populated by young adults. Therefore, any prevention program for this community must be specifically designed for this group. Toward these goals, Texas Tech University of Lubbock, Texas, has created a holistic intervention/relapse prevention program known as The Collegiate Recovery Community (CRC). This program is administered through The Center for Addiction Recovery. The CRC supports recovering students in many ways. It provides education, community support, scholarship money, and fellowship. Eligibility in the program depends on a minimum of 12 months of sobriety, participation in the community 12-step recovery program, and registration in and passing a 1 credit college course on addiction. In addition, the Center provides study hall space for peer tutoring programs for students who are struggling with courses. Center participants are expected to help each other upon request. Contribution to the community is required for participation in the Center. They report that the GPA for participants averages 3.4–3.6 on a 4-point GPA scale. The Academic scholarship ranges from $500 to $5,000 per semester. Candidates for the scholarship must maintain a 3.0 GPA and must be registered in 12 credit hours undergraduate and 9 hours in graduate school. This recovery community provides a peer group for college students in recovery so that they have friends and an extensive support network that do not use and abuse drugs/alcohol. It is also an alternative to the community standard of drug and alcohol use and abuse (Harris, Baker, & Cleveland, 2010). The CRC maintains a relapse rate of 4.4% each semester, which means the 94% of the participants maintain sobriety (Wiebe et al., 2010). The Center was founded under a SAMSHA grant in 2004. Since then, a total of 27 colleges and universities have established CRCs. Thirteen of these colleges and universities are participating in the collection of data on relapse and recovery and resiliency of college students participating in the program. This data will provide information regarding the natural progress of college students in recovery. It will also give information on the efficacy of this holistic recovery program.

PREVENTION AND TREATMENT PROGRAMS FOR PREGNANT ADOLESCENTS AND ADULTS

There is no level of alcohol or drug use that is considered safe for a developing fetus. Therefore drugs are prescribed for pregnant women very cautiously. Information on the risks of alcohol use is available on every bottle of alcohol in the United States. It is generally understood that pregnant women should not smoke tobacco products, use opiates or illicit drugs, or drink alcohol. However, 10.8% of pregnant American women continue to drink alcohol (3.7% binge drink), 4.4% use illicit drugs, and 16.3% smoke cigarettes (SAMHSA, 2013a). The younger the pregnant female, the more likely she was to use drugs during her pregnancy (Behnke et al., 2013). Pregnant women admitted for substance abuse treatment were more likely to be less educated, to have fewer financial resources, and to have used methamphetamine or amphetamines (SAMHSA, 2013b). A different study showed that the outcomes for children living with mothers who continue using substances show developmental delays (Schuler, Nair, & Kettinger, 2003). This is further evidence of the values of drug treatment and intervention with mothers.

Home Visit Programs

The United States is about to embark on wide-scale home visitation programs targeting vulnerable populations funded by the Affordable Care Act of 2010 (PL 111-148) (DHHS, 2014). According to the public law, states will design maternal, infant, and early childhood intervention programs utilizing home visits, coordinate services within at-risk communities, and provide comprehensive services with the goal of helping families and their members of reaching their full potential and to strengthen the family. The bill calls for regular home visits to expectant mothers, fathers, and caregivers, new parents, by "nurses, social workers, parent educators, or other paraprofessional" until the child is 5 years old. The statute requires that most of the funding goes to evidenced-based maternal, infant, and early childhood home visitation and case management interventions. These programs will provide a continuity of care for expectant mothers, through delivery, and postpartum and early childhood development. These kinds of programs have been shown to have a lasting impact on the future lives of the mothers as well as the children.

These programs are built upon models that have been in practice on a smaller scale. These can be classified as educational, skill building, and in-home monitoring with continuous assessment and referral. An example of education-based prevention includes Clean Start, a program designed to increase awareness among medical care practitioners about the risks of drug use and diagnostic assessments for addiction and abuse during pregnancy. Clean Start is a subsidiary of Healthy Start, which is a national initiative funded by the Department of Health and Human Services. Healthy Start targets at-risk mothers and families. The program provides educational materials for pregnant women and infants, referrals to medical practitioners and other support agencies, and case management. Information on Clean Start may be found at the end of this chapter under "Useful Websites." In addition, home visits are made by either a child development specialist or a health care provider. Another federal initiative providing home visits is known as the Maternal, Infant, and Early Childhood Home Visit Program (MIECHVP). The goals of the program are as follows:

- Improved maternal and newborn health;
- Prevention of child injuries, child abuse, neglect, or maltreatment, and reduction of emergency department visits;
- Improvement in school readiness and achievement;
- Reduction in crime or domestic violence;
- Improvements in family economic self-sufficiency; and
- Improvements in the coordination and referrals for other community resources and supports.

The program protocol calls for all substance-abusing pregnant women to receive education regarding the impact of drugs on the fetus, referral for treatment, continued drug use assessment, individual counseling, and treatment case management. There is strong evidence to show that the best way to impact lasting changes with children is by making changes in the family system. The evidence indicates that the earlier the interventions are made, the greater the outcome is for the child. Early intervention can improve the outcomes for all of the following: prenatal care, reduction of maternal drug use, and protection of the health and safety of the fetus.

Outcome measures from the Home Visitation by Nurses Program demonstrate that positive impacts begin in utero and continue through the child's second birthday. In this program, the same nurse visits the young mother and her family in her home twice monthly during the pregnancy and weekly following childbirth. The nurse advises the mother, monitors her health during the pregnancy, and monitors the child's health and development following delivery. A 15-year follow-up on this intervention/prevention program resulted in healthier behavior during pregnancy; cessation of smoking and drinking while pregnant; significantly fewer cases of child abuse, neglect, and injuries to the children; reduction in welfare dependence; and reduction in substance abuse and illegal behavior. This program impacts the outcome of the children in the next generation. They have significantly fewer arrests and convictions, and lower alcohol consumption. It is also very cost beneficial. For every dollar spent on this program, 4 dollars are saved. It is estimated that by the time the child is 4, the cost of the program is already recovered. The benefits are also extended to future children born to these mothers in later years (Lawler, 2000; Olds, Hill, Mihalic, & O'Brien, 1998; DHHS, 2001).

ADDICTION PREVENTION PROGRAMS FOR MILITARY PERSONNEL, VETERANS, AND THEIR FAMILIES

Military Personnel

Substance use and abuse has been a concern among military personnel since the American Revolutionary War, where it was known as the "soldier's disease." Then, as now, addiction to pain medication such as opiates became epidemic among injured military personnel and returning veterans. The increased stress of combat, linked with the culture that punishes people seeking substance abuse treatment, sustains rather than combats addiction (National Institute on Drug Abuse [NIDA], 2013).

The U.S. military utilizes a primary drug and alcohol use/abuse prevention program based upon drug screening and random drug testing. Since 1984, all military personnel know that they will be tested periodically when on duty. Positive drug tests result in dishonorable discharge or criminal prosecution. These screenings reveal that active duty personnel use illegal substances at a much lower rate than the civilian population (2.3% military compared with 12% civilian) (NIDA, 2013). A weakness of these on-duty screening programs is that they do not deter off-duty use/abuse of legal substances such as alcohol and prescription drugs. A concern has been the ready availability of alcohol on military bases at low cost (IOM, 2013) and the increased rate of prescription narcotics for pain-only management (NIDA, 2013). In 2002, only 2% of military personnel admitted to abusing prescription medication as compared with 11% in 2008. There has been a steady increase of binge drinking while off duty, with rates of 27% of combat veterans reporting that they had experienced binge drinking every "weekend" for the past month (NIDA, 2013).

The IOM (2012) made several recommendations intended to combat these issues. These include limiting access to alcohol on the military bases, increased access to drug and alcohol treatment while in the service and after discharge, implementation of research-based substance abuse prevention programs, and the destigmatizing and decriminalizing of the need for treatment so that people will access services sooner.

The IOM (2012) suggests managing behavior of the individual through managing the community environment. The Institute proposes controlling abuse through creating policies that manage the supply side. The IOM recommends four policy changes, including the following:

1. Increasing the cost of alcohol on the military bases, where alcohol has traditionally been inexpensive. Research shows that increase in costs yields less consumption. A meta-analysis indicated that this is the most effective means of preventing use (Wagenaar, Salois, & Komro, 2009).

2. Making alcohol less available by restricting the amount of time that the clubs on base are open and enforcing the age limitations for use. This is considered a highly effective means of reducing use (Wagenaar & Toomey, 2002).
3. The imposition of "server interventions," where servers refuse service to customers who are intoxicated or under age (Rammohan et al., 2011).
    a. Enforcement of laws and policies against driving under the influence. This would include driving under the influence (DUI) checkpoints with field sobriety tests. Research shows that increased law enforcement has resulted in a reduction of injuries and death rates due to impaired drivers (Treno, Gruenewald, Lee, & Remer, 2007).

Interestingly, none of these interventions change attitudes just the policies. In addition, the alcohol use is managed by others instead of teaching self-management.

Veterans

Because the United States has been at war for more than 10 years, more military service personnel and returning veterans have experienced separation from their family and loved ones, and have undergone physical and emotional trauma (IOM, 2013; NIDA, 2011). As a result, there have been concerns about the veterans' physical and mental health. In order to discover if the veterans were exhibiting more binge drinking, Bohnert et al. (2012) reviewed the data from the 2004 Behavioral Risk Factor Surveillance System. Surprisingly, they found that there were no significant differences between veterans and nonveterans for binge drinking rates, except for the veterans aged 50–60 years old (Vietnam War era veterans). The Vietnam War era veterans have continued to have higher than expected drug and alcohol problems. It is possible that the results can be explained because analyzing data from 2004 missed the majority of veterans involved in the current war.

In contrast, a 2008 Department of Defense Health Behavior Survey reported that prescription drug use had nearly tripled between 2005 and 2008, while there was an increase in alcohol abuse for the same time period among military personnel. The U.S. military reported that within the first 4 months of returning from deployment, 27% of the veterans meet the criteria for substance abuse but are rarely referred for treatment. The younger veterans are more likely to have drug and mental health disorders, with one-fourth of these veterans meeting the criteria for a substance use disorder.

The military has been confronting the high rate of suicide among active duty military and veterans. An investigation by the U.S. Army reported alcohol was present in the blood of 30% of the soldiers who completed suicide and 45% of the soldiers who attempted suicide (NIDA, 2011). An element in the reduction of suicide is the reduction of drug and alcohol abuse among the enlisted and veterans.

PREVENTION PROGRAMS FOR SENIOR ADULTS

The problems associated with the nonmedical use of prescription drugs have received recent attention. The inappropriate use of prescription medication more than doubled from 907,000 to 2,375,000, or from 2.7% to 5.8% among the elderly population from 2002 to 2010 (Dailey & Cravedi, 2012).

There are very few prevention programs for senior and older adults. The programs that do exist are in the form of education for health care providers, senior adults, and their families. The concerns are with the abuse of prescription medications.

The website from National Institute of Health advises older adults to be honest when asked by the health care provider about their alcohol use, ask questions of their pharmacist, only take medications as prescribed, and never take anyone else's prescriptions. The website lists the following warning signs of substance abuse among the elderly: mood swings; increases in the amount of medication used, demands for refills of medicines sooner than the prescription allows, changes in personality; signs of an altered mental state, "doctor shopping" to obtain multiple prescriptions without informing the health provider about the other prescriptions, use of more than one pharmacy, false or forged prescriptions, and taking another person's prescription for other than medical reasons ("Prescription and Illicit Drug Abuse," 2014).

SUBSTANCE ABUSE PREVENTION OUTCOMES

Determining the effectiveness of prevention programs is difficult because the successful ones either reduce or keep something from happening. It is much easier to measure what happens, rather than what does not happen. Further, in the rush to reduce the terrible impact of substance abuse, many programs are instituted without valid evaluation measures in place, or that lack evaluation as part of the design. For example, many are implemented without constructing a comparison/control group.

With this in mind, there is evidence to show that school-based programs are effective in preventing some students from experimentation and drug use. The effective programs have several components in common. They include social-skills training, parental involvement, peers as educators and mediators, and partnerships with community members (Goldberg, 2006).

Prevention programs that attempt to solve the global problems of addictions by focusing on single factors or by teaching a few specific skills are ineffective. Single-episode exposure methods, such as 20 minutes of drug education regarding the health risks of tobacco, increased students' knowledge regarding the health risks of drug use, but failed to deter students from experimenting with drugs (Tobler, 1996).

For most participants in prevention programs, several methods with a series of contacts over time are required. Because many factors result in drug abuse, effective prevention programs must first identify the risk factors, decide who will participate in the program, and create a multimodal approach with several contacts over time. The process should address the most important factors associated with addiction because they work together to transition people from sobriety to addiction (Ellickson & Morton, 1999; Hawkins et al., 2002).

Shin (2001) reviewed effective programs and discovered five essential components: (1) adequate contact hours in the program, with exposure lasting at least 3 years; (2) the involvement of peers; (3) an emphasis on refusal skills, social-skills, and decision-making skills; (4) changes in students' expectations and definitions of "normal behavior"; and (5) cooperation and involvement of parents, peers, and community members.

It is essential that outcome data be used for evaluation of program effectiveness because some programs have been found to increase rather than decrease targeted behaviors. For example, programs that attempt to normalize drug use so that students will be more open about

Five essential components of effective prevention programs are (1) contact hours, (2) peers, (3) skills, (4) change in "normal behavior," and (5) cooperative involvement. Effective intervention programs are valuable because the later the onset of substance abuse, the later people begin using substances, the less time they use, the less amounts they use, and the greater the impact on prevention of serious and pervasive negative consequences.

discussing their problems, may result in increased use by increasing participants' belief that "everyone is doing it." Programs utilizing scare tactics may have the opposite effect by inadvertently piquing the interest of thrill seekers (Carter, Stewart, Dunn, & Fairburn, 1997).

Skara and Sussman (2003) performed a meta-analysis of the long-term results of 25 adolescent substance abuse prevention programs. Analysis of this data was difficult because the programs vary widely from each other. For example, the programs ranged from 5 sessions to 384 sessions over 3 months to 3 years. Most studies indicated that the treatment programs were effective in preventing some participants from smoking cigarettes. These effects (9–14% reduction rate) lasted up to 15 years in some cases. Out of nine programs that assessed use of alcohol and marijuana, the five that had booster sessions the next year or two following initial training had a positive long-term impact on the participants. These studies showed that approximately 71% of the participants used less alcohol than the control group, findings that indicate comprehensive programs with more intervention sessions, as well as booster follow-up sessions, had greater long-term impact on the substance use reduction. None of these programs are as effective as inoculations against addictions. However, given the dire consequences from the experimentation, use, and abuse of tobacco, alcohol, and other intoxicating substances, any delay or reduction in use is worth the effort. This is because the earlier people begin using substances, the longer they use, and the larger amounts they use, the more serious and pervasive the negative consequences (Skara & Sussman, 2003).

Summary and Some Final Notations

Abuse of tobacco, alcohol, narcotics, and other substances are a major public health hazard, contributing to crime (CASA, 2004), poverty, child abuse, neglect (The Executive Office of the President, 2001), mental and physical disability, premature birth, and premature death (Behnke et al., 2013; NCCDPHP, 2002; Volkow & Li, 2005; Wuetrich, 2001). Many people are exposed prenatally and are born with addictions. Some will suffer life-long consequences to varying degrees. Most people who abuse substances began as children or adolescents; some are exposed before they are even born. The rate of substance abuse among children, adolescents, young adults, and returning combat veterans has risen to epidemic proportions. In response to this public health nightmare, educators, lawmakers, and public health and mental health professionals rushed to develop prevention programs. Most were initiated without the inclusion of an evaluation component. Some promised miraculous results that could not be realized. Some of these programs target the most vulnerable youth (Callas et al., 2004); others are inclusive of individuals and their families.

Many different types of abuse prevention programs exist (Biederman et al., 2000; CASA, 2004, 2007; Dishion & Kavanagh, 2000; Hser et al., 2003; Marlatt & Witkiewitz, 2002; Wiebe et al., 2010). Some focus on educating people about the risks of drug abuse; others train participants to refuse peer pressure to experiment with substances; still others use a multimodal approach training parents (to improve communication and behavior management), school personnel, peers, and students (to improve refusal skills, self-esteem, problem-solving skills, and stress reduction). The programs demonstrating the greatest impact are multimodal in their approach, working with the student, family, school/institution of higher education, and community. Some of these multimodal programs demonstrated lasting results during 15 years of follow-up study (Skara & Sussman, 2003). Given the severity and lifelong negative consequences of substance use, any positive outcome from these prevention programs is welcomed. However, more rigorous research is needed to develop prevention programs that are most effective and efficient in delivery of their information with the greatest outcomes.

MyCounselingLab

Visit the MyCounselingLab site for *Foundations of Addictions Counseling,* Third Edition to enhance your understanding of concepts. You'll have the opportunity to practice your skills through video- and case-based exercises. You will find sets of questions to help you prepare for your certification exam with *Licensure Quizzes.* There is also a Video Library that provides taped counseling sessions, ethical scenarios, and interviews with helpers and clients.

Useful Websites

The following websites provide additional information relating to the chapter topics:

American College Counseling Association
www.collegecounseling.org/

American Counseling Association
www.counseling.org/

American Psychological Association
www.apa.org/topics/topicaddict.html

American School Counseling Association
www.schoolcounselor.org/

Healthy Start of Sarasota
healthystartsarasota.org/start/resources/pregnant/are-you-pregnant/

The Partnership at Drugfree.org
www.drugfree.org/prevent

Join Together
www.drugfree.org/join-together

Substance Abuse and Mental Health Services Administration
store.samhsa.gov/facet/Treatment-Prevention-Recovery

NIDA for Teens
teens.drugabuse.gov/

National Institute on Aging: National Institutes of Health
www.nia.nih.gov/newsroom/2012/06/prescription-and-illicit-drug-abuse-timely-new-topic-nihseniorhealthgov

National Institutes of Health Senior Health (NIH)
nihseniorhealth.gov/drugabuse/preventingsubstanceabuse/01.html

Preventing Drug Abuse Among Children and Adolescents
www.drugabuse.gov/publications/preventing-drug-abuse-among-children-adolescents-in-brief/chapter-4-examples-research-based-drug-abuse-prevention-programs

National Institutes of Health National Institute on Drug Abuse
www.drugabuse.gov/?NIDA_Notes/NNVol12N4/steroid.html

Steroid Prevention Program Scores with High School Athletes
www.drugabuse.gov/publications/research-reports/anabolic-steroid-abuse/nida-funded-prevention-research-helps-reduce-steroid-abuse

Tobacco Use Prevention
www.cdc.gov/TOBACCO/

Stop Underage Drinking
www.stopalcoholabuse.gov/default.aspx

Substance Abuse and the Military
www.drugabuse.gov/publications/topics-in-brief/substance-abuse-among-military-veterans-their-families

References

Arthur, M., & Blitz, C. (2000). Bridging the gap between science and practice in drug abuse prevention through needs assessment and strategic community planning. *Journal of Community Psychology, 28*(3), 241–255.

Becker R. F., Little, C. R., & King, J. E. (1968). Experimental studies on nicotine absorption in rats during pregnancy: Effect of subcutaneous injection of small chronic doses upon mother, fetus, and neonate. *American Journal of Obstetrics and Gynecology, 100*(7), 957–968.

Behnke, M., Smith, V., & Committee on Substance Abuse and Committee on Fetus and Newborn. (2013). Short- and long-term effects on the exposed fetus. *Pediatrics, 131,* e1009–1020.

Biederman, J., Faraone, S., Wozniak, J., & Monteaux, M. (2000). Parsing the association between bipolar, conduct, and substance use disorders: A familial risk analysis. *Biological Psychiatry, 48,* 1037–1044.

Birkeland, S., Murphy-Graham, E., & Weiss, C. (2005). Good reasons for ignoring good evaluation: The case of the Drug Abuse Resistance Education (DARE) program. *Evaluation and Program Planning, 28,* 247–256.

Bohnert, A., Ilgen, M., Bossarte, R., Britton, P., Chermack, S., et al. (2012, February). Veteran status and alcohol use in men in the United States. *Military Medicine, 177*(2), 198–203.

Botvin, G. (2000). Preventing drug abuse in schools: Social and competence enhanced approaches targeting individual-level etiological factors. *Addictive Behaviors, 25*(6), 887–897.

Botvin, G., Griffin, K., Diaz, T., Scheier, L., Williams, C., & Epstein, J. (2000). Preventing illicit drug use in adolescents: Long-term follow-up data from a randomized control trial of school population. *Addictive Behaviors, 24*(5), 769–774.

Bousman, C., Blumberg, E., Shillington, A., Hovell, M., Lehman, S., & Clapp, J. (2005). Predictors of substance use among homeless youth in San Diego. *Addictive Behaviors, 30,* 1100–1110.

Callas, P., Flynn, B., & Worden, J. (2004). Potentially modifiable psychosocial factors associated with alcohol use during early adolescence. *Addictive Behaviors, 29,* 1503–1515.

Capone, C., Wood, M. D., Borsari, B., & Laird, R. D. (2007). A prospective examination of relations between fraternity/sorority involvement, social influences and alcohol use among college students: Evidence for reciprocal influences. *Psychology of Addictive Behaviors, 21,* 316–327.

Carey, K., Henson, J., Carey, M., & Maisto, S. (2009). Computer versus in-person intervention for students violating campus alcohol policy. *Journal of Consulting and Clinical Psychology, 77*(1), 74–87.

Carter, J., Stewart, D., Dunn, V., & Fairburn, C. (1997). Primary prevention of eating disorders: Might it do more harm than good? *International Journal of Eating Disorders, 22,* 167–172.

Catalano, R. F., & Hawkins, J. D. (1996). The social development model: A theory of antisocial behavior. In J. D. Hawkins (Ed.), *Delinquency, crime: Current theories* (pp. 149–219). New York, NY: Cambridge University Press.

Centers for Disease Control and Prevention. (2005). *HIV prevention strategic plan through 2005.* Atlanta, GA: Division of HIV/AIDS Prevention, National Center for HIV, STD, and TB Prevention, Centers for Disease Control and Prevention.

Centers for Disease Control and Prevention. (2012). http://www.cdc.gov/chronicdisease/overview/index.htm

Chasnoff, I. J., Burns, W. J., Schnoll, S. H., & Burns, K. A. (1985). Cocaine use in pregnancy. *New England Journal of Medicine, 313*(11), 666–669.

Clayton, R., Cattarello, A., & Johnstone, B. (1996). The effectiveness of drug resistance education (Project DARE): 5-year follow-up results. *Preventive Medicine, 25,* 307–318.

Compton, W., Stein, J., Robertson, E., Pintello, D., Pringle, B., & Volkow, N. (2005). Charting a course for health services research at the National Institute on Drug Abuse. *Journal of Substance Abuse Treatment, 29,* 167–172.

Compton, W., & Volkow, N. (2006). Major increases in opioid analgesic abuse in the United States: Concerns and strategies. *Drug and Alcohol Dependence, 81*(2), 103–107.

Cooper, S. (1999). Changing the campus drinking culture: An initiator—catalyst consultation approach. *Consulting Psychology Journal: Practice and Research, 51*(3), 160–169.

Culberson, J. W., & Ziska, M. (2008). Prescription drug misuse/abuse in the elderly. *Geriatrics, 63*(9), 22–31.

Dailey, S., & Cravedi, K. (2012). *Prescription and illicit drug abuse is timely new topic on NIHSeniorHealth.gov: Information on worrisome trend among older adults; tips on prevention, treatment.* National Institute on Aging, National Institutes of Health. Retrieved on March 17, 2014, from http://www.nia.nih.gov/newsroom/2012/06/prescription-and-illicit-drug-abuse-timely-new-topic-nihseniorhealthgov

Dawson, D. A., Grant, B. F., Stinson, F. S., & Chou, P. S. (2004). Another look at heavy episodic drinking and alcohol use disorders among college and noncollege youth. *Journal of Studies on Alcohol, 65,* 477–488.

DeJong, W. (1987). A short term evaluation of project DARE (Drug Abuse Resistance Education). *Journal of Drug Education, 17,* 279–294.

Department of Health and Human Services. (2001). Youth violence: A report of the Surgeon General: Executive summary. *American Journal of Health Education, 32,* 169–174.

Department of Health and Human Services. (2004). *National drug control strategy.* Washington, DC: Government Printing Office.

Department of Health and Human Services. (2014). *Catalog of federal domestic assistance.* Affordable Care Act (ACA). Maternal, Infant, and Early Childhood Home Visiting Program. MECHV # 93 505.

Department of Justice, Bureau of Justice Assistance. (1991). *Program brief: An introduction to DARE: Drug Abuse Resistance Education* (2nd ed.). Washington, DC: Bureau of Justice Assistance.

Dimeff, L., Baer, J., Kivlahan, D., & Marlatt, G. A. (1999). The alcohol screening program. *Brief alcohol screening and intervention for college students* (pp. 18–25). New York, NY: Guilford Press.

Dishion, T., Capaldi, D., & Yoerger, K. (1999). Middle childhood antecedents to progression in male adolescent substance use: An ecological analysis of risk protection. *Journal of Adolescent Research, 14,* 175–206.

Dishion, T., & Kavanagh, K. (2000). A multilevel approach to family-centered prevention in schools: Process and outcome. *Addictive Behaviors, 25*(6), 899–911.

Dwyer, S., Nicholson, J., Battistutta, D., & Oldenburg, B. (2005). Teacher's knowledge of children's exposure to family risk factors: Accuracy and usefulness. *Journal of School Psychology, 43,* 23–38.

Ellickson, P., & Morton, S. (1999). Identifying adolescents at risk for hard drug use: Racial/ethnic variations. *Journal of Adolescent Health, 25,* 382–395.

Elliot, D., Goldberg, L., Moe, E., DeFrancesco, C., Durham, M., & Hix-Small, H. (2004). Preventing substance use and disordered eating. *Archives of Pediatric Adolescent Medicine, 158,* 1043–1049.

Executive Office of the President: Office of Drug Control Policy. (2001). *Economic costs of drug abuse in the United States 1992–1998.* Washington, DC: Author.

Fals-Stewart, W., & Lucente, S. (1994). Treating obsessive-compulsive disorder among substance abusers: A guide. *Psychology of Addictive Behaviors, 8,* 14–23.

Fendrich, M., & Rosenbaum, D. (2003). Recanting of substance use reports in a longitudinal prevention study. *Drug and Alcohol Dependence, 70,* 241–253.

Finnegan, L. P. (1979). Pathophysiological and behavioural effects of the transplacental transfer of narcotic drugs to the fetuses and neonates of narcotic-dependent mothers. *Bulletin of Narcotics, 31*(3-4), 1–58.

Gallaghar, R. (2009). National Survey of Counseling Center Directors 2009. Retrieved February, 13, 2010, from http://www.collegecounseling.org/pdf/nsccd_final_v1.pdf

Gogtay, N., Giedd, J., Lusk, L., Hayashi, K., Greenstein, D., Vaituzis, A., et al. (2004). Dynamic mapping of the human cortical development during childhood through early adulthood. *Proceedings of the National Academy of Science USA, 101*(21), 8174–8179.

Goldberg, R. (2006). Drugs and the law. In *Drugs across the spectrum* (5th ed., pp. 71–89). Belmont, CA: Thompson, Wadsworth.

Goldberg, L., Elliot, D., MacKinnon, D., Moe, E., Kuehl, K., Nohre, L., et al. (2003). Drug testing athletes to prevent substance abuse: Background and pilot study results of the SATURN (Student Athlete Testing Using Random Notification) study. *Journal of Adolescent Health, 32*(16), 116–125.

Golub, A., & Johnson, B. (2002). The misuse of the "gateway theory" in US policy on drug abuse control: A secondary analysis of the muddled deduction. *International Journal of Drug Policy, 13,* 5–19.

Grant, B. F., Dawson, D. A., Stinson, F. S., Chou, S., Dufour, M. C., & Pickering, R. P. (2004). The 12-month prevalence and trends in DSM-IV alcohol abuse and dependence: United States, 1991–1992 and 2001–2002. *Drug & Alcohol Dependence, 74,* 223–234.

Griffin, K., Botvin, G., Nichols, T., & Doyle, M. (2003). Effectiveness of a universal drug abuse prevention approach for youth at high risk for substance use initiation. *Preventive Medicine, 36*(1), 1–7.

Han, B., Gfroerer, J. C., Colliver, J. D., & Penne, J. D. (2009). Substance use disorder among older adults in the US in 2020. *Addiction, 104*(1), 88–96.

Harmon, M. (1993). Reducing the risk of drug involvement among early adolescents: An evaluation of Drug Abuse Resistance Education (DARE). *Evaluation Review, 17,* 221–239.

Harris, K., Baker, A., & Cleveland, H. (2010). Collegiate recovery community: What they are and how they support recovery. In H. Harrington, K. Harris, & R. Wiebe (Eds.), *Substance abuse recovery in college: Community supported abstinence* (pp. 9–22). New York, NY: Springer.

Hawkins, J., Catalano, R., & Arthur, M. (2002). Promoting science-based prevention in communities. *Addictive Behaviors, 27,* 951–976.

Hornik, R., Maklan, D., Cadell, D., Barmada, C., Jacobsohn, L., . . ., Steele, D. (2003). *Evaluation of the national youth anti-drug media campaign-executive summary.* Rockville, MD: National Institute on Drug Abuse. Retrieved September 9, 2014, from http://www.drugpolicy.org/docUploads/nida_2003_ondcp_eval.pdf

Hser, Y., Grella, C., Collins, C., & Teruya, C. (2003). Drug-use initiation and conduct disorder among adolescents in drug treatment. *Journal of Adolescence, 26,* 331–345.

Institute of Medicine. (2013). *Substance use disorders in the U.S. armed forces.* Washington, DC: The National Academies Press.

Iwamoto, K., Corbin, W., Lejuez, C., & MacPherson, L. (2014). College men and alcohol use: Positive alcohol expectancies as a mediator between distinct masculine norms and alcohol use. *Psychology of Men & Masculinity, 15*(1), 29–39.

James, R., & Gilliland, B. (2001). Off the couch and into the streets. In *Crisis intervention strategies* (4th ed., pp. 649–680). Belmont, CA: Brooks/Cole.

James-Burdumy, S., Goesling, B., Deke, J., & Einspruch, E. (2010). *The effectiveness of mandatory-random student drug testing* (NCEE 2010-4025). Washington, DC: National Center for Education Evaluation and Regional Assistance, Institute of Education Sciences, U.S. Department of Education.

Johnston, L. D., O'Malley, P. M., & Bachman, J. G. (1996). *National survey results on drug use from the Monitoring the Future Study, 1975-1995. Volume I: Secondary school students* (NIH Pub. No. 97–4139). Rockville, MD: National Institute on Drug Abuse.

Johnston, L. D., O'Malley, P. M., & Bachman, J. G. (2003). *National survey results on drug use from the Monitoring the Future Study, 1975-2002. Volume I: Secondary school students* (NIH Pub. No. 03–5375). Rockville, MD: National Institute on Drug Abuse.

Johnston, L. D., O'Malley, P. M., Bachman, J. G., & Schulenberg, J. E. (2005). *Monitoring the Future national results on adolescent drug use: Overview of key findings, 2004* (NIH Publication No. 05–5726). Bethesda, MD: National Institute on Drug Abuse.

Jones, K. L., & Smith, D.W. (1973). Recognition of the fetal alcohol syndrome in early infancy. *Lancet, 302* (7836), 999–1001.

Kilpatrick, D. G., Acierno, R., Saunders, B., Resnick, H., Best, C., & Schnurr, P. (2000). Risk factors for adolescent substance abuse and dependence: Data from a national sample. *Journal of Consulting and Clinical Psychology, 68,* 19–30.

Knight, J. R., Wechsler, H., Kuo, M., Seibring, M., Weitzman, E. R., & Schuckit, M. A. (2002). Alcohol abuse and dependence among U.S. college students. *Journal of Studies on Alcohol, 63,* 263–270.

Kurtzman, K., Otsuka, K., & Wahl, R. (2001). Inhalant abuse by adolescents. *Journal of Adolescent Health, 28,* 170–180.

LaBrie, J., Lewis, M., Atkins, D., Neighbors, C., Zheng, C., Kenny, S., . . ., Larimer, M. (2013). RCT of web-based personalized normative feedback for college drinking prevention: Are typical student norms good enough? *Journal of Consulting and Clinical Psychology, 81*(6), 1074–1086.

Lawler, M. (2000). School-based violence prevention programs: What works? In D. Sandhu & C. Aspy (Eds.), *Violence in American schools: A practical guide for counselors* (pp. 247–266). Alexandria, VA: American Counseling Association.

Lynam, D., Milich, R., Zimmerman, R., Novak, S., Logan, T., Leukefield, C., & Clayto, R. (1999). Project DARE: No effects at 10-year follow-up. *Journal of Consulting and Clinical Psychology, 67*(4), 590–593.

Lynskey, M., Heath, A., Bucholz, K., Slutske, W., Maddon, P., Nelson, E., . . ., Martin, N. (2003). Escalation of drug use among early cannabis users vs. co-twin controls. *Journal of the American Medical Association, 289*(4), 427–433.

Marlatt, G., & Witkiewitz, K. (2002). Harm reduction approaches to alcohol use: Health promotion, prevention, and treatment. *Addictive Behaviors, 27,* 267–287.

Mayo Clinic. (2007). Performance-enhancing drugs and your teen athletes. Retrieved May 2, 2007, from *www.mayoclinic.com/health/perfarmance-enhancing-drugs/sm00045*

McAuliffe, W., Woodworth, R., Zhang, C., & Dunn, R. (2002). Identifying substance abuse treatment gaps in substate areas. *Journal of Substance Abuse Treatment, 23*(3), 199–208.

McCabe, S., Boyd, C., & Teter, C. (2005). Illicit use of opioid analgesics by high school seniors. *Journal of Substance Abuse Treatment, 28,* 225–230.

McCoy, C. B., Lai, S., Metsch, S., Messiah, S., & Zhao, W. (2004). Injection drug use and crack cocaine smoking: Independent and dual risk behaviors for HIV infection. *Annals of Epidemiology, 14*(8), 535–542.

McDonald, C., Roberts, S., & Descheemaeker, N. (2000). Intentions to quit in substance-abusing teens exposed to a tobacco program. *Journal of Substance Abuse Treatment, 18,* 291–308.

Miller, T., & Hendrie, D. (2009). *Substance abuse prevention dollars and cents: A cost-benefit analysis* (DHHS Pub. No. [SMA] 07-4298). Rockville, MD: Center for Substance Abuse Prevention, Substance Abuse and Mental Health Services Administration.

Minami, T., Davies, D. R., Tierney, S. C., Bettmann, J., McAward, S., Averill, L., . . ., Wampold, B. (2009). Preliminary evidence on the effectiveness of psychological treatments delivered at a university counseling center. *Journal of Counseling Psychology, 56*(2), 309–320.

Morgan, O. (2005). Prevention. In P. Stevens & R. Smith (Eds.), *Substance abuse counseling: Theory and practice* (3rd ed., pp. 314–338). Upper Saddle River, NJ: Pearson, Merrill Prentice Hall.

MSNBC. (2005). Binge drinking reaches deep across America. Retrieved May 4, 2007, from http://www.msnbc.com/id/7179876/

National Center for Chronic Disease Prevention and Health Promotion. (2002). *Adolescent and school health: Injury.* Retrieved October 10, 2005, from http://www.cdc.gov/nccdphp/dash/injury.htm

National Center on Addiction and Substance Abuse at Columbia University. (2004). *Criminal neglect: Substance abuse, juvenile justice and the children left behind.* New York NY: Author.

National Center on Addiction and Substance Abuse at Columbia University. (2007). *Wasting the best and the brightest: Substance abuse at America's colleges and universities.* New York, NY: Author.

National Drug Intelligence Center. (2011). *The economic impact of illicit drug use on American society.* Washington DC: United States Department of Justice.

National Institute of Justice. (2000). *1999 annual report on drug use among adult and juvenile arrests* (Publication No. NCJ 181426). Washington, DC: Author.

National Institute on Drug Abuse. (2003). Evaluation of the National Youth Anti-drug Media Campaign—Executive summary. Retrieved September 8, 2014, from http://archives.drugabuse.gov/initiatives/westat/exec_summ2.html

National Institute on Drug Abuse. (2011). Substance abuse among the military, veterans, and their families. Retrieved February 16, 2014, http//www.drugabuse.gov/publications/topics-in-brief/substance-abuse-among-military-veterans-their-families

National Institute on Drug Abuse. (2013, March 1–3). Substance abuse in the military. *Topics in Brief: Drug Facts.* Retrieved February 19, 2014, http://www.drugabuse.gov/publications/drugfacts/substance-abuse-in-military

Naylor, A., Gardner, D., & Zaichkowsky, L. (2001). Drug use patterns among high school athletes and non athletes. *Adolescence, 36,* 627–639.

New York Times Knowledge Network. (2003). Early action against teen drug use: Teens as communicators to their peers. Retrieved November 1, 2005, from *www.nytimes.com/learning*

Office of National Drug Control Policy. (2001). *Evidence-based principles for substance abuse prevention.* Washington, DC: Author. Retrieved December 12, 2013, from https://www.ncjrs.gov/ondcppubs/publications/prevent/evidence_based_eng.html

Office of National Drug Control Policy. (2002). *What you need to know about drug testing in schools* (Report NO NCJ-195522). Washington, DC: Author. Retrieved from http://www.whitehousedrugpolicy.gov/index.html

Olds, D., Hill, P., Mihalic, S., & O'Brien, R. (1998). *Blueprints for violence prevention: Book 7: Prenatal and home visitation by nurses.* Boulder, CO: Center for Study and Prevention of Violence.

Park, A., Sher, K., Wood, P., & Krull, J. (2009). Dual mechanisms underlying accentuation of risky drinking via fraternity/sorority affiliation: The role of personality, peer norms, and alcohol availability. *Journal of Abnormal Psychology, 118*(2), 241–255.

Poulin, C., & Nicholson, J. (2005). Should harm minimization as an approach to adolescent substance use be embraced by junior and senior high schools? *International Journal of Drug Policy, 16*(6), 403–414.

Prescription and illicit drug abuse: Preventing substance abuse. (2012). Retrieved March 19, 2014, from: http://www.nia.nih.gov/newsroom/2012/06/prescription-and-illicit-drug-abuse-timely-new-topic-nihsenior-healthgov

Rammohan, V., Hahn, R. A., Elder, R., Brewer, R., Fielding, J., Naimi, T. S., . . ., Chattopadhyay, S. K. (2011). Effects of dram shop liability and enhanced overservice law enforcement initiatives on excessive alcohol consumption and related harms: Two community guide systematic reviews. *American Journal of Preventive Medicine, 41*(3), 334–343.

Ringwalt, C., Ennett, S., & Holt, K. (1991). An outcome evaluation of Project DARE (Drug Abuse Resistance Education). *Health Education Research, 6,* 327–337.

Rosenbaum, D., & Hanson, G. (1998). Assessing the effects of school based drug education: A six year multilevel analysis of Project DARE. *Journal of Research in Crime and Delinquency, 35*(4), 381–412.

Sales, A. (2004). *Preventing abuse: A guide for school counselors.* Washington, DC: Office of Educational Research and Improvement.

Sanders, M. (2000). Community-based parenting and family support interventions and the prevention of drug abuse. *Addictive Behaviors, 25*(6), 929–942.

Santrock, J. (2009). The science of life-span development. *Life-Span Development* (12th ed., pp. 38–73). New York, NY: McGraw Hill.

Schuler, M., Nair, P., & Kettinger, L. (2003). Drug exposed infants and developmental outcome effects of home intervention and ongoing maternal drug use. *Archives of Pediatric Medicine, 157,* 133–138.

Shin, H. (2001). A review of school-based drug prevention program evaluations in 1990's. *American Journal of Health Education, 32,* 139–147.

Simoni-Wastila, S., & Yang, H. (2006). Psychoactive drug abuse among older adults. *American Journal of Geriatric Pharmacotherapy, 4* (4), 380–394.

Skara, S., & Sussman, S. (2003). A review of 25 long-term adolescent tobacco and other drug use prevention program evaluations. *Preventive Medicine, 37,* 451–474.

Slutske, W. S. (2005). Alcohol use disorders among US college students and their non-college-attending peers. *Archives of General Psychiatry, 62,* 321–327.

Slutske, W. S., Hunt-Carter, E. E., Nabors-Oberg, R. E., Sher, K. J., Bucholz, K. K., Madden, P. A., . . ., Heath, A. (2004). Do college students drink more than their non-college-attending peers? Evidence from a population-based longitudinal female twin study. *Journal of Abnormal Psychology, 113,* 530–540.

Substance Abuse and Mental Health Services Administration. (2013a). *Results from the 2012 National Survey on Drug Use and Health: Summary of National Findings* (NSDUH Series H-46, HHS Publication No. [SMA] 13-4795). Rockville, MD: Author. http://samhsa.gov/data/NSDUH/2012SummNatFindDetTables/NationalFindings/NSDUHresults2012.htm#ch1.1

Substance Abuse and Mental Health Services Administration, Center for Behavioral Health Statistics and Quality. (2013b, May 9). *The TEDS Report: Characteristics of pregnant teen substance abuse treatment admissions.* Rockville, MD: Author.

Suchman, N., Mayes, L., Conti, J., Slade, A., & Runsaville, B. (2004). Rethinking parenting interventions for drug-dependent mothers: From behavior management to fostering emotional bonds. *Journal of Substance Abuse Treatment, 27*(3), 176–189.

Sung, H., Richter, L., Vaughan, R., Johnson, P., & Thom, B. (2005). Nonmedical use of prescription opioids among teenagers in the United States: Trends and correlates. *Journal of Adolescent Health, 37,* 44–51.

Teplin, L., Abram, K., McClelland, G., Dulcan, M., & Mericle, A. (2002). Psychiatric disorders in youth in juvenile detention. *Archives of General Psychiatry, 59*(12), 1133–1143.

Tobler, N. (1996). Meta-analysis of 143 adolescent drug prevention programs: Quantitative outcome results of program participants compared to a control or comparison group. *Journal of Drug Issues, 16,* 537–567.

Toumbourou, J., Stockwell, T., Neighbor, C., Marlott, G., Sturge, J., & Rehm, J. (2007). Interventions to reduce harm associated with adolescent substance use. *Lancet, 9570* (369), 1391–1401.

Treno, A. J., Gruenewald, P. J., Lee, J. P., & Remer, L. G. (2007). The Sacramento neighborhood Alcohol Prevention Project: Outcomes from a community prevention trial. *Journal of Studies on Alcohol and Drugs, 68*(2), 197–207.

van Wormer, K., & Davis, D. (2003). *Addiction treatment: A strength perspective.* Pacific Grove, CA: Brooks/Cole.

Vaughan, E., Corbin, W., & Fromme, K. (2009). Academic and social motives and drinking behavior. *Psychology of Addictive Behaviors, 23*(4), 564–576.

Vermonia School District 47 v. *Acton,* 15 S Ct 2386 (1995).

Volkow, N., & Li, T. (2005). Drugs and alcohol: Treating and preventing abuse, addiction, and their medical consequences. *Pharmacology & Therapeutics, 108,* 3–17.

Wagenaar, A. C., Salois, M. J., & Komro, K. A. (2009). Effects of beverage alcohol price and tax levels on drinking: A meta-analysis of 1003 estimates from 112 studies. *Addiction 104*(2), 179–190.

Wagenaar, A. C., & Toomey, T. L. (2002). Effects of minimum drinking age laws: Review and analyses of the literature from 1960 to 2000. *Journal of Studies on Alcohol 14*(Suppl.), 206–225.

Wechsler, H., Lee, J., Kuo, M., & Lee, H. (2000). College binge drinking in the 1990s: A continuing problem: Results of the Harvard School of Public Health 1999 College alcohol study. *Journal of American College Health, 48,* 199–210.

Wiebe, R., Clevelans, H., & Dean, L. (2010) Maintaining abstinence in college: Temptations and tactics. In H. Harrington, K. Harris, & R. Wiebe (Eds.), *Substance abuse recovery in college: Community supported abstinence* (pp. 57–76). New York, NY: Springer

World Health Organization. (2001). *The World Health Organization Report, 2001—Mental Health: New understanding, new hope.* Geneva, Switzerland: Author.

Wu, L.T., & Blazer, D. (2011). Illicit and non-medical drug use among older adults: A review. *Journal of Aging and Health, 12*(3), 481–504.

Wuetrich, B. (2001). Getting stupid. *Discover, 22*(3), 56–63.

Wysong, E., & Wright, D. (1995). A decade of DARE: Efficacy politics and drug education. *Sociological Focus, 28*(3), 283–311.

Zeitlin, H. (1999). Psychiatric comorbidity with substance misuse in children and teenagers. *Drug and Alcohol Dependence, 55,* 225–234.

Chapter 17

Cross-Cultural Counseling: Engaging Ethnic Diversity

Jane E. Rheineck
Northern Illinois University

Melissa M. Lugo
Northern Illinois University

The substance abuse treatment field has begun more, and increasingly sophisticated, discussions of multicultural issues in recent years. As research into the etiology and consequences of addiction has expanded, so too has the understanding of significant differences in use and abuse by, and treatment of chemical dependency for, diverse cultural, racial, and ethnic groups in the United States. This chapter will discuss current perspectives on substance abuse and treatment for Native American/Alaska Natives, Asian American/Pacific Islanders, Latinos, African American/Black and multiracial persons, as well as the use of culturally competent practices when providing services.

An examination of who is using drugs and alcohol, becoming addicted, and being treated reveals startling differences among cultural, racial, and ethnic groups. Until recently, little has been written about this in the research and treatment literature. What is more often emphasized in mainstream news media is the active role of non-Whites in the illegal sale, distribution, and incarceration for—and addiction to—drugs in the United States, contributing to the development of stereotyped perceptions (Chideya, 1995). Figure 17.1 illustrates the stratification of both illicit drug and alcohol dependence among the different races over the course of the previous month (ages 12 years and up). Clearly, there are disproportionate numbers compared to the overall population of each group. Native Americans have the highest rate of illicit drug use at 7.6%, followed by multiracial persons at 4.2%. The rate for African American/Blacks is 4.1%, Latinos, 2.8%, Whites, 2.7%, while the rate for Pacific Islanders and Asian Americans is 2.3% and 6%, respectively. In regard to alcohol use, Native Americans rank the highest at 17.3%, Latinos at 7.3%, multiracial persons and Whites at 7%, and African American/Blacks at 6.2%. Rounding out the numbers, Pacific Islanders were at 3.7% and Asian Americans at 2.9% (Substance Abuse and Mental Health Services Administration [SAMSHA], 2012). While female use of alcohol did not increase in this time period (2011 to 2012), overall use among both genders did increase across race with the highest increase among Native Americans followed by African American/Blacks and Latinos (SAMHSA, 2012).

Race/Ethnicity	Illicit Drug Use in Percent	Alcohol Use in Percent
Native Americans	7.6	17.3
Multiracial	4.2	7.0
African American/Black	4.1	6.2
Latino/a	2.8	7.3
White	2.7	7.0
Pacific Islander	2.3	3.7
Asian American	6.0	2.9

FIGURE 17.1 National Survey on Drug Use & Health: Illicit Drug and Alcohol Dependence (2012)
Source: Substance Abuse and Mental Health Services Administration (2012).

WHY DOES CULTURE MATTER IN SUBSTANCE ABUSE TREATMENT?

Contrary to popular belief, substance use and abuse is not an equal opportunity phenomenon. Persons use, abuse, and become addicted to substances in significantly different ways. Research has established that patterns and perceptions of substance use vary widely by gender and cultural group, adversely affecting some groups while largely overlooking others (Beckett, Nyrop, Pfingst, & Bowen, 2005; Chen, Lee, & Iwamoto, 2012; National Institute on Drug Abuse [NIDA], 2003; SAMHSA, 2012). Differences in cultural norms, practices, and beliefs have been shown to affect rates of use (NIDA, 2003; SAMHSA, 2012), as well as perceptions about each group. As a result, significantly different consequences of drug and alcohol use exist for persons from each cultural group in this country. Some groups are highlighted more publicly, incarcerated more often, and have less access to sources of assistance (Beckett et al., 2005; Field, Caetano, Harris, Frankowski, & Roudsari, 2009). Understanding the reasons behind these differences and working to erase these disparities is an important thrust of current research activity.

The "drug wars," as they have come to be known in federal policy parlance, are being fought at various levels and with varying degrees of commitment. Government policy and action on this critical health issue is racially, culturally, and politically driven, and shifts in accord with the beliefs of those who seek election to public office. Interdiction, longer prison sentences, and occasionally treatment are interchangeably discussed and promoted as short-term solutions to this long-term problem that has social and economic, not political, roots.

An examination of who is providing and receiving treatment reveals racial stratification that is reflective of American society as a whole. Treatment providers—those who work "in the trenches" of recovery in hospitals, treatment centers, and therapeutic communities—are largely divided along race and class lines. Professional staff members—counselors, social workers, psychologists, psychiatrists, physicians, nurses, treatment center directors—are overwhelmingly White. Paraprofessional staff members, many of whom are recovering addicts, serve as addiction counselors and as intake and aftercare assistants, and are largely non-White. Drug abuse researchers and academicians, reporting on the field's phenomena, are predominantly White (Marger, 1994; NIAAA, 2013). The SAMSHA commissioned the Annapolis Coalition, mental and behavioral experts, to study the needs within the mental health disciplines. The published report found not only the need to address the workforce size but also the lack of racial and cultural diversity among the mental health disciplines. It was reported that approximately 90% of mental and behavioral professionals are non-Hispanic Whites; while the U.S. Census Bureau (2004) reported that 30% of the U.S. population was racial or ethnic minorities (American Psychological Association, 2008).

Each cultural, racial, and ethnic group has its own history, experience, and cultural perspective on the use of alcohol and illicit substances. Because of the breadth and depth of this topic and the importance of understanding the context of each group, we recommend additional sources to provide a more comprehensive understanding of addiction with racial minorities. This chapter will provide an overview and discuss the substance-related experiences of African Americans, Latinos, Asian Americans, and Native Americans, and will place that information into the context of substance abuse counseling and treatment today.

DEFINITIONS

This chapter will adhere to definitions of these terms used in the American Counseling Association's Multicultural Counseling Competencies as operationalized (Arredondo et al., 1996; Sue, Arredondo, & McDavis, 1992). In this context, cultural groupings in the United States refer to persons with similar historic and geographic origins as well as racial heritage. The United States, as the reference point for this chapter, is considered a multicultural society consisting of members of five major cultural groups: African/Black, Asian, Caucasian/European, Hispanic/Latino, and Native American or indigenous groups.

As perspectives on these concepts have matured, research in substance abuse has begun to appreciate the need to treat ethnicity, race, and culture as multidimensional constructs. In the past, these concepts have been treated as dichotomous, descriptive categories, which obscure relevant information—e.g., different races exist within an ethnic group, and psychological identification with racial or ethnic groups can vary significantly.

How Did We Get to This Point?

Consistent with other areas of counseling, racial and ethnic issues in substance abuse treatment were largely absent from research and clinical perspectives until the 1970s. Despite significant differences in substance and treatment utilization, neither race nor ethnicity was included in characterizations of substance abusers until the 1970s. Tucker (1985) discussed the negation of these issues, indicating that "In 1963 the field displayed shockingly little concern for ethnic [racial] issues, and existing work was often embedded in the context of the 'White middle-class' values that characterized social and biomedical science at the time" (p. 1038).

Consistent with the mental health model and major psychological theorists, race and culture, as salient aspects of personality, were largely ignored in the addiction community. Under the nonracial paradigm, it was argued that the emphasis in addiction treatment must single-mindedly focus on sobriety in order to devote full attention to the arduous process of preventing relapse into drug or alcohol abuse.

A passive negation of culture and race in the treatment literature evolved into the use of a colorblind doctrine in clinical practice. Racial and cultural issues, if acknowledged at all, were often seen as diversionary matters, subsumed under the larger issue of staying sober. One of the longest-lasting forms of nonprofessional treatment in the addiction field, the 12-step program of Alcoholics Anonymous, espoused this nonracial paradigm. Under the umbrella of anonymity, demographic and personal characteristics were sublimated to the overarching concern of maintaining another day's sobriety.

Early researchers (Brisbane & Womble, 1985; Gary & Gary, 1985) argued against the colorblind paradigm, citing its ineffectiveness with African-American alcoholic clients. Colorblindness, it was believed, worked against the interests of African-American clients because it assumed that race and skin color were not relevant aspects of the self brought into treatment.

As awareness of racial, ethnic, and cultural group differences in drug and alcohol use and treatment were documented, culturally sensitive or racially focused treatment issues and outcomes began to infuse the treatment literature (Barr, Farrell, Barnes, & Welte, 1993; Boyd, Blow, & Orgain, 1993; D'Avanzo, 1997; Harris-Offit, 1992; Ja & Aoki, 1993; Rowe & Grills, 1993; Wallace, 1993). Often the rationale for incorporating race and culture into treatment was based on a growing recognition that members of differing groups entered treatment with distinctly different perspectives due to their sociopolitical status as members of historically denigrated groups in this society. Thus, treatment interventions were developed to recognize and build on cultural differences in order to improve treatment outcomes.

Typically, attempts were made to modify existing treatment approaches by incorporating the belief systems, cultural values, and practices of a particular racial group. For example, Pena and Koss-Chioino (1992) advocated modifying family systems approaches in drug treatment to incorporate the "bicultural" nature of the African-American experience, utilizing modifications based on Boyd-Franklin's (2003) approach—for example, incorporating the extended kinship networks, spiritual values, and appreciating role flexibility in the African-American family (Boyd-Franklin, 2003).

Other approaches have since advocated the development of new treatment models altogether, arguing that existing practices, based on Eurocentric ideas, are incompatible with, or dismissive of, other cultural perspectives (Harris-Offit, 1992; Longshore, Grills, Annon, & Grady, 1998; Rowe & Grills, 1993). African-centered, Muslim-based, Asian- or Native-American-centered cultural perspectives that emphasize acquisition of power (e.g., spiritual, communal, personal) instead of notions of powerlessness espoused in traditional 12-step approaches, have been created. Programs in which emphasis is placed on group and communal healing; interdependence instead of individualized treatment plans; and use of reciprocity and relational respect instead of confrontational, unequal positions between staff and client have been suggested (Rowe & Grills, 1993; Moore, Madison-Colmore, & Moore, 2003).

Unfortunately, consistent with other work in drug treatment at the time, many culturally based treatment approaches have suffered from a lack of empirical support (Hanson, 1985; Heath, 1991; Tucker, 1985). Current research also supports that a discrepancy among ethnic minorities and successful treatment still exists (Crawford, Rudolph, & Fuller, 2014; Luger, 2011). Thus, there does not appear to be consensus regarding whether or not such efforts are more effective than modes that do not consider culture as a treatment variable. Lowery (1998) has argued that successful recovery for Native-American substance abusers must encompass cultural teachings that are spiritual, relational, and intergenerational; Washington and Moxley (2001) have successfully integrated prayer into recovery efforts with African-American women; while Lewis (2004) applied a Womanist theory (a social theory deeply rooted in the racial and gender oppression of black women) approach that proved successful. In addition, culturally specific programs have successfully been implemented for Southern Asian immigrants in New York (Sachs, 1999) and Asian-American adolescents in San Francisco (Yuen & Nakano-Matsumoto, 1998). The result has been the creation of a body of work that appears to be relevant and useful for clients, but which needs a stronger research foundation upon which to build (Beauvais, 1998).

TREATMENT NEEDS AND ISSUES FOR RACIAL AND ETHNIC MINORITIES

As efforts to diversify and professionalize substance abuse treatment services continue to expand, there is growing recognition of the need to incorporate cultural knowledge into an understanding of all clients, but particularly racial minority clients (Luger, 2011). While there are many reasons to broaden our understanding of racial minorities, what is known about the efficacy of drug treatment for various cultural, racial, and ethnic groups today is sufficient to suggest that new paradigms are needed. Some groups, most notably African Americans, have more alcohol-related problems than Whites (e.g., health, criminality), even though research indicates that African Americans do not drink more than Whites (especially at younger ages), and have a higher proportion of alcohol abstainers (Barr et al., 1993; Lee, Mavis, & Stoffelmayr, 1991; National Institute on Alcohol Abuse and Alcoholism [NIAAA], 2013; Zapolski, Pedersen, McCarthy, & Smith, 2014). This would suggest that addiction treatment plans for visible racial and ethnic groups ought to be more specific and focused in order to address the increased level of severity of addiction and its related difficulties.

Improving the relationship between clients and counselors is at the core of improving treatment outcomes. Relationship formation is critical to the psychotherapeutic process (Rogers, 1951). Current clinical research concurs with this view, and contends that racial, cultural, and ethnic issues are not just demographic facts, but are in fact psychological phenomena that influence the therapeutic interaction between client and counselor (Carter, 1995; Constantine & Sue, 2005; Helms, 1990, 1995, 1999; Sue & Sue, 2012). Several clinicians and researchers suggest that, instead of marginalizing or ignoring cultural/race issues in the therapeutic dyad, therapy can and should alter those assumptions by assuming that culture and race is always present and operating in the lives of both client and counselor. Within this paradigm, the emphasis then shifts to building the relationship, rather than addressing racial issues, in order to be culturally sensitive. Cultural, ethnic, and racial issues may or may not be salient for clients, depending on a variety of factors. Assessing for cultural factors should therefore be incorporated into counseling practices in order to determine salience while building the relationship.

DISPARITIES IN USE AND ACCESS TO TREATMENT

Every large cultural group in the United States consists of different racial/ethnic subgroups, each with its own customs and values pertaining to substance use and abuse. The variations within each group are such that generalizations about any specific culture would lead to erroneous beliefs negatively affecting judgment, perception, and action. The following information about substance use and treatment access will present a brief summary of information about racial minorities and substance use in this country to provide a base of knowledge for the counselor in training. (See also Figure 17.2.)

Racial and Ethnic Minorities

NATIVE AMERICANS AND ALASKAN NATIVES As of July 2010, the Native American population was estimated at just over 3 million people (U.S. Census Bureau, 2010). Today nearly two-thirds of Native Americans live away from traditional native communities, also known as reservations (Robbins, 1994). The experience of life on reservations has historically contributed to significant health disparities experienced by many Native Americans. The long-term impact of forced relocations, lack of economic opportunity on many reservations, and family division

Race/Ethnicity	Percentage of Admissions
White	59.8
African American/Black	20.9
Latino/a	13.7
Native American/Alaskan Native	2.3
Asian/Pacific Islander	1.0
Other	2.3

FIGURE 17.2 Admissions to Publicly Funded Substance Abuse Treatment Programs (2008)
Source: National Institute on Alcohol Abuse and Alcoholism (2008).

brought about by the U.S. government's boarding-school policies for Native children (phased out in the mid-1900s) has generated conditions of grinding poverty and limited access to health care. Access to and use of illegal drugs and alcohol is reinforced by these difficult conditions, as well as by the limited availability of prevention and treatment services to stem the tide of use (Szlemko, Wood, & Thurman, 2006).

As of 2010, there were just over 3 million Native American/Alaska natives living in the United States (U.S. Census Bureau, 2010), a figure that has increased tenfold since the beginning of the 20th century. These individuals, representing more than 550 federally recognized tribes including Alaskan Natives, share a common cultural heritage but are extremely diverse in the ethnic and racial manifestations of that culture.

Alcohol, drug, and tobacco usage patterns and related illness and death rates are collectively higher for many Native Americans than for other population groups. In fact, "Native Americans as a group have the highest rates of alcohol-related deaths of all ethnicities in the United States" (Ehlers, 2007, p. 14). Chen, Balan, and Price (2012) also suggested that Native Americans have the highest risk for substance use of any racial minority group. Even so, promising community-based interventions have been described in treatment literature in recent years (Szlemko et al., 2006). Cultural belief systems in many Native American tribes may incorporate values that differ significantly from broader American patterns. The following are some attributes and skills that counselors need to be aware of when working with Native Americans (Cliff, 2005; Szlemko et al., 2006).

Attributes:
- Cultural stereotypes and generalizations.
- Chronic, historical trauma that has built up through generations and as a result, distrust of the White, dominant culture.
- Institutional racism; treatment programs often do not meet cultural needs.
- Spiritual differences different from the dominant culture.
- Perspectives on collectivism.
- Views of human interrelatedness with nature.

- Respect for spiritual and elder wisdom that may differ sharply from American values of individualism.
- Emphasis on youth.

Skills:

- Include extended kin for support of identity formation, a sense of belonging, and a shared history of survival of the group.
- Integration of spirituality.
- Integrate traditional ceremonial and healing customs.
- Understand communalism and its importance in recovery. (Cliff, 2005; Szlemko et al., 2006)

Thus, behavior change for Native Americans confronting substance abuse may emerge more naturally from collaboration, ceremony, and spiritual renewal rather than confrontation, as is often practiced in more traditional substance abuse treatment programs.

What emerges clearly from studies of Native-American substance use and treatment patterns is the understanding that, despite the significant impact of substance use among indigenous communities in the United States, a variety of culturally congruent interventions is in place and available for treatment providers to draw upon.

ASIAN AMERICANS/PACIFIC ISLANDERS According to the U.S. Census Bureau (2010), the population of Asian/Pacific Islanders was approximately 14 million in 2010. Information about alcohol and drug abuse by Asian/Pacific Islanders has been fairly sparse until recently, when broader national surveys have been able to capture larger sample sizes. Until that time, Asians were often relegated to the Census category of "other," which contributed to the underreporting of clear information.

The picture that has emerged of Asian/Pacific Islanders today is of significantly different substance use patterns among subgroups. As an entire group, the estimate of illicit drug use is 3.7% (SAMHSA, 2012) yet the estimate for some Asian subgroups is 6.9%, higher than the average for all persons in the United States (NIDA, 2003).

Persons having origins in the Far East, Southeast Asia, the Indian subcontinent, or Hawaii, Guam, Samoa, or other Pacific Islands constitute the incredibly diverse cultural/racial group known broadly as Asian American/Pacific Islanders. More than 30 Asian and 21 Pacific Islander ethnic groups are included, suggesting that sweeping generalizations about Asian American practices and behaviors have little value. The U.S. Census Bureau (2010) reported approximately 14 million persons of Asian/Pacific Islanders living in the United States in 2010.

Alcohol consumption patterns among Asian/Pacific Islanders may also be affected by physiological factors. An often-reported finding is that the effects of alcohol ingestion may be felt more strongly and cause facial flushing, nausea, and headache among some Asian subgroups (Luczak, Elvine-Kreis, Shea, Carr, & Wall, 2002; van Wormer & Davis, 2003). This physiological reaction, caused by the absence of aldehyde dehydrogenase, an enzyme needed to metabolize alcohol and safely remove it from the body, is estimated to occur in 47%–85% of Asians, as opposed to some 3%–29% of Whites (Chan, 1986).

Religious affiliations of Asian/Pacific Islanders are broad (e.g., Buddhism, Hinduism, Christianity, Muslim), and may incorporate beliefs that restrict or prohibit the use of alcohol or other mind-altering substances (Franklin & Markarian, 2005).

Finally, as with all other cultural groups, acculturation and length of exposure to American cultural patterns can have a significant impact on substance use patterns among Asian/Pacific Islanders. Greater degrees of acculturation are generally associated with increased use of illicit substances in many groups, and Asian/Pacific Islanders are no exception. The following are some attributes and counseling skills that counselors need to be aware of when working with Asian/Pacific Islanders (Hosley, Gensheimer, & Yang, 2003; Shea & Yeh, 2008).

Attributes:

- Language barriers.
- The stigma attached to seeking professional help.
- Treatment as a form of acculturation.
- Acculturation in treatment can be coercive.
- Some Asian Americans believe in genetic etiology while others believe in psychosocial etiology.
- Asian cultures often emphasize family hierarchy, emotional restraint, and avoidance of shame (Zane & Yeh, 2002).
- Despite lower incident rates, Asian American women experience higher rates of poor mental health than Asian American men (Chen et al., 2012).
- Eastern philosophical influences may contradict with traditional western approaches; not focusing on personal issues to preserve social harmony (Yeh, 2000).

Skills:

- Initiate outreach and collaboration with ethnic churches and ethnic organizations' health services.
- Provide explanations for symptoms and possible treatment.
- Psychoeducational groups.
- Provide avenues for anonymity (online discussion groups), especially for Asian males, who have more negative attitudes toward treatment (Chang, Yeh, & Krumboltz, 2001).

LATINOS The Latino population has become the fastest growing ethnic minority in the United States, with a current population of just over 50 million and an expected 24% by 2050 (NIDA, 2003; U.S. Census Bureau, 2010). Currently, this group has recently surpassed African Americans to become the largest minority population within the United States (U.S. Census Bureau, 2009).

Although the encompassing term *Latino* is used, it is important to recognize the heterogeneity of this population, distinguishing various subculture heritages such as Cuban, Mexican, Puerto Rican, or other countries from South and Central America.

As with any identified minority group, differences within the group are far more diverse than those between groups. For example, one study conducted by Katz and Ulbrich (as cited in NIDA, 2003) reported no relationship between family structure and drug and alcohol use among Cubans, while persons of Mexican and Puerto Rican descent had more drug and alcohol use in homes headed by women. A previous study by Nielsen (as cited in NIDA, 2003) also indicated that Mexican American men and women may be more likely than their other Latino counterparts to engage in alcohol use.

Latinos currently account for over 50 million people in the United States. The NIDA additionally reported that the Latino population comprises the largest segment of the adolescent population, with a median age of 26.6 years, compared with the overall median age of 35.9 years.

The NIDA further reported that young Latinos had a higher prevalence of drug use (other than alcohol) compared to their non-Latino peers. Mexican American men and women may be more likely than their other Latino counterparts to engage in alcohol use. Delgado (as cited in NIDA, 2003) postulated that "stresses associated with what often are more constrained economic conditions, combined with lower educational attainment, generally a higher degree of drug availability, and the possible impact of racism on self-esteem are believed to make Latinos particularly vulnerable to alcohol and other drug use and associated problems" (p. 12).

The following are selected attributes of and counseling skills directed to Latino Americans (Torres-Rivera, Wilbur, Phan, Maddux, & Roberts-Wilbur, 2004).

Attributes:
- Potential language barriers.
- Understand the "power" of the Latino family.
- Substance abuse problems for Latinos are multidimensional and complex (Torres-Rivera et al., 2004).
- The sociopolitical history of racism and discrimination of the Latino culture.
- Awareness of important survival skills (i.e., distrust of the White culture).
- Most Latinos are social-centric; self-esteem and self-definition are a result of family influence (Arredondo, 1995).
- As a whole, compared to other ethnic groups in the United States, Latinos are a young group characterized by a large "within-group" diversity (Vaughan, Kratz, Escobar, & Middendorf, 2013).
- The hierarchy of gender.

Skills:
- Collaboration with the whole family.
- Group and psychoeducational interventions.
- Avoid helping Latinos adjust to the dominant culture. Rather, investigate the system of values, beliefs, and attitudes of those who are "using."
- Integrate spiritual, cultural, and family values of the client. This may include indigenous healing practices.
- Supportive confrontation.
- Provide explanations for symptoms and possible treatment.
- Encourage honesty and expression of emotion, which are highly valued in the Latino culture.

AFRICAN AMERICANS African Americans, who constitute approximately 39 million of the U.S. population, claim ancestry from Africa and the Caribbean as well as many parts of Central and South America. Persons born and raised in the United States and persons born in South America or the Caribbean before emigrating here share common racial and cultural characteristics, but may differ widely in their perspectives on other factors (U.S. Census Bureau, 2010).

The arrival of Africans onto the shores of America stands apart from all other cultural, ethnic, and racial groups who began new lives in this country. While every other group arrived voluntarily, Africans were uprooted and brought to America involuntarily as slaves. This cultural upheaval has had profound sociocultural, economic, and psychological effects on the experience of African Americans ever since, resulting in traumatic cultural losses and significant disparities in access to education, employment, health care, and financial services. The racism inherent in the practice of slavery has, hundreds of years later, continued to subtly shape policies and practices while limiting access to the ladder of success.

> As of 2010, there were approximately 39 million African Americans living in the United States. Rates of poverty, family dissolution, unemployment, incarceration, ill health, and shortened life span are much greater for African Americans than their White counterparts (U.S. Department of Health and Human Services [DHHS], 2001). Substance use and abuse among African Americans must be considered within this historical and contemporary context.

Today, substance use in African-American communities continues to contribute to disproportionate rates of violence and health difficulties (Luchansky et al., 2006). An additional contextual factor is the extent to which African American urban communities are targeted for liquor and tobacco advertising. The private sector has contributed to alcohol and tobacco addiction in many non-White communities of this country. These companies and their advertisers have historically targeted African-American and Latino communities, boldly seeking to encourage and promote the use of liquor and tobacco. Visits to any urban community of visible racial/ethnic group members will reveal billboards; bodega advertisements; sponsorship of community events; free lighters, T-shirts, and caps; and financial and other donations to neighborhood initiatives, all provided by alcohol and tobacco companies. These same items are simply not found in middle- and upper-middle-class White neighborhoods. The public health community's promotional efforts, drawn from the one-third of the federal drug budget directed toward prevention and treatment, are no match for the millions of dollars annually poured into these neighborhoods in an effort to encourage use and addiction (Alaniz, 1998; Yancey et al., 2009).

The following are selected attributes and counseling skills to be aware of within the African-American community (Lewis, 2004; Roberts, Jackson, & Carlton-LaNey, 2000).

Attributes:

- Awareness of the racist historical background that still shapes policy today.
- Negative experiences with society (White dominant culture) have made African Americans resistant to treatment that is typically provided by the dominant culture (DHHS, 2001).
- May have different beliefs, attitudes, and behaviors toward health (Campbell & Alexander, 2002).
- May have more external stressors that impede treatment (socioeconomic status, family influences).
- African Americans have lower rates of use but higher rates of problems associated with alcohol such as HIV/AIDS, incarceration, and higher mortality rates (Mukka, Benson, Alam, Richie, & Bailey, 2012; Zapolski, Pedersen, McCarthy, & Smith, 2013).
- Disproportionate rates of poverty, family dissolution, unemployment, incarceration, ill health, and shortened life span.
- African-American women are more affected by negative images of themselves (compared to other racial groups) and tend to internalize these images (hooks, 1984; Taylor, 1999).
- Communally based; therefore, look to community or religious leaders when seeking help.

Skills:
- For African-American women in particular, integrating the impact of race, gender, and sexual orientation (Womanist/Feminist theory) and how these factors can create material consequences in the lives of African-American women (Collins, 2000).
- Life-skills training.
- Integrating religion and/or spirituality.
- Fellowship; family, friends, religious leaders.
- Having treatment programs with counselors and staff of color.
- Provide an ethic of caring; the sharing of one's (counselor) own experiences. In particular, counselors who have had their own success in recovery (Collins, 2000).

MULTIRACIAL PERSONS From 2000 to 2010, the number of Americans who considered themselves multiracial grew faster than any individual who identified as a single race. The largest gains come in the once racially segregated South and among those who identify as both White and Black (U.S. Census Bureau, 2010).

Those identifying with multiple races grew by 32% over the decade (2000–2010) for a total of 9 million. Single-race identifiers grew by just 9.2% (2010). Ninety-two percent of those who reported being multiracial checked two races on the Census questionnaire, while 7.5% identified three races and less than 1% reported four or more races. According to the U.S. Census Bureau, this was also the slowest overall population growth since the Great Depression.

THEORETICAL FRAMEWORKS
Racial and Cultural Identity Models

Theories of racial identity development (Cross, 1971, 1978; Helms, 1990) have been in existence for approximately the last 30 years. Racial and cultural identity theories view race as a psychological, not demographic, variable, which exists in a race-based culture. Like ego identity, racial identity formation is also seen as a dynamic, lifelong developmental process of racial self-actualization (Thompson & Carter, 1997). Rather than accounting for behavior on the basis of sweeping, racially based group generalizations, racial identity theories view race as a within-group variable, thereby allowing for the examination of an individual's identification with his or her racial group. For racial minorities, the development of racial identity involves a transformative process that reflects attitudes and behaviors of internalized racism. For Whites, the process involves recognition and psychic movement away from identification with racism at individual, institutional, and cultural levels (Helms, 1995).

In its earlier conception (Cross, 1971, 1978), racial identity was seen as a staged developmental process of psychological movement from less developed to healthier stages of identification with and internalization of one's racial group membership. Helms (1990) has since described each stage as representing a "worldview," through which racial information about self, other, and institutions is organized. The theory views racial identity as an aspect of ego status and includes thoughts, feelings, and behaviors exhibited toward oneself as a member of a racial group, as well as toward other groups. Such a view includes specific cognitive, affective, and behavioral expressions organized into schemata, which govern one's outlook and interaction with others.

Racial identity theory has been empirically investigated in numerous studies that have identified relationships between racial identity status and affective, personality, and counseling

Helm's Racial Identity (1990)

Pre-encounter: Identification with Whites is a source of approval.
Encounter: Recognition of one's ability to attain success in White society.
Immersion-Emersion: To immerse oneself in all aspects of learning about African-American culture.
Internalization: When aspects of Black identity are merged; individuals feel comfortable with their own race and also respect and interact comfortably with Whites.

variables (Austin, Carter, & Vaux, 1990; Goodstein & Ponterotto, 1997; Martin & Nagayama Hall, 1992; Munford, 1994; Nghe & Mahalik, 2001; Parham & Helms, 1985a, 1985b; Pyant & Yanico, 1991; Richardson & Helms, 1994). Studies of Black racial identity development and its relationship to other aspects of psychological functioning have identified several consistent findings in college and employment settings. To date, racial identity theory has had more limited use in clinical settings. Pena, Bland, Shervington, Rice, and Foulks (2000) conducted a factor analytic study of the use of the Black racial identity attitude scale with a sample of 294 African American men in treatment for cocaine dependence. This study, utilizing a four-factor solution, provided structural validity for the use of this instrument in this sample of substance abusers. More recently, Alleyne (2004), in her study of treatment motivation and racial identity in African Americans seeking substance abuse treatment, found that racial identity statuses were related to type of treatment motivation and treatment retention. Persons with internalized racial identity were more likely to feel confident about their choice of substance abuse treatment and were engaged in treatment for longer periods. Externally motivated persons who were immersed in their racial identity tended to leave treatment earlier than other groups.

Association of Multicultural Counseling and Development (AMCD) Multicultural Counseling Competencies

In working with racial minorities, it is imperative to understand that all people are culture bound and that effective counseling must reflect the client's culture (Torres-Rivera et al., 2004; Torres-Rivera, Wilbur, & Roberts-Wilbur, 1998). The Multicultural Counseling Competencies (MCC) provides such a framework for best practices when working with racial minorities. The MCC consists of three domains: (a) Counselor Awareness of Own Cultural Values and Biases, (b) Counselor Awareness of Client's Worldview, and (c) Culturally Appropriate Intervention Strategies. Within each domain, there are three subskills: (a) Beliefs and Attitudes, (b) Knowledge, and (c) Skills (Arredondo et al., 1996). This framework is comprehensive and provides appropriate structure to work with various clients in substance abuse counseling. The following will focus on the three domains and their application in treatment of racial minorities.

COUNSELOR AWARENESS OF OWN CULTURAL VALUES AND BIASES Effective counseling with racial minorities mandates that counselors develop the specific awareness, knowledge, and skills associated with a particular racial or ethnic minority, but also requires awareness of one's own cultural attitudes and beliefs. In a study conducted by Hoare, as cited in Baruth and Manning (1999), "a well grounded, mature psychosocial identity is necessary for the acceptance of culturally different persons and clients who may have different perceptions of reality. Identity is a complex and multifaceted entity which can be perceived in terms of culture, development, and gender, and directly influences how counselors perceive situations, as well as their counseling effectiveness" (p. 30). In addition, counselors who increase their multicultural competence will better understand how their own personal dimensions affect their perception and understanding of the personal dimension of their client, which will translate to culturally appropriate treatment (Arredondo et al., 1996). Self-awareness improves the delivery of services, the continuity of treatment, and ultimately the success rate of the culturally diverse client (Richardson & Molinaro, 1996).

Arredondo et al. (1996) identified "counselor awareness of own cultural values and biases" as an important focus in their discussion of the American Counseling Association's Multicultural Competencies. Culturally skilled counselors believe, understand, and integrate their self-awareness as well as awareness of racism, sexism, and poverty. They value individual differences as well as collective cultures, and understand that diversity goes beyond race and ethnicity. Arredondo et al. (1996) identified the following as crucial steps for the competent multicultural counselor to take in regard to awareness of culture and sensitivity to cultural heritage:

- Identify culture(s) to which they belong.
- Identify specific cultural groups from which they derived fundamental culture heritage and significant beliefs and attitudes.
- Recognize the impact of their beliefs on their ability to respect others.
- Identify specific attitudes, beliefs, and values from their own cultural heritage that support behaviors demonstrating respect and valuing.
- Engage in an ongoing process of challenging their beliefs and attitudes that do not support respecting and valuing differences.
- Appreciate and articulate positive aspects of their heritage that provide them with strengths and understanding of differences.
- Recognize the influence of other personal dimensions of identity and their role in self-awareness.

To establish the awareness, knowledge, and skills pertaining to cultures different from one's own, it makes sense that understanding one's self is critical. Sue et al. (1992) stated that counselors must be able to identify their specific cultural group and the beliefs and attitudes derived from it. They must recognize the impact these beliefs, attitudes, and consequently, assumptions have on their ability to interact, communicate, and ultimately provide interventions to persons who are culturally different. Counselors must actively challenge the beliefs, attitudes, and assumptions that may hinder effective treatment for culturally different clients, but also recognize the culturally specific attributes of self that provide empathy toward and understanding of cultural differences. This emphasis on awareness and individual change promotes effective counseling techniques, interventions, and treatment modalities.

COUNSELOR AWARENESS OF CLIENT'S WORLDVIEW AND CULTURALLY APPROPRIATE INTERVENTION STRATEGIES The final two domains of the MCC examine the worldview of the client and interventions suitable for ethnically diverse clients. Counselors should be aware of their own emotional reactions to a cross-cultural counseling experience and gain knowledge of the particular group or groups they are working with. Going beyond the counseling session in obtaining that knowledge and information is an integral component of multicultural competence, as well as understanding those cultural and institutional barriers that may hinder access to treatment. Finally, culturally competent counselors educate their clients, as well as the community at large, in an attempt to eliminate the biases, prejudices, and discrimination perpetuated in our culture (Arredondo et al., 1996).

Association for Multicultural Counseling and Development (MCCs)

1. Counselor awareness of own cultural values and biases.
2. Counselor awareness of client's worldview.
3. Culturally appropriate intervention strategies.

CASE SCENARIOS

Lawrence

Lawrence is a 46-year-old African-American male who has been addicted to cocaine for 16 years. He has supported his drug addiction with crimes including burglary, theft, and pimping. He has two children—Jamar, 19, and DaNelle, 24. He has minimal contact with his children and has been in and out of their lives for the past 15 years. Although he has been involved in 10 different treatment programs (all court mandated), none has been successful. Currently, Lawrence is living with a female associate and has convinced her to engage in prostitution to support their substance abuse addiction. Lawrence has reported for treatment (court mandated). How would you approach treatment using the MCC model?

Jorgé

Jorgé is a 25-year-old Latino male. He is currently a college student; however, his grades have slipped because of his addiction to alcohol and marijuana. He smokes daily and drinks heavily on the weekends. Jorgé has been using since he was 16 years old. His marijuana and alcohol use began as a "rite of passage" to fit in with the older kids in the neighborhood. He has a girlfriend who is currently pregnant with their first child. His substance use has increased since he found out about the pregnancy. Since his family has a strong Latin cultural foundation, he feels he is being pressured to "do the right thing" and marry his girlfriend. His addiction has caused him to lose his employment and he was recently issued his third violation for drinking under the influence. The court has ordered counseling as part of his restitution.

LaDonna

LaDonna is a 20-year-old Native-American female. Although she did not grow up on the reservation, her parents participated in and practiced many of the ancient rituals. She has had strong ties to Navajo people through her grandparents and other extended kin. She is the oldest daughter and has four younger siblings. After high school, she went away to college to get a "well-rounded experience." LaDonna was the first in her family to attend college and has become a role model of sorts to her younger siblings as well as many of the other Navajo children. After arriving on campus approximately 2 years ago, she has had a difficult time adjusting to life away from her family. To "fit in" and make new friends, she began to "party" as soon as she arrived. LaDonna now drinks almost daily and never passes up a "good" party. In fact, she admits that alcohol helps her cope and alleviates the stress and frustration of not knowing what direction to take her life. Her grades over the last year have declined and she's now concerned that her undergraduate grade point average may not be good enough to attend graduate school. LaDonna has come to the university counseling center to help her get life "back on track." Utilizing the MCC, how would you approach your counseling sessions with LaDonna?

Carl

Carl Zhang was born and raised in Beijing, China. He is a 30-year-old single male now living in Atlanta, Georgia. He came to the United States to attend college on the West Coast. He did well in school, earning good grades and becoming involved with the Asian-American community on campus. He had many friends and enjoyed the university culture. He also adopted his "American" name to "fit in." After receiving his graduate degree from the same university, he took a position with a firm in Atlanta (approximately 6 years ago). Since graduating and relocating, Carl has been lonely, reports feeling isolated and like "he just doesn't fit in." He is an only child and feels a tremendous amount of pressure to be successful and to "honor" his family back in Beijing. As a result, he reports that he drinks alcohol to "calm" himself. He recently overdosed on prescription medication and alcohol, which prompted him to see a professional counselor. He reports feeling "hopeless" and "out of control" and reluctantly shares with you that he thinks he might be gay. Utilizing the MCC, how would you establish a counseling relationship with Carl?

Alicia

Alicia is a 14-year-old half Puerto Rican and half Mexican female. Her parents have recently decided to divorce, prompting a move from a Puerto Rican neighborhood to the suburbs, attending a predominantly Caucasian school. Alicia had been picked on by her classmates in her previous school, often called a half-breed and told that she did not belong because she cannot speak Spanish and sounds funny when she tries. In her new school, she finds it difficult to connect with people in her classes and has struggled with making friends in school. However, she has been able to make a few friends in after school clubs and is invited to parties. Her mother has started to notice that she is missing money and received a call from the school about Alicia's truancy. When meeting with a counselor, Alicia does not think there is a problem missing a few classes. When asked about drug use in her high school, she admits to trying marijuana and having been to a couple "Skittles" parties, but would never do "hard core drugs" like heroine. (A Skittles party is when each teen brings a variety of prescription medication, such as Ritalin or Tylenol with Codeine, to a party. The pills are tossed into a container, then party-goers reach in, pull out a random pill, and swallow it.) Utilizing the MCC, how would you approach your counseling sessions with Alicia?

Table 17.1 will assist you in the decision-making and problem-solving process when working with the four identified multicultural groups. The authors have provided some examples for Lawrence's case. Now go through the cases of Jorgé, LaDonna, Carl, and Alicia using the MCC model.

TABLE 17.1 Culturally Appropriate Intervention Strategies

Attitudes and Beliefs	Lawrence	Jorgé	LaDonna	Carl	Alicia
Culturally skilled counselors are aware of their negative and positive reactions toward other racial and ethnic groups that may prove detrimental to the counseling relationship.	What kind of thoughts and emotions come when you realize Lawrence is breaking the law? Has little to no relationship with his children? How do you feel about him "pimping" and encouraging women to prostitute?	What are positive and negative reactions you have toward Jorgé?	What are some positive and negative reactions you have toward LaDonna?	What are some positive and negative reactions you have toward Carl?	What are some positive and negative reactions you have toward Alicia?
Culturally skilled counselors are aware of stereotypes and preconceived notions they may hold toward other racial and ethnic groups.	Do you think that all African Americans are criminals?	What stereotypes do you have about the Latino culture?	Do you have any preconceived notions regarding the Native-American population?	Do you hold the "model minority" belief that Asian Americans have been successful, function well, and have few cultural adjustments?	Do you think all Latino cultures are the same?

Knowledge

	Lawrence	Jorgé	LaDonna	Carl	Alicia
Possess specific knowledge and information about the particular group with which they are working. They are aware of life experiences, cultural heritage, and historical background. This particular competency is linked to "minority identity development models."	African Americans have been oppressed and discriminated against since the days of slavery. Overall, African Americans have a lower socioeconomic status than White Americans. At what stage is Lawrence in the Helms Racial Identity model?	What is the historical and cultural background of Latinos? Do you know the differences between Latino subgroups?	How is LaDonna's background different than that of her non–Native American peers? What might be her adjustment issues to college?	What are the attributes of Chinese Americans? Why was Carl's adjustment to college relatively uneventful compared to his relocation to Atlanta?	Do you know the differences between Latino subgroups? What are some of those differences?

Culturally skilled counselors understand how race, culture, and ethnicity may affect personality formation, vocational choices, manifestation of psychological disorders, help-seeking behavior, and beliefs in appropriateness or inappropriateness of counseling.	Poverty, illiteracy, lack of education, limited job opportunities, and urban stressors are prevalent in the African-American community. African Americans have a high incidence of mental health misdiagnosis (Baker & Bell, 1999).	How might Jorgé feel about counseling and why?	How might LaDonna feel about counseling and why?	How might Carl feel about counseling and why?	How might Alicia feel about counseling and why?
Culturally skilled counselors understand and have knowledge of the sociopolitical influences that impinge upon the lives of minorities. Immigration issues, poverty, racism, stereotyping, and powerlessness may impact self-esteem and self-concept in the counseling process.	40% of the nation's prison population is African American males. African-American women in particular struggle with lower self-esteem than any other racial group. Per capita income for African Americans is less than any other group (U.S. Department of Health and Human Services, 2001).	Does Jorgé have immigration issues? What about poverty and racism?	What would you estimate LaDonna's self-esteem to be? What impact does her culture and the transition away from her family have on that?	How might being gay impact his cultural background and beliefs? How does family "pressure" affect his self-esteem? His autonomy?	What would you estimate Alicia's cultural identity to be? What impact does her culture and language have?

Skills

Culturally skilled counselors should familiarize themselves with relevant research and the latest findings on mental health that affect various ethnic and racial groups. They should actively seek out educational experiences that enrich their knowledge, understanding, and cross-cultural skills for more effective counseling behavior.	Read professional journals and scholarly books. Attend workshops and conferences. Do course work related to the topic. Consult with experts.	Read professional journals and scholarly books. Attend workshops and conferences. Do course work related to the topic. Consult with experts.	Read professional journals and scholarly books. Attend workshops and conferences. Do course work related to the topic. Consult with experts.	Read professional journals and scholarly books. Attend workshops and conferences. Do course work related to the topic. Consult with experts.	Read professional journals and scholarly books. Attend workshops and conferences. Do course work related to the topic. Consult with experts.

(continued)

TABLE 17.1 Continued

Attitudes and Beliefs	Lawrence	Jorgé	LaDonna	Carl	Alicia
	Become actively involved with minority individuals outside the counseling setting so that the perspective of minorities is seen as more than an academic helping exercise.	Church, sporting events, community benefits, political functions, social functions.			
Beliefs and Attitudes					
	Respect for religious and/or spiritual beliefs because they affect worldview and psychosocial functioning. Respect for indigenous helping practices. Value bilingualism and do not view another language as an impediment.				
Knowledge					
	Have clear knowledge and understanding of the generic characteristics of counseling and therapy (culture bound, class bound, monolingual) and how they may clash with other cultures. Are aware of institutional barriers that prevent minorities from using mental health services. Have knowledge of potential biases in assessment instruments. Have knowledge of family structures, hierarchies, values, and beliefs from various cultures. Are aware of discriminatory practices at the social service and community level that may affect the psychological welfare of the population being served.				
Skills					
	Engage in verbal and nonverbal helping responses. Counselors should not be tied down to just one modality but should have the ability to modify their approach. Exercise institutional intervention skills on behalf of their clients. Seek consultation with traditional healers or religious and spiritual healers. Interact in the language requested or find appropriate referrals. Have training and expertise in assessment and understand the cultural limitations and adjust accordingly. Attend to, as well as work to eliminate, biases, prejudices, and discriminatory contexts in conducting evaluations and providing interventions. Should develop sensitivity to issues of oppression, sexism, heterosexism, elitism, and racism.				

Summary and Some Final Notations

The success of intervention with any population is understanding that it is culture bound. The formula for success begins with culture-appropriate awareness, knowledge, and skills, as a result of which trust and rapport (essential components to therapeutic success) will develop. The paradigms for effective and operational counseling will also evolve as the populations we serve change. Counselors must remain open and aware as treatment modalities also grow and change. These paradigms explore domains such as worldviews, cultural values, belief systems, and racial identities. The prerequisite to developing multicultural competencies is counselor self-awareness, and a counselor who understands his or her racial identity can then provide a positive influence on the counseling process and its outcome (Richardson & Molinaro, 1996).

Understanding the developmental process and cultural attributes of specific racial and ethnic minorities (as well as their subgroups) is essential to understanding the treatment needs of these populations. Developmental models such as Helms's Black Racial Identity Model provide structure and assistance for skill development, which can promote effective treatment when working with people of color. As awareness, knowledge, and skills increase, multicultural competencies will also increase. The counselors' own self-awareness of their culture cannot be neglected. It is an important component of the successful treatment equation. Without this self-awareness and understanding of one's own culture, the counseling relationship is incomplete and effective treatment will be elusive.

MyCounselingLab

Visit the MyCounselingLab site for *Foundations of Addictions Counseling,* Third Edition to enhance your understanding of concepts. You'll have the opportunity to practice your skills through video- and case-based exercises. You will find sets of questions to help you prepare for your certification exam with *Licensure Quizzes*. There is also a Video Library that provides taped counseling sessions, ethical scenarios, and interviews with helpers and clients.

Useful Websites

The following websites provide additional information relating to the chapter topics:

Association for Multicultural Counseling and Development
www.amcdaca.org

Motivational Interviewing—Resources for Clinicians, Researchers, and Trainers
www.motivationalinterviewing.org

National Institute on Alcohol Abuse and Alcoholism
www.niaaa.nih.gov

National Institute on Drug Abuse
www.drugabuse.gov

Substance Abuse and Mental Health Services Administration
www.samhsa.gov

References

Alaniz, M. (1998). Alcohol availability and targeted advertising in racial/ethnic minority communities. *Alcohol Health & Research World, 22*(4), 286–289. Retrieved June 6, 2007, from PsychInfo database.

Alleyne, V. (2004). The relationship between Black racial identity, motivation, and retention in substance abuse treatment. *Dissertation Abstracts International: Section B: Sciences and Engineering, 64*(10-B), 5204.

American Psychological Association. (2008). *Health disparities and mental/behavioral health*. Retrieved from http://www.apa.org/about/gr/issues/workforce/disparity.aspx

Arredondo, P. (1995). MTC theory and Latina(o)-American population. In D. W. Sue, A. E. Ivey, & P. B. Pedersen (Eds.), *A theory of multicultural counseling and therapy* (pp. 217–235). Pacific Grove, CA: Brooks/Cole.

Arredondo, P., Toporek, R., Brown, S. P., Jones, J., Locke, D. C., Sanchez, J. et al. (1996). Operationalization of the multicultural counseling competencies. *Journal of Multicultural Counseling and Development, 24*(1), 42–78.

Austin, N. L., Carter, R. T., & Vaux, A. (1990). The role of racial identity in Black students' attitudes toward counseling and counseling centers. *Journal of College Student Development, 31*, 237–244.

Barr, K. E. M., Farrell, M. P., Barnes, G. M., & Welte, J. W. (1993). Race, class and gender differences in substance abuse: Evidence of middle class/underclass polarization among Black males. *Social Problems, 40*(3), 314–326.

Baruth, L. G., & Manning, M. L. (1999). *Multicultural counseling and psychotherapy: A lifespan perspective* (2nd ed.). Upper Saddle River, NJ: Merrill.

Beauvais, F. (1998). American Indians and alcohol. *Alcohol Health Research World, 22*(4), 253–259.

Beckett, K., Nyrop, K., Pfingst, L., & Bowen, M. (2005). Drug use, drug possession arrests, and the question of race: Lessons from Seattle. *Social Problems, 52*(3).

Boyd, C. J., Blow, F., & Orgain, L. S. (1993). Gender differences among African-American substance abusers. *Journal of Psychoactive Drugs, 25*(4), 301–305.

Boyd-Franklin, N. (2003). *Black families in therapy: Understanding the African American experience*. New York, NY: Guilford Press.

Brisbane, F. L., & Womble, M. (1985). Afterthoughts and recommendations. *Alcoholism Treatment Quarterly, 2*(3/4), 249–258.

Campbell, C. I., & Alexander, J. A. (2002). Culturally competent treatment practices and ancillary service use in outpatient substance abuse treatment. *Journal of Substance Abuse Treatment, 11*, 325–337.

Carter, R. T. (1995). *The influence of race and racial identity in psychotherapy*. New York, NY: John Wiley & Sons.

Chan, A. W. (1986). Racial differences in alcohol sensitivity. *Alcohol and Alcoholism, 21*(1), 93–104.

Chang, T., Yeh, C. J., & Krumboltz, J. D. (2001). Processes and outcome evaluation of an online support group for Asian American male college students. *Journal of Counseling Psychology, 48*, 319–329.

Chen, H.-J., Balan, S., & Price, R. K. (2012). Association of contextual factors with drug use and binge drinking among White, Native American, and Mixed-Race adolescents in the general population. *Journal of Youth and Adolescence, 41*(11), 1426–1441. doi:10.1007/s10964-012-9789-0

Cheng, A. W., Lee, C. S., & Iwamoto, D. K. (2012). Heavy drinking, poor mental health, and substance use among Asian Americans in the NLAAS: A gender-based comparison. *Asian American Journal of Psychology, 3*(3), 160–167. doi:10.1037/a0028306

Chideya, F. (1995). *Don't believe the hype: Fighting cultural misinformation about African Americans*. New York, NY: Penguin Books.

Cliff, S. (2005). Culturally sensitive substance abuse treatment for Native Americans. Retrieved from http://www.wellbriety-nci.org/Publications/CulturallySensitiveSubAbuseTX.doc

Collins, P. H. (2000). *Black feminist thought: Knowledge, consciousness, and the politics of empowerment* (2nd ed.). New York, NY: Routledge.

Constantine, M. G., & Sue, D. W. (2005). *Strategies for building multicultural competence in mental health and educational settings*. Hoboken, NJ: John Wiley & Sons.

Crawford, N. D., Rudolph, A. E., & Fuller, C. M. (2014). Racial/ethnic differences in recent drug detoxification enrollment and the role of discrimination and neighborhood factors. *Substance Use and Misuse, 49*, 124–133. doi:10.3109/10826084.2013.824469

Cross, W. E. (1971). The Negro-to-Black conversion experience: Toward a psychology of Black liberation. *Black World, 20*(9), 13–27.

Cross, W. E. (1978). Models of psychological nigrescence: A literature review. *Journal of Black Psychology, 5*(1), 13–31.

D'Avanzo, C. E. (1997). Southeast Asians: Asian-Pacific Americans at risk for substance misuse. *Substance Use and Misuse, 32*(7), 829–848.

Ehlers, C. L. (2007). Variations in ADH and ALDH in southwest California Indians. *Alcohol Research and Health, 30*, 14–17.

Field, C. A., Caetano, R., Harris, T. R., Frankowski, R., & Roudsari, B. (2009). Ethnic differences in drinking outcomes following a brief alcohol intervention in the trauma care setting. *Society for the Study of Addiction, 105*, 62–73. doi:10.1111/j.1360-0443.2009.02737

Franklin, J., & Markarian, M. (2005). Substance abuse in minority populations. In R. J. Frances, S. I. Miller, & A. H. Mack (Eds.), *Clinical textbook of addictive disorders* (pp. 321–339). New York, NY: The Guilford Press.

Gary, L. E., & Gary, R. B. (1985). Treatment needs of Black alcoholic women. *Alcoholism Treatment Quarterly, 2*(3/4), 97–113.

Goodstein, R., & Ponterotto, J. G. (1997). Racial and ethnic identity: Their relationship and their contribution to self-esteem. *Journal of Black Psychology, 23*(3), 275–292.

Hanson, B. (1985). Drug treatment effectiveness: The case of racial and ethnic minorities in America—Some research questions and proposals. *The International Journal of the Addictions, 20*(1), 99–137.

Harris-Offitt, R. (1992). Cultural factors in the assessment and treatment of African-American addicts: Afrocentric considerations. In B. C. Wallace (Ed.), *The chemically dependent: Phases of treatment and recovery* (pp. 289–297). New York, NY: Brunner/Mazel.

Heath, D. B. (1991). Uses and misuses of the concept of ethnicity in alcohol studies: An essay in deconstruction. *The International Journal of the Addictions, 25*(5A & 6A), 607–628.

Helms, J. E. (1990). *Black and White racial identity: Theory, research, and practice.* New York, NY: Greenwood Press.

Helms, J. E. (1995). An update of Helm's White and people of color racial identity models. In J. G. Ponterotto & J. M. Casas (Eds.), *Handbook of multicultural counseling* (pp. 181–198). Thousand Oaks, CA: Sage.

Helms, J. E. (1999). Another meta-analysis of the White Racial Identity Attitude Scale's Cronbach alphas: Implications for validity. *Measurement & Evaluation in Counseling & Development, 32*(3), 122–137.

hooks, B. (1984). *Feminist theory: From margin to center.* Boston, MA: South End Press.

Hosley, C. A., Gensheimer, L., & Yang, M. (2003). Building effective working relationships across culturally and ethnically diverse communities. *Child Welfare, 82*, 157–168.

Ja, D. Y., & Aoki, B. (1993). Substance abuse treatment: Cultural barriers in the Asian-American community. *Journal of Psychoactive Drugs, 25*(1), 61–71.

Lee, J. A., Mavis, B. E., & Stoffelmayr, B. E. (1991). A comparison of problems-of-life for Blacks and Whites entering substance abuse treatment programs. *Journal of Psychoactive Drugs, 23*(3), 233–239.

Lewis, L. E. (2004). Culturally appropriate substance abuse treatment for parenting African American women. *Issues in Mental Health Nursing, 25*, 451–472. doi: 10.1080/0161284049443437

Longshore, D. G., Grills, C., Annon, K., & Grady, R. (1998). Promoting recovery from drug abuse: An Africentric intervention. *Journal of Black Studies, 28*(3), 319–333.

Lowery, C. T. (1998). American Indian perspectives on addiction and recovery. *Health and Social Work, 23*(2), 127–135.

Luchansky, B., Nordlund, D., Estes, S., Lund, P., Krupski, A., & Stark, K. (2006). Substance abuse treatment and criminal justice involvement for SSI recipients: Results from Washington State. *American Journal on Addictions, 15*, 370–379.

Luczak, S. E., Elvine-Kreis, B., Shea, S. H., Carr, L. G., & Wall, T. L. (2002). Genetic risk for alcoholism relates to level of response to alcohol in Asian-American men and women. *Journal of Studies in Alcohol, 63*, 74–83.

Luger, L. (2011). Enhancing cultural competence in staff working with people with drug and alcohol problems—A multidimensional approach to evaluating the impact of education. *Social Work Education, 30*(2), 223–235. doi:10.1080/02615479.2011.540398

Marger, M. H. (1994). *Race and ethnic relations: American and global perspectives* (3rd ed.). Belmont, CA: Wadsworth Publishing.

Martin, J. K., & Nagayama Hall, G. C. (1992). Thinking black, thinking internal, thinking feminist. *Journal of Counseling Psychology, 39*, 509–514.

Moore, S. E., Madison-Colmore, O., & Moore, J. L. (2003). An Afrocentric approach to substance abuse treatment with adolescent African American males: Two case examples. *The Western Journal of Black Studies, 27*(4), 219–230.

Mukku, V. K., Benson, T. G., Alam, F., Richie, W. D., & Bailey, R. K. (2012). Overview of substance use disorders and incarceration of African American males. *Frontiers in Psychiatry, 3.* doi:10.3389/fpsyt.2012.00098

Munford, M. B. (1994). Relationship of gender, self-esteem, social class, and racial identity to depression in Blacks. *Journal of Black Psychology, 20*(2), 157–174.

National Institute of Drug Abuse. (2003). *Drug use among racial/ethnic minorities: Revised* (DHHS Publication No. 03-3888). Washington, DC: U.S. Government Printing Office.

National Institute on Alcohol Abuse and Alcoholism. (2013). *Minority health and health disparities.* Retrieved from http://www.niaaa.nih.gov/alcohol-health/special-populations-co-occuring-disorders/minority-health-and-healthdisparities.

Nghe, L. T., & Mahalik, J. R. (2001). Examining racial identity statuses as predictors of psychological defenses in African American college students. *Journal of Counseling Psychology, 48*, 10–16.

Parham, T. A., & Helms, J. E. (1985a). Attitudes of racial identity and self-esteem of Black students: An exploratory investigation. *Journal of College Student Personnel, 26*(2), 143–147.

Parham, T. A., & Helms, J. E. (1985b). Relation of racial identity attitudes to self-actualization and affective states of Black students. *Journal of Counseling Psychology, 32*(3), 431–440.

Pena, J. M., Bland, I. J., Shervington, D., Rice, J. C., & Foulks, E. F. (2000). Racial identity and its assessment in a sample of African American men in treatment for cocaine dependence. *American Journal of Drug and Alcohol Abuse, 26,* 97–112.

Pena, J. M., & Koss-Chioino, J. D. (1992). Cultural sensitivity in drug treatment research with African American males. *Drugs & Society, 6*(1–2), 157–179.

Pyant, C. T., & Yanico, B. J. (1991). Relationship of racial identity and gender-role attitudes to Black women's psychological well-being. *Journal of Counseling Psychology, 38*(3), 315–322.

Richardson, T. Q., & Helms, J. E. (1994). The relationship of racial identity attitudes of black men to perceptions of "parallel" counseling dyads. *Journal of Counseling and Development, 73*(2), 172–178.

Richardson, T. Q., & Molinaro, K. L. (1996). White counselor self-awareness: A prerequisite for developing multicultural competence. *Journal of Counseling and Development, 74,* 238–242.

Robbins, M. L. (1994). Native American perspective. In J. U. Gordon (Ed.), *Managing multiculturalism in substance abuse services.* Thousand Oaks, CA: Sage Publications.

Roberts, A., Jackson, M., & Carlton-LaNey, I. (2000). Revisiting the need for feminism and Afrocentric theory when treating African-American female substance abusers. *Journal of Drug Issues, 30*(4), 901–917.

Rogers, C. R. (1951). *Client-centered therapy: Its practice, implications and theory.* Boston, MA: Houghton Mifflin.

Rowe, D., & Grills, C. (1993). African-centered drug treatment: An alternative conceptual paradigm for drug counseling with African-American clients. *Journal of Psychoactive Drugs, 25*(1), 21–33.

Sachs, S. (1999, June 16). Tying drug and alcohol programs to immigrants' backgrounds. *New York Times,* late edition (East Coast), 1–2.

Shea, M., & Yeh, C. J. (2008). Asian American students' cultural values, stigma, and relational self-construal: Correlates of attitudes toward professional help seeking. *Journal of Mental Health Counseling, 30,* 157–172.

Substance Abuse and Mental Health Services Administration—Department of Health and Human Services. (2012). *Center for Behavioral Health Statistics and Quality, National Survey on Drug Use and Health.* Retrieved from http://www.samhsa.gov/data/NSDUH/2012SummNatFindDetTables/DetTabs/NSDUH-DetTabsSect5peTabs1to56-2012.htm

Sue, D. W., Arredondo, P., & McDavis, R. J. (1992). Multicultural counseling and standards: A call to the profession. *Journal of Multicultural Counseling and Development, 20*(2), 64–89.

Sue, D. W., & Sue, D. (2012). *Counseling the culturally diverse: Theory and practice* (6th ed.). Hoboken, NJ: John Wiley & Sons.

Szlemko, W. J., Wood, J. W., & Thurman, P. J. (2006). Native Americans and alcohol: Past, present and future. *The Journal of General Psychology, 133*(4), 435–451.

Taylor, J. Y. (1999). Colonizing images and diagnostic labels: Oppressive mechanisms for African American women's health. *Advances in Nursing Science, 21*(3), 32–45.

Thompson, C. E., & Carter, R. T. (Eds.). (1997). *Racial identity theory: Applications to individual, group and organizational interventions.* Mahwah, NJ: Lawrence Erlbaum Associates.

Torres-Rivera, E., Wilbur, M., Phan, L., Maddux, C., & Roberts-Wilbur, J. (2004). Counseling Latinos with substance abuse problems. *Journal of Addictions & Offender Counseling, 25,* 26–42.

Torres-Rivera, E., Wilbur, M. P., & Roberts-Wilbur, J. (1998). The Puerto Rican prison experience: A multicultural understanding of values, beliefs, and attitudes. *Journal of Addictions & Offender Counseling, 18,* 63–77.

Tucker, M. B. (1985). U.S. Ethnic minorities and drug abuse: An assessment of the science and practice. *The International Journal of the Addictions, 20*(6 & 7), 1021–1047.

U.S. Census Bureau. (2010). *2010 census home.* Retrieved from http://www.census.gov/2010census

U.S. Department of Health and Human Services. (2001). *Mental health: Culture, race, & ethnicity—A supplement to mental health: A report of the Surgeon General.* Rockville, MD: U.S. Department of Health and Human Services, Substance Abuse and Mental Health Services Administration, Center for Mental Health Services.

van Wormer, K., & Davis, D. (2003). *Addiction treatment: A strengths perspective.* Pacific Grove, CA: Brooks/Cole.

Vaughan, E. L., Kratz, L. M., Escobar, O. S., & Middendorf, K. G. (2013). Latino subgroup as a moderator of the relationship between language usage and alcohol use in a national sample of Latino emerging adults. *Journal of Latina/o Psychology, 1*(3), 182–194. doi:10.1037/a0033384

Wallace, B. C. (1993). Cross cultural counseling with the chemically dependent: Preparing for service delivery within our culture of violence. *Journal of Psychoactive Drugs, 24*(3), 9–20.

Washington, O. G. M., & Moxley, D. P. (2001). The use of prayer in group work with African American women recovering from chemical dependency. *Families and Society, 82,* 49–59.

Yancey, A. K., Cole, B. L., Brown, R., Williams, J. D., Hillier, A., Kline, R. S., . . ., McCarthy, W. J. (2009).

A cross-sectional prevalence study of ethnically targeted and general audience outdoor obesity-related advertising. *The Milbank Quarterly, 87,* 155–184.

Yeh, C. J. (2000). Depathologizing Asian-American perspectives of health and healing. *Asian American and Pacific Islander Journal of Health, 8,* 138–149.

Yuen, F., & Nakano-Matsumoto, N. (1998). Effective substance abuse treatment for Asian American adolescents. *Early Child Development and Care, 147,* 43–54.

Zane, N., & Yeh, M. (2002). Asian American mental health: Assessment theories and methods. In K. Kurasaki, S. Okazaki, & S. Stanley (Eds.), In *The use of culturally-based variables in assessment* (pp. 123–138). New York, NY: Kluwer Academic/Plenum.

Zapolski, T. C. B., Pedersen, S. L., McCarthy, D. M., & Smith, G. T. (2014). Less drinking, yet more problems: Understanding African American drinking and related problems. *Psychological Bulletin, 140*(1), 188–223. doi:10.1037/a0032113

Chapter 18

Gender, Sex, and Addictions

Cynthia A. Briggs
Walden University

INTRODUCTION

Understanding addiction is no easy task. Addiction confounds, frustrates, and challenges the most skilled counselors in part because of its devastating effects across demographic boundaries, and because no one method of treatment has proven effective for all clients. Counseling professionals and counselor educators strive to better understand addicted clients, introducing new therapies and ideas via research and practice. In this chapter, the influence of gender and sex on, and the development of, addiction and treatment outcomes are examined. First, an historical overview of the complex relationship between gender, sex, and addiction is presented. Second, the biological, psychological, and social impacts of alcohol and drug dependence are viewed through a gendered lens. Finally, treatment paradigms and counseling recommendations are discussed.

Prior to beginning a discussion about the impact of gender and sex on the development of addiction in humans, it is important to distinguish the difference between these two terms. *Gender* and *sex* are related concepts, but not the same.

Gender refers to one's identity on the spectrum of female to male, and is determined by one's biological sex, culture of socialization, and personal identity and preferences. Gender is externally defined by how feminine or masculine one appears, based on expectations, norms, and stereotypes within a given culture, and varies widely throughout the world. For example, in some Western African countries, extreme corpulence is seen as beautiful (and feminine) for women, a sign of a husband's wealth and ability to provide for his family (Lips, 2006). Obesity as beauty stands in strong contrast to the American perspective of thinness as the ultimate feminine goal. In addition, attributes such as nice, thin, and modest serve as cultural hallmarks of femininity in the United States (Brown, 2012). In contrast, masculinity in the United States is socially characterized by the following: "winning, emotional control, risk-taking, violence, dominance, playboy, self-reliance, primacy of work, power over women, disdain for homosexuality, and pursuit of status" (Brown, 2012, p. 107). Gender as a social construct differs from culture to culture, but universally creates interpersonal demands that may result in intrapsychic disharmony and conflict. These social constructs can both trap us in roles that artificially demand our subordination or dominance, or create conflict within ourselves if our personal sense of gender conflicts with the prevailing norms. Regardless, oppressive gender stereotypes cultivate rich soil for mental health and addiction issues throughout the life span.

Sex refers to the physical anatomy of a person, that which identifies one as either male or female from a biological perspective. In humans, we most often identify females and males via their reproductive organs, yet in other species (e.g., invertebrates such as earthworms and oysters) two separate sexes do not always exist, as these organisms have both types of sexual organs. Thus even within the animal kingdom, sex is not always a cut and dried definition (Crawford & Unger, 2004).

The interaction between gender and sex varies from person to person. Individuals gender-identify within a spectrum from female to male as defined by the social constructs within the culture where they live. A *transgendered* person is one who experiences discomfort within the conventional expectation of his/her sex and chooses to live part or full time within the constructs of the opposite sex. One who is *transsexual* feels that his/her gender identity does not match his/her sex and desires to make physical modifications, including hormone treatment and surgery, in order to align with the other sex. A person who identifies as *intersex* possesses a mixture of anatomical features typically identified as male and female (Lips, 2006).

Addiction research focused primarily on male clients until the early 1970s. Since that time, research has expanded to include women, but very little research has been conducted on the development of addiction within the transgendered, transsexual, and intersex populations. This chapter reflects the research available at the time of publication, and the author strives to be as inclusive as contemporary research literature allows.

GENDER, ALCOHOL, AND DRUG USE AND ABUSE IN THE UNITED STATES

Throughout history, gendered societal norms and stereotypes with regard to alcohol and drug use have impacted the development of addiction across the gender spectrum. Because the historical research literature chooses a binary gender approach (i.e., men and women), little information exists about the experience of people who identify outside of this duality. Thus, within this historical analysis, the terms *men* and *women* will be used to describe gender differences through a historical lens.

Alcohol use in colonial times was "pervasive," a part of almost every aspect of daily life, – and was consumed by men, women, and children alike (Straussner & Attia, 2002). Alcohol has long been used in the United States as a part of ritual, as a social rite, as medicine, and as a coping mechanism. However, though it was socially acceptable for men to imbibe, the use of alcohol by women began to draw criticism in the 1830s when author Harriet Martineau identified only four reasons why women might drink: cultural oppression, vacuousness, self-medication, and prescribed medication (Straussner & Attia, 2002). Thus, the notion of women as social drinkers was culturally discouraged. Alcohol was seen as a man's means to inebriation, and unladylike for women to consume. Women who became addicted to alcohol were subject to societal distain, imprisonment, and in extreme cases, sterilization as "treatment" (Straussner & Attia, 2002).

An increase of moral and religious influence in government led to the temperance movement in the late 1800s and early 1900s. A pervasive cultural myth fueled prohibition: The plight of helpless women abused by angry, drunken husbands. While this social concern did (of course) possess some truth, women were portrayed either as victims of alcohol if their spouses drank, or as prostitutes if women themselves drank (Straussner & Attia, 2002). The moralization of alcohol use became ingrained in societal thinking: women were whores, saints, or helpless victims, depending on the apparent role alcohol played in their lives (North Carolina Association of School Administrators, 2006), while alcoholic men were stereotyped as drunken abusers (Straussner & Attia, 2002). The relationship between gender and alcohol became increasingly complex and difficult to navigate.

To understand the pervasive nature of societal gender norms, try this experiment: Close your eyes, and imagine a typical bar scene—people gathered around the bar, chatting with the bartender, playing pool, talking and laughing in crowded booths. Now, imagine a typical man in this scene. Imagine him holding a brown beer bottle, taking a big swig. He orders several shots of whiskey for him and his male friends, and on the count of three they all down the shots together, laughing loudly and following the shots with beer chasers. Our man orders another round for his friends, and they have a noisy toast before again downing whiskey shots followed by more beer.

Imagining this, what feelings come up for you? What perceptions do you have of this group of men? What words would you use to describe them?

Now imagine the exact same scene, except with a group of women downing shots and guzzling beer straight from the bottle. What changes about your perceptions? What words would you (or others) use to define them? Are there any judgments that come up for you? What are they?

The complicated relationship between gender and drinking behaviors continues today. There remain subtle messages about a woman's virtue or a man's masculinity based on drinking behaviors. However, in birth cohorts since World War II, statistics demonstrate a shrinking demographic difference between male and female drinking behaviors (Keyes, Grant, & Hasin, 2007). One disturbing trend in modern times is the emergence of binge drinking as a pastime for young men and women, particularly during the college years. Consuming five to six drinks in rapid succession becomes a competitive act, as women try to "keep up with the boys" by drinking as heavily and rapidly as their male counterparts. This is dangerous practice, as women suffer the negative effects of excessive alcohol use more quickly and severely than men (Briggs & Pepperell, 2009).

Counseling research literature has long considered problem drinking worthy of study. However, only 29 studies on women alcoholics appeared in the English language research literature between 1929 and 1970. Male-only population samples were used, as alcoholism was perceived to be a "man's problem" (Bride, 2001; Greenfield, 2002; Lynch, Roth, & Carroll, 2002). This changed during the 1970s and 1980s, when government and societal attention to problem drinking for women reached a peak, and the number of research studies increased rapidly. In recent years, interest in this subject has waned, replaced by concern about illicit drug use, reflecting government funding preferences (Straussner & Attia, 2002).

The relationship between gender and drug use is similarly complex, driven by cultural impressions and moral thinking. In the 1800s, prescription medications often contained addictive substances including opium, cocaine, or cannabis (Gordon, 2002; Straussner & Attia, 2002). Laudanum, liquid opium dissolved in alcohol, was often prescribed, particularly to women, to treat a variety of vague symptoms (Straussner & Attia, 2002). Ultimately, women were among the primary consumers of opiates and cocaine in the 19th century as these drugs were added to pain medications and remedies specifically targeted toward them (Gordon, 2002). At that time, lawmakers and prophets assumed that the "numberless dope fiends" in the United States were men, laid low by drug use. However, the typical opium addict was a middle-aged, southern White woman taking medication prescribed by her doctor (Gray, 1998). When women taking prescription medication began displaying signs of addiction, they were often given new medications to help alleviate symptoms (Gordon, 2002). Thus, their addictive problems were minimized or ignored, and men were considered the primary consumers and abusers of illicit drugs.

Into the modern age, men and women continued to use drugs, often in very different ways. For women, drugs of abuse and dependence were more often prescribed (Nelson-Zlupko, Kauffman, & Dore, 1995). In the 1950s, barbiturate abuse became prevalent as these drugs were prescribed for sleep, while amphetamines were prescribed for weight loss. Tranquilizers and sedatives such as Valium were prescribed to women to reduce anxiety (Straussner & Attia, 2002). The use of cocaine increased in the 1980s as women sought its appetite-suppressing effects. The less-expensive derivative, crack cocaine, became prevalent in poorer African-American and Hispanic communities. The social backlash against mothers who used crack cocaine, especially while pregnant, resulted in legal action against many women, rather than treatment (Straussner & Attia, 2002).

Time for another perception check: Imagine you're a drug addiction counselor, and a new female client comes to your office. She describes regular crack cocaine use, alcohol use, and abuse of prescription medication. She also smokes marijuana occasionally. What perceptions would you hold of this woman? What assumptions might you make? Now imagine she is a mother, with small children at home while she uses. How does your perception of her change? Are there different or new assumptions you'd make about her?

And finally, if this client were a man, a father, would your assumptions about him be the same or different?

Today, women's use of drugs and alcohol continues to be quite pervasive. Nationwide, it is estimated that 6.5% of women aged 12 years and older abuse illicit drugs, and 47.1% of women aged 12 and older identify as "current drinkers" of alcohol. In most categories of drug and alcohol use, men are more likely to use and abuse than women. However, women's abuse of prescription drugs, including pain medication, tranquilizers, and stimulants, tends to be equal to or exceeds that of men (Substance Abuse and Mental Health Services Administration [SAMHSA], 2012).

During the past 30 years, alcohol use disorders rose for women: In the early 1980s, surveys showed a lifetime prevalence of 5.17 men experiencing alcohol-use disorders to each woman. By the early 1990s, that gap had closed to 2.45 men to each woman (Greenfield, 2002). Similarly, in the 1950s, the age of initiation to alcohol for adolescent girls and boys aged 10–14 showed a male-to-female ratio of 4:1. In other words, for every girl who took her first drink between the ages of 10 and 14, four boys took their first drinks. By the early 1990s, this ratio was 1:1 (Greenfield, 2002): Girls and boys are now equivalent in their early drinking behaviors (for girls and boys under 12 years of age, the rate of alcohol use is 13.3% for both genders) (SAMHSA, 2012). The gender difference in alcohol use behaviors among adults is also shrinking (Keyes et al., 2007).

However, in the United States, men continue to be the primary consumers and abusers of alcohol and other drugs. The 2011 National Survey on Drug Use and Health determined that 11.1% of men 12 and older used illicit drugs, and boys aged 12–17 years old were more likely to use illicit drugs than were girls of the same age (10.8% vs. 9.3%). With regard to alcohol use, 56.8% of men and boys aged 12 years and older identified as current users. Men also tend to become addicted to substances as a higher rate than women, about twice as often (10.4% vs. 5.7%). Among youth ages 12–17 years old, the rates of substance addiction were the same (6.9%) (SAMHSA, 2012).

With regard to tobacco use, 32% of men and 21% of women 12 and older reported tobacco use (most often cigarettes), although these numbers have been on the decline over the past decade. In 2002, for example, 12.3% of boys aged 12–17 years old were current tobacco users. In 2001, this percentage had dropped to 8.2%. Because most smokers are initiated into tobacco use before age 18, these statistics are promising (SAMHSA, 2012). With regard to treatment for substance abuse and addiction, men tend to outnumber women in treatment programs, often at a rate of 3 or 4 to 1 (Greenfield, 2002; Veach, Remley, Kippers, & Sorg, 2000).

Clearly, the relationship between gender, alcohol, and drug addiction is complex, affected by moral climate, legal precedence, and gender roles. To more fully understand the experience of addiction, it is necessary to explore addiction from multiple perspectives: biological, psychological, and social. In the following sections, each will be discussed from a gendered perspective.

WOMEN AND ADDICTION

Until recently, the complex experience of addicted women remained largely unexamined from both a scientific and cultural perspective. Although women have long struggled with addiction to drugs and alcohol, the counseling community largely ignored their unique needs and experiences. Scientifically speaking, most research studies on addiction featured all-male samples (Friedman, 2003). Subsequently, most treatment strategies and milieus targeted the needs of men (Cook, Epperson, & Gariti, 2005; Gordon, 2002). The following sections will examine the specific biological, psychological, and social needs of women addicts.

Biological Considerations

Women metabolize alcohol and drugs differently than men. For example, with regard to alcohol, women are intoxicated after consuming only half as much as men, metabolize alcohol differently (Angove & Fothergill, 2003), develop cirrhosis of the liver more quickly, and are at greater risk of death due to alcohol-related violence or accidents (Greenfield, 2002). Also, women begin problem drinking later than men, drink smaller quantities, and are less frequent drinkers. However, the time between onset of problem drinking and physical problems is shorter than that of men (Gordon, 2002; Greenfield, 2002). This phenomenon is commonly referred to as *telescoping* (Parks, Hesselbrock, Hesselbrock, & Segal, 2003). Telescoping occurs in part because women's bodies have a higher fat-to-water ratio than men's (Angove & Fothergill, 2003); therefore, alcohol becomes more concentrated in the female system and ethanol becomes concentrated in all body parts, including the liver and brain (Greenfield, 2002). Additionally, alcohol dependence in women increases the risk of death five times (compared to nonalcohol-dependent women) versus three times for alcohol-dependent men (Greenfield, 2002). Alcohol-dependent women are also more susceptible than men to liver damage, heart problems (Angove & Fothergill, 2003; Haseltine, 2000), osteoporosis, cardiovascular disease, and breast cancer (Gordon, 2002).

With regard to drug use, again, women tend to use more heavily and become addicted more quickly than their male counterparts (Nelson-Zlupko et al., 1995). While drug use carries the risk of damage to health for all abusers, there are problems specific to women that are important to consider. These include malnourishment, hypertension, and sexually transmitted diseases, to which women are particularly susceptible (Gordon, 2002). There are also health risks for female substance abusers related to age. For example, younger women are most at risk of accidental death or injury, suicide, and overdose related to their drug use; middle-aged women are more likely to develop breast cancer or osteoporosis; and older women who abuse substances are prone to bone fractures, such as the hip, due to accidents or falls (Gordon, 2002). Additionally, the death rate for female addicts is higher than that of male addicts (Cook et al., 2005).

Hormones appear to play a significant role in the development of addiction for women, particularly with regard to the menstrual cycle. For example, during preovulation, when estrogen is high, addicted women experience stronger effects from stimulants such as cocaine or amphetamines. However, during postovulation, when estrogen is lower and progesterone is higher, women addicted to alcohol or nicotine experience enhanced effects from those drugs. Helping women understand the relapse risks related to the menstrual cycle is an important psychoeducational element of addictions counseling (Briggs & Pepperell, 2009; Lynch et al., 2002).

Unfortunately, addicted women are more likely to contract sexually transmitted diseases than their male counterparts, especially HIV. Specifically, addicted women are less likely to use condoms during sex, thus increasing their vulnerability to sexually transmitted diseases (STDs) (Dudish & Hatsukami, 1996). Studies on incarcerated, addicted women also show a greater likelihood of sexually risky behaviors and HIV infection (Guyon, Brochu, Parent, & Desjardins, 1999). Women using intravenous drugs are more likely to acquire HIV as well (Lynch et al., 2002), as they are more likely than men to share needles with their partners.

CASE STUDY

Introducing Sandra

Case studies for this chapter are based on the author's experiences as an addictions counselor. Identifying information and names have been altered to protect clients' anonymity.

Sandra is a 33-year-old woman who identifies herself as Caucasian and lesbian. She is court-ordered to treatment after an arrest for possession of crack cocaine. Sandra began using crack about three years ago when she began dating a woman who also used the drug. Sandra reports that "within just a few weeks" her use went from casual to compulsive, and she now feels the drugs "own" her and "make me do terrible things." She is deeply ashamed about her behavior and states that "my parents and God are so disappointed in me."

If you were Sandra's counselor, how would you apply the biological concepts presented in this section to her case? How would you use this information to educate her about the etiology and risks of her drug use?

Psychological Considerations

Psychological problems go hand-in-hand with addiction. In fact, every diagnosis found in the *Diagnostic Statistical Manual* (4th ed., text revision) (DSM-IV-TR) is more likely to be found in an addicted woman than in a nonaddicted woman (Gordon, 2002). For example, 78% of men and 86% of women with alcohol dependence also meet the criteria for at least one other psychiatric diagnosis (Sonne, Back, Zuniga, Randall, & Brady, 2003). In particular, addicted women are most likely to suffer from affective disorders such as depression and anxiety. In this regard, women differ from men—specifically, they appear more likely to develop an affective disorder prior to the addiction, while men are more likely to experience the dependency first (Bride, 2001; Gordon, 2002). In general, it appears that individuals who have difficulty "expressing, tolerating, or modulating" strong emotions are more vulnerable to developing addiction disorders

(McKechnie & Hill, 2009, p. 109). Often, women begin abusing alcohol or drugs following a traumatic event (Nelson-Zlupko et al., 1995), including childhood sexual abuse (Bride, 2001; McKechnie & Hill, 2009). Thus, alcohol treatment alone may be enough to remit an alcohol-dependent man's affective disorder, while women may require ongoing treatment to alleviate their co-occurring psychiatric condition.

Depression that occurs with alcohol dependence can lead to suicidal ideation. For example, alcoholic women are five times more likely to attempt suicide than are nonalcoholic women. In fact, the rate of alcoholic women who die from a suicide attempt is equal to that of alcoholic men who attempt suicide (Gordon, 2002). To understand how significant this is, compare it with the fact that among nonalcoholics, men complete suicide at a rate of four times that of women (Centers for Disease Control [CDC], 2010). Women addicted to crack cocaine also experienced higher rates of suicidal ideation (Dudish & Hatsukami, 1996). "Suicide thoughts, attempts, and completions are highly related to substance abuse, particularly with co-morbid depression. Substance abuse has been related to a greater frequency of suicide attempts, repeat suicide attempts, and more serious ideation" (Wilke, 2004, p. 232).

In addition to affective disorders such as anxiety and suicidality, women experience other gender-specific psychological phenomena with regard to substance abuse. Specifically, they are more likely than are men to use drugs to cope with negative moods, to internalize childhood problems, and to self-medicate with drugs or alcohol as a coping mechanism (Haseltine, 2000; Hegamin, Anglin, & Farabee, 2001). Addicted women are also more likely than are men to experience sexual dysfunction, bulimia, and low self-esteem (Angove & Fothergill, 2003; Gordon, 2002).

CASE STUDY

Sandra

Sandra experiences intense shame and guilt about her behavior. As a result, she avoids her parents, whom she describes as "loving and supportive." Some days, her depression is debilitating and she struggles to get out of bed. By the weekend, though, her desire for crack overwhelms her, and she finds herself bingeing with her friends and her girlfriend. She also admits to you that while attending college in her early twenties, she was raped at a party. "I was so drunk, I had no idea what was going on. I should have known better." After the rape she dropped out of college and moved home, lapsing into a long depressive phase. She admits she has suicidal thoughts, and sees few alternatives to "getting out" of this situation.

How would you apply the psychological concepts presented in this section to her case? How would you use this information to educate her about the etiology and risks of her drug use?

Social Considerations

As described in the historical overview that began this chapter, women are affected by social norms around alcohol and drug use. Social factors may influence how women seek treatment for addiction and affect their likelihood of becoming addicted in the first place. According to Angove and Fothergill, "Society is responsible for pushing some women into chemical solutions" (2003, p. 215). For example, women's development of problem drinking appears inextricably linked to relationships. Women with a family history of alcoholism or drug dependence are at greater risk of becoming dependent themselves (Gordon, 2002; Kaskutas, Zhang, French, & Witbrodt, 2005; Nelson-Zlupko et al., 1995). Also, addicted women experience over-responsibility within their families of origin, experience high levels of familial strife, and are often discouraged from seeking treatment by their family members (Nelson-Zlupko et al., 1995). Women seem more susceptible than are men to social pressure to drink or use drugs, and are more likely to have a substance-abusing partner (Gordon, 2002). For example, women heroin addicts are more likely to be introduced to the drug by a male friend, while men are more likely to be introduced to heroin by other men. Also, these women are more likely to buy heroin from their male partners, to support their drug habits with their partners, and to share needles with their partners, than are men are with their female partners (Cook et al., 2005; Gordon, 2002).

On a broader cultural level, society tends to judge women's problem drinking and drug use more harshly than men's (Angove & Fothergill, 2003; Haseltine, 2000; Lynch et al., 2002; Kaskutas et al., 2005; Matthews & Lorah, 2005). Thus, women often feel compelled to hide their drinking from family and social supports out of a sense of guilt and shame (Angove & Fothergill, 2003), and may hesitate to seek treatment (Roeloffs, Fink, Unutzer, Tang, & Wells, 2001). Women entering treatment for addiction are less likely than are men to have family support, and are more likely to have a lower socioeconomic status, less education, and to be unemployed (Gordon, 2002; Haseltine, 2000; McCance-Katz, Carroll, & Rounsaville, 1999).

Special Considerations for Addicted Women

WOMEN WHO PARENT Women have particular concerns with regard to their children, both during and after pregnancy. Pregnant women who abuse alcohol put their babies at risk of developing fetal alcohol syndrome (FAS), the most preventable form of mental retardation. In fact, as many as one-third of women who drink six drinks a day or more may give birth to a child with FAS (Gordon, 2002). Children born with this syndrome suffer developmental delays, behavioral problems, and facial and neurological abnormalities (Gordon, 2002). Addicted pregnant women might also deliver prematurely, experience vaginal infections, or suffer miscarriages (Nelson-Zlupko et al., 1995).

Women with children might also perceive barriers to addiction treatment. They may be hesitant to enter treatment for fear of retribution or investigation by social services (Gordon, 2002). Addicted women already in the criminal justice system often internalize shame, perceiving themselves as "bad mothers" (Hegamin et al., 2001). For example, women who are single parents and are referred to treatment through the court system may internalize complex feelings of inadequacy if parenting young children. Additionally, they may fear losing their children if they seek treatment for dependence (Greenfield, 2002). In other words, addicted women may perceive the court system and treatment community as punitive rather than restorative.

Finally, for women who are the sole or primary parent, a lack of child care can be a barrier to treatment. Research has shown that women are more likely to be successful in addictions treatment if ancillary services are available to specifically address their social and gender-related needs, such as child care. Unfortunately, most service providers seem to lack the awareness or resources necessary to provide gender-specific care, including services for women with infants and young children (Fendrich, Hubbell, & Lurigio, 2006). In fact, only 41% of U.S. treatment facilities that accept women clients offer special programs or groups for women; of these, only

18% offer child care (Drug and Alcohol Services Information System, 2005). Addicted women thus perceive treatment as hostile or unsupportive of their needs, and are unable to receive the care necessary for recovery (Fendrich et al., 2006).

WOMEN, ADDICTION, AND VIOLENCE Women suffer unique social consequences for their drinking and drug use behaviors. For example, they may believe that drinking improves sexual performance. In fact, the opposite is true: Sexual appetites are generally decreased by alcohol use (Gordon, 2002). The cultural stereotype that women who drink are more likely to have sex may be part of the reason that women are often the victims of sexual assault while under the influence (Gordon, 2002). Men who are sexually aggressive toward women impaired by substances may justify their attacks by implying that the victim "wanted" to have sex (Gordon, 2002). With regard to physical violence, it appears excessive alcohol use also contributes to women's likelihood of attack, as an intoxicated woman may appear vulnerable to an attacker, or may herself behave aggressively, initiating a violent exchange (Wells et al., 2007).

Increasingly, practitioners and researchers alike are becoming aware of the dangerous intersection of addiction and violence against women. This relationship appears to be bidirectional—women who experience violence are more likely to become addicted, and addicted women are more likely to experience violence (Gordon, 2002; Matthews & Lorah, 2005). The numbers of women addicted to alcohol or drugs who are also victims of violence are shocking: As many as 90% of women with drug abuse and dependence problems report being sexually abused at least once in their lifetime, and 40–74% of alcoholic women have been victimized by sexual assault, incest, or rape (Gordon, 2002). Women who were violated during childhood are particularly vulnerable to developing mental health problems, personality disorders, suicidality, and addiction (Schafer, Verthein, Oechsler, Deneke, Riedel-Heller, & Martens, 2009). These numbers are far higher than the general population, where it is estimated that one in five women has been the victim of rape or attempted rape (Black et al., 2011).

Women who have experienced the repeated violence of sexual assault appear to be at higher risk for abusing drugs and/or alcohol than their peers (Cook et al., 2005; Gordon, 2002). In addition, they are more likely to develop mental health problems and to have contracted HIV/AIDS than women who have not experienced chronic violence. With regard to childhood abuse, approximately 23% of female alcoholics report a history of childhood sexual abuse, compared to 11% in the general population. Similarly, women who are alcohol or drug dependent are also more likely to be victimized by their partners (Cook et al., 2005; Gordon, 2002).

WOMEN AND TOBACCO USE The negative impact of nicotine on the lives of Americans is often eclipsed by our focus on other drug and alcohol dependence. However, the Centers for Disease Control (CDC) reports that 480,000 people each year die from tobacco-related illnesses (U.S. Department of Health and Human Services, 2014), compared to 80,000 alcohol-related deaths (Kanny, Garvin, & Balluz, 2012) and 38,000 drug-related deaths (Jones, Mack, & Poulazzi, 2013). Although men made up the majority of smokers until World War II, since the 1950s the number of women using nicotine has increased to rates higher than those of men (Gordon, 2002). Also, it appears more difficult for women to stop smoking than it is for men, as cravings are linked to a woman's menstrual cycle, and they receive less partner support for quitting smoking than men (Gordon, 2002).

For all people, smoking increases rates of lung cancer, heart disease, and cancer of the larynx, oral cavity, and esophagus. Specifically for women, smoking increases the likelihood of contracting cancer of the cervix as well as heart disease, especially when paired with an oral contraceptive. With regard to pregnancy, nicotine has been linked to increased rates of spontaneous abortion, perinatal mortality, premature birth, low birth weight, and behavioral problems in infants (Gordon, 2002).

CASE STUDY
Sandra

Sandra describes her relationship with her crack-cocaine-using girlfriend as "on again, off again." "There is so much drama," she reports to you with a sigh. She describes frequent, verbal arguments that occasionally become physical, followed by tearful apologies and reconciliation. Sandra says she knows this pattern is destructive, and the relationship is hindering her recovery, but can't seem to break away from her girlfriend. "She loves me so much. I worry if I stop using with her, she'll leave me for good."

If you were Sandra's counselor, how would you apply the social concepts presented in this section to her case? How would you use this information to educate her about the etiology and risks of her drug use?

MEN AND ADDICTION

Women are not alone in suffering due to the impact of addiction to drugs or alcohol. Men also experience gender-specific consequences from substance abuse and dependence. In the following section, the biological, psychological, and social impacts of addiction on men are examined.

Biological Considerations

Men continue to be the primary consumers of alcohol and drugs (SAMHSA, 2012). Bearing this in mind, it becomes particularly important to understand the physical effects of alcohol and drug abuse on men. In the case of alcohol, while recent studies have shown that light-to-moderate alcohol consumption can benefit heart health, heavy or chronic drinking can lead to increased heart problems (Haseltine, 2000), as well as to stroke and high blood pressure, for men (Rantakömi, Laukkanen, Sivenius, Kauhanen, & Kurl, 2013). Men with a family history of alcoholism may be particularly susceptible to developing the disease, as some studies demonstrate a genetic link for alcoholism, particularly for sons of alcoholic fathers (Nelson-Zlupko et al., 1995; Straussner, 1997). Young men aged 18–29 are most at risk for developing alcohol dependence, and young to middle-aged men who drink heavily or develop alcoholism have an elevated chance of mortality compared to their nondrinking counterparts (Banks, Pandiani, Schacht, & Gauvin, 2000). Older men, however, experience a decrease in risk of mortality due to alcohol abuse compared to their younger counterparts, but that risk is still elevated compared to their nondrinking peers (Banks et al., 2000).

While many studies explore gender differences in patterns of alcohol abuse, fewer studies closely examine gendered drug abuse and dependence. Although empirical data is limited, some interesting statistics have emerged from research. For example, men are three times more likely to abuse marijuana on a weekly basis than women. Men are also more likely to smoke cigarettes, use nonprescription opiates (particularly heroin), abuse inhalants, and suffer more severe complications from cocaine use than are women (Straussner, 1997). Biologically speaking, some studies have shown that aggressive boys, who may have an imbalance of testosterone, are more likely to abuse substances than are their nonaggressive peers (Straussner, 1997). Also, men who abuse cocaine are more likely to be diagnosed with attention deficit hyperactivity disorder (McCance-Katz et al., 1999).

CASE STUDY

Tom

Tom is a 53-year-old African-American heterosexual male. He is court-ordered to treatment following his second Driving While Intoxicated (DWI) charge. As a result, his driver's license has been revoked for 1 year and his current forms of transportation are city bus and moped. He is currently separated from his second wife. "She left me because of my drinking," he admits, "because she's afraid it's going to kill me." Diagnosed with hypertension, Tom's doctor has advised him to cut down on his drinking if he wants to avoid future heart problems and early mortality. "I've been drinking beer every day since I was 15. What am I supposed to do about it? Plus my buddies tell me alcohol is good for your heart."

If you were Tom's counselor, how would you apply the biological concepts presented in this section to his case? How would you use this information to educate him about the etiology and risks of his drug use?

Psychological Considerations

Psychological needs and reinforcement contribute to addictive behavior for both men and women. However, there are significant gender differences worth exploration. While women often abuse drugs and alcohol for relational reasons or as a result of negative emotions, men tend to abuse drugs and alcohol in an effort to stimulate or suppress feelings (Haseltine, 2000; Hegamin et al., 2001). For example, men might use to get high, to feel more relaxed in social situations, to stimulate emotion, or to experience a feeling of adventure (Haseltine, 2000; Straussner, 1997). Paradoxically, men may also abuse substances to suppress feelings, such as using marijuana or heroin to control feelings of anger or violence (Straussner, 1997). Finally, they may abuse substances, such as alcohol or cocaine, to increase their perception of personal power in their lives (Straussner, 1997; Wade, 1994). Thus, while women use in reaction to emotions (such as depression or anxiety), men use to manipulate emotions—either to heighten positive feelings or suppress negative ones (McKechnie & Hill, 2009; Wade, 1994).

While addicted women tend to present with affective disorders such as depression, men are more likely to exhibit sociopathology (Haseltine, 2000; Landheim, Bakken, & Vaglum, 2003), engage in criminal behavior (Nelson-Zlupko et al., 1995), and engage in violent behavior (Dudish & Hatsukami, 1996; Hoaken & Pihl, 2000; McKechnie & Hill, 2009) more often than do their sober peers. They are also more likely to express overconfidence and rationalization with regard to their addiction treatment (Haseltine, 2000) and to be in denial about the extent of their substance abuse problems (Nelson-Zlupko et al., 1995). Additionally, while women tend to internalize or self-blame for their problems with alcohol and drugs, men tend to externalize, or blame others (Straussner, 1997). All of these factors need to be taken into consideration when counseling addicted men. On a lighter note, addicted men tend to have a more positive outlook on their lives and future potential than do addicted women (Nelson-Zlupko et al., 1995).

CASE STUDY

Tom

Tom admits he drinks to feel good. "I just love it. My buddies and I, we sit around the garage, or in the basement, watch football, and down a couple of cases of beer. What am I supposed to do if I stop drinking?" He readily acknowledges that alcohol elevates his mood and makes him feel in control of life. "I guess it came from watching my dad, you know? He was a big guy, a strong guy, and I always wanted to be just like him. He always had a beer in his hand, his whole life . . . he died of a heart attack when he was about my age."

How would you apply the psychological concepts presented in this section to his case? How would you use this information to educate Tom about the etiology and risks of his drug use?

Social Considerations

Socially speaking, men and women abuse and become addicted to substances for different reasons. For example, drug-dependent men are more likely to use alcohol or drugs to socialize, often in bars or other social settings (Nelson-Zlupko et al., 1995) and in conjunction with positive emotional experiences (Gordon, 2002). Thus, men appear to use substances in an effort to create community and to feel connected. Heavy drinking may be considered a way of building camaraderie among men (Straussner, 1997; Wade, 1994). Developmentally speaking, while adolescent girls and boys tend to abuse substances at similar rates through experimentation, young men tend to demonstrate problem drinking and drug use behaviors earlier than do young women (Palmer, Young, Hopfer, Corley, Stallings, Crowley, & Hewitt, 2009). Thus what appears "typical" adolescent experimentation for boys ("boys will be boys") may actually be a precursor to dangerous and health-compromising addiction by the early 20s.

Unlike women, men also tend to have social support from their family members once they decide to seek treatment for their substance abuse problems (Nelson-Zlupko et al., 1995). Men also receive more social support from the court system to receive treatment, as they are more likely to be mandated to treatment (Parks et al., 2003). Subsequently, men tended to report more legal problems due to their alcohol use than did women (Banks et al., 2000; Brown, Alterman, Rutherford, Cacciola, & Zaballero, 1993).

Like women, men are more likely to be the victims of violent attacks while under the influence of alcohol. Men who are under the influence and who have been drinking heavily may be targeted as vulnerable by an attacking party or may themselves incite aggression through violent behaviors. The likelihood of physical assault (not sexual) may be more significant for men than for women, as evidenced by emergency room data on reported injuries (Wells et al., 2007). However, study results have been mixed.

Finally, men suffering from unemployment experience shame similar to that of addicted mothers, as described in the previous section. Conventional social roles identify men as the primary breadwinner within a family structure. Thus, those who find themselves unemployed may possess a deep-seated sense of guilt and self-loathing as they are unable to financially support their loved ones. These men may turn to drugs and alcohol as a means of suppressing their shameful feelings (Straussner, 1997; Wade, 1994).

CASE STUDY

Tom

Tom's motivation to seek counseling treatment lies both in his desire to regain his license and clear his legal record, and in his hope of saving his marriage. "She stood with me after the first DWI," Tom reports. "She's a good woman. She said she'd take me back if I stop drinking." Tom also states that he has lost his job as a delivery driver because he lost his license. Not having employment has been tough on him, and he has few educational or vocational resources to draw on. "What am I supposed to do? I've got no money, no job, no wife, and no license. What kind of man is that?"

If you were Tom's counselor, how would you apply the social concepts presented in this section to his case? How would you use this information to educate him about the etiology and risks of his drug use?

TREATMENT CONSIDERATIONS

The purpose of this section is to evaluate treatment strategies from the perspective of gender. A brief review of commonly used treatment paradigms is provided. Also, general treatment conditions are identified as effective components of treatment for men and women. Specific treatment concerns, treatment outcomes, and relapse prevention for women and men are reviewed. Finally, case studies and sample treatment interventions are presented.

Treatment Overview and History

Since the 1940s, the Minnesota model of treatment provided the backbone for addictions counseling. Currently about 95% of treatment programs in the United States are based on this model, which incorporates residential treatment with education about the disease model of addiction and attendance at 12-step meetings (Veach et al., 2000). In this age of managed care, inpatient treatment lacks cost-effectiveness, so outpatient treatment has become the treatment of choice (Pagliaro & Pagliaro, 2000). However, most treatment centers continue to use the Minnesota model modified for outpatient treatment, paying particular attention to the character and spirituality of clients (Matthews & Lorah, 2005).

Despite the fact that this model has a long history of use by addictions counselors, it is not necessarily the best treatment for all clients, particularly women. It is important to remember that Caucasian men developed both the Minnesota model and Alcoholics Anonymous (AA) (Matthews & Lorah, 2005). Because these models reflect middle-class, male, Caucasian values, they may fail to take into account the unique needs of women (Matthews & Lorah, 2005).

In this section, treatment qualities that address gender difference will be described. One such quality is the counselor/client relationship. Regardless of theoretical orientation, the relationship between counselor and client is the single greatest predictor of treatment success (Fiorentine & Hillhouse, 1999). If clients do not feel empathy from and connection with their counselors, the likelihood that they will leave treatment before completion is high. The same holds true for clients seeking addictions counseling. One way to improve the odds of a successful counseling relationship is to pair clients and counselors on cultural features such as gender

(Fiorentine & Hillhouse, 1999). Also, regardless of clients' gender, addictions counselors can increase the odds of client success by

- Addressing gender issues as integral to the counseling process
- Examining client problems in a societal context
- Acting as an advocate for clients experiencing gender oppression
- Engaging in collaborative counseling
- Facilitating clients' freedom to choose success (Straussner, 1997)

The following sections describe additional gender-specific treatment needs for women and men.

Gender-Specific Treatment Needs: Women

Although the Minnesota model is the current benchmark for addictions treatment, it does not necessarily meet the needs of all clients, particularly women. For example, confrontation, a hallmark of this treatment philosophy, has been shown to be less effective for women clients, who prefer a more collaborative treatment modality (Beckerman & Fontana, 2001). Also, the Minnesota model places clinical focus on individual pathology. Thus, societal conditions such as discrimination, oppression, abuse, and sexism are not taken into account as factors in women clients' battle with addiction (Matthews & Lorah, 2005). Finally, the structure of the Minnesota model is hierarchical and nonmutual. Women may find this type of system alienating, preferring collective models of treatment (Matthews & Lorah, 2005).

Often, treatment centers pair the Minnesota model with 12-step practices. In the 12-step progression, clients are encouraged to acknowledge their personal powerlessness (Alcoholics Anonymous, 2002). Recall that two men began the 12-step movement. Dr. Bob and Bill W. enjoyed privileged lifestyles, and as a result found their personal power and ego kept them from sobriety. For these two men, giving up power facilitated their recovery (Matthews & Lorah, 2005). However, for women, personal power is often in short supply. Thus, the 12 steps may actually further minimize women who are in a position of powerlessness prior to entering treatment (Matthews & Lorah, 2005). In other words, women may perceive the treatment system as perpetuating a culture that is already oppressive.

It appears that the most prevalent treatment modalities in use today are not as effective for women as they are for men. However, as the research literature has focused almost exclusively on men, identifying more effective treatment modalities is difficult. For example, since 1984, only one randomized study has been published in which mixed-gender versus single-sex (female) groups are compared for treatment outcomes and success (Kaskutas et al., 2005). Furthermore, because most addictions studies have been conducted with all-male participants, misperceptions about substance abuse for women flourish—for example, that women are less likely to suffer from alcohol and drug problems, that researching women is significantly more complicated than studying men, and that no gender difference exists for women with alcohol disorders (Greenfield, 2002; Roeloffs et al., 2001).

In reality, women are less frequently studied than are men, as they experience greater reluctance to seek addiction-specific treatment (Bride, 2001; McCance-Katz et al., 1999). Women are more likely to seek the advice of a physician, counselor, or OB/GYN for substance abuse problems (Greenfield, 2002), perhaps out of shame (Cook et al., 2005). In these settings, they are more likely to be misdiagnosed and less likely to be referred to counseling for treatment (Greenfield, 2002). In a compelling qualitative study, Shaughney (2009) describes a process of "hailing," or repeated calls from concerned others, that ultimately compels an addicted woman into treatment. Hailing might originate from authority figures, friends, family members, co-workers, medical professionals, counselors, or concerned others, and repeated hailing over time may facilitate women's readiness to enter treatment. Shaughney asserts that coming to grips with the term *addict* is not a one-time event, but a progression over time, as addicted women come to internalize addiction as a part of their identity.

Once they are referred to a counselor for addictions treatment, women may experience additional barriers—lack of child care, mistrust of social services, sexism, financial limitations, and cultural stigma around women's addiction—which all play a role in attrition rates for addicted women (Roeloffs et al., 2001; Nelson-Zlupko et al., 1995). Also, low numbers of female addictions counselors mean women clients lack role models through the treatment process (Nelson-Zlupko et al., 1995). Finally, women are more likely to present with psychiatric symptoms than are men, further complicating the course of counseling treatment (Parks et al., 2003).

To attract and retain addicted women clients in treatment, some have suggested offering alternatives to traditional modes of therapy, which often include mixed-gender group treatment. Mixed-gender groups offer the following potential barriers to women: first, male group members tend to dominate the group discussion; second, women are more reluctant to discuss deeply personal issues in a mixed group; and third, women are more likely to acquiesce to the topical preferences of male group members (NeSmith, Wilcoxon, & Satcher, 2000). Also, they may be less likely to discuss aspects of their personal lives, including sex, with men (Kaskutas et al., 2005). It appears that women in a mixed-gender group may comply with societal gender roles rather than feeling empowered to assert their wishes and needs for the group. However, positive outcomes may emerge from mixed-gender groups as well. For example, for many women it may be their first opportunity to relate to men in a healthy, safe environment. Also, being in a mixed-gender group is more realistic with regard to the socialization issues women will face upon leaving the group (NeSmith et al., 2000).

However, women-only groups offer benefits as well. Particularly when working with women who have been sexually abused, or have struggled with an eating disorder, female-only groups provide a safe place for women to attempt recovery (Nelson-Zlupko et al., 1995; NeSmith et al., 2000). Additionally, women who have been sexually or violently assaulted may be reluctant to seek assistance in mixed-gender facilities (Greenfield, 2002) and may experience greater difficulties with relapse and treatment completion (Schafer et al., 2009). Women choosing female-only treatment programs were more likely to have dependent children, to identify as lesbian, to have a family history of substance abuse problems, and to have suffered sexual abuse (Greenfield, 2002). One reason women may be more likely to attend a women-only treatment facility or program is that these programs appear more likely to offer ancillary services specifically for them, including case management, child care, and other health services (Fendrich et al., 2006).

CASE STUDIES

Sandra and Tom

Review the case study details for Sandra and Tom. Based on what you've learned in this section about mixed-gender vs. single-gender treatment, which do you feel would be best for Sandra? Why? Which would be best for Tom? Why? Imagine them attending the same addiction treatment group. How would they fare? What obstacles or supports would they offer to one another?

Working with same-sex counselors also appears to be important, as women state a preference for women counselors (Hegamin et al., 2001). Although limited information exists about the efficacy of women-oriented addictions treatment, it does appear that women who might otherwise avoid treatment may feel drawn to a program that is designed for women only (Gordon, 2002; Weisner, 2005) and that some studies demonstrate current treatment modalities (including mixed-gender groups) are less effective for women (Bride, 2001). Regardless of treatment paradigm or gender makeup of treatment groups, counselors should increase their awareness of and sensitivity to women-specific considerations. For example, focusing on overcoming personal disadvantage, understanding oppression, and strength building appears more important for women than for men (Nelson-Zlupko et al., 1995). Other elements of treatment for women should include:

- Addressing complications from incest, sexual assault, or sexual abuse
- Collaborative counseling rather than hierarchy
- Attention to general and reproductive health
- Available child care during treatment
- Parenting classes
- Access to individual counseling
- Access to female counselors (Bride, 2001; Nelson-Zlupko et al., 1995)

Finally, counselors should be open to exploring alternative, cutting-edge therapies, including holistic healing methods such as yoga, meditation, and mindfulness training; expressive arts including music or art therapy; and acupuncture as a supplemental treatment. While little empirical research to date exists on the effectiveness of these therapies, they show promise when integrated into a comprehensive counseling program (Briggs & Pepperell, 2009).

Gender-Specific Treatment Needs: Men

Men tend to outnumber women in addictions treatment at a rate of 4:1, to acknowledge problem alcohol use earlier than women, and to benefit more from addictions counseling than do women clients (Nelson-Zlupko et al., 1995; Parks et al., 2003). Thus, counselors entering the field of addictions must be ready to meet the needs of male clients. Just as the Minnesota and 12-step models may not meet the complex needs of women, men require special consideration when designing counseling interventions. For example, traditional counseling, which often focuses on expression of feelings, may not be an entirely appropriate intervention for men, particularly in the early stages of treatment (Wade, 1994). As men often use drugs and alcohol to suppress their emotions (Straussner, 1997), they may find it difficult, threatening, or impossible to divulge emotions from the outset of treatment (Straussner, 1997; Wade, 1994). In fact, if men in the early stages of addictions counseling experience pressure to share emotions before they are ready to do so, counselors may find clients' resistance to treatment increasing, making headway difficult (DiClemente, 2003). Instead, interventions such as goal setting, creating lists and contracts, and homework assignments may be more beneficial in drawing men into the counseling process (Wade, 1994). These techniques help men to draw boundaries around the counseling process, making it feel safer for them to eventually delve into deeper emotional issues. Similarly, openly addressing how counseling may seem "unmasculine" to male clients is also important. Men may perceive a loss of manhood as they seek help and talking about this issue assists them in overcoming their fears (Wade, 1994). One goal of addictions counseling is to assist men in building effective coping and communication skills (Cook et al., 2005).

For both men and women, addictions counseling must address the whole client, as opposed to just the addicted behaviors. For men specifically, focusing early on concrete concerns around employment, health, and family issues acknowledges their needs outside of the addiction. By addressing these issues early on, the counselor demonstrates awareness of the client's needs, and offers evidence that counseling will be effective for the client in the long run (Wade, 1994). Other factors specific to men that may contribute to a positive treatment outcome include:

- Health education
- Anger management skill training
- Social-skills training
- Recreational and leisure opportunity development (Wade, 1994)

Finally, it is important for addictions counselors to be aware that men are more likely than women to be mandated to treatment by the legal system (Parks et al., 2003). As drug laws become increasingly stringent, counselors will increasingly receive clients from this source (Beckerman & Fontana, 2001; Gray, 1998). Court-ordered clients present particular challenges to counseling professionals. It has been demonstrated that court-ordered clients with low socioeconomic status, prior convictions, and a history of heroin use are less likely to succeed in mandated treatment (Rempel et al., 2003). Also, clients mandated to treatment, as opposed to those entering voluntarily, do not possess the same levels of self-motivation to complete treatment. It is thus the responsibility of the counselor to assess clients' strengths and barriers, and to determine their level of motivation for change (DiClemente, 2003).

Treatment for court-ordered clients is worthy of examination also. Most court-ordered treatment occurs in large, heterogeneous groups. Clients of all ages, genders, races, and addictions are combined, and generally group meetings are conducted in a psychoeducational format (Beckerman & Fontana, 2001). In this type of setting, it is easy for individual counseling needs to be overlooked, and for clients to feel lost in the system. Beckerman and Fontana (2001) discuss a gender-specific model in which clients were separated into all-male or all-female groups, where individual member needs (as described earlier) were acknowledged. Group members were offered case management services, free child care during treatment sessions, individual contact with counselors, and support-services needs assessment. Overall, both groups demonstrated greater success in abstaining from alcohol and drugs, as evidenced by urinalysis test results (Beckerman & Fontana, 2001). Thus single-sex groups that focus on gender-specific client needs may benefit both male and female clients.

It is important to note that both men and women suffer from the stereotyped gender roles that pervade U.S. cultural values. With regard to identity development, it was long assumed that men and women developed gender identity in similar ways. Feminist research has determined that while men develop male identity features based on cultural norms such as autonomy and independence, women tend to establish their identities in connection with others, through community. Thus, group counseling may feel like "coming home" for women, as it allows them to connect with others in meaningful ways. For men, group counseling may feel threatening or foreign, as they are less acculturated to sharing feelings with others. Counselors must be sensitive to both genders, understanding the cultural supports and barriers that may enhance or hinder progress in treatment (Briggs & Pepperell, 2009; Gilligan, Ward, & Taylor, 1988).

Gender-Specific Treatment Needs: Transgendered Clients

There exists a dearth of research regarding transgendered or transsexual people and substance use. Two factors contribute to the lack of attention to this specific population. First, as mentioned previously, until the 1970s nearly all addiction research focused on men exclusively. Over the past 40 years, women have been included in research study, but most research participants remain in the heterosexual, gender-normative demographic (Benotch et al., 2013). Second, the transgendered demographic is often lumped in with the gay, lesbian, and bisexual community for addiction research purposes. For example, Hunt (2012) reports that "twenty-five percent of gay and transgender people abuse alcohol, compared to 5 to 10 percent of the general population" (p. 2). But what does this statistic mean? Does it mean that 25% of the transgendered population abuses alcohol, or that 25% of the entire gay, lesbian, bisexual, and transgenedered population abuses alcohol? The answer is unclear. While statistics like these demonstrate the transgendered population appears more likely to develop certain substance abuse problems than does the general population, without accurate data it is impossible to grasp the scope of the problem.

General guidelines for counselors working with transgendered clients do exist and can provide a roadmap for creating innovative treatment planning for transgendered clients struggling with addiction issues. From a social justice perspective, counselors must be aware that transgendered clients suffer from alarming social discrimination, including extreme poverty, harrassment and discrimination in education and employment, housing discrimination and homelessness, discrimination in access to public services, discrimination in health care and poor health outcomes, and high rates of suicidality (41% compared to 1.6% of the general population) (Grant, Mottet, & Tanis, 2011).

The American Counseling Association (ACA) and the World Professional Association for Transgender Health's Standards of Care both offer competencies for health care providers who serve transgendered clients. These competencies include more expansive gender-fluid language, movement away from diagnosis of gender identity as a "disorder," increased self-awareness on the part of the practitioner with regard to biases and stereotyping, increased awareness of the myriad social discriminations placed upon the transgendered population, and overall enhanced positivity toward the expression of gender in all its forms (ACA, 2010; Lev, 2009). Grant and colleagues (2011) identified tremendous resilience in the transgendered population surveyed: "Despite all of the harassment, mistreatment, discrimination and violence faced by respondents, study participants also demonstrated determination, resourcefulness and perseverance" (p. 6). Counselors must draw upon these many strengths as a part of treatment planning.

Gender-Specific Treatment Needs: Intersex Clients

Similar to the transgendered population, little literature exists regarding addiction and addiction counseling with intersex clients. Like transgendered clients, intersex clients may experience gender identity confusion, shame, concern about sexuality, and social stigma (MacKenzie, Huntington, & Gilmour, 2009). These conditions, as they would for any group outside the dominant culture, can lead to emotional trauma and symptoms of depression or anxiety, or substance use, to cope. Intersex clients, like transgendered clients, report experiencing relief when finally able to talk about their true identity, often with the help of a skilled counselor in adulthood. Intersex client resilience is likely: One study of 41 intersex individuals found that 100% of participants expressed some sense of gratitude for being born intersex stigma (MacKenzie et al., 2009).

In general, counselors are encouraged to seek specific training about intersex medical and psychological needs, to explore their own internal beliefs about intersex individuals, to develop cultural understanding of the intersex community including social stigma, to develop relationships with physicians and other helpers in an intersex client's life, to provide community education and advocate on behalf of intersex clients, and to be willing to openly discuss issues of gender and gender identity with these clients (Guth, Witchel, Witchel, & Lee, 2006).

Treatment Outcomes and Relapse Prevention

Gender differences also exist with regard to treatment outcomes. In one study, among patients who completed a 30-day treatment program, women were more likely to relapse than were men (Greenfield, 2002). They were also more likely to drop out of outpatient treatment after the first session than were men (Greenfield, 2002). Possible predictors for the attrition of women in treatment are history of sexual abuse or physical assault, co-occurring affective disorders such as depression or anxiety, and self-referral, as they are more likely to self-refer to treatment (Greenfield, 2002; Haseltine, 2000; Schäfer et al., 2009). Men, on the other hand, are more likely to enter treatment because of family opposition to use or court order (Haseltine, 2000; Parks et al., 2003). With regard to re-entry to treatment following attrition or relapse, men were more likely to return to treatment following pressure from social institutions including place of employment, the criminal justice system, or family, while women were more likely to re-enter at the encouragement of a social worker or counselor (Haseltine, 2000).

Summary and Some Final Notations

Addiction affects women and men very differently. In order to be truly effective, counselors must understand the biological, psychological, and social impact of addiction on all their clients, both male and female. Gender-sensitive treatment is essential to client success.

MyCounselingLab

Visit the MyCounselingLab site for *Foundations of Addictions Counseling,* Third Edition to enhance your understanding of concepts. You'll have the opportunity to practice your skills through video- and case-based exercises. You will find sets of questions to help you prepare for your certification exam with *Licensure Quizzes.* There is also a Video Library that provides taped counseling sessions, ethical scenarios, and interviews with helpers and clients.

Useful Websites

The following websites provide additional information relating to the chapter topics:

Gender Spectrum
www.genderspectrum.org/
Gender Spectrum provides education, training, and support to help create a gender-sensitive and inclusive environment for all children and teens.

International Lesbian, Gay, Bisexual, Trans, and Intersex Association
ilga.org/ilga/en/index.html
The international advocacy and information network for people across the gender and sex spectrum.

National Institute on Drug Abuse (NIDA)
www.drugabuse.gov/
Infofact sheets, provided by the National Institute on Drug Abuse (NIDA), gives information specific to various issues related to addiction, including gender and sex.

Stephanie Covington
www.stephaniecovington.com/
Dr. Covington is a pioneer and leader in women's issues and addiction in counseling. Her integrative, holistic treatment approaches epitomize effective gender-sensitive counseling practices. Many books, workshops, and materials are available through her site.

U.S. Department of Health and Human Services (USDHHS)
womenshealth.gov/
This website, supported by the USDHHS, provides addiction and health information for both men and women.

Women for Sobriety
www.womenforsobriety.org/
Women for Sobriety offers a gender-sensitive alternative to the 12-step program for women suffering from addiction. The organization is strength-based, community focused, and positive. Groups are only open to women addicts and alcoholics.

Women, Girls, and Addiction: Celebrating the Feminine in Counseling Treatment and Recovery
www.routledge.com/books/Women-Girls-and-Addiction-isbn9780415993524
This landmark text presents a feminist perspective on addiction treatment for women and girls, and explores with depth the developmental, psychological, sociological, and biological components of the addiction process. Holistic and comprehensive treatment options are discussed.

References

Alcoholics Anonymous. (2002). *The twelve steps*. AA World Services. Retrieved on March 16, 2014, from http://www.aa.org/en_pdfs/smf-121_en.pdf

American Counseling Association. (2010). American Counseling Association competencies for counseling with transgender clients. *Journal of LGBT Issues in Counseling, 4*(3), 135–139.

Angove, R., & Fothergill, A. (2003). Women and alcohol: Misrepresented and misunderstood. *Journal of Psychiatric and Mental Health Nursing, 10,* 213–219.

Banks, S. M., Pandiani, J. A., Schacht, L. M., & Gauvin, L. M. (2000). Age and mortality among white male problem drinkers. *Addiction, 95,* 1249–1254.

Beckerman, A., & Fontana, L. (2001). Issues of race and gender in court-ordered substance abuse treatment. In J. J. Hennessy & N. J. Pallone (Eds.), *Drug courts in operation: Current research* (pp. 45–61). New York, NY: Haworth Press.

Benotsch, E. G., Zimmerman, R., Cathers, L., McNulty, S., Pierce, J., Heck, T., . . ., Snipes, D. (2013). Non-medical use of prescription drugs, polysubstance use, and mental health in transgendered adults. *Drug and Alcohol Dependence, 132,* 391–394.

Black, M. C., Basile, K. C., Breiding, M. J., Smith, S. G., Walters, M. L., Merrick, M. T., & , Stevens, M. R. (2011). *The National Intimate Partner and Sexual Violence Survey (NISVS): 2010 summary report*. Atlanta, GA: National Center for Injury Prevention and Control, Centers for Disease Control and Prevention.

Bride, B. E. (2001). Single-gender treatment of substance abuse: Effect on treatment retention and completion. *Social Work Research, 25,* 223–232.

Briggs, C. A., & Pepperell, J. P. (2009). *Women, girls and addiction: Celebrating the feminine in counseling treatment and recovery*. New York, NY: Routledge.

Brown, B. (2012). *Daring greatly: How the courage to be vulnerable transforms the way we live, love, parent, and lead*. New York, NY: Penguin Group.

Brown, L. S., Alterman, A. I., Rutherford, M. J., Cacciola, J. S., & Zaballero, A. R. (1993). Addiction severity index scores of four racial/ethnic and gender groups of methadone maintenance patients. *Journal of Substance Abuse, 5,* 269–279.

Centers for Disease Control and Prevention, National Center for Injury Prevention and Control. (2010). Web-based Injury Statistics Query and Reporting System (WISQARS) [online]. Available from www.cdc.gov/injury/wisqars/index.html

Cook, L. S., Epperson, L., & Gariti, P. (2005). Determining the need for gender-specific chemical dependence treatment: Assessment of treatment variables. *The American Journal on Addictions, 14,* 328–338.

Crawford, M., & Unger, R. (2004). *Women and gender: A feminist psychology* (4th ed.). New York, NY: McGraw-Hill.

DiClemente, C. C. (2003). *Addiction and change: How addictions develop and addicted people recover*. New York, NY: The Guilford Press.

Drug and Alcohol Services Information System. (2005). Report. Retrieved November 17, 2006, from http://oas.samhsa.gov/2k6/womenTx/womenTX.htm

Dudish, S. A., & Hatsukami, D. K. (1996). Gender differences in crack users who are research volunteers. *Drug & Alcohol Treatment, 42,* 55–63.

Fendrich, M., Hubbell, A., & Lurigio, A. J. (2006). Providers' perceptions of gender-specific drug treatment. *Journal of Drug Issues, 36,* 667–686.

Fiorentine, R., & Hillhouse, M. P. (1999). Drug treatment effectiveness and client-counselor empathy: Exploring the effects of gender and ethnic congruency. *Journal of Drug Issues, 29,* 59–74.

Friedman, S. R. (2003). Harm reduction among post-treatment men: Some reflections. *Addiction Research and Theory, 11,* 163–165.

Gilligan, C., Ward, J. V., & Taylor, J. M. (1988). *Mapping the moral domain.* Boston, MA: Harvard University Press.

Gordon, S. M. (2002). *Women & addiction: Gender issues in abuse and treatment* (Report No. CG031857). Wernersville, PA: Caron Foundation. (ERIC Document Reproduction Service No. ED466897)

Grant, J. M., Mottet, L. A., & Tanis, J. (2011). *Injustice at every turn: A report of the National Transgendered Discrimination Survey, executive summary.* Washington, DC: National Center for Transgender Equality and National Gay and Lesbian Task Force.

Gray, M. (1998). *Drug crazy.* New York, NY: Random House.

Greenfield, S. F. (2002). Women and alcohol use disorders. *Harvard Review of Psychiatry, 10,* 76–85.

Guth, L. J., Witchel, R. I., Witchel, S. F., & Lee, P. A. (2006). Relationships, sexuality, gender identity, gender roles, and self-concept of individuals who have congenital adrenal hyperplasia: A qualitative investigation. *Journal of Gay & Lesbian Psychotherapy, 10*(2), 57–75.

Guyon, L., Brochu, S., Parent, I., & Desjardins, L. (1999). At-risk behaviors with regard to HIV and addiction among women in prison. *Women & Health, 29,* 49–66.

Haseltine, F. P. (2000). Gender differences in addiction and recovery. *Journal of Women's Health & Gender-Based Medicine, 9,* 579–583.

Hegamin, A., Anglin, G., & Farabee, D. (2001). Gender differences in the perception of drug user treatment: Assessing drug user treatment for youthful offenders. *Substance Use & Misuse, 36,* 2159–2170.

Hoaken, P. N. S., & Pihl, R. O. (2000). The effects of alcohol intoxication on aggressive responses in men and women. *Alcohol and Alcoholism, 35,* 471–477.

Hunt, J. (2012, March 9). Why the gay and transgender population experiences higher rates of substance use. *Center for American Progress.* Retrieved on March 11, 2014, from http://www.americanprogress.org/wp-content/uploads/issues/2012/03/pdf/lgbt_substance_abuse.pdf

Jones, C. M., Mack, K. A., & Paulozzi, L. J. (2013). Pharmaceutical overdose deaths, United States, 2010. *Journal of the American Medical Association, 309*(7), 658.

Kanny, D., Garvin, W. S., & Balluz, L. (2012). Vital signs: Binge drinking prevalence, frequency, and intensity among adults—United States, 2010. *Morbidity and Mortality Weekly Report, 61*(1), 14.

Kaskutas, L. A., Zhang, L., French, M. T., & Witbrodt, J. (2005). Women's programs versus mixed-gender day treatment: Results from a randomized study. *Addiction, 100,* 60–69.

Keyes, K. M., Grant, B. F., & Hasin, D. S. (2007). Evidence for a closing gender gap in alcohol use, abuse, and dependence in the United States population. *Drug and Alcohol Dependence, 93,* 21–29.

Landheim, A. S., Bakken, K., & Vaglum, P. (2003). Gender differences in the prevalence of symptom disorders and personality disorders among poly-substance abusers and pure alcoholics. *European Addiction Research, 9,* 8–17.

Lev, A. I. (2009). The ten tasks of the mental health provider: Recommendations for the revision of the World Professional Association for Transgender Health's standards of care. *International Journal of Transgenderism, 11*(2), 74–99.

Lips, H. M. (2006). *A new psychology of women: Gender, culture, and ethnicity.* New York, NY: McGraw-Hill.

Lynch, W. J., Roth, M. E., & Carroll, M. E. (2002). Biological basis of sex differences in drug abuse: Preclinical and clinical studies. *Psychopharmacology, 164,* 121–137.

MacKenzie, D., Huntington, A., & Gilmour, J. A. (2009). The experiences of people with an intersex condition: A journey from silence to voice. *Journal of Clinical Nursing, 18,* 1775–1783.

Matthews, C. R., & Lorah, P. (2005). An examination of addiction treatment completion by gender and ethnicity. *Journal of Addictions & Offender Counseling, 25,* 114–125.

McCance-Katz, E. F., Carroll, K. M., & Rounsaville, B. J. (1999). Gender differences in treatment-seeking cocaine abusers: Implications for treatment and prognosis. *The American Journal on Addictions, 8,* 300–311.

McKechnie, J., & Hill, E. M. (2009). Alcoholism in older women religious. *Substance Abuse, 30,* 107–117.

Nelson-Zlupko, L., Kauffman, E., & Dore, M. M. (1995). Gender differences in drug addiction and treatment: Implications for social work intervention with substance-abusing women. *Social Work, 40,* 45–54.

NeSmith, C. L., Wilcoxon, S. A., & Satcher, J. F. (2000). Male leadership in an addicted women's group: An empirical approach. *Journal of Addictions & Offender Counseling, 20,* 75–83.

North Carolina Association of School Administrators. (2006). *Women under the influence.* Baltimore, MD: The Johns Hopkins University Press.

Pagliaro, A. M., & Pagliaro, L. S. (2000). *Substance use among women: A reference and resource guide.* Philadelphia, PA: Brunner/Mazel.

Palmer, R. H. C., Young, S. E., Hopfer, C. J., Corley, R. P., Stallings, M. C., Crowley, T. J., & Hewitt, J. K. (2009). Developmental epidemiology of drug use and abuse in adolescent and young adulthood: Evidence of generalized risk. *Drug and Alcohol Dependence, 102,* 78–87.

Parks, C. A., Hesselbrock, M. N., Hesselbrock, V. M., & Segal, B. (2003). Factors affecting entry into substance abuse treatment: Gender differences among alcohol-dependent Alaska Natives. *Social Work Research, 27,* 151–161.

Rantakömi, S., Laukkanen, J., Sivenius, J., Kauhanen, J., & Kurl, S. (2013). Alcohol consumption and the risk of stroke among hypertensive and overweight men. *Journal of Neurology, 260*(2), 534–539.

Rempel, M., Fox-Kralstein, D., Cissner, A., Cohen, R., Labriola, M., Farole, D., et al. (2003). *The New York State Adult Drug Court Evaluation: Policies, participants, and impacts.* New York, NY: Center for Court Innovation.

Roeloffs, C. A., Fink, A., Unutzer, J., Tang, L., & Wells, K. B. (2001). Problematic substance use, depressive symptoms, and gender in primary care. *Psychiatric Services, 52,* 1251–1253.

Schäfer, I., Verthein, U., Oechsler, H., Deneke, C., Riedel-Heller, S., & Martens, M. (2009). What are the needs of alcohol dependent patients with a history of sexual violence? A case-register study in a metropolitan region. *Drug and Alcohol Dependence, 105,* 118–125.

Shaughney, A. (2009). Identities under construction: Women hailed as addicts. *Health, 13*(6), 611–628.

Sonne, S. C., Back, S. E., Zuniga, C. D., Randall, C. L., & Brady, K. T. (2003). Gender differences in individuals with comorbid alcohol dependence and post-traumatic stress disorder. *The American Journal on Addictions, 12,* 412–423.

Straussner, S. L. A. (1997). Gender and substance abuse. In S. L. A. Straussner & E. Zelvin (Eds.), *Gender and addictions* (pp. 3–27). Northvale, NJ: Jason Aronson Inc.

Straussner, S. L. A., & Attia, P. R. (2002). Women's addiction and treatment through a historical lens. In S. L. A. Straussner & S. Brown (Eds.), *The handbook of addiction treatment for women* (pp. 3–25). San Francisco, CA: Jossey-Bass.

Substance Abuse and Mental Health Services Administration. (2012). *Results from the 2011 National Survey on Drug Use and Health.* U.S. Department of Health and Human Services.

U.S. Department of Health and Human Services. (2014). *The health consequences of smoking—50 years of progress: A report of the Surgeon General.* Retrieved on March 16, 2014, from http://www.cdc.gov/tobacco/data_statistics/sgr/50th-anniversary/index.htm

Veach, L. J., Remley, T. P., Kippers, S. M., & Sorg, J. D. (2000). Retention predictors related to intensive outpatient programs for substance use disorders. *American Journal of Drug & Alcohol Abuse, 26,* 417–428.

Wade, J. C. (1994). Substance abuse: Implications for counseling African American men. *Journal of Mental Health Counseling, 16,* 415–433.

Weisner, C. (2005). Substance misuse: What place for women-only treatment programs? *Addictions, 100,* 7–8.

Wells, S. W., Thompson, J. M., Cherpitel, C., MacDonald, S., Marais, S., & Borges, G. (2007). Gender differences in the relationship between alcohol and violent injury: An analysis of cross-national emergency department data. *Journal of Studies on Alcohol and Drugs, 68,* 824–833.

Wilke, D. J. (2004). Predicting suicide ideation for substance abusers: The role of self-esteem, abstinence, and attendance at 12-step meetings. *Addiction Research and Theory, 12*(3), 231–240.

Chapter 19

Lesbian, Gay, Bisexual, Transgender, and Queer Affirmative Addictions Treatment

Anneliese A. Singh
The University of Georgia

Pamela S. Lassiter
The University of North Carolina at Charlotte

Sexual orientation, gender identity, and gender expression are critical issues to consider in addictions counseling with lesbian, gay, bisexual, transgender, and queer (LGBTQ) clients. Although closely interrelated constructs, there are some important distinctions of which counselors should be aware. *Sexual orientation* is typically defined in the counseling literature as one's same-sex attractions. People who have same-sex attractions may self-define as lesbian, gay, bisexual, queer, questioning, or other self-generated labels. *Gender identity* refers to one's sense of being masculine or feminine (or both), while *gender expression* refers to how one expresses one's gender to others (Singh, Boyd, & Whitman, 2010). *Transgender* is an umbrella term that may include people who identify as *transsexual, genderqueer, gender-bending*, or other terms that define one's gender variance or nonconforming identity and expression (American Counseling Association [ACA], 2010). Addictions counselors should also be familiar with the term *cisgender*, which refers to people whose gender identity is in alignment with their sex assigned at birth (Singh et al., 2010). Cisgender people, similar to straight people, have privileges that transgender people do not hold (ACA, 2010). For a more in-depth discussion of language and terminology appropriate to use with LGBTQ people, we refer readers to the glossary in *Bending the Mold* (Lambda Legal, n.d.). In this chapter, we provide an overview of LGBTQ issues in addictions counseling; however, while not unimportant to address, our discussion of issues related to transgender people and substance abuse will necessarily be limited, because of the sparse literature available with this group.

Prevalence rates of addiction in the LGBTQ community are difficult to approximate (Matthews, Selvidge, & Fisher, 2005). While estimating the percentage of the general population who identify as LGBTQ is complex (ACA, 2010; Association of LGBT Issues in Counseling [ALGBTIC], 2013), understanding rates of substance abuse and addiction among the LGBTQ population is even more difficult. Some researchers have reported rates of alcohol abuse as high as 33% (Saghir, Robins, Walbran, & Gentry, 1970; Weinburg & Williams, 1974), while others have found no significant difference in rates of use when comparing heterosexual women with lesbian or bisexual women (McKirnan & Peterson, 1989). A meta-analysis of adolescent substance abuse research suggested sexual orientation becomes a serious risk factor, with LGB youth more likely to abuse substances (e.g., alcohol, tobacco) than their heterosexual peers (Marshal et al., 2008). Historically, there have been few studies concerning the rates of alcoholism in the LGBTQ population (Cabaj, 1997; Hughes & Wilsnack, 1997). In those studies, frequencies may be inflated due to sampling issues (Cabaj, 1997; Drabble, Midanik, & Trocki, 2005; Friedman & Downey, 1994). Many studies that reported higher rates of substance abuse problems for the LGBTQ community relied on recruiting participants from gay bars. Those potential participants who are more hidden within society are not adequately included in the data, while those who would be more likely to abuse chemicals might be more likely to attend gay bars. To further complicate estimates of abuse, many studies extrapolate lesbian substance use based on studies conducted with gay men.

Despite these methodology issues, it is estimated that 28–35% of gay men and lesbians have engaged in some form of recreational drug use, compared to 10–12% of the heterosexual population (Drabble et al., 2005; Ungvarski & Grossman, 1999). The importance of bars as social gathering places for sexual minorities may contribute to increased levels of substance abuse (Trocki, Drabble, & Midanik, 2005). Based on these estimates, it is critical for counselors to develop culturally competent treatment skills for this population.

To gain competence in this area, counselors must not only be familiar with addictions issues in general, but they also must examine the systems of heterosexism and homoprejudice that affect the lives of LGBTQ individuals. *Heterosexism* has been defined as an ideological system that assumes that all individuals are heterosexual and that heterosexuality is a "normal" model of sexual identity (ACA, 2010; Singh et al., 2010). Using heterosexuality as normative in this manner is problematic for LGBTQ individuals because heterosexism is also used to devalue, or legitimize ignorance of, LGBTQ people and their concerns. Because heterosexism is insidious and permeates every part of society, it will certainly appear in addictions treatment settings. For instance, heterosexist assumptions about addictions work would include recovery relapse interventions that do not recognize and include LGBTQ individuals' support systems as important, or ignore and pathologize LGBTQ identities while leading addictions groups.

While heterosexism is defined as the invisibility or devaluation of LGBTQ people, *homoprejudice* is the irrational hatred and fear of LGB individuals (ACA, 2010). Logan (1996) asserted that the word *homoprejudice* implies a fear of LGB people and does not adequately encapsulate the active prejudice and discrimination that LGB people experience. Instead, she encourages counselors to use the word *homoprejudice*. *Transprejudice* is often forgotten about in the LGB community, so it is critically important for addictions counselors to also recognize that transprejudice (hatred and fear of individuals with nontraditional gender expression) exists, and that transgender people may feel rejected by both LGB and heterosexual communities (Singh et al., 2010).

Heterosexism, homoprejudice, and transprejudice are systems of oppression that have negative consequences for LGBTQ people and provide significant stressors in their lives. Because a major role of the addictions counselor is to assess stress and coping factors in the lives of people struggling with addiction, it is important to develop attitudes, knowledge, and skills with LGBTQ issues. For instance, a gay man may have begun using alcohol as a teenager to cope with his sexual identity and the feeling that he would be ostracized from his family for being gay. On the other hand, a transgender woman may have used drugs to numb the pain of feeling the disconnection between the sex she was assigned at birth (male) and her gender identity as a woman.

Counselors should understand that homoprejudice and transprejudice may be internalized, causing LGBTQ clients to hold negative attitudes about their own sexual identity (Szymanski, Kashubeck-West, & Meyer, 2008) and/or gender identity (Singh, Hays, & Watson, 2011). This internalization can appear in the form of guilt, shame, and negative self-concept about one's gender or sexual identity. These negative feelings can greatly affect addiction treatment, as LGBTQ individuals may be vulnerable to alcohol and drug use and relapse when attempting to cope with their sexual orientation, gender identity, and/or expression.

Because of the damaging impact heterosexism, homoprejudice, and transprejudice have on the mental health of LGBTQ individuals, LGBTQ-affirmative treatment has become the standard of care for counselors to provide to this population (ALGBTIC, 2013). Addictions counselors should be aware that there are recent competencies specific to LGB, intersex, and ally competencies endorsed by the LGBTQI C, a division of the ACA. In addition, specific counseling competencies for those working with transgender clients also exist and have been endorsed by the ACA (2010). LGBTQ-affirmative therapies seek to explore and validate how LGBTQ people experience and understand universal issues, such as family and social systems, religion and spirituality, career and life planning, and thoughts and feelings about oneself. The purpose of this chapter is to provide the reader with culturally relevant and helpful information that counselors may incorporate in the assessment and treatment of LGBTQ individuals living with addiction.

COMMON TERMS FOR AND MYTHS ABOUT LGBTQ PEOPLE

The field of counseling and mental health has a long history of viewing "homosexuality" and nontraditional gender expression as a disorder (ACA, 2010). In fact, homosexuality was categorized as a mental disorder as recently as 1973 in the *Diagnostic and Statistical Manual of Mental Disorders* (American Psychiatric Association [APA], 1973). Because of its history of pathology, it is no longer best practice to use this word to refer to LGBQ people. Furthermore, although an LGBQ identity is no longer considered pathological, transgender people continue to face the stigma of diagnosis because Gender Dysphoria remains a classification in the current edition of this same manual (APA, 2013). Transgender activists, scholars, and practitioners have advocated for the removal of this diagnostic label because of their view that transgender identity is a medical condition rather than a psychological one (Lev, 2007).

Because of the evolving terminology used by individuals in the LGBQ community, becoming competent with treatment of this population requires knowledge of current and past uses of terms, along with their definitions. Addictions counselors should be curious and have knowledge about how these terms are used differently within specific ethnic/racial groups in order to understand how LGBTQ individuals define themselves ethnically or racially. For the purposes of this chapter, common terms are listed in the following sidebar.

- *Sexual orientation* describes the attractions (e.g., romantic, emotional, physical) that an individual has to gender(s), such as bisexual, heterosexual, asexual, and homosexual. A *lesbian* has attractions primarily to females, a *gay man* is attracted primarily to males, and *bisexuals* have attractions to both men and women.
- *Gender* refers to the ideological system that categorizes humans into a binary system of "male" or "female," and *gender identity* describes how people self-identify their gender (e.g., transgender, woman, man). *Transgender* is an umbrella term used to describe people who have gender identities and gender expressions that are outside of the limited gender binary (e.g., transsexual, transman, drag queen).
- *Queer* is a term that is being reclaimed by the LGBTQ community to refer to people who challenge the restrictive system of heterosexuality and traditional gender norms. This word was once used to denigrate LGBTQ people; therefore, LGBTQ people of an older generation may find the term problematic. When clients use the word *queer*, they are typically using this word to reflect being politicized and to denote a sense of pride and inclusion of all LGBTQ people.

In addition to having a strong grasp of the appropriate terms and definitions used to describe the LGBTQ community, it is also important to be aware of the myths that surround this population. Similar to other populations who hold marginalized identities, the energy that

LGBTQ individuals use to counter or ignore pervasive myths about being LGBTQ is time-consuming and stressful. For instance, bisexual people are often targeted with the myth that they are "confused" and "want to have their cake and eat it too" (Horowitz & Newcomb, 1999). These myths, such as the myth that bisexual individuals are "over-sexed," can be pervasive as they may be held by members of both the straight *and* queer community. Gay men are similarly targeted as being overly sexual, and along with this may come the myth that all gay men live with HIV/AIDS or are sexual predators. These myths are problematic because gay men have to struggle to be seen as people who want to engage in long-term partnerships and/or raise children. On the other hand, lesbians face the myths that they are "trying to be men," not interested in sex, and are more interested in pursuing stereotypically male jobs. In addition to myths bound specifically to each group, there are widely held stereotypes about all of the groups. These include stereotypes that LGBTQ people want to "recruit" heterosexuals into being homosexual and that being LGBTQ is a mental disorder or is not "normal."

The most important myth for addictions counselors to be aware of in treatment is that LGBTQ people can "choose" their gender or sexual identity. This stereotype is especially concerning because it has historical roots in the counseling and psychological professions and is practiced by some counselors as *reparative* or *conversion therapy*. In these therapies, counselors attempt to convert LGB people to being heterosexual. It is important to know that these therapies have been deemed unethical, because LGB identity is no longer defined as an abnormal sexual identity (Amadio & Perez, 2008). However, because survey research suggests counselors continue to hold negative and/or stereotypic beliefs about LGBTQ individuals (Bidell, 2013), addictions counselors may work with clients who have suffered harm in reparative therapy programs or have been in treatment programs in which heterosexism and homoprejudice were endorsed. In these cases, counselors need to educate clients about the ethical guidelines and standards of care in the counseling profession that demand affirmative practice with LGBTQ individuals, in addition to intentionally creating an LGBTQ-affirmative environment in addictions treatment.

COMING OUT, CULTURAL DIFFERENCES, AND ADDICTION

Coming out is a term used to describe the process of sexual identity development for lesbian, gay, and bisexual people. Although transgender individuals are not typically included when counselors and academics discuss the coming-out process, research has shown that there is a process of gender identity development that exists for transgender people as well (Singh et al., 2011). There are numerous coming-out models for LGBTQ clients (Cass, 1984; Lev, 2007; McCarn & Fassinger, 1996; Troiden, 1998). Because the stages of coming out may stress significant relationships that LGBTQ people have with their family, friends, and community (D'Augelli, 2006), it is important that addictions counselors assess what stage of sexual identity development the client is in to provide culturally competent addiction treatment. This treatment must recognize and assess the extensive energy that LGBTQ people expend on the coming-out process in their personal and professional lives. LGBTQ people must manage being mindful about their sexual identity and/or gender identity on multiple levels: how they think about themselves, how the world thinks about them, and the discrepancy between the two (Singh et al., 2010).

Counselors should also know that there are many sexual identity models to draw from in working with LGBTQ clients (Cass, 1979; Cox & Gallois, 1996; Lev, 2007; Troiden, 1998). Kus and Latcovich's (1994) coming-out model delineates four stages that counselors may easily use to assess sexual identity stage for a client seeking addiction treatment. The four stages include *identification* (using terms such as *lesbian, gay,* and *bisexual,* and identifying one's attraction to the same sex), *cognitive changes* (accessing community resources and activities in the LGB community), *acceptance* (giving oneself permission to be LGB), and *action* (sharing about one's LGB identity with family, friends, and others, and embracing one's sexual identity). Because bars are often viewed by the LGBTQ community as the only safe places for them to explore and validate their sexual identity, assessment of a client's coming-out stage is important historically and currently to understand their social support systems. For instance, if a gay man living with alcohol addiction is recently identifying his attraction to men in the identification stage of coming out, he may increase his use of alcohol to manage internalized homoprejudice and/or explore his sexual identity in the LGBTQ bar scene. A culturally competent counselor working with this client should be adept in normalizing and affirming his sexual identity, as well as identifying LGBTQ-affirmative addiction recovery systems in the community.

However, when assessing the coming-out process as it relates to addiction (see the section LGBTQ-Affirmative Addiction Treatment and Assessment for more specific information), it is also critical to understand that different cultural groups (e.g., race/ethnicity, religious/spiritual affiliation) may have coming-out processes that are very different (Singh, 2012). For instance, research has shown that Asian Americans' coming-out process typically occurs in predominantly White LGBTQ communities, and they often experience racism and discrimination in these spaces (Chung & Singh, 2008). Additionally, African-American, Native-American, and Latin-American LGBTQ people must also manage societal racism (Bridges, Selvidge, & Matthews, 2003) in addition to heterosexism as they move through the addiction and recovery process. Therefore, counselors must be adept in assessing not only LGBTQ-community support for people of color in addictions treatment, but also the safety level of their connections to their families and community. Chernin and Johnson (2002) recommend that counselors raise questions with LGBTQ clients of color in order to clarify support networks and assist in clarifying how clients think and feel about their sexual and ethnic/racial identity, through the following questions: "With which groups do I identify most clearly? What role does sexual orientation play in my life? How open am I willing to be?" (p. 35).

Advice to Addictions Counselors About Clients' "Coming-Out" Processes

- Do not assume every client is straight or gender-conforming. This can place pressure on LGBTQ people to self-disclose about their sexual orientation and/or gender identity.
- Create an environment in all counseling modalities (e.g., individual, partners, group) where at the beginning of each intake session, an affirmative stance is stated about all multicultural identities (e.g., race/ethnicity, gender identity and expression, sexual orientation, socioeconomic status, disability).
- If and when LGBTQ clients come out about their sexual orientation and/or gender identity, respond in an affirmative manner about this disclosure. Explore how this (or these) identities might shape counseling goals or needs.
- Do not "out" clients to others involved in treatment (e.g., family, friends, employers, co-workers) unless there is specific permission granted from the client. Because of the extensive heterosexism, homoprejudice, and transprejudice that exist in society, the consequences for outing an LGBTQ client can place the client in harm's way.
- Do not highlight a client's sexual orientation and/or gender identity and expression in client conceptualization, case supervision, and consultation unless this is a significant aspect of their treatment. With heterosexual and cisgender clients, be sure to explore their gender identity and/or sexual orientation as well in case consultation and client conceptualization.

CASE STUDY

Coming Out and Cultural Issues in Addictions Treatment

Asim is a 36-year-old Muslim male of South Asian heritage who presents for individual counseling and who reports abusing alcohol and marijuana. When you ask about precipitants to his drinking behavior, Asim shares that he began abusing substances after the end of a difficult relationship 3 years ago. When you ask for more information about this relationship, Asim hesitates and you notice that Asim is not using any identifying pronouns about this individual. Asim suddenly changes the subject and asks whether it is possible to be attracted to people of both genders.

1. How will you answer Asim's question in a manner that honors both his cultural and sexual identities?
2. What are interventions you could utilize that would invite Asim to share more about his past relationship and sexual orientation?
3. What are cultural issues that may bring strengths and challenges to Asim's treatment in addiction counseling?

LGBTQ-AFFIRMATIVE ADDICTION TREATMENT AND ASSESSMENT

Culturally relevant assessment and interventions with LGBTQ people living with addiction issues must recognize the unique context in which they live. Because LGBTQ people are an invisible minority group due to the pervasiveness of heterosexism, and the resulting assumption of a heteronormative standard in society (ALGBTIC, 2013), this same invisibility is present when attempting to understand the unique addictions concerns of this population. Therefore, it is not surprising that rates of alcohol and drug abuse for this population are difficult to estimate (SAMHSA, 2012). In a qualitative study of mental health professionals with LGBTQ expertise, participants suggested that because many helping professionals do not receive adequate LGBTQ training, counselors must intentionally seek professional development on LGBTQ issues in order to develop competence with LGBTQ clients (Rutherford, McIntyre, Daley, & Ross, 2012).

Counselors should be aware that the LGBTQ community is often divided in its social networks along gender lines (Fassinger, 1991). Therefore, the types of drugs abused, location of abuse, and potential triggers for relapse can look quite different depending on the population. The following is an abbreviated list of the ways alcohol and drug addiction may vary across LGBTQ communities:

- *Transgender* people may face challenges in being underemployed (Grant et al., 2011), or overrepresented in entertainment environments such as drag shows, or as sex workers (Bockting & Avery, 2005). These environments may be dangerous, and research has shown that it is particularly important to provide transgender individuals working in these settings psychoeducation about HIV/AIDS prevention, safer sex, and sexual assault due to lack of knowledge about these risks (Bockting & Avery, 2005). Transgender people experience high rates of substance abuse and face treatment issues that include external and internal transprejudice, hate crimes, job and career loss, family estrangement, isolation, lack of medical care, and low self-esteem. They also may distrust counselors due to previous bad experiences with health care providers. Further, transgender people may choose hormone therapy, which may affect mood and serve as relapse triggers, including self-injection requirements simulating illicit drug use (SAMHSA, 2012).

- *Gay men* may abuse anabolic steroids due to the body image pressure that exists particularly within White gay male cultures; the use of steroids may also be associated with higher risk for contracting HIV/AIDS (Bolding, Sherr, Maguire, & Elford, 1999). In urban areas, gay men may attend all-night circuit parties or dance venues where "party" or designer drugs, such as crystal methamphetamine, Ecstasy (methylenedioxymethamphetamine), special K (ketamine hydrochloride), and γ-hydroxybutyrate (GHB), are taken to "last through the night." Gay men also demonstrate high rates of addiction to the Internet, which researchers believe is linked to the homoprejudice and invisibility they face in society and the increasing access to a gay male community online (Chaney & Chang, 2005). Gay men have also been shown to potentially rely on gay bars and parties for social and sexual connections; may or may not connect sex and intimacy; face HIV/AIDS as a daily reality, with rates of contraction rising again for men of color and young men; and may experience additional shame and targeting for being "too effeminate" (SAMHSA, 2012).
- *Lesbian women* have been shown to abuse alcohol at higher rates than do their heterosexual counterparts (Drabble, Trocki, Hughes, Korcha, & Lown, 2013), and research has shown that alcohol abuse may begin as a way to cope with their emerging sexual identity (McNally & Finnegan, 1992). In addition, survey data shows that lesbian and bisexual women use marijuana at significantly higher rates than do their heterosexual counterparts (Trocki, Drabble, & Midanik, 2009). SAMHSA (2012) has also shown that lesbians have higher rates of alcoholism than do heterosexual women and that their use of alcohol tends to show less decline with age; may attend LGB bars, which provide safe space for them to socialize and find support; and manage stress related to possible trauma history, coming-out issues, and "passing" as heterosexual.
- *Bisexual* people are typically underrepresented in studies examining queer populations (Moradi et al., 2009), which suggests that we have little information on their addiction patterns. Others may view bisexual identity as a behavior rather than as a sexual orientation, and bisexuals may face identity and self-acceptance issues that could complicate addictions treatment. They may also be labeled by some providers as immature, living with borderline personality disorder, or as "acting out" with their sexual behavior (SAMHSA, 2012).
- *Queer or Questioning Youth* may use substances for the same reasons as nongay youth, but may also use to soothe effects of shame and social isolation, to help deny feelings of same-sex attractions, and/or to cope with ridicule. They may also face challenging sexual development issues in isolation. Many experience first sexual attractions at age 10, have first sexual experiences between 13 and 15, and begin to identify orientation from 15 to 16 years. Transgender and queer youth of color are at the highest risk for violence (SAMHSA, 2012).

LGBTQ-Specific Assessment of Addiction

Every sound clinical assessment process begins with relationship building. This is particularly important when working with LGBTQ clients. Without a strong therapeutic alliance, individuals will not want to begin the journey toward recovery and will not be motivated to stay engaged in treatment through more challenging times. Trust is particularly important with groups who experience discrimination and oppression as a daily part of living. Assessment procedures with people who abuse substances typically involve clinical interviews with the client and with people who may be in their family of origin or members of their support group in combination with objective assessment instruments. Potential barriers to a strong therapeutic alliance include interviews that assume heterosexuality and assessment tools laden with heterosexist bias. Counselors should ask about family and other relationships in a manner that communicates acceptance to people of all sexual identities. Each client, regardless of cultural context, should be asked about sexual orientation in a relaxed, matter-of-fact manner as a normal part of the assessment procedure. Additionally, inclusion of partners in the assessment process is crucial.

Affirmative Assessment with LGBTQ Clients

It is important to use open-ended questions when assessing clients' sexual orientation and/or gender identity. For instance, rather than asking if a client is married (since not all LGBTQ people have access to marriage rights in the United States and globally), a counselor could ask the following: "Tell me about your relationship history" and "Share about the partners you have had in your life."

- What other open-ended questions typically used in addictions assessment should be changed to demonstrate respect and a welcoming environment for LGBTQ clients?

AFFIRMATIVE USE OF LANGUAGE WITH LGBTQ CLIENTS A basic consideration when assessing and treating sexual and gender minorities who are struggling with substance abuse and with their families is the counselor's use of language. It is important for the counselor to be knowledgeable and aware of relevant terms for this culture in order to facilitate trust and credibility with sexual minority clients. For example, the term *homosexual* suggests that this community is just about sex when, in fact, sexuality plays the same role in all of our lives regardless of sexual orientation. Gay men and lesbians are no more sexual than nongay people. The words *gay* and *lesbian* suggest these are the only two groups within the larger community of sexual minorities, but bisexual and transgender people are also represented in the gay community. Although they exist in smaller numbers, the kind of discrimination and oppression they experience is like that of gay men and lesbians.

The term *sexual preference*, commonly used by uninformed people, is considered to be offensive by many LGB people and their allies. A more correct term is *sexual orientation*, as "preference" suggests that LGB people have a choice about their sexual identity. Gay people, like nongay people, discover their sexual orientation in terms of their attractions to the same gender. Gay men and lesbians *come out* as a statement of integrity. They are simply being who they are. The only choice they make is how to integrate this part of their being into their lives. The term *coming out* infers an event or a single action that one performs, when in reality this is a complex process that occurs repeatedly over a lifetime and can actually be required many times within a single day. Because people are generally assumed to be heterosexual, LGB people have to decide when, where, and with whom they disclose their sexual orientation on an ongoing basis with varying consequences (e.g., acceptance, rejection, or physical harm) for this disclosure. This management of sexual identity can be extremely difficult to negotiate while also attempting to become clean and sober. Often the client seeking recovery is "young" in his or her sexual identity development and new to a recovery identity. Managing both identities can be complicated and overwhelming. With regard to working with transgender clients, it is most appropriate to use the terms that transgender people use to describe themselves—from use of pronouns, names, and other gender identity and expression markers. Do not use words like "the name she prefers" or use the pronouns related to the sex a transgender client was assigned at birth. See the ACA's (2010) "Competencies for Counseling with Transgender Clients" for further information on best practices with transgender clients. It is important to note that transgender-affirmative counselors serve more as facilitators and advocates in providing mental health services, rather than solely as gatekeepers (Singh & Burnes, 2010).

In addition to assessing substance abuse issues, counselors will need to be well versed in different models of sexual identity development to better understand the interplay between recovery identity development and sexual identity development (SAMSHA, 2012). Just as a person from a sexual minority group evolves into self-acceptance of their sexual orientation, a client will need to move from an identity as an addict to identity as a recovering person. Often multiple levels of identity development will intersect in terms of race, age, gender, ability status, socioeconomic status, religious/spiritual affiliation, and recovery. It will take a skilled and aware counselor to assist clients in managing these multiple identities.

PSYCHOSOCIAL HISTORY A complete psychosocial history should be gathered about relevant information in multiple areas to get a complete picture of an LGBTQ individual's life. The counselor should gather this information from both the client and significant others about patterns of alcohol and other drug (AOD) use, including frequency, acute dose, duration, tolerance, and co-occurring physical signs and symptoms of addiction. Patterns of use should include contextual information about where, when, and with whom the client uses most often. If this history indicates the client uses more frequently at bars, the treatment goals will need to reflect alternative social outlets within the LGBTQ community. The history should also include information about the client's family history of addiction, degree of outness, family support for sexual orientation, family addiction history, dating and relationship history (including history of partners with substance abuse issues), and a detailed account of how substance use has affected the client's significant relationships. Information should be gathered concerning communicable disease (e.g., HIV/sexually transmitted disease [STD], Hepatitis C) status, safer sex practice issues especially related to substance use, and patterns of drug administration (e.g., needle sharing). For some LGBTQ clients, as with heterosexual counterparts, use of mood-altering chemicals may lead to unprotected sexual activity.

It is also important for counselors to be aware that signs and symptoms of substance abuse in older LGBTQ populations may mimic the symptoms of aging (Briggs, Magnus, Lassiter, Patterson, & Smith, 2011). For example, memory loss, impaired motor function, disorientation, depression, and changes in hygiene can all be symptoms of both aging and substance abuse and can lead to a misdiagnosis. In addition, counselors should be prepared to gather information concerning employment history (paying special attention to the impact of sexual orientation and gender identity and expression on career issues), legal history, history of mental illness, sexual and physical abuse history, and mental status information. Higher rates of suicide and eating disorders (Kane, 2010) are other factors to assess when working with LGBTQ clients.

Spirituality may also be a vital part of the recovery process for an LGBTQ person, and therefore may be an important part of the assessment. Counselors should explore the client's concepts of spirituality, including religious history and the intersections between faith and sexual identity particular to the client. The client's openness to spiritually focused 12-step ancillary programs will be greatly affected by past experiences with organized religion, especially around sexual identity. Religiously sanctioned prejudice and condemnation toward sexual minorities may obstruct the client's willingness to find spiritual fellowship with other recovering people. In order to set an open tone around spirituality during the assessment process, counselors may want to use the phrase "spiritual community center" instead of "church." Assessment questions centered on life purpose or meaning may help the clinician to access spiritual dimensions, without creating defensiveness related to past experiences with religious condemnation.

Often psychometric instruments are used in assessing substance abuse and dependence. Counselors should scrutinize assessment instruments for heterosexist bias and gender bias. It is recommended that all assessment tools use gender-neutral language. This helps set a positive tone for future therapeutic work. Many can be modified to use inclusive language without affecting their validity and reliability. Additionally, counselors will need to be familiar with psychometric instruments that assess internalized homonegativity, especially considering the importance of guilt and shame in the recovery process for addicts. Intersecting identities may necessitate additional dimensions for the assessment process. The coming-out process may be different for people of color, people living in poverty, and people of varying ages, ability status, and socioeconomic levels. Every unique identity will bring different stressors and joys in each stage.

CASE STUDY

Lesbian Client Coming Out in a Support Group

Sharon is a 23-year-old woman who identifies as a lesbian and reports abusing alcohol for the past 8 years. She has been in both individual and group addictions counseling for the past month, and has been attending Alcoholics Anonymous (AA) meetings. Traditional Christian prayers have been used to close many of the AA meetings she has attended. Sharon describes "being out" in other areas of her life (e.g., family, friends, work), but says she feels uncomfortable disclosing her sexual orientation to her sponsor and in other friendships she is developing in the support group. She asks you what she should do and if she should disclose her sexual orientation to the group.

1. What would you say to Sharon that would be affirmative of her sexual orientation and validate her concerns?
2. How will you explore challenges that Sharon may face if she does decide to disclose her sexual orientation to the group?

LGBTQ-Specific Treatment of Addiction

Sexual and gender identity issues should be integrated into the substance abuse client's treatment plan as appropriate. Counselors should focus on those problems most important to the client, and treatment plans should be created collaboratively. According to Cabaj (2008), each of the following factors should be considered when developing a treatment plan with a sexual or gender minority client: life stage; coming-out process; support available; current and past relationships; degree of comfort with sexual identity; and issues related to career, finances, and health. In nurturing a therapeutic relationship, SAMHSA (2012) recommends counselors become aware of certain underlying assumptions regarding sexual or gender minority groups. These assumptions include:

- Each person's unique life story, including the person's circumstances and experiences, may affect recovery and should be explored by the counselor.
- Legal prohibitions against LGB behavior limits social outlets to settings such as LGBTQ bars, homes, or clubs where AODs may be central.

- LGBTQ people may have experienced discrimination as a result of their gender or sexual identity, and may have internalized homonegativity as a result.
- LGBTQ people may have been victims of antigay violence or hate crimes.
- Increasing numbers of LGBTQ individuals are becoming parents.
- LGBTQ-sensitive and affirmative treatments are more likely to have successful outcomes with this population.

Modality Issues

Substance abuse treatment modalities include individual therapy, couples and family counseling, group counseling, and a variety of therapeutic community milieus. Higher treatment success rates have been associated with family involvement, and group therapy is often the modality of choice in treatment settings (Capuzzi, Gross, & Stauffer, 2010; Feldstein & Miller, 2006; Hogue, Dauber, Samuolis, & Liddle, 2006; Watkins et al., 2012). However, special considerations need to be taken when working with an LGBTQ client in these settings.

Partners should be invited to attend treatment along with the client, but it is also important to consider that they may not feel comfortable or want to openly discuss sexual orientation and/or gender identity and expression concerns in a group setting with primarily heterosexual and/or gender-conforming members. Many LGBTQ clients will have "chosen" families comprised of close friends; it may be appropriate to include them in the treatment process. It may also be appropriate to begin with single-unit family therapy and psychoeducational experiences before referring them to a family group environment. Likewise, an LGBTQ individual may not feel comfortable disclosing his or her orientation in a heterosexual group. These issues should be discussed with the client prior to prescribing any treatment modality.

In group and community treatment settings, clients need guidance and support when deciding where and when to "come out." This is especially true if the client is early in the sexual and/or gender identity development process *and* is early in recovery. Often, LGBTQ clients early in their sexual identity experience "pink cloud" altruism, disclosing their sexual and/or gender identity in settings in which they are unprepared to manage the potential consequences and are then unable to cope with potential negative consequences. Most residential or inpatient treatment communities set up living quarters based on binary gender models, which may complicate daily life for LGBTQ clients seeking recovery. For example, many substance abuse treatment centers struggle deciding which dormitory (male or female) would be most appropriate for a transgender person. For some, the client's treatment stay may range from awkward to dangerous. LGBTQ stigma management is also an important coping skill for LGBTQ clients to develop when they are early in their sexual identity and/or gender identity and recovery. Counselors need to prepare clients for the potential rejection and discrimination they will experience as a result of living a more open life as an LGBTQ person.

Counselors may also need to educate non-LGBTQ clients in treatment about treating every community or group member with respect, including setting ground rules that discrimination and disrespect of members will not be tolerated. It can be healing for LGBTQ clients to obtain acceptance and support from heterosexual and gender-conforming group members, and this acceptance may be the first time they experience safety sharing their LGBTQ identity in a group setting. Regardless of the treatment modality, LGBTQ clients need to be treated with respect and dignity.

LGBTQ people who abuse substances also need assistance identifying social and recovery support communities that are both safe and affirmative of their identity. This may be difficult in rural settings, where sexual minorities are even more hidden. Some urban areas may offer

LGBTQ-specific 12-step meetings. Counselors should know the details about these resources, including the relative "health" of the LGBTQ groups in the community. Clients should learn how to identify healthy, safe recovery meetings and sponsors. It will also be valuable to help LGBTQ clients view 12-step meetings as support for recovery, and not an avenue for dating. Sponsorship should be with someone of differing sexual and/or gender identities from the client, especially initially. For example, a gay man may choose a lesbian sponsor. Just as a heterosexual man would not sponsor a woman, this helps eliminate the dual role attraction might create. If LGBTQ-specific 12-step groups do not exist in the client's community, the counselor will need to prepare the client for possible prejudice and discrimination in traditional self-help settings. Finally, counselors should be aware that some LGBTQ clients show reluctance to become involved in 12-step fellowships due to experiences of discrimination from organized religion. Assisting clients to explore the wounds inflicted by some of these experiences may help formulate or identify a chosen, more autonomous spirituality. Finding and learning to nurture a healthy spiritual life can be crucial to recovery for LGBTQ people.

Despite warnings to stay away from social settings where alcohol and other drugs are present, many LGBTQ clients will continue to socialize in bars and at LGBTQ parties in order to connect with the LGBTQ community. Counselors need to help clients address this concern openly and strategize about how to handle this situation without relapse. Recovery skills such as sponsorship, relaxation, visualization, meditation, and journaling may all be valuable coping strategies in helping the client maintain sobriety. Role-playing various social settings that are potential triggers for relapse while in the counseling office may also help prepare the client to guard against it.

Relapse Prevention

Relapse prevention is an important part of any recovery treatment plan. Unique triggers exist for LGBTQ clients, which require unique strategies. Counselors should help clients identify triggers that may cause relapse, as well as ways to counteract those triggers based on the individual's situation. Some common relapse precursors for LGBTQ clients are coming-out issues, experience of shame, low self-esteem, internalized homonegativity and/or transnegativity, verbal and physical attacks, grief and loss due to HIV/AIDS, learning about HIV status, and social situations where AODs are present. Treatment and prevention plans should provide clients with the skills and strategies to overcome these potential triggers, as well as empower the client to become more resilient in the face of unique challenges to long-term recovery.

CASE STUDY

A Gay Transgender Man with a Relapse Crisis

Kasey is an African-American man (who was assigned the sex of female at birth but who identifies as a male) in his early thirties. While in inpatient treatment for his alcoholism, he learned he is HIV positive. Now that he has returned home, he is afraid he will never have another relationship and is unsure of how to negotiate his HIV status with potential partners. Kasey feels he should tell his close-knit family about his health status in order to get the support he needs, but has never disclosed his sexual orientation or his gender identity to them. It was hard enough to admit his alcoholism. Although he left treatment feeling a great deal of hope for his life, he has begun to doubt his self-worth and whether his sobriety is worth all the effort. He is overwhelmed with thoughts of using and has begun to connect with old drinking buddies.

1. As Kasey's counselor, how would you help him sort out the disclosure issues he is struggling with?
2. How would you help him find the support he needs to avert this relapse? What recovery skills would you help him develop to cope with this crisis?
3. How would you help Kasey utilize this crisis to enhance his overall recovery? What competencies can you identify that might contribute to his personal resiliency?
4. How would you address the intersections of Kasey's gender identity and sexual orientation in counseling? How would you discuss these intersections of identity in addition to his diagnosis of HIV?

Resilience strategies are particularly helpful with a population that experiences multiple levels of societal oppression (e.g., substance abuser, sexual minority, gender difference, race diversity) (Singh et al., 2011). Ten strategies to build resilience, adapted from the Discovery Health Channel and the American Psychological Association (as cited in Miller, 2005), are:

1. Make connections.
2. Avoid seeing crises as insurmountable problems.
3. Accept that change is a part of living.
4. Move toward one's goals.
5. Take decisive actions.
6. Look for opportunities for self-discovery.
7. Nurture a positive view of self.
8. Keep things in perspective.
9. Maintain a hopeful outlook.
10. Take care of one's self.

Helping LGBTQ clients discover their own resiliency, often born out of adversity, survival, and adaptation, can be one of the most fulfilling aspects of recovery. Claiming this source of inner strength can help establish a foundation on which to build a healthy life.

Role of Addictions Counselors Working with LGBTQ Clients

Regardless of the treatment setting, counselors will work with LGBTQ clients, and have a unique opportunity to powerfully impact the lives of LGBTQ clients seeking help with substance abuse issues. It is the counselor's responsibility to follow best-practice guidelines and to become competent when working with this population. The following list highlights some important principles for culturally competent treatment provision:

- Remember every client has the right to be treated with sensitivity and respect.
- Become knowledgeable and competently trained to work with LGBTQ issues.
- Be aware of the myths and realities regarding LGBTQ people.
- Display LGBTQ cultural symbols such as the rainbow flag and LGBTQ 12-step literature in your office as a sign of affirmation.
- Become knowledgeable and aware of the Stages of Change Model (Prochaska & Norcross, 2002) and how these stages might be affected by the client's stage of sexual identity development.
- Do not confront sexual and/or gender identity and expression identity—explore, work collaboratively, and use empowerment strategies.

- Challenge agency discrimination and prejudice against this population, including exclusionary language in treatment-team processes and agency policies.
- Remember that LGBTQ clients live in a heterosexual and gender-conforming world and are not afforded the same legal protections and privileges (e.g., marriage) as their heterosexual counterparts.
- Clients should not be required to discuss sexual and/or gender identity or relationship issues in mixed groups if they are uncomfortable doing so.
- If counselors are uncomfortable working with LGBTQ clients, they should acknowledge this lack of competence and refer to counselors who are LGBTQ-friendly.
- Do not try to change the sexual orientation and/or gender identity of the client.
- Self-monitor countertransference issues. Examine your own biases and reactions with a counselor, colleague, or supervisor.
- Be diligent in exploring your own heterosexist assumptions and language.
- Remain flexible and individualize treatment strategies based on the unique contexts of the client.

Creating a Safe Environment for LGBTQ People

Because LGBTQ individuals have extensive, and often daily, experiences with prejudice due to their sexual orientation or gender identity and expression, it is important for counselors to ensure that their counseling office and the organization in which they work send a clear message that the environment is safe for them to disclose their struggles. Keeping LGBTQ magazines (e.g., *The Advocate, Curve, Girlfriends*) and LGBTQ books (e.g., *My Gender Workbook* by Kate Bornstein) in the waiting room and in counseling offices is one way to send this affirmative message. Another, more significant way to send a welcoming message to LGBTQ people is to display a "Safe Zone" or rainbow sticker on the front door of the building, reception desk, and/or counseling office, as such a symbol can be a universal message of welcome and safety that LGBTQ people recognize. It is important, however, to seriously assess the safety of the counseling environment before deciding to display such a symbol. Counselors may want to consider organizing a "Safe Zone" committee to assess not only LGBTQ attitudes within the workplace, but also to consider offering LGBTQ trainings. In addition, counselors should have brochures on hand for organizations that are affirmative of LGBTQ clients and their families and friends, should they need additional support outside of addictions counseling. Recent research has suggested that gay and bisexual men in LGBTQ-specific substance abuse treatment programs have more positive outcomes than those in traditional substance abuse treatment programs (Senreich, 2010). Although the research in this area is nascent, it is important to collaboratively explore with LGBTQ clients whether LGBTQ-specific substance abuse treatment may be a better fit for their recovery. An example of LGBTQ-specific treatment—the Pride Institute—is shown in the following.

The Pride Institute: An Example of LGBTQ-Focused Addiction Treatment

"How can you recover when you can't be yourself? Begin your recovery where you can be yourself" (Pride Institute, 2006). This is the basis of the philosophy of the Pride Institute, an organization dedicated to providing culturally relevant and appropriate addictions treatment for LGBTQ people. Individuals seeking treatment first call a central office; they receive a phone assessment and a referral to a treatment center (located in Minneapolis, Dallas, Fort Lauderdale, Chicago, and New York City). The Pride Institute offers individual and group counseling modalities and provides treatment for issues comorbid with addiction (e.g., depression, anxiety).

The Pride Institute appears to achieve positive recovery outcomes with its LGBTQ clients due to assumptions of its safety and freedom from homoprejudice and heterosexism; encouragement to discuss how coming out and other issues that affect LGBTQ people (e.g., HIV/AIDS, domestic partnership) can influence the addiction process; an LGBTQ-friendly staff; creation of an LGBTQ community of treatment and recovery; and counseling modalities specifically geared toward LGBTQ people. Addictions counselors may use any of these strategies to enhance their cultural competence with LGBTQ individuals, which may entail moving from valuing the client's cultural identity to actually doing LGBTQ social advocacy.

How to Be an Advocate for LGBTQ-Affirmative Treatment

Social advocacy on behalf of LGBTQ people is one of the most important roles that addictions counselors may hold when working with clients who struggle with addictions issues. With social justice named as the fifth force in counseling (Ratts, D'Andrea, & Arredondo, 2004) and the endorsement of the Advocacy Competencies by the American Counseling Association (Counselors for Social Justice, 2003), best practices for counselors working with this population include a careful assessment of how they incorporate affirmative counseling in their work with LGBTQ people living with addiction. In addition, the movement for social justice in counseling urges counselors to recognize how systems of privilege and oppression affect the mental well-being of clients. For counselors working with LGBTQ people living with addictions issues, this translates to moving beyond the traditional counseling role to advocating on behalf of the LGBTQ population for culturally relevant addiction treatment. In order to support addictions counselors in their advocacy efforts, we suggest five major ways in which they can intervene on behalf of LGBTQ clients seeking addiction treatment:

1. *Create a "zero" tolerance policy about heterosexist behaviors and language.* Counselors may enlist their fellow staff members to create a policy directing agency personnel to deliver LGBTQ-affirmative and LGBTQ-inclusive addiction treatment. Including LGBTQ staff and clients in this process may provide additional insight into the effectiveness of the resulting policy, as well as ensure that it is enforceable and meaningful and accounts for overt (e.g., LGBTQ-demeaning jokes) and covert (e.g., excluding LGBTQ clients and/or staff from access to resources) prejudicial acts. Counselors can advocate for sexual orientation, as well as gender identity and expression, to become part of a larger nondiscrimination clause the organization may have to address its mission of serving diverse clients. In addition, counselors may access materials from The National Gay and Lesbian Task Force (*ngltf.org*) and the Human Rights Campaign (*hrc.org/*), both of which have guidelines on how to create LGBTQ-positive work environments.
2. *Create a team to conduct an assessment of how LGBTQ-friendly the addiction setting appears to others.* Sending a clear message that LGBTQ people are valued and understood is critical to establishing an LGBTQ-affirmative environment. How many LGBTQ magazines are in the reception area? What types of LGBTQ books and pride symbols are on the bookshelves of counselor offices and group-treatment rooms? Having a team assess and answer these questions will ensure a more welcoming environment for this population, as well as sending a clear message to other clients and staff that heterosexism, homoprejudice, and transprejudice are not acceptable.

3. *Hold focus groups and workshops in the LGBTQ community.* Although the bar scene may feel like the safest place for LGBTQ people to interact and socialize within the queer community, counselors may play a significant role in education about the importance of alcohol- and drug-free spaces and support networks in the community. Holding focus groups in the LGBTQ community may also enhance understanding of the local queer culture. In addition, providing LGBTQ-centered addiction and recovery is a way to outreach in a nonthreatening manner to LGBTQ people who distrust counseling and psychological professionals.
4. *Write letters to representatives and local straight and queer newspapers about LGBTQ issues in addiction.* Counselors witness firsthand how heterosexism, homoprejudice, and transprejudice feed the addictive cycle, in addition to how these systems are internalized by clients in the form of negative attitudes. Writing letters to demand equitable treatment of LGBTQ people in the mental health system, as well as asking representatives and local newspapers to highlight LGBTQ issues, are advocacy activities that directly challenge and counter heterosexism in the fields of mental health and substance abuse.
5. *Use your knowledge of local addiction, mental health, and LGBTQ community resources to raise awareness about LGBTQ issues in addiction.* Counselors may seek out local resources to ensure their addiction work utilizes the most current information on LGBTQ-friendly 12-step programs, treatment centers, and other community organizations. Counselors may take their advocacy one step further by compiling and distributing an LGBTQ addiction resource guide that includes this information as a service to the community. In compiling this guide, a team of local counselors, LGBTQ allies, and LGBTQ community leaders could be convened to lead this effort collaboratively.

Top 10 Ways Addictions Counselors Can Advocate for LGBTQ People

1. Include LGBTQ magazines (e.g., *The Advocate, Curve, Girlfriends*) in the reception area.
2. Post a list of LGBTQ-friendly 12-step meetings in the local, regional, and national area.
3. Develop a statement that heterosexism, homoprejudice, and transprejudice will not be tolerated while in treatment.
4. Ensure that all paperwork is LGBTQ-inclusive and free of heterosexist language (use gender-neutral language, such as "partner" rather than "spouse") and includes "transgender" as a gender box or allows clients to write in their gender as opposed to checking a box.
5. Train fellow counselors and staff on LGBTQ culture (e.g., media, language, resources) to ensure an LGBTQ-friendly environment at all levels of treatment.
6. Hire openly LGBTQ staff to serve so that others may see them as role models.
7. Write letters to representatives at the local, state, and national level to advocate on behalf of issues important to LGBTQ people.
8. Be aware that the LGBTQ community is more heterogeneous than homogeneous (e.g., political awareness, coming-out stages, language, gender, race/ethnicity, disability status, socioeconomic status, religious/spiritual affiliation).
9. Provide psychoeducation on LGBTQ people and addictions issues in the LGBTQ community (e.g., bars, parks, pride festivals, social organizations, nonprofits, Internet).
10. Constantly monitor one's level of awareness, knowledge, and skills in working with LGBTQ people living with addiction in order to increase one's competence with these issues.

CASE STUDY

The Story of Sonali

This story weaves together the complex intersection of race/ethnicity, gender identity and expression, socioeconomic status, disability, and religious/spiritual affiliation. As you read through this case study, think about the opportunities for culturally competent treatment with Sonali, as well as the ways that you may engage in advocacy efforts both within the treatment center and outside of the office. Questions about the case study follow this short description:

What Would You Do?

Sonali, a first-generation student of South Asian heritage who is struggling with alcohol addiction, presents in your office and asks you "to help save her." She reports that she found your addiction treatment center's information on the Internet, and that she has been court-ordered to a 90-day treatment program for alcohol addiction due to a DUI she received 2 weeks ago. She is tearful in her presentation and reports many depressive symptoms (e.g., loss of weight, insomnia, anhedonia, isolation from others, hopelessness). She repeats over and over how scared she is that her parents "will find out" about her drinking habits, and doesn't know how she will pay for treatment because she is living on financial aid. She also shares with you that she has "secrets that cannot be told" to her family about who she loves, and reports relationship difficulties with her best friend. She shares that she needs to do a "puja" at her temple as soon as possible in order to "get better."

You assess Sonali's consumption of alcohol; she has recently increased her drinking to a six-pack of beer nightly for the past month. When you ask about the escalation of her alcohol abuse, she shares that she is not ready to face her parents over the winter holiday break and that she and her best friend will be in two different cities. She reports that she first began drinking about 2 years ago, when she started sneaking into a local bar to "hang out with good friends." When you ask about the nature of her relationship with her best friend, she gets fidgety and has minimal eye contact. She repeatedly asks you to help her "solve her problems" and "make the pain go away."

Questions

1. What additional information do you need to gather about Sonali in order to provide culturally competent addictions treatment?
2. How will you assess Sonali's stage of sexual identity development? What questions would be important to ask, and what questions might be inappropriate?
3. What are the subtle messages that Sonali will receive about her multiple identities (e.g., sexual identity, gender identity and expression, class identity, racial/ethnic identity) as she enters the addiction treatment center's lobby and your personal office? How can you structure an inviting and nonheterosexist environment?
4. As you read Sonali's intake before she comes to your office, what information will you use to begin building good rapport?
5. How will you ensure that you deliver culturally competent assessment and treatment to Sonali in regard to her sexual identity? How will you explore the intersection between her sexual identity and her racial/ethnic identity?
6. What are the opportunities for advocacy prior, during, and after treatment with Sonali? How might you engage your fellow counselors in these advocacy efforts? Are there ways that you could bring these advocacy efforts to the local, regional, national, and international counseling organizations of which you are a member?

Summary and Some Final Notations

Counselors must address issues of heterosexism, homoprejudice, and transprejudice in order to work effectively with LGBTQ people seeking recovery from alcohol and drug abuse. Because they must constantly make decisions about coming out in their family, friend, and work relationships, counselors must recognize that the same hesitancy to come out may exist in an addictions treatment setting. Accurate assessment and treatment interventions with alcohol and drug abuse that include acknowledgment of society's devaluation of LGBTQ identities by counselors allow a more accurate and honest rapport to build between counselor and the client in recovery. Because counselors are privy to the intimate ways that LGBTQ mental health is shaped by heterosexism, homoprejudice, and transprejudice, it is important to use this knowledge in advocacy and social justice efforts on behalf of LGBTQ people both within and outside the counseling office.

Regardless of the complexity of issues, abstinence and sobriety should be a priority in assisting the LGBTQ person living with substance abuse. Establishing a safe, affirmative environment will help in developing a strong therapeutic alliance. Collateral issues may include alienation from family, multiple identity management issues, trauma history, HIV/AIDS, suicide potential, domestic violence, trust issues, and parenting issues. Alienation from family and friends due to a combination of social damage from addictive behavior and sexual orientation stigma create complex barriers for the LGBTQ substance abuser to overcome. Culturally competent treatment strategies provide the best opportunity for sexual minority clients to overcome addiction and lead fulfilling, healthy lives. The websites listed in the next section provide additional information relating to the chapter topics.

MyCounselingLab

Visit the MyCounselingLab site for *Foundations of Addictions Counseling,* Third Edition to enhance your understanding of concepts. You'll have the opportunity to practice your skills through video- and case-based exercises. You will find sets of questions to help you prepare for your certification exam with *Licensure Quizzes.* There is also a Video Library that provides taped counseling sessions, ethical scenarios, and interviews with helpers and clients.

Useful Websites

The following websites provide additional information relating to the chapter topics:

Amigas Latinas
www.amigaslatinas.org

Association for LGBT Issues in Counseling (ALGBTIC)
www.aLGBTic.org

Children of Lesbians and Gays Everywhere
www.colage.org

Communities United Against Violence
cuav.org

Deaf Queer Resource Center
www.deafqueer.org

Gay and Lesbian Alliance Against Defamation
glaad.org

Gay and Lesbian Medical Association
glma.org

Gay Parent Magazine Online
www.gayparentmag.com

Human Rights Campaign
www.hrc.org

Lambda Legal Defense and Education Fund
www.lambdalegal.org

National Gay and Lesbian Task Force
www.thetaskforce.org

National Minority AIDS Council
www.nmac.org

National Native American AIDS Prevention Center
www.nnaapc.org

Parents, Families and Friends of Lesbians and Gays (PFLAG)
www.pflag.org

People of Color Against AIDS Network
www.sasgcc.org/links/peopleofcolor

Pride Institute
www.pride-institute.com

Religious Tolerance
www.religioustolerance.org

Soulforce
www.soulforce.org

Substance Abuse and Mental Health Services Administration (SAMHSA)
www.samhsa.gov

Transgender Forum's Resource Guide
www.3dcom.com/tgfr.html

Trikone: Lesbian, Gay, Bisexual and Transgender South Asians
www.trikone.org

Zuna Institute (African American Lesbians)
www.zunainstitute.org

References

Amadio, D. M., & Perez, M. (2008). Affirmative counseling and psychotherapy with lesbian, gay, bisexual, and transgender clients. In C. Negy (Ed.), *Cross-cultural psychotherapy: Toward a critical understanding of diverse clients* (2nd ed., pp. 363–399). Reno, NC: Bent Tree Press.

American Counseling Association. (2010). Competencies for counseling with transgender clients. *Journal of LGBTQ Issues in Counseling, 4,* 135–159.

American Psychiatric Association. (1973). *Diagnostic and statistical manual of mental disorders* (3rd ed.). Washington, DC: Author.

American Psychiatric Association. (2013). *Diagnostic and statistical manual of mental disorders* (5th ed.). Washington, DC: Author.

Association of LGBT Issues in Counseling. (2013) Association for Lesbian, Gay, Bisexual, and Transgender Issues in Counseling competencies for counseling with lesbian, gay, bisexual, queer, questioning, intersex, and ally individuals. *Journal of LGBT Issues in Counseling, 7*(1), 2–43.

Bidell, M. P. (2013). Addressing disparities: The impact of a lesbian, gay, bisexual, and transgender graduate counseling course. *Counselling & Psychotherapy Research, 13*(4), 300–307.

Bockting, W. O., & Avery, E. (Eds.). (2005). *Transgender health and HIV prevention: Needs assessment studies from transgender communities across the United States.* Binghamton, NY: Haworth.

Bolding, G., Sherr, L., Maguire, M., & Elford, J. (1999). HIV risk behaviours among gay men who use anabolic steroids. *Addiction, 94,* 1829–1835.

Bridges, S. K., Selvidge, M. D., & Matthews, C. R. (2003). Lesbian women of color: Therapeutic issues and challenges. *Multicultural Counseling & Development, 31,* 113–131.

Briggs, W., Magnus, G., Lassiter, P., Patterson, A., & Smith, L. (2011). Substance use, misuse, and abuse among older adults: Implications for clinical mental health counselors. *Journal of Mental Health Counseling, 33*(22), 112–127.

Cabaj, R. J. (2008). Gay men and lesbians. In M. Galanter & H. Kleber (Eds.), *The American Psychiatric Publishing textbook of substance abuse treatment* (4th ed., pp. 623–638). Arlington, VA: American Psychiatric Publishing.

Capuzzi, D., Gross, D., & Stauffer, M. D. (Eds.). (2010). *Introduction to groupwork* (5th ed.). Boulder, CO: Love Publishing.

Cass, V. C. (1979). Homosexual identity formation: A theoretical model. *Journal of Homosexuality, 4,* 219–235.

Chaney, M. P., & Chang, C. Y. (2005). A trio of turmoil for Internet sexually addicted men who have sex with men: Boredom proneness, social connectedness, and dissociation. *Sexual Addiction and Compulsivity, 12,* 3–18.

Chernin, J. N., & Johnson, M. R. (2002). *Affirmative psychotherapy and counseling for lesbians and gay men.* Thousand Oaks, CA: Sage.

Chung, Y. B., & Singh, A. A. (2009). Lesbian, gay, bisexual, and transgender Asian Americans. In A. Alvarez & N. Tewari (Eds.), *Asian American psychology: Current perspectives* (pp. 233–246). New York, NY: Taylor & Francis.

Counselors for Social Justice. (2004). *Advocacy competencies*. Retrieved November 5, 2005, from http://www.counseling.org/resources/competencies/advocacy_competencies.pdf

Cox, S., & Gallois, C. (1996). Gay and lesbian development: A social identity perspective. *Journal of Homosexuality, 30,* 1–30.

D'Augelli, A. R. (2006). Developmental and contextual factors and mental health among lesbian, gay, and bisexual youths. In A. E. Omoto & H. M. Kurtzman (Eds.), *Sexual orientation and mental health: Examining identity and development in lesbian, gay, and bisexual people* (pp. 37–53). Washington, DC: APA Books.

Drabble, L., Midanik, L., & Trocki, K. (2005). Reports of alcohol consumption and alcohol-related problems among homosexual, bisexual, and heterosexual respondents: Results from the 2000 National Alcohol Survey. *Journal of Studies on Alcohol, 66*(1), 111–120.

Drabble, L., Trocki, K., Hughes, T. Korcha, R., & Lown, A. (2013). Sexual orientation differences in the relationship between victimization and hazardous drinking among women in the National Alcohol Survey. *Psychology of Addictive Behaviors, 27*(3), 639–648.

Fassinger, R. E. (1991). The hidden minority: Issues and challenges in working with lesbian women and gay men. *The Counseling Psychologist, 19,* 157–176.

Feldstein, S., & Miller, W. (2006). Substance use and risk-taking among adolescents. *Journal of Mental Health, 15,* 633–643.

Friedman, R. C., & Downey, J. I. (1994). Homosexuality. *The New England Journal of Medicine, 331,* 923–930.

Grant, J. M., Mottet, L. A., Tanis, J., Harrison, J., Herman, J. L., & Kiesling, M. (2011). *Injustice at every turn: A report of the national transgender discrimination survey*. Washington, DC: National Center for Transgender Equality & National Gay and Lesbian Task Force.

Hogue, A., Dauber, S., Samuolis, J., & Liddle, H. (2006). Treatment techniques and outcomes in multidimensional family therapy for adolescent behavior problems. *Journal of Family Psychology, 20,* 535–543.

Horowitz, J. L., & Newcomb, M. D. (1999). Bisexuality, not homosexuality: Counseling issues and treatment approaches. *Journal of College Counseling, 2,* 148–164.

Hughes, T. L., & Wilsnack, S. C. (1997). Use of alcohol among lesbians: Research and clinical implications. *American Journal of Orthopsychiatry, 67,* 20–36.

Kus, R. J., & Latcovich, M. A. (1994). Special interest groups in Alcoholics Anonymous: A focus on gay men's groups. *Journal of Gay and Lesbian Social Services, 2,* 67–82.

Lambda Legal. (n.d.). *Bending the mold: An action kit for transgender youth*. Retrieved from http://www.lambdalegal.org

Lev, A. (2007). Transgender communities: Developing identity through connection. In K. Bieschke, R. Perez, & K. DeBord (Eds.), *Handbook of counseling and psychotherapy with lesbian, gay, bisexual, and transgender clients* (2nd ed., pp. 147–175). Washington, DC: American Psychological Association.

Logan, C. R. (1996). Homophobia? No, homoprejudice. *Journal of Homosexuality, 31*(3), 31–53.

Marshal, M. P., Friedman, M. S., Stall, R., King, K. M., Miles, J., Gold, M. A., . . . , Morse, J. Q. (2008). Sexual orientation and adolescent substance use: A meta-analysis and methodological review. *Addiction, 103,* 546–556.

Matthews, C. R., Selvidge, M. M. D., & Fisher, K. (2005). Addictions counselors' attitudes and behaviors towards gay, lesbian, and bisexual clients. *Journal of Counseling and Development, 83,* 57–65.

McCarn, S. R., & Fassinger, R. E. (1996). Re-visioning sexual minority identity formation: A new model of lesbian identity and its implications for counseling and research. *The Counseling Psychologist, 24*(3), 508–534.

McKirnan, D. J., & Peterson, P. L. (1989). Alcohol and drug use among homosexual men and women: Epidemiology and population characteristics. *Addictive Behaviors, 14,* 545.

McNally, E. B., & Finnegan, D. G. (1992). Lesbian recovering alcoholics: A qualitative study of identity transformation—A report on research and applications to treatment. In D. L. Weinstein (Ed.), *Lesbian and gay men: Chemical dependence and treatment issues* (pp. 93–104). New York, NY: The Haworth Press.

Miller, G. (2005). *Learning the language of addiction counseling*. Hoboken, NJ: Wiley.

Moradi, B., Mohr, J. J., Worthington, R. L., & Fassinger, R. E. (2009). Counseling psychology research on sexual (orientation) minority issues: Conceptual and methodological challenges and opportunities. *Journal of Counseling Psychology, 56,* 5-22.

Pride Institute. (2006). *The Pride Institute*. Retrieved from http://www.pride-institute.com

Prochaska, J. O., & Norcross, J. C. (2002). Stages of change. In J. C. Norcross (Ed.), *Psychotherapy relationships that work: Therapist contributions and responsiveness to patients* (pp. 303–313). New York, NY: Oxford University Press.

Ratts, M., D'Andrea, M., & Arredondo, P. (2004, July). Social justice counseling: Fifth force in counseling. *Counseling Today*, pp. 28–30.

Rutherford, K., McIntyre, J., Daley, A., & Ross, L., E. (2012). Development of expertise in mental health service provision for lesbian, gay, bisexual and transgender communities. *Medical Education, 46*(9), 903–913. doi:10.1111/j.1365-2923.2012.04272.x

Saghir, M. T., Robins, E., Walbran, B., & Gentry, K. A. (1970). Psychiatric disorders and disability in the female homosexual. *American Journal of Psychiatry, 127,* 147–154.

Senreich, E. (2010). Are specialized LGBT program components helpful for gay and bisexual men in substance abuse treatment? *Substance Use & Misuse, 45*(7-8), 1077–1096. doi:10.3109/10826080903483855

Singh, A. A. (2012, March). Transgender youth of color and resilience: Negotiating oppression, finding support. *Sex Roles: A Journal of Research,* pp. 1–13.

Singh, A. A., Boyd, C. J., & Whitman, J. S. (2010). Counseling competency with transgender and intersex individuals. In J. Cornish, L. Nadkarni, B. Schreier, & E. Rodolfa (Eds.), *Handbook of multicultural competencies* (pp. 415–442). New York, NY: Wiley & Sons.

Singh, A. A., & Burnes, T. R. (2010). Shifting the counselor role from gatekeeping to advocacy: Ten strategies for using the *ACA Competencies for Counseling with Transgender Clients* into counseling, practice, research, and advocacy. *Journal of LGBTQ Issues in Counseling, 3/4,* 126–134.

Singh, A. A., Hays, D. G., & Watson, L. (2011). The resilience experiences of transgender individuals. *Journal of Counseling and Development, 89*(1), 20–27.

Substance Abuse and Mental Health Services Administration. (2012). *A provider's introduction to substance abuse treatment for lesbian, gay, bisexual, and transgender individuals* (DHHS Publication No. SMA 03-3819). Rockville, MD: Author.

Szymanski, D. M., Kashubeck-West, S., & Meyer, J. (2008). Internalized heterosexim: A historical and theoretical overview. *The Counseling Psychologist, 36*(4), 510–524.

Trocki, K. F., Drabble, L., & Midanik, L. (2005). Use of heavier drinking contexts among heterosexuals, homosexuals and bisexuals: Results from a national household probability survey. *Journal of Studies on Alcohol, 66,* 105–110.

Trocki, K. F., Drabble, L., & Midanik, L. (2009). Tobacco, marijuana use and sensation-seeking: Comparisons across gay, lesbian, bisexual and heterosexual groups. *Psychology of Addictive Behavior, 23*(4), 620–631.

Troiden, R. R. (1998). *Gay and lesbian identity: A sociological analysis.* New York, NY: General Hall.

Ungvarski, P. J., & Grossman, A. H. (1999). Health problems of gay and bisexual men. *Nursing Clinics of North America, 34,* 313–326.

Watkins, K., Hunter, S., Hepner, K., Paddock, S., Zhou, A., & de la Cruz, E. (2012). Group cognitive-behavioral therapy for clients with major depression in residential substance abuse treatment. *Psychiatric Services, 63*(6), 608–611. doi:10.1176/appi.ps.201100201

Weinburg, M. S., & Williams, C. J. (1974). *Male homosexuals: Their problems and adaptations.* New York, NY: Oxford University Press.

Chapter 20

Inpatient and Outpatient Addiction Treatment

Richard J. Cicchetti
Walden University

Gary M. Szirony
Walden University

INTRODUCTION

As the field of addiction treatment continues to rely upon more evidence-based intervention, clients can benefit from inpatient services, outpatient services, or a combination of both (Ducharme, Knudsen, Roman, & Johnson, 2007). Individuals presenting with substance use and addiction disorders can be referred from a variety of sources. To guide inpatient placement into an inpatient setting, outpatient setting, or a combination of both, screening and diagnosis is followed by assessing six dimensions of patient characteristics of pertinent biopsychosocial aspects of addiction. These dimensions, also known as *problem areas,* have been found to be salient to the formation of an effective individualized plan for treatment. Immediate and long-term needs are considered in determining treatment options from a variety of possible interventions. Considered to be the last step in a multidimensional assessment, the choice and intensity of services are intended to match an *individualized treatment plan* (ITP). The intent is to help clinicians determine treatment planning by these criteria rather than by insurance reimbursement limitations, ideology, or other nonpatient-oriented criteria.

According to Substance Abuse and Mental Health Services Administration (SAMHSA) (2009), most referrals for treatment come through the criminal justice system. Understanding the options, choices, benefits, and challenges to both inpatient and outpatient treatment are essential for clinicians. When clinicians work with clients who have substance abuse issues, many times clients are referred to inpatient settings. Since inpatient substance abuse rehabilitation can significantly alter a client's life, counselors need to know how to help clients by making effective choices that best serve the client. They need to be familiar with addiction rehabilitation treatment options, sources, and referral choices in an effort to reduce recidivism and curb the excessive impact of addiction. The impact of substance abuse and treatment is staggering, affecting individuals, families, friends, community, and the world of work. The economic cost to society is in the billions. Substance abuse rehabilitation might remain a mystery for many counselors, as they have not experienced it themselves; therefore, the first half of the chapter will discuss:

- Levels of care
- How a clinician best makes a decision for inpatient versus outpatient treatment
- The tools used to make this determination
- How a counselor might determine if a client is truly interested in treatment, or cleansing to continue use

- How to determine the right inpatient treatment setting
- How rehabilitation centers might work with dually diagnosed clients
- What clients, families, and referring clinicians might expect during inpatient treatment, and what challenges the inpatient setting might incur when working with clients
- What clients, clinicians, and family might expect as follow-up services after inpatient treatment
- Recidivism rates for those entering inpatient treatment

The second half of the chapter will examine:

- Rehabilitation treatment versus incarceration/prison
- The perceptions of Americans regarding rehabilitation versus prison
- Historical perspective of drug policies in the United States
- Cost of federal and state prison for each year versus treatment
- Recidivism rates for prison versus treatment
- Other options to prison
- Loss of freedoms for ex-felons
- Advocacy and societal errors in rehabilitation

INPATIENT TREATMENT

Levels of Care

A *continuum of care* refers to "a treatment system in which clients enter treatment at a level appropriate to their needs and then step up to a more intense treatment or down to less intense treatment as needed" (Center for Substance Abuse Treatment [CSAT], 2005, p. 17). An effective continuum of care consists of a series of levels. Various systems can be used to assess levels of care appropriate to particular individuals with substance use problems. The term *level of care* refers to a series of points within a continuum of care, providing consistency and flexibility in the spectrum, intensity and duration of addiction treatment (CSAT, 2005). For example, the Center for Substance Abuse Treatment (CSAT, 2005), an agency with SAMHSA, consists of categorizing levels of care into a classification system consisting of basic, intermediate, advanced, and fully integrated treatment approaches. The basic approach provides treatment for a single disorder, but screens for other disorders. The intermediate level addresses two disorders, but focuses on one primary disorder. The advanced level provides services for both disorders in an integrated manner. A fully integrated program provides treatment for multiple disorders by the same clinicians trained in multiple treatment strategies, and is primarily intended for comorbid use of substances combined with mental diagnoses.

One of the most commonly employed systems, known as the *ASAM Patient Placement Criteria (PPC)*, consists of five levels of care. The ASAM PPC comes from the American Society of Addiction Medicine's Patient Placement Criteria (ASAM). Levels of care are organized by the degree to which medical management, structure, security, and treatment intensity are required. Treatment matching occurs at three levels: admission, continued stay, and discharge. The second edition of the ASAM, revised to include criteria for co-occurring substance use and mental health disorders, can also help to determine the needs of patients with dual diagnoses, providing a broad range of incorporating a multidimensional approach. The validity and cost-effectiveness of the ASAM PPC are supported, although the PPC's decision tree has been described as complex and sophisticated (Gastfriend & Mee-Lee, 2011).

Levels are assessed through qualitative assessment of each dimension. For example, in dimension one, intoxication or withdrawal potential, at the early intervention level (0.5), the patient would not be seen as presenting at risk of withdrawal. Dimension two for that same early intervention level would result in no biomedical conditions or complications, with the patient being diagnosed as stable. In dimension three of the first level, emotional, behavioral, cognitive conditions, or complications would also be seen as none or very stable. Dimension four is used to assess readiness to change. As an example, in the early intervention level (0.5), the patient would be seen as willing to explore how drug use could affect personal goals. Dimension five of that same first level, an assessment of relapse, continued use, or continued problem potential will result in a patient needing an explanation or understanding of the skills necessary to change. The last dimension, dimension six, assessing the recovery environment, would be rated at that first level (0.5) as the patient having a deleterious social support network and other factors that would increase the risk of personal conflict about substance use (Mee-Lee, Shulman, & Fishman, 2001). Each risk dimension is called *The Multidimensional Risk Profile*. Each risk description provides both a numeric and narrative description of risk in terms of signs and symptoms that indicate severity of level of function in each dimension.

Originally, and until about 2001, ASAM and other institutions recommended bundling of care for those who had substance abuse issues (Lee & Schulman, 2003). *Bundling of care* describes an approach that combines or encompasses many services included for a client. For example, a client might go to an agency to receive services for a combination of issues associated with substance abuse. The problem with bundling is many times the services required by a client are not available at an agency, or a client has to wait to receive services. This can leave a client frustrated and contribute to relapse. Realizing this might not be the most efficient and effective manner to serve a client, around 2001 ASAM began recommending services to be unbundled. The benefit of unbundling services has benefit in that the client receives treatment based on the needs of the client, rather than being limited to what is provided by an agency. This approach meant clients would now seek services required, when required, avoiding the problem of long waiting lists for services. Clients who were ready for change could seek immediate treatment.

The philosophy behind bundling was that clients would benefit from treatment beyond the substance abuse issues alone, extending into associated medical, psychological, social, vocational, and legal problems as well. Treating substance abuse issues might be similar to any other emotional or physical discomfort. Thus, the ASAM criteria was created for the purpose of outlining outcome-based and results-oriented care in the treatment of addiction (American Society of Addiction Medicine [ASAM], 2014). The criteria consisted of principles ASAM recognized as important for potential treatment success. Those principles were goals of treatment, individualized treatment plans, choice of treatment levels, continuum of care, progressing through levels of care, length of stay, clinical versus reimbursement considerations, and treatment failure. Once the principles were identified, this led to the identification of problem areas, which were important for creating an effective ITP, along with identifying patient placement options (Mee-Lee et al., 2001).

The problem areas identified by ASAM are referred to as *assessment dimensions,* which can be used when creating an ITP. The six ASAM dimensions are Acute Intoxication and/or Withdrawal Potential; Biomedical Conditions and Complications; Emotional, Behavioral, or Cognitive Conditions and Complications; Readiness to Change; Relapse, Continued Use, or Continued Problem Potential; and Recovery Environment (see Table 20.1). The goal is to assess clients within each dimension on an independent basis, and to assess based upon how one dimension might relate to another dimension. For example, when examining acute intoxication or withdrawal potential within the recovery environment, it might be determined, because of a client's

TABLE 20.1 ASAM Dimensions

Dimension	Criterion
1	Acute Intoxication and/or Withdrawal Potential
2	Biomedical Conditions and Complications
3	Emotional, Behavioral, or Cognitive Conditions and Complications
4	Readiness to Change
5	Relapse, Continued Use, or Continued Problem Potential
6	Recovery Environment

greater likelihood of intoxication and lack of a supportive social system, that the client might best be served in a Level III.1—a Clinically Managed Low Intensity Residential setting. This is a setting where the client receives a structured treatment program by clinically trained personnel with a minimum of 5 hours of individual or group sessions per week.

When a clinician anticipates a client's need for inpatient treatment, one of the requirements is to ensure the patient is placed in the proper treatment setting. This process is referred to as "placement matching." Modality matching describes a specific treatment approach whereby the modality meets the specific needs of the client (2003). Without matching, chances are good the client will not receive the most appropriate treatment for her or his substance use or related issue(s), possibly contributing to relapse (Lee & Schulman, 2003). As a result, ASAM proposed a system of levels of care.

As noted earlier, different systems can be used to assess levels of care appropriate to individuals with substance use problems. According to ASAM, the most widely accepted method consists of five levels of care. The levels range from the least intensive form of treatment, Level 0.5, Early Intervention, to the most intensive Level IV, Medically Managed Intensive Inpatient Treatment (see Table 20.2).

Within each ASAM level beginning with Level I, decimal ratings indicate intensity sublevel of treatment required. The sublevels range from .1 to .9, with the higher range requiring more intensive treatment within the level. In the following, we will discuss the various levels and ranges of care. The first level is *Level 0.5, Early Intervention*. In this level, intervention services are provided for clients at risk or those who might have a substance-related problem. In this initial stage, there is rarely sufficient information to effectively diagnose a substance-related issue. This is a discovery stage in which information is gathered to make a determination for further diagnosis. That information could come from intake interviews, assessments, interviews with family and other members of a client's support system, records from clinicians, or from other health care providers.

TABLE 20.2 American Society of Addiction Medicine's Patient Placement Criteria (ASAM) Levels of Care

No.	Level	ASAM Levels of Care
1	Level 0.5	Early Intervention
2	Level I	Outpatient Treatment
3	Level II	Intensive Outpatient or Partial Hospitalization
4	Level III	Residential or Inpatient
5	Level IV	Medically Managed Inpatient Care

The next level, Level I, *Outpatient Treatment*, consists of nonresidential services, which are organized and can be delivered in a variety of settings. Clinicians trained in the field of substance abuse or other mental health professionals will provide evaluations and various modes of treatment. This is in the form of scheduled sessions, which might include individual and group settings, and are usually established topics or issues related to the client's level of discomfort. Medical interventions might also be included. The basic tenet of Level I is to work with the client on his/her level of severity and to aid in achieving desired goals in relation to his/her substance use behaviors and mental functioning. The scope of services includes behavioral issues, attitude issues, and lifestyle of the client. The goal is to work with the client to identify issues that might trigger use, work through these discomforts, and identify required tools that will aid in the ability to live without self-medicating, replacing dysfunctional systems with functional, healthier systems. Recently, Level I has been adapted to include those who are dually diagnosed with substance use and mental health disorders, clients who might not be motivated, mandated clients, and clients who previously had agreed to intensive treatment approaches. The adaptation acknowledges approaches such as stages of change, motivational interviewing, and solution-focused brief therapy (SFBT). These therapeutic interventions might be appropriate for those clients who are possibly in denial, or are deemed unmotivated for treatment. The intent is to keep clients in treatment, and thus improve chances of recovery (Klostermann & O'Farrell, 2013; Miller & Rollnick, 2012; Tryon & Winograd, 2011).

Level II is *Intensive Outpatient Treatment*. This is usually in an outpatient setting and can be delivered before or after work and school, during weekdays, or on weekends. Programs in this level might provide biopsychosocial evaluations, co-creation of treatment plans with clients, and the development of measurable goals and objectives. Many times these programs will have case managers who work with clients to obtain required social supports such as vocational rehabilitation, child care, and transportation to and from the setting. The daily program can be as long as 6 hours and can include treatment as well as psychoeducational classes, delivered in individual or group settings. Clients can apply what they have learned in real-life settings. Psychiatric and medical consultation, physical examinations, psychopharmacological consults, medication management, and access to a 24-hour crisis line might also be arranged in this type of programming.

Level III, *Residential Inpatient Treatment*, is a 24-hour residential (live-in) setting in which services are provided by mental health professionals and addiction treatment counselors. Inpatient treatment consists of a regimented style of care in which the client is required to obey a given set of procedures and policies. Staff remains on site 24 hours a day. Within Level III are four areas of programs. As discussed earlier, the higher the level of care, the more intense the treatment program. The main tenet of Level III's residential treatment programming is to provide a safe, stable living environment in an effort to help the client co-create, develop, and enhance recovery skills. Table 20.3 lists sublevels within Level III.

TABLE 20.3 Sublevels Within Level III

Sublevel	Treatment Modality
Level III.1	Clinically Managed Low-Intensity Residential Treatment
Level III.3	Clinically Managed Medium-Intensity Residential Treatment
Level III.5	Clinically Managed High-Intensity Residential Treatment
Level III.7	Medically Monitored Inpatient Treatment

Level IV, *Medically Managed Intensive Inpatient Treatment*, is designed to provide 24-hour medically managed evaluation and treatment. Clients in this level are often diagnosed with substance use and mental health related issues. Staffing at Level IV can include psychiatrists, nurses, primary care physicians, substance abuse counselors, and other mental health clinicians who work in an integrated team setting with the client. Services can include substance abuse counseling, hospital services, psychiatric services, and medical services if required. These integrated services allow for comprehensive treatment of biomedical conditions the client might be experiencing or issues that need to be addressed.

Types of Inpatient Services

According to SAMHSA (Lee & Schulman, 2003), some clients require only detoxification, while others might require detoxification with inpatient treatment. This section will describe the various classifications of detoxification, along with the requirements for each classification. Ambulatory Detoxification with Extended On Site Monitoring is a Level II-D classification, meaning that the client is not at this moment in need of inpatient services, is experiencing moderate discomforts from detoxification, and is able to go home to family and social support, with 24-hour assistance at the ready, if required.

The next, Levels of Detoxification, which are Level III and Level IV, require an Inpatient Treatment Setting. Clinically Managed Residential Detoxification is at Level III.2-D, where a client might be experiencing moderated symptoms of withdrawal, requiring all-day support to complete detoxification. The client in this sublevel requires continue treatment for recovery. In Level III.7D, Medically Monitored Inpatient Detoxification, a client is experiencing withdrawal symptoms that are severe and requires 24-hour nursing aid and periodic visits from a physician. Usually, if the client does not obtain this assistance, detoxification is not successful. The final classification of detoxification is Level IV- D, Medically Managed Inpatient Detoxification. This level diagnoses a client experiencing severe withdrawal symptoms and possibly unstable medical conditions related to detoxification. Nursing monitoring is required 24 hours a day, physician visits daily as required, and medical assistance is possibly needed to achieve detoxification.

This section will explore Levels III and IV of Inpatient Treatment along with details of each classification. In Level III.1, Clinically Managed Low Intensity Residential, the client receives a structured treatment program by clinically trained personnel with a minimum of 5 hours of individual or group sessions per week. Level III.3, Clinically Managed Medical, Intensity Residential Treatment, consists of 24 hours of structured care with trained counseling professionals. Multi-dimensional treatment is provided to stabilize dangers associated with substance abuse and withdrawal. The program consists of less intense treatment for those with some cognitive or other disabilities, whereby a more intensive treatment setting might not be beneficial. Level III.5 is also a 24-hour structured Residential Treatment program consisting of a more intensive inpatient and group setting offered by trained professional counselors. Other portions of the program consist of stabilization designed to reduce the threat of imminent danger associated with substance abuse and preparation for outpatient treatment. Level III.7 is an even more intense Residential setting, where 24-hour nursing and physician care is available for detoxification. In this level, professionally trained counselors, psychologists, and psychiatrists might be on staff to work with clients regarding substance abuse related issues, biopsychosocial issues, and preparation for treatment. The highest level, Level IV, Medically Managed Intensive Impatient Treatment, is a program for those who require daily physician care, 24-hour nursing care, counseling care for those who experience unstable issues related to detoxification, substance abuse, and other biopsychosocial issues.

Clinician Determination of Inpatient Treatment

Bernstein et al. (1998) posited an approach that could be used by hospital emergency departments in the care of patients with substance use and behavioral disorders. Noting that millions visit emergent care centers each year due to substance use or behavioral disorders, creating a strain on the health care system, the high patient volumes and limited capacity to treat these individuals can be daunting and might not be sustainable. Instead, the authors suggested an approach known as **S**creening, **B**rief **I**ntervention, and **R**eferral to **T**reatment, or SBIRT. The three-step SBIRT (approach typically takes between 5 and 10 minutes, beginning with a brief screening instrument or questionnaire, most commonly the Substance Abuse Subtle Screening Inventory (SASSI) (Miller, 1985), the Michigan Alcohol Screening Test (MAST) (Selzer, 1971), or the Drug Abuse Screening Test (DAST) (Skinner, 1982). Brief Intervention can incorporate principles of Motivational Interviewing (MI) in combination with humanistic approaches including empathy, reflective listening, and behavioral aspects of positive reframing. Intervention can begin at the time of screening or later. Benefits of a system such as SBIRT include cost-effectiveness and rapid intervention in dealing with individuals facing emergent care. This approach could become a coordinated effort by health care systems, providing the opportunity to improve the health of millions (Babor et al., 2007; Bernstein & D'Onofrio, 2013; Kraemer, 2007). The SBIRT phases can be seen in Table 20.4 and in the diagram seen in Figure 20.1 – The SBIRT Cycle.

TABLE 20.4 SBIRT Phases

SBIRT	Phases	SBIRT Component
1	Screening	Screen for alcohol use/drug use; alcohol problems/drug problems; risk factors. Determines if intervention is needed using a validated brief questionnaire, such as the MAST, DAST, SASSI
2	Brief Intervention	Can involve Motivational Interviewing (MI) in combination with humanistic approaches including empathy, reflective listening, and behavioral aspects of positive reframing
3	Referral to Treatment	For moderate- to high-risk assessment, referral to inpatient or outpatient setting may result

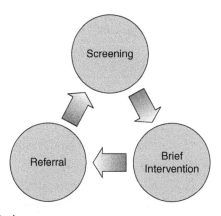

FIGURE 20.1 The SBIRT Cycle.

When a clinician anticipates that a client might be in need of inpatient treatment, the requirements as previously stated in the chapter are to match the client with the proper Inpatient Treatment Setting and Modality to ensure the patient receives a specific treatment approach that meets his or her specific needs (Lee & Schulman, 2003). The clinician most likely will conduct a biopsychosocial intake, obtain a client release to talk to members of the family or other members of the client's social support network, and use other assessments such as the MAST, SASSI, DAST, Alcohol Use Inventory (AUI), Addiction Severity Index (ASI), or the Minnesota Multiphasic Personality Inventory-2 (MMPI-2) to determine if a problem exists, and to help assess the severity of the problem. To aid in determining a proper Inpatient Treatment Setting and Modality, clinicians and other health care professionals might rely on the ASAM PPC.

Use of Motivational Interviewing to Assess Readiness to Change

MI can be used in the identification of motivation to change in persons with substance use disorders and can be helpful in making decisions related to the required level of care. It is crucial, according to McKay and Sturmhofel (2011), to identify the most desirable incentive that will lead to active engagement in treatment and remaining in therapy. MI is a directive, person-centered approach that has been shown to be effective in enhancing intrinsic motivation to change (Miller & Rollnick, 2012; Moyers & Rollnick, 2002). Based on Prochaska and DiClemente's five-stage model (Prochaska, Norcross, & DiClemente, 2013), MI can be used as a guideline in working with individuals who may be considering change, but display ambivalence at early stages of change, and to help determine at which stage of motivation the client might be at the time. (See Table 20.4.)

Clients presenting for substance use treatment hail from a variety of referral sources, as mentioned earlier. Determining whether a client is ready for services or is interested in and motivated toward change can be challenging. DiClemente & Prochaska (1982) presented the Transtheoretical Model of Change, an approach initially designed to help determine at which stage an individual might be in relation to preparation to change. Within this model, five levels or stages were identified. Those stages were (1) Precontemplation, (2) Contemplation, (3) Preparation, (4) Action, and (5) Maintenance. In the first stage, Precontemplation, individuals generally display no intent to change. In the Contemplation stage, people were most likely to respond to feedback and education as sources of information regarding aspects of change. The Preparation stage is committed to changing, seeking a plan of action. Within the Action and Maintenance stages, people actively pursue change, including the environments that so strongly deter change. Those who had relapsed were found to cycle back into earlier stages as they geared up to quit again. Application of these stages to rehabilitation can be seen in Table 20.5. Based on this

TABLE 20.5 Importance of Transtheoretical Stages to Rehabilitation

Motivational Interviewing Stages

Stage	Description
1 Precontemplation	No intended change behavior
2 Contemplation	Awareness of problem with no commitment to change
3 Preparation	Intent to change
4 Action	Steps taken to modify behavior
5 Maintenance	Continuing commitment to and action toward change

research, counselors can better understand not only how people change, but also how to assist those who desire to change habits, and in particular, addictive behaviors.

Van Horn and Bux (2001) tested MI as a brief therapeutic approach in an inpatient setting with dual diagnoses. Active substance abuse and psychiatric conditions were common among the participants. The thought behind the research was to take advantage of group psychotherapy interventions in order to facilitate inpatient diagnosis and treatment aimed in large part at cost containment and efficacy. The authors test piloted an MI group and found the group to be proactive and engaged. Addressing ambivalence was a major concern, and the results of the study seemed to support the fact that one of the benefits involved client exploration of ambivalence regarding motivation to change.

Challenges Facing Rehabilitation Centers

According to van Wormer and Davis (2013), given the large percentage of individuals with substance use and addiction problems, "most of them will never step foot in a treatment center" (p. 11). For those who do, less than half obtain funding from insurance sources (Buck, 2010). Treatment centers have faced several challenges over the years, and although the horizon is changing, many still do today. According to Buck (2010), the majority of addiction treatment centers have operated predominately in the specialty sector, outside of bounds of conventional medical settings. Treatment for addiction disorders was reported to have occurred more than twice as often in rehabilitation centers than in private physician offices (SAMHSA, 2010a). Most addiction treatment is delivered through private, not-for-profit facilities or through government treatment centers. Funding problems have challenged substance use treatment for years, relegating care to individuals who were limited in licensure or training. Described by Broome, Knight, Joe, and Flynn (2012) as a "constellation of challenges" (p. 4), focusing on clinical activities, average duration of stay, and counseling hours, the primary significant predictor of costs associated with treatment center programming was found to be estimated counselors' time spent conducting counseling sessions. Although higher costs were found to be associated with longer treatment stays, the authors supported the importance of treatment matching. According to Mark, Levit, Vandivort-Warren, Buck, and Coffey (2011), factors facing rehabilitation centers included limited funding, spending patterns, and policy. Others factors can include public perception, staffing, proximity, and availability. Recent changes in legislation have had and are likely to continue to have an effect on treatment options. The Mental Health Parity and Addiction Equity Act and the Affordable Care Act, however, may have a more positive effect on substance use treatment and care.

In their research, Mark et al. (2011) noted the rise in treatment spending over that last decade or so, with Medicaid's share growing from 17% in 1986 to 28% in 2005, although as a share of all health spending, mental health and substance use spending grew at a slightly slower rate than the gross domestic product. The potential for the new legislation to improve access to behavioral health services and help to increase spending on treatment is hopeful. Mark et al. described the impact of the Affordable Care Act in conjunction with the Mental Health Parity Act as having what they termed "tremendous potential" (p. 284) to improve access to health care for millions who previously had spending caps or limits on their psychiatric and substance use insurance benefits.

Jiménez, Lam, Marot, and Delgado (2004) noted length of stay to be a salient factor in relation to efficiency in psychiatric inpatient treatment. However, in a recent study by Shaffer, Hartman, Listwan, Howell, and Latessa (2011), even though the drug court model and the concern over type of drug of choice have prevailed, recidivism rates do not seem to be correlated with type of drug used. Although individuals who have shorter wait times tended to stay longer in programs, wait time is inversely proportional to length of stay. Attempts toward increases in quality of addiction services also seemed to result in shorter wait times, possibly contributing to increased length of stay. However, longer lengths of stay do not seem to be associated with better outcomes (Harris, Kivlahan, Barnett, & Finney, 2012). In spite of efforts, recidivism rates remain high (Travis, 2005).

Client Inpatient Experience

A client inpatient experience might vary based on level of care and whether administered in a public or private sector. Any client is free to leave at any time. Most public inpatient treatment programs serve mostly the indigent, the uninsured, or the underinsured. Medicaid and private insurance may be accepted, but most funding is underwritten from local, state, and federal assistance programs. There can be a waiting list of at least 6 months based on the community, public sector funding, available space in a program, and/or services required. A typical inpatient program is 28 days in length. In some cases, the program might be longer if detoxification is required. The program can also be shorter, 10 days once stabilized, with transfer to an intensive outpatient program. The outpatient program might be in a residential treatment center if living arrangements are required or a community-based intensive outpatient treatment center (SAMHSA, 2010b).

Many of the public programs are generic in nature, meaning they are not client specific to individuated needs. Clients might be housed in a dorm setting or in a room with three to four beds. Clients are not encouraged to bring personal belongings, although some treatment centers will allow clients to bring personal belongings as long as they are stored in a padlocked footlocker. Services might include medically monitored or managed detoxification at a hospital setting, followed by transfer to an inpatient setting. Based on level of care, dually diagnosed versus single diagnosis, movement might be restricted and regimented. Many settings are not fully staffed 24 hours per day, 7 days per week. Programs might be generic in nature, consisting of substance abuse psychoeducation classes, individual, and group sessions. The program might not be holistic in nature, as one might find in a private inpatient center.

Private inpatient center programs can generally range from 30 to 90 days, depending on the level of care required by the client. This may or may not include detoxification, which is contingent on whether an agency supplies the services. If not, a program might include another 5–10 days for detoxification. Programs might be fully or partially covered through private insurance. Some private treatment centers might accept Medicaid. Others might not. Many accept Medicare and associated supplemental insurance plans.

FIRST STEP Upon entering the facility, in the initial phase, a client will most likely meet with a clinician, one who will be in charge of the treatment program. The next process is usually a quick medical evaluation, followed by more introductions and being escorted to a dorm room for the night. The next day, a room might be assigned, where a client is encouraged to bring personal belongings and pictures of loved ones. The purpose of the program is to be very structured to aid in creating a disciplined routine and boundaries. Most programs do not allow correspondence via email, but calling is usually permitted after the first week to 10 days.

The next portion of treatment is the active phase. In this active cycle, a client will have access to and utilize various treatment modalities and services. These services within the active cycle can include some or all of the following treatment components, presented via individual and/or group counseling sessions:

- Learning about the physical and psychological aspects of addiction
- Identifying and learning to work through addiction triggers
- Exercise routines, eating healthy, and medication.
- Coping skills, social skills, working through anger and grief of addiction.
- Stress and anger management.
- Activities of daily living, including cleaning one's room, doing laundry, and completing assigned chores.

Sleeping is regimented and relationships are forbidden. In the final phase, sometimes referred to as the "release" or "discharge cycle," preparation for release from inpatient treatment is initiated. Plans are created for an aftercare program. Referral to an outpatient community or residential treatment center serves as a central component of this final phase. Housing, education, and work issues are addressed. Educational advancement, such as completing a GED or pursuing a college degree, or job training and placement are often considered as part of the discharge cycle. Goals and plans for reentry are set. Fears and apprehensions are discussed with clinicians in group or individual settings.

REFERRING CLINICIAN AND FAMILY ROLES A referring clinician's role is often limited while a client is in inpatient therapy. A clinician might be asked by an agency to share any significant case notes, which could be beneficial in treatment. Of course, the client is required to sign a release of information. Some agencies with permission from the client might give the clinician updates in the treatment progress of the client. Some might give the client a discharge plan to review with the outpatient clinician, and there might be an instance where the referring clinician is not asked for input, given updates, or involved in any aspect of the inpatient treatment.

Families are encouraged to visit and to become involved with the client through phone calls and participation in family group counseling sessions. The family also might be working through anger, grief, and feelings of helplessness associated with the loved one's addiction. During this time, the family might be "walking on eggshells" with fear that the loved one might drop out, leaving the program prematurely. Families are encouraged to prepare the home for the return of the loved one, include searching for and removing any "stashes" the loved one left behind, ridding the home of any alcohol or unused prescription drugs. Many families start attending support groups to learn about their roles associated with the loved one's addiction, how to set boundaries, and how to build healthy communication patterns.

WHAT CLIENT, CLINICIAN, AND FAMILY MIGHT EXPERIENCE AFTER INPATIENT REFERRAL After inpatient referral, clients might experience periods of feeling lost, lonely, and sometimes depressed. They might also have difficulty sleeping—some have experienced night sweats and periods of hyperanxiety. Clients are encouraged to reconnect with their clinicians to schedule regular counseling sessions. They are encouraged to discuss their recovery programs with their families and employers. Clients should not be too quick to jump back into family routines and employment, although they can include this into their recovery plan. The key is for them not to feel overwhelmed. Many treatment centers encourage clients to attend 12-step meetings and find a sponsor. Clients should create time for meditation or relaxation, finding or reacquainting with friends who do not use. They should discover new area of pleasure, acknowledge their accomplishments, but avoid becoming overconfident.

Family members might feel apprehensive about asking the loved one questions about treatment. It is all right to ask, but not to push. Families can set boundaries, discuss expectations, and reinforce consequences for actions. They should use language that is supportive and be aware of not coming off as authoritarian. Families might also notice their loved ones are more assertive, not requiring as much caring or enabling. Treatment, or the whole of addiction itself, might be a very new experience for loved ones, so patience is valued. Families might also become involved in family therapy and can participate in continued support groups.

For clinicians, there are many factors that complicate addiction treatment. Clients can come back motivated to continue with their treatment, but also might be experiencing the feeling of being the expert because of having gone through treatment. Clients might be one moment very agreeable and the next, somewhat challenging. Clinicians might need to stay in contact with clients if they start missing sessions, become too overconfident, or notice old patterns starting to emerge.

CASE STUDY

The following demonstrates what a counselor might be faced with when referring for detox treatment, inpatient, or intensive outpatient therapy.

Jane is a 39-year-old divorced female who works in a large law office. She stops on her way home each week to meet with associates from work for dinner and a few drinks. On the way home, feeling drowsy, she loses control of her car and slides off the road, barely avoiding a major collision. The incident serves as a personal wakeup call and results in her seeking counseling through her employer's Employee Assistance Program (EAP). She contacts your counseling center. After reviewing the intake forms and completing a brief intake interview, you note that she is taking hydrocodone p.r.n. for back pain related to extensive computer work on her job at the law office, a selective serotonin reuptake inhibitor (SSRI) for depression; she also reports taking ibuprofen for frequent headaches. During the initial intake interview, you additionally ascertain that she has no pets, no longer plays tennis due to the back pain, has some family living a considerable distance away, but does enjoy watching TV. She agrees to begin the three counseling sessions covered by her EAP, but does not seem overly enthusiastic. The following week, your counseling center makes a routine reminder call to the patient and confirms that she does plan to attend, but is having second thoughts, wondering what the counseling sessions would actually accomplish. What might be your next step? What approach would be helpful? What stage of change does she seem to be in? Think about your options in recommending treatment: detox, inpatient, intensive outpatient therapy, a combination of inpatient or outpatient treatment options, or continue with limited EAP sessions. How best can you make that determination? What tools might be helpful in ascertaining the best route to take with Jane?

OUTPATIENT TREATMENT

In this section, we will explore the historical perspectives of substance use and addiction. Issues covered will include:

- Perception of the population regarding treatment versus prison.
- Cost to federal and state prisons versus treatment. Recidivism rate for prison versus treatment.

- Cost to society for families who have loved ones in prison.
- Cost for court cost for drug offender cases.
- How many families seek federal assistance when loved one is sent to prison.
- Advocacy and societal errors in the past.

Drug and Alcohol Legislation Affecting Treatment

For decades, the policies of alcohol or other drug treatment (AOD), abolition or control, in the United States have been dictated by political ideology and governmental policy. This can be traced back to the temperance movement in the early 1800s, the federal government's role in banning importation of opium by Chinese immigrants in 1887, and the ongoing "war on drugs." The temperance movement established alcohol as an inherently addictive substance, which weakened the moral centers of the brain, reduced a drinker's control over her or his behavior, promoted animalistic behavior, and weakened the entire moral and mental faculties of the country (Levine, 1984). Pressures from temperance groups led to the passage of prohibition laws in many states. Although these laws were eventually overturned, the tone of the evils of alcohol had been firmly established in the United States. Despite countless efforts, alcohol use is at an all-time high (Cooper, 2012).

The U.S. war on drugs policy has also dictated treatment. Currently, the accepted practice of treatment for drug and alcohol abuse and dependence is abstinence. This theory of treatment is the predominant format taught to many counselors for the treatment of a client who has a substance use problem, although defining abstinence as treatment is questionable at best (Pattison, 1966). Driven by U.S. ideology, treatment centers and private practitioners cater to clients who rely on federal subsidies, use an abstinence-based treatment program, or they are not be reimbursed for their clients' treatment (Denning, 2000).

From the Anti-Drug Abuse Act of 1986 and beyond, minimum sentences for the distribution of cocaine and crack cocaine were mandated, resulting in higher incarceration rates. Shortly thereafter, the law became more inclusive, dictating mandatory minimum 5-year sentences for anyone in possession of cocaine, which included first-time offenders and those convicted of intent to sell or distribute (Humphreys & Rappaport, 1993). During the early 2000s, Attorney General John Ashcroft, who was appointed by President George W. Bush, made a determination resulting in stricter enforcement of mandatory minimum sentencing requirements: "the Ashcroft Justice Department demands the harshest prison terms and goes out of its way to track federal judges who do not give them" (von Zielbauer, 2003, p. 1). Penalties for manufactured drugs were made stricter. For example:

- Conviction was now possible for a drug offense involving 5 grams of crack cocaine or 500 grams of powdered cocaine, resulting in at least 5 years in prison.
- Conviction of a drug offense involving 50 grams of crack or 5,000 grams of powdered cocaine can result in a minimum of 10 years in prison.
- Possession of more than 5 grams of crack would result in a felony conviction punishable by at least 5 years in prison.

Public perception can be based on the laws enacted, which are perceived to protect, even though public opinion might not be in favor of the legislation. For example, in 1982, less than 2% of the public viewed drugs as the most important issue facing the nation, yet President Ronald Reagan at the time began to push the war on drugs to new levels (Rock, 2003). From this momentum to the current day war or drugs, much of what is provided for in addiction intervention has been and continues to be driven by political action and social perception.

Alex Ashcroft, then 25, and his brother Adam, 19, were arrested and charged with production and possession of marijuana after police raided their home in January 1992. A housemate, Kevin Sheely, then 24, was also arrested. Officials said approximately 60 marijuana plants were found growing in a basement crawl space, and growlights, irrigation, and security systems were also discovered. Although growing more than 50 plants often triggers federal prosecution, and results in jail time—thanks to federal mandatory minimum sentencing laws John Ashcroft fought to toughen as senator—Alex Ashcroft was prosecuted on a state charge and received probation (Forbes, 2001).

As with many mandates or laws, evaluation of the effectiveness or lack thereof is not determined until years later. As the data are collected regarding people imprisoned for drug offenses, research on effectiveness of incarceration, and the cost associated to states and the federal government, evaluations are made and public opinion is heard. Each year from 2002 to 2012, for example, over 80% of those incarcerated for drug-related offenses were incarcerated for use, and not for intent to distribute or manufacture. As of 2010, more than 51% of prisoners in the federal system were serving time for drug offenses (Guerino, Harrison, & Sabol, 2012). It is estimated that the United States had, for instance, more than 1.6 million prisoners behind bars. The imprisonment rate in 2007 was 500 inmates for every 100,000 in population. According to the U.S. Department of Justice, in 2005, the recidivism rate for those arrested for a drug offense was given as 76.9% within 5 years (Durose, Cooper, & Snyder, 2014). Although there is a major disparity between Caucasian, African American, and Hispanic men and women, it might seem most everyone could be subjected to mandatory minimums if incarcerated for a drug offense. See Table 20.6 for a breakdown of incarceration rates published by the U.S. Department of Justice, Bureau of Justice Statistics by ethnicity and gender (Guerino et al., 2012).

REHABILITATION VERSUS INCARCERATION The United States has one of the highest, if not the highest, incarceration rates in the world (Tsai & Scommegna, 2012). More people are arrested in the United States than in nearly all other nations. Although the United States consists of 5% of the world's population, the United States incarcerates 25% of the world's prisoners. During the time between 1996 and 2010, the U.S. population grew by almost 12%, but the number of incarcerated adults in prisons and jails grew by about 33% to almost 2.25 million. The adult population of inmates who were incarcerated for substance abuse issues grew by 42% to almost 1.7 million, although a decrease in drug offense imprisonment was seen between 2006 and 2011. Incarceration affects virtually every member of society. From the Opium Wars

TABLE 20.6 Estimated Incarceration Rates by Ethnicity or Race and Gender in 2010

Race/Gender	Ratio
African-American males	3,074 per 100,000
Hispanic males	1,258 per 100,000
Caucasian males	459 per 100,000
African-American females	133 per 100,000
Hispanic females	77 per 100,000
Caucasian females	47 per 100,000

to modern day military overt and clandestine operations, drug trafficking and addiction persist, contributing to substance use disorders in returning veterans, particularly from Vietnam and the Middle East, and extending on into society (Bergen-Cico, 2012).

Public perception varies regarding criminal prosecution. The Sentencing Project (n.d.), a media source that serves to inform the public, summarized studies conducted about crime, punishment, and public opinion. Policy makers, when asked to estimate support for alternative sentencing for drug offenses, for example, estimated that support to be at 12%, when it actually was 66%. Even though the majority supported or favored alternative sentencing, and did not perceive drugs as the most serious problem in the nation, the administration at that time enforced stricter drug policies.

Analysis of the effectiveness of a program and public opinion are not always examined until data is studied, and sometimes when this is evaluated, politicians, judges, and other leaders discuss publicly their opinions regarding the policy or law. Finally, when a program becomes financially cumbersome, a cost–benefit analysis is conducted to evaluate the cost and benefit of the program and to explore possible alternatives.

Sometimes the public might get tired of the affluent not being subject to the same policies and laws as those in lower socioeconomic settings. It is more likely people who are in a lower socioeconomic setting are given longer prison terms than those of higher socioeconomic setting (Perez & Smith, 2010). This allows socioeconomic discrimination to occur at every stage of the process (Brown, 2002).

In May of 2001, twins Barbara and Jenna Bush were cited by Austin, Texas, police for misdemeanors when they attempted to order alcohol at a local Mexican restaurant. Jenna Bush was cited for misrepresentation of age for allegedly using a false ID, which would have resulted in multiple offenses. Ironically, the offenses would have occurred shortly after then Governor George Bush signed into law harsher penalties for underage drinking (ABC News, n.d.).

Shortly after, Noelle Bush, daughter of President Bush's younger brother, Jeb Bush, was arrested for attempting to fill a forged drug prescription for Xanax in Tallahassee, Florida. The store's pharmacist, Carlos Zimmerman, had reported receiving messages from someone identifying herself as Dr. Noelle Scidmore. The pharmacist became suspicious and reported contacting the doctor's office to verify the authenticity of the prescription. Noelle Bush has been cited for several traffic violations and was involved in at least 3 car crashes, according to news media ("Jeb Bush's Daughter," 2002).

Eric Holder, the Attorney General under President Barack Obama's administration, suggested that it is time for mandatory minimum reform because there are too many people with drug-related offenses in prison. There is a bipartisan effort to revamp federal mandatory minimum laws (Drug Policy Alliance, 2013). "By a shift in focus to maximization of the public good, greater societal and political support can be generated for evidence-based measures that avoid the detrimental effects of the marginalization of drug users by, among other strategies, the imposing of severe criminal penalties" (Strang, Babor, Caulkins, Fischer, Foxcroft, & Humphreys, 2012, p. 80).

Although there has been a decline in the past 10 years for violent crimes, incarcerations for substance abuse issues have increased. Overall, it is estimated of the almost 2.25 million prisoners, 1.7 million (about two-thirds) meet the *Diagnostic Statistical Manual of Mental Disorders* (DSM) criteria for substance abuse (Califano, 2010). See Table 20.7 for a breakdown of the numbers of inmates by type of prison (Guerino et al., 2012). Of those incarcerated for substance-related issues, only about 11% have received any type of treatment, much of which barely meets the minimum required drug treatment standards.

TABLE 20.7 2010 Incarcerated Individuals in Federal, State, and Local Prison Convicted of Substance-Related Crimes

Type of Prison	Inmates
Federal Prisons	164,521
State Prisons	989,352
Local Prisons	548,644
Total	1,702,517

Inmates who abuse substances are four times more likely to have received income from illegal activities. They are almost twice as likely to have at least one parent who has abused alcohol and more than likely have some history of family crime. Almost 30% are less likely to have at minimum a high school diploma. Almost 20% are unemployed a month before incarceration. Almost 54% are more likely to recidivate—to be incarcerated again—and being arrested as a juvenile for using drugs or alcohol, or juvenile delinquent behavior, both contributed to recidivism (LaVigne & Samuels, 2012). It was estimated in 2008 that almost 1 million parents were incarcerated, leaving 2.2 million children living in a one-parent household or less. Minor children who have at least one parent who is an inmate are at higher risk for juvenile delinquency, committing adult crimes, and having substance abuse issues.

A substantial portion of the general population of those who experience substance use problems also have a treatable mental health condition—the most common dually diagnosed condition is alcohol use in combination with mood disorders (Cridland, Deane, Hsu, & Kelly, 2012).

According to a study by the National Survey of Substance Abuse Treatment Services (SAMHSA, 2011), almost 43% of clients treated for substance use disorders have a co-occurring mental health disorder. An estimated 33% of the total incarcerated population, those who had co-occurring substance-related issues, also had mental health issues. Although many inmates experience comorbidity, only half of the incarcerated population received treatment for mental health issues (National Center on Addiction and Substance Abuse, 2010). Table 20.8 helps to illustrate the breakdown of race/ethnicity with comorbidity issues.

Societal costs associated with drug abuse are staggering. In 2012, estimated costs associated with substance abuse in the United States exceeded 600 billion dollars (National Institute on Drug Abuse [NIDA], 2013). Costs associated with substance abuse can include lost productivity in the employment sector, insurance claims and fraud, crime, investigation of activities

TABLE 20.8 Percentage of Inmate Population Experiencing Comorbidity by Race/Ethnicity

Race	%
White	35.4
Black	40.8
Hispanic	18.4
Native American	3.9
Other	1.4

associated with substance-related crime, incarceration, substance abuse treatment, education, and probation. Court costs to adjudicate a defendant can vary depending on whether there is a plea agreement or a jury trial. If there is a plea agreement, the cost could range from $9,000 to $28,000 based on the severity of the case. If the case goes to trial, the amount might increase by another $30,000 for personal costs. These items could include the cost of research, court reporters, expert witnesses along with travel and expense reimbursement, translators (if needed), or possible sequestering of the jury (The Pew Charitable Trusts, 2009). The low end of the cost scale correlates with a defendant plea bargain, and the higher end is reached if the defendant goes to trial. Twenty-four and a half billion dollars were spent in 2012 for preventing illicit drug use, public safety and reintegration associated programs, countering production and trafficking, protecting borders, and international drug trafficking and distribution prevention partnerships (NIDA, 2013).

It is estimated that about 1.5 million children have at least one parent who is incarcerated in a federal or state prison. Ten million more children are living with a parent who has undergone supervision from either the courts or prison upon release. It is estimated that about 10% of children with mothers who were incarcerated and 2% of children with fathers who were incarcerated live in foster homes. Almost 75% of women who are incarcerated are mothers and over 50% have children under the age of 18. The cost for a child to maintain contact with an incarcerated parent might be costly and can serve as a barrier to family connectedness. Other barriers associated with incarceration might include financial instability, emotional instability, shame, and social stigmas (Bouchet, n.d.). Many families who have loved ones in prison seek assistance from relatives and close friends. Divorce rates for men who have been or are incarcerated are approximately 25% greater than the national average. If the man was unemployed before going to prison, the chance of divorce is greater than 33% of the national average (Western, 2004).

When serving prison time for a felony conviction, loss of personal freedom along with forfeiture of property is possible. Drug-related crimes could be subject to loss or seizure of assets and property. A personal residence can be lost, bank accounts frozen or drained, a business closed, cars repossessed, and/or recreational material may be lost to civil forfeiture proceedings. Since these are civil proceedings, state and federal governments do not have to prove their cases beyond a reasonable doubt. The burden falls on the accused to prove that the assets were not involved in criminal activities. Property can be seized even if criminal charges are not filed. It can take years for assets to be returned (The Pew Charitable Trusts, 2009).

Felons can lose the right to vote, the right to carry firearms, or be in possession of ammunition or explosives if sentenced to prison for more than 1 year. In some states, there also is a restriction to being within a certain distance of a firearm. This might restrict living arrangements if someone in the household owns a firearm. Guidelines vary by state regarding the right to travel to foreign countries, a restriction enacted by the foreign country, and the right to apply for Medicaid. If a person was convicted of a felony while enrolled in school and receiving federal aid, eligibility to receive federal student loans and grants is suspended. If convicted while not receiving federal assistance for school, the right to apply for federal aid for school might be denied or limited. The same is true for the right to live in or receive aid for government subsidized housing. If a felon is living with a person who receives or is living in federal subsidized housing, the person can be evicted from the housing or lose the subsidy. Felons also cannot serve on a federal grand jury unless their civil rights have been restored. Many states also restrict felons from serving on any jury. Felons cannot enlist in the armed forces. A person who received military benefits will lose those benefits while in prison.

Felons, as with most applying for a job, must endure a background check. It is estimated between 5 and 7 out of every 10 ex-felons is unemployed. In a study conducted by Schmitt and Warner (2010), it was estimated in 2008 that there were between 12.3 and 13.9 million ex-felons in the United States. It was also estimated about 1 in 15 working-age adults were ex-felons. Lost productivity to the U.S. economy from felon unemployment in 2008 was estimated to have been between 57 and 65 billion dollars.

Residential Drug Abuse Program

The Federal Bureau of Prisons has many treatment programs for inmates who have substance-related issues. Programs generally consist of drug abuse education classes, which provide education about substance abuse and identify inmates who might require additional treatment. Nonresidential drug abuse treatment consists of a 12-week cognitive behavioral group program for inmates who have short sentences, do not meet requirements for the Residential Drug Abuse Program (RDAP), are awaiting entry into the RDAP program, are transitioning into the community, or have tested positive for drugs. The RDAP uses cognitive behavior therapy as its primary approach. Inmates live in a modified environment, separated from the general population. Inmates experience half a day of treatment programs and either a half day of school or vocational training. The program is generally 9 months in length. The final program is Community Treatment Services, which provides care for offenders placed in Residential Reentry Centers and in Home Confinement (Federal Bureau of Prisons, 2013). As of 2013, there were 451,339 inmates participating in Drug Education, 202,236 inmates participating in Nonresidential treatment, 270,449 participating in Residential treatment, and 219,089 inmates participating in Community Transition programs. See Table 20.9 for details (Federal Bureau of Prisons, 2013).

Before entering the RDAP program, an inmate must meet eligibility requirements. An inmate must have proof of a substance abuse problem, and this can be substantiated from a previous treatment provider, probation, or parole officer, or previous problem verified by the Bureau of Prisons medical staff. The Bureau of Prisons has to make a determination of substance abuse or dependency per the DSM. The inmate must have at least 24 months left on the sentence. If an inmate had previously participated in a drug treatment program, that inmate does not qualify. The warden must give consent. If testing positive while in the program, an inmate is returned to general population and does not qualify for the RDAP reduction of sentence.

According to a study conducted by Sung, Richter, Vaughn, and Foster (2013), in 2011 more than 51,000 inmates were on a waiting list for the RDAP program. The program was vastly overcrowded and more areas for the program were needed. Only 11% of inmates with a substance abuse issue received sufficient treatment. If all inmates who did not receive treatment were to receive evidence-based treatment and aftercare, the United States would break even on

TABLE 20.9 Residential Drug Abuse Program (RDAP) Participation in 2013

Program	Participants
Drug Education	451,339
Nonresidential Treatment	202,236
Residential Treatment	270,449
Community Transition	219,089

the investment if only 10% remained abstinent, crime free, substance free, and employed. For each additional year of maintaining sobriety, the U.S. economy would reap $90,953,000 in benefits from reduced crime, lower arrest rate, prosecution, incarceration, health care costs, benefits such as taxation, and consumption of goods.

Criminalization of drug users has been the mainstay of the system for at least the last 30 years, having remained relatively stable until about the 1970s (Tripodi, Kim, & Bender, 2010). Babor (2010) wrote, "At both the international and national levels, drug control efforts have also been aimed at the user by criminalizing or otherwise punishing possession or use of illicit drugs" (p. 163). Babor went on to add that as of 2010, little had changed. Governments, he suggested, are still "flying blind." According to Grissom (2008), investing in treatment can reduce substance-related burden by 12 to 1. For every dollar spent on treatment, there is a reduction of 12 dollars in criminal justice and health cost. Prison employees who work in a prison where drug treatment is supplied report a less stressful work environment, more job satisfaction, lower rates of sick leave, and fewer employee firings.

According to NIDA (2010), surveys have shown most Americans are in support of addiction treatment, and oppose the idea of returning inmates to incarceration without making an effort to treat the substance abuse issue, which might reduce recidivism. Also 78.5% of the population believe non-violent drug abusers belong in treatment and counseling instead of prison.

The first drug court program was instituted in Miami, Florida, in 1989 (King & Pasquarella, 2009). Drug courts are an alternative to incarceration for nonviolent substance abuse offenders. Today there are approximately 2,750 drug courts in the United States. Two types of drug courts exist: deferred prosecution and postprosecution. In the deferred prosecution system, defendants are not required to plead and are mandated to substance abuse treatment. If the defendant successfully completes the program, the defendant is free. If not, the defendant is sent to prison. In the postprosecution system, the defendant pleads and sentences are deferred or suspended pending outcome of the program. If successful, the defendant's sentence is either reduced or waived, or probation is ordered. If the defendant does not successfully complete the program, the defendant is returned to a criminal court setting to be sentenced for the guilty plea. The eligibility requirements are such that the defendant is charged with a nonviolent substance abuse crime, the defendant has tested positive for drug use, or a substance abuse issue has been established through diagnostic criteria according to the DSM. If a defendant has a prior history of violence, the Federal Bureau of Prisons will not fund the case (King & Pasquarella, 2009).

Programs are usually between 6 and 12 months in length. Defendants participate in an evidence-based substance abuse program, one that is frequently monitored by the prosecution and judge. The defendant is also regularly tested for drugs. If a defendant happens to relapse, the judge can decide to have the defendant continue the program or be sent to criminal court for sentencing. Many times the judge might seek input from the prosecuting attorney, the defense attorney, and the substance abuse counselor. The defendant is required to have an attendance sheet signed by the counselor on days the defendant attends the program. This information is brought to court on specified days of monitoring required by the judge. The cost of drug court can range from between $9,500 and $12,000, plus the cost of therapy. Usually the clinician agrees to a specified "per visit" group and individual counseling fee, which is often below normal rates for service. Economically advantageous, the estimated saving between drug court and incarceration is around $3,000–$13,000 per client (National Association of Drug Court Professionals, 2012).

In a study conducted by King and Pasquarella (2009), 76 drug courts found a 10% reduction in rearrests with defendants who were deferred prosecution, and a 13% reduction of overall rearrests. A review of 30 drug courts disclosed a 13% decline in convictions for a new crime. There was a report that disclosed postprogram recidivism rates between 4% and 25% in 13 of 17 courts polled. Economically advantageous, the estimated saving between drug court and incarceration is around $3,000–$13,000 per client (National Association of Drug Court Professionals, 2012). According to McVay, Schiraldi, and Ziedenberg (2004), two out of three individuals released from state prisons for drug-related offenses will be rearrested within 3 years. The results of their analysis of governmental agencies, surveys, and conclusions made by think tanks in the State of Maryland showed that treatment was found to be far more cost-effective than cycling individuals in and out of prison.

During the 1970s and the initial stages of the war on drugs, it was estimated that 3%–5% of the population had a substance abuse problem. Today, after spending a trillion dollars on the war on drugs, it is estimated that 3%–5% of the population has a substance abuse problem. Scholars have argued that the war on drugs has failed and instead has focused attention away from prevention and treatment options (Buckley et al., 1996). It might seem we have maintained a constant, but the population has actually increased over the past 40 years. Although the percentage has been maintained, the actual numbers have increased. When a person decides to enter treatment, there are many choices based on the level of care. The balance of this section will break down the possible choices and associated costs.

Therapeutic outpatient sessions can cost between $1,500 and $5,000 per year or more. If considered to be intensive outpatient, the price can range between $5,000 and $9,000 per year. If partial hospitalization or detoxification is required, costs can run between $800 and $1,200 per day, depending on hospitalization or private rehabilitation setting. Inpatient settings can cost between $2,000 and $7,000 per month, and reach as much as $15,000 per month for the affluent. Treatment of a client who is dually diagnosed can be considerably higher. Some private centers could charge as much as $7,000 to $10,000 per month. (Most of these costs were obtained by calling various rehab centers in the United States.)

Medicare will help pay the cost of inpatient and outpatient rehabilitation if the primary care physician determines that treatment is necessary. The attending physician creates a treatment plan and the facility is required to be Medicare approved. Medicare deductibles apply. Medicaid covers outpatient treatment for drug abuse in the same way it covers outpatient mental health treatment. The exact coverage varies from state to state. Covered treatment may include individual counseling, group counseling, educational programs, marital counseling, family counseling, case management, and social services. Medicaid covers inpatient treatment for drug abuse when a physician or other treatment provider deems inpatient care medically necessary.

On October 3, 2009, the Paul Wellstone and Pete Domenici Mental Health Parity and Addiction Equity Act of 2008 (MHPAEA) became law (Sussman, 2009). Commonly known as the Parity Act or Mental Health Parity Act (MHPA), this law now requires health insurance providers to cover both mental and physical health equally. Under this law, insurance companies can no longer arbitrarily limit the number of hospital days or outpatient treatment sessions, or assign higher copayments or deductibles for those in need of psychological services (American Psychological Association, 2008). At that time, approximately 70%–80% of the estimated 113 million American adults and children who had mental illness disorders, who were in need of mental health services, did not receive help, due mainly to discriminatory practices by insurers. The new law, after a long fought battle, addressed this issue in an effort to make mental health care equal to medical and surgical care, although exemptions and definitions reduce its efficacy. The MHPA became effective after January 1, 2010. With the high percentage of overlap between mental health and substance use disorders, this act is expected to have a substantial effect.

According to SAMHSA (2009), alcohol relapse rates hover around 86% of those entering alcohol recovery programs, returning to dependency within 5 years. Heroin, which is a highly addictive opiate, has a relapse rate of 87% after 1 year of treatment. Crack cocaine has a relapse rate of 87% after 1 year of treatment, and cocaine, 55% after 1 year of treatment. PCP, inhalants, and hallucinogens have a 43% relapse rate after 5 years. Methamphetamine users relapsed at a rate of 54% after 5 years, and those addicted to "downers" (i.e., depressants, such as such as benzodiazepines, barbiturates, valium, GBH, heroin, opium, etc.) relapsed at a rate of 51% after 5 years. A breakdown of drug of choice and related relapse rates can be found in Table 20.10 (SAMHSA, 2009).

Many factors contribute to relapse, including length of use, type of drug, severity of addiction, unemployment, lack of education, and social supports. These and other factors, such as the strength of the drug, whether it is prescribed or obtained illegally, and the physical and mental condition of the person using the drug, serve to complicate the issue considerably. Add to that one of the hallmarks of substance use and abuse—denial—and problems exponentiate.

During the initial stages of the "War on Drugs," it was estimated that 3 to 5 percent of the population had a substance abuse problem. Nearly half a century later, after spending a trillion dollars on the "War on Drugs," it is estimated that 3 to 5 percent of the population has a substance abuse problem.

Advocacy

As we look at advocacy for those who have substance abuse issues and their families, we might best be served to look at our policies for the past 40–50 years. For more than 40 years, our government has gotten tough on addiction using the correctional system to combat abuse. This net widening approach has resulted in overcrowding of prisons, deterioration of families, and high unemployment rates for felons; in addition, it has strained the federal budget as well as the budgets of states, cities, and municipalities across the nation. Our policies have moved from compassion and rehabilitation to becoming punitive in nature. Other contributing factors were the closing of institutions for those with mental health issues and the budget cuts to social services, which has also contributed to warehousing those with mental health and comorbidity issues. In communities that are lower in socioeconomic status and minority based, males are more likely to be incarcerated, thus contributing to deteriorating stable relationships (Rich, Wakeman, & Dickman, 2011).

TABLE 20.10 SAMHSA Relapse Rates by Drug Type

Drug of Choice	Relapse Rate
Alcohol	86% within 5 years
Heroin	87% after 1 year
Crack Cocaine	87% after 1 year
Cocaine	55% after 1 year
PCP, inhalants, hallucinogens	43% after 5 years
Methamphetamine	54% after 5 years
Depressants	51% after 5 years

Summary and Some Final Notations

In spite of efforts, drug use continues and alcohol use is at an all-time high (Cooper, 2012). Five states are now spending less on higher education than on incarceration. Even though evidence-based addiction treatment is more effective, many politicians are reluctant to endorse treatment over incarceration, since they do not want to be seen as soft on crime (Rich et al., 2011). In an analysis of what has worked and what has not worked, let us explore ways to advocate for more efficient and effective approaches to substance abuse treatment. As a society, we are morally obligated to advocate for those who do not have a voice. As clinicians, we are morally and ethically obligated to advocate for efficacious treatment that is beneficial to client and society alike.

Locking up millions of people for drug-related crimes has failed as a public-safety strategy and has harmed public health in the communities to which these men and women return. A new evidence-based approach is desperately needed. We believe that in addition to capitalizing on the public health opportunities that incarceration presents, the medical community and policymakers must advocate for alternatives to imprisonment, drug-policy reform, and increased public awareness of this crisis in order to reduce mass incarceration. (Rich et al., 2011, p. 3)

MyCounselingLab

Visit the MyCounselingLab site for *Foundations of Addictions Counseling,* Third Edition to enhance your understanding of concepts. You'll have the opportunity to practice your skills through video- and case-based exercises. You will find sets of questions to help you prepare for your certification exam with *Licensure Quizzes*. There is also a Video Library that provides taped counseling sessions, ethical scenarios, and interviews with helpers and clients.

Useful Websites

American Counseling Association
www.counseling.org/

American Rehabilitation Counseling Association
www.arcaweb.org/

American Society for Addiction Medicine (ASAM) Criteria
www.asam.org/publications/the-asam-criteria

Drug and Alcohol Dependence Journal
www.drugandalcoholdependence.com/home

Food and Drug Administration
www.fda.gov/Drugs/

FDA Drug Law History
www.fda.gov/aboutfda/whatwedo/history/milestones/ucm128305.htm

Health and Human Services
www.hhs.gov

Medline Plus
www.nlm.nih.gov/medlineplus/

National Institute of Drug Abuse
www.nida.nih.gov

National Institute on Disability and Rehabilitation Research (NIDRR)
www2.ed.gov/programs/nidrr/

National Institutes of Health
www.nih.gov

Office of Drug and Alcohol Policy and Compliance
http://www.dot.gov/odapc

Substance Abuse and Mental Health Services Administration
www.samhsa.gov/

Veterans Affairs Alcohol and Drug Misuse and Dependence
www.mentalhealth.va.gov/substanceabuse.asp

References

ABC News. (n.d.). Jeb Bush's daughter accused of prescription fraud. Retrieved from http://abcnews.go.com/US/story?id=91959&page=1

American Psychological Association. (2008). *Mental Health Parity and Addiction Equity Act*. Washington, DC: Author.

American Society of Addiction Medicine. (2014). Understanding the basic concept and theory of ASAM. Retrieved from: http://www.mh.alabama.gov/Video/ASAMtraining.aspx

Babor, T. (2010). *Drug policy and the public good*. New York, NY: Oxford University Press.

Babor, T. F., McRee, B. G., Kassebaum, P. A., Grimaldi, P. L., Ahmed, K., & Bray, J. (2007). Screening, Brief Intervention, and Referral to Treatment (SBIRT): Toward a public health approach to the management of substance abuse. *Substance Abuse, 28*(3), 7–30.

Bergen-Cico, D. (2012). *The role of military conflict in the development of substance abuse*. Boulder, CO: Paradigm.

Bernstein, S. L., & D'Onofrio, G. (2013). A promising approach for emergency departments to care for patients with substance use and behavioral disorders. *Health Affairs, 32*(12), 2122–2128.

Bouchet, S. (n.d.). *Children of families with incarcerated parents*. Baltimore, MD: Annie E. Casey Foundation.

Broome, K. M., Knight, D. K., Joe, G. W., & Flynn, P. M. (2012). Treatment program operations and costs. *Journal of Substance Abuse Treatment, 42*(2), 125–133.

Brown, C. M., II, Lane, J. E., & Rogers, K. R. (2002). Walking a policy tightrope: Balancing educational opportunity and criminal justice in federal student financial aid. *Journal of Negro Education, 71*(3), 233–242. doi:10.2307/3211239

Buck, J. A. (2011). The looming expansion and transformation of public substance abuse treatment under the Affordable Care Act. *Health Affairs, 30*(8), 1402–1410.

Buckley W. F., Jr., Nadelmann, E. A., Schmoke, K., McNamara, J. D., Sweet, R. W., Szasz, T., & Duke, S. B. (1996). The war on drugs is lost. *National Review, 48*(2), 34–48.

Califano, J. A. (2010). Criminally unjust: Why America's prison policy needs repair. *New York Times*. Retrieved from http://americamagazine.org/node/149760

Center for Substance Abuse Treatment. (2005). *Data for substance abuse treatment*. Washington, DC: Author.

Cridland, E., Deane, F., Hsu, C., & Kelly, P. (2012). A comparison of treatment outcomes for individuals with substance use disorder alone and individuals with probable dual diagnosis. *International Journal of Mental Health & Addiction, 10*(5), 670–683. doi:10.1007/s11469-011-9364z

Denning, P. (2000). *Practicing harm reduction psychotherapy: An alternative approach to addiction*. New York, NY: Guilford.

DiClemente, C. C., & Prochaska, J. O. (1982). Self-change and therapy change of smoking behavior: A comparison of processes of change in cessation and maintenance. *Addictive Behaviors, 7*, 133–142.

D'Onofrio, G., Bernstein, E., Bernstein, J., Woolard, R. H., Brewer, P. A., Craig, S. A., & Zink, B. J. (1998). Patients with alcohol problems in the emergency department, Part 1: Improving detection. *Academic Emergency Medicine, 5*(12), 1200–1209.

Drug Policy Alliance. (2013). Attorney General Eric Holder calls for major sentencing reform. Retrieved from: http://www.drugpolicy.org/news/2013/08/attorney-general-eric-holder-calls-major-sentencing-reform

Ducharme, L. J., Knudsen, H. K., Roman, P. M., & Johnson, J. A. (2007). Innovation adoption in substance abuse treatment: Exposure, trialability, and the Clinical Trials Network. *Journal of Substance Abuse Treatment, 32*(4), 321–329.

Durose, M. R., Cooper, A. D., & Snyder, H. N. (2014). *Recidivism of prisoners released in 30 states in 2005: Patterns from 2005–2010*. Washington, DC: Bureau of Justice Statistics.

Federal Bureau of Prisons. (2013). *Report on substance abuse treatment and programs*. Washington, DC: Author.

Forbes, D. (2001). Ashcroft's nephew got probation after major pot bust. *Salon*. Retrieved from http://www.salon.com/2001/01/13/ashcroft_nephew/

Gastfriend, D. R., & Mee-Lee, D. (2011). Patient placement criteria. In M. Galanter & H. D. Kleber (Eds.), *Psychotherapy for the treatment of substance abuse* (pp. 99–124). Arlington, VA: American Psychiatric Publishing.

Grissom, J. N. G. (2008). Economic benefit of chemical dependency to employers. *Journal of Substance Abuse Treatment, 34*(30), 311–319.

Guerino, P., Harrison, P. M., & Sabol, W. J. (2012). *Prisoners in 2010*. Washington, DC: Bureau of Justice Statistics.

Harris, A. H., Kivlahan, D., Barnett, P. G., & Finney, J. W. (2012). Longer length of stay is not associated with better outcomes in VHA's substance abuse residential rehabilitation treatment programs. *The Journal of Behavioral Health Services & Research, 39*(1), 68–79.

Humphreys, K., & Rappaport, J. (1993). From the community mental health movement to the war on drugs: A study of the definition of social problems. *American Psychologist, 48*(8), 892–901.

Jeb Bush's daughter charged with prescription fraud. (2002). *USA Today*. Retrieved from http://usatoday30.usatoday.com/news/nation/2002/01/29/noelle-bush.htm

Jiménez, R. E., Lam, R. M., Marot, M., & Delgado, A. (2004). Observed-predicted length of stay for an acute psychiatric department, as an indicator of inpatient care inefficiencies. Retrospective case-series study. *BMC Health Services Research, 4*(1), 4.

King, R., S., & Pasquarella, J. (2009). *Drug courts: A review of the evidence*. Washington, DC: The Sentencing Project.

Klostermann, K., & O'Farrell, T. J. (2013). Treating substance abuse: Partner and family approaches. *Social Work in Public Health, 28*(3-4), 234–247.

Kraemer, K. L. (2007). The cost-effectiveness and cost-benefit of screening and brief intervention for unhealthy alcohol use in medical settings. *Substance Abuse, 28*(3), 67–77.

Lavigne, N., & Samuels, S. (2012). The growth, and increasing cost of the federal prison system: Drivers and potential solutions. Urban Institute Justice Policy Center. Retrieved from http://www.urban.org/UploadedPDF/412693-The-Growth-and-Increasing-Cost-of-the-Federal-Prison-System.pdf

Lee, D. M., & Shulman, G. R. (2003). *The ASAM placement criteria and matching patients to treatment* (3rd ed.). Chevy Chase, MD: American Society of Addiction Medicine.

Levine, H. G. (1984). What is an alcohol related problem? *Journal of Drug Issues, 13*(3), 100–115.

Mark, T. L., Levit, K. R., Vandivort-Warren, R., Buck, J. A., & Coffey, R. M. (2011). Changes in US spending on mental health and substance abuse treatment, 1986–2005, and implications for policy. *Health Affairs, 30*(2), 284–292.

McKay, J. R., & Hiller-Sturmhoefel, S. (2011). Treating alcoholism as a chronic disease: Approaches to long-term continuing care. *Alcohol Abuse and Alcoholism, 33*(4), 356–370.

McVay, D., Schiraldi, V., & Ziedenberg, J. (2004). *Treatment or incarceration. National and state findings on the efficacy and cost savings of drug treatment versus imprisonment*. Washington, DC: Justice Policy Institute.

Mee-Lee, D., Shulman, G. D., & Fishman, M. (2001). ASAM patient placement criteria for the treatment of substance-related disorders—revised (ASAM PPC-2R). Chevy Chase, MD: American Society of Addiction Medicine.

Miller, G. A. (1985). *The Substance Abuse Subtle Screening Inventory (SASSI) manual*. Springville, IN: SASSI Institute.

Miller, W. R., & Rollnick, S. (2012). *Motivational interviewing: Helping people change*. New York, NY: Guilford Press.

Moyers, T. B., & Rollnick, S. (2002). Motivational interviewing prospective resistance in psychotherapy. *Journal of Clinical Psychotherapy, 58*(2), 185–193.

National Association of Drug Court Professionals. (2012). *Drug courts work*. Alexandria, VA: Author.

National Center on Addiction and Substance Abuse. (2010). *Substance abuse and mental health concerns*. Washington, DC: Author.

National Institute on Drug Abuse. (2010). *Analysis of perceptions of addiction versus prison*. Washington, DC: Author.

National Institute on Drug Abuse. (2013). *NIDA funding strategy for fiscal year 2013*. Washington, DC: Author.

National Institute on Drug Abuse. (2014). *National Institute of Drug Abuse organizational structure*. Washington, DC: Author.

Pattison, M. E. (1966). A critique of alcoholism treatment concepts with special reference to abstinence. *Quarterly Journal of Studies on Alcohol, 27*(1), 49–71.

Perez, J. S., & Smith, R. A. (2010). *Issue brief: Social economic status/class criminal justice in the U.S. Columbia University Academic Commons*. New York, NY: Columbia University Academic Commons.

The Pew Charitable Trusts. (2009). *The long reach of American convictions*. Washington, DC: Author.

Prochaska, J. O., Norcross, J. C., & DiClemente, C. C. (2013). Applying the stages of change. *Psychotherapy in Australia, 19*(2), 10–15.

Rich, J. D., Wakeman, S. E., & Dickman, S. L. (2011). Medicine and the epidemic of incarceration in the United States. *New England Journal of Medicine, 364*(22), 2081–2083.

Rock, M. (2003). Mandatory minimums: Where do they come from? *Criminal Injustice*. Retrieved from http://criminalinjusticeblog.wordpress.com/2013/04/22/mandatory-minimums-where-do-they-come-from/

The Sentencing Project. (n.d.). *Crime, punishment and public opinion: A summary of recent studies and their implications for sentencing policy*. Washington, DC: Author.

Schmitt, J., & Warner, K. (2010). *Ex-offenders and the labor market*. Center for Washington, DC: Economic and Policy Research.

Selzer, M. L. (1971). The Michigan Alcoholism Screening Test: The quest for a new diagnostic instrument. *American Journal of Psychiatry, 127*(12), 1653–1658.

Shaffer, D. K., Hartman, J. L., Listwan, S. J., Howell, T., & Latessa, E. J. (2011). Outcomes among drug court participants: Does drug of choice matter? *International Journal of Offender Therapy and Comparative Criminology, 55*(1), 155–174.

Skinner, H. A. (1982). The drug abuse screening test. *Addictive behaviors, 7*(4), 363–371.

Strang, J., Babor, T., Caulkins, J., Fischer, B., Foxcroft, D., & Humphreys, K. (2012). Drug policy and the public good: evidence for effective interventions. *The Lancet, 379*(9810), 71–83.

Substance Abuse and Mental Health Services Administration. (2009). *Registry of evidenced based programs and practices.* Washington, DC: Author.

Substance Abuse and Mental Health Services Administration. (2010a). *National Mental Health Services Survey (N-MHSS): 2010. Data on Mental Health Treatment Facilities.* BHSIS Series S-69, HHS Publication No. Rockville, MD: Author.

Substance Abuse and Mental Health Services Administration. (2010b). *Results from the 2009 National Survey on Drug Use and Health. Vol. 1.* (HHS Publication No. SMA 10-4586). Rockville, MD: Author.

Substance Abuse and Mental Health Services Administration. (2011). *National Survey of Substance Abuse Treatment Services (N-SSATS): 2010. Data on substance abuse treatment facilities* (DASIS Series S-59, HHS Publication No. [SMA] 11-4665). Rockville, MD: Author.

Sung, H. E., Richter, L., Vaughn, R., & Foster, S. E. (2013). Substance abuse addictions and prisons and jailed inmates. In L. Gideon (Ed.), *Special needs offenders in correctional institutions* (pp. 459–494). Newbury, CA: Sage.

Sussman, N. (2009). Mental Health Parity Act becomes the law on October 3, 2009. *Primary Psychiatry, 16*(10), 10–11.

Travis, J. (2005). *But they all come back: Facing the challenges of prisoner reentry.* Washington, DC: Urban Institute.

Tripodi, S. J., Kim, J. S., & Bender, K. (2010). Is employment associated with reduced recidivism? The complex relationship between employment and crime. *International Journal of Offender Therapy and Comparative Criminology, 54*(5), 706–720.

Tryon, G. S., & Winograd, G. (2011). Goal consensus and collaboration. *Psychotherapy, 48*(1), 50–57. doi:10.1037/a0022061

Tsai, T., & Scommegna, P. (2012). *U.S. has world's highest incarceration rate.* Washington, DC: Population Reference Bureau.

Van Horn, D. H., & Bux, D. A., Jr. (2001). A pilot test of motivational interviewing groups for dually diagnosed inpatients. *Journal of Substance Abuse Treatment, 20*(2), 191–195.

van Wormer, K., & Davis, D. R. (2013). *Addiction treatment: A strengths perspective* (3rd ed.). Belmont, CA: Brooks Cole.

von Zielbauer, P. (2003). Rethinking the Key Thrown Away; as Ashcroft Cracks Down, States Cut Prison Terms, *New York Times.* Retrieved from http://www.nytimes.com/2003/09/28/nyregion/rethinking-the-key-thrown-away-as-ashcroft-cracks-down-states-cut-prison-terms.html

Western, B. (2004). *Incarceration, marriage, and family life.* Princeton, NJ: Princeton University.

INDEX

A

Aalto, M., 129
Aanes, D. L., 269
Aasheim, Lisa Langfuss, 147
Aasland, O. G., 125
Abenavoli, L., 249
AbolMagd, S., 9
Abraham, A. J., 165, 167
Abram, K., 361
abstinence
  as accepted practice, 461
  alternatives to, 6
  as goal of addicts, 10, 165, 286
  harm reduction and, 185
  mental disorders and, 194
  recovering counselors and, 74
abstinence eventually, 185
abstinence violation effect, 293–294, 299
acamprosate, 253
acceptance and commitment therapy (ACT), 174
access risk factors, 338–339
access to care. See barriers to care
accreditation, 80
acculturation, 199, 384
acetylcholine (ACH), 256
Ackerman, D., 229
Acosta, K. M., 55
Acri, M. C., 68
action stage of change, 148
Adams, J., 37
Adderall, 39
addiction, 18–47. See also process addictions; specific drugs
  commonly abused drug chart, 24–25
  explanation of, 18
  history of (See history of addiction)
  neurobiology and physiology of, 19–26
  psychopharmacological perspective of, 241
  rate of, 18
  substances of, 26–43
Addiction Acknowledgement Scale (AAS), 132–133
addiction causes, 6–14
  biological models, 11–12
  developmental model, 11
  disease model, 10
  family models, 9
  moral model and, 7–8
  multicausal models, 13–14
  psychological models, 7–9
  public health model, 10–11
  sociocultural models, 12–13
Addiction Potential Scale (APS), 132
Addiction Severity Index (ASI), 136–137, 197
Addolorato, G., 249

Adger, H., 123
Adler, L., 37
adolescents
  ADHD medication and, 38–39
  alcohol use and, 30
  brain damage due to drug use, 356
  counseling during hospitalizations, 29
  counselor issues and, 68
  gender differences, 409
  Juvenile Drug Court (JDC) for, 4, 358, 360
  LGBTQ issues, 428, 434
  marijuana use and, 41
  opioid use of, 356
  pregnancy, prevention during, 353, 371–373
  prescription medication abuse and, 37
  prevention programs for, 360–371
  solution-focused integration and, 179
  stimulant use of, 37
  support groups for, 266, 267, 270
  tobacco use and, 35–36
Adolescent Transition Program (ATP), 367
Adult Children of Alcoholics (ACOA), 231, 314
adverse childhood events, 111
advocacy, 94–95, 442–443, 469
Advocacy Competencies, 442
advocacy talk, 158–159
affirmation of clients, 156, 434–435
Affordable Care Act of 2010, 81, 372, 457
African Americans, 391–393. See also race
aftercare concerns, 235
aftercare groups, 218
Ager, J. W., 125, 126
age restrictions, alcohol, 5
agonist, 241
agonist substitution pharmacotherapy, 256
Agrawal, A., 110
agreeing with a twist, 160
Ahmed, S. H., 48, 60, 61
Aissen, K., 89, 90, 92, 112
Alaniz, M., 392
Al-Anon, 231, 265
Alateen, 231, 266
Alcohol, Drug Abuse, and Mental Health Administration (ADAMHA), 4
alcohol and alcohol use disorder
  family and (See family, impact of addiction on)
  gender and, 407
  history of, 2–4, 27, 407
  neurobiology of addiction, 22–23
  pharmacotherapy for, 251–252
  physiology of addiction, 26–33
  prevention policies, 5–6
  relapse rate for, 285
  relapse rates for, 469

tobacco use and, 36
Alcohol and Drug Consequences Questionnaire (ADCQ), 108
Alcohol Expectancy Questionnaire (AEQ), 107–108
alcoholic personality, 9
Alcoholics Anonymous
  comorbid conditions and, 202–203
  counselor beliefs and, 165
  culture and, 385
  on disease of addiction, 94
  goal of, 10
  history and development of, 263–264
  neuroscience of, 19
  recovering counselors and, 74
  spirituality and, 112–113
Alcoholics Anonymous for Atheists and Agnostics (Quad A), 267
alcohol poisoning, 368–369
Alcohol Problems Scale (ALC), 133–134
Alcohol Use Disorders Identification Test (AUDIT), 126, 129–130
Alcohol Use Inventory (AUI), 130
Alcohol Withdrawal Syndrome, 251–252
Alexander, J. A., 392
Alexander, T., 129
Alford, G. S., 270
Alford, K. M., 309
Alho, H., 129
Ali, R., 255
Allen, J. P., 98
Alleyne, V., 383, 394
alpha 2 receptor, 256
alprazolam, 33
Alterman, A. I., 136, 417
alternative medications, 255
Altman, D. G., 123
Alverson, H. S., 306
Amadio, D. M., 431
Amador, H., 203
Amaro, H., 176
Amato, P. R., 313
ambivalence, 153–154
Amen, D. G., 19, 22, 33
American Association for Marriage and Family Therapy (AAMFT), 50, 80
American Board of Addiction Medicine (ABAM), 72
American College of Obstetricians and Gynecologists (ACOG), 137
American College of Surgeons, 29
American Counseling Association (ACA)
  Advocacy Competencies, 442
  code of ethics, 67, 75, 96, 223, 224
  counselors in recovery, 75
  diversity issues, 13
  ethical care, 70

International Association for Addiction and Offender Counselors (IAAOC), 77
  LGBTQ clients, 429, 436
  Multicultural Counseling Competencies, 385, 395
  transgendered clients, 423, 428
American Psychiatric Association (APA)
  on caffeine addiction, 36
  on cocaine use, 39–40
  on denial of substance abuse, 121
  DSM (*See Diagnostic and Statistical Manual of Mental Disorders* [5th edition; DSM-5])
  on interpersonal skills, 221
  on marijuana use, 41
  on process addictions, 48, 51, 52, 60, 61
  on rate of substance abuse disorders, 18
  on substance use disorders, 197
American Psychological Association, 80, 81, 385, 468
American Sign Language (ASL), 338
American Society of Addiction Medicine (ASAM), 81, 98–99, 101, 252, 342, 450–452
Americans with Disabilities Act (ADA), 333
Ammon, L. N., 270
amobarbital with secobarbital, 34
Amodia, D. S., 14
Amos, S., 52, 53, 56
Amour, D. J., 285
amphetamines, 37–39, 409
amplified reflection, 159
ANAD National Association of Anorexia Nervosa and Associated Disorders (ANAD), 49, 61
Anderson, K. G., 111
Andrews, N. R., 167
Angermeyer, M. C., 250
Anglin, G., 412
Anglin, M., 68, 112
Angove, R., 410, 412, 413
anhedonia, 26
Ankenmann, R. D., 56
Annapolis Coalition, 384
Annis, H., 291, 292
Annon, J., 112
Annon, K., 386
anonymity in group therapy, 278–279
anorexia nervosa, 61
Anorexics Anonymous, 61
Antabuse, 251
antagonist, 241, 247
anterior cingulated cortex (ACC), 21–22
anticonvulsants, 256
Anti-Drug Abuse Prevention Act of 1986, 4, 461
Anton, R. F., 168, 249
Antonini, V. P., 81
anxiety treatment, 33
anxiolytics, 256
Aoki, B., 386
Apodaca, T. R., 153, 308
applications, interventions as, 166
arguing, 158, 227

Armor-Garb, A., 201
Arnau, J., 317
Arndt, S., 345
Arredondo, P., 96, 227, 228, 277, 385, 391, 394–396, 442
Arredondo, R., 132
Arria, A., 199
Arthur, M., 359
ASAM Patient Placement Criteria (PPC), 450–452
Asanjo, B., 276
Asay, T. P., 110
ASGW, 224
Ashcroft, John, 461–462
Ashton, H., 246
Asian Americans/Pacific Islanders, 389–391. *See also* race
assertiveness training, 234
assessment, 89–146
  addicted family systems, 319–322
  Addiction Severity Index (ASI), 136–137
  alcohol misuse during pregnancy, 137–139
  Alcohol Use Disorders Identification Test (AUDIT), 129–130
  Alcohol Use Inventory (AUI), 130
  background and contextual information, 103–108, 110
  best practices, 93, 96
  CAGE, 128–129
  change theory stage, 108–109
  for college students, 369
  of communities, 359
  comorbid conditions, 197–200
  construction of, 122
  coping skills, 111
  cost-efficiency, 124
  counselor-initiated, 135–137
  counselor role in, 95
  diagnosis and, 123, 124–125
  dimensions of, 451–452
  evaluating, 123–124
  family and peer relationships, 110–111
  high risk behavior, 111
  human assessment measures, 95–98
  interviews, 100–103
  for level of care, 450–456
  for LGBTQ clients, 433–444
  Michigan Alcoholism Screening Test (MAST), 127–128
  personality assessments, 130–135
  philosophical foundations, 90–95
  prior treatment, 109–110
  for process addiction, 49
  process of, 98–100
  readiness for change, 102, 108
  reliability and validity, 124
  screening, 123
  self-administered screening, 126–130
  sensitivity and specificity, 123–124
  spirituality, 112–113
  standardized assessments, use of, 121–122
  Substance Abuse Subtle Screening Inventory-3 (SASSI-3), 126–127
  treatment specific, 108–113
  work and vocation, 112
Association for Addiction Professionals (AAP), 79
Association for Assessment in Counseling, 96
Association of Multicultural Counseling and Development (AMCD), 394–396
Association of Recovery Community Organizations, 83
Astone, N. M., 111
Astromovich, R. L., 1
ATHENA (Athletes Targeting Healthy Exercise and Nutrition Alternatives), 366
athletes
  alcohol consumption of, 23
  amphetamine use of, 37
  high school, drug use and, 365–366
Ativan, 356–357
Atkins, D., 355
Atlas of Psychiatric Pharmacotherapy (Shiloh), 240
attention deficit hyperactivity disorder (ADHD), 38
Attia, P. R., 407–409
Austin, N. L., 394
Avena, N. M., 60, 61
Avery, E., 433
avoiding topics, 158
axon, 256
ayahuasca, 255
Azrin, N. H., 333

B

Babits, N., 90
Babor, T., 455, 463, 467
Babor, T. F., 125, 129
bachelor's degrees, 72
Bachman, J. G., 354, 356
Bachman, S. S., 329, 332, 335, 343, 344
Back, S. E., 411
background information for assessment, 103–108
baclofen, 253
Bacon, M. K., 12
Baer, J. S., 175, 204, 369
Baffour, T. D., 178
Bailey, C. E., 50
Baiocco, R., 9
Baker, A., 371
Baker, S., 81
Bakken, K., 416
Balan, S., 388
Baldwin, S. A., 319
Baler, R. D., 19–20, 22
Bales, B. F., 12
Balkin, R. S., 66
Ballack, A. S., 162
Balluz, L., 414
Bancroft, J., 51
Bandura, A., 8, 148, 161, 168, 287
Banks, S. M., 415, 417
Barber, J. G., 69
barbiturates, 33, 409

Barbuti, A. M., 172
Bargh, J. A., 150
Barmada, C., 370
Barnes, C. P., 331
Barnes, G. M., 386
Barnett, P. G., 458
Barnett, R., 311
Barnhill, A., 328, 331
Barnow, B. S., 332
Baron, D., 9
Barr, K. E., 386
Barr, K. E. M., 386, 387
Barrett, S. P., 68
Barrick, C., 69
Barrick, M. R., 122
barriers to care
　complications and red tape, 99
　criminal justice system, 343
　culture and, 387–393
　disabilities, persons with, 330, 335
　education of clients, 251
　location, 278
　for women, 413, 420
Baruth, L. G., 394
Basford, J. R., 331, 333
BASICS program, 175–176
"bath salts" (MDMA), 43
Battistutta, D., 359
Bauman, S., 127
Baumeister, R. F., 278
Beals, J., 340
Beam, H. P., 274
Bean, R., 319
Beattie, M., 80
Beattie, R., 68
Beauvais, F., 386
Beck Depression Inventory (BDI), 197
Becker, R. F., 353
Beckerman, A., 419, 422
Beckett, K., 384
Begg, M., 256
behavioral addictions. *See* process addictions
behavioral approaches. *See* cognitive-behavioral approaches
behavioral contracting, 172–173
behavioral medical management programs, 168
behavioral models, 9
behavioral sensitization, 256
behaviors, assessment of, 105–106
Behl, M., 119
Behnke, M., 371
Beiderman, J., 362
Belding, M. A., 177
Bell, P., 273
Bellini, J. L., 329
Belsky, J., 317
Bender, K., 467
Benishek, L. A., 167
Bennett, L., 311
Bennett, L. A., 316
Bennett, M. E., 167
Ben-Porath, Y. S., 131–133
Benton, S. L., 128

Beneviste, R. J., 43
benzodiazepines, 33–34, 252, 356–357, 469
Berg, I. K., 176–177, 180
Bergen, R. K., 345
Berger, P. L., 93
Bergin, A. E., 112
Bergin, L., 91
Berkeljon, A., 319
Berlin, R., 311
Bernstein, S. L., 455
best practices, 73, 93, 96, 200
Beveridge, S., 329
Bevilacqua, L., 11
Bhutia, A. M., 172
bias
　in diagnosing, 199–200
　in pharmacotherapy, 240
biculturalism, 386
Bidell, M. P., 431
Biebel, E. P., 70
Biederman, J., 360
Bilal, R., 273
Bina, R., 69, 72
Binder, P., 90
binge drinking
　college students and, 30, 354–355
　explanation of, 369
　gender and, 408
　race and, 29
　of veterans, 374
binge eating, 61
biological considerations, gender and, 410–411, 415–416
biological models, 11–12
biomedical conditions, 102
biopsychosocial model, 55
Birchler, G. R., 312, 313
Birkeland, S., 363, 364
bisexual people, 434. *See also* lesbian, gay, bisexual, transgender, and queer (LGBTQ) clients
Bishop, M., 328
Bissell, L., 74
Black, C., 305, 309, 310
Black, M. C., 414
Black, M. M., 311
Blais, M. A., 133
blame, 235
blaming trap, 160
Bland, I. J., 394
Bland, J. M., 123
Blayney, J. A., 7
Blazer, D., 357
Blevins, G. A., 298
Blitz, C., 359
Blore, R. L., 314
Blow, A. J., 312
Blow, F. C., 128, 312, 386
Blum, T. C., 274
Blume, A. W., 185
Bockow, T. B., 336
Bockting, W. O., 433

body awareness techniques, 299–300
Bogenschutz, M., 254
Bohart, A. C., 153
Bohnert, A., 374
Bois, C., 94
Bolding, G., 434
Bombardier, C. H., 332
Bond, J., 80
Bonebright, C. A., 56, 58
Bonenfant, E., 252, 254
Bonhomme, J., 340
Bonuccelli, U., 51
Boomsina, D. L., 11
Boone, D., 134
Booth, B. M, 111
border control, illegal drug import and, 4–5
Bornstein, K., 441
Borsari, B., 107, 367
Bottlender, M., 110
Botvin, G., 361, 362, 364
Bouchet, S., 465
boundaries, families and, 308–309, 316
boundary crossings, 226
boundary violations, 70, 73
Bousman, C., 362
Bowen, M., 384
Bowen, S., 22, 111, 174–175, 292, 295
Boyd, C., 356
Boyd, C. J., 386, 428
Boyd, J. W., 176
Boyd-Franklin, N., 386
Boye, M. W., 126
Bradley, K. A., 129, 137, 138
Bradley, L., 221
Brady, B. R., 58
Brady, K. T., 411
Braiker, H. B., 285
brain. *See also* memory; reward pathway in brain
　benzodiazepines and, 33
　children, drug use and, 356
　disorders, 102
　hallucinogen use and, 41–42
　methamphetamine use and, 37
　neurobiology of addiction, 12, 19–26
brain plasticity, 19
Braithwaite, R., 340
brand name, 256
Brandon, T. H., 288
Branson, C. E., 172
Brault, M. W., 329, 332, 333, 337
Braun, K., 165
Brave Heart, M., 340
breathalyzer instruments, 28–29
Breggin, P. R., 38
Brems, C., 192, 193, 199, 200
Bride, B. E., 408, 419, 421
Bride, C. A., 411
Bridges, S. K., 432
Brief Alcohol Screening and Intervention for College Students (BASICS) program, 369
brief interventions, 175–176, 455

Brief Symptom Inventory, 197
Briggs, C. A., 34, 406, 408, 411, 421, 422, 436
Briggs, W., 436
Brigham, G. S., 165
Brink, W. V. D., 248, 249, 253
Brisbane, F. L., 386
Bristow-Braitman, A., 275
Brochu, S., 411
Brodey, B. B., 136
Brook, D. W., 316, 317
Brooks, C. S., 309, 310, 318
Brooks, M. K., 126
Brown, C. M., II, 463
Brown, J., 151
Brown, L. S., 417
Brown, R., 119
Brown, S., 269, 270, 317, 319, 406
Brown, S. A., 108, 111, 274
Brownell, C., 162
Brownell, K. D., 60
Brucker, D., 329–331, 335, 343
Brucker, D. L., 333
Brys, S., 77
Buchanan, R. L., 340
Buck, J. A., 457
Buck, T., 52, 53, 56
Buckley, W. F., 468
Buckley-Walker, K., 91
Budman, S. H., 165
Bukstein, O. G., 136
bulimia nervosa, 61
Bulimics Anonymous, 61
bundling of care, 451
buprenorphine, 35
Bupropion, 36
Burck, A. M., 126
Bureau of Labor Statistics, 72, 76, 80
Burgard, J. F., 333
Burke, B. L., 162
Burnes, T. R., 436
Burnett, J. A., 50
burnout of counselors, 75–76
Burns, K. A., 353
Burns, W. J., 353
Bush, Barbara, 463
Bush, George H., 6
Bush, George W., 6, 463
Bush, Jenna, 463
Bush, K. R., 129, 138
Bush, Noelle, 463
Butcher, J. N., 130–132
Butler, S. F., 136
Buu, A., 13
Bux, D. A., Jr., 457
Buxton, M., 273

C

Cabaj, R. J., 428, 437
Cacciola, J. S., 136, 417
Cadell, D., 370
Caetano, R., 312, 316, 384
caffeine, 36, 328
 physiology of addiction and, 36
CAGE, 128–129

Caldwell, P. E., 279
Califano, J. A., 463
Callas, P., 362
Calmes, S. A., 119
Calsyn, D., 111, 135
Cameron, J., 111
Campbell, C., 270
Campbell, C. I., 392
Campbell, L., 218, 220
Campinha-Bacote, J., 244
Campos-Holland, A. L., 345
Campral, 253
cancer risk
 alcohol and, 23, 410
 substance abuse and, 410
cannabinoids, 256. *See also* marijuana
cannabis use disorder, 41
Cannatella, A., 71
Cano, N., 14
Capaldi, D., 370
Caplehorn, J. R. M., 165
Capone, C., 367
Caputi, P., 91
Capuzzi, D., 1, 89, 438
carbamzepine, 253
car crashes, 29–30
cardiovascular health
 ADHD medication and, 39
 alcohol and, 23
 women and alcohol, 410
Cardoso, E., 343
caretaker role, 9, 312
Carey, K., 358
Carey, M., 358
Carlson, R. G., 111
Carlton-LaNey, I., 392
Carmichael Olson, H., 316
Carnes, Patrick, 50, 51
Carr, L. G., 389
Carrier, J. W., 81
Carroll, J., 51
Carroll, K. M., 81–82, 167, 413
Carroll, M. E., 244, 408
cartels, drug, 5
Carter, J., 376
Carter, R. T., 387, 393, 394
Case, B., 50
case managers, 205–206
case studies
 addiction and families, 307, 313, 319
 alcohol use and abuse, 30–31
 cocaine abuse, 40
 comorbidity, 194, 195–197, 201–204, 208–214
 compulsive buying, 60
 culture, 396–401
 disabilities, persons with, 334–335, 339–340
 disordered eating, 62
 gambling addiction, 54
 gender and addiction, 411, 412, 415–418, 420
 group therapy, 231–236
 LGBTQ clients, 433, 437, 439–440, 444
 methamphetamine abuse, 39
 motivational interviewing, 155–156

OxyContin addiction, 35
 pharmacotherapy, 245–246, 252–255
 relapse prevention, 296–301
 sedative abuse, 34
 sexual addiction, 51–52
 solution-focused counseling, 182
 stages of change model, 148–151
 tobacco use, 36
 12-step groups, 274, 277
 work addiction, 59
Cashel, M. L., 127
Cashwell, C. S., 161
Caspi, Y., 222
Cass, D., 240
Cass, V. C., 431
Castaneda, R., 271
Catalano, R., 359
Catalano, R. F., 359
Catanzaro, P., 9
Cattarello, A., 363
Caulkins, J., 463
causes of addiction. *See* addiction causes
Cavanaugh, J. C., 345
Celio, M., 129
cell phone use, 55
Center for Addiction Recovery, 371
Center for Substance Abuse Prevention
 (CSAP), 4
Center for Substance Abuse Treatment
 (CSAT), 72, 450
Centers for Disease Control (CDC)
 on alcohol fatalities, 29
 on domestic violence, 313
 on drinking dangers, 26
 on high-risk behavior, 357
 on rate of substance abuse, 353
 on suicide, 412
 on tobacco deaths, 414
 on underage drinking, 30
central nervous system, depressants and, 34
Cepeda, L. M, 178
Ceravolo, R., 51
certification, 76–77, 206
certified addiction counselor (CAD), 79
Chamberlain, C. M., 56, 58–59
Chamberlain, L., 308, 320, 321
Chan, A. W., 389
Chan, F., 329, 332
Chandler, M. C., 177
Chandler, N., 66, 69, 72, 75
Chaney, M. P., 434
Chang, C. Y., 434
Chang, F. C., 111
Chang, G., 137–138
Chang, I., 130
Chang, T., 390
change
 clients, achieving, 152–154
 explanation of, 151
 motivational interviewing and, 151–152
change of subject in conversation, 158
change plan, 162
Change Readiness and Treatment Eagerness
 Scales (SOCRATES), 311

change talk, 153, 157
change theory stage, 108–109
Chapman, J. E., 81
Chappel, J., 273
character defects, 234
Chartas, N. D., 200, 201
Chasek, C. L., 69, 72
Chasnoff, I. J., 316, 353
Chassler, D., 103
Chaudhry, C., 244
Chawla, N., 174
Chedrese, P. J., 257
chemical addiction, 256, 355. *See also* addiction
Chen, C., 244
Chen, H. -J., 388
Cheng, A. W., 384
Cheon, J., 91
Chermack, S. T., 312
Chernin, J. N., 432
Cherpitel, C. J., 138
Chi, F., 270
Chi, F. W., 81
Chiauzzi, E. J., 297
Chideya, F., 383
children. *See also* parenting
 of addicts, 311–312, 353, 371
 ADHD medication and, 38–39, 197–198
 adverse childhood events and, 111
 alcohol addiction of family member and, 315–319
 brain damage due to drug use, 356
 counseling, family dynamics and, 306–310
 counselor issues and, 68
 developmental model and, 11
 fetal alcohol syndrome and, 137, 316, 353, 413
 first exposure to addiction and, 106
 genetic model and, 11
 of incarcerated parents, 464–465
 prevention programs for, 220, 360–371
 sexual assault and, 414
 solution-focused integration and, 179
 stimulant use of, 37
 support groups for, 267
 trauma and mental health of, 30
 work addiction of parents and, 58
choice, moral model and, 7
Chou, C. C., 329, 332
Chou, P. S., 354
Christian, S., 319
Christiansen, B. A., 108
Christo, G., 270
Christopher, S., 83
Christopoulos, A., 241
Chung, Y. B., 431
Ciaccio, C. P., 331
Cicchetti, R. J., 449
Cifu, D. X., 330, 335
cigarettes. *See* tobacco
Cingel, P. A., 192
cisgender, 428
Clark, C., 72
Clark, L., 48, 51

Clark, S. M., 60
Clay, D. L., 56
Clayton, R., 363
Clean Start, 372
Cleland, C. M., 271
Clements, R., 132, 133
Clemmey, P., 172
Cleveland, H., 111, 371
Cleveland, H. H., 312
clients. *See also specific types of clients*
 affirmation of, 156, 434–435
 background and contextual information of, 103–108
 barriers of (*See* barriers to care)
 change, achieving, 152–154
 collaboration with, 94, 180
 commitment of, 162
 confidence of, 161
 confidentiality (*See* confidentiality)
 education of, 98, 251
 empowering, 181
 expectations of, 107–108, 288
 inpatient experience, 458–460
 language use of, 180–181
 motivating, 93–94
 protection of welfare and information, 95
 traps, resistance and, 160–161
Cliff, S., 388–389
Clinically Managed Low Intensity Residential settings, 451–452, 454
clinician determination of treatment, 455–456
cocaine
 gender differences and, 409
 history of, 3–4
 neurobiology of addiction, 20–21
 neurosurgical procedures for, 22
 physiology of addiction and, 39–40
 relapse rates for, 469
Cochran, S. D., 229
Cocores, J. A., 60
codependence, 314
Co-Dependents Anonymous, 265
codes of ethics
 boundary violations and, 70
 competence, 75, 96
 confidentiality and, 68, 225
 on culture, 96
 group counseling and, 223
 referrals and, 67
 screening group participants, 224–225
Cofey, R. M., 457
Cogley, C. B., 217
cognitive-behavioral approaches
 contingency management and behavioral contracting, 172–173
 functional analysis, 169–170
 for inmates, 466
 overview, 168–169
 relapse prevention, 174–175
 triggers, targeting, 170–172
cognitive-behavioral models, 7–8
cognitive dissonance, 153–154
cognitive interventions, 171

cognitive limitations, 194, 201
cognitive therapy, 292
Cohen, D., 38
Cohen, J., 80
Cohen, R. J., 122
Cohen, W., 292
Cohen, W. E., 39, 105
Coll, K., 197
Coll, K. M., 126
collaboration with clients, 94, 180
collecting summaries, 156
college students
 alcohol use of, 29–30, 354–355, 367
 gaming addiction and, 53
 interventions for, 175–176
 prevention programs for, 367–368
 recovery programs for, 371
Collegiate Recovery Community (CRC), 371
Collins, C., 360, 393
Collins, K. A., 108
Collins, P. H., 392
Collins, R. L., 313
Colliver, J. D., 357
combined behavioral intervention (CBI), 168, 170
coming out, 431, 435
commendations, 183
commitment of clients, 162
Committee on Substance Abuse and Committee on Fetus and Newborn, 353
commonly abused drug chart, 24–25
communication of assessment procedures and results, 98
Community Reinforcement and Family Training (CRAFT), 173–174
community reinforcement approach (CRA), 173–174
community resources, 199
comorbidity, 192–216
 in adolescents, 360–361
 assessment, 197–200
 counselor competence for, 67–68
 disabilities, persons with, 330
 group therapy, 200
 in incarcerated population, 464
 issues-based diagnostic summary, 212–214
 multidisciplinary treatment team, 205–206
 prevalence of, 193–195
 process addictions and, 49, 53
 treatment and care needs, 200–201
 treatment models, 202–205
 treatment planning, 206–207
comparing clients, 159
competence
 in assessment instruments, 96
 counselors, non-users, 75
 on culture, 13
 ethics, 70
 LGBTQ issues, 429
 multicultural, 96
complainant-type therapeutic relationship, 180

Index **479**

compliance, 250–251
complications, medical, 102
Composite International Diagnostic Interview (CIDI-Core), 105
Compton, W., 356, 358
compulsive behavior, 8, 21, 198. *See also* process addictions
compulsive buying (CB), 59–60
Concerta, 37–39
confidence of clients, 161
confidentiality
　of assessment results, 95
　of criminal justice system, 343
　group therapy and, 225–226, 278–279
confrontational/denial trap, 160
Conner, B., 112
Connors, G. J., 109, 270
consequences, 107
Constantine, M. G., 387
consultation, 279
contemplative neuroscience, 22
contextual information for assessment, 103–108
contingency management, 172–173
continuing education, 76
continuity of care, 95
continuum of care, 450
Controlled Substance Act of 1970, 4
conversion therapy, 431
co-occurring competency, 68
co-occurring conditions. *See* comorbidity
Coocher, G. P., 167
Cook, C. C. H., 285, 295
Cook, L. S., 410, 411, 413, 421
Cooke, C. G., 308
Cooney, J. L., 172
Cooper, A. D., 462
Cooper, S., 367
Copello, A., 312
coping skills, 111
　interventions for, 170–172
　modeling, 235
　relapse prevention and, 288–289, 291, 294, 298
Corbin, W., 367
Corbin, W. R., 60
Corcoran, J., 177, 179
Corey, C., 219
Corey, G., 202, 217–220, 224–226, 271
Corey, M. S., 219, 227, 271
Corley, R. P., 417
Cornelius, J. R., 312
Cornelius, M. D., 312
Correia, C. J., 107
cortico-basal ganglia network, 21–22
cost-efficiency of screenings, 124
Costenbader, E. C, 111
cost of interventions, 167
Cotton, N. A., 11
Council for Accreditation of Counseling and Related Educational Programs (CACREP), 72, 224
Council on Rehabilitation Education (CORE), 80

Counselor License Resources, 76
counselors
　accreditation of, 80
　assessments initiated by, 135–137
　assessor role of, 95
　beliefs and behaviors of, 165–166
　boundary violations, 70
　comorbidity, 67–68
　continuing education, 76
　credentialing, 68, 76–79
　cultural and racial diversity of, 384–385
　cultural awareness of, personal, 394–395
　education, 72–73
　empathy of, 22
　gender of, 420–421
　licensure, 79–80
　Multicultural Counseling Competencies, 96, 394
　multiculturalism, 70–72
　non-users, 75
　in recovery, 73–75, 205
　role in inpatient care, 459
　role in pharmacotherapy, 250–251
　role with LGBTQ clients, 440–441
　self-care, 75–76
　self-evaluation, 207
　specific populations, 68
　Twelve Step programs, role in, 275–279
countertransference, 70, 74–75, 301
Cousins, S. J., 81
Cox, R. B., 312, 313
Cox, S., 431
crack cocaine, 39, 409. *See also* cocaine
Craig, R. J., 132
Crane, E. H., 34
Cranford, J. A., 313
Crape, B. L., 271
cravings, 248–255, 288
Crawford, M., 406
Crawford, M. J., 29
Crawford, N. D., 386
Creager, C., 128
credentialing, 68, 72, 76–79
Crews, F. T., 22
Crews, T. M., 128
Cridland, E., 464
Cridland, E. K., 67
crime
　alcohol related, 5
　of juveniles, 361
　to obtain drugs, 198
　penalties for drug use, 461–469
criminal justice barriers, 343
crisis intervention, 100
criterion-keyed scales, 122
Crits-Christoph, P., 275
Cronbach alphas, 136
Cronkite, R. C., 312
Cross, W. E., 393
Croughan, J., 132
Crowe, T., 91
Crowell, J. A., 318

Crowley, N., 296
Crowley, T. J., 417
Crozier, M. K., 331
CSAT Treatment Improvement Protocol, 103
Cucciare, M. A., 73
Culberson, J. W., 357
Culbreth, J. R., 200, 201
Cullen, J., 70, 73–74
culture, 383–405. *See also* ethnicity; race
　access to treatment and, 387–393
　assessment and treatment, 70–71, 96, 198–200
　attitudes towards alcohol, 12
　case studies, 396–401
　continuing education for, 76
　counselor competence on, 13
　definitions, 385–386
　diversity in group settings and, 227–230
　expectations of adolescents, 368
　gender roles an, 422
　importance of in treatment, 384–385
　as risk factor, 340
　theoretical frameworks and, 393–396
　treatment issues, 387
　twelve-step programs and, 273
culture-specific models, 12–13
Cunningham, J. A., 94, 108
Cunningham, M. S., 96
Cunradi, C. B., 312, 316
curriculum standards, 72
Curtis, R., 197
Curtis, R. C., 126
Curtiss, G., 134
customer-type relationship, 180
cybersex, 50
cyclooxygenase (COX), 256

D

Dahlstrom, W. G., 130
Daisy, F., 135
Dakof, G. A., 307
Daleiden, E. L., 134
Daley, A., 433
Daley, D. C., 81, 342
Daley, M., 81–82
Dana, R. Q., 298
D'Andrea, M., 442
D'Andrea, M. A., 95
Daniels, J. A., 95
Darredeau, C., 68
date-rape drugs, 34
Dauber, S., 438
D'Augelli, A. R., 431
Daughhetee, C., 76
D'Avanzo, C. E., 386
Davenport, D. S., 178
Davidson, L. D., 81
Davidson, R., 9
Davis, A. K., 186
Davis, C., 292
Davis, C. R., 56
Davis, D., 356, 358, 370, 389
Davis, D. R., 23, 26, 28, 273, 309, 457
Davis, H. G., 132

Davis, R., 130, 134
Davis, R. B., 311
Davis, S. J., 73
Dawson, D. A., 354
DEA, 38, 39
deaf population, 338–339
Dean, H. Y., 153
Deane, F., 464
Deane, F. P., 67
Dear, G. E., 314
Debtors Anonymous, 59
Decisional Balance, 157
decision making, boundary crossing and, 71
Deck, D., 329
Deck, D. D., 330
Deegan, P. E., 250
Defense Department, 99
deferred prosecution, 467
DeFrancesco, C., 366
Degree Directory, 79
DeJong, W., 363
Deke, J., 365
de la Fuente, J. R., 125
Delaney, S. I., 266
Delanty, N., 251
De Leon, G., 108
Delgado, A., 457
Dellor, E., 30
Del Toro, I. M., 274
Delucci, K., 273
de Menil, V. P., 217
Dempster, M., 129
dendrites, 257
Deneke, C., 414
denial, 50, 234, 310–311
Denis, C. M., 136
Denning, P., 461
Dennis, C. B., 275
Depade, 253–254
Department of Health and Human Services (DHHS), 123, 360, 372, 392
Department of Justice, 363
dependence on group therapy, 272
DePompolo, R. W., 331
depressants, 26–33. *See also specific types*
depression
 comorbidity and, 193
 disabilities, persons with, 332, 337
 pharmacotherapy for, 254
 women and, 412
Derevensky, J., 52
Descheemaeker, N., 358
de Shazer, S., 176–178, 182, 185
Desjardins, L., 411
Desoxyn, 39
detoxification, 100, 454
developmental model, 11
developmental risk factors, 340
de Villeneuve, Arnauld, 27
de Waart, R., 174
De Witte, P., 257
dexamphetamine, 39
dextroamphetamine, 39

diagnosis, assessments for, 119–146. *See also* assessment
Diagnostic and Statistical Manual of Mental Disorders (4th edition; DSM-4), 48, 52
Diagnostic and Statistical Manual of Mental Disorders (5th edition; DSM-5)
 on caffeine addiction, 36
 on comorbidity, 48–49
 for diagnosis, 119
 on disabilities, 330
 on gambling addiction, 52–53
 on Gender Dysphoria, 430
 on marijuana use, 41
 purpose of, 124
 reliance on, 92–93
 revisions in, 48–49, 192
 on sexual addiction, 51
dialectical behavior therapy (DBT), 174
Diamond, G., 319
diathesis-stress model, 316–317
Diaz, R., 317
Diaz, S., 331
diazepam, 33, 252
Dickinson, K. A., 133
Dickman, S. L., 469
DiClemente, C. C., 69, 108–109, 162, 289, 311, 421, 422, 456
Dierberger, A., 275
dieting, 61
Diguer, L., 275
Dildine, R., 126
Dimeff, L. A., 175, 369
DiNitto, D. M., 5, 7, 13, 129
disabilities, persons with, 328–352
 case studies, 334–335, 339–340
 characteristics and status of, 332–334
 intervention, rehabilitation settings, 343–347
 overview of, 328–332
 risk factors for addiction, 335–339
 treatment utilization and outcomes, 341–343
discrepancy, motivational interviewing and, 153–154
discrimination, 423, 463, 468
disease concept model, 10, 165–166, 202–203
Dishion, T., 367, 370, 376
disinhibition-based craving, 249
dissonance, 157
distribution control, 5
distrust days, 321
disulfiram, 251
Ditchman, N., 329, 332
diversity
 assessment and treatment, 70–71
 of counselors, 384–385
 in group settings, 227–230
 multicultural competence and, 96
 pharmacotherapy and, 243–245
divorce, 313
Dodgen, C. E., 9, 11
Doman, K., 314

domestic violence, 200–201, 312–313
Donnelly, M., 129
D'Onofrio, G., 455
Donohue, B., 333
Donovan, D., 254
Donovan, D. M., 81, 97, 106, 109, 168, 171, 270, 277, 292
dopamine, 20, 257
Dore, M. M., 409
Dorsman, J., 266
double-sided reflection, 159
Doughtry, G. P., 340
Douglas, H., 295
Douglas, K. R., 111
Doukas, N., 70, 73–74
Dow, S. J., 68
Dowd, E. T., 228
Dow-Edwards, D. L., 258
Doweiko, H. E., 23, 26, 28, 33, 35–39, 43, 220–222, 235, 236, 263–268, 285, 329, 331, 335, 341, 343
Downey, J. I., 428
downregulation, 257
Doyle, K., 74
Doyle, M., 362
Dozois, D. J. A., 108
Drabble, L., 428, 429, 434
Draijer, N., 316
Drainoni, M., 329
Drake, R. E., 165, 166, 306
Draus, P. J., 111
Drobes, D. J., 288
Drug Abuse Awareness and Resistance Education (D.A.R.E.), 363–364
Drug Abuse Resistance Education (D.A.R.E.), 220
Drug Abuse Screening Test (DAST), 455
drug courts, 4, 358, 467–468
drug metabolism, 244
Drug Policy Alliance, 463
Drug Problems Scale (DRG), 134
drug testing, 365
drug use. *See specific drugs by name*
drug wars. *See war on drugs*
"dry" option for states, 5
DSM. *See Diagnostic and Statistical Manual of Mental Disorders* (5th edition; DSM-5)
dual diagnosis personality disorder, 306
Dube, S. R., 111
Ducharme, L. J., 165, 172, 250, 449
Dudish, S. A., 411, 412, 416
Dufault, K., 91
Duffy, M., 198
Dugosh, K. L., 167
DUI convictions, 5–6
DUI laws, 29
Dulcan, M., 361
Duncan, B. L., 177
Dunn, C., 29
Dunn, R., 361
Dunn, V., 376
duplication of services, 201
DuPont, R., 273

Durham, M., 366
Durose, M. R., 462
Dutta, A., 329, 332
Dwyer, S., 359
Dykeman, C., 240, 250
Dziegielewski, S. F., 35

E

Earleywine, M., 275
Early Action Against Teen Drug Use, 364–365
early diagnosis, 360–361
early intervention, 452–453
eating disorders, 60–62
Ebama, M. S., 312
Ebener, D. J., 330
Ecological Systems Theory, 367
economic risk factors, 336–337
ecstasy (MDMA), 42–43
Edleson, J. L., 345
education, 72–73
　of clients, 98, 251
　continuing, counselor, 76
　of inmates, 466
　of pregnant women, 372
Edwards, G., 285
Edwards, J. T., 305
efficacy of treatment, 81–82
Egan, G., 153
Ehde, D. M., 336
Ehlers, C. L., 388
Ehrmann, L., 132
Einspruch, E., 365
elderly adults, substance abuse of, 357, 374–375, 436
Elford, J., 434
El-Guebaly, N., 77–78
Eliason, M. J., 14
Ellickson, P., 362, 370, 375
Elliot, D., 366
Elliot, R., 153
Ellis, D. A., 317
Ellis, L., 312
El Rakhawy, M., 9
Elvine-Kreis, B., 389
Emmelkamp, P. M. G., 315
Emmerling, M. E., 150, 152
emotional desert, 321
emotional interventions, 170–171
emotional stress, 288, 290
empathy, 22, 75, 97, 153
employment
　alcohol effect on, 29
　assessment information on, 112
　disabilities, persons with, 332
　felons and, 465
　relapse prevention and, 68
　as risk factor, 336–337
　transgendered people and, 434
　unemployment, 71, 295, 336–337, 417, 465
empowering clients, 181
Emrick, C. D., 270, 271
enabling, 314
endogenous, 257
Engel, J. M., 336

Ennett, S., 363
environment
　cause of addiction and, 13–14
　family systems addiction and, 321
　for LGBTQ clients, 441
　for recovery, 102–103
environmental interventions, 170
ephedrine, 37–39
Epperson, L., 410
Epstein, E. E., 165, 307, 313, 321
Epstein, M., 91
Epston, D., 171, 181
Erfan, S., 9
Erickson, C. K., 316
Erickson, M., 176
Erickson, S., 27, 33, 34, 42
Erickson, W., 328
Espeland, B., 306
Essic, E. J., 18, 48
ethanol, 27–28, 410
ethics. *See also* codes of ethics
　boundary violation issues and, 70–72
　children, working with, 68
　continuing education and, 76
　group therapy and, 223–226
　managed care and, 80–81
　recovering counselors and, 74
ethnicity. *See also* culture
　assessment and treatment, 70–71
　comorbidity and, 199, 464
　drug use and, 3
　group therapy and, 228
　pharmacotherapy and, 243–245
ethnic psychopharmacology, 257
etiology of addiction. *See* addiction causes
evaluating during treatment, 207
evaluating screenings and assessments, 123–124
evidence-based practices, 69, 81–83, 166–168, 358–359
Ewing, J. A., 125, 128
Examination for Master Addiction Counselors (EMAC), 77
exams, 77–79
exceptions to problem, 181–182
Executive Office of the President, 356
expert trap, 160
external consequences, 107
external motivation, 93–94
external triggers, 106–107

F

Fabian, E., 329
Faces and Voices of Recovery, 83
Fahy, A., 74
Fairburn, C., 376
Fala, N. C., 167
Falkowski, C. L., 28, 34
Fallot, R. D., 345
false positives and negatives, assessments, 123–124
Fals-Stewart, W., 134, 308, 311–313, 360
family, impact of addiction on, 305–327
　case studies, 307, 313, 319
　children, 315–319 (*See also* children)
　concerned significant other (CSO), working with, 173–174
　counseling, family dynamics and, 306–310
　counseling and treatment for, 319–322
　couple relationships, 312–315
　fetal alcohol syndrome, 137, 316, 353, 413
　group therapy and, 230–231
　incarcerated parents and, 464–465
　overview, 305–306
　parenting, 311–312
　pregnancy, substance abuse during, 137–139, 252–254, 316, 353, 371–373
　relapse and, 299–300
　role in inpatient care, 459
　stages in family systems, 310–311
　work addiction, 58–59
family and peer relationships, 110–111
family disease model, 9
family models, 9
family support. *See* social support
family systems model, 9
Farabee, D., 412
Faraone, S., 360, 362
Farentinos, C., 66
Faria, R., 256
Farrell, M. P., 386
Farrell, N., 329, 330
Fassel, D., 49, 56, 58
Fassinger, R. E., 431, 433
Fassler, A., 178
Fast Alcohol Screening Test (FAST), 129
fatalities
　car crashes, 29
　huffing and, 355
　overintoxication, 28, 357, 368
　tobacco use and, 35
　violence and, 410
Federal Bureau of Prisons, 466
Federal Drug Administration, 39
Feldstein, S., 438
Feldstein, S. W., 127
felons, 465
femininity, 406
Fendrich, M., 364, 413, 420
Fenton, M., 252, 254
Ferderman, E. B., 136
Ferentzy, P., 7, 10–11
Fernando, D. M., 178
Ferraro, N., 43
Festinger, L., 153
fetal alcohol syndrome, 137, 316, 353, 413
Field, C. A., 384
Fields, R., 309, 316–318
Fielling, D. A., 129
Fihn, S. D., 129
Filomensky, T. Z., 59, 60
Fincham, F. D., 311
Fink, A., 413
Finn, A., 353
Finn, S. E., 94, 98
Finnegan, D. G., 434
Finnegan, L. P., 353

Finney, J. W., 136, 266, 312, 342, 458
Fiorentine, R., 418–419
Fioritti, A., 149
firearms, restrictions on, 465
first exposure to addiction, 106
first-line agent, 257
Fischer, B., 463
Fischer, J. L., 312
Fisher, D., 192
Fisher, G. L., 1, 10, 81, 301, 331, 340, 343, 345
Fisher, K., 428
Fishman, M., 97, 451
Fitzgerald, E., 80
Fitzgerald, H. A., 317
Fitzgerald, H. E., 311, 316, 317
Fleming, M. F., 128
Fletcher, K., 255
Flicker, S. M., 308
flow of assessment, 98–100
Floyd, F. J., 313
flunitrazepam, 34
Flynn, B., 362
Follette, V. M., 174
Foltz, R., 10
Fong, T. W., 54
Fontana, L., 419, 422
food addiction, 60–62
Food Addicts in Recovery Anonymous, 61
Forbes, D., 462
Forcehimes, A. A., 175, 305
Forman, R. F., 341
Forman-Hoffman, V., 289
formative process evaluation, 207
formative product evaluation, 207
Fosados, R., 340
Foster, M., 130
Foster, S. E., 466
Fothergill, A., 410, 412, 413
Foulks, E. F., 394
Fournier, E., 222
Fox, T. S., 165
Foxcroft, D., 463
FRAMES perspective, 184–185
Frances, R. J., 228
Franck, J., 287
Franco, H., 271
Franey, C., 270
Franklin, J., 389
Frankowski, R., 384
Freimuth, M., 96, 276
French, M. T., 413
Frey, R. M., 165
Friedman, A. S., 319
Friedman, R. C., 428
Friedman, S. R., 410
Friedrich, W. N., 127
"Friends Don't Let Friends Drive Drunk" campaign, 369
Fromme, K., 367
Frosini, D., 51
Frusti, D. K., 148
Frye, M. A., 251
Fuhrmann, J. C., 257
Fuller, B. E., 312
Fuller, C. M., 386

functional analysis, 169–170
functioning of client, 104–105
funding for treatment, 80–81, 457
Fung, T. S., 108
Furst, J., 271, 275
Fusillo, S., 37
Fussell, H. E., 81–82

G

GABA (γ-aminobutyric acid), 257
Gabriel, R., 329, 330
Gabrielsen, K. R., 1
Gage, A., 253
Galanter, M., 271, 346
Gallagher, R., 367
Gallati, R. J., 53, 54
Gallois, C., 431
Gamblers Anonymous (GA), 54
gambling addiction, 52–54
gaming addiction, 53
gamma-amino butyric acid (GABA), 20–21
Garbutt, J., 251, 253
García, M., 317
Gardner, D., 365
Gargon, N., 54
Gariti, P., 410
Garry, J. K. F., 108
Garvin, W. S., 414
Gary, L. E., 386
Gary, R. B., 386
Gasbarrini, G., 249
Gass, J., 255
Gastfriend, D. R., 97, 136, 450
gateway drugs, 362
Gaume, J., 153
Gauvin, L. M., 415
gay men, 434. *See also* lesbian, gay, bisexual, transgender, and queer (LGBTQ) clients
Gazda, G. M., 224, 228, 229
Gearhardt, A. N., 60
Geerlings, P., 248, 253
gender, explanation of, 430
gender-bending, 428
gender differences
  of addicts, 34
  alcohol and drug use and, 407–409
  alcohol tolerance and, 28
  amphetamine use and, 37
  benzodiazepines and, 33
  case studies, 411, 412, 415–418, 420
  codependence and, 314
  college students, high-risk behaviors of, 367–368
  development of addictions and, 319–320
  disabilities, people with, 332
  divorce and, 313
  drug abuse and, 244–245
  effects of alcohol and, 137
  explanation of, 406
  gambling addiction and, 53
  group therapy and, 228–229
  men and addiction, 415–418
  parenting and, 311–312
  sexual addiction, 50

twelve-step programs and, 273
violence and alcohol, 312
women and addiction, 410–415
Gender Dysphoria, 430
gender expression, 428
gender identity, 428, 431
gender queer, 428
generic name, 257
genetic models, 11–12
Geniza, C., 253
genogram, 220, 320
Gensheimer, L., 390
Gentilello, L., 29
Gentry, K. A., 428
George, A. A., 271
George, W., 286, 293
George, W. H., 287
Gershenfeld, M. K., 228
Gervey, R., 329, 332
Gfroerer, J. C., 357
Giannandrea, P., 220
Gilberston, R., 28
Gilchrist, G., 111
Gill, C., 67
Gillham, J., 80
Gillig, S. W., 192, 198, 201
Gilligan, C., 422
Gilliland, B., 357
Gilliland, B. E., 18, 221, 230, 234
Gilmour, J. A., 423
Gima, K., 342
Gingerich, W. J., 176, 177, 180
Ginter, E. J., 224
Gladding, S. T., 220, 227
Glantz, M. D., 11, 320, 321
Glenn, M. K., 329, 331
Glik, D. C., 68
glutamate, 257
goals
  failure and, 340
  of treatment, 178
  of twelve step programs, 267–268
Godfrey, M., 70
Godkin, J., 340
Goesling, B., 365
Goffman, E., 93
Gogel, L. P., 68
Gogtay, N., 356
Gold, M. S., 60, 61
Gold, R., 108
Goldberg, L., 365, 366
Goldberg, R., 362, 375
Golden, J., 311
Golden, J. C., 308
Golden, S. H., 66
Goldman, D., 11
Goldman, M. S., 108
Gollwitzer, P. M., 150
Golub, A., 363
Gonzales, R., 68
Gonzales, R. A., 12
Gonzalez, C., 127
Goode, E., 12
Goode, J. L., 35
Goodhart, R. L., 345

Goodheart, C. D., 166
Goodman, A., 241
Goodman, C., 240
Goodstein, R., 394
Goodwin, D. W., 11
Goodwin, L. R., 331, 343
Gordon, J., 287, 297
Gordon, J. R., 174–175, 290
Gordon, S. M., 410–415, 417, 421
Gorman, D., 220
Gorski, T. T., 296, 298
gradualism, 185
Grady, R., 386
Graham, C. W., 330, 335
Graham, J., 211
Graham, J. R., 130, 131, 133
Graham, K., 94
Graham, M. D., 112
Graham, N. A., 60
Graham, V., 338
Grant, B. F., 316, 354, 408
Grant, J., 256
Grant, J. M., 423
Grant, M., 125
Grasso, B. C., 177
Grawe, R. W., 306
Gray, B. T., 126
Gray, M., 408, 422
Greason, P. B., 161
Greenbaum, P. E., 307
Greenberg, L. S., 153
Greene, R. L., 132
Greenfield, S. F., 408–410, 413, 415, 419, 420, 424
Greiner, J., 51
Grella, C., 192, 360, 362
grief, 234
Griffin, K., 362
Griffith, J. H., 97
Griffiths, M., 50
Griffiths, M. D., 306
Griffiths, R. R., 328
Grills, C., 386
Grilo, C. M., 49, 60
Grisham, J. R., 59
Grissom, J. N. G., 467
Gross, D., 438
Grossman, A. H., 429
Grothaus, D., 1
Groth-Marnat, G., 123, 124, 131, 135
Grotmol, K., 107
group therapy, 217–239. *See also* Twelve Step programs
 addiction treatment and, 218
 case study, 231–236
 conflict in, 227
 diversity, managing, 227–230
 ethical and legal issues, 223–226
 family members of addicts, 230–239, 306–310
 in inpatient setting, 459
 mixed-gender, 416, 420
 psychoeducational groups, 219–220
 psychotherapeutic groups, 220–222
 self-help groups, 222–223
 strategies for, 236–237
 theory behind, 217–218
 women and, 420
Groves, P., 295
Grunewald, P. J., 374
Grzywacz, J. G., 313
Gual, A., 317
Guerino, P., 462
Guillem, K., 48
Guldager, S., 134–135
Guth, L. J., 424
Guthmann, D., 338
Guyon, L., 411
Gwaltney, C. J., 288

H

Haber, P. S., 250
Habing, B., 136
Haddock, L. R., 217
Hage, R., 306
Hagedorn, W. B., 48–50, 316
hailing, 419–420
Haley, M., 66, 81
half-life, 257
Hall, J., 37
Hall, S. M., 290
Hall, W., 108
Hallinan, P., 129
hallucinogens, 41–43, 469
Halme, J. T., 129
Halter, M. J., 43
Hamilton, M., 270
Hamm, T., 68, 69, 77
Hammer, R. R., 12
Han, B., 357
hangovers, 26
Hanson, B., 386
Hanson, G., 363
Harley, D. A., 328, 334
Harmon, M., 363
harm reduction, 184–187, 368–369
Harned, M. S., 169
Harp, K. H., 70
Harper, H., 126
Harrell, E., 337
Harrell, P. T., 36
Harrington, D., 311
Harris, A. H., 458
Harris, K., 111, 371
Harris, M., 345
Harris, S. K., 176
Harris, T. R., 312, 384
Harris-Offit, R., 386
Harrison, G. L., 301
Harrison, P. M., 462
Harrison, T. C., 1, 10, 81, 331, 340, 343, 345
Harrison Act of 1914, 4, 39
Hartel, C. R., 320, 321
Hartley, P., 320
Hartman, J. L., 457–458
Haseltine, F. P., 410, 412, 413, 415, 416, 424
Hasin, D. S., 408
Hatsukami, D. K., 411, 412, 416
Havassy, B. E., 290
Hawkins, J., 359, 370, 375
Hawkins, J. D., 359
Hawley, C. E., 331
Hayes, S. C., 174
Hays, D. G., 429
Hayyan, Jabir ibn, 27
health systems, evolution of, 192–193
Healy, J., 42
Hearon, G. A., 168
Heath, A. W., 320, 321
Heath, D. B., 386
Heather, N., 108, 175
Heatherton, T. F., 278
Hedlund, J., 127
Hegamin, A., 412, 413, 416, 421
Heil, S. H., 172
Heintz, J. M., 132, 133
Helms, J. E., 387, 393, 394
Helm's racial identity theory, 393–394
Helzer, J. E., 132
Hendershot, C. S., 287
Henderson, C. E., 307
Hendricks, B., 221
Hendrie, D., 362
Henkel, D., 337
Henson, B. R., 136
Henson, J., 358
Hepner, K. A., 222
Herbeck, D. M., 177
Herlihy, B., 95, 100
Herman, J., 172
heroin, 34–35
 consumption rate of, 4
 history of, 4, 34
 relapse rates for, 469
Herrera, V. M., 312
Herringer, L. G., 270
Herzog, T. A., 340
Hesse, M., 134–135
Hesselbrock, M. N., 410
Hesselbrock, V. M., 410
Hester, R. K., 165, 166
heterosexism, 429
Hettema, J., 154, 162
Hettema, J. E., 167
Hewitt, J. K., 417
Heyward, C., 273
Hickling, F. W., 70
Higgins, T. S., 172
Higgins-Biddle, J. C., 129
high-risk behavior, 111, 200, 357, 367–369, 411
high-risk situations, relapse and, 290–292
Hill, E. M., 411, 416
Hill, P., 373
Hill, S., 11
Hiller-Sturmhofel, S., 271, 456
Hillhouse, M. P., 418–419
Hine, D. W., 314
Hirsch, L. S., 307
Hispanics. *See* Latinos
historical trauma, 340
history of addiction, 1–6
 cocaine, 40
 policies and, 5–6
 prevention in U.S., 2–5
Hitzemann, R., 22

484 Index

HIV/AIDS, 357, 411, 414, 434
Hix-Small, H., 366
Hoaken, P. N. S., 416
Hodgkins, C. G., 81
Hodgson, R. J., 129
Hoebel, B. G., 60
Hoffman, H., 131
Hogan, J. A., 1
Hoge, M. A., 73
Hogue, A., 438
Holck, P., 199
Holder, Eric, 463
Hollar, D., 329, 332
Holm Linneberg, I., 134–135
Holt, K., 363
homeostasis of families, 307–308
Home Visitation by Nurses Program, 372–373
home visit programs, 372
Homish, G. C., 69
Homish, G. G., 312
homoprejudice, 429
homosexuality. *See* lesbian, gay, bisexual, transgender, and queer (LGBTQ) clients
Hook, M. K., 305
hooks, b., 392
hope, 90–91, 180–181
Hopfer, C. J., 417
hormones, addiction and, 411, 415–416
hormones, cravings and, 249
hormones, explanation of, 257
Horn, J., 130
Horne, A. M., 224
Hornik, R., 370
Horowitz, J. L., 431
Horrigan, T. J., 119
Horst, T., 274
Horton, E. G., 35
Horton, N., 94
Horvath, A. T., 81
Hoskins, W. J., 1
Hosley, C. A., 390
hospitalization, for alcohol related injuries, 29
hospital settings, 31–33
hostile behavior, 227
Howell, T., 457–458
Hser, Y., 177, 360–362
Hsu, C., 67, 464
Hsu, S., 53
Hsu, S. H., 295
Hubbell, A., 413
Hubble, M. A., 177
Huber, G. L., 69
Huber, M. J., 329
Hübner, C. A., 257
Huey, L. Y., 73
huffing, 355
Hughes, J. R., 328
Hughes, S., 108
Hughes, T., 434
Hughes, T. L., 428
human assessment measures, 95–98
Human Genome Project, 11–12

Humfleet, G. L., 290
Humphreys, K., 264, 276, 461, 463
Hunt, J., 423
Hunt, L. M., 244
Hunter, S. B., 222
Huntington, A., 423
Huntley, E. D., 36
Husband, S. D., 177
hypnotics, 33–34
hypothetical change, 161

I

Iacono, W. G., 60
Iarussi, M. M, 1
ibogaine, 255
ice (methamphetamine), 38
identity models, 393–394
ignoring, 158, 227
Iguchi, M. Y., 177
Imm, P. S., 314
immigrants
  drug use of, 3
  illegal, 5
immunotherapy, 257
Importance Ruler, 157
importation of illegal drugs, 4–5
impulse control, 51, 61
Inaba, D., 292
Inaba, D. S., 39, 105
incarceration vs. rehabilitation, 462–466
INCASE, 72
Inciardi, J. A., 26, 27–28, 35, 43
informed consent, 95, 225
informed eclecticism model, 166
Ingersoll, R. E., 256, 258
inhalants, 355
inhibitory pathway, 21
inpatient and outpatient treatment, 449–473
  inpatient programs
    case study, 460
    client experience, 458–460
    clinician determination of treatment, 455–456
    inpatient, levels of care, 450–454
    motivational interviewing for, 456–457
    rehabilitation center challenges, 457–458
    types of, 454
  outpatient programs
    advocacy, 469
    explanation of, 453
    legislation affecting, 461–466
    overview, 460–461
    residential, 466–469
  persons with disabilities and, 341–343
Institute of Medicine (IOM), 355, 373
institutes of higher education (IHEs), 367–368, 371. *See also* college students
insurance
  background information and, 103
  of college students, 368
  inpatient care and, 457, 458
  laws for, 6

legislation for, 468–469
outpatient care and, 468
provider reimbursement, 80–81
treatment coverage, 10
intake procedures, 71
integral model, 14
intensive outpatient treatment, 453
internal consequences, 107
internal motivation, 93–94
internal triggers, 106–107
International Association for Addiction and Offender Counselors (IAAOC), 77
International Association of Addictions, 48
International Certification Reciprocity Consortium (IC & RC), 77–79
Internet
  gambling addiction and, 52–53
  gaming addiction and, 53
  self-help groups, 263
  sexual addiction and, 50
interpersonal risk factors, 337
interrupting, 158, 227
intersex persons, 407, 423–424
interventions
  brief, 175–176
  culturally appropriate, 398–400
  disabilities, persons with, 343–347
  evidence-based, 166–167
  twelve-step programs as, 274
interviews
  affirmative assessment, LGBT clients, 435
  assessment, 91
  Composite International Diagnostic Interview (CIDI-Core), 105
  Diagnostic Interview Schedule, 132
  for family counseling, 320
  motivational interviewing, 147–164 (*See also* motivational interviewing)
  structured, semi-structured, unstructured, 100–103
intravenous drug use (IDU), 357, 411
Inventory of Drinking Situations, 291
involuntary group therapy, 226
Ioannidis, J. P. A., 252
ion channels, 257
Irwig, L., 165
Isebaert, L., 177–178, 185
issues-based diagnostic summary, 212–214
IV drug use, 111
Iwamoto, D. K., 384
Iwamoto, K., 367

J

Ja, D. Y., 386
Jackson, D. D., 300
Jackson, K. M., 106
Jackson, M., 392
Jacob, C., 12
Jacobsohn, L., 370
Jacobson, G. R., 128
Jaffee, W. B., 217
James, R., 357
James, R. K., 18, 221, 230, 234
James-Burduny, S., 365, 366

Janis, I. L., 107
Jansen, G. G., 273
Jansson, L. M., 80
Jastreboff, A. M., 60
Jayaram-Lindstrom, N., 287
Jellinek's curve, 109–110
Jellinek, E. M., 10
Jenkinson, G., 296
Jensen, M. P., 336
Jentsch, T. J., 257
Jew, C. L., 308, 320, 321
Jiménez, R. E., 457
Joanning, H., 319
Joe, G. W., 136
Johansen, G. J. E., 129
Johansen, J., 127
Johnsen, E., 270
Johnson, A. L., 263
Johnson, B., 363
Johnson, B. A., 83
Johnson, J., 220
Johnson, J. A., 449
Johnson, J. D., 314
Johnson, J. L., 217, 218, 235, 236
Johnson, M., 192, 193, 197, 200
Johnson, M. R., 432
Johnson, P., 356
Johnson, P. N., 275
Johnson, S. L., 98, 103, 106
Johnson, T. P., 107
Johnson-Green, D., 128
Johnston, L. D., 37, 354, 356
Johnstone, B., 363
Jones, E., 221
Jones, H., 80
Jones, K. D., 67, 341
Jones, K. L., 353
Jorgensen, M., 69
journaling, 321
Joutsenniemi, K., 312
Juhnke, G., 197
Juhnke, G. A., 48–50, 126, 316
Juliano, L. M., 328
Julien, R. M., 241, 247, 257
Jung, Y., 329
Juvenile Drug Court (JDC), 4, 358
juveniles. *See* adolescents

K

Kadish, W., 321
Kaemmer, B., 130
Kahler, C. W., 288
Kahn, D. E., 43
Kaij, L., 11
Kail, R. V., 345
Kalinichev, M., 250
Kalivas, P. W., 20, 22
Kalyoncu, A., 255
Kaminer, Y., 99, 136
Kammeier, M. L., 131
Kanny, D., 414
Kaplan, H. B., 128
Kashdan, T. B., 313
Kashubeck-West, S., 329

Kaskutas, L. A., 274, 278, 413, 419
Kat (methamphetamine), 38
Kauffman, E., 409
Kauhanen, J., 415
Kavanagh, K., 367, 376
Kazdin, A. E., 166
Kearns-Bodkin, J. N., 318
Keferl, J., 329, 331
Kehl-Fie, K. A., 133
Keith-Spiegel, P., 71
Kelch, B. P., 227
Kellet, S., 59, 60
Kelley, M. A., 311
Kelley, M. L., 308, 314
Kellogg, S. H., 185
Kelly, J. F., 68, 250, 269, 270, 274
Kelly, P., 464
Kelly, P. J., 67
Kenakin, T., 241
Kenna, G., 252, 254
Kennedy, S., 250
Kenny, S., 355
Kessler, F., 136
Ketcham, K., 19, 40
Ketner, J. S., 312
Kettinger, L., 311, 371
Keyes, K. M., 408, 409
Keziah, T. B., 72
Khantzian, E. J., 275
Kidman, R., 52
Kiefer, F., 251
Kilpatrick, D. G., 370
Kim, J. S., 166, 177, 467
Kim-Berg, I., 204
King, J. E., 353
King, R. S., 467
Kinney, J., 307, 316–318, 329, 335, 336, 346, 349
Kippers, S. M., 410
Kirby, K. C., 167
Kirkpatric, J., 266
Kishline, A., 267
Kishline, S., 267
Kitchens, J. M., 128
Kivlahan, D., 369, 458
Kivlahan, D. R., 66, 129, 175
Kleber, H. D., 346, 347
Klostermann, K., 453
Knack, W. A., 270
Knapp, C., 23, 26
Knight, E. L., 271
Knight, J. R., 176, 354–355
Knight, K., 136
Knopf, A., 79
Knowlton, A. R., 271
Knudsen, H. K., 165, 250, 449
Kocarnick, J., 66
Koch, D. S., 73
Koehler, R. A., 270
Koeter, M. W. J., 253
Kolakowsky-Hayner, S. A., 333
Kolb, B., 256
Kole, J., 328, 331
Komro, K. A., 373
Koopmans, J. R., 11

Koppelman, K. L., 345
Korcha, R., 434
Korman, H., 176, 180
Koss-Chioino, J. D., 386
Kosten, T., 66, 257, 260
Kotova, E., 126
Kozlowski, L. T., 312
Kraemer, K. L., 455
Krahn, G., 329, 330, 343, 345
Kranzler, H., 253
Kranzler, H. R., 12, 18, 49, 172
Krebs, P. M., 288
Krege, B., 152
Kreiner, M. J., 244
Krentzman, A. R., 83
Kristen, R. B., 138
Krull, J., 367
Krumboltz, J. D., 384
Kubler-Ross, E., 234
Kubler-Ross Model, 234
kudzu, 255
Kunkel, L. E., 81
Kunz, C., 162
Kuo, M., 369
Kuorelahti, M., 91
Kurl, S., 415
Kurtzman, K., 356
Kus, R. J., 431
Kvam, M. H., 338, 339
Kyzas, P., 252

L

labeling trap, 160
Labouvie, E., 165
LaBrie, J., 355
labs for drug making, 38
Lai, S., 355
Lainas, H., 55
Laird, R. D., 367
Lakin, R., 220
Lam, R. M., 457
Lamb, R. J., 177
Lambert, M. J., 110
Lamictal, 255
lamotrigine, 255
Landheim, A. S., 416
Lane, T., 329
Langås, A., 67
Langeland, W., 316
Langlois, J. A., 333
language
 affirmative, 434–435
 used by clients, 180–181
language deficiencies, 340
Lapham, S. C., 130
Lappalainen, K., 91
lapses
 prevention techniques, 298–299
 relapses vs., 286, 294
Larimer, M., 355
Laris, A. S., 271
La Rouche, M. J., 83
Larson, D. B., 112
Larson, M., 94

Larson, S. S., 112
Lassiter, P., 436
Lassiter, P. S., 428, 436
Latcovich, M. A., 431
Latessa, E. J., 457–458
Latinos, 390–391. *See also* race
Latkin, C. A., 111, 271
Laudet, A., 273, 275, 276
Laudet, A. B., 263, 271, 272, 275, 279
Laukkanen, J., 415
Laux, J. M., 119, 126–128, 131
Lavigne, N., 464
Lawhon, D., 290
Lawler, M., 373
Lawson, A., 316
Lawson, A. W., 269, 308, 309, 317
Lawson, G., 316
Lawson, G. W., 269–272, 275, 308, 309, 317
Lawson, S., 270, 271
Lazowski, L. E., 126, 127
leaders
  competence of, 224
  role of, 222
learning models, 8
Leary, J. D., 340
Lee, C., 328
Lee, C. S., 384
Lee, D. M., 451, 452, 454
Lee, D. R., 81
Lee, H., 369
Lee, J., 75, 369
Lee, J. A., 387
Lee, J. P., 374
Lee, M. Y., 181
Lee, P. A., 424
Lee, S., 59, 60, 75
legal issues
  boundary violations, 70
  children, working with, 68
  group therapy and, 223–226
legalization of drugs, 6
Leggio, L., 249, 252, 254
legislation, 461–466. *See also specific acts*
Lehert, P., 253
Leierer, S. J., 343
Lejuez, C., 367
Lemanski, N., 34
Lemkau, Paul, 10–11
Leonard, J., 270
Leonard, J. C., 72
Leonard, K. E., 312, 313, 318
Leonhard, C., 136
Leontiva, L., 29
lesbian, gay, bisexual, transgender, and queer (LGBTQ) clients, 428–448
  case studies, 433, 437, 439–440, 444
  coming out, 431–433
  overview, 428–430
  terms and myths, 430–431
  treatment and assessment, 433–444
lesbian women, 434
Leszcz, M., 225
Letourneau, E. J., 81
Leukefeld, C. G., 111

Leukefeld, C. G., 94
Lev, A., 430, 431
level of care, 101–103, 450–454
Levenson, H., 165
Levin, J. D., 13
Levine, C., 43
Levine, H. G., 461
Levit, K. R., 457
Levy, D. T., 30
Levy-Stern, D., 310
Lewis, J., 95
Lewis, J. A., 277, 298
Lewis, L. E., 386, 392
Lewis, M. D., 95, 355
Lewis, T. F., 152, 178
Lewy, C. S., 81
Leykin, Y., 73, 75
LGBTQ clients. *See* lesbian, gay, bisexual, transgender, and queer (LGBTQ) clients
Li, T., 12, 49, 356, 366
Li, T. K., 18
liability laws, 6
Licensed Addiction Counselor (LAC), 79–80
licensure, 1–2, 67, 77, 79–80
Liddle, H., 438
Liddle, H. A., 307, 319
Liepman, M. R., 127
Liese, B. S., 169
lifestyle changes, 287, 295–297, 301
Lilienfeld, S. O., 167
Limbrick-Oldfield, E. H., 48, 51
Lin, K., 244
Lin, K. M., 243, 244, 257
Lin, Y., 136
Lindgren, K. P., 7
Linehan, M. M., 171, 174
Link, T., 250
linking summaries, 156
Linney, K. D., 306, 308, 313, 321
Linton, J. M., 75, 177
Lioresal, 253
Lipkin, C., 250
Lips, H. M., 406, 407
Lisha, N., 50
Lisman, S. A., 129
listening, reflective, 155
Listwan, S. J., 457–458
Little, C. R., 353
Liu, Y., 60
liver health, 28, 410
locus of control, 340
Loeb, M., 338
Loesch, L., 204
Loftsgard, S. O., 127
Logan, C. R., 429
log of ongoing use, 106
Logsdon, T., 311
Long, L. L., 50, 51
Longabaugh, R., 153
Longshore, D., 112
Longshore, D. G., 386
Lonsdale, J., 103
Looking Back/Forward techniques, 157

Loos, M. D., 205
Loper, R. G., 131
Lopez, E. N., 288
Lorah, P., 413, 414, 418, 419
Lorber, W., 308
Lovato, L. V., 185
Lovinger, D. M., 20–21, 23
Lowery, C. T., 386
Lown, A., 434
LSD, 3
Lu, L., 23
Lubman, D. I., 19, 20–21
Lubman, D. L., 8
Luborsky, L., 134, 275
Lucente, S., 360
Luchansky, B., 392
Luck, R. S., 330, 331
Luckman, T., 93
Luczak, S. E., 389
Luger, L., 70, 386, 387
Lugo, M. M., 383
Lumley, R. S., 165
Luna, N., 1
Lundahl, B. W., 162
Lundgren, L., 69, 81–82, 103
Lundqvist, T., 105
Lurigio, A. J., 413
Lustky, M. K., 295
Lustyk, M. K., 22
Lyman, R., 42
Lynam, D., 363
Lynch, K. G., 136
Lynch, W. J., 244, 408, 411, 413
Lynde, D. W., 166
Lynskey M., 110, 362

M

MacAndrew, C., 9, 131
MacAndrew Alcoholism Scale—Revised, 131
Mack, J. E., 275
MacKenzie, D., 423
Mackinnon, S. V., 113
MacPherson, L., 367
Madden, T. E., 66
Maddux, C., 391
Madill, A., 70
Madison-Colmore, O., 386
Magill, M., 269, 274
Magnus, G., 436
Maguire, M., 434
Magura, S., 271
Mahajan, V. K., 69
Mahalik, J. R., 394
maintenance programs. *See* relapse prevention
maintenance stage of change, 150
Maisto, S., 358
Majoor, B., 185
Mäkelä, K., 136
Making Alcoholics Anonymous Easier (MAAEZ), 278
Maklan, D., 370
Malt, U., 67
managed care, 80–81
management plan for relapse prevention, 296

Index

mandated treatment, 422
mandatory sentencing, 4, 5, 360, 463
Manis, M., 128
Mann, K., 251
Mann, L., 107
Manning, M. L., 394
Manuel, J. K., 174
Marecek, J., 80
Marel, R., 53, 54
Marger, M. H., 384
marijuana
   college student use of, 355
   history of, 3
   legalization of, 42
   physiology of addiction and, 41
Marinkovic, K., 21, 22, 28
Mark, T. L., 457
Markarian, M., 389
Marks, A. D. G., 314
Marks, N. F., 313
Marlatt, A., 111, 292
Marlatt, G., 286, 293, 297, 358
Marlatt, G. A., 97, 106, 171, 174–175, 184–185, 204, 287, 290, 299, 342, 368, 369
Marot, M., 457
Marsh, D. T., 135
Marshal, M. P., 28, 312
Martens, M., 414
Martier, S. S., 125, 126
Martin, B., 172
Martin, C., 70
Martin, C. S., 127
Martin, J. K., 394
Martin, M. K., 220
Martin, N., 126
Martino, S., 167
Martocchio, B. C., 91
masculinity, 406, 421
Masheb, R. M., 60
Maslar, E. M., 267, 274
Mason, M. J., 148, 153
Mason, W. H., 177, 180
Mason-John, V., 295
mass media campaigns, 369–370
master's degrees, 69, 72, 77–80
Masyn, K., 343
Maternal, Infant, and Early Childhood Home Visit Program (MIECHVP), 372
Matschinger, H., 250
Matsuda, M., 250
Matthews, C. R., 413, 414, 418, 419, 428, 432
Matthews, H., 67
Matto, H., 178
Mattson, M. E., 98
Mavis, B. E., 387
Maxon, T., 69
Mayeda, S., 218, 227, 236, 237
Mayman, M., 128
Mayo Clinic, 366
Mays, V. M., 229
McAuliffe, W., 361
McAweeney, M., 329, 332
McBride, J., 52
McCabe, S., 356

McCambridge, J., 175
McCance-Katz, E., 175, 413, 416, 419
McCance-Katz, E. F., 413, 415–416
McCarn, S. R., 431
McCart, M. R., 81
McCarthy, D. M., 387
McCarty, D., 66, 81, 222
McCaul, M. D., 271, 275
McCaul, M. E., 128
McClellan, A. T., 136
McClelland, G., 361
McCollum, V. J. C. See ethnicity
McCord, J., 311
McCoy, C. B., 355, 357
McCrady, B. S., 165, 263, 266, 307, 313, 321
McDaniel, P., 80
McDavis, R. J., 277, 385
McDonald, C., 358
McDonell, M. B., 129
McElrath, K., 43
McGillicuddy, N. B., 333
McGilloway, S., 129
McGovern, M. P., 165, 166
McGrath, J., 41
McGrew, J., 132
McGue, M., 60
McHugh, R. K., 168
McIntyre, J., 433
McIntyre, J. R., 91, 305, 311, 320, 321
McKay, J. R., 82, 456
McKay, M., 269
McKechnie, J., 411, 416
McKenna, T., 131, 132
McKeon, A., 251
McKergow, M., 176, 180
McKinney, C. M., 312
McKirnan, D. J., 428
McLellan, A. T., 134–136, 275
McMullen, J. W., 48
McNally, E. B., 434
McNeese, C. A., 5, 7, 13
McNeil, R., 184
McNulty, J. L., 133
McVay, D., 468
MDMA, 42–43
MDMA ("bath salts"), 43
Meason, P., 136
Medicaid, 457, 458
Medicaid and Medicare, 468
medical histories, 244
medically managed intensive inpatient treatment, 454
medical marijuana, 42
medication. See specific drugs
Meeks, T. W., 253
Meekums, B., 70
Mee-Lee, D., 97, 98, 101, 342, 343, 450–452
Mejta, C. L., 267, 274
memory
   alcohol's effects on, 21
   benzodiazepine and, 34
   marijuana's effect on, 41
   methamphetamine and, 38
   as substance abuse symptom, 436

men. *See also* gender differences
   addiction and, 415–418
   college students, high-risk behavior of, 367–368
   group therapy and, 228–229
   treatment needs of, 421–422
Mendoza, R., 257
mental health
   childhood trauma and, 30
   comorbitiy and, 67–68 (*See also* comorbidity)
   co-occuring with addiction, 102
   marijuana use and, 41
   prescription drug abuse and, 330–331
Mental Health Parity and Addiction Equity Act, 457
Mental Health Parity and Addiction Equity Act of 2008 (MHPAEA), 468–469
mental illness, 162, 468
mental status exam (MSE), 104
Meredith, S. E., 328
Mericle, A., 199, 361
Merrens, M. R., 166
Merta, R. J., 127
Messer, G., 316
Messiah, S., 355
metabolic defects, 11
metabolic tolerance, 23, 410
methadone, 35
methamphetamine, 37–39, 469
methaqualone, 34
methcathinone, 38
methylphenidate, 38–39
Metrik, J., 288
Metsch, S., 355
Meyer, J., 329
Meyers, R. J., 173, 308
Michigan Alcoholism Screening Test (MAST), 126, 127–128, 197, 455
Midanik, L., 428, 429, 434
Mihalic, S., 373
Milford, J. L., 173
military personnel, 355
   prevention programs for, 373–374
Milivojevic, D., 9
Miller, B. A., 127, 128
Miller, F. G., 125, 126
Miller, G., 51, 72, 77, 79, 267, 275, 278, 438
Miller, G. A., 108, 111, 126, 127, 132, 455
Miller, J. D., 12
Miller, K. B., 132, 246
Miller, M. A., 23, 37
Miller, M. D., 32
Miller, P. M., 166
Miller, P. R., 29
Miller, S., 204
Miller, S. D., 176, 177, 180, 181
Miller, S. I., 228
Miller, T., 362
Miller, T. R., 30
Miller, W., 147, 152, 440
Miller, W. R., 108, 147, 148, 151–160, 162, 165–170, 173, 175, 185, 201, 263, 270, 305, 311, 453, 456

Millon, C., 130, 134
Millon, T., 130, 134, 135
Millon Clinical Multiaxial Inventory—III (MCMI-III), 134–135
Minami, T., 367
mind-altering drugs, 7
mindfulness-based relapse prevention (MBRP), 22, 174–175
mindfulness training, 22
minimization, 235
Minnesota Multiphasic Personality Inventory—2 (MMPI-2), 131, 197
minorities. *See specific types of minorities*
minors. *See* adolescents; children
miracle question, 182
Mirijello, A., 249
Mitchell, J. E., 49
mnemonic devices, 299–300
modality, LGBTQ issues and, 438–439
modality matching, 452
Moderation Management (MM), 266–267
Moe, E., 366
Molinaro, K. L., 395, 401
Moline, M. E., 224
"Molly" (MDMA), 43
Molnar, A., 176, 182
Moltu, C., 90
monotherapy, 257
Montague, P., 122
Monteaux, M., 360, 362
Monteiro, M. G., 129
Monterosso, J., 250
mood disorders, 464
Moore, D., 329, 332
Moore, J. L., 386
Moore, M. R., 336
Moore, S. E., 386
Moos, R. H., 136, 264, 312, 342
Moradi, B., 434
Morey, L. C., 130, 133, 134
Morgan, O., 370
Morgenstern, J., 82, 165
Moro, R. R., 18, 48
morphine addiction, 4, 34–35
Morral, A. R., 177
Morrissette, P. J., 313
Morton, S., 362, 370, 375
Moss, R., 285
motivation, 93–94, 288, 315
motivational interviewing, 147–164
  advantages and disadvantages, 162–163
  change and resistance, 151–152
  clients, achieving change, 152–154
  explanation of, 152
  for inpatient programs, 455, 456–457
  overview, 147–148
  primary principles of, 153–154
  resistance, 151–152, 157–161
  Stages of Change Model, 148–151
  techniques, 154–157, 161–162
motivation for drug use. *See* addiction causes
motivation of clients, 108
Mott, J. A., 106
Mount, M. K., 122

Moxley, D. P., 386
Moyer, M., 100
Moyers, T. B., 165, 456
Moyers, W. C., 19, 39, 40
Muchowski, P., 310
Mueser, K. T., 306
Muid, O., 340
Mullen, R., 319
Mullins, P. M., 7
Mulloy, J. M., 134
multicausal models, 13–14
multicultural counseling competence, 96, 394
multiculturalism, 70–72
Multidimensional Risk Profile, 451
multidisciplinary approach, 94
multidisciplinary treatment team, 205–206
multimodal prevention programs, 366–367
multiple addictions, 49. *See also* comorbidity
multiple sclerosis (MS), 332
multiracial persons, 393
Mulvey, K., 136
Mun, E.-Y., 317
Munford, M. B., 394
Munoz, R. F., 165, 290
Murphy, C. M., 311, 312, 315
Murphy, J. G., 107
Murphy, J. W., 4
Murphy, M., 315
Murphy-Graham, E., 363
Myerholtz, L. E., 126
Myers, P. L., 72
Myers, R., 340
Myers, R. W., 128
Mysyk, A., 59, 60

N

Nagayama Hall, G. C., 394
Nagy, P. D., 341
Nair, P., 311, 371
Najavits, L. M., 66, 69, 81–82, 169, 170, 275
Nakano-Matsumoto, N., 386
naltrexone, 253–254
Namyniuk, L. L., 192, 193, 199, 200
Napier, R. W., 228
Nar-Anon, 231
Narcotics Anonymous, 265
Nathanson, L. S., 122
National Addiction Studies Accreditation Commission (NASAC), 72
National Association of Addiction Professionals (NAAP), 67–68
National Association of Alcoholism and Drug Abuse Counselors (NAADAC)
  addictive disorder understanding, 69
  comorbidity, 68
  continuing education, 76
  credentialing, 76–77
  cultural competency, 68, 71–72
  development of, 72
  on diversity, 96
  exam content areas, 79
  recovering counselors and, 74
  standards of, 75

National Association of Children of Alcoholics (NACoA), 266–267
National Association of Drug Court Professionals, 467–468
National Board of Certified Counselors (NBCC), 77–78
National Center for Chronic Disease Prevention and Health Promotion (NCCDPHP), 353
National Center on Addiction and Substance Abuse (CASA), 354, 355, 357, 360, 361, 368, 464
National Certification Commission (NCC), 79
National Certification Commission for Addiction Professionals, 77
National Collegiate Athlete Association (NCAA), 37
National Council on Problem Gambling (NCPG), 53, 54
National Drug Abuse Institute, 365
National Drug Abuse Treatment Clinical Trials Network (CTN), 81
National Eating Disorders Association (NEDA), 61
National Highway Traffic Safety Administration (NHTSA), 29
National Institute of Justice (NIJ), 361
National Institute on Alcohol Abuse and Alcoholism (NIAAA), 4, 26, 387
National Institute on Drug Abuse, 369
National Institute on Drug Abuse (NIDA)
  addiction research, 19, 20, 22–23, 26, 33, 35–38, 43
  addiction treatments, 467
  Adolescent Transition Program, 367
  caffeine use, 329
  cost of drug abuse, 464–465
  establishment of, 4
  prevention programs, 373
  professional issues, 67
  race, 389, 390–391
  treatment, 341
  veterans, substance abuse of, 374
National Institute on Substance Use and Addiction Disorders, 83
National Institutes of Health (NIH), 4
National Registry of Evidence-based Programs and Practices (NREPP), 166
National Survey on Drug Use and Health (NSDUH), 357, 409
Native Americans and Alaskan Natives, 387–389. *See also* race
natural consequences, 174
Navarra, R., 312
Naylor, A., 365, 366
Naylor, C. L., 267, 274
needle/syringe exchange programs, 7, 175
negating problems, 158
negative consequences, 107
Neighbors, C., 7, 355
Neighbors, C. J., 165
Nelson, J. R., 250

Nelson, L. S., 43
Nelson-Zlupko, L., 409, 410, 412, 413, 415, 417, 420, 421
nervous system injuries, 333
NeSmith, C. L., 229, 420
Neubig, R. R., 241
neurobiological models, 12
neurobiology of addiction, 19–26
neurogenesis, 22
neuroimaging studies, 22
neurology in pharmacotherapy, 241–243
neurons, 258
neurotransmitters, 20, 241, 246
Newcomb, M., 106
Newcomb, M. D., 431
Newman, I., 119
New Roads exercise, 169–170
Newton-Taylor, B., 165
New York Times in Education Program, 364
Nghe, L. T, 394
Niaura, R., 288
Nicholas, K., 316, 317
Nichols, T., 362
Nicholson, J., 359, 371
nicotine. *See* tobacco
NIDA. *See* National Institute on Drug Abuse
Nielsen, G., 90
Nixon, Richard, 360
Nixon, S. J., 28, 60
n methyl d aspartate (NMDA), 258
Noel, N. E., 314
nonabstinence as treatment. *See* harm reduction
nonaccredited training, 72
nonbarbiturates, 33
nonconfrontational approach, 193
Noonan, D., 311
Norcross, J. C., 108, 148, 167, 275, 288, 456
norephinephrine, 258
Nosen, E., 150
noticing differences in clients, 182–183
No Wrong Door Policy, 201
Ntais, C., 252
Nugent, F. A., 341
Nunnally, E., 181
nursing care, 454
Nutt, D., 241, 247
Nyrop, K., 384

O

Oberbeck, D., 22
Oberste, E. A., 278
obesity, 61, 406
O'Brien, C., 204
O'Brien, C. P., 49, 134, 240
O'Brien, M. C., 29, 32
O'Brien, R., 373
obsessive behavior. *See* process addictions
O'Connell, M. J., 73
O'Connor, M. J., 316
O'Connor, P. G., 128, 129
Oechsler, H., 414
O'Farrell, T. J., 311–313, 315, 319, 453
Offender Counselors Committee on Process Addictions, 48

Office for Substance Abuse Prevention (OSAP). *See* Center for Substance Abuse Prevention (CSAP)
Office of National Drug Control Policy (ONDCP), 4, 356, 358, 364, 365
Office on Disability, 330
Ogborne, A. C., 165
O'Hanlon, W., 176
Oldenburg, B., 359
Olds, D., 373
Olive, M., 253
Olive, M. F., 255
Olmstead, M. E., 318
Olmstead, T. A., 167, 172
Olson, M. E., 148
Olthuis, J. V., 68
O'Malley, P. M., 354, 356
O'Malley, S. S., 49
Ong, C., 68
oniomania, 59
open-ended questions, 154–155, 434
opioids, 34–35, 258, 330–331
opium, history of, 3–4
Opjordsmoen, S., 67
orbitofrontal cortex (OFC), 21
Oregon Health & Science University, 366
Orford, J., 285
Orgain, L. S., 386
Osborn, C., 204
Osborn, C. J., 152, 165, 179
Oscar-Berman, M., 21, 22, 28
Oser, C. B., 70
osteoporosis, 23, 410–411
Otto, M. W., 168
Ouimette, P. C., 266, 342
outcome expectancies, 288
outcomes, measuring, 81–83
outcomes of prevention programs, 375–376
outcomes of treatment programs, 424
outpatient treatment programs. *See* inpatient and outpatient treatment
Overeaters Anonymous, Inc., 61
overintoxication, 28
over-the-counter drugs. *See specific drugs*
over-the-counter drugs, history of, 3–4
Owens, S. M., 257
OxyContin, 35

P

Paddock, S. M., 222
Padovano, A., 167
Page, A. C., 185
Page, R., 218, 220
Pagliaro, A. M., 418
Pagliaro, L. S., 418
painkillers, nonmedical use of, 4, 355
Pakos, E., 252
Paleg, K., 269
Palmer, R. H. C., 417
Panas, L., 222
Pandiani, J. A., 415
Pankow, J., 136
Pantelis, C., 8, 19
paraphilic disorders, 51

Paredes, D., 197
Paredes, D. M., 126
Parent, I., 411
parentification of children, 309
parenting
    in addicted family systems, 311–312
    effect on drug use of children, 370
    teens, substance abuse and, 367
    training in, 370–371
    women, addiction and, 413–414
Pargament, K. I., 220
Parham, T. A., 394
Park, A., 367
Parker, G., 255
Parker, J. D., 134
Parkinson's disease, 51
Parks, C. A., 410, 417, 420–422, 424
Parr, G., 221
Parsons, K. J., 128
partial agonist, 258
Pascoe, W., 320
Pascual, F., 317
Pasquarella, J., 467
PATHOS, 51
Patient Placement Criteria (PPC), 99
Patient Protection and Affordable Care Act of 2010, 81, 457
Patterson, A., 436
Pattison, M. E., 461
Paul Wellstone and Pete Domenici Mental Health Parity and Addiction Equity Act of 2008 (MHPAEA), 81, 468–469
Pearlin, L., 111
Pechacek, T. F., 169
Pedersen, S. L., 387
Peele, S., 329
peer counselors, 175
Peller, J. E., 185
Pena, J. M., 386, 394
Penne, J. D., 357
people with disabilities (PWDs). *See* disabilities, persons with
Pepperell, J. L., 34
Pepperell, J. P., 408, 411, 421, 422
Perepiczka, M., 66
Perera-Diltz, D. M., 119, 126, 127
Perez, J. S., 463
Perez, M., 431
perfectionism, 56
Perjessy, C. C., 1
Perl, H., 81
Perron, B. E., 333, 345
Perry, J., 127
Personality Assessment Inventory (PAI), 133–134
personality assessments, 130–135
personality theory models, 9
personal power, 419
Peselow, E., 253, 254
Peteet, J., 273
Peterson, L. T., 177
Peterson, P. L., 428
Petry, N. M., 49, 172
Pettinati, H., 254

Index

Pettinati, H. M., 250
Pfefferbaum, A., 22, 27
Pfingst, L., 384
Phan, L., 391
pharmacotherapy, 168, 240–262
   alcohol addiction, 251–252
   case studies, 245–246, 252–255
   counselor's role in, 250–251
   craving, theory of, 248–250
   disabilities, persons with, 336
   diversity and, 243–245
   glossary of terms, 256–258
   neurology, key concepts, 246
   neurotransmitters, 264
   pharmacodynamics, 247–248, 258
   pharmacokinetics, 247, 258
   for relapse prevention, 287
   terms and concepts, 241–243
Phelps, G. L., 275
Phillips, K. T., 186
Phillips, R. E., 220
philosophical foundations
   advocacy, 94–95
   client collaboration, 94
   hope, 90–91
   of instrument construction, 122
   motivation, 93–94
   multidisciplinary approach, 94
   strength-based approaches, 91–92
   whole person approach, 92–93
physical interventions, 171–172
Physician's Desk Reference (PDR), 38
physiological risk factors, 340
physiology of addiction
   alcohol, 26–33
   cannabinoids, 41
   cocaine, 39–40
   depressants, 26–33
   ephedrine and amphetamines, 37–39
   hallucinogens, 41–43
   opioids, 34–35
   overview, 19–26
   sedatives and hypnotics, 33–34
   stimulants, 35–36
   tobacco, 35–36
Piazza, N. J., 119, 123, 124, 126–128, 227
Pici, M., 289
Pietrzykowski, A. Z., 23
Pihl, R. O., 416
Pilkinton, M., 71
Pillai, V., 177
Pincus, A. L., 133
Piotrowski, C., 59
Platt, J. J., 94
Pluess, M., 317
Pokhrel, P., 340
Pokorny, A. D., 128
Poland, R. E., 243, 257
Polich, J. M., 285
policies for prevention, 5–6, 373–374
Pollock, M., 68
polysubstance abuse, 68–69
polytherapy, 257
Ponterotto, J. G., 394

Poon, E., 317
Pope, K. S., 71
pornography, 50
positive behavior. *See* solution-focused counseling
positive emotions, relapses and, 290
positive psychology, 83
positron emission tomography (PET), 21–22
postprosecution, 467
postsecondary trauma, 75–76
post-traumatic stress disorder (PTSD), 139
Poulin, C., 371
Powell, B., 11
Powers, M. B., 315
Prater, C., 246
Prather, R., 28
prayer, 386
precontemplation of change, 148
pregnancy, substance abuse during, 137–139, 252–254, 316, 353, 371–373
prenatal alcohol exposure, 316. *See also* fetal alcohol syndrome
Prentice, W. E., 36, 41
prescription drugs. *See also* pharmacotherapy
   adolescent abuse of, 356
   nonmedical use of, 4, 35, 374–375
   veterans' use of, 374
presentation of client, 104–105
Preston, J. D., 241, 247, 251, 258
prevention programs, 353–382
   age groups, targeting, 360
   children and adolescents, 360–371
   evidence-based programs, 358–359
   group counseling and, 218, 220
   military personnel, 373–374
   mindfulness-based relapse prevention (MBRP), 22, 174–175
   need for, 353–357
   outcomes, 375–376
   policies influencing, 2–5
   pregnant adolescents and adults, 371–373
   public health prevention program model, 357–358
   senior adults, 374–375
   strategies for, 29
   types of, 359–360
Previti, D., 313
Price, R. H., 267
Price, R. K., 388
Pride Institute, 441–442
primary prevention programs, 357–358
Prince, V., 251
prior treatment, 109–110
process addictions, 48–65
   compulsive buying, 59–60
   explanation of, 48
   food addiction, 60–62
   gambling addiction, 52–54
   sexual addiction, 50–52
   technology addiction, 55
   twelve-step programs for, 276
   work addiction, 56–59
Prochaska, J. M., 69

Prochaska, J. O., 108, 109, 147, 148, 289, 456
professional issues, 66–88
   accreditation, 80
   boundary violations, 70
   comorbidity, skills for, 67–68
   continuing education, 76
   counselors, never been users, 75
   counselors in recovery, 73–75
   credentialing, 76–79
   education, 72–73
   future trends, 83
   licensure, 79–80
   managed care and treatment funding, 80–81
   Multicultural Counseling Competencies, 96, 394
   multiculturalism, 70–72
   outcomes, measuring, 81–83
   overview, 66
   polysubstance abuse, skills for, 68–69
   self-care, 75–76
   specific populations, skills for, 68
   theory, treatment, and recovery models, knowledge of, 69–70
Prohibition, 3
Project COMBINE, 168, 169–170
proof, beverage strength, 28
property seizure, 465
pros and cons of addiction, 107
Prosser, J. M., 43
provider reimbursement, 80–81
psychedelics, 41–43
psychiatric disorders. *See* comorbidity
psychiatrists, on-site, 205–206
psychoeducational groups, 219–220, 223
psychological considerations, addiction and, 411–412, 416–417
psychological models, 7–9
psychological risk factors, 336–337
psychological traps, 292–294
psychosis, 41
psychotherapeutic approaches, 165–191
   brief interventions, 175–176
   cognitive-behavioral approaches
      community reinforcement approach, 173–174
      contingency management and behavioral contracting, 172–173
      functional analysis, 169–170
      overview, 168–169
      relapse prevention, 174–175
      triggers, targeting, 170–172
   counselor beliefs and behaviors, 165–166
   evidence-based practices, 166–168
   harm reduction, 184–187
   solution-focused counseling
      assumptions and practices, 180–184
      integration, 179
      overview of, 176–177
      research on, 177–179
psychotherapeutic groups, 220–223
public, prevention programs for, 369–370
public health model, 10–11

public health prevention program model, 357–358
Pueleo, S., 76
Pullen, E., 70
Pure Food and Drug Act of 1906, 4
Puttler, I. I., 317
Pyant, C. T., 394

Q

Quaalude, 34
queer, explanation of, 430
queer or questioning people, 434. *See also* lesbian, gay, bisexual, transgender, and queer (LGBTQ) clients
querying extremes, 157
question/answer trap, 160
questions, motivational interviewing and, 154–155
Quick Drinking Screen (QDS), 106
Quigley, L. A., 204
Quinn, W., 319
Quintero, M., 341

R

race. *See also* culture
  alcohol use and, 29
  amphetamine use and, 37–38
  assessment and treatment, 70–71
  comorbidity and, 199, 464
  disabilities, people with, 332
  drug use and, 3, 71
  gambling addiction and, 54
  LGBTQ clients and, 432
  self-administered screenings and, 127
  twelve-step groups and, 273
racial and cultural identity theories, 393–394
Rada, P., 60
Rafferty, P., 320
Rainone, G., 53, 54
Raistrick, D., 9
Rak, C. F., 256, 258
Rammohan, V., 374
Ramo, D. E., 111
Rand, L., 267
Randall, C. L., 411
Ranganathan, S., 316
Rantakömi, S., 415
Rao, N., 250
rape, 34, 414
Rappaport, J., 461
rapport, 90, 97
Rasmussen, E., 316, 317
Ratcliff, K. S., 132
rationalization, 235
Rational Recovery (RR), 266
Ratts, M., 442
Rawson, R. A., 81
Ray, S., 67
readiness for change and treatment, 102, 108, 288, 456–457
Readiness to Change Questionnaire (RTCQ), 108
Reagan, Ronald, 461
Reagan administration, 6

Reboussin, B., 29, 32
receptors, 241
recidivism rates, 457–458, 462
recovering addicts, counselors as, 73–75
recovery environment, 102–103
recovery-oriented system of care (ROSC), 81
recovery vs. recovered, 10
Reed, S. W., 1
referrals, 67, 206, 275, 345, 449
reflection responses, 159–160
reflective listening, 155
reframing, 160
reframing exceptions, 182
rehabilitation center challenges, 457–458
rehabilitation vs. incarceration, 462–466
Reid, C. M., 129
Reid, S., 250
reimbursement, provider, 80–81
Reinert, D. F., 112
Reiness, G., 246
Reiss, D., 316
relapse
  of counselors in recovery, 74
  explanation of, 285–286
  group therapy and, 235
  of LGBTQ clients, 439
  mindfulness-based prevention, 174–175
  preventing, 102
  rates of, 469
  reversion as, 150
relapse prevention, 285–304
  abstinence violation effect, 293–294
  case study, 296–301
  explanation of, 286–287
  high-risk situations, 290–292
  of LGBTQ clients, 439
  management plan for, 296
  model for, 287–290
  overview of, 285–287
  reality of, 301
  seemingly irrelevant decisions (SIDs), 292–293
relationships. *See* family, impact of addiction on
relationship with counselor, 75, 90, 97
reliability of screenings, 124
religion. *See* spirituality and religion
remedial groups, 218
Remer, L. G., 374
Remley, T. P., 95, 100, 410
Rempel, M., 422
Renzetti, C. M., 345
reparative therapy, 431
research
  outcomes, measuring, 81–83
  on twelve step programs, 279
resentment, 235
residency programs, 72
Residential Drug Abuse Program (RDAP), 466
residential inpatient programs, 453, 454
residential outpatient programs, 466–469
resistance
  motivational interviewing and, 151–152, 154, 157–161
  reversion as, 150

resistance talk, 158
restricting access to drugs, 360
reuptake, 241
Reus, V. I., 290
Reuss, N. H., 177, 180
ReVia, 253–254
reward pathway in brain, 20–21, 34, 40
Rheineck, Jane E., 383
Rice, J. C., 394
Rice, K. F., 309, 310, 317, 318
Rich, J. D., 469
Richardson, T. Q., 394, 395, 401
Richman, J. A., 311, 321
Richter, L., 356, 466
Rieckmann, T., 66, 69, 72, 81
Riedel-Heller, S., 414
Riedel-Heller, S. G., 250
Riegal, A. C., 20, 22
Rieger, E., 153
Rigg, K. K., 4
Riley, W., 289
Ringwalt, C., 363
Riordan, R. J., 275
risk factors for addiction, 335–339, 362
Ritalin, 37–39, 197–198
Ritchie, M., 126
Rivas, R. F., 220
Rivera, J., 185
Rivers, C., 311
Rivers, P. C., 269
Robbins, M., 165
Robbins, M. L., 387
Roberts, A., 392
Roberts, C. M., 314
Roberts, J., 126
Roberts, L. J., 306, 308, 313, 321
Roberts, S., 358
Roberts-Wilbur, J., 391, 394
Robins, E., 428
Robins, L. N., 105, 132
Robinson, B. E., 58
Robinson, S., 253
Rock, M., 461
Rodgers-Bonaccorsy, R. A., 331
Roeloffs, C. A., 413, 416, 419, 420
Roger, E. M., 69–70
Roger, P., 128
Rogers, B., 220
Rogers, C., 70
Rogers, C. R., 387
Rogers, J. L., 18, 48
Rogers, R., 127
Rohe, D. E., 331
Rohrbach, L. A., 340
Rohypnol, 34
Roizen, R., 83
role-playing, 194, 364
roles in families, 309
Rollnick, S., 108, 147, 148, 151–160, 162, 453, 456
Roman, P. M., 165, 167, 250, 274, 449
Roots, L. E., 269
Roozen, H. G., 173–174
Roseman, C., 127

Rosen, C. S., 136
Rosen, W., 18, 34, 37, 41
Rosenbaum, D., 363, 364
Rosenberg, H., 126, 186
Rospenda, K. M., 311
Ross, L. E., 433
Ross, M. W., 229
Ross, S., 253, 254
Rossi, C., 51
Rossi, G., 135
Roth, M. E., 244, 408
Rotrosen, J., 37
Rotunda, R., 58, 314
Rotunda, R. J., 320, 322
Rouaud, T., 22
Roudsari, B., 384
Rounsaville, B. J., 167, 306, 413
Rouse, S. V., 132, 133
Rowan-Szal, G. A., 136
Rowe, C. L., 231, 307, 319
Rowe, D., 386
Roy, M., 105
Royce, J. E., 74
Rubin, D. H., 317, 318
Rudolph, A. E., 386
Rugle, L., 228
Ruiz, M. A., 133
Ruiz, P., 217
rules in families, 309–310
Rush, Benjamin, 2, 10
Russell, M., 125, 138
Rutherford, K., 433
Rutherford, M. J., 417
Rutland-Brown, W., 333
Ryan, R. M., 94

S

Sabol, W. J., 462
Sachs, S., 386
Safe Zone, 441
Saghir, M. T., 428
Saitz, R., 76, 94
Salamone, P. R., 56
Sales, A., 359
salience, 294
Salois, M. J., 373
Salyers, K. M., 126, 127
Samet, J. H., 76, 94
SAMHSA. *See* Substance Abuse and Mental Health Services Administration (SAMHSA)
Samuels, S., 464
Samuelson, M., 108
Samuolis, J., 438
Sanchez, V. C., 175
Sanchez-Craig, M., 176
Sanders, M., 218, 227, 236, 370
Sannibale, C., 250
Santrock, J., 366
Satcher, J. F., 229, 420
Satterfield, J., 175
Sattler, J. M., 94, 95, 98, 101
SATURN (Student Testing Using Random Notification), 365–366

Saules, K. K., 60, 127
Saunders, E. C., 166
Saunders, J., 93
Saunders, J. B., 125, 129
Savolainen, H., 91
Sawrie, S. M., 132
Sawtell, R., 37
Saxon, A., 135
Sayette, M. A., 288
SBIRT (Screening, Brief Intervention, and Referral to Treatment), 175, 455
Scarborough, J., 72
scare tactics, 370, 376
Schacht, L. M., 415
Schaef, A. W., 49, 56, 58
Schäfer, I., 414, 420, 424
Schafer, J., 312, 316
Schairer, L. C., 30
Schaufeli, W. B., 56
Scherer, D. G., 314
Schik, G., 251, 253
Schinka, J. A., 133, 134
Schiraldi, V., 468
Schmid, J., 319
Schmidt, C., 316
Schmitt, J., 466
Schnabel, J., 19
Schneekloth, T. D., 288
Schneider, J. P., 50, 192, 193, 197, 198, 201, 306
Schnoll, S. H., 353
school-based prevention programs, 362–371
school counselors, 219, 306
Schooler, C., 111
Schottenfeld, R. S., 128
Schuckit, M. A., 9
Schulenberg, J. E., 313, 356
Schuler, M., 371
Schuler, M. E., 311
Schulman, G. D., 451, 452, 454
Schumm, J. A., 312, 313
Sciacca, K., 193
Scommegna, P., 462
scope of practice, 67, 95
Scott, E. G., 192
Scott, M. S., 38
Scoular, J., 111
Screening, Brief Intervention, and Referral to Treatment (SBIRT), 175, 455
screenings
  assessment and, 99–100
  comorbidity and, 67
  explanation of, 99
  for group participants, 224–225, 272
  for sexual addiction, 51
  tools for, 197
secondary prevention programs, 358
second-line agent, 258
Secular Organization of Sobriety (SOS), 266, 275
sedatives, 33–34
Seegers, J. A., 50
seemingly irrelevant decisions (SIDs), 292–293
Segal, B., 410
Seifert, C. J., 133, 134

seizures, 26
Selekman, M. D., 182
self-acceptance, 58
self-administered screenings, 126–130
self-care, 75–76
self-disclosure, 74–75, 320
self-efficacy, 148, 154, 161, 204, 287–288
self-evaluation, 207
self-help groups. *See also* Twelve Step programs
  group counseling and, 222–223
  unity among, 83
self-inventory, 170
self-monitoring, 297–298
self-verification, 98
Seligman, D., 275
Selvidge, M. D., 428
Selvidge, M. M. D., 432
Selzer, J. A., 165, 455
Selzer, M. L, 125, 127, 135
semistructured interviews, 100–101
senior adults, substance abuse of, 357, 374–375, 436
sensitivity to screenings, 123
sensitization, 258
Sentencing Project, 463
Seppa, K., 129
serotonin, 258
set-ups, 292
Sewell, K. W., 127
sex, explanation of, 406–407
sexaholic, 50
Sexaholics Anonymous, Inc. (SA), 50
Sexton, R. L., 111
sexual abuse, 316
sexual addiction, 50–52
sexual assault, 34, 414, 420
sexual behavior, high-risk, 111, 355, 357
sexual identity development, 436
sexually transmitted infections, 357, 411
sexual minorities, group therapy and, 229–230
sexual orientation, 430, 435
sexual preference, 435
Seybold, K. C., 56
Seymour, R., 273
Sgambati, S., 37
Shabad, P., 90
Shadish, W. R., 319
Shaffer, D. K., 457–458
Shaffer, H. J., 14, 52
Shaffer, J. J., 165
SHAPe Curriculum (Success, Health, and Peace), 367
shaping strategy, 177
Sharpe, C., 1
Shaughney, A., 419–420
Shea, M., 390
Shea, S. H., 389
Shea, W. M., 9, 11
Shealy, A. E., 107
Shedler, J., 128
Sheeran, P., 150
Sheidow, A. J., 81
Sheperis, D. S., 217

Sheppard, K., 60–61
Sher, K., 367
Sher, K. J., 128
Sherer, R. A., 333
Sherr, L., 434
Shervington, D., 394
Shiffman, S., 288, 292
shifting focus, 160
Shiloh, R., 241, 243, 247, 258
Shimazu, A., 56
Shin, H., 375
shopping, compulsive, 59–60
Shulman, G. D., 97
Shwartz, M., 136
Siegal, H. A., 26, 27–28
Silasi, G., 256
Silkworth, W., 290
Silverman, K., 172
Simoni-Wastila, S., 357
simple reflection, 159
Simpson, C. A., 134
Simpson, D., 136
Sinclair, S. J., 133, 134
Singh, A. A., 428, 429, 431, 432, 436, 440
Sinha, R., 49, 60
Sivenius, J., 415
Skala, K., 254
Skara, S., 376
Skinner, W. F., 455
Slayter, E. M., 330
Slesnick, N., 308
Sligar, S. R., 331
Sloboda, Z., 11
Sloore, H., 135
Slutske, W. S., 354
SMART Recovery, 223
Smedema, S. M., 330
Smirnoff, J., 126
Smith, D., 273
Smith, D. E., 81
Smith, D. W., 353
Smith, G. T., 387
Smith, J. E., 173
Smith, L., 436
Smith, M. W., 257
Smith, R. A., 463
Smith, R. L., 13, 346
Smith, Robert Holbrook, 263
Smock, S. A., 177, 178
smoking. *See* marijuana; tobacco
Smokowski, P. R., 340
Sneed, Z., 73
Snow, M., 128
Snyder, H. N., 462
SOBER breathing space, 174–175
sobriety. *See* abstinence
sobriety sampling, 185
social considerations, addiction and, 412–413, 417–418
social controls of treatment, 93
social interventions, 170
social pressures, 291
social risk factors, 337
social support, 200, 289–290

social workers, 69
Society of Credentialed Addiction Professionals (SCAP), 79
sociocultural models, 12–13
sociocultural risk factors, 340
socioeconomic status, 71
sodium oxybate-SMO, 254
Sokol, R. J., 125, 126, 128
soldier's disease, 373
Solomon, J., 149
solution-focused counseling, 171
  as alternative model, 204–205
  assumptions and practices, 180–184
  integration, 179
  overview of, 176–177
  research on, 177–179
Sonne, S. C., 411
Sorensen, J. L., 165
Sorg, J. D., 410
Sovereign, R. G., 152
Soyka, M., 110
speakeasies, 3
specificity of screenings, 123
specific populations, 68
Spedding, M., 241
Speed, J., 165
speed (methamphetamine), 37
Spicer, J., 27
Spicer, R. S., 30
Spilsbury, G., 177
spinal cord injury (SCI), 333
Spirito, A., 20
spirituality and religion
  of Asian Americans, 389
  background information and, 112–113
  LGBTQ people and, 436–437
  moral model of addiction and, 7
  recovery and, 386
  in recovery programs, 235
  as remedy for alcoholism, 2–3
  treatment approach and, 295–296
  twelve-step groups and, 273
  women and, 273
Sponsors for twelve step programs, 269–270
Stage of Change Theory, 108–109
stages in addicted family systems, 310–311
Stages of Change Model, 148–151, 456
Stages of Change Readiness and Treatment Eagerness Scales (SOCRATES), 108
Stahl, S. M., 251, 255, 256
Stallings, M. C., 417
standardized assessments, 121–122
Stanton, M., 315
Stanton, M. D., 320, 321
Stauffer, M. D., 1, 89, 438
Steele, J., 154
Steenrod, S. A., 75
Stein, D. B., 10
Stein, L. A. R., 127, 133
Steinberg, M. L., 307, 315
Steiner, R., 127
Steinglass, P., 316, 319–321
Stephens, T., 340
stereotypes

cultural, 13
gender and, 407, 414
multicultural competence and, 96
of persons with disabilities, 333
Sterling, S., 81, 270
Sternberg, R. J., 166
steroids, 365–366, 434
Steven-Jones, P., 270
Stevens, P., 13, 34, 36, 38, 39, 346
Stewart, D., 376
stigma. *See also* stereotypes
  disease model and, 10
  transgender people and, 430
Stile, S. A., 135
stimulants, 35–41, 355
Stinnett, R. E., 128
Stinson, F. S., 354
Stippikohl, B., 106
Stoeber, J., 56, 58
Stoffelmayr, B. E., 387
Stolerman, I. P., 248
Storey, G., 270
Stoughton, N. L., 135
Stout, R. L., 269, 274
Strain, R., 217
Strang, J., 463
Strassner, S. L. A., 320
Straussner, S. L. A., 96, 407–409, 415–417, 419, 421
Streiner, D. L., 133
strength-based approaches, 91–92, 176–177, 345
strengths, examining, 161, 423
stress
  children of addicts and, 316–317
  disabilities and, 336
  lifestyle and, 295
  parenting and, 311
  postsecondary trauma and, 75–76
  replapse prevention and, 288
  work addiction and, 56, 58
stress-reduction-based craving, 249
Strickland, I., 193
Strickland, T. L., 257
Strosahl, K. D., 174
structured interviews, 100–101
Strupp, H. H., 90
Stryjer, R., 241
students. *See* adolescents
Sturmhofel, S., 456
Subbaraman, M. S., 274
subcultural models, 13
subject changing, in conversation, 158
Substance Abuse and Mental Health Services Administration (SAMHSA)
  addiction research, 26, 29, 30, 34–36, 38, 41, 42
  Annapolis Coalition, 384
  assessment and diagnosis, 91, 92, 94, 95, 97, 99, 103–106, 112, 119
  children, drug use of, 356
  comorbid conditions, 192–195, 198–199, 203, 208
  criminal justice barriers, 343

Substance Abuse and Mental Health Services Administration (*continued*)
  disabilities, persons with, 328, 336, 337
  gender differences, 409, 415
  inpatient treatment, 454
  interventions, 166, 186
  LGBT clients, 434, 437
  prevention programs, 371
  race, drug use and, 383, 389
  recovery-oriented system of care (ROSC) of, 81
  referrals, 449
  relapse rates, 469
  standards for knowledge, 72
  treatment, 274
Substance Abuse Subtle Screening Inventory-3 (SASSI-3), 126–127, 197
substance use disorder, term, 192
successes, reviewing, 161
Suchinsky, R., 136
Suchman, N., 371
Sue, D., 273, 340, 387
Sue, D. W., 273, 277, 340, 385, 387, 395
sugar, addiction to, 61
suicide, 193, 306, 374, 412
Suissa, A. J., 51, 54
Sullivan, E. V., 22, 27
Sullivan, L. M., 76
summaries, collecting, 156
summarization, 156
summative evaluation, 207–208
Sun, P., 340
Sung, H., 356
Sung, H. E., 466
supervision of counselors, 79, 167
support
  community, 199
  relapse and, 299–300
  social, 200
supracultural models, 12
Supreme Court on drug testing, 365
Suris, N., 35
Sussman, A. N., 48, 49
Sussman, N., 468
Sussman, S., 48–51, 56, 58, 59, 340, 376
Sutter-Hernandez, J., 314
Suvak, M. K., 311
Svanum, S., 132, 133
Svikis, D. S., 80
Sweet, R. I., 127
Swendsen, J., 67
Swerdlik, M. E., 122
Swift, R., 252, 254
syndrome model, 14
Szirony, G. M., 449
Szlemko, W. J., 388–389
Szymanski, D. M., 329

T

taboos, 49
T-ACE, 126, 137–138
Tafa, M., 9
Taffe, M. A., 22
Taft, C. T., 311
Tambs, K., 338
Tang, L., 413
Taormina-Weiss, W., 336, 337
Ta Park, V., 199
tapering down, 185
Taris, T. W., 56
Tarter, R. E., 11, 98
Tarter, R. L., 136
Tatarsky, A., 185, 186
Tate, S. R., 274
taxation of alcohol, 5
Taylor, D. M., 30
Taylor, J. B., 19, 21
Taylor, J. M., 422
Taylor, J. Y., 392
teachable moments, 32, 175
techniques for motivational interviewing, 154–157, 161–162
technology addiction (TA), 55, 434
teens. *See* adolescents
Teesson, M., 250
Tegretol, 253
Teichner, G., 333
telescoping, 28, 410
Telford, E., 316
Tellegen, A., 130
temperance movement, 2–3, 407, 461
temptation, relapses and, 291
Teplin, L., 361
tertiary prevention programs, 358
Teruya, C., 177, 360, 362
testing behaviors, 235
Teter, C., 356
text messaging, 55
Theno, S., 192
theory, treatment, and recovery models, 69–70
third-party payers, 81
Thom, B., 356
Thom, D. J., 274
Thomas, F., 319
Thomas, K. E., 333
Thomas, R. V., 50
Thombs, D. L., 165
Thompson, C. E., 393
Thompson, J. K., 288
Thornton, C. E., 153
Thrower, E., 76
Thurber, S., 128
Thurman, P. J., 388
Tice, D. M., 278
Tidblom, I., 129
Tillotson, C. J., 66
Time-Line Followback for Alcohol (TFLB-Alcohol), 105–106
Timney, C. B., 94
Tims, F. M., 94
Tiro, L., 328
tobacco
  fetus, effect on, 353
  gender differences and, 410
  physiology of addiction and, 35–36
  prevention programs for, 357–358
  women and, 414–415
Tobias, C., 329
Tobler, N., 375
Tobler, N. S., 110, 111
tolerance
  of alcohol, 22–23
  medical conditions reducing, 336
  to methamphetamine, 38
  withdrawal and, 26
Tollefson, D., 162
Tomko, I. A., 319
Tonigan, J. S., 108, 250, 254, 270–272, 311
Tonsager, M. E., 94, 98
Tontchev, G. V., 69, 72
Toomey, T. L., 374
Toriello, P. J., 343
Torres-Reverón, A., 258
Torres-Rivera, E., 391, 394
Toseland, R. W., 220
Toumbourou, J. W., 29, 270, 369
Touyz, S. W., 153
Townley, J., 56
Tracy, S. W., 166
training
  on comorbidity, 193–194, 206
  for evidence-based practice, 167
  of group leaders, 224
  for parents, 370–371
  standardization of, 72
tranquilizers, 33, 409
transference, 70, 301
transgendered persons, 407, 423, 428, 433–434. *See also* lesbian, gay, bisexual, transgender, and queer (LGBTQ) clients
transitional summaries, 156
transprejudice, 429
transsexual, 407
Transtheoretical Model of Change (TTM), 69, 456
traps, client resistance and, 160–161
traumatic alcohol-related injuries, 29
traumatic brain injury (TBI), 333
treatment funding, 80–81
Treatment Intervention Protocol (TIP), 112
treatment programs. *See also* inpatient and outpatient treatment; *specific programs by name*
  comorbidity and, 200–207
  disabilities, persons with, 341–343, 346–347
  funding and policies for, 5, 80–81, 457
  gender and, 418–424
  goals of, 178
  legal consent for, 68
  for LGBTQ clients, 433–444
  motivation for entering, 93–94
  for process addiction, 49
  work schedules and, 112
treatment team, 205–206
Treistman, S. N., 23
Treno, A. J., 374
trial moderation, 185
triggers, 106, 169, 170–172, 439
Trimpey, Jack, 266

Tripodi, S. J., 467
Trocki, K., 428, 429, 434
Troiden, R. R., 431
Trout-Landen, B. L., 135
Tryon, G. S., 453
Tsai, T., 462
Tsuang, J., 54
Tubman, J. G., 316, 318
Tucker, J. A., 271
Tucker, M. B., 385, 386
Tucker, S., 148
Tuinal, 34
Turner, N. E., 7, 10–11
Turpin, K., 251
TWEAK, 138–139
Twelve Step programs, 263–284. *See also specific programs by name*
    advantages and disadvantages of, 271–274
    for compulsive buying, 60
    counselor role in, 275–277
    culture and, 385
    for food addiction, 61
    for gambling addiction, 54
    goals of, 267–268
    group dynamics, 269
    history and development of, 263–267
    leaders, role of, 222
    learning more about, 279
    for LGBTQ clients, 439
    self-help groups based on, 222–223
    for sexual addiction, 50
    spirituality and, 112–113
    sponsors for, 269–270
    success of, 270–271
    suggestions for, 277–279
    as treatment adjunct, 202, 274–275
    twelve steps and traditions, 264–265, 268
    for work addiction, 59
Twenty-First Amendment, 5
twins, alcoholism and, 11
Tyson, E. H., 178

U

unemployment, 71, 295, 336–337, 417, 465
Unger, J. B., 70, 71
Unger, R., 406
Ungvarski, P. J., 429
United States Department of Health and Human Services (USDHHS), 71
University of Rhode Island Change Assessment Scale (URICA), 108
unstructured interviews, 100–101
Unutzer, J., 413
upregulation, 258
Urbanoski, K., 270
U'Ren, A., 270
urge-surfing, 292
Utada, A., 319
Utzinger, L., 37

V

Vacc, N., 193, 197
Vacc, N. A., 126
Vaglum, P., 416

Valentine, S. R., 340
validity of screenings, 124
Valium, 252, 356–357
van Bael, M., 75
Vandaele, Y., 48
van den Brink, W., 316
van der Ark, L., 135
van der Kolk, B. A., 321
van der Kroft, P., 174
Vandivort-Warren, R., 457
Van Horn, D. H., 457
van Wormer, K., 23, 28, 309, 356, 358, 370, 389, 457
Varenicline, 36
Vasquez, J., 119
Vaughan, E., 367
Vaughan, R., 356
Vaughn, R., 466
Vaux, A., 394
Veach, L. J., 18, 29, 32, 48, 55, 410, 418
Vedel, E., 315
Velasquez, M. M., 311
Velez, M., 80
Velez, M. B., 345
Venner, K. L., 71
Verheul, R., 248, 249, 253
Vermonia School District 47 v. Acton, 1995, 365
Verthein, U., 414
veterans, 355, 374
Vetter-O'Hagen, C. S., 129
Viamontes, J., 11
Vieweg, B., 127
Villanueva, M., 173
Villarroel, N. A., 288
Violato, C., 77–78
violence
    alcohol related, 30
    children and, 316
    domestic violence, 200–201, 312–313
    fatalities resulting from, 410
    physical assault, 417
    women and, 414
visitor-type relationship, 180
vitamin deficiencies, 11
Vodanovich, S. J., 58, 59
Vogel, H. S., 271
Volkow, N., 356, 366
Volkow, N. D., 19–20, 22
Volpicelli, J. R., 250
Volstead Act of 1920, 3
voluntary group therapy, 226
von Deneen, K. M., 60, 61
Von Eye, A., 317
von Ranson, K. M., 60, 61
von Schrader, S., 328
Von Steen, P., 193
von Zielbauer, P., 461
voting rights, 465
Vukadinovic, Z., 51

W

Wabeke, T., 176, 180
Wade, J. C., 416, 421, 422

Wagenaar, A. C., 373, 374
Wahl, R., 356
wait times for inpatient care, 458
Wakeman, S. E., 469
Walbran, B., 428
Walfish, S., 133
Walitzer, K. S., 319
Wall, A., 312, 316
Wall, T. L., 389
Wallace, B. C., 386
Wallace, S., 75–76
Wallach, M. A., 306
Wallbrown, F. H., 128
Walsh, L., 275
Walsh, S., 91
Walter, J. L., 185
Wanberg, K. W., 130
Ward, J. V., 422
Warner, K., 466
war on drugs, 360, 384, 461–462, 468–469
Washington, O. G. M., 386
Washingtonian Total Abstinence Society, 2
Washousky, R., 310
Washton, A. M., 218
Wasserman, D. A., 290
Waters, E., 318
Watkins, K., 438
Watkins, K. E., 222
Watkins, L. E., 311
Watson, J. C., 23, 153
Watson, L., 429
Wechsler, H., 369
Wedgerfield, K., 94
Weed, N. C., 131, 132
Wegscheider, S., 310
Weiden, P. J., 250
Weil, A., 18, 34, 37, 41
Weinburg, M. S., 428
Weiner-Davis, M., 176
Weingardt, K. R., 73
Weinstein, L., 119
Weisner, C., 81, 270, 421
Weiss, C., 363
Weiss, R. D., 217, 218, 220
Weizman, A., 241, 247
Wekerle, C., 312, 316
Wells, A. M, 316
Wells, E. A., 270, 277
Wells, K., 276
Wells, K. B., 413
Wells, K. M., 69
Wells, R., 192
Wells, S. W., 414, 417
Wells, T. D., 69
Welte, J. W., 386
Wen, M., 53
Wenger, S., 267
Werner, M. J., 123
Wertz, J. M., 288
West, P. L., 68, 69, 77
West, R., 151
West, S. L., 330, 331, 335, 337, 338, 342, 343
Westerman, A. T., 36
Western, B., 465

Westra, H. A., 108
Wexler, H. K., 167
Whelton, W. J., 150, 152
White, M., 171, 181
White, M. A., 60
White, W., 201
White, W. L., 8, 10, 13, 19, 74–75, 263, 272, 275, 343
Whitfill, J., 128
Whiting, P., 221
Whitley, C. E. M., 68, 69, 72
Whitman, J. S., 428
Whittinghill, D., 204
Whittinghill, L. R, 204
whole person approach, 92–93
Wiedland, D. M., 43
Wiersma, J. D., 312
Wilbourne, P. L., 167
Wilbur, K., 14
Wilbur, M., 391, 394
Wilcox, R. E., 12
Wilcoxon, S. A., 229, 420
Wild, T. C., 93–94, 165
Wildroot, C., 301
Wilens, T., 37
Wilke, D., 128
Wilke, D. J., 412
Williams, A. D., 59
Williams, C., 110
Williams, C. J., 428
Williams, G. T., 224
Wilsnack, S. C., 428
Wilson, Bill, 263–264
Wilson, K. G., 174
Windle, M., 316, 318
Winograd, G., 453
Winter, M., 94
Wisdom, J. P., 68
Wise, E. A., 133, 134
Witbrodt, J., 273, 413
Witchel, R. I., 424
Witchel, S. F., 424
withdrawal
  causes of, 8
  inpatient services for, 454
  of marijuana, 41
  pharmacotherapy for, 251–252
  tolerance and, 26
withdrawal management, 99, 102
Witkiewitz, K., 22, 111, 184, 185, 222, 287, 288, 295, 343, 358, 368, 369
Wolf, A. W., 343

Wolf, M. E., 256
Wolin, S., 311
Wolin, S. J., 316
Womanist theory, 386
Womble, M., 386
women. *See also* gender differences
  addiction and, 410–415
  alcohol, effect on, 23, 137
  benzodiazepines and, 33
  with disabilities, 345
  historic role of, 407
  pregnancy, substance abuse during, 137–139, 252–254, 316, 353, 371–373
  prenatal alcohol exposure, 316 (*See also* fetal alcohol syndrome)
  spirituality and religion and, 273
  treatment needs of, 419–420
  violence and alcohol, 312
Women for Sobriety (WFS), 266–267, 275
Women's Christian Temperance Movement, 2
Wood, J. W., 388
Wood, M. D., 367
Wood, P., 367
Woodwarth, R., 361
Woody, G., 275
Woody, G. E., 134
Woody, S. R., 150
word choice, 180–181
Worden, J., 362
work addiction, 56–59
Workaholics Anonymous, 59
workaholism, 56
work and vocation, assessment information, 112
World Health Organization (WHO), 129, 369
worldviews, 393, 395–396
Worley, M. J., 274
Wozniak, J., 360, 362
Wright, D., 363
Wright-Bell, A., 329
Wu, L. T., 357
Wu, M., 53
Wu, N. S., 30
Wuetrich, B., 356
Wysong, E., 363

X
Xanax, 33
Xie, H., 165
Xyrem, 254

Y
Yalisove, D., 346
Yalom, I. D., 217, 225
Yancey, A. K., 392
Yang, H., 311, 357
Yang, M., 390
Yanico, B. J., 394
Yeh, C. J., 390
Yeh, M., 390
Yeterian, J., 81
Yin, H. H., 19, 22
Yoerger, K., 370
Young, C. M., 127
Young, K., 53
Young, S. E., 417
youth. *See* adolescents; children
Yücel, M., 8, 19
Yuen, F., 386

Z
Zaballero, A. R., 417
Zaichkowsky, L., 365
Zamora, D., 50
Zapf, J. L., 51
Zapolski, T. C. B., 387
Zaskutas, L. A., 270
Zavodnick, A. D., 255
Zeitlin, H., 360–362
Zelvin, E., 314, 320
Zemore, S. E., 270, 273
zero tolerance policies, 6, 442
Zhang, C., 361
Zhang, L., 413
Zhang, N., 56, 58–59
Zhao, W., 355
Zheng, C., 355
Zickler, P., 38
Ziedenberg, J., 468
Zimmerman, Carlos, 463
Ziska, M., 357
Zmuda, N., 51
Zubenko, N., 343, 345
Zucker, R. A., 311, 313, 317
Zuniga, C. D., 411
Zweben, A., 175, 305
Zweben, J. E., 218, 263
Zylstra, R., 246